FOCUS ON SOCIETY

An introduction to sociology *SECOND EDITION*

NORMAN W. STORER

Bernard M. Baruch College
City University of New York

ADDISON-WESLEY PUBLISHING COMPANY

Reading, Massachusetts
Menlo Park, California
London
Amsterdam
Don Mills, Ontario
Sydney

FOR MARY

301
ST7f
133389
Sept. 1985

This book is in the
ADDISON-WESLEY SERIES IN SOCIOLOGY.

Library of Congress Cataloging in Publication Data

Storer, Norman W.
  Focus on society.

  Bibliography: p.
  Includes index.
  1. Sociology. I. Title.
HM51.S899 1980   301   79–26376
ISBN 0-201-07337-4

ISBN 0-201-07337-4
ABCDEFGHIJ-HA-89876543210

Preface

No text can ever fully achieve its author's aims, but the reader deserves an account of those aims if only for the sake of orientation. The preface to the first edition of this book (1973) began with the statement that the book was meant to be an *introduction* to the field of sociology rather than an encyclopedic summary of its entire body of knowledge. I intend this to be true of the second edition as well.

I believe that an introduction should be inviting as well as instructive; it should be a cordial welcome to the new topic as well as a survey of what it includes. Just as a host owes a visitor every hospitality, so I believe that the author of an introductory text should make every effort to make the reader feel at home in the new field of knowledge. This means in particular that the book should help the reader to achieve a sense of familiarity with each new topic as it is introduced. No one, after all, feels very comfortable in new surroundings if he or she is made to feel inferior to the host or incompetent to handle the situation.

Coming for the first time to a new field, any student may well feel bewildered: "How can I possibly get acquainted with all this strange material?" I have tried to keep this uncertainty in mind and to do my best to ease the reader's initial fear that the book's contents will be too complex ever to understand. Thus, as with the first edition, I have tried to write for the beginning student rather than for the professional sociologist.

This does not mean that I have compromised any intellectual standards. No attempts are made here to be "cute" or to pander to the student who is not willing to make a serious effort to become familiar with sociology. A college student should be prepared to do college-level work. But I have done my best to be clear, to provide helpful examples, and to organize each chapter so that its parts build toward a meaningful overview of its contents.

It should be noted that this edition differs substantially from its predecessor. Two chapters (on socialization and on changing sex roles) are entirely new, many others have been completely rewritten, and the remainder have been expanded to provide more comprehensive and up-to-date coverage of their topics. In addition, new chapters on sociological research and sociological theory have been included as appendixes so that individual instructors will have maximum flexibility in determining just when during the introductory course they should be introduced.

In response to colleagues' suggestions, more attention has been paid to the sources of particular facts and ideas, and efforts have been made to provide additional graphic illustrations of key concepts. I am satisfied that this second edition represents a tangible improvement over the first edition.

In addition to being informed of the aims of the book, the reader should also be aware of my particular perspective on the field of sociology. The discipline today is divided among several perspectives, some of them apparently incompatible with one another; the one embodied here should not be viewed as the only one or as one with which all of my colleagues are in full sympathy. My own point of view is best identified as a modified structural-functional perspective, and it can be contrasted with others such as are provided by conflict theory and the symbolic-interactionism perspective. (The meanings of these terms are explained briefly in Chapter 1 and in more detail in Appendix 2, "Sociological Theory.")

For example, this text does not concentrate on social injustices or on the ways that human beings "create" society by building shared mental pictures of it. I assume that the first job of sociology is to describe and explain what *is* and that it is not the sociologist's responsibility to prescribe either explicitly or implicitly what *ought to be.* I assume further that society exists "out there" in reality rather than mostly in our heads and that we can do a reasonably useful job of describing it in the same way that geologists describe rock formations and biochemists describe molecular structures. Obviously, I believe that this perspective is legitimate and deserves a hearing. The student, however, should be aware that it is by no means the only legitimate approach to understanding society. I have tried to give other perspectives their due where appropriate, and I trust that students who are interested in them can find other sociologists who can provide additional instruction in them.

In conclusion, I must confess the obvious: No author writes in a vacuum. Therefore, I must record my intellectual indebtedness to four senior sociologists who have taught me either formally or informally: Charles K. Warriner, Robin M. Williams, Jr., Talcott Parsons, and Robert K. Merton. Colleagues and students—past and present—have commented on my work with questions and criticisms that have continually expanded my horizons. A number of anonymous reviewers, together with the editors at Addison-Wesley, have contributed further to the shaping of the present text, and I am grateful to them.

Finally, my wife, Professor Mary Hiatt, has prodded, questioned, suggested, and supplied the endless encouragement I needed while I was struggling to find the clearest and most effective ways to improve this book. I look forward to the coming years as they will provide continuing opportunities to acknowledge my debt to her.

New York City   N. W. S.
November 1979

Contents

APPENDIXES: RESEARCH AND THEORY—THE MEANS
AND ENDS OF SOCIOLOGY

1 SOCIOLOGICAL RESEARCH

2 SOCIOLOGICAL THEORY

Introduction

Sociology is the science that focuses on society. As such, sociology is the systematic study of human groups as natural phenomena in their own right. A society is the largest type of group there is, so studying it must include studying its parts—the various types of groups that together make up a society.

Sociology is not a science because sociologists wear white lab coats and carry out experiments, or because they explain their findings in complicated mathematical terms, or because they have established a complete set of laws of social behavior. Rather, sociology is a science because sociologists are *trying* to be systematic and objective in their work. They, like scientists in other fields, are trying to develop generalizations that can yield valid predictions. This is as much as we can ask of any science.

More important than how "scientific" sociology is, however, is the sociological perspective. This view of society assumes that human groups can be treated as things that are just as real as stones, automobiles, molecules, roses, thunderstorms, and individual human beings. Perhaps the most important thing an introductory course in sociology can accomplish is to demonstrate that this is indeed a useful assumption and that it can expand our awareness and appreciation of society.

For most students, the course in which they read this book will be their first intensive exposure to the field of sociology. But it will not be their first acquaintance with the word *sociology*, for in recent years the sociologist has become a standard authority. Whenever a national scandal occurs or a social problem is treated "in depth," sociologists are sure to be quoted in magazine and newspaper articles on that topic.

But the student's image of the field is blurred and uncertain. Who *are* these characters who go around observing people, asking them questions, carrying out experiments with groups, and writing books and articles about what they have found?

A standard introductory course in sociology does not usually tell the student much about the personal habits and interests of individual sociologists. Rather, it means to introduce the student to the body of knowledge with which these people are concerned. He or she is taken on a relatively short tour of a specialized body of knowledge that sociologists, past and present, have put together and that exists as a part of the intellectual world called the liberal arts.

There are many ways in which a student can be introduced to a new field of academic knowledge. One is to emphasize its historical development, introducing the famous names and research achievements of the past and showing how they have contributed to the field as it is today. Another is to emphasize the methods of research used to produce and validate new knowledge in the field. A third is to stress the field's relevance to understanding and perhaps helping to solve current social problems. Each approach is sure to be especially attractive to some students.

This book represents a fourth approach—an attempt to acquaint the student with the *way of thinking* that characterizes the sociologist's attempts to understand the makeup and workings of human society. It seeks to demonstrate that each of the major areas of interest within sociology can be analyzed and understood systematically. Although it is written primarily in a "functionalist" perspective (see the section entitled "Schools of Thought Within Sociology" in Chapter 1), the book does not advocate this as the only approach to understanding society.

In the end, it is hoped that the student will develop a sense of confidence that even such a complex and confusing thing as society itself can be mastered intellectually. This book will try to show that the component parts and processes of society can be pictured in a meaningful way and that the sociological enterprise may be worthy of further investigation in advanced courses.

The *Focus* section introduced at the beginning of each chapter provides a central idea, or theme, for the chapter. The purpose of the *Focus* is to provide a sense of the basic phenomenon or question that is central to the topic under discussion. To the extent that it illuminates the chapter's central concern and helps to crystallize its content, the *Focus* will have been successful in building the feeling of intellectual mastery that is the book's purpose.

Section I deals with the nature of sociology itself. After a brief history of the discipline and illustrations of the sociological perspective (Chapter 1), there is a chapter on the basic concepts sociologists use to talk about social relationships and processes. It may be true, as some have joked, that "sociology isn't a science, it's a language," but this merely indicates the need to

understand the central concepts of any field before one can begin to grasp its
content. You may know, for instance, how to get from your home to a particular movie theater, but if you did not have names for the directions, streets,
landmarks, and distances involved, you would find it impossible to tell someone else how to get there. In the same way, sociology is more than just individual understanding. It is public knowledge, and we must be able to discuss it,
question it, and correct it when necessary. Learning the basic vocabulary of
sociology, then, must come first.

Chapter 3 looks at culture—the shared "maps of the world," both as it is
and as it should be, that underlie the coordination of all social behavior.
Chapter 4 covers socialization, the process through which human beings become capable of social behavior, and the social structures in which it takes
place. Section I concludes with an examination (Chapter 5) of how and why
sex roles are changing today, giving the student a chance to see in a concrete
way how the basic concepts developed in preceding chapters can be applied to
a current issue that is of general interest.

Section II of the book covers the various types of human groupings that
are recognized by sociologists: social classes (Chapter 6), racial and ethnic
groups (Chapter 7), human communities (Chapter 8), and formal organizations such as factories, hospitals, and prisons (Chapter 9).

In Section III (Chapters 10–14), the idea of social exchange is introduced
as a key to understanding the nature and functioning of social institutions—the basic social structures through which the members of society seek
to satisfy their individual and collective needs.

A number of important social processes are the concern of Section IV
(Chapters 15–18). Considered here are the types of and reasons for deviant behavior, the ways in which society tries to maintain order through various
methods of social control, the dynamics of public opinion and collective behavior, and, finally, the processes of social change.

A complete appreciation of sociology, as both a body of knowledge and
an academic profession, is impossible unless one is familiar with the methods
of research employed by sociologists and with the theories of society they have
developed. Yet it is not necessarily the case that one should acquire such a
thorough acquaintance with the discipline in the course of a single term's introduction to it. Some professors believe that a familiarity with research methods
and with theory is fundamental to the introductory course; others assume that
these professional concerns are better left to subsequent courses. For this reason, detailed treatments of these topics are provided in Appendixes 1 and 2 for
immediate use or for reference later on. The student who is intellectually ad-
venturous, of course, will explore them regardless of the professor's decision.

Suggestions for further reading follow each chapter, along with a glossary
of the principal concepts used throughout the chapter.

SOCIOLOGY: THE BASIC IDEAS

The study of human beings, as individuals and in groups, is probably the most challenging task to which scholars can address themselves. The path of a falling stone can be understood by considering only a handful of factors: gravitational pull, air resistance, wind, and so on. Understanding the growth of a simple plant requires the scientist to consider many more possible influences, ranging from genetic endowment to solar radiation. The number of things that may influence an individual's behavior is even greater, and those that must be taken into consideration if we are to understand an entire society are still greater in number.

Viewed in this way, it is no wonder that the social sciences are at least three hundred years behind the physical sciences in understanding their subject matter and certainly a century behind the biological sciences. The more complex the topic being studied, the more time is required to conceptualize it effectively and to begin to trace the cause-and-effect relationships that shape it. Yet the social sciences are making progress more rapidly now than at any time in the past. Whatever frustration one may feel when considering how much work remains to be done should be more than balanced by the knowledge that so much intellectual excitement still lies ahead.

Fortunately, no one has to do the whole job. Because humankind is so complex, a number of distinct social science disciplines have grown up around the study of its most important features:

- *Psychology* takes the individual *homo sapiens* as its target of investigation, concentrating on both emotional and cognitive processes and aberrations in them. Those aspects of psychology more relevant to sociology are taken up in Chapter 4, on socialization.

- *Economics* examines the mechanisms through which material goods and services are produced and distributed. The sociologist's view of the economic institution is covered in Chapter II.

- *Political science* focuses on the role of power and authority in social life, both in the analysis and comparison of different political systems and in the study of political philosophy. Chapter 12 provides a sociological analysis of the political institution of society.

- *Geography* is concerned with the role of physical space in social relationships; some aspects of it are brought out in Chapter 8, on communities.

- *Linguistics,* a field that is only now emerging from the fields of psychology and anthropology, investigates human communication and covers both the physiological aspects and the contents of this process. The nature and importance of language are discussed in Chapter 3, on culture.

- *History,* the determination and interpretation of what went on in the past, is often classified as a social science. In one sense it stands as a major source of information in which sociologists are interested, but it also commands interest through the sheer fascination of trying to ascertain more and more completely what our ancestors did and how they lived.

- *Statistics,* a branch of mathematics, is sometimes included among the social sciences simply because of its special application to the sorts of data with which sociologists and other social scientists deal. Appendix 1, on research methods, amplifies this point.

It seems fair to say that the remaining social sciences—*sociology* and *anthropology*—are converging toward a common perspective that views societies as natural entities in their own right. The fact that they are identified as separate disciplines reflects their different origins more than their concern with different phenomena. Anthropology has traditionally involved the study of entire, relatively primitive (that is, nonliterate) societies around the world. Entering such a society, one is likely to be struck primarily by the people's way of life as a whole because it is so different from the observer's own society. Out of this sort of experience has come the anthropologist's central concern with culture as the key to a society's way of life. The sociologist, on the other hand, most often studies advanced, complex societies (usually his or her own). Knowing generally what his or her own culture involves, the sociologist is thus more interested in discovering the patterned relationships that lie beneath the surface of a familiar society and places less emphasis on the idea of culture.

Because this book is about sociology in particular, we begin in Chapter 1 with a general discussion of the sociological perspective—the nature of the field and its history, the central assumptions sociologists bring to their work today, and some examples of how this perspective can help make sense of what we observe around us every day.

Chapter 2 is a concentrated introduction to the basic conceptual tools of the sociologist. Here we will become familiar with the central ideas that enable the sociologist to talk about social relationships, structures, and processes, and how these concepts are interrelated.

The idea of culture as a distinctive aspect of society, intangible and yet providing the foundation for the regular social relationships that make up society, is taken up in Chapter 3. Chapter 4 concentrates on the ways in which people are socialized, or develop a sense of themselves in relation to others so that they can participate successfully in social relationships. Finally, showing how these basic concepts, culture, and socialization are all involved in a problem of widespread interest today, the case of changing sex roles is analyzed in Chapter 5.

1
Sociology: The Field and Its Concerns

FOCUS:

ACADEMIC KNOWLEDGE

Often called a discipline, a body of **academic knowledge** *is a large number of facts, ideas, interpretations, formulas, and other units of information that are recorded and systematically related to one another.* Thus a body of knowledge is quite different from a person's private knowledge of last night's dreams or people's shared knowledge of the latest political scandal. The subject matter of most college courses, other than those which teach skills, is a body of academic knowledge: history, chemistry, philosophy, Spanish literature, and, of course, sociology. (The occasional use of the term "academic" to mean "irrelevant" clearly stems from the fact that a generalized, organized body of knowledge is usually of less value in helping one get through the day's immediate problems than is the detailed but *ad hoc* [that is, "to the point, but unorganized"] knowledge that one develops through private experience.)

We can point to three aspects of any body of knowledge. At the foundation is knowledge of *how* knowledge is produced in a particular discipline: laboratory techniques, research skills, or, more generally, *methodology*. Second, there is the field's detailed knowledge of its subject matter: what happened in pre-Revolutionary France, how DNA molecules are coded, what Kant said about aesthetics, the central themes in Garcia Lorca's poems, and how child-rearing practices vary among social classes.

Finally, there is all of the material that is concerned with the body of knowledge itself: critiques of the discipline, histories of its development, attempts to link it to other bodies of knowledge, and efforts to reorganize its contents in new configurations. A body of knowledge, then, is made up of answers to the *hows, whats,* and *whys* that may be asked about its subject matter.

To become familiar with a particular body of academic knowledge, one must get acquainted with the perspective, or mental framework, that is shared by the people who are engaged in adding to that knowledge and in teaching it to others. An introduction to a body of academic knowledge, therefore, is something like a first visit to a new city. No one ever knew his or her way around on the first visit, but with repeated exposure to the city's main streets and landmarks, the visitor eventually comes to feel "at home" there. Sooner or later, one begins to feel like a native.

An introductory textbook should be the equivalent of a sympathetic guide on one's first visit to a new city. It should allow the visitor to explore things at a reasonable pace, pointing out the most prominent features of the area before going into complicated discussions of, say, the history of a particular neighborhood. This chapter attempts to serve as such a guide for your first visit to a new body of academic knowledge, Sociology City.

Sociologists are concerned primarily with ▶
social relationships within and among
groups of people, rather than with the
behavior of separate individuals such as
these men and women in Plains, Georgia.
(Owen Franken/Stock, Boston)

DEFINING SOCIOLOGY

This book is about the structure and dynamics of human society and of its major parts as they are viewed by the academic discipline called sociology. It was noted in the Introduction that **sociology** *is the study of human groups as natural phenomena* in their own right, or as things that exist in the real world and can be analyzed and described objectively. Some sociologists define their field as the study of *human interaction;* others say that it is the study of *life in groups;* still others emphasize its central interest in *social order.* No matter which specific words are used in a definition, however, it is important to remember that the central subject matter of sociology is the relationships *among* people rather than their behavior as separate individuals.

Here at the beginning, we want to provide a sense of the sociological perspective—the basic assumptions and kinds of questions that the sociologist has in mind while studying social relationships. This is not to say that there is only one perspective in sociology, for today there is lively and sometimes heated debate among sociologists as to just which basic assumptions, research methods, and final purposes should characterize their work.

For some, sociology should emulate the natural sciences such as physics and chemistry, striving for quantified, dispassionate understanding of how so-

ciety works. For others, sociology should aim for a humane, personal understanding of why social relationships are the way they are, so that people can take more effective control of their own lives. And there are other sociologists who want the discipline to take on a much more active character, exposing injustices and using sociological findings to make society better for everyone. Yet whether one wants sociology to be objective or subjective, "pure" or "applied," it is necessary first to develop a clear idea of what really exists.

Sociology, like any other branch of learning, is an activity as well as a body of knowledge. Sociology is more than a definition; it is what sociologists *do*. They investigate and analyze and develop theories about all sorts of social relationships and the groups within which they are found: families, work groups, towns and cities, voluntary associations, categories of people such as "the middle class" and "Mexican-Americans," social institutions such as religion, and complete societies as well. Some sociologists make a career of studying particular types of groups; others specialize in studying particular social processes in various social contexts. (The various methods used in these studies are discussed in Appendix 1, on sociological research methods.)

What is the relation between human groups and society? It lies in the fact that a human **society**—which we often think of as a nation, a country, a people, or a state—*is the most nearly complete type of human group there is, and it is made up of many smaller groups*. Each of these smaller groups (for instance, families, governments, corporations, neighborhoods, ethnic groups, and so on) exists within society and is best understood in this context. Therefore, although the sociologist may devote attention to a particular type of group, the major reference is to society itself.

"But," you may ask at this point, "doesn't this mean that sociology is just a kind of mass psychology? After all, groups are made up of individuals, and the study of individuals is really the job of the psychologist." The sociologist must answer this question with a gentle no, for sociologists work from quite a different perspective.

There is indeed a good deal of interaction between the personalities of individuals and the nature of the groups to which they belong, but it would be wrong to say that a group is simply the sum of its members. A human group may also be viewed as an entity—as an object itself, worthy of study in its own right—and the sociologist feels that this is a reasonable and fruitful point of view.

For instance, groups have many characteristics that cannot be reduced to the qualities of their individual members. The type of political structure a nation has is a matter of the relationships *among* its citizens rather than of their personal psychological characteristics. The relative number of males and females in a group or their distribution among different age groups is an aspect of the group itself. Different groups have different homicide and suicide rates, which remain remarkably stable from one year to the next. Even though these are individual acts, the fact that the suicide rate in the United States is usually around eleven per 100,000 per year, whereas in Hungary it is nearly thirty per 100,000 per year (DeVos, 1968), suggests that there are significant differences between these nations as human groups. Similarly, homicide rates in different states in this country vary considerably (for instance, from 0.3 in Vermont to 10.3 in Georgia during 1962 [Bedau, 1964, p. 68]), although they change very little over time.

Forms of organization, then, together with various types of distributions and rates, are distinctive attributes of groups that cannot be determined or explained by examining the psychological makeup of their individual members. This is not to say that the sociologist ignores these individuals, for they are, of course, the visible components of groups, but his or her interest is in describing the social relationships in which they participate rather than the participants themselves.

It may be helpful to think of a continuum that extends from a sharp focus on the individual (psychology) to a distinctive interest in the group itself (sociology), with the midpoint being the concern of a hybrid field called social psychology. This third discipline concentrates both on how groups are influenced by their individual members and on how membership in groups influences the individual.

So the sociologist is interested primarily in groups—their structures, processes, and relationships. He or she views groups as things that have their own special qualities and dimensions. Frequently, these can be discovered only by observing and questioning their individual members, but the sociologist's central purpose is always to analyze groups *as groups*.

The Usefulness of Sociology

It is quite appropriate for you to ask at this point, "What good is it for me to study sociology?" And it is only fair to answer by noting first some of the things it will *not* do for the student. First, it will not necessarily make anyone more brilliant or effective in personal relationships with others. At best, it can eventually give a person more insight into why and how things happen as they do in groups, but sociology holds no magic formulas or techniques that will enable someone to manipulate others or to suddenly become more popular.

Second, the study of sociology will not necessarily enable you to solve social problems in your home, community, dormitory, or campus. Here, as in most real-life situations, "book-larnin'" is no substitute for experience and energy, even though in combination with these indispensable factors, it may help people to direct their energies more effectively.

As with the study of European history, astronomy, or the works of Chaucer, the study of sociology is not very practical in either an economic or a personal-skills sense. Rather, its value lies in how it can expand the student's perspective on life in society. Sociology should broaden and deepen one's understanding of the ways in which people organize themselves into groups and societies. And through demonstrating that social relationships do exhibit regularities that may not be immediately apparent, sociology can perhaps give the student greater confidence that he or she can find meaning in a sometimes chaotic world.

It is thus suggested that you will be introduced here to a relatively new framework for viewing society. Facts about social life take on added meaning when placed in an appropriate context of basic ideas, just as a picture can look much more beautiful when properly framed. The purpose of this book is to give you a new context which will give certain facts new and different meanings. Studying sociology, then, means more than just learning answers to questions; it means learning to ask new questions through getting acquainted with a new perspective. The study of sociology is thus properly in the tradition of the liberal arts. It is an enterprise intended to broaden our understanding and appreciation of the world and of human beings and their works.

THE HISTORICAL DEVELOPMENT OF SOCIOLOGY

At the beginning of this chapter it was noted that sociology is a relatively new field of knowledge. Actually, like most academic disciplines, it can trace its origins far back into antiquity in terms of substance if not of name and organization. But as a recognized area of scholarly endeavor, sociology has existed only since the middle of the nineteenth century. The word *sociology* itself was coined about 1836 by a French scholar, Auguste Comte, who naturally enough is now called "the father of sociology."

Comte had originally wanted to call the new field "social physics," but that term had already been used by a Belgian, Adolfe Quetelet, as a name for what we now call social statistics. So Comte had to join a Latin base to a Greek suffix to produce a name for his new branch of knowledge. Thus there has been a trace of validity in the occasional charge that sociology is a mongrel science—even though etymological illegitimacy is really irrelevant to the purpose and quality of the work of the sociologist. The substantive contributions of Comte and others to the development of sociology are related in more detail in Appendix 2, on sociological theory.

It was not until the 1880s that much in the way of significant sociology was produced. Karl Marx's works had been written by then, but were not initially recognized as contributions to the field of sociology. Emile Durkheim in France and Max Weber in Germany wrote books both before and after the turn of the century that are acknowledged as classics today. Probably the most important popularizer of sociology in the last quarter of the nineteenth century was the British philosopher Herbert Spencer, even though today there is little recognition of his substantive contributions.

The first formal department of sociology was established at the University of Chicago in 1896, although for the next forty years it was often taught in departments of economics, political science, and philosophy. The discipline gradually acquired departmental status of its own throughout this country and is being increasingly recognized over the rest of the world as an independent field of learning.

The American Sociological Society was formed in 1906, but as late as the 1940s it had fewer than one thousand members. Today, however, the group (since renamed the American Sociological Association—partly, some say, to rid itself of an unfortunate acronym) has close to 14,000 professional and student members. About four-fifths of them are employed in college-level teaching, with the remainder engaged primarily in social research for private and governmental organizations.

THE SOCIOLOGICAL VIEW OF HUMAN NATURE

As a background to the sociological perspective, it will be useful at this point to say something about how the discipline views the question of whether a "science of society" is possible and how it sees the relationship between individuals and groups.

Free Will versus Determinism

"If sociology is a science," someone will ask, "trying to develop valid, empirical knowledge of human groups, doesn't this mean that sociologists are trying to *predict* human behavior?" (Smiling, the professor nods in agreement.) "And doesn't this mean," the questioner continues, "that the sociologist assumes that human beings are *predictable*—and that their behavior is therefore *determined?*" (Again, but with a faint frown indicating important qualifications, the answer must be yes.)

Here, obviously, we have hit on the old question of free will versus determinism. Do people make their own choices about what they will do, or are they just puppets being jerked about by forces of which they are only dimly aware? It does seem that the sociologist must assume that people lack free will, for otherwise he or she could have no faith that people's behavior can ever be predicted. We cannot have it both ways: If behavior is *caused* by external events (whether in the immediate situation or dating back to the individual's childhood), the idea of **free will,** *or the freedom to choose what one will do next,* becomes meaningless.

Much of this apparent dilemma lies in our assumption that the opposite of **determinism,** *or being caused,* is randomness, or complete *un*predictability. But as we shall see, this assumption is not warranted. The question is not so simple as it first appears.

Critics of sociology sometimes charge that the sociologist is a fool, because people do have free will and therefore can never be subject to "scientific" laws. They may complain also that the sociologist is a would-be-dictator, seeking to predict behavior so that it can be controlled. The two criticisms are clearly inconsistent with each other. (Moreover, it should not be presumed that prediction and control always go hand in hand. Astronomers can predict an eclipse of the sun because they understand what is involved, but they certainly cannot *make* it happen. On the other hand, we may be able to make someone obey our command to "stick 'em up," even though we cannot explain in detail exactly why he or she responded as we wished just because we had a pistol in our hand.)

The question, though, concerns the sociologist's view of free will. Actually, there is no inevitable conflict between free will and determinism. The sociologist assumes, as we all do, that people have goals—that there are things that people want to achieve or acquire in the future. It is also assumed that people live in the "real world," where wishing does not ordinarily make things come true.

If we accept these additional assumptions, we can see that a person can achieve goals only if she or he takes into account the given facts in a situation. In other words, a person must behave "reasonably" (and thus predictably) with respect to such things as the law of gravity, the location of grocery stores, the existence of wild animals, and the sorts of things other people are likely to do. The individual must thus choose to behave *as though* he or she is determined, for the sake of achieving those goals. And so the question of free will becomes "academic" as far as the sociologist is concerned. He or she is interested in what other people actually do, rather than in what they might do in the absence of all constraints.

This is not meant to imply that sociologists expect people to behave rationally all the time. Their interest in groups, and thus in *patterns* of social relationships, means that they are interested in how *most* people behave *most* of the time; their faith in the validity of their work, then, is not undermined when a few people seem, with apparently irrational unconcern for the consequences, to exercise their free will. And as we shall see in the next chapter, people generally take a very negative attitude toward those who behave unpredictably, so that "determined" behavior is very much the rule for human beings.

Social Facts

Another important aspect of the sociologist's view of human nature is that it is often irrelevant to the explanation of social phenomena. In fact, Emile Durkheim's attempt to establish the independent foundations for a science of society led him to suggest that a **social fact** *(a statement referring directly to a group rather than to individuals)* can be explained only in terms of other social facts. He suggested, for instance, that a country's suicide *rate* (a characteristic of that

Individuals are often motivated by intangible concepts such as "patriotism" and "honor," even to the point of sacrificing their own lives. These Israeli soldiers carry the body of a Palestinian commando killed in an attack on Nahariya Beach. (William Karel/Sygma)

group rather of its individual members) can be accounted for only by certain other characteristics of that group—in this case, by the extent to which the group's members are integrated into the whole. (Durkheim's study of suicide is examined at greater length in Appendix 2, on sociological theory.)

Related to Durkheim's concept of social fact is the tendency for individuals to react to generalizations and to their expectations about the future as though they are just as "real" as the concrete experience of stubbing one's toe, eating a meal, or seeing an auto accident. Animals do not panic in response to rumors, plants do not grow lush because the gardener promises to add fertilizer to the soil next week, and stones do not roll uphill because other stones believe it more prestigious to be located higher on the mountain. Only human beings react to their perceptions of social reality, which exists above and apart from the individuals who make up society. Even if this social reality has arisen only as a kind of summary of individuals' separate, concrete experiences, it becomes independent of them and exerts appreciable influence on their relations with one another.

The reality of this "unreal" factor in society is seen through its causal power, or in the fact that only by assuming its existence can we explain why people do many of the things they do and enter into the patterned relationships that we observe. So long as men and women behave as though "society," "honor," "the buying public," and a host of other intangibles are real things, the sociologist must accept and study the existence of those things.

Occasionally the things that people assume to be real actually become real later on; this process is discussed in Chapter 17, on public opinion and collective behavior, under the concept of the self-fulfilling prophecy. Here, however, we are concerned with refuting **reductionism,** *the belief that the characteristics of society itself can be explained merely by understanding the characteristics of its members.* Reductionism has proved effective, however, in the understanding of inanimate nature and of basic biological phenomena. But since mutual expectations are involved in social interaction and social behavior is influenced by long-range goals as well as immediate circumstances, the sociologist argues that social structures cannot be understood or predicted on the basis of biological, geographical, or even psychological analyses. Society as a phenomenon, in other words, is a reality *sui generis* (created by itself), and special research techniques and special concepts are needed for its investigation and description.

SCHOOLS OF THOUGHT WITHIN SOCIOLOGY

As noted above, sociologists are by no means in full agreement on either the essential nature of society or the basic questions that should be asked about it. Nor is there complete agreement on *why* sociologists should study society. Rather than being totally disorganized, however, sociologists tend to identify themselves with one of a few vaguely defined (but clearly distinctive) schools of thought. These are often called theories, or approaches. Each is based on a handful of basic assumptions about the central character of society, and they in turn suggest the major questions to be asked about it and some ideas about why and how sociologists should go about their business.

In this section we will provide brief descriptions of three major schools of thought in sociology today, hoping to give you some idea of the various ways in which sociology can be defined as an intellectual enterprise and thus a broader orientation to the discipline as a whole. The history and current array of sociological theories are taken up in more detail in Appendix 2.

The Structural-Functional Approach

This view of society, often simply called **functionalism,** takes as its starting point *the assumption that society is best viewed as a system composed of interrelated parts.* Each of these parts—whether a political structure, a form of family organization, or a particular economic practice—is assumed to have one or more **functions,** or *ways in which it contributes to the continued existence of the larger system.* By contrast, **dysfunctions** are a part's disruptive consequences for other parts, or ones that tend to harm the system.

This view of society goes back at least to Comte. Since his time, it has been extended and modified by Spencer, Durkheim, and Weber, among others, and so can claim to have perhaps the most impressive pedigree in sociology. Among present-day sociologists associated with functionalism are Talcott Parsons (1951), Robert K. Merton (1957), and Kingsley Davis (1948).

The concept of society-as-system implies that it has an objective existence and thus can be studied as objectively as the subject matter of any other science. Emphasizing the idea of "system" as an appropriate model of society, however, has meant that misleading analogies between societies and biological organisms have been easy to draw (as, it is charged, Spencer did) and also that there is a continuing temptation to think of society as a living thing that has its own needs and somehow sees that they are satisfied. But the fact that the concept of system has proved so fruitful in other sciences enables functionalists to argue that such excesses are not intrinsic to the approach and that the perspective remains valid despite occasional misuse.

The central questions highlighted by the functional approach to society relate to the ways in which social order is maintained and the circumstances under which order is threatened. Since the system's very existence depends on the maintenance of orderly relations among its parts, the questions asked by functionalists must eventually refer back to the idea of social order, or equilibrium.

The adherents of other approaches claim that this emphasis carries with it the unavoidable implication that maintaining the status quo is preferable to any sort of social change, so that functionalists tend to be politically conservative. Carrying this further, it is sometimes charged that they thus contribute to the continuing dominance of today's political and economic elites. But this is a criticism of the potential social consequences of the functionalist position rather than of its merits as an approach to studying society. More to the point, in terms of scientific adequacy, has been the criticism that the functionalists are ill-equipped to study social change because of their emphasis on social equilibrium. As we shall see in Chapter 18, however, this criticism is not necessarily valid.

The structural-functional approach dominated American sociology until perhaps the mid-1960s, but since then it has come under increasing attack from at least two other schools of thought. The one most directly in opposition to it is generally referred to as conflict theory.

The Conflict Approach

Stemming originally from the works of Karl Marx, **conflict theory** *is anchored on the assumption that change rather than stability is the central characteristic of society.* It assumes further that the chief cause of change is continuing conflict among different groups in society. For Marx, the major struggle was between social classes and was essentially economic in nature. For today's conflict theorists, competition for prestige, for the power to determine organizational goals, and even for such things as religious legitimacy are also viewed as demonstrating the validity of this approach.

The questions that flow naturally from these assumptions generally have reference to "Who gets what and why?" rather than to how social order is maintained. Periods of social stability are assumed to be simply times when one group has temporarily succeeded in dominating others to the point where continued conflict seems useless. Because the unequal distribution of wealth, power, and prestige produces different social classes, the study of social stratification is of central importance in the conflict approach.

Although claiming to be just as "scientific" as the functionalists, sociologists identified with conflict theory tend also to advocate a much more active role for themselves in society. They stress the injustices of "the system," point out the ways in which the haves exploit the have-nots, and recommend active involvement by sociologists in correcting these evils. At times, the distinction between sociology as a body of knowledge and sociology as an ideology of political activism becomes blurred or even erased.

If the functionalists are criticized for ignoring conflict and change, the conflict theorists are faulted for paying too little attention to cooperation and social order. They may also be charged with overemphasizing the more unpleasant aspects of human nature: greed, selfishness, aggression, and so on. Yet conflict is clearly present throughout society in one form or another, and only by seeing it as natural rather than as pathological can sociology make progress in understanding society. Perhaps the disagreements between functionalists and conflict theorists stem more from the fact that the need to establish distinctive approaches to the study of society leads to oversimplification than that one school must be right and the other wrong.

Contemporary sociologists identified with the conflict approach include Ralf Dahrendorf (1959), C. Wright Mills (1956), and Lewis A. Coser (1956).

The Symbolic-Interactionist Approach

Whereas both the functionalists and conflict theorists concern themselves with society as a whole, a third school of thought, **symbolic interactionism,** *concentrates on the complexities of individual social relationships.* The interactionists, as we may refer to what is actually a collection of several specialized points of view, share the central assumption that the reality of society lies essentially in the perceptions of its participants rather than its objective existence in time and space. To understand society, they argue, we must understand how people assign meaning to their own and others' behavior and develop shared images of society that enable them to interact effectively.

Symbolic interaction refers to people's coordinating their activities through the use of symbols, and so it must involve shared assumptions about motives, expectations, and goals. Since there would be no society without communication, the interactionists believe that the foundation of sociology must lie in understanding the mental processes that make interaction possible.

They trace their roots back to Max Weber's discussion of *verstehen* (a way of understanding the meaning of people's behavior by "standing in their place"), and additional contributions to this approach have come from philosophers such as Alfred Schutz (1962) as well as from George Herbert Mead (1934) and Herbert Blumer (1969), who are more clearly identified as sociologists. Although there is no fully developed interactionist theory of society as a whole, its concentration on the thoughts and feelings of individuals gives it a pronounced humanistic character that appeals to many sociologists.

Specialized approaches within the interactionist framework include analyzing social relationships in terms of drama (Goffman, 1959, and Berger, 1963), the negotiation of shared meanings (Garfinkel, 1967, and others who call themselves ethnomethodologists), and social exchange (Homans, 1950, and Blau, 1964). At present, social exchange shows the greatest promise of developing a full-scale view of society that can serve as an alternative to the functionalist and conflict-theory views, although it has not yet fulfilled this promise.

Summing Up

Despite their differences, sociologists identified with each of these schools of thought tend to take a common perspective when observing social behavior. Perhaps the simplest way to explain this is to say that they try to be aware of the social context within which observable social phenomena occur. Several examples of this are offered in the next section of this chapter.

THE SOCIOLOGICAL PERSPECTIVE

It was mentioned before that the study of sociology involves learning a new conceptual framework, or a new perspective on social life. To illustrate this, we present here some examples of sociological perspective.

Let us begin with an analogy—the tailpipe of a standard American automobile. The tailpipe twists and turns most peculiarly, yet its purpose is simply to carry the exhaust gases away from the car's engine. Why won't a straight pipe do? Why all these funny twists and angles? A straight pipe would be simpler and easier to manufacture, but it is unlikely that you will ever find one as standard equipment for an automobile (we must, naturally, ignore rear-engine cars here for the sake of the analogy). The reason the pipe is bent so strangely is that it must fit in with the other parts of the car—the frame, the axle, the gas tank, and so on. And these parts, in turn, are where they are because they must fit in with still other parts.

Of course, you could probably build an entire automobile around a straight tailpipe. You could redesign the rest of the car so that none of the other parts would be in the way of a straight pipe. But this would very likely be more expensive and less efficient than building a car according to present designs. Further, even if the redesigned car were in fact more efficient, it would involve so much expense to change over to producing it that the extra efficiency probably wouldn't be worth the extra cost.

When we look at the tailpipe apart from the rest of the car, then, it looks funny. It doesn't look very practical, given its purpose with respect to the proper functioning of the car. But when we look at how it fits with the rest of the car, we can see that its peculiar shape makes good sense.

The sociologist looks at patterns of social behavior in much the same way, asking not only "What is the purpose of this pattern of behavior?" but also "How does it fit in with the *other* patterns of behavior that characterize this group of people?" It is obvious that different patterns of behavior within a particular group are interdependent, directly or indirectly, and so we must conclude that it is important to ask this sort of question.

Why the Soldiers Are Drilling

For example, let us look at a company of soldiers as they spend a hot Thursday afternoon practicing dismounted drill (that is, marching) in the hot sun. This is not a particularly pleasant thing to be doing—they already know how to march—and yet here they are, forward-marching and right-facing. Some numbskull has goofed again, and there is a lot of griping and unmannerly language to be heard. Why must they engage in this useless, tiresome activity?

In sociological perspective, this activity is part of the broader set of patterns of behavior called "the Army." It is like a particular twist in the tailpipe. From the Army's point of view, this bend is here so that the broader pattern—the whole tailpipe, if you will—does not get in the way of some of the other patterns that make up the Army. Something else besides dismounted drill could have been scheduled for these soldiers, certainly, but that might require the use of personnel or materials that are being used more efficiently elsewhere this afternoon. To have the soldiers doing nothing at all would set an undesirable precedent; members of adjacent companies would be asking for time off when they should be doing other things, and morale would drop a bit when they were refused. It is possible, too, that with a free afternoon these soldiers might develop some patterns of behavior that were definitely in conflict with the other patterns making up the Army. Thus although the drill may not be very valuable in itself and does depress morale to a minor extent, it is apparently the activity least likely to conflict with other Army activities on this particular afternoon.

This is not meant to suggest that large organizations are always completely rational or efficient in scheduling various patterns of behavior; rather, there may be reasons for the twists in the behavioral tailpipe that are not immediately apparent. The point is simply that the sociologist tries to see the other parts of the car as well as just the tailpipe. She or he tries to see how a particular pattern of behavior fits in with and contributes to the larger set of regular activities of which it is a part. To be sure, we all do this from time to time, but it is an important and explicit part of the sociologist's approach to understanding social behavior, and he or she tries to be systematic about it.

This perspective, it is true, might be thought of as favoring the status quo or as assuming that we live in the best of all possible worlds. But we need not believe that an activity, a group, or a society is good simply because we want to know how it is organized, any more than we need to assume that this is a good car just because we want to know how its tailpipe fits into it. The fact is that the car exists. And disease exists, too—so the medical researcher studies the ways that germs live and reproduce, even though disapproving of the effects they produce. Studying how something works is quite different from deciding whether it is good or not; the sociologist studies the nature and organization of groups, whereas the citizen must decide which groups or patterns of behavior are desirable and which are not.

Why the Doctor Is Respected

For another illustration of the sociological perspective, let us look at the role of the doctor in society. The physician's purpose, obviously, is to help other people get well—to cure their illnesses, patch up their injuries, and help them avoid getting sick or hurt in the first place. But the doctor also has another function in society as well, performing activities that have a different set of consequences for the group.

This second function is the doctor's *certification* that someone is sick (Parsons, 1951, Chapter X). It is the doctor's statement, backed by training and experience that we all respect, that legitimates the condition of "being sick." Once this condition has been certified by the doctor, it is all right for the person not to go to work and to avoid meeting other obligations. The sick person is excused from these normal responsibilities because the doctor has, in effect, declared that regardless of what this person *should* or *would like* to do, he or she is unable to engage in these activities without some risk to personal well-being or to the health of others.

Why is this important to society? It tells others to change their expectations of the sick person. Since they no longer expect him or her to come to work, they can make arrangements to have someone else do the work. Without having illness certified in this manner, the person's employer or co-

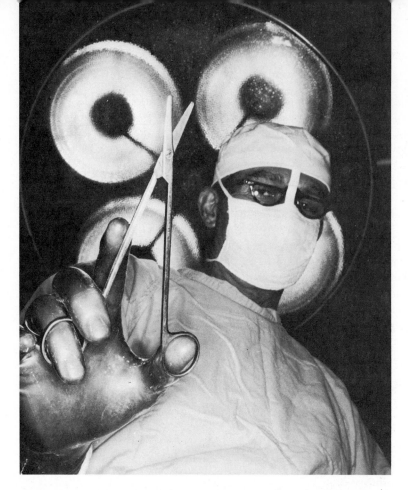

One of the doctor's functions in society is to certify that an individual is sick. Endowed with a certain authority and prestige, the physician's certification that someone is ill also has consequences for other members of society. (Elliott Erwitt/Magnum Photos)

workers might well wonder whether the unsupported self-diagnosis of illness isn't simply being used as an excuse to avoid an unpleasant task or to spend a long weekend out of town. Suspicions of this sort are damaging to the fabric of social relationships, and the doctor's impartial certification of illness prevents them. It is for this reason that students need medical excuses if they have missed an exam and want to make it up and why employees need similar statements from their physicians in order to have absences counted against sick leave.

This discussion of the doctor's functions in society certainly does not tell us something we didn't know before, but it does put things in a new perspective and can perhaps explain some interesting aspects of the doctor's position in society. The generally high level of prestige that the doctor enjoys is based not only on our occasional need for medical attention, but on the fact that his or her activities are important to us even when we are not sick. In declaring that someone is ill, the doctor helps define the situation for all of us and thus helps us keep our relationships with others free of suspicion. It is important to each of us that the doctor continue to enjoy this prestige so that his or her verdict will be accepted by everyone whenever someone is declared to be officially sick.

Our occasional reluctance to see the doctor is better explained, too, if we understand this aspect of the doctor's role. We don't avoid a physician because we *want* to be sick, but because she or he has the power to rule us out of the game for a while when we would rather continue playing it, even if we don't feel very well. Without an official declaration that we are ill, we are free to decide for ourselves whether we want to go to the dance or stay in bed.

Because the doctor has this authority, he or she must be particularly concerned with medical ethics, or with the professional rules that prohibit the use of medical authority for personal advantage. The medical profession has known, since at least 400 B.C., when Hippocrates drew up his famous Oath, that the public will trust an expert only when it is sure that he or she will not exploit this expertise. If people are to follow "doctor's orders," in other words, they must be assured that the doctor is not going to take advantage of them. And since doctors cannot expect to cure people if their advice is not followed, they must take pains to assure the public that they are in fact trustworthy. So, collectively, the medical profession licenses its members and the schools where they are trained, sets forth standards of behavior, and works hard to expose frauds and quacks—all for the sake of protecting the doctor's reputation so that he or she can go about the business of not only preventing and curing illness, but also helping the rest of us maintain orderly social relationships.

Why the Sociologist Uses Jargon

As a final example of the sociological perspective, let us turn it on one aspect of sociology itself—one that has occasionally brought the profession in for some criticism. This is the problem of sociological jargon, the complicated terms that sociologists use and that sometimes seem to be unnecessarily complicated or precious:

1. Cross-cutting reference groups

2. Latent dysfunctions

3. Horizontal occupational mobility

4. Consummatory orientation

It is quite possible that you will run across these phrases, or others similar to them, in more advanced works by sociologists. And it is true that some sociologists, like some historians and some biologists, do not write as clearly as we might wish they would. But the sociologists seem occasionally to invent new terms for familiar things. It is claimed that they are being confusing on purpose in order to make others think that they know more than they do. Indeed, it is possible to translate these esoteric phrases into simpler language:

1. A situation in which few people look to exactly the same groups all the time for standards by which to judge issues, events, and even themselves, so that even though two people may disagree greatly on one point, they are likely to agree on some other point.

2. Patterns of behavior that have unrecognized but harmful consequences for one's group or society.

3. A change in occupation that does not involve any real change in one's social-class ranking, such as someone's moving from the job of truck driver to that of auto mechanic, or from college president to the presidency of a private foundation.

4. To look on something as an end in itself rather than as a means to a more distant goal. For example, a family out for a Sunday drive is enjoying the travel for itself, whereas the person driving to work thinks of travel simply as a necessity.

It may be true in some cases that such phrases are used to beef up the sociologist's claim that he or she commands a mysterious and difficult body of knowledge, but before we can conclude that this is the only explanation, we should look at some of the less obvious purposes of language. Special phrases like those given above serve not only to simplify communication, but also to indicate the group to which the speaker belongs (or would like to belong). To use phrases taken from jazz musicians, Wall Street lawyers, or computer programmers allows us to inform our listeners of a particular social identity that we claim for ourselves, as well as the contents of our thoughts.

This fact holds true for sociologists as well as for the members of any other group. Like anyone else, sociologists use certain terms and phrases to identify themselves, even when their use may seem silly or pretentious to someone who does not recognize this implicit purpose or respect the group that they claim membership in.

The use of jargon is not something we can do much about. Just as you should learn to speak French if you want to have a good time in Paris, so you should learn the sociologist's vocabulary if you want to have an easy time studying sociology. Although sociologists enjoy making up new words or using them in specialized ways as much as anyone else does, the number of specialized terms used in this book will be held to a minimum.

Those terms that are introduced, of course, will do more than simply enable you to talk like a sociologist. They will serve as convenient ways to refer to things for which our common language has no words, or they will indicate sets of things that are not ordinarily called to mind by a single term. To the extent that a field of knowledge requires its own specialized vocabulary for communication as well as for social identity, students will find it necessary to master these terms before they can honestly say that they know what sociology is all about.

CONCLUSION

This, then, is sociology. In some ways, it is a new way of looking at things with which we are already familiar. More broadly, it is an academic discipline that makes up one part of a liberal arts education. Most of all, it is a subject that will repay many times over in excitement and intellectual satisfaction the effort that is put into understanding it.

SUGGESTED READINGS

The American Sociologist. Published since 1965 by the American Sociological Association, this journal features articles and comments on the profession of sociology. The association also published *Footnotes,* a monthly newsletter that keeps members abreast of current events in the discipline.

Careers in Sociology (Washington, D.C.: American Sociological Association, 1977). This useful booklet provides a good look at the various sorts of jobs held by professional sociologists and also some detailed advice about how to enter the profession.

Gouldner, Alvin W., *The Coming Crisis of Western Sociology* (New York: Basic Books, 1970). Gouldner writes from an explicitly ideological viewpoint, criticizing sociology's "conservatism" and supporting his analysis with a sparkling display of scholarship.

Sills, David L., ed., *International Encyclopedia of the Social Sciences* (New York: Macmillan and Free Press, 1968). These seventeen massive volumes, excellently cross-indexed, provide authoritative coverage of nearly everything one could want to know about sociology and the other social sciences.

Mills, C. Wright, *The Sociological Imagination* (New York: Oxford University Press, 1959). Mills was something of a maverick in his day, but this book is more and more recognized today as a trenchant criticism of the discipline. The concluding essay, "On Intellectual Craftsmanship," is especially valuable to anyone planning a career in academia.

Parsons, Talcott, ed., *American Sociology: Problems, Perspectives, Methods* (New York: Basic Books, 1968). A collection of twenty-four short, nontechnical articles originally prepared for a series of overseas broadcasts by the Voice of America, this book offers a quick overview of many of the major sociological specialties.

Reynolds, Larry T., and Janice M. Reynolds, *The Sociology of Sociology* (New York: McKay, 1970). Since sociologists are themselves a group, it is no wonder that they have turned their analytical skills on themselves. This book contains twenty-two articles, often critical, about the structure of the discipline and its future.

Glossary

Conflict theory The perspective within sociology that views competition for the scarce necessities of life—wealth, power, and prestige—as the central fact of social life. (See Appendix 2 for further discussion.)

Determinism The assumption that all behavior is caused by external forces, even though they cannot always be pinpointed, so that the sense of being in command of one's own actions is a delusion.

Dysfunction The consequences of a pattern of social relationships which, if it is continued, are thought to be ultimately harmful to the continued existence of the society in which it occurs. Any particular pattern, of course, can have both harmful and beneficial consequences (see **Function** below).

Free will The assumption that human beings are free to choose how they will behave at any given time, thus denying that their actions are caused by external forces.

Function The consequences of a pattern of social relationships that are thought to be ultimately beneficial for the continued existence of the society in which they occur (see **Dysfunction** above).

Functionalism The perspective within sociology that views society as a system of interrelated parts whose continued existence depends on the contributions of those parts (their "functions") to the system. (See Appendix 2 for further discussion.)

Knowledge, academic A body of information whose parts—facts, ideas, interpretations, formulas, etc.—are recorded and systematically related to one another. No body of academic knowledge is ever fully complete or free of all internal inconsistencies, but all of them develop in the direction of greater completeness and consistency.

Reductionism The assumption that a phenomenon can be most effectively understood by studying the characteristics of its component parts. This strategy has proved effective in the physical and biological sciences, but its value for the social sciences is questionable.

Social fact A statement describing some aspect of a human group directly, such as its suicide rate or its form of political organization, that can be explained only by relating it to other social facts. Emile Durkheim coined the term in 1895.

Society The most nearly self-sufficient type of human group, a society is made up of many smaller and overlapping groups that exhibit some overall unified identity.

This identity may be based on the use of a common language, the occupancy of a particular territory, allegiance to a specific political system, or a combination of these and other things. There are many cases, however, in which such an identity is perceived more by outsiders than by those who are supposed to be members of a society.

Sociology The systematic study of human groups and societies as natural phenomena. Their reality thus lies in the social relationships *among* people rather than in people's behavior as separate individuals.

Symbolic interactionism The perspective within sociology that emphasizes the importance of human communication, both as it makes social relationships possible and as our "picture of reality" (our symbols) influence these relationships. (See Appendix 2 for further discussion.)

2
Basic Sociological Concepts

SOCIAL RELATIONSHIP

Sociology is the study of societies and of the groups that make up societies. Yet we cannot "see" groups directly. All we can see are the concrete individuals whose repeated relationships with one another enable us to identify them as participating in groups. A group, then, consists of people behaving in relation to one another. These **social relationships**—*the patterns of interaction among individuals*—lie at the heart of sociology's subject matter.

To speak of a relation is to speak of a connection between two or more things that allows us to say something about both of them in a single sentence (Harry loves Jill; I asked him a question; She called the meeting to order; The professor will grade our exams; Max will vote for Debbie). These are all statements about social relationships.

But unique, concrete relationships, such as "Harry loves Jill," are not the sociologist's major concern. Instead, it is the *type,* or *form,* of relationship that is the central interest, for these occur again and again and form the basis for generalizations about human groups.

The sociological concepts introduced in this chapter are important because together they provide a generalized language for talking about social relationships. Just as *intersect, right angle, parallel,* and *congruent* are generalized words used in talking about geometrical figures, each being defined directly or indirectly in terms of the others, so the words or concepts introduced here are necessary if we are going to talk clearly about the social relationships that are the essence of human groups.

THE SOCIOLOGICAL VOCABULARY

Students studying biology for the first time may have difficulty *remembering* new terms and their meanings, but at least they are spared the *confusion* that would arise if they had previously used these terms in other ways or had used different words to mean the same things. Few of the students have had reason to use the terms *gene, mitosis, DNA,* and *phylum* in everyday conversation or to use familiar words to mean the same things.

When students study social sciences, however, two particular difficulties may appear. One is that these sciences tend to use familiar terms more precisely than most people are used to. The word *crowd,* for instance, is not used very precisely in ordinary conversation, but the sociologist whose special interest is in collective behavior (see Chapter 17) will use the word to identify something that differs in specific ways from a group, a public, and an aggregation. Naturally, students who are used to talking generally about "my crowd" or "the crowd in the bus station" will find it confusing and perhaps frustrating to learn that this word may not be used so freely in a sociology exam.

The second difficulty can arise when students feel that they are being asked to learn new terms for things that they have been perfectly familiar with under different names. After all, they have got along pretty well in society so far with the language they already know, and sometimes it seems a bit pseudo-sophisticated to have to use new words for no obvious reason. It complicates things unnecessarily to have to talk about not only people's feelings, but also their norms, values, attitudes, and orientations. Or, conversely, it oversimplifies things too much to discuss "institutionalized patterns of deviance" as a single topic when the term obviously covers so many different types of behavior. Sociological concepts sometimes create differences that seem to make no difference, and sometimes they lump things together that seem too different to have anything important in common.

Yet the proof of the pudding is in the eating, and the utility of a set of concepts can be evaluated only after they have been established and then put to the task of analyzing and explaining the phenomena to which they refer. This chapter lays out the basic set of concepts around which most of sociology is organized. We also present some illustrations intended to clarify the concepts and to indicate their potential usefulness in taking a fresh look at society.

Interaction

Ms. Martian Sociologist, equipped with a hyperfragilistic invisibility shield, would begin the job of learning about the inhabitants of Earth by observing them. Even without knowing their language, she could learn a good deal simply by watching and taking notes on what they do. Let us see how she might go about this.

Let's assume that she selects Mr. Earthly Male at random and follows him through the day. Early in the morning her subject can be found in a dwelling—a small building separated from similar buildings by patches of crabgrass and dandelions—together with two other creatures. One is about his size but wears a different sort of garment, and the other is markedly smaller. The first is probably his mate; the second, their offspring.

Our Martian friend observes that although there is a lot of talk among these three creatures, the subject behaves differently toward the other two. For instance, just before he leaves, he kisses the other big one, but only pats the head of the smaller one.

Then the male leaves the dwelling and climbs into a large vehicle with many windows. Without saying anything he hands a piece of green paper to the operator of the vehicle, who in turn hands him several round pieces of metal and allows him to sit down.

Still later, the man leaves the vehicle and goes into a large building where there are many other people. He ignores most of them—and they ignore him—but with a few of them he engages in different sorts of behavior: nodding to one, giving directions to another, and listening respectfully to a third. Finally, he goes into a small room and sits behind a desk.

What has our Martian sociologist learned so far? For one thing, she has noticed that her subject's actions are interwoven with those of others. The man pays attention to what some other people do and makes his behavior "mesh" with theirs, but his behavior seems to bear no relationship at all to what certain other people do (even though for brief periods he is physically close to them).

Certain other people, in turn, seem to know how to respond to what he has just done or said. His goodbye kiss with his mate went smoothly; each person knew what to do in that situation. Even without the use of words, he knew what to do in relation to the busdriver, and the driver seemed to respond appropriately to his behavior. At his office, he and several other people did different things in relation to each other, but in each case the actions of both parties fitted smoothly together.

When any two people were behaving in relation to each other, their actions were *inter*dependent. This interdependence, in fact, seemed to be the essence of these people's behavior: being aware of and responding to each other's actions. This is why people's behavior in groups is called *inter*action.

This statement is so simple that it seems almost unnecessary to mention it, and yet it is important that we be explicitly aware of this basic fact of social life. Interdependence, for instance, requires that each party understand the other, in terms of what each one means by his or her language and gestures and in terms of what each one understands to be appropriate to the occasion.

Spotting this as the most important thing she has observed so far, the visiting sociologist has developed her first concept—that of *interaction*. She (and we) can define **interaction** as *the purposeful, reciprocal influencing of two or more people by each other;* it is generally carried out through the use of symbols rather than physical contact.

The concept of interaction takes a great deal for granted. We have tried here to examine some of the prior assumptions involved so that it can become not only meaningful for us, but also suggestive of further questions.

The problem of shared meanings will be treated in Chapter 3, on culture; for now, we must consider what it is that produces different types of interaction. Why is it, for example, that the person our Martian sociologist was observing kissed one person but not another, gave money to one but not another, and obeyed one person's orders but not another's?

Social Status

Let us assume that Ms. Martian Sociologist spends a month observing different earthlings. As soon as she looks over her notes, she begins to see that there is a good deal of similarity in what different people do when they are in similar situations. This seems to be the case regardless of physical appearance or the personal habits that show up when these individuals are alone. Most of them kiss their spouses goodbye in the morning, give money to the busdriver or the conductor on the train, and follow the suggestions of one or more people where they work.

She has discovered, in short, that she can predict different types of behavior—of interaction—better by knowing something about the nature of the situation (where, when, and who else is involved) than she can by knowing something about the individual's psychological makeup. She has found that the young and the old, the grouchy and the friendly, all go through roughly the same patterns of interaction when they are saying goodbye at home in the morning, buying a newspaper, answering the telephone, being introduced to a stranger, and so on. To be sure, there are subtle differences in how they do these things, but these would become apparent only after the observer had become quite familiar with the general pattern in each case.

(Rather than wait for her to become completely familiar with our earthly customs, we can assume at this point that our Martian has served her didactic purposes and can be sent home. From here on, we're by ourselves again.)

Next comes the question of how it is that a person knows *how* to interact with a particular person. What is it about the other person that tells him or her what to do and what the other person is likely to do?

It turns out that people use a number of different clues to tell them what sort of behavior is appropriate—what the other person, and still others as well, will welcome or at least tolerate as behavior on their part. The sex of the other person, the particular situation they are in, the time of day, the other person's clothing—all these provide a good deal of guidance in the matter.

We often make judgments about what people are like and how to interact with them on the basis of visual clues such as clothing, mannerisms, and sex. Here Queen Elizabeth encounters a Bunny Girl on Derby Day at Epsom Downs. (Wide World Photos)

For instance, one assumes that the person standing behind the counter in a bakery during the daytime and wearing a white garment, whether male or female, is a salesclerk. On the basis of these three clues alone, one has a pretty good idea of what to expect of this person and what he or she expects in return. This person is there to take the customer's money and to see that the customer is satisfied. There will be little difficulty for either party in carrying out an efficient and satisfactory pattern of interaction here.

Similarly, the person in the blue uniform, standing at the intersection, is undoubtedly a police officer. You know what to expect of the officer and what he or she expects of you. Place and clothing have given you all of the information you need.

It should be noted that we have summed up this information by giving the person in question a name: *salesclerk, police officer.* But there are many occasions when observable clues will not be enough to tell us how to interact with someone. So we must ask what to expect, and we do this by asking the name of the person's social position rather than his personal name. When a stranger knocks on our door, we ask "Who is it?" but we mean "What is your social position?" rather than "What is your name?"

The stranger knows what we mean by "Who is it?" and will answer, "Meter reader," "Police officer," or "Special delivery." It would foolish for someone to reply, "My name is William Jones," for this would not be appropriate; it would tell us nothing about what to expect of this person or what he or she expects of us. Sometimes the person must even make up a position, as in the answer "I'm a stranger; my car has broken down in front of your house."

In each of these cases, once we have figured out or been told what social position the other person is occupying, we know generally how to interact with him or her. This is our second central concept—the idea of social position. One way to distinguish between the psychologist and the sociologist is that the latter is interested in the individual primarily *as he or she occupies a social position.* It was noted earlier that Mr. Earthly Male changed his ways of interacting with others as he moved from the home to the bus to the office, and we can say now that he changed from one status to another as he entered each new situation. At first he was a husband (and also a father), then he was a passenger (a particular type of customer), and finally he assumed the social position, or status, of employee.

A **status**, then, is actually the name of a social position; it *identifies a bundle of rights and obligations that go together and are more or less assigned to anyone who occupies that position.* Most of us have had the uncomfortable experience of being thrust into a new status whose rights and obligations we are unsure of, for we have worried about whether we could carry off the performance expected of us by others. Presiding over a committee meeting for the first time, giving a speech before a class, starting on one's first job—remembering any of these experiences reminds us of the distinction between individual and status and of our awareness that different statuses entail different sets of rights and obligations.

It should be noted that there is likely to be confusion between the idea of status as *social position* and the more common use of the word "status" to indicate *relative prestige.* It is perfectly possible to talk about someone's holding a "high" status, meaning that he or she somehow deserves more respect than someone in a "low" status, but we cannot talk about someone's having "more" status than anyone else. *Governor* Julio Perez occupies a status, just as *pharmacist* Julio Perez does, but neither has any *more* status than the other. The ideas of status and of "social honor," then, should be kept separate.

Two further aspects of status should be noted here. One is the degree to which a status is formalized, or to which its associated rights and obligations are precisely stated. The status of bank president, for instance, is governed by a number of federal and state laws, as well as by the bank's charter and bylaws, and so a person's behavior while occupying this status is determined to a substantial extent by fairly clear-cut rules. On the other hand, the informal status of "class clown" is extremely vague; no one can point to a widely accepted set of rules that should govern someone in this status, nor is it clear exactly how someone comes to occupy it or when he or she has left it to occupy another status.

As a rule of thumb, we might say that the more formalized a status is, the easier it is to determine who is occupying it and when and to recognize a situation when it is vacant. This is because more precise rights and obligations link a status more closely to other, related statuses, and their occupants will be clearly aware of it when this status is unoccupied.

This brings us to the second aspect of status—how people come to occupy statuses in the first place. Sometimes it is a matter of choice. A person may choose whether he or she wants to get married, so it is a matter of individual decision whether that person comes to occupy the status of husband or wife. Occupational statuses, providing that the individual is capable of carrying out the activities associated with them, are also matters of choice.

Other statuses, however, are not a matter of choice. People cannot choose whether to be born female or male, black or white, or in 1920 or 1960, but regardless of personal preference, they do occupy sex, racial or ethnic, and age statuses.

To speak of an **achieved status** is to *indicate that the person has a choice about whether or not to occupy that status.* An **ascribed status,** on the other hand, *is one in which the person has no choice in the matter.* In the latter case, the status is in effect *assigned* to the individual by others: "You're a male"; "You're an old woman"; "You are a white person."

But the distinction between achieved and ascribed statuses is not really this simple. Some statuses, even if ascribed at birth, can be changed. One can lie about one's age, may be able to "pass" as a member of a different racial or ethnic group, and even have a sex-change operation. On the other hand, some achieved statuses later become ascribed to the person: an Olympic champion, for example, may have difficulty shedding that status even when he or she would prefer not to have strangers seeking autographs all the time. The status of "prison convict" (presumably an achieved status because one chose to commit a crime) will follow someone long after his or her debt to society has been paid in full.

The importance of the distinction between achieved and ascribed statuses, despite these definitional problems, lies in the individual's attitude toward the rights and obligations that go with each. An achieved status is usually sought because the person expects to find some satisfaction in assuming the rights and obligations associated with it. The rights and obligations assigned to an ascribed status, however, may be distinctly unpleasant, although this is by no means true in all cases. (Chapter 4, on socialization, discusses how most of us come to accept and enjoy most of our ascribed statuses.) After a consideration of the relationship between status and group, we will go on to examine the nature of the rules (norms) that define the rights and obligations that are associated with different statuses.

Particularly in an achievement-oriented society like our own, however, ascribed statuses are increasingly defined as conferring either unfair advantages or unfair disadvantages on their occupants and thus as contradicting the ideals of equal opportunity and human rights. The implications of ascribed statuses are taken up in more detail in Chapter 5, on changing sex roles; Chapter 6, on social stratification; and Chapter 7, on intergroup relations.

Group

If people did not interact with one another regularly according to a relatively stable set of rules (whether or not they were conscious of them), there could be no sociology. There could be no patterns of social interaction and thus no groups and no societies. There would be only isolated individuals.

The word *group* may refer to a number of things. It sometimes indicates a set of objects or people assembled in one place—e.g., a group of china teacups, a group of lakes, or a group of spectators. It can indicate a category, all of whose members share one or more characteristics—the "group" of all professional soccer players or of all carnivorous mammals. In sociology, however, the term is given a more specific definition.

For the sociologist, a **group** *is a set of people occupying interrelated statuses.* Even more fundamentally, it is the interrelated statuses themselves. An example of the validity of this latter point is that we recognize a group's existence even when its component statuses are unoccupied at a particular time. The statuses that make up a bowling league team, for example, are unoccupied during most of the week, yet we recognize the team as a group. A particular family remains a group even when the father is on a business trip, the mother is attending a convention, and the children are away at college. And a baseball team retains its identity during the winter, when most of the members have scattered to their home towns and the rest are playing ball in Puerto Rico or Venezuela.

A group's existence, then, lies in the statuses that are its parts and in the existence of people who are ready to occupy those statuses at particular times. In some instances, specific individuals are almost equated with their statuses in certain groups. A family is an excellent example. To its members, a family would not be the same group if the father died and were replaced by a step-father, even though they would build their relationships with the new member largely in accord with the same rules that governed their interactions with the original father.

A baseball team affords a much better example of the distinction between the statuses that make up a group and the individuals who occupy them. The team retains its identity even after there has been a complete turnover in players, because there is always someone to occupy each of the statuses of which it is composed. The meaningless trivia often provided by baseball announcers ("Lifetime, Smithers has 21 wins and 11 losses against the Braves") are useless as far as predicting Smithers's future performance against the Braves is concerned; he has pitched against many different batters in compiling that record, but is unlikely to face more than one or two of them at most when he goes against them tomorrow. Here, clearly, the team is *its statuses* rather than its individual players.

The distinction between formal and informal statuses helps us to understand the difference between formal and informal groups. A formal group usually consists of a number of clearly defined statuses, all of which must be occupied if the group is to carry out its activities most effectively. An informal group, on the other hand, is much looser in terms of both specific statuses and their rights and obligations in relation to one another. In this sense, the statuses that make up a friendship group are barely more than the personal identities of its members, even though the individuals do develop relationships with one another that are roughly comparable to those that exist among different statuses in more formal groups.

In looking at the relationship between *status* and an individual *status occupant*, we should remark that the idea of "personality" is in one way much like that of status, in that it sums up a bundle of expectations about a person. We have an idea, for example, of what we can expect of someone with an aggressive personality, regardless of the status she or he may be occupying. But a given personality is not related by particular rules to other types of personalities, nor does the individual necessarily change his or her personality each time a new status is occupied. Personality is, instead, subordinate to status. It is attached to the individual and goes with him or her from one status to the next. Although personality may provide clues as to the *style* of behavior an individual will exhibit while occupying a particular status and may even tell us something about which statuses he or she would *prefer* to occupy, it will not add very much to our ability to predict the *kinds* of behavior he or she will engage in while occupying a particular status. Both the aggressive and the shy salesperson will wait on customers; both the optimistic and the pessimistic political candidate will run for office; and both the trusting and the suspicious patron in a restaurant will use the same table manners.

How do we distinguish one group from another? Primarily, the boundaries between groups are drawn on the basis of which statuses are related to which other statuses. People occupying statuses in one group have rights and obligations to one another that they do not have in relation to people occupying statuses in other groups. A woman, for instance, does not ordinarily have the right to spank a neighbor's child; a man does not usually expect a stranger to loan him money in time of need the way his brother ought to; and a student at one high school should not cheer for another school's team the way he or she should cheer for the local team.

Different groups, of course, have different sets of rights and obligations among their members. The important thing, whether these relationships are based entirely on statuses (a baseball team) or on the identities of specific individuals (a friendship group), is that "groupness" itself exists because of the readiness of people to interact with one another in certain ways that are not characteristic of their interactions with other people.

Norms

So far we have introduced three important concepts. First, there is the idea of *interaction*—people responding to one another in sequence, presumably with the aim of achieving something, whether the giving and receiving of expressions of friendship, buying something, asking directions, or planning a meeting.

Second is the concept of *status*, the name of a social position whose occupant is ready to engage in certain types of interaction with those occupying certain other statuses. Someone who claims to occupy a particular status ("I'm the coach here") or is in a situation that seems to define him or her as occupying one (the stranger who enters a store during business hours is assumed to be a potential customer) is, presumably, ready to undertake the set of rights and obligations that are ordinarily associated with that status. And those rights and obligations, within broad limits, pertain to anyone who is occupying the status, so that they are attached to a social position rather than to a specific individual. (The fact that different individuals may vary in how faithfully they live up to these rights and obligations or in how skillfully they do what they are expected to do is an aspect of status that we will discuss later under the heading of "role.")

Finally, we introduced the idea of *group*, which we defined as people who occupy a set of statuses, formal or informal, among which a distinctive set of relationships exists. The basic thing about a group is that its members carry these particular expectations about one another around in their heads. However, a group is not simply a number of people who happen to interact with one another. Thus two warring gangs of juvenile delinquents do not constitute a single group. Rather, one of the particular aspects of belonging to a group is that one has an idea of how to interact with outsiders.

But these three concepts leave us with two fairly obvious questions. What are the rules that set forth the rights and obligations associated with a status? How does a person move from one status to another?

Since any one status may be occupied by many people, the rights and obligations associated with it must be somewhat vague, so that there is room for individual variation. The rights and obligations give the broad outlines of what the status occupant may and may not do and of what he or she can expect from others, but they cannot be too detailed. For instance, someone occupying the status of pitcher on a professional baseball team knows generally what he is to do most of the time, but his obligations do not specify precisely how he should deliver his pitches or how much effort he should make to stop a line drive through the box. There is opportunity, in other words, for him to behave somewhat differently from another pitcher, even though both of them are governed by the general rules that pertain to the status of pitcher.

These rules are called *norms*, and behavior that is generally in accord with them is called *normative behavior.* We can think of **norms** as *shared expectations of what a person ought, may, and ought not to do while occupying a particular status*—expectations held by most other people and usually also by the person occupying that status. In the traditional American family of the past, for instance, there was widespread agreement that the mother ought to prepare the family dinner. This was an obligation that went with the status of "mother." While she was engaged in cooking dinner, then, she was engaging in normative behavior; if she neglected this obligation, she was violating one of the norms pertaining to her status.

It is true, of course, that the norms governing a particular status can change over time, so that we cannot think of specific norms as eternally attached to particular statuses. The normative obligations of mothers are certainly changing today, and Chapter 5 examines this process as part of the broader topic of changing sex roles.

If we think of norms as rules, we can treat them as though they are written down as laws—and indeed, sometimes they are. Although Congress has not passed a law specifically describing the normative obligations of mothers, it has passed laws defining what an ambassador should and should not do and what the recipient of a research grant from the National Science Foundation may and may not do with the money. Not all laws embody norms, however, in the sense that they express most people's ideas about proper behavior. The laws that require us to pay income taxes and that prohibit us from parking in certain places are certainly not reflections of what most of us fervently believe others should do. But norms and laws are similar in that they concern the rights and obligations of people as they occupy social statuses.

Norms may be classified in a number of ways. We may ask how many people a particular norm applies to (better, how many statuses it applies to) and can see that a basic norm such as "Be polite to strangers" applies to nearly everyone, or to nearly all statuses. On the other hand, a norm such as "Try to strike out the batter" applies only to baseball pitchers; it is much more limited in its application.

Another means of classifying norms is to ask how many people are aware of them. Some norms such as "Wash your hands before eating," are very widely known; others, such as "The pitcher should cover home plate if the catcher has to chase a wild pitch when there is a runner at third base," are known to relatively few people.

Still another way to classify norms is to determine the amount of importance that is attached to them. If some norms are violated, the response from other people can be quite severe, as when someone violates the norm "Thou shalt not kill." In other cases, such as "A gentleman should rise when a lady enters the room," very few people are seriously upset if the norm is violated.

Finally, there is the matter of whether a norm encourages or discourages a specific type of behavior and how firmly. Here we have what might be called "the four Ps"—norms that *prescribe, prefer, permit,* or *proscribe* particular sorts of behavior.

For example, a parent *should* take care of a sick child. This is *prescribed* behavior, and few exceptions to it are made. Second, there is preferred behavior: It is *preferred* that a parent keep the children clean and well dressed. (Note that not quite the same amount of moral obligation is involved here.) Third, there is *permitted* behavior: A parent *may* let the children stay up late on a school night to watch a particular television show. Finally, there is *proscribed* behavior, the things that a person should not do at all. A parent *should not* let the children play with a loaded gun or beat them with a whip. Here, as with prescribed behavior, it would take an unusually good excuse to enable a parent to escape responsibility for living up to the norm.

A convenient way to distinguish between relatively "weak" norms (those whose violation elicits little or no punitive response) and relatively "strong" norms (whose violation calls forth severe sanctions) is the use of the terms *folkways* and *mores.* These words, first used by William Graham Sumner around the turn of the century, are still popular today. Folkways, for instance, would be norms governing the proper use of silverware at meals, and mores would be norms such as the prohibition of murder.

The point of this discussion is to demonstrate that we can think of norms objectively. We can analyze the rights and obligations that pertain to different statuses and in this way begin to develop some systematic understanding of social relationships. Although the concept of norms will not be used explicitly in the following chapters, it underlies much of the material in the same way that the concept of addition underlies all advanced courses in accounting; norms are a fundamental part of sociological analysis.

The question of the relationship between norms and *real* behavior is, however, of further concern to us. Some people, for instance, may choose not

Definitions of acceptable and unacceptable behavior vary from society to society. Participants in the *Sioux Sun Dance*, depicted below, were pulled into the air to worship the sun, by means of a rope hooked into the muscles of the chest wall. To the Indians this ritual was beautiful and holy, but it shocked the early missionaries who witnessed it. (Painting by Oscar Howe, Philbrook Art Center, Tulsa, Oklahoma)

A folkway is a weakly enforced norm, such as the proper serving of a meal and the placement and use of silverware at the table. (Ellis Herwig/Stock, Boston)

to obey the norms that pertain to the statuses they occupy, and others may not be able to live up to them on all occasions. Normative behavior, in other words, can be thought of as ideal behavior, or as a set of standards that people may or may not live up to at all times. We will have more to say along this line later.

Role

Taken together, the norms that govern the occupant of a particular status when he or she is interacting with someone in a related status are said to define that person's *role*. If *status* is the name of the social position, **role** is the word we use to indicate *what the occupant of a given status should do while in that position.* The distinction between the two terms is not always very clear, and some sociologists either speak of "status-role" as though it were a single idea or use the term "role" to mean both the position and the activities that are associated with it. For our purposes, though, it seems better to distinguish between the static aspects of social behavior (status) and the dynamic aspects (role).

We are all familiar with the idea of role as it is used in the theater. An actor plays a role, and the sociologist uses the term to mean essentially the same thing. Just as an actor may speak of "the role of Hamlet," so a sociologist may speak of "the role of the husband" or "the role of the baseball pitcher."

And just as an actor can play Hamlet or Ophelia well or poorly, so an individual can play his or her real-life roles well or poorly. One can be a good pitcher or a poor one, a good mayor or a bad one, an effective teacher or an ineffective one. What someone actually does while occupying a status is called that person's *role performance.* This distinction between role and role performance, or between normative expectations and actual behavior, is quite important. It allows us to be aware of the relationship between the two and thus to see that the rules by which people try to guide their behavior are not simply descriptions of what really happens. Instead, norms represent standards that people try to live up to (or at least think that others ought to live up to), and because they are real in that they influence people's behavior, the sociologist must think of them as though they they exist in the real world, just as houses and trees do.

PUTTING THE CONCEPTS TOGETHER

Throughout this chapter we have emphasized the distinction between real human beings on the one hand and social statuses on the other. Yet statuses would be meaningless if there were not people to occupy them occasionally (that is, to interact with others in accordance with the norms governing those statuses). It is important, therefore, to look systematically at the relationships between individuals and statuses.

Status Set

Earlier, a few references were made to "moving from one status to another." This suggests that people may occupy many statuses during a given span of time. At the same time, it is clear that no one can occupy, over any period of time, *all* of the statuses that are recognized in a society. So we must seek a way to describe all of the statuses that *are* open for occupancy by a particular individual.

Status set is a convenient name for *all of the statuses a particular person can occupy legitimately* (that is, with other people's approval). Our Martian sociologist observed at least four or five different statuses that her subject occupied—husband, father, passenger, employee, and supervisor—and we can easily name more: voter, taxpayer, neighbor, pedestrian, musician, college graduate, and so on. All of these statuses, plus a good many more, make up that particular person's status set for the present. If we were to consider all those he could occupy throughout his lifetime, it would naturally include many more: infant, kindergartner, sick person, senior citizen, etc.

It is interesting that most of these statuses could also be occupied by his wife, since fewer and fewer statuses are restricted to one sex or the other these days. Yet there are certain constraints on the makeup of every individual's status set, and because statuses exist only in relation to other statuses, most of these constraints are based on the "mutual exclusivity" of certain complementary statuses.

If a certain status is included in one's status set, this means that certain other statuses cannot be part of it. Sometimes this is because a person simply cannot be in two places at the same time. A person who attends a Methodist church service at 11:00 on a Sunday morning cannot also participate in a Baptist service at that time. If one holds a full-time 9:00–5:00 job with an insurance company, he or she cannot also be a full-time daytime employee of a construction company.

Certain statuses, too, are mutually exclusive because they involve differences within ascriptive categories. One cannot be both male and female, Greek and Chinese, or a teenager and a senior citizen. In other words, a person can occupy only one status in terms of sex, ethnicity, or age group.

A third constraint involves conflicts of interest. A judge will ordinarily refuse to be involved in an accused relative's court proceeding. A purchasing officer for a corporation should not also be a stockholder in a company that is bidding on a contract, for he or she might be influenced by personal financial considerations rather than by the quality of that company's product. Even if it would be to the person's advantage to include both statuses (judge and family member, or buyer and seller) in his or her status set, others would object.

Finally, there is the question or how much discrepancy there is between the apparent goals of two different statuses. An avowed pacifist, for instance, would hardly want to hold a position with a company that manufactures bombs, and a vegetarian would find it stressful to be employed as a butcher. These limitations are generally self-imposed, however, for they have to do with the individual's sense of internal consistency in life rather than with any restrictions imposed by others.

Status Conflict

Still, it occasionally happens that a person experiences **status conflict**—*is caught between two statuses,* perhaps being personally uncertain as to which of them he or she should be occupying or perhaps being pressured by one person to occupy one status and another person to occupy the other. An example of the former type of status conflict can be found in the familiar movie plot in which a young police officer catches a childhood chum in the act of robbing a store: Should the officer define himself as occupying the status of "friend" and let the thief go, or must he continue to occupy the status of "police officer" and arrest his old pal?

Even more unpleasant is the latter type of status conflict. If a young woman's boyfriend wants her to go to a midnight concert with him, but her parents want her home at midnight, which obligation—or which status to which the obligation is attached—should take precedence? In both cases the individual suffering the status conflict seems to be in a no-win situation. To choose to occupy either status is to disappoint those who want one to occupy the other, or at least to feel some uncertainty about the wisdom of one's decision.

Because status conflict is unpleasant for everyone concerned, people try to avoid it whenever possible. We will conclude this section, then, with a brief review of the various strategies people have developed to avoid or to resolve status conflict.

Handling status conflict   First of all, we are usually able to prevent such problems by segregating in time and/or space those situations in which two potentially conflicting statuses are ordinarily occupied by the same person. Two high school teachers may find it difficult to act as close friends when they are in the presence of their students, but in the teachers' lounge they can occupy these other statuses without conflict. The man who says gruffly to his wife on the telephone, "I *told* you not to call me at the office, dear!" is trying to keep his occupational and family statuses entirely separate. Those who support state "blue laws" are trying to make sure that it is not possible for others to choose between the statuses of "shopper" and "churchgoer" on Sunday mornings.

When status conflict cannot be avoided, there are three ways in which it can be resolved. First, those involved can refer to shared values which make one of the statuses more important than the other: "Look, I [or you] took an oath that I [you] would enforce the law." Or, they can cite those aspects of the immediate situation that make one status more appropriate than the other: "You're supposed to be working here, aren't you? So how about a little service instead of spending all day on the phone with your girlfriend?"

Second, power can be used to resolve the conflict. Whether this is simply greater physical strength or the force of numbers, in the absence of clear-cut values or situational factors that can help decide which status should be occupied, power can be used. "No, you *can't* be the leader of this gang; my friends and I won't let you!" Even more bluntly, an unwilling citizen can be forced to occupy the status of holdup victim: "Hand over your money, Mac, or this gun might go off!"

But the use of naked force in social relationships is relatively rare; therefore, an appeal to values or to situational cues is most often the method used to resolve status conflicts. There is, however, a third way out of the dilemma: the person experiencing conflict can withdraw, or "resign," from one status or the other. A person can resign from a job if its requirements conflict too severely with his or her family responsibilities, or an adolescent can run away from home (withdrawing from the parent-child relationship) if there is too much conflict between parents' and friends' demands.

Cases of status conflict are usually dramatic, sometimes poignant, and always uncomfortable for the person caught in one. Their being dramatic, however, is partly a result of their being relatively rare—which is testimony to the ingenuity human beings have shown in working out their social structures so that such situations do not happen more often.

Role Set

Not only does everyone have a status set, but it should be clear that each of these statuses involves several relationships with other related statuses. For example, the rights and obligations of "son" (that is, the son's role) in relation to "father" differ somewhat from those in relation to "mother." A "professor" has different role relationships with a "student," a "colleague," and a "dean," respectively. The role a priest plays in relation to a parishioner is different from the priest's role in relation to a bishop. Almost always, then, more than one role is attached to a single status.

The **role set** of a status consists of *all of the roles that one can play while occupying a particular status.* Each individual thus has a status set, and in turn each of these statuses has a role set. Each of these roles, finally, is outlined by a set of norms that guides the interaction between the occupants of two statuses. As in the case of statuses, however, things do not always run smoothly with role sets.

Role Strain

What happens, for instance, when a father faces conflicting demands from his wife and his son about what the family will do next weekend? What happens when a military doctor must decide which of two seriously wounded soldiers should be attended to first? What happens when a daughter must decide whether she will continue with her college studies, as her mother wishes, or get a job, as her father wishes? In none of these cases is there a problem of which *status* the individual is occupying. Rather, the problem is one of **role**

strain—*determining which of two or more roles he or she should play at the moment.*

To avoid confusion, we will call this situation role strain rather than role conflict. Role strain is ordinarily avoided or resolved through the same techniques that people use in situations of status conflict. One usually tries to separate potentially stressful role relationships in time and/or space, as when a lieutenant criticizes a sergeant behind closed doors rather than in front of the troops, or when a sex-education specialist schedules separate meetings with high school girls and boys rather than lecture to both groups at the same time.

If role strain cannot be resolved this way, the person suffering from it can bring the problem into the open and ask that those making the conflicting demands try to compromise their differing expectations so that both roles can be played without strain. Role strain is thus essentially the result of disagreement among people in related statuses about the relative importance of different roles attached to a single status, and its resolution is up to them rather than to the person experiencing the strain.

SUMMARY

This chapter has been devoted to laying out the central terms or concepts needed if we are to talk systematically about social relationships. Groups can exist only as people develop patterns of interaction among themselves, and these patterns must be based on shared expectations. These expectations— norms—are keyed to social statuses rather than to concrete individuals, and collectively they define the roles to be played by the occupant of a status. Because everyone occupies a number of statuses throughout the day, he or she can be said to have a status set. Each status, further, has a role relationship with several other statuses, so associated with each one is a role set.

When questions arise as to which status an individual should occupy at a given time, a condition of status conflict exists. If, on the other hand, a problem arises as to which of two or more roles one should play while occupying a particular status, it is called role strain.

Table 2.1 summarizes these concepts, and Fig. 2.1 shows how they are interrelated.

TABLE 2.1   THE BASIC CONCEPTS

Individual	Some statuses in status set	Related statuses	Relevant norms	Possible status conflict	Possible role strain
Debbie (wife of Charles, mother of Pat)	Writer	Critic/Editor	Write clearly, Receive royalties		Writer: write to please critic or editor?
	Wife/Mother	Husband/Child	Love husband, Guide child	Mother/Church member: attend services *or* stay home with sick child?	
	Church member	Minister/Usher	Attend services, Sit where directed		
Pat (child of of Debbie and Charles)	Playmate	Playmates	Share toys, Don't fight		
	Child	Mother/Father	Obey both, Get help with studies	Playmate/Student: study *or* go out to play?	Child: obey mother *or* father?
	Student	Teacher/Principal	Go to school, Do homework, Don't misbehave		
Charles (husband of Debbie, father of Pat)	Voter	Candidate/Party Leader	Vote in primaries and election		Voter: support party candidate *or* "best" candidate?
	Husband/Father	Wife/Child	Support both, Take out garbage	Husband/Employee: work late *or* go home to dinner?	
	Employee	Assistant/Boss	Give job training, Do job as ordered		

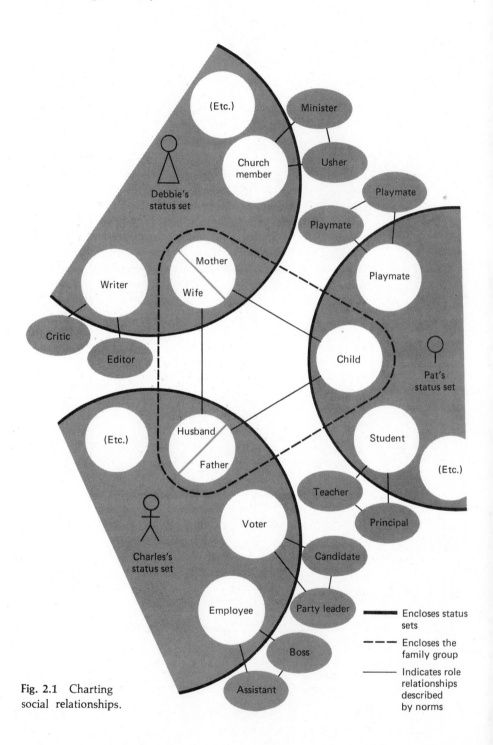

Fig. 2.1 Charting social relationships.

SUGGESTED READINGS

Goffman, Erving, *The Presentation of Self In Everyday Life* (New York: Anchor, 1959). One of the most sensitive and insightful analysts of social interaction, Goffman presents here many of the techniques that we use in fitting ourselves into different statuses and in avoiding both status conflict and role strain.

Hare, A. Paul, Robert F. Bales, and Edgar F. Borgatta, eds., *Small Groups,* rev. ed. (New York: Knopf, 1965). Although the field of small-groups research has become less popular in recent years, a substantial amount of research on the topic has been done. This collection of articles covers both research findings and theoretical interpretations of people's behavior in face-to-face groups.

Homans, George C., *The Human Group* (New York: Harcourt Brace Jovanovich, 1950). One of America's leading sociologists attempts here to develop a systematic set of propositions about the ways that groups are formed and maintained. His attempt is not fully successful, but it is stimulating and thoughtful.

Merton, Robert K., "Continuities in the Theory of Reference Groups and Social Structure," in his *Social Theory and Social Structure,* rev. ed. (New York: Free Press, 1957), pp. 281–386. Toward the end of the lengthy article, Merton finds it necessary to develop the concepts of status set and role set to expand our understanding of various problems in social relationships. This is a thorough exploration of the topic and written in the author's delightfully elegant style.

Sumner, William Graham, *Folkways* [1906] (Boston: Ginn, 3rd ed., 1960). This book by one of America's first great sociologists may seem a bit stiff by today's standards, but it is worth looking into for the insight it offers into earlier perspectives on norms.

Williams, Robin M., Jr., *American Society,* 3rd ed. (New York: Knopf, 1970). In establishing the conceptual background for this unsurpassed sociological analysis of our own society, Williams presents here a thorough discussion of the basic ideas necessary to describe any society.

Glossary

Achieved status A social position whose occupancy is (at least at one point) a matter of the individual's own choice. Occupational statuses are good examples. Once achieved, however, some of these statuses may take on the characteristics of ascribed statuses (see below).

Ascribed status A social position to which someone is assigned by others without regard for his or her wishes. Sex, age, and racial or ethnic statuses are prominent examples. If others insist on treating someone as movie star (an achieved status) even when he or she would rather be treated as, say, an ordinary shopper, the achieved status has temporarily become an ascribed status.

Folkway A relatively minor or unimportant norm (see **Norm,** below) whose violation does not elicit severe reactions from others. Introduced by William Graham Sumner in 1906, the term is vague but still in use. (See **Mores,** below.)

Group A set of people occupying interrelated statuses. The set's "groupness" lies in the relationships among these statuses rather than in the people as a collection of concrete individuals. To the extent that these statuses are formal (their roles [see **Role,** below] are explicitly defined) and their occupants can be replaced, as in a baseball team or garment factory, the group is basically composed of the statuses themselves. If the statuses are informal and their occupants cannot be duplicated by replacements, as in a friendship group, the individuals, in effect, *are* the statuses.

Interaction The purposeful, reciprocal influencing of two or more people by each other, usually carried out through the use of symbols rather than physical contact. When a particular series of such actions is repeated regularly, such as the actions involved in buying a newspaper from a newsdealer, it becomes a *pattern* of interaction and thus part of the social structure.

Mores Sumner's term for important norms or rules of behavior whose violations are treated by others as very serious acts that deserve severe punishment. (See **Folkway,** above.)

Norm A rule that in some way describes the way the occupant of a status should (or should not) behave in interacting with someone in a related status. It can be stated positively ("A private must obey a sergeant") or negatively ("A banker must not embezzle the depositors' money") and may be stated as something permitted or preferred rather than as strictly prescribed or proscribed ("Professors are allowed to wear beards"; "A motorist should blow the horn only in an emergency"). Taken together, the norms that describe the proper relationship between one status and another describe a "role" (see below). Behavior that conforms to these norms is called *normative behavior.*

Role All of the normatively appropriate behaviors one must, may, and must not engage in while interacting with someone in a related status. A role is thus an ideal that one is ordinarily expected to try to live up to; what one actually does in interaction is called one's *role performance,* and it can be judged in terms of how closely it approximates the ideal. It is possible, then, for someone to play a role (say, as a clerk in a bakery store) either well or poorly.

Role set All of the roles that one may play while occupying a particular status. Someone in the status of student, for instance, has one role in relation to the teacher, another in relation to the librarian, and a third in relation to a fellow student. Each role is governed by a separate set of norms, although there may be considerable overlap among them.

Role strain A situation in which the occupant of a status is uncertain as to which of two or more roles he or she should play at a given time. If a soldier is given one order by one sergeant and a conflicting order by another sergeant, for example, he or she experiences role strain.

Social relationship A pattern of interaction among two or more statuses, which can be viewed as the junction or two or more roles. The husband's and wife's roles in relation to each other make up a social relationship, as do the doctor's and patient's roles when they are interacting.

Status The name of a social position which connotes (reminds people of) the normative rights and obligations that should govern the behavior of anyone who occupies that position. The fact that the norms associated with a status can change (see Chapter 5, on changing sex roles) makes us aware that a status is more than simply the norms that govern its occupants. (It is true that the word "status" sometimes means "relative social honor," or "prestige," but except in discussing social stratification, we shall use it here to refer to any social position, regardless of its relative prestige.)

Status conflict A situation in which a person has difficulty deciding which of two or more statuses he or she should occupy at a particular time. The conflict is sensed primarily when the roles incumbent on each status call for contradictory behavior and when there is pressure from some people to occupy one of the statuses and from others to occupy the other status.

Status set All of the statuses that an individual can legitimately (that is, with others' approval) occupy during a given period of time such as a week or month.

3
Culture

FOCUS:

THE COORDINATION OF BEHAVIOR

Human beings are obviously separate physical entities who are self-directed and capable of independent behavior. It is equally apparent, however, that the members of society communicate with one another, predict one another's likes and dislikes, and anticipate others' responses to their own actions so that they can successfully coordinate their activities, or *interact*. There must be, then, some intangible linkage among human beings that makes this knowledge of one another (and thus interaction) possible.

There must be something that these individuals hold in common, even though it is not itself physical. Part of that something is a code—a shared method of translating symbols into meanings so that communication is possible. Part of it is a map—a shared picture of society and its setting in the world that provides a common orientation for everyone. And part of it is a set of values—a shared set of standards by which past, present, and future situations are evaluated in terms of their desirability. Further, people must be aware that all of these things *are* shared, for patterns of interaction could not develop if people did not have confidence that they could communicate and coordinate their activities with at least some effectiveness.

These invisible but shared codes, maps, and values are crucial to the development and continued existence of any society; without them, there could be little, if any, dependable coordination of behavior. Together, they make up *culture*, and it is impossible to understand society without an appreciation of the nature and characteristics of this unique and indispensable component of social life.

THE IDEA OF CULTURE

There are times when human beings cannot help recognizing the existence of something huge and complex, but quite invisible, that provides structure and meaning for their lives in society. A visitor to another society is struck not only by the fact that the people there speak and interact quite differently from the members of his or her own society, but that they all do these different things together, voluntarily, and think it entirely good and proper that they act in these ways. If it were not that they look like regular human beings, the visitor might be tempted to believe that they are members of an entirely different species. After all, pigs and horses are different species, and they certainly live different kinds of lives: Perhaps the differences among societies are biological in origin.

Indeed, throughout much of history, human beings have regarded the members of different societies as subhuman, if not altogether nonhuman. The names that most primitive human groups give themselves tend to be a variant of the idea of "the people"—implying that all other groups are not really "people" at all. **Ethnocentrism,** *the readiness to glorify one's own group—to make this group "the center"—at the expense of others,* is a basic characteristic of virtually every society.

But experience undermines the biological explanation of societal differences, even if it cannot persuade people that other societies' ways of life are as good as their own. A baby born in one society but raised in another will resemble in thought and behavior the members of the host society. And as one becomes more familiar with another society, one can find meaning and order that make it very much a *human* society, even though it differs from one's own. The differences, then, must be due to something other than biology, for they cannot be traced to anything that people have inherited genetically.

How, then, shall we talk about whatever this "thing" is that makes one society different from another? Even early in history, some people were apparently content to say simply that each society has a different "character," or *ethos* (from the Greek, meaning "moral custom") and to let it go at that. But as the social sciences developed and people became more curious about this "stuff"—its component parts, its organization, its origins and consequences—they began to call it *culture.*

This word, adopted from its earlier usage to refer to the content of what we would call highbrow sophistication, is from the Latin *cultus,* meaning "tilled" or "plowed." In its more general form, "culture" indicates anything grown or produced by society, and culture is certainly a product of human society, for it obviously cannot exist without society. Yet analyzing culture apart from the other aspects of society is extremely difficult, and the job has not yet been accomplished to everyone's satisfaction.

There is, for example, the problem of distinguishing between actual, observable behavior and the thoughts and ideas that apparently lie behind it. Do people interact in certain ways (say, taking part in a political campaign) because there is a blueprint in their heads that tells them how to do it, or is the behavior *itself* culture? Those who prefer the latter sort of perspective are likely to define culture as "the total way of life of a people" or as "learned patterns of behavior."

But if behavior is learned—passed on from one person to another in some nongenetic way—there must be something that is acquired by people and somehow stored so that it can be used again and again. Whether or not people are conscious of this process, incidentally, is irrelevant. So long as they do learn to prefer some foods and to avoid others, how to greet a stranger, how to ride a bicycle, and which goals are worth striving for, it is not important whether they are fully aware of how this has happened. The important thing is that something has been "put into their heads" by something other than genetic inheritance and that it thereafter influences their behavior.

The first formal definition of culture was given in 1871 by a British anthropologist, Edward B. Tylor, in his book *Primitive Culture*. He wrote: "Culture or civilization . . . is that complex whole which includes knowledge, belief, art, morals, law, custom, and other capabilities acquired by man as a member of society."

More recently, two leading anthropologists, Alfred L. Kroeber and Clyde Kluckhohn (1963, p. 357), defined culture in the following way:

> Culture consists of patterns, explicit and implicit, of and for behavior acquired and transmitted by people, constituting the distinctive achievement of human groups, including their embodiment in artifacts; the essential core of culture consists of traditional (i.e., historically derived and selected) ideas and especially their attached values; culture systems may, on the one hand, be considered as products of action, on the other as conditioning elements of further action.

If the former definition seems a bit vague and the latter too complex, our own definition of the concept shall be developed later on. First, however, we must take up two fundamental questions about the nature of culture: what it is composed of and what part it plays in society.

THE NATURE OF CULTURE

A society's culture, first of all, must be composed of many parts. Learned patterns of interaction between husband and wife and between buyer and seller are different, so culture cannot be simply an undifferentiated mass of *something*. If, further, these parts are intangible and yet can be transmitted (that is, taught and learned) and also stored, they must exist in some physical form.

This is not the place for a treatise on the neurophysiological basis of thought, but it may be sufficient to indicate that the physical foundations of thought are probably to be found in tiny, subtle differences in the synaptic connections among brain cells, which determine the pathways through which small electrical currents flow in our brains. If a different pathway means a different thought, "learning" consists of the process of making changes in these submicroscopic connections so that new pathways are created. Rather than go on with speculations about the biological bases of thought, however, we shall assume that the "units" of thought are symbols and thus that a large part of culture is made up of symbols.

Symbols

The most obvious example of a symbol is a word, either spoken or written. A **symbol** *is something that reminds us of something else*: an object, a feeling, an event, a quality, a relationship, an action; that something else is its *referent*. Yet there is no natural similarity or intrinsic relationship between a symbol and its referent. There is, for example, no physical connection between the sound "automobile" (or the series of printed marks on this page that remind you of the sound) and the four-wheeled machine that you drive around in.

There are other kinds of symbols besides words, of course. Gestures, sounds, objects, signs, and even colors can serve as symbols. But because words are our most important symbols, particularly when they are linked together to make language, we shall pay attention primarily to them.

Gestures, objects, and words are all symbols, or reminders of something else. This delegate to the 1976 Democratic convention wears on her head the symbol of that party—the donkey.
(H. Bureau/Sygma)

Having at our disposal a large number of different symbols, we can engage in *thinking*—that is, putting symbols together in different ways so that we create "pictures in our heads" of different things, even in the absence of the symbols' referents. We can recall and symbolize previous experiences (both our own and those we have learned from others), we can take parts of those experiences and put them together in new ways, and we can use them to arrive at conclusions: *"If* this and *if* that, then *thus."* Using symbols in this way, human beings become "time-binding animals," recalling the past in order to anticipate the future and using these pictures as a guide to behavior in the present.

But if symbols are to be useful in this way, they must have two important characteristics. First, we must be able to link them together into meaningful patterns—into sentences, if you wish. An isolated symbol is virtually worthless because its referent has no context; it floats in empty space and is incapable by itself of creating a complete picture that can lead to a conclusion or guide our behavior.

> last

Without being linked to other symbols,
this one is useless.

But how shall we fit our symbols together? Clearly we need rules, for without standards by which to decide which symbols may and may not be put next to each other, any and all sequences of symbols would be equally acceptable—and so none would be meaningful. This is not to say that such rules must be explicit. As a matter of fact, most of the rules we use to determine why one sentence makes sense and another is nonsense are unknown to us. It seems almost a matter of intuition that we know that a sentence such as "The hit boy ball the" means nothing, even though "The boy hit the ball" (or "The ball hit the boy," for that matter) is a perfectly acceptable sentence. Rather than go into linguistic theory here, we must be satisfied to know that we *do* have rules by which we organize our symbols to create "complete thoughts." These rules make up the syntax of a language.

Symbols also have a second important characteristic. Symbols must be reasonably accurate reminders of their referents. They cannot be so *inaccurate* that they continually mislead us. A swimmer for whom the symbol *shark* does not carry a reminder of "danger" could get into trouble; a student for whom the symbol *examination* does not carry a reminder of "study" and "grade" can also run into problems.

The rule-guided relationships among symbols are extremely important in helping us to detect inaccurate or misleading or false statements. Although people can and do tell lies, we can usually identify a lie sooner or later because in some way or other it does not "fit" with other statements that we know to be true. The logical inconsistency between the statements "Jimmy is hungry" and "Jimmy just ate two whole pizzas" alerts us to the fact that one or the other of these sets of symbols is probably not an accurate guide to reality.

Until now, we have concentrated on the importance of symbols to individuals as they are used in the thinking process and in guiding behavior. A great deal of thinking, of course, does not make use of words, for we can "think" in pictures, musical sounds, in vague images that cannot be classified as either sounds or pictures, and even in muscular sensations. An example of this last type of thinking is the way we "drive by the seat of our pants"—letting our physical senses of balance and of muscular tension tell us how fast we can drive around a sharp turn and never putting this "thinking" into words at all.

But when we want to communicate with others, we must depend largely on words. And since social interaction is carried out mainly through the use of symbols, as noted in the previous chapter, a further problem arises. People must *share* symbols if those symbols are to be of any value in carrying out the process of interaction. Unless we reduce interaction to mere pushing and shoving and using grunts as crude indicators of our intentions, we must agree that sharedness is essential if symbols are to be useful to us. A large number of people must hold a large number of symbols in common if they are to develop the patterns of interaction that make up groups and societies.

Culture is not *all* symbols, as we shall see, yet they are vital to people's ability to think, to plan, and to communicate so that interaction is possible. And so long as the symbols shared by people are reasonably well organized in terms of shared rules and reasonably accurate as pictures of the real world, they are the *sine qua non* (the "without which, nothing") of social life. But although they are necessary, they are not sufficient, for people need preferences as well as symbols, or destinations as well as roadmaps. The standards by which preferences are determined are called values.

Values

Feelings of like and dislike, opinions of what is good and bad, and judgments of moral and immoral are as necessary to social life as are methods of communication. Such emotions are not themselves symbols, even though they can be symbolized (as in "Stealing is bad"), but they are necessary to help us make choices. And we must make choices almost every minute of every day. Shall I stay in bed or go to class? Shall I report all of last year's tips on my income tax return? Shall I ignore that insult or make an issue of it?

In a world without values, we would have no guidance at all in answering such questions. Our behavior would become random—without direction and without predictability. Other people, then, would not know how to interact with us, for they could not know which actions on their part would elicit which responses from us. **Values,** which we may think of as *conceptions of the desirable,* are thus necessary to both individuals and society.

In the pure sense, symbols are "neutral," for they are simply reminders of their referents. Yet they ordinarily have emotional weightings as well as referents in the objective sense. Some people react quite negatively to the symbol "homosexual," and others quite positively to the symbol "Jesus." The symbol "democracy" usually calls forth a positive feeling in Americans; the symbol "Nazi," a distinctly negative one. And we must use symbols in order to talk about values: good and bad, love and hate, right and wrong. Yet it is important to keep these two components of culture analytically separate so that we can talk more intelligibly about the makeup of culture.

Values as well as symbols must be organized, or systematically interrelated. Just as symbols are organized according to linguistic rules, values are organized on the basis of their relative importance and in terms of their logical compatibility. Let us look at these two principles of value organization more closely.

Some values, clearly, must be more valuable than others if they are to help us make choices and to predict others' preferences. For example, even though "Be kind to animals" is a value, it may be necessary in some cases to be extremely cruel to an animal, particularly if it is engaged in gnawing on someone's leg. Here we will agree that it is more important, or of *more* value, to save a human being from injury than to be kind to an animal; the former value is higher on our scale of priorities than the latter. Culture thus contains not only values, but also what we might call *meta*values, or values *concerning* values. Perhaps it is because levels of relative importance are harder to establish with precision for values than is the accuracy or inaccuracy of symbols that we generally have more problems in agreeing on goals than on the meaning of speech.

Values should also be logically compatible; that is, the goals or desirable situations that they identify should not be mutually exclusive. It is difficult, for instance, to believe in equal opportunity for all and at the same time to believe that employers should be free to discriminate on the basis of race or sex. To support the realization of one value means that one cannot also support the realization of the other. Similarly, there is obvious conflict between valuing freedom of speech and valuing the community's right to censor "offensive" films and literature.

There are, of course, degrees of compatibility. Certain sets of values can be more easily realized together than others. There is little difficulty in simultaneously placing a high value on private property, on free enterprise, and on economic growth, but some compromises must be made if one also feels it desirable to protect the environment and to provide public assistance for the poor and the unemployed.

Yet it is not always possible to see clearly just when the achievement of one value will indeed preclude the achievement of another. The sudden wealth one has won in a state lottery, for example, may make it impossible to maintain friendly relationships with one's neighbors or even one's relatives; to pass laws protecting the environment may force higher prices for consumers or lead to higher unemployment as some companies cut back on production.

The point is that neither of the ways by which society attempts to keep its values organized—assigning different priorities to different values and recognizing differences in logical compatibility—is as precise as are the rules by which we keep our symbols organized. Yet we can no more tolerate an unorganized set of values than we can tolerate gibberish in place of language, for each would seriously weaken our abilities to interact successfully with others.

A distinction should be made at this point between personal values and cultural values. A personal value, obviously, is an individual preference. A cultural value, on the other hand, is one which the members of a society are *expected* to hold. One person, for instance, may prefer fried eggs for breakfast, whereas another likes them scrambled; these are different personal values, but both are acceptable within our cultural definition of "decent food." If one of these people, however, expressed a preference for baked mouse embryos or grasshopper stew for breakfast, she or he would be well outside the range of foods that are valued by our culture and could expect to meet strong expressions of disapproval from others.

But if in most cases cultural values are less specific than personal values, they are also less a matter of free choice, for they must be shared if people are to be able to predict one another's actions. Because this is so important, we do more than just try to discover others' conceptions of the desirable (and undesirable); we make active attempts to ensure that they *do* hold the values of our culture. We train our children to "know right from wrong," we preach the central values of our culture to others, and we punish those whose actions suggest that they do not hold these values. Just as people must share symbols if they are to communicate with one another, so too they must share values if they are to be able to anticipate one another's preferences and thus interact effectively.

Since these anticipations have a certain moral strength behind them, it should be clear that they have precisely the same characteristics as norms. Norms, then, as learned expectations of what people in particular statuses should do in particular situations, make up an important part of culture. To the extent that we verbalize norms, of course, they are symbolized, but since they carry a heavy component of "should/should not" feelings as well, they also represent values.

Material Culture

Although we have argued that culture is entirely intangible, made up solely of symbols and values, a number of anthropologists believe that it should also include **artifacts,** *all physical objects that have been altered or created by* *human intention.* A stone axe is an artifact, a teakettle is an artifact, and a roadway is an artifact, just as are skyscrapers and saxophones, pots and pans, jewelry and Jeeps; thus **material culture** *is that aspect of culture which is made up of artifacts.*

Because they have physical existence and endure over time, artifacts do influence people's behavior and can be passed down from one generation to the next. We would argue, though, that their importance lies in their *meaning* to people rather than in their physical existence. Who would know, for instance, without having learned and remembered it through the use of symbols, what a corkscrew is for, or a ski pole, or a shoehorn? To the extent that they are formed and consciously used by people, artifacts are certainly *products* of culture. But it seems unnecessary to complicate the concept by having to include such a broad category of qualitatively distinct components along with symbols and values in our definition of culture.

A Definition of Culture

On the basis of the foregoing discussion and understanding that it is absolutely indispensable to patterns of interaction, and thus to the existence of society itself, we can now define **culture** as *the complete, organized complex of symbols and values that the members of society share and feel that they have a right to expect other members to know and accept.*

CULTURE AS A PROPERTY OF SOCIETY

People need to share symbols and values if they are to constitute a society, and it has been suggested that people are aware of this. This feeling—that to be a member of a society, one must share its language and value system—seems to be largely responsible for the continued existence of human societies. It encourages their members to "keep up with things," to "stay in tune" with other members, and in a broader sense it is this feeling that makes parents try so hard to teach their children how to speak, how to behave, and how to think about the world. (The ways in which this is accomplished are discussed in Chapter 4, on socialization.)

If someone who is supposedly a member of a group, as indicated by dress, residence, or specific claim, demonstrates through language or behavior that he or she does not share the group's culture, others will question the legitimacy of this person's membership. For example, if a man in a naval uniform goes aboard a ship and begins to talk about the ship's walls, floors, stairs, and windows (instead of its bulkheads, decks, ladders, and portholes), the other people on the ship might reasonably wonder whether this fellow is really a sailor and a member of their group.

This principle seems to appear also in the familiar statement: "Ignorance of the law is no excuse." From one point of view, we could never fairly convict anyone of a crime if ignorance of the law were to be accepted as an excuse, for how can "nonignorance" be demonstrated? But this principle is a reasonable defense against the "ignorance" excuse because of the underlying assumption that if one is a member of the group—this town, this state, this nation—one should know the law. The argument that "if you know the culture, you are probably a member of the group" has been turned around: "If you are defined as a member of the group or claim membership in it, you should know the group's culture—including its laws."

This may, of course, be a quite unrealistic assumption in reality, but it does provide a kind of moral support for enforcing the law that is not supplied by simple utilitarian necessity. The political customs which exempt foreign diplomats from our traffic regulations, although probably rooted in political expediency, are given some support by this reasoning: Since these people are, by definition, not members of our society, it is unfair for us to expect them to know our traffic laws.

Culture and Subculture

It is inevitable that some members of a society will interact more with one another than they will with others. As this continues over time, they will probably come to develop special symbols and values that are not part of their society's "common culture." Perhaps they will need special symbols and values to help them deal with particular problems that others do not face, or to help distinguish themselves from other members of their society, or even to keep certain things secret from others. No matter what the origin of these new symbols and values, whenever they come to make up something approaching a *culture within a culture*, we say that they make up a **subculture**.

The same thing appears whenever a number of people emigrate to another society, bringing with them the symbols and values of the society from which they came. For at least two generations, this group of people will be easily distinguishable from other members of their new society, even though they become citizens, because their language and values differ from those of their neighbors. These people, too, form a subculture.

To the extent that a family develops a lifestyle that differs appreciably from that of other families nearby, it has developed a miniature subculture. The specialized jargon and values that characterize a streetcorner gang, or those who play professional football, or the members of the medical profession, also may be viewed as subcultures. No one, of course, ever knows *all* of his or her society's culture (how many strange words do you find whenever you look in a dictionary?), nor is everyone a member of a distinctive subculture in addition to being a member of the larger society. Most of us, however, can probably lay claim to a fairly thorough acquaintance with at least one subculture, even if we do not claim personal membership in it or identify it as a subculture.

The point at which a distinct subculture comes into being or is to be distinguished from either society's common culture or another subculture is difficult to define clearly. A good rule of thumb is that a subculture must define at least a substantial part of its members' lifestyles and patterns of behavior before it can merit this designation. Two lovers who share a few secret terms of endearment do not share a subculture; the men serving in a Navy underwater-demolition team may develop a subculture; the people who came to America from Italy at the turn of the century and settled in the same neighborhoods quite clearly did form a subculture. (Some additional aspects of subcultures, both their origins and their consequences, are brought out in the discussion of social classes, Chapter 6, and of racial and ethnic groups, Chapter 7.)

Reference should also be made at this point to the concept of **contraculture,** which is *one type of subculture.* A contraculture is distinguished by the fact that those who share it are in some ways sharply opposed to the values of the larger society. A band of terrorists whose beliefs lead them to commit acts of violence can obviously be termed a contraculture. Less clearly, perhaps, a gang of juvenile delinquents and a commune whose members reject the material values of American society might also be called contracultures. The term is applicable whenever the opposition to the larger culture is clear-cut and leads those who share it to either attack society or withdraw their commitment to it.

CULTURE AND REALITY

One more point should be made about culture, one that will make clear that culture can indeed be treated as a separate entity—as a system in its own right that has its own special dynamics—even if it is completely intangible. Culture contains a picture of the world, both as it is and as it should be; the anthropologist Ralph Linton (1936), in fact, speaks of culture as a set of "blueprints for behavior." We have noted that it must be both accurate and organized, even though in reality we never find a culture that is completely accurate or perfectly organized. There are always some discrepancies, inaccuracies, and fuzzy areas in any culture.

For example, we sometimes explain two people's friendship by saying, "Birds of a feather flock together"; at other times we may say with equal conviction, "Opposites attract." Clearly, both statements cannot be true at the same time, for they are logically contradictory, yet we treat each one as though it were a general explanation of why people are attracted to each other. Here, then, is a small inconsistency in our culture's picture of the world.

More frequent are cases in which we say one thing but do another. The traffic laws now limit highway speed to fifty-five miles per hour, even though many drivers regularly exceed this limit. If, after driving along a stretch of road at sixty-five miles an hour (as we have seen everyone else do for months), we are arrested for traveling too fast, we may complain that we were only driving as fast as the rest of the traffic. We might even argue that the speed limit should be raised to sixty-five, but we can hardly ask the law to be a hypocrite. We can hardly ask a judge to say officially, "The law *says* you should drive no faster than fifty-five, but it really *means* sixty-five." Such an announcement would introduce a logical inconsistency into the law that would be as bad as the present discrepancy between what we say we should do (what we write into law) and what we actually do. Our dilemma here lies in having to decide between changing either our behavior so that it matches our culture's picture of what it should be or our culture so that it is again an accurate picture of what we are actually doing.

Cultural Lag

On a broader scale, it is important to understand how culture can become an inaccurate picture of reality. The key fact is that symbols and values do not erode, wear out, or necessarily change with the passage of time. The real world, on the other hand, is continually changing. Although our culture may at one time have been a quite accurate reflection of reality, we cannot expect it automatically to change as the world changes. This was pointed out more than fifty years ago by the sociologist William F. Ogburn (1922), who termed it **cultural lag,** *or the ways that advances in technology* (say, the invention of the automobile) *bring about discrepancies between what is really going on in the world and the ways that our culture directs us to behave.*

Ogburn suggested, for instance, that traffic congestion is the result of our culture's failure to help us adjust to the presence of more and more cars. In seeking individually to maximize the value of convenient personal transportation, we have not at the same time made changes in our culture that would enable us to deal effectively with the consequences of this change in our material circumstances. (For more on this concept, see Chapter 18, on social change.)

Although technological advances may be one of the most important sources of change in the real world today, other types of change can also reduce the "fit" of culture to reality. Changes in population (both in numbers and in the relative size of different age groups), in the quality of the environment, and even in the goals and resources of other societies can all contribute to a decline in the accuracy—and thus the usefulness—of our culture.

But one of the basic dynamics of culture is that it *should* be accurate, and for this very practical reason we are continually trying to adjust our maps of

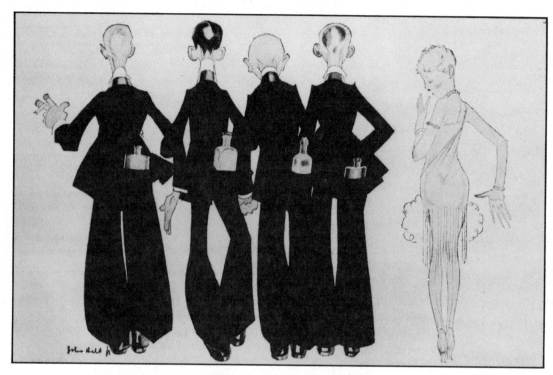

Cultural lag exists when our culture directs us to behave in a way inconsistent with reality. During Prohibition, the drinking public defied the Eighteenth Amendment, which prohibited the manufacture, transportation, and sale of alcohol, by obtaining liquor illegally, in speakeasies. (Courtesy of the New-York Historical Society, New York City)

reality so that they can be effective guides to behavior. The difficulty comes when we must make a choice between keeping our symbols logically consistent with one another and keeping each of them an accurate guide to its referent.

The Great Depression of the 1930s provides an example. Before that time, our shared picture of the world told us that anyone who looked hard enough for a job could find one. This had generally been true during the industrial expansion of the previous century. But when millions of people were unemployed, it became extremely difficult to accuse all of them of sheer laziness. Our picture of the world was inaccurate, of course, but the logical conclusion it led us to was that no one should try to help the unemployed, because laziness should not be rewarded.

It required the "revolution" of the New Deal to change our basic picture of the economic system so that it became logical and proper for the government to establish programs like the WPA and Social Security. With this adjustment in our common picture of the world, we no longer needed to conclude that people standing in breadlines were lazy, and we could agree that it was both reasonable and moral for the government to help them. We continued to maintain, of course, that the government should not assist people who were simply too lazy to help themselves, but we dissociated unemployment from laziness and were able to reach new conclusions that led to effective action.

It is impossible to describe the *best* relationship between culture and reality or to prescribe one method as the most effective way to reduce cultural lag. There will always be some gap between the symbols we share and the reality they are supposed to describe, and it is unlikely that we will ever be in full agreement on which should be changed to fit the other. Sometimes, as in the case described above, we must change our picture of reality so that it can be a more effective guide to behavior. At other times we may decide that it is more important to change reality (as, for example, when we undertake an urban-renewal program) so that it will correspond more closely to the dictates of our culture.

The one thing we can agree on is that if we had no culture, we would not have society. Despite its complexity and the problematic nature of its relation to reality, culture is the indispensable foundation of the patterns of coordinated behavior—that is, social interaction—that constitute society.

SUMMARY

Differences among societies, once attributed to biological differences among their members, are actually based on differences in the symbols and values that their members share. Since these intangible things are both shared and passed on to the next generation, they can be viewed as making up an organized complex that is a distinctive component of society. Today it is called *culture.*

Culture is composed of *symbols* (sounds, gestures, signs, etc., that remind us of their referents) and *values* (conceptions of the desirable). Human communication depends not only on the sharing of symbols, but also on the existence of shared rules for fitting them together; symbols must also be reasonably accurate in reminding us of the characteristics of their referents. Values, too, must be shared so that people can anticipate one another's likes and dislikes. Values must be sufficiently organized so that people can agree on the relative importance of different values, and they must be sufficiently compatible with one another so that people do not continually find that achieving one value makes it impossible to achieve another value of equal importance.

Personal values—that is, individual preferences—are ordinarily more specific than cultural values, but they cannot conflict with cultural values without incurring problems. Some social scientists believe it important to treat artifacts as part of culture; this text, however, takes the position that although artifacts are products of culturally directed behavior, they should not be treated themselves as part of culture.

Membership in a society presupposes knowledge and acceptance of its culture. People defined as members are expected to have this familiarity, and those who claim membership but demonstrate unfamiliarity may be suspect. Ignorance of the law (part of culture) is no excuse, then, for a member of society, whereas ignorance is *expected* of those who are defined as nonmembers.

The fact that some groups within a society hold symbols and values that are not part of that society's common culture leads us to the concept of *subculture*. To the extent that a group—racial, ethnic, social class, or regional—has a distinctive lifestyle that is the product of its members' sharing particular symbols and values, it can be said to be a subculture. If a subculture is in important ways directly opposed to the culture of the larger society, it can be termed a *contraculture.*

Although society's members need their culture to be shared, organized, and an accurate picture of reality so that they can continue to interact successfully, no culture ever satisfies these needs perfectly. Every culture contains some internal contradictions and some inaccuracies in its portrayal of reality. When such flaws develop because culture has failed to change as the real world changes, they are the result of *cultural lag.* On some occasions when such problems develop, we find it more effective to redraw our cultural maps so that they can guide our behavior more effectively. On other occasions we will instead seek to bring reality back into correspondence with the map provided by our culture.

For all of its complexities and problems, however, culture is essential to society, for only culture can enable people to communicate, plan for the future, and anticipate one another's actions so that they can develop the patterns of interaction that make up society.

SUGGESTED READINGS

Berger, Peter L., and Thomas Luckmann, *The Social Construction of Reality* (Garden City, N.Y.: Doubleday, 1966). Although the word "culture" appears only rarely in this book, the concept of culture developed in this chapter has been heavily influenced by Berger and Luckmann's phenomenological analysis of the emergence of bodies of meaning in society.

Kroeber, Alfred L., and Clyde Kluckhohn, *Culture: A Critical Review of Concepts and Definitions* (New York: Vintage Books, 1963). Probably as complete a review of the various ways in which the concept has been used as one can find. This book, however, can be supplemented by reference to the article "The Concept of Culture" in the *International Encyclopedia of the Social Sciences,* referred to at the end of Chapter 1.

Ogburn, William F., *Social Change* [1922] (New York: Viking, 1950). Although perhaps this book should be cited at the end of Chapter 18, on social change, Ogburn's analysis of culture in this classic work has probably been of more lasting value than his analysis of change.

Tylor, Edward B., *The Origins of Culture* [1871] (New York: Harper, 1958). This important work by a British anthropologist contains his famous definition of culture and was highly influential in the development of anthropology in Britain. Tylor later served as president of the British Anthropological Association and was Oxford University's first professor of anthropology.

White, Leslie A., *The Evolution of Culture* (New York: McGraw-Hill, 1959). White's definition of culture is rather different from that in this book. Giving technology and artifacts a prominent place in his conception of the topic, he argues, in fact, that culture is chiefly influenced in its content and organization by the level of a society's technology.

Williams, Robin M., Jr., *American Society: A Sociological Interpretation*, 3rd ed. (New York: Knopf, 1970). One of the most interesting parts of this comprehensive and impressive book is Williams's characterization of the central themes in American culture.

Glossary

Artifact Any physical object that has been altered or created by human intention. Because artifacts are products of culturally shaped intentions and because their existence then influences people's behavior, some social scientists refer to them as material culture (see below) and treat them as a distinctive component of culture.

Contraculture A type of subculture (see below) which in some important way is opposed to the larger culture within which it exists. This opposition leads its members to attack the surrounding society (e.g., a band of terrorists) or to withdraw from it (e.g., a strict religious sect).

Cultural lag A situation in which one part of culture (say, medical technology) has changed more rapidly than another part (say, the norms and values concerning sickness and death) so that there is a discrepancy between what people are actually doing and the guidelines for behavior provided by the rest of their culture.

Culture The complete, organized complex of symbols and values that the members of society share and feel that they have a right to expect other members to know and accept. Some social scientists include artifacts (see above) as a part of culture, along with symbols and values, but this text does not. In relation to the concepts of subculture and contraculture, the definition offered here can be taken to refer primarily to a society's "common culture," although if the word "group" is substituted for "society," it can cover subculture and contraculture just as well.

Ethnocentrism The belief that one's own group or society is superior to all others, even though others may surpass it in such specific areas as size, wealth, military power, technological achievements, etc.

Material culture That part of culture which, some social scientists say, is composed of artifacts (see above). The concept is discussed in this chapter, but not treated as an intrinsic component of culture.

Subculture A specialized "culture within a culture." It may be so complete as to make it difficult for those who share it to interact easily with other members of the surrounding society (as in the case of a group of immigrants), or it may consist of particular symbols and values "added on" to the common culture (as in the case of a group of circus performers). We may apply the term whenever a substantial part of a group's lifestyle and patterns of interaction are distinctly different from those of the other members of their society. A contraculture (see above) is a particular type of subculture.

Symbol Anything that consistently makes us think of (or "stands for") something else. A word is perhaps the clearest example of a symbol because it is relatively precise, but gestures, signs, objects, markings, noises, and colors may also serve as symbols. The printed marks that you read as "pig" on this page make you think of a certain kind of animal (curly tail, *oink,* likes mud, source of bacon, etc.); the printed or spoken word *pig* is the symbol; the animal itself is the symbol's *referent.*

Value A conception of the desirable or of a condition or situation that an individual or group wants to achieve. Values provide guidance for behavior by helping us choose between alternative courses of action and, when we know others' values, by helping us predict their responses to our actions. *Cultural values* are those values that the members of a society expect one another to know and accept, whereas *personal values* are individuals' conceptions of the desirable; the former ordinarily determine the latter. A society's values are organized (1) on the basis of their relative importance, and (2) in terms of their relative compatability (that is, not being mutually exclusive in the sense that achieving one will prevent the achievement of another).

4
Socialization

FOCUS: *THE SELF*

To speak of "my*self*" implies that I am aware of my own existence—that I am an object of my own attention. This fact does not strike us as strange or unusual, for all of us are aware of our*selves*, but its implications for the understanding of human groups are enormous.

In order to interact successfully with others, a person must have a reasonably accurate idea of what others expect and thus of how they will respond to particular statements and acts. This is possible only if one can view oneself as others do. Yet the newborn child is completely lacking in self-awareness. Each individual's development of a *self*, then, is crucial to his or her ability to participate in social relationships. This chapter deals with the processes through which society helps each of its members develop a *self*.

"As the twig is bent, so is the tree inclined." This statement summarizes our belief that what happens to a living organism early in life will influence its character later on. If we look at a baby as a "twig," however, we cannot be content to know only that its early experiences *will* influence its subsequent development. We also want to know *what* these experiences are, *how* they will influence it, and how it came to have these experiences in the first place.

The psychologist, focusing on the individual, usually calls this twig-bending process "child development." But the sociologist is not interested in the individual per se, for the focus of sociology is the group, and the basic building block of the group is the social status rather than the biological human being. So the sociologist calls this process **socialization** and defines it as *the series of experiences through which the human being is made "social," or capable (in terms of both knowledge and motivation) of participating in the patterns of interaction that make up society.* More specifically, the concept refers to both the process through which the individual internalizes his or her group's culture, thereby developing a self, and also the social arrangements that facilitate this process. (It should be remembered that for the sociologist, socialization does *not* mean the process through which a government assumes ownership of private property or through which a population is converted to the political ideology called socialism.)

SOCIALIZATION AND SOCIETY

Even though ultimately interested in human groups, the sociologist must obviously make many assumptions about the individuals who occupy the social statuses that make up groups. Social statuses must be occupied before groups can be studied, and so individual human beings must be able (and, usually, willing) to occupy them. Thus the process of socialization is in one sense prior to the existence of groups, and understanding it can contribute much to our knowledge of them.

Although we are concerned with individual abilities and limitations (for these certainly influence people's expectations of one another), our interest here is directed primarily toward the ways in which society arranges for its members to have those experiences that will "bend" them so that they will *want* to participate in social relationships and also know pretty well *how* to do this. We take for granted that a society cannot exist unless its members are able to occupy most of its statuses most of the time without severe strain. (No status, for instance, routinely requires its occupant to jump twenty feet in the air, and no status requires that its occupant regularly ignore basic biological needs for air, water, and food.) If we accept this as one fact about society, though, we must also accept another: that human needs, perceptions, and abilities are shaped to a considerable extent *by* society. Over the long run, society must adjust to the general range of its members' needs and abilities, but in the short run, it is the individual who must adjust to society's demands. Each person, in other words, is born into a group that is already functioning with at least minimal success, and so he or she must fit into this ongoing structure effectively enough to at least stay alive.

The vast amount of variation we find among human societies attests to both the remarkable plasticity of human beings (that is, to the fact that the members of this single biological species can be "bent" in so many different ways) and the efficacy with which each society is able to shape its new members so that they can fit smoothly into its particular social structure. If this were not so, we would find much less distinction between one society and the next and very little social change in any society. The fact that we do find differences over time within one society, as well as differences among societies, is possible only because human beings can be "bent" in so many different ways.

It is clear, then, that as far as the sociologist is concerned, **nurture** *(what happens to the child after birth)* is much more important than **nature** *(what the child "brings with it" in terms of heredity)*. But the relative importance of nature (heredity) and nurture (all of the influences that come to bear on the child after birth) is still debated, and it will be useful here to pay some attention to this question.

Nature versus Nurture

No matter how much we may think that heredity determines one's interests, abilities, or character—even one's physical appearance—it is obvious that inherited tendencies may or may not be fulfilled, depending on one's experiences after birth. Even such things as height, weight, and coloring can be influenced by diet. A hereditary talent for mathematics or for art can be stifled or helped to blossom by the range of opportunities that society makes available to the individual. And such things as ideals, ambitions, and everyday social skills seem to be determined almost entirely by training rather than by genetics.

There must, of course, be some genetically imposed limitations on what any given individual is capable of. But what one *might* do and what one *does* do are quite separate things, and we can assume that only in rare instances do individuals ever reach the limits of what they *could* do. Someone, for instance, might be born with a high potential for both athletic excellence and musical creativity, but devoting the time and energy necessary to developing one will probably result in the other's remaining relatively underdeveloped. It is quite likely, then, that for the most part, "nurture" *masks* "nature" by interfering with the realization of inherited potentials.

The problem of distinguishing between the effects of nature and of nurture is compounded by the fact that after certain individual characteristics have been "set" by early experience, they may be extremely difficult to change later in life. If, for example, one has suffered substantial malnutrition as a young child, it is unlikely that a better diet later on will make up for the effects

The nature/nurture controversy is illustrated in the case of Roger Brooks (left) and Anthony Milasi (right), identical twins who were separated at birth and raised a thousand miles apart by two culturally different families. Reunited by chance at age 24, the two brothers displayed behavioral similarities that were probably genetic, such as holding a coffee cup the same way, having similar speech mannerisms, and giving identical answers in a psychological test. However, Roger displayed greater emotional maturity and sensitivity, whereas Anthony was more dependent on his family and always looked for a magical, happy ending. A psychologist attributed these differences to environmental influence. (Wide World Photos)

this deprivation has had on physical and even mental growth. Or, if a child has been raised by parents who were emotionally "distant" and relied largely on harsh physical discipline for control, it is unlikely that the "personality" developed under these conditions can be greatly changed later in life, no matter what is done to, for, or with that person. In other words, it is easy to understand the reasons for our tendency to think that the "unchanging" characteristics of people are due to heredity rather than to experience, even though they may lead to the unrealistic belief that genetic endowment accounts for a great deal of what we observe in others.

Implications of Answering the Nature/Nurture Problem

The question of whether nature or nurture carries the greater weight in explaining behavior is important because of its implications for the ways we treat others and thus for the social policies adopted by our governments. If, for instance, we believe that genetic inheritance is responsible for most of the differences we find among human beings, we must conclude that there is little we can do now, even with very young children, to improve them. On the other hand, if we assume that most differences among people have been caused by how they were brought up, perhaps a great deal can be done to help the next generation overcome whatever handicaps seem to have prevented the present generation from leading fuller, happier lives.

An important component of racist theories of human nature is their reliance on the former sort of reasoning. Such theories, or ideologies, are sometimes carried to the point of declaring that certain people are *un*human—so that ethics and morality should be irrelevant to how they are treated by other individuals and by governments. We have only to look at how the Jews were treated in Nazi Germany or how most Indians have been treated in this country to see the consequences of such reasoning.

"Liberal" social-welfare programs are based on the other reasoning: If we can change the circumstances under which children are raised and in which many adults live today, perhaps we can help them to be more successful in life. Even if imperfect knowledge of how "nurture" actually works and/or imperfect implementation of such programs produce frequent failure in terms of their stated goals, the facts in the case seem to support the belief that nurture is more important than nature in determining the individual's ability to lead a meaningful, satisfying life.

This question, clearly, is not confined to the halls of academic discussion. *Which* theory of human nature is accepted by a society will have important implications for its members, so that those who are likely to profit from a particular theory (the "haves" if nature is accepted as the dominant force, or the "have-nots" if nurture is taken to be more important) have a personal stake in its validity. This means that a person will probably resist *any* "facts," scientific or otherwise, if they seem to dispute the validity of his or her position. It would be urealistic, then, to expect that social scientists' findings on this question will be accepted readily and without controversy.

For our purposes, though, we can consider that the individual's genetic endowment is considerably less important to the understanding of society than are the experiences to which she or he is exposed after birth. These experiences, in turn, are determined largely by the society into which the individual is born.

THE INGREDIENTS OF SOCIALIZATION

No child is born knowing how to be a son or daughter, a student, a tennis player, or a banker—or wanting to be one. The newborn child does not even know how to communicate with other human beings; it is, in fact, not even aware at first that other human beings exist. If it is to become an effective member of society, then, the newborn child must acquire a vast amount of knowledge during the first stages of life. The process through which this knowledge (*and* motivation) is acquired is, of course, socialization, and we recognize it as the foundation of order and continuity in society. Without socialization, there would be nothing called "society" for us to study. But the process of socialization is both complex and problematical, and many aspects of it are still so vaguely understood that it is one of the genuinely fascinating and challenging parts of sociology as well as of psychology.

Cognitive and Affective Aspects of Socialization

One of the most fundamental distinctions we make in talking about social behavior is that between the cognitive (or "knowing") and the affective (or "feeling") components. Although there is considerable interdependence between the two, it is clear from the way we tend to conceptualize the world that an individual ordinarily will not do something unless he or she both knows *how* to do it and *wants* to do it. (One may, of course, achieve something through luck or accident rather than through understanding, and one may "want" to do something only because it is the least unpleasant course of action available in a given situation. For the most part, though, we assume that people need both appropriate knowledge *and* motivation if they are to participate successfully in social relationships.)

Another way to put this is to say that all human behavior is tinged with emotion. We react emotionally to whatever we—and others—do, and these emotions help to guide our future behavior. Without the scale of preferences provided by our emotions (usually in the form of *values*), we would be unable to decide what we want to do next or what we would like others to do. From society's point of view, the most successful individual is one whose personal preferences coincide entirely with those prescribed by his or her culture, for this individual *wants* to live up to others' culturally determined expectations. It should be clear that no society can continue to exist if its members do not come reasonably close to this sort of correspondence between personal motives and cultural expectations.

On the other hand, though, each individual is a separate organism; his or her pleasures and pains, sense of meaning in the world, and even physical survival need not be closely correlated with the survival of society itself. The unabashed "me-first" emotional orientation of the infant, then, must somehow be modified so that "me" and "society" come to be quite similar. If my interests continually opposed those of society or if the two coincided only randomly, it would be extremely difficult for others to trust me to respect property rights, keep appointments, restrain my occasional tendencies toward violence, and otherwise to behave predictably in my relations with them. Thus **affective development**—*the way in which one comes to want to fit into society*—is a crucial component of the socialization process.

Cognitive development, *or the intellectual aspects of socialization,* is not so directly important to the continued existence of society. A child may or may not be able to do long division (or, these days, to operate a pocket calculator), but lack of mathematical skill is not viewed as a positive danger to others. Although we view improper motivation as dangerous, a lack of knowledge is ordinarily thought of only as deplorable. Incorrect knowledge is unfortunate, to be sure, but we never assume that someone *wants* to know that ice is hot, that $6+6=7$, or that a red traffic light means "go." We may take it for granted that people are motivated to learn, or we may worry about how to instill this motivation, but thereafter the business of teaching facts and skills is treated as essentially a matter of technique rather than of values or morality.

Personal needs, interests, and preferences certainly influence the kinds of knowledge one acquires, as when a student decides to major in economics because this topic seems especially gratifying. But it is also true that the knowledge one has acquired can often influence one's preferences. Having learned a good deal about auto mechanics, for instance, a person can be expected to place more value on owning a particularly fine automobile than if he or she knows only that you have to put gasoline into a car from time to time in order to keep it running.

In terms of our current knowledge of socialization, though, these two aspects of human development are usually treated separately rather than together. Tests of intelligence and tests of psychoneurotic symptoms are separate; schools are organized with respect to their pupils' cognitive needs rather than their emotional needs; and psychiatrists rarely focus on their patients' intellectual abilities when treating them for emotional disorders. Although it is evident that sooner or later the cognitive and affective components of human development must be reconceptualized in a new synthesis, for the moment we must accept the fact that they are treated separately by most students of socialization.

If a judgment must be made, it would seem that the individual's emotional development carries more weight in determining the direction and extent of his or her cognitive development than vice-versa. For this reason, we shall pay more attention in what follows to personality than to intellect, despite the apparently greater susceptibility of the latter to quantitative, "scientific" analysis.

Human Contact

The human infant is completely helpless at birth. If it is to live at all and become a member of society, it must undergo **social development,** *the contacts with other human beings that help shape the self.* This fact is so obvious that it hardly seems worth mentioning. But because it is so self-evident, it means that we have had few, if any, opportunities to see what happens to children who have *not* had such contact. An abandoned baby is almost certain to die, so no examples are available for us to compare abandoned babies with those who have had human contacts during infancy and childhood. There have been, however, documented cases of *minimal* human contact, and these are sufficient to demonstrate the crucial importance of close, continuing relationships with others for the child's mental and social development as well as for its physical survival.

Although stories of "feral children" in India (children supposedly reared by wolves after having been abandoned by their parents) seem questionable (MacLean, 1978), two cases of "extreme isolation," described in the late 1930s by the sociologist Kingsley Davis (1948, pp. 204–208), provide convincing evidence of the vital role that human contact plays in socialization. Anna, born illegitimately and kept out of sight in an upstairs room by an embarrassed family, apparently received barely enough attention to stay alive. When she was discovered at the age of six, she could not walk or talk and at first gave the impression of being deaf and perhaps blind as well. Isabelle, born under similar circumstances but to a deaf-mute mother who did spend considerable time with her in a darkened room, showed the same characteristics: no speech, clumsy movements, and almost no sensible awareness of her surroundings.

In both cases, socialization had to begin at the age of six rather than immediately after birth. Anna died before she was eleven, having made only modest progress in terms of language and the ability to interact with others; it was concluded, though, that she was probably congenitally retarded (her mother was found to have an IQ of 50), so that relatively little should have been expected of her under any circumstances. Isabelle, on the other hand, being normal and having had close (although limited) contact with her deaf-mute mother since birth, made rapid progress. Her acquisition of language came quickly, and by her ninth birthday she showed only minor differences from other children of her age. The fact that both girls had been deprived of the give and take of ordinary social relationships is the obvious explanation for their seeming so severely retarded when they were found.

It is apparent, then, that although the infant comes equipped with a tool—the brain—which can develop under proper circumstances to the point where it can enable the individual to behave effectively (to get along with others), this development can occur only when the brain is stimulated by contact with others. The case of Isabelle in particular demonstrates that a great deal of catching up can be done even when such stimulation has been missing for several years. But it is doubtful that the individual can become a fully normal adult later on if this stimulation comes too late in life.

The importance of interaction   Stimulation (from the Latin *stimulare*, meaning "to goad on") is important to the child because it is basic to learning about cause-and-effect relationships. Equipped only with the ability to sense changes in its internal state and its immediate environment, together with some vague criteria of what constitutes satisfactory (that is, pleasant) and unsatisfactory (unpleasant or painful) feelings, the child is ready to begin learning about its relationships with the rest of the world.

As its brain develops physically so that events can be remembered, the child begins to learn that its own feelings and actions are related to other events. An unpleasant feeling in the stomach (hunger) leads to crying, which (as far as the baby is concerned) "causes" the presence of someone else, which in turn is accompanied by the opportunity to suck something—which finally relieves the hunger pangs. Conversely, the presence of someone else, if responded to in the proper fashion, can lead to the pleasure of being held and fondled. Eventually the lesson is learned: There is a definite relationship between what the child does and what happens next, and the presence of someone else is usually necessary if what happens next is to be pleasant.

For the most part, *only* other human beings can provide the prompt, specific feedback that is fundamental to this learning process. A pet dog or cat cannot do much to relieve a baby's discomfort, nor will it respond to the child's actions consistently. Without other human beings, then, the child has little opportunity to engage in the same patterns of interaction over and over again until it has learned to identify and remember them.

As the child's store of experience grows and as it develops greater control over its own actions, its knowledge of *which* acts tend to produce *which* results expands tremendously. Sooner or later the child finds it easier to remember these various relationships through pretending to *be* the other person—through learning to look at oneself as the other person seems to. It is at this point that the self comes into being, as will be explained in more detail in the next section.

Language As Chapter 3 stressed, the ability to use symbols is fundamental to the ability to think, to remember, to discriminate among different experiences, and to plan. But a baby is not born with language; speech must be acquired. There is still a lively controversy in the field of linguistics over whether the human brain is "naturally" adapted to learning speech or whether it is learned strictly on a trial-and-error basis (with rewards for effective speech serving to reinforce this kind of learning just as they encourage learning to use a spoon or drink from a cup) (Chomsky, 1972; Hockett, 1968). Whatever the basis, though, we can assume that because vocal behavior (crying, cooing, screaming, etc.) was important in the very beginning in eliciting desired responses from others, the child is particularly sensitive to the advantages of verbal communication.

As distinctive sounds come to be associated with specific people and objects, the child learns that language can make memory and thinking more effective. Further, words can be tremendously more effective than other kinds of actions in influencing the behavior of others. But more than practical advantage is involved. The cognitive mastery of the world that is made possible by the use of symbols is intrinsically gratifying. Anyone who has ever heard a small child naming objects again and again or talking in a private singsong about what he or she is doing can recognize the pleasure and wonder the child finds in this new form of behavior.

It is of particular importance to note the role of language in the development of the self. The child not only hears (and, increasingly, understands) what others say to it, but can also say the same things to itself. "Now it's time for bed," a three-year-old will say, copying what Mommy or Daddy usually says, and through this experiment in "being" the parent, the child learns to look at himself or herself as the parents do. Eventually the child achieves a more detailed and realistic picture of itself as others see it and thus becomes able to participate in more complex, extended patterns of interaction with others. This brings us to the details of the processes through which several components of the self develop.

STAGES OF DEVELOPMENT

A person's **self**—*the object of his or her self-awareness*—is made up of not only a sense of how others perceive one, but also knowledge of one's own needs, abilities, and preferences. If the self consisted *only* of others' expectations, it would lack standards by which to decide which expectations were more important than others or which situations (and social relationships) should be sought and which should be avoided. It would lack, in other words, any sense of initiative and of the ability to make choices.

The self, then, must include an awareness of one's own being as an actor as well as of the probable relationships between one's actions and their effects on others. A baseball player, for example, must have a realistic sense of how expert he is at stealing bases (and of how important a stolen base may be in a given situation) and at the same time a clear understanding of his responsibility to the team as a whole. A slow-footed player will play a conservative game when he is on base rather than risk an attempted steal that might win the game, despite his desire to help win it. His decision not to try to steal second is based on his awareness of what he *can* do, what he *wants* to do, and what others *expect* him to do.

Part of socialization thus involves coming to terms with oneself as a biological organism—with one's physical and intellectual passions, fears, strengths, and weaknesses. The other part, equally important, involves learning to see oneself as others do; eventually, one constructs an objective "picture" of one's relationships with others, almost in the same way that we can point to a map of our hometown and say, "My house is located *here*."

If there is a typical pathway from infancy to adulthood, measured in terms of the development of the self and increasing social competence, we should be able to speak of it in some systematic way. This is ordinarily done by dividing the process into stages, or successive periods of life during which different problems, challenges, and abilities are particularly prominent. A number of theories of development—not necessarily contradicting one another, but concentrating on different components of the self—have been devised, and they require our attention here.

Freud's Psychosexual Model

Sigmund Freud (1856–1939) was the originator of psychoanalysis and of the most important theory of personality we have today (for a good introduction, see Wollheim, 1971). Freud's analysis of the process of personality development focuses, as we shall see, on how the individual learns to deal with his or her own physical needs as they come into conflict with the demands and prohibitions imposed by other people.

Freud assumes that the **libido** (*the fundamental desire for pleasure*) is extremely diffuse and can become "attached" to different parts of the person's own body as well as to different individuals and objects outside the person. In the beginning, he says, the child's attention is focused primarily on the mouth and on sucking, for this part of the body is most closely associated with the satisfaction of hunger (and with anxieties over the relief of hunger that predominate during the first year or so of the child's life). This is the *oral* stage of development.

Later, as toilet training is initiated and the child is caught between the need to defecate and the need to satisfy parents in terms of when and where this act is permissible, it is the *anal* region that becomes the most important center of attention. The child is also faced with conflicting definitions of feces during this period; most of the time, fecal matter is defined as "dirty" and "disgusting," but at the proper time and place it is a "good" thing and may even be rewarded with extra love and approval.

Finally, the capacity for genital pleasure comes to the fore, both because this is inevitable with physical growth and because anxieties over oral and anal needs have been "solved" (either through learning that these needs can be satisfied routinely or by suppressing into the unconscious whatever conflicts and uncertainties remain associated with them). The self must expand to include an awareness of one's sexuality. Sexual needs, transformed now from the infant's original desire to "possess" the parent in every respect into much more specific attachments and patterns of behavior, must be recognized and fitted in with other components of the self so that it remains realistic and whole.

In general, Freud views the process of physical maturation—and the changing demands placed on the growing child by parents and others—as unstoppable, even though the child's personality development depends very much on *how* his or her experiences with these sequential needs and anxieties have been shaped by others. Unresolved anxieties related to any of these stages, Freud says, can turn up in disguise in later life. The residue of worries about the timing of bowel movements, for instance, can be expressed through a neurotic compulsion to be neat; unresolved anxieties over being fed may lead to compulsive eating or other oral activities such as smoking. Failure to understand one's sexual needs properly, or to be able to accept them, can distort one's relations with others in many ways.

Freud thus finds the basic determinants of the self in how the individual has experienced and dealt with these crucial problems during childhood. Although he stresses the child's relationships with the parents, his theory tends to view social interaction as shaped largely by individual psychosexual needs rather than as an attribute of human groups, and he tends to take intellectual development and the learning of social roles for granted.

Piaget: Cognitive Development

Just as Freud concentrated on the individual's emotional development, so the eminent Swiss child psychologist Jean Piaget (b. 1896) has given us a comprehensive explanation of the stages through which the child's intellectual abilities develop. He distinguishes four principal stages, each characterized by a distinctive form of cognitive organization; although the particular ages at which one stage or another is predominant may vary from one society to another, their sequence seems reasonably well established (Piaget, 1954).

Learning, for Piaget, involves direct interaction between the knower and the known. It is not enough, he says, for the child to develop a mental picture of an object; the child must also have the experience of how its actions and those of the object (animate or inanimate) are related. Thus the physical manipulation of things is essential to the child's learning; touch is quite as important as sight and hearing.

The infant begins, of course, with no meaningful awareness that it exists in an environment. The first stage of its intellectual development, therefore, *the sensorimotor stage,* involves learning that its own physical actions have consequences for things outside its own skin and that these things exist independently of the infant. The simplest awareness of cause and effect is acquired together with what Piaget calls "object permanence"—the knowledge that something (say, a ball, or even a parent) continues to exist even when it is out of reach and out of sight and hearing. This stage lasts, at least for most children in Western societies, until the age of eighteen to twenty-four months.

The second stage, the *preoperational,* or *intuitive,* stage, occurs roughly between the ages of two and seven years. The acquisition of language is the most important event during this period, together with the advances in intellectual development that language makes possible. Words are taken fairly literally, and the connections between the static existence of things and the processes of transformation in them (for instance, falling, ripening, changes in shape) are not well understood. Although the child can conceive of ice and of water, for example, it is not ordinarily capable of grasping the idea that the processes of melting and freezing are equally "objective" and understandable. During this period the child also moves from a predominantly *egocentric* view of the world to a view that he or she is not the center of all relationships, but simply one component of a system of relationships. (This aspect of socialization is viewed in more distinctly sociological terms by Cooley and Mead, whose work is discussed below.)

The third stage, that of *concrete operations*, lasts from the age of seven or eight until about the child's twelfth year. During this period the ideas of qualities, measurements, and properties come to be more fully understood as meaningful abstractions. During the preoperational stage, a child often believes that the *amount* of water increases when it is poured from a wide, shallow glass into a tall, slender glass; during the third stage, however, the child is able to understand that there is a difference between shape and volume, so that the former may change while the latter remains the same. The child's ability to deal with abstractions increases a great deal during this stage, but is still tied to direct experience with the objects involved. In other words, the child can grasp relatively complicated chains of cause and effect, but continues to have difficulty dealing with them in the absence of concrete examples.

Finally, by the age of twelve or so, the child has ordinarily developed in intellectual terms to the point where he or she can deal directly with abstract principles. Now the child can think about thinking, or handle symbols and their relationships, in the same way that earlier he or she could handle wooden blocks. By this time, too, the essentially *general* nature of rules is recognized, so that the child can "take the role of the other" in a game without undue difficulty. He or she can now begin to understand the relationship between two other people in the same terms that his or her relationship to each of them is understood. Piaget calls this final development the stage of *formal operations*.

By the early teens, then, the individual has ordinarily developed the emotional balance and the intellectual abilities that are minimally necessary for full-fledged participation in society. Specific kinds of knowledge continue to be acquired, of course, but hereafter socialization is mainly the process of extending one's acquaintance with society and of refining one's skills and one's self. The ability to grasp the principles that underlie both social and physical relationships has now been achieved.

Mead and Cooley: The Social Self

George Herbert Mead (1863–1931) and Charles Horton Cooley (1864–1929) are generally recognized as the originators of the first genuinely sociological analysis of the socialization process, even though this judgment is based on the intellectual convergence of their separate works rather than on any actual collaboration between them (Mead, 1934; Cooley, 1902).

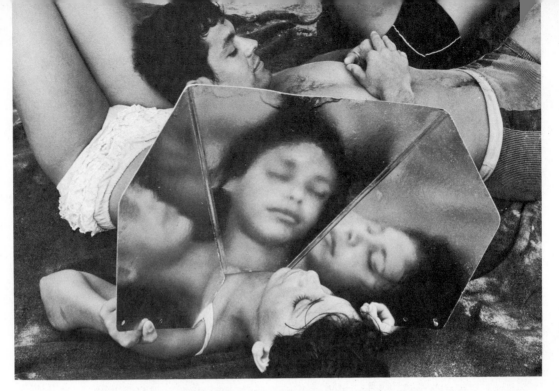

According to the concept of the "looking-glass self," we define ourselves as we see our images reflected back by others, especially those within our primary groups. (Burk Uzzle/Magnum Photos)

Each was concerned with how the individual's sense of self develops through interaction with others, emphasizing the importance of learning how others perceive one. An unrealistic sense of "who I am," after all, will make it difficult to interact successfully with others. Someone with delusions of grandeur or a serious inferiority complex will be continually frustrated because others do not respond in the ways that are expected. We may wonder, further, whether such a person is suffering from psychological difficulties, since it is difficult to believe that anyone would *choose* to be consistently wrong in predicting others' reactions to his or her behavior.

Cooley's key contribution here is the concept of *the looking-glass self*, or the idea that we develop our self-images on the basis of how others react to us. We see ourselves reflected in others, Cooley suggests, and so come to define ourselves as others do. This process is most effective within the "primary group"—another of Cooley's contributions—since a person is most sensitive to the attitudes of those with whom she or he has close, continuing relationships. The family, of course, is the major primary group for nearly everyone, so Cooley's perspective adds sociological emphasis to the importance of the family in socialization.

Mead, a philosopher and social psychologist, adds detail to the process through which the self develops. He divides the personality between the "I" and the "me," viewing the "I" as the individual who is acting *now* and the "me" as the sum of the individual's past experiences with others. The "I," then, turns to the "me" in order to get an idea of how others will respond to the "I's" future behavior. One useful deduction from this analysis is that our tendency to behave "in character," or in a way that is consistent with our previous behavior, is due to our tendency to expect of ourselves what we have learned that others expect of us.

Mead calls the members of our primary groups "significant others," and he too stresses their importance in helping us to develop a clearly defined self. But complete social maturity comes only when we have learned also to appreciate the relationships among others. Learning to play games is important to children, he says, because the child must eventually learn not only what others expect of it but also of one another. One cannot perform effectively as a guard in a basketball game, for instance, without knowing what the other players expect of one another. The ability to "take the role of the other," both with respect to oneself and to third parties, is thus a critically important goal of socialization.

In neither man's work do we find a complete theory of socialization or one that identifies particular stages of social development with precision. Both, however, emphasize the importance of interaction in the formation of the self and of the groups within which this occurs. With their distinctly sociological perspective on the process, both Mead and Cooley stress the fact that socialization is a social as well as a psychological process.

Erikson: The Self and Others Through the Life Cycle

Erik H. Erikson (b. 1902), a student of Freud's and widely known for his contributions to the field of psychohistory, has suggested an elaboration of the Freudian model. Erikson's model covers the entire life cycle and places greater emphasis on the individual's relations with others as they contribute to the growth of the self. He identifies eight successive problems that each person faces in encountering new social relationships in the process of growing older, and his model identifies the "dimension of the self" in terms of which each problem is resolved (Erikson, 1952). It points out, in other words, the extremes of satisfactory and unsatisfactory (psychologically "good" and "bad") resolutions of each problem.

The earliest "conclusion" the infant comes to in its relations with others is cast in terms of basic *trust or mistrust.* To the extent that its needs are cared for with warmth and consistency, the baby develops an attitude of generalized trust. As it senses greater inconsistency in others' behavior and attitudes toward it, however, its fundamental attitude will verge toward mistrust.

Later, as the child begins to explore the world around it, the way that its early adventures are defined as successful or as failures contributes to its sense of either *autonomy* or of *shame and doubt* about its own abilities. Still later, between the ages of four and five, when the child becomes more sensitive to others' responses to its behavior, its personality is further elaborated in terms of confidence in its own *initiative* or (at the other extreme) a sense of *guilt*—the feeling that its own actions are essentially unworthy, so that it is safer to be passive rather than active.

After the age of six, when the child's social environment expands to include the school, the critical problem in self-definition is cast in terms of *industry* or *inferiority:* Are the child's accomplishments rewarded, so that confidence in the ability to perform more sophisticated tasks is established, or is the child led to conclude that he or she is really unequal to these challenges?

During adolescence, roughly from twelve to eighteen years of age, the individual's central need is to answer the question "Who am I?" Erikson suggests that one's **peer group** *(one's equals)* is particularly important at this stage in helping to determine whether one emerges from this stage with a firm sense of *identity* or else of *role confusion.* To the extent that a person has developed a clearly defined, unambiguous self by the end of adolescence, he or she will be more capable of meeting the major problem of young adulthood—that of the willingness and ability to "open" oneself to another person. This is the challenge of *intimacy versus isolation,* and it is posed more directly as one explores the joys and sorrows that come with loving someone else.

Over the next twenty to forty years, the adult's personality is further shaped by the degree to which a sense of *generativity* (the feeling of accomplishment, contribution, and continuing growth) predominates over a sense of *stagnation.* The "crisis of middle age" apparently revolves about this problem, although the specific criteria by which each individual resolves it in his or her life are difficult to identify. Finally, in old age (beginning, say, in one's sixties) there is the ultimate characterization one achieves of himself or herself. Erikson sees this as the distinction between *integrity* (an acceptance of oneself and a sense of the wholeness of one's life) and *despair* (a basic sorrow over previous failures and the impossibility of "straightening out" one's past).

Erikson thus envisions a continuous interplay between the individual and others throughout life, in which the personality's growth takes different turns as new problems in defining one's self are met and answered in one way or another. He does not say that failure to resolve one challenge satisfactorily dooms one to failure in answering all of the successive problems, but it is clear that a less successful conclusion to one stage of self-definition will make it more difficult for a person to resolve the next one successfully.

Some Reflections on Theories of Development

Although a neat, systematic model of the entire socialization process is not yet available in a form acceptable to all social scientists, we can at least identify the major phenomena it will have to include. These are the emotional and cognitive components of the self and the social relationships that shape their development.

Each of these three aspects of socialization has distinct qualities, involves different aspects of the individual, and presumably must be measured in different ways. We assume, for instance, that emotional development begins with the person's ability to experience physical pleasure and pain. On this foundation are built more and more complex definitions of "good" and "bad," shaped largely by culture and emerging finally as values. These values, in turn, provide not only motivation, but also standards for evaluating the self. Cognitive development, the increasing ability to use symbols more effectively, seems quite a separate process. These two aspects of socialization, however, are intricately interdependent, and neither can be understood in the absence of the other.

Finally, there is the input of society to this process. One's relationships with others shape one's needs, motives, and sense of self; they determine to a great extent the content of one's knowledge of the world as well as the kinds of intellectual abilities that will be encouraged. We know that neither emotional nor cognitive growth can occur in the absence of social relationships, and yet they influence each other within the individual in ways that are apparently independent of social influences.

We have at minimum, then, a triangular relationship among three conceptually distinct components of the socialization process, each of which is partially independent of the others but is at the same time greatly influenced by them. Freud, Piaget, Cooley, Mead, and Erikson have led us by different routes to an appreciation of how complex the process of socialization is. A *complete* theory of socialization, however, must await further developments: more useful ways to conceptualize these components and increased knowledge of the ways and sequences in which they encourage, inhibit, and redirect one another's development.

SOCIETY'S ARRANGEMENTS FOR SOCIALIZATION

It was stressed earlier that the newborn child arrives in the midst of an ongoing society. Since the birth of children is a relatively routine event in society (despite the excitement of individual parents), we can expect that regular arrangements have been made—some social structures have been prepared—to care for the new arrivals. Since the beginnings of human society, the principal structure to which this task has been assigned has been the family. This does not mean, of course, that the family was consciously designed for the purpose of socializing society's new members. But so long as a baby has value to others—whether this is based on mother-love, the father's pride in his virility, or the potential economic importance of a child to the group—there is motivation to look after it. And, as with other continuing human interests, this motivation has led to the establishment of particular social relationships through which it can be implemented.

The Family: Society's Major Socialization Structure

The family is one of the principal institutions of society. It is discussed as a social institution in Chapter 13, where it is shown to have developed as the result of several different human and social needs. Here, our interest in the family will be restricted to its importance as the major site of the initial socialization process. Occupying a cluster of closely interrelated statuses, the family's members naturally spend a good deal of time together, usually in the household. The child spends most of its early life within this primary group, and so its experiences within the family ordinarily carry the greatest weight in shaping the child's self.

Until quite recently in human history, however, there was little awareness on the part of parents that there was more to bringing up children than keeping them fed, healthy, and out of trouble. Indeed, child rearing for most of the world's population is still largely a matter of unreflective behavior: coping with the child's needs in mostly the same ways that one's own parents did and instilling in the child (both consciously and unconsciously) the values and attitudes of one's particular society, ethnic group, and social class.

Until recently, also, a child was usually defined as simply a small adult, and there was little, if any, conception of adolescence as a special period of life. A child as young as three or four can make useful contributions to the family, tribe, or village, even if its strength and judgment are not equal to those of adults. Throughout most of history, then, conscious attempts at socialization consisted mainly of teaching the child how to participate usefully in the group's economic and religious activities. Collective problems of survival were usually so severe that there was no opportunity to leave children free of full-time obligations; the postponement of adulthood until the age of sixteen or later is predominantly a relatively recent characteristic of modern, industrialized societies.

Although the family is found in every society, the activities and relationships that go on within the family, particularly as they influence the growing child, can vary considerably. Toilet training may begin early or late, and it may be harsh or casual; similar variations are found in weaning. The amount of physical freedom allowed the child is another dimension of variation, as is the determination of which older members of the family take major responsibility for the child. Punishment for misbehavior may be severe or almost nonexistent. The line between childhood and adulthood may be sharp or quite hazy. The age at which the child undertakes full-time work may vary by as much as twenty years, and both the kinds of work and the extent to which they are defined as appropriate to one sex or the other can vary considerably as well.

Yet we do not find clear-cut relationships between specific child-rearing patterns and particular personality types. There is not, for instance, a high correlation between the age at which toilet training was begun and particular adult personality traits, or between the amount of exploratory behavior allowed a child and the kind of career to which he or she will be attracted later on. The incredible *number* of experiences that each person has during childhood, the differing order in which they occur for each individual, and the different ways each person makes sense of his or her experiences mean that the shaping of the self is far too complex for us to reduce it to a few simple cause-and-effect relationships.

We do, however, find large clusters of child-rearing patterns that tend to go together and that tend to produce individuals with different types of selves. If a mother stresses early toilet training, for instance, it is likely that she will also employ physical punishment (as contrasted with verbal punishment —scolding) in coping with misbehavior and that she will value behavioral conformity more than intellectual growth. Such combinations of specific practices and goals are in turn related to the family's social class and probably to ethnic or regional subcultures as well. They seem to reflect the basic conditions in which the family lives and the ways that have been found most effective in dealing with these conditions.

For example, if the breadwinner's job requires taking orders rather than exercising independent judgment and remaining at the mercy of changing economic conditions (a miner, factory worker, or longshoreman, for instance), conformity in the child will be seen as more important than individual initiative and creativity. If, on the other hand, the family's circumstances encourage greater independence of action (as when the breadwinner is a lawyer, editor, business executive, or scientist), the child is likely to grow up in an atmosphere that stresses curiosity, self-expression, and personal responsibility (Kohn, 1969).

Out of such broadly differing families tend to come differing selves —selves that are particularly shaped to continue the kinds of lives that their parents led. This is true despite the fact that there is always a certain amount of intergenerational conflict, or what has been called the generation gap. One might argue, in fact, that such conflicts are the result of there being such similarities in the selves of parents and children, for conflicts are sharpest when disagreements are set against the participants' need for one another and when they are aware that they are actually very much alike.

Socialization thus ensures a good deal of continuity within society, particularly in terms of its ethnic, class, and regional subcultures. The specific attitudes, values, and expectations of self that develop within the family continue into the next generation. In one sense, these act as restraints or blinders, limiting the extent to which the individual can adopt a different lifestyle later in life and thus slowing the overall rate of social mobility within society (see Chapter 6, on social stratification). In another sense, though, by encouraging the continuity of different lifestyles, socialization tends to sustain the identities of different groups within society. In the long run, this means the the majority of people are given opportunity to develop more detailed, integrated selves than would be possible if their only group identity were that of "citizen."

(It is perhaps for this reason that the idea of "mass society" is so often criticized. In a completely standardized world in which childhood experiences and adult lifestyles are common to all, interesting variation among people would certainly be much lessened. Worse, people's selves would be boringly similar; the sense of individuality, or of the uniqueness of one's self, would be missing, and an important American value would be lost.)

The Peer Group

To the child, any older person is someone with greater power and authority. Until the age of ten or twelve, even a year's difference in age between two children usually means that the older one is significantly superior in social and physical skills. It is quite realistic, then, for the child to equate "older" with "better." These differences are accentuated within the family, where older children are often put in charge of the younger ones, and in school, where age groups are segregated by grade, and higher grades have progressively more prestige.

For the first several years of life, the child's social experiences are usually colored by others' greater power and authority. The child is controlled by others, and its self-image incorporates this fact. After the age of three, however, as he or she becomes more independent, there is increasing opportunity to interact with others of about the same age. Now, for the first time, the child is equal to others, and it is in the peer group that the child's relations with others are not influenced by their built-in superiority.

In the early years of school, of course, and even playing in the neighborhood, children are usually under close adult supervision. But this decreases as they grow older, and they are increasingly exposed to the kinds of relationships that will occupy most of their adult lives—relationships with equals rather than with superiors.

Since one's peers lack the *authority* to control one's activities (even though brute strength and, later, leadership abilities will make some children "more equal" than others), one has more freedom with them—and a chance to be evaluated on grounds other than those of conformance to adults' rules. The child is reflected in a new kind of mirror, so to speak, and this can be quite rewarding. Behavior forbidden by adults may be rewarded by peers; the self expands as new qualities and abilities are recognized by others.

As the young person spends more and more time with peers, he or she must (and wants to) learn to get along with them; the developing self, in other words, must take account more and more of peers' expectations as well as those of parents, teachers, and other adults. During adolescence, the peer group develops a more clearly defined subculture, aided by both the structure of the schools and the image of "youth" that is presented by advertisers and by the mass media. Thus the chances increase that the teenager will experience conflict between what adults expect and what peers expect. The self may have a rough time for a while as the question of "Who am I?" becomes more difficult to answer. (This is the period, in Erikson's analysis, when the essential choice is between identity and role confusion.)

But as the individual slowly settles into the status of adult and his or her identity is more clearly defined by family and occupational responsibilities (whether or not the Eriksonian question of identity has been fully resolved), the peer group loses its importance as a special group. Instead, it gradually expands to become the individual's entire social environment. And with the establishment of a new family and the arrival of children, the cycle begins all over again.

Thus the self is increasingly shaped by the responses of one's equals rather than by those of authority figures. Because the change in the nature of one's "significant others" begins in late childhood and is largely completed by the end of adolescence, we tend to think of this period as the one during which the peer group is of greatest importance. Actually, however, all of one's adult life is lived with the peer group (in the broadest sense); its significance for socialization declines simply because the process has been mostly completed by the time one reaches maturity.

The School

Although the child's peer group tends to be composed primarily of school classmates, we distinguish between the peer group and the school because the latter is quite different in structure. As an organized set of interrelated statuses, the school is the principal social structure through which consciously planned socialization is carried out. The peer group, on the other hand, tends to be informal and unplanned, even though it often exists within the larger, planned structure of the school.

The school (from the Greek *skhole*, meaning "leisure devoted to learning") is essentially an extension of the family, for it specializes in advanced socialization and plays an important part in placing the child in society. As soon as any society develops specialized occupations that have their own subcultures (the priesthood and the military are major examples that date back thousands of years), it is often the case that a youngster must undergo intensive training before he or she can enter that occupation. Arrangements for such training constituted the earliest formal "schools."

Earlier than that, of course, specialized training outside the family was not unknown. An older member of the tribe, for instance, might make a regular practice of telling myths and stories to groups of village children; a pottery maker would instruct apprentices in the art of firing clay. Gradually, the school was recognized as a distinct new part of the social structure.

Although today we tend to think that schools are devoted mainly to cognitive skills ("readin', 'ritin', and 'rithmetic"), in earlier times they often devoted considerable attention to training in motivation and ideals. Vestiges of this remain today in the way our schools seek to instill patriotism, honesty, and "good work habits." But with the development of universal public education in the nineteenth century, differences over *which* values should be taught (particularly because schoolchildren form a captive audience) have been resolved by keeping the ideological content of public schooling to a minimum. The ban on prayers in public schools is, of course, a logical extension of the legal separation of church and state, but in a broader sense it is a good illustration of this process.

Parochial schools and others at which attendance is voluntary (that is, they may be chosen by a child's parents as an alternative to public school) have much more freedom in this respect. And since all college attendance is voluntary, the extent to which colleges try to train students in particular values and motivations depends largely on student demand.

In general, then, we may say that the schools carry primary responsibility for cognitive socialization, ranging from the basic intellectual skills (the "three Rs" noted above) to advanced occupational skills such as medicine, law, and scientific research. To the extent, however, that the cognitive components of socialization are less important than the affective, or emotional, in the development of the self, we must conclude that the school is less important than the family in this basic social process.

This is not to say that the schools have no impact on children. The classroom provides a new set of adults with whom they must learn to interact and, correspondingly, new significant others whose responses help to mold their selves. Beyond this, as new intellectual skills open the doors to new activities and social relationships, the school can have even more important consequences for socialization. It is through this, in fact, that formal education helps to offset the "conservative" influence of the family and encourages social mobility by expanding the self beyond those definitions provided by family and peers.

As the formal certification of students' education becomes increasingly important, however—and this is the fundamental reason for grades, transcripts, and diplomas—the school may be seen to contribute more to the effective operation of other social structures than it does to the direct socialization of individual students. Yet it remains society's major structure for the advanced socialization of its members, and the sociology of education has become an important area of specialization within sociology.

Adult Socialization

It should be obvious, finally, that the socialization process does not necessarily come to a halt at the age of fifteen or even twenty-five, although basic changes in adults' selves tend to be the exception rather than the rule. **Adult socialization** *occurs when one enters an important new status,* such as husband, wife, supervisor, or senator, *or when one assumes subsequent statuses* such as unemployed person, divorced or widowed person, or retired worker, *or in some other way is reshaped.* The most common form of purposeful adult socialization, even though it ordinarily involves little change in the self, is found in advanced education—vocational programs, college, postgraduate work, and professional "refresher courses." For most people, such changes represent additions *to* the self rather than radical changes *in* the self. Yet there are circumstances under which far-reaching personality change occurs. A brief examination of such situations will throw more light on the nature of the socialization process.

First, there are times when an adult *wants* to change his or her personality, or at least gets into a desirable new situation and then finds that his or her self has been extensively changed in the process. A person who enters psychotherapy or a drug addict who joins a therapeutic community is pretty well aware that the help he or she needs will require basic personality changes. A person entering medical school may not do so for the express purpose of changing her or his self, but will find this happening as medical training proceeds. Out of the former situation will come, it is hoped, a better person; out of the latter will come someone with a new, firm professional identity (Becker, *et al.,* 1961).

The adult self may also be changed *against* the individual's will. Because involuntary personality change is unpleasant, however, it generally occurs only when the individual is reluctant or unable to leave the situation that is producing the change—when he or she is in prison, a mental hospital, a boarding school, basic training in the armed forces, etc.

How does this process of adult socialization (or, actually, *re*socialization) work? If we accept the fact that a fully developed self is already in existence, it is clear that this self must be broken down before it can be significantly changed. But the individual ordinarily resists this, for the existing self is both valuable and useful. It *is* one's identity; the distress one feels at the prospect of having *no* identity or no answer to the question "Who am I?" should demon-

The adult self may be changed through: (1) separation of the individual from old relationships and activities; and/or (2) systematic devaluation of the "old self" in a new environment. These marines will be made to desire a "new self" by being forced to engage in demeaning activities and to endure criticism and insults. (Burk Uzzle/ Magnum Photos)

strate its central value to the individual. Further, as was pointed out earlier, the self provides guidance in one's relations with others. To break down the self, then, requires that both of these positive aspects be undermined.

To undermine the utility of the already established self, the individual must be sharply cut off from the relationships, settings, and activities in which it was previously useful and must be prevented from recreating them. This occurs most completely when one enters prison (Cressey, 1961) or a mental hospital (Goffman, 1961), but happens on a lesser scale whenever one moves into a completely new situation: a college dormitory, a branch of the armed forces, or a new job far from home. If the move is accompanied by mandatory changes in personal appearance (a GI haircut, for example, or a new kind of clothing), the break with the past is made even more complete.

Beyond this, an additional experience is necessary: the severe, systematic devaluation of the "old self" by others in the new situation. Being forced to engage in demeaning activities (the hazing a new fraternity member may go through, or assignment to KP during basic training) and being made the object of insults that stress how "bad" the old self was, the individual comes to *want* to develop a new self. Simply for the sake of survival as an integrated person, the old self must be discarded, and a new one, appropriate to the new situation, must be created. The process of devaluing the old self may involve no more than someone's saying impatiently, "You're not a kid anymore"; it may be a drill sergeant's relentless criticisms and insults; and in extreme cases it can extend to enforced public self-criticism, as occurred in the brainwashing techniques employed in prisoner-of-war camps during the Korean War (Schein, 1971).

After a new self has developed, the individual is likely to be just as attached to it as he or she was to the previous self—and just as resistant to having it changed. This fact takes on poignant meaning when we read of people who have been "converted" to a religious movement and then broken contact with their parents and former friends. It may be claimed that they have been brainwashed and thus "psychologically kidnapped," but they often resist attempts to change them back to their former selves. The possession of a reasonably whole self, regardless of its specific nature, seems of greater importance than the particular details of its makeup, and we can understand why these people, once converted, are so resistant to change.

Although extreme or dramatic instances of adult socialization are relatively rare in society, their occurrence should make us aware that less striking examples of the same process occur much more frequently in adult life and that they work in the same ways, although more slowly, to produce changes in the adult self. The important difference, of course, between childhood socialization and adult socialization is that in the former, the individual develops a self out of nothing. Adult socialization requires the additional step of breaking down, or at least loosening up, a self that has already been formed. To the extent that the self seeks to protect itself or to resist being changed, adult socialization tends to occur in situations of major change and when the self's defenses have been weakened. If this were not so, a large part of the continuity of social life would be lost.

SUMMARY

The shaping of individuals so that they both want to participate in social relationships and know how to do this is accomplished through the process of socialization: the development of each person's *self*. A person's self is essentially his or her social identity—a combination of the awareness of one's own needs and abilities together with a generalized definition of one as an individual, based on how others have responded to one in the past. The study of socialization includes attention to both the inner development of the self and the outer, or social, arrangements that facilitate and influence this process.

Although the individual's genetic endowment naturally sets limits to what he or she is capable of, the fact that "nurture" so often masks "nature" leads the sociologist to concentrate on the former. The self develops through interaction with others, although it is shaped also by the physical, intellectual, and emotional changes that go on during the first two decades of life. Several theories of the development of the self, each emphasizing a different aspect of the process, have been formulated. Those of Freud (psychosexual development), Piaget (cognitive development), Cooley and Mead (social development), and Erikson (the self throughout the life cycle) were described here.

The family is the principal social structure within which socialization takes place, and the experiences of the child in the family usually work to produce an individual especially suited to carrying on that family's lifestyle in the next generation. A good deal of society's continuity over time can be traced to this fact.

The peer group provides the child's first opportunity to interact with equals and assumes greater and greater importance as he or she grows older. The school represents a specialized extension of the family's responsibilities for advanced cognitive training and subsequent occupational placement and may balance the "conservative" influences of the family in terms of facilitating greater social mobility.

Finally, our discussion of adult socialization reemphasizes the basic components of the socialization process and reminds us that the self changes throughout life, although generally at a much slower pace than it develops initially during childhood.

SUGGESTED READINGS

Aries, Phillipe, *Centuries of Childhood: A Social History of Family Life* (New York: Vintage, 1962). Translated from the French, this is a fascinating survey of changing definitions of childhood over the past several hundred years and the accompanying changes in the ways children have been treated as members of the family.

Elkin, Frederick, and Gerald Handel, *The Child and Society: The Process of Socialization*, 2d ed. (New York: Random House, 1972). An excellent introduction to the topic, well written and much more detailed than this chapter.

Erikson, Erik H., *Childhood and Society* (New York: Norton, 1952). In this book Erikson develops the model of socialization described at greater length in this chapter. His writing is clear and persuasive, and one can see here the foundations of his later studies of Martin Luther and Mahatma Gandhi.

Goffman, Erving, *Asylums* (Garden City, N.Y.: Doubleday/Anchor, 1961). This insightful volume provides a meaningful analysis of the painful process of adult socialization that goes on in "total institutions" such as prisons and mental hospitals.

Jencks, Christopher, *et al.*, *Inequality: A Reassessment of the Effect of Schooling in America* (New York: Basic Books, 1972). Here, Jencks and his colleagues consider some aspects of the nature/nurture argument and conclude that luck plays a much larger part in "success" than is usually supposed. The book is also relevant to social stratification (Chapter 6), but is cited here because of its importance in helping to clarify the relations among family socialization, schooling, and how people fare as adults.

Glossary

Adult socialization The processes through which the self (see below) is reshaped during adulthood. Even in cases of radical change in the self, this may be voluntary (for example, seeking psychotherapy or assistance in giving up drug addiction) or involuntary (as when one is subjected to brainwashing [see below]). In less extreme form, it involves mainly acquiring additional skills and/or elaborating one's self-image rather than changing the basic character of one's self.

Affective development The aspect of socialization that involves the shaping of one's emotional self, in contrast to the development of cognitive and social abilities. A prominent effort to understand affective development is Freud's theory of the stages of psychosexual development.

Brainwashing The process of systematically breaking down a person's previously established self, usually against his or her will, so that a new self must be constructed that will more closely suit the requirements of the brainwashers. This involves both depriving the person of social support for that self (for instance, cutting off contact with previous friends and situations) and making it seem undesirable (through insults, enforced self-criticism, etc.). Since the process can be quite unpleasant, it generally occurs either when someone cannot escape from it or when its outcome promises to be especially rewarding. After a new self has been shaped by those administering the process, the person may well come to value it and to believe that the outcome fully justifies the experience.

Cognitive development The aspect of socialization that involves the shaping of the intellectual aspects of one's self (such as IQ and the power of reasoning). This is to be distinguished from affective and social development. The work of Piaget has been concerned primarily with the stages of cognitive development.

Libido Freud's name for the basic, generalized desire for pleasure that exists in all human beings. As socialization progresses, the libido becomes more differentiated and focuses first on specific parts of one's body and then on other people.

Nature As used in discussing socialization, *nature* refers to the newborn child's genetic inheritance, or everything that is already "built in" at the time of birth. It is thus to be distinguished from everything that happens to the child and influences it after birth (see **Nurture**).

Nurture As used in discussing socialization, *nurture* refers to all of the influences one experiences after birth that contribute to one's affective, cognitive, and social development (see **Nature**, above).

Peer group Any group made up of one's equals. The term usually refers to a child's friends and classmates who are about the same age, but it can refer also to an adult's circle of friends and acquaintances. The key quality of the peer group is that its members are not clearly distinguished by differences in power or authority.

Self The individual as the object of his or her own awareness. The self is composed of an awareness of not only one's own needs, desires, abilities, and limitations, but also how one seems to appear to others (as judged by their responses to one). A healthy, realistic self (or self-image) is the end result of a successful process of socialization. To the extent that one's self-image is poorly integrated or unrealistic, interaction with others is more difficult and less satisfying.

Social development The aspect of socialization that involves one's relations with other people and particularly the ways that the development of one's self is influenced by these relationships. The theories of Cooley, Mead, and Erikson emphasize this facet of the socialization process.

Socialization A general term covering the processes of cognitive and affective development within the individual and also the social structures and patterns of interaction involving the individual which facilitate his or her social development. A satisfactory model of the relationships among these three aspects of socialization is yet to be developed, but the end result of socialization is a *self* which makes the individual capable of effective and satisfactory participation in society.

5
The Case of Changing Sex Roles

FOCUS: *ROLE CHANGE*
Because the roles associated with social statuses are delineated by norms, role change obviously involves changes in norms. And because norms exist as expectations, **role change** *means changes in people's assumptions about the rights and obligations that should be accepted by anyone who occupies a particular status.*

Role change is possible, of course, because there is no intrinsic relationship between the initial reasons that people come to occupy statuses and the specific roles they are expected to play. If a status were no more than the roles played by its occupant, we would have to recognize new statuses continually—because a change in role would mean, strictly speaking, a change in status. But since the *names* of statuses do not change as rapidly as do the *norms associated with them*, we ordinarily think of statuses as having a social reality apart from the specific roles currently "assigned" to them.

The study of role change is thus the study of not only how and why norms change, but also how people come to occupy statuses in the first place and how their roles come to be defined and maintained. In this chapter we shall be particularly concerned with changes in the roles associated with the statuses of "male" and "female." The phenomenon of role change in general, however, extends far beyond sex roles, so that concentration on them will also serve to illustrate the broader process.

BASIC ASPECTS OF ROLE CHANGE

Role change may occur slowly or rapidly, and it may or may not be due to the conscious efforts of those involved. Changes in the rights and obligations of children, for instance, have taken place slowly over several centuries, and the changes from one generation to the next have been so slight that only the work of social historians has made us clearly aware of them. Changes in the roles of black Americans, on the other hand, have come with relative rapidity over the past twenty-five years—and only after a great deal of conscious protest and legal action.

Four aspects of the process of role change require our attention if we are to explore and understand it systematically. First, we need to know how people have come to occupy a particular status. Second, we want to know how the norms currently governing this status developed and have been maintained. Third, we must pay attention to the social conditions that have produced either actual change in the roles associated with it or at least the desire that they change. Finally, we should examine the various mechanisms through which role change actually takes place.

The topic is obviously complex. It will be useful, then, to consider these four questions in a general way before we apply them to the specific problem of changes in sex roles.

Occupying Statuses

People occupy statuses (as discussed in Chapter 2) because they have either chosen to occupy them (achieved statuses) or been assigned to them by others (ascribed statuses). In the case of achieved statuses, we may assume that most people are reasonably satisfied with the rights and obligations that go with these statuses, since otherwise they would not have chosen to occupy them in the first place. There are, of course, exceptions to this rule. Whenever occupancy of an achieved status is less than fully voluntary (as when a woman marries in order to escape spinsterhood, a man enlists in the Army because he cannot find employment in civilian life, or a business executive accepts an assignment to an unpleasant location because she wants to continue to rise in the corporation), it is not automatically true that he or she will be entirely satisfied with the rights and obligations that go with the new status.

Ascribed statuses, however, are not always occupied willingly. They are assigned to people by others, regardless of the assignees's wishes, and may entail an undesirable combination of few rights and many obligations. Because most people cannot easily escape from their ascribed statuses, it is understandable that the roles attached to these statuses are more often the focus of conscious attempts to bring about role change.

This does not mean to say that all ascribed statuses are burdensome. People begin their lives, after all, with ascribed statuses—sex, age, and family membership (which entails ethnic and social-class identities as well)—and these come to make up an important part of the self (see Chapter 4). To the extent that a person neither desires additional rights nor rejects the obligations normatively associated with an ascribed status, there will be little conscious interest in role change. Further, because the sense of self (the individual's concept of "who I am") is rooted more deeply in ascribed than in achieved statuses, there may be considerable resistance to role change if this seems to threaten the integrity of the self that has already been established.

Still, role change does occur. And this means that one or more roles must already exist—else there would be nothing to change *from*.

The Establishment of Roles

The various activities required for human survival certainly provided the initial basis for identifying statuses and establishing the norms that governed their occupants. It is, of course, possible for an isolated individual to undertake all of the activities needed for personal survival, but since people are born into groups and ordinarily spend their lives in the company of others, a rudimentary division of labor has been characteristic of the human species since its emergence on the earth. In particular, the fact that humans are not parthenogenic—that is, they are not capable of self-fertilization, but instead are divided into two sexes whose cooperation is necessary if the species is to be perpetuated—forms the single most important basis for the division of labor. This fact will come in for more intensive discussion later.

Beyond the distinction between male and female, which in fact is of crucial importance in the social organization of nearly all nonhuman species as well, we may suppose that even in the earliest human groups, some people came to engage in certain activities more than others did. These activities acquired names, and those names came to identify statuses. The activities of hunting, gathering, planting, weaving, healing, leading, story telling, etc., must have formed the basis for some of the earliest social statuses.

But the ascribed statuses of age, sex, and lineage were certainly of central importance, for they were crucial in defining broader and more fundamental social relationships. Expectations defining mutual obligations were based primarily on family relationships. Expectations regarding what one might be able or required to do now and in the future because of certain visible characteristics (again—sex, age, and parentage) defined different roles. Ascribed statuses thus assumed greater significance than achieved statuses because they defined ahead of time the kinds of activities that individuals could be expected to engage in later on. Beginning at birth, then, people were trained to play the roles associated with their ascribed statuses, and their self-expectations (that is, their *selves*) were shaped accordingly.

Because roles are interrelated and because people seem to need a fair amount of predictability in their lives, it is logical that people needed not only to "invent" statuses based on current and anticipated future behavior, but also to *confine* people to the roles associated with their statuses. The advantages gained through the identification of social statuses have thus required the "fixing" of roles, and violations of normative expectations (that is, of roles) have been met with negative sanctions (unpleasant responses) since the beginnings of human groups. In general, then, role change tends to be viewed as undesirable, unless it is to everyone's advantage, and this is rarely clear to everyone involved.

Sources of Role Change

The fact that roles are interrelated (for example, the wife's rights are the husband's obligations, and vice-versa) means that role change is not something that the occupant of given status can accomplish unilaterally. Role change requires the cooperation of others in related statuses, and the circumstances under which such cooperation can be obtained provide a convenient way to discuss the various sources of role change.

We can think of three distinct circumstances in which role change may occur through conscious human intent. First, the occupant of a more powerful status may require changes in the role played by the occupant of a subordinate status. A manager, for instance, may change the job specifications of a worker, or the rights of the members of a minority group may be increasingly limited by the threats or actions of the more powerful majority group. In the former case, role change is enforced by the conditions of continued employment; in the latter, it is based on threatened or actual physical coercion.

Sometimes such changes are initiated because a change in technology or resources makes it possible or necessary. As banks have come to depend more on computers, for example, their employees have had to learn how to use them if they want to keep their jobs. If, in the antebellum South, a plantation's land lost its fertility and a new kind of crop had to be grown, the slave owner would require the slaves to adapt their roles to the requirements of the new crop. Here, change in the roles associated with particular statuses came about because it was to the advantage of the occupants of related statuses, and it was achieved because the other statuses commanded greater power.

Second, the occupants of interrelated statuses may see, although often not too clearly, that it will be to their mutual advantage to change their reciprocal rights and obligations. This might occur when a wife finds full-time employment; it will be more satisfying for both of them if the husband takes more responsibility for the housework and if she participates fully in decisions about spending *their* money. Historically and on a broader scale, children's roles in this country changed slowly, as mandatory public schooling spread during the late nineteenth century and as children's economic value to the family decreased. The physician's role has changed (with the cooperation of patients)

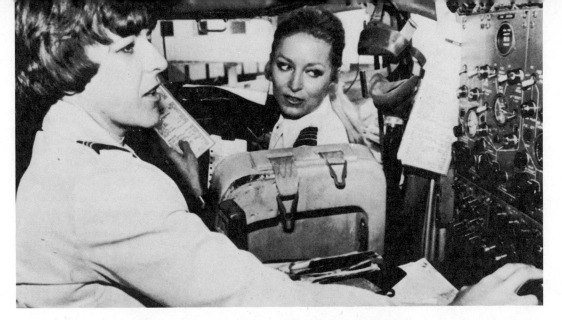

First Officer Valerie Petrie and Second Officer Cindy Rucker, preparing to take off from Los Angeles International Airport, are the first two female pilots to occupy the same cockpit on a scheduled commercial jet flight. In the past, women were assigned to duties considered appropriate for females; today, however, expectations are changing, and more women are filling positions formerly restricted to men. (U.P.I.)

as medical care has become more specialized and as preventive medicine has become a more important part of the physician's responsibilities.

As new social structures come into being and as new technologies open the doors to new activities and relationships, the need for role change is often perceived by everyone. Such changes are usually viewed simply as sensible adaptations to new circumstances, and the problems that accompany role change tend to be those of coordinating the shift to new expectations rather than of conflict over whether change should occur at all.

Third, the occupants of certain statuses may work actively to change their *own* roles, even when those in related statuses do not wish to cooperate. Changes in the relationships between Jews and Christians, between blacks and whites, and between men and women illustrate this type of role change. It is the opposite of the first source described above, for here the initiative comes from those who are currently unhappy with the roles imposed on them by others rather than from those who will profit from the changes they impose on others.

Under what circumstances do people come to want change in their roles or in the roles of related statuses? In the case of *imposed* role change, we may suppose that people occupying the more powerful status discover new ways to profit at the expense of those occupying the weaker status. Thus they enforce changes that will be to their advantage. If the repeal of laws recognizing the rights of labor unions were to be accomplished, this would be a victory for business interests and would diminish the rights of those occupying the status of worker.

On the other hand, the roles of some statuses have always been acknowledged to be unpleasant, but their occupants do not actively seek role change until they see it as a realistic possibility. The roles imposed on slaves in ancient Rome and in the antebellum South, for example, were certainly known to everyone as distinctly unpleasant, but the enforcers of those roles were too powerful to be disobeyed successfully. When, however, the slave population grew so large that a successful revolt became a distinct possibility, forcible efforts to escape from or to destroy those who had imposed the slave role were occasionally attempted. A change in the relative power of the occupants of interrelated statuses, then, may be an occasion for the disadvantaged parties to seek role change.

A change in cultural values can be a second source of the motivation to seek change in one's own roles. Roles that were formerly defined as entirely fair and reasonable can be redefined, from the perspective of new values, as unfair and unjust. What was formerly acceptable becomes unacceptable, and the new evaluation becomes the basis for seeking change. A change in social circumstances can contribute importantly to this. When conditions change so that the occupant of one status takes on new obligations but is not accorded commensurate rights by the occupant of a related status, the sense of unfairness is brought into the open.

The roles played by women during the nineteenth century in this country were largely accepted by both men and women. However, as women began to enter the work force in increasing numbers and as the family slowly became less central in the American social structure (so that men's and women's interdependence became less important), more attention was focused on the concept of equality, and the disadvantages of women's roles became more clearly recognized. Even in the early 1800s, of course, a small minority of women were certainly aware of the limits imposed on them by their "women's roles," but this awareness spread only slowly until after 1900. (Landmarks in the quickening movement to change women's roles are discussed later in this chapter.)

Mechanisms of Role Change

Change in one status's rights and obligations necessarily requires change in the rights and obligations of related statuses. Rarely, however, do we find a situation in which all those who occupy related statuses agree entirely on the need for, or the details of, a change in the norms governing their relationship. It ordinarily requires persuasion at least, and often power—either acquired by those who would initiate change or else gained through the intervention of third parties—to achieve enduring change in those norms.

Persuasion to accept change is usually based on demonstrating the practical advantages to be gained by all through change and/or arguments citing the "moral superiority" of the new norms in relation to the old. As the result of a new union contract, for instance, employees in certain positions may accept new responsibilities in return for higher wages, or managers may grant additional rights to employees in return for higher productivity. In both cases all parties accept the changes because it is to their advantage to do so.

The civil rights movement, on the other hand, has succeeded in winning acceptance of changes in the relations between whites and various minority groups largely because these changes came to be defined as embodying more clearly the basic values to which all Americans should subscribe. In particular, relationships involving systematic discrimination on the basis of racial and ethnic statuses were eventually interpreted as being at odds with the values expressed in the Constitution. Not only were laws that supported discrimination declared invalid, but also new laws were passed which made the imposition of such role relationships illegal. Here the power of the weaker status was enhanced by the intervention of a third party—the courts, backed by the strength of the state—so that morality was used to secure the aid of a powerful third party.

Power, of course, is not always legitimate. If it is the power of the state, guided by law, we must consider it legitimate, whether or not we think it is fair. Racial discrimination was supported and even required by legitimate power in America until the middle of this century, but since then it has been defined as illegal. Earlier patterns of discrimination were also enforced by the illegitimate power of lynch mobs and other forms of private intimidation. The difference is that legitimate power is the power of the state and is supposed to command the support of all citizens; illegitimate power does not have these characteristics and is itself, in principle at least, illegal.

Whether legitimate or not, power may be used to maintain the imposition of unwanted roles on certain statuses or to force unwanted role change on the occupants of certain statuses, whether this is to the increased advantage of the stronger or the weaker of the statuses involved. The control of power is thus of continuing concern in every society (see Chapter 12, on the political institution), particularly because of its importance in determining role relationships.

The acceptance of change by all those who may occupy two or more interrelated statuses, however, is only half the problem. Whether role change is accepted on the basis of moral persuasion or simply because those who wish it are too powerful to be resisted, there remains the problem of making sure that everyone involved knows that everyone else knows and accepts the change—and then of coordinating the shift to the new role relationships.

To the extent that people are unsure that others know and are willing to abide by the new norms, they will be reluctant to switch to new roles. The greater the number of people who may occupy a particular set of interrelated statuses (for instance, all those in a society who may occupy the statuses of husband, wife, and mother-in-law or those of employer, employee, and labor-relations arbitrator), the more difficult it will be for each of them to be certain that those occupying related statuses are aware of and will accept the changes in their relationships.

The ways in which people become aware of what others are thinking are discussed in more detail in Chapter 17, on public opinion and collective behavior. It is enough to say here that with the advent of the mass media and of near-universal literacy, the task of publicizing role change is much easier than it was even a few decades ago. Both private and public communications are so much more effective today that news of impending role changes spreads much more rapidly—and is likely to be accepted more readily.

Summing Up

The initial reasons that people come to occupy certain statuses determine in large part how much they or others will seek role change; the occupants of ascribed statuses are more likely to try to change their roles than are those who occupy achieved statuses.

The roles assigned to statuses develop on the basis of what their occupants are doing or may be expected to do in the future and in terms of their rights and obligations in relation to others. Most of the time, people accept their ascribed roles because they have been socialized to think of them as natural and satisfying. The rights and obligations that go with their sex, age, and family statuses make up a large part of their selves, so that to a large extent people *are* their ascribed statuses.

Role change, then, tends to happen under three circumstances: when it is imposed on certain statuses by the occupants of stronger, related statuses; when it is to the mutual advantage of the occupants of two or more interrelated statuses; and when the occupants of a particular status dislike their assigned roles and are able (through recognizing the possibility of change and then employing persuasion and/or power) to bring others to accept the changes they want.

THE ESTABLISHMENT OF SEX ROLES

Although no discussion can cover all of the factors that may have contributed to the establishment of sex roles in different times and places, it is at least possible to identify several that have been of major importance. There is, of course, no intrinsic link between one's anatomy and the rights and obligations one assumes as a result of this. Being "feminine" (that is, exhibiting the attitudes, interests, and activities expected of anyone occupying the status of "female") may in one society mean being flirtatious, ambitious, and selfish; in

another, just the opposite. But we cannot ignore the fact of strong though indirect linkages between anatomical sex differences and the norms that have
governed sex roles.

The Essential Situation

To begin with, it is of fundamental importance that there are only *two* sexes
and that they have a strong, continuing interest in each other. The nature of
sexual attraction, futhermore, ordinarily results in pairings—the establishment
of two-member groups. Such groups, called dyads, as we know from Simmel
(1950) (see Appendix 2, on sociological theory), have particular characteristics, especially the fact that their members must work out reciprocal rights and
obligations or else break up, leaving only isolated individuals.

The human need for such pairings has another important implication: The
two sexes cannot ordinarily be separated geographically for long. Thus, males
and females are usually distributed evenly throughout a society's territory.
There is little chance, in other words, that the sexes will be segregated spatially
on a permanent basis. Given, therefore, the existence of multiple male/female
pairs throughout a society and the fact that these pairs spend a substantial
amount of time alone together rather than in the presence of others, the pressures are strong and continuous for them to develop and maintain complementary roles.

There is another consequence of the fact that virtually everyone is assigned to one of only two sexual identities: No one can be accepted as
"neutral," or without vested interests in the norms defining sex roles. Labor
and management can turn to arbitrators for neutral advice on resolving their
differences; two nations on the verge of war can seek help in negotiations from
an uninvolved third nation; but in the case of the sexes, no such disinterested
third party exists. No matter who advocates either change in sex roles or their
maintenance without change, it must always be a "he" or a "she," and this
means (at least in the eyes of most people) that the advice must be tainted with
vested interests. As a result, sex roles have probably been more resistant to
conscious change than any other roles in humankind's history.

With the inescapable need for the two sexes to work out complementary
relationships *without* the help of third parties, factors related to physical differences and to the nature of the sex drive have taken on central importance in
determining the content of these relationships.

Anatomical Differences

The physical differences between males and females, apparent at birth in nearly all cases, are of critical importance to society. One's anatomical femaleness
or maleness determines which of the two basic, complementary parts one will

play in the reproductive process and thus which status one will occupy in the family. Because the family is the primary social unit within society and because, despite current concern about the population explosion, the birth of children is almost universally desired, one's sexual identity has generally been and remains of greater importance to society than any other single status one may hold. Each society throughout history has therefore ascribed a sexual status to each of its members, which means that every society has imposed particular normative expectations on its members because of their anatomies.

It is the female rather than the male who bears children and who is physically capable of nursing them after birth. Throughout most of history, further, infant mortality rates were quite high, children were viewed as being of considerable economic value, and reliable contraceptives did not exist. We may thus reason that a high proportion of adult women tended to be either preg-

Historically, there has been a tendency to relate the female's anatomy to activities centered on child bearing, child care, and the home. (The Bettman Archive)

nant or responsible for young children during almost all of their fertile years. This meant that they were frequently unavailable for long hunting trips or organized warfare.

Statistically, then, the tendency was to relate one's anatomical femaleness to activities centered in and close to the household. After all, if the maintenance of the family group required both "outside" activities—hunting, defense, warfare, large-scale tribal projects, etc.—and "inside" activities—cooking, weaving, child care, gardening, etc.—it must have seemed eminently sensible to assign the former responsibilities to males and the latter to females.

Differences in Size

A second correlate of sexual identity is that females tend to be smaller than males. The average adult American male today, for instance, is about 4½ inches taller than the average American female (5′9″ and 5′4½″, respectively). This difference has existed over at least the past hundred years, even though the average height of each sex has increased by about four inches over that period. Not surprisingly, this difference is associated with an average difference in weight of between thirty and forty pounds. We have reason to believe that on the average, males have been larger than females in most human populations since the emergence of *homo sapiens*.

Since the capacity for physical work is partly a function of size, many of the tasks on which human survival depended in the past thus came to be assigned to males: hunting, plowing with horses or oxen, building, and warfare. *Relative* physical weakness, then, together with occasional unavailability for certain activities because of pregnancy and child-care responsibilities, combined to sharpen the distinctions between the roles assigned to males and to females (Friedl, 1978).

Sexual Initiative

Two aspects of the sexual relationship itself have almost certainly contributed additionally to the definition of sex roles. For one thing, the specific physiology of sexual union means that the immediate initiative ordinarily rests with the male: He must be physically aroused before coitus can take place, but this is not true of the female. If female arousal were necessary before coitus could occur, the crime of heterosexual rape would not exist.

There is thus a kind of imbalance in the sexual "leadership" relationship between male and female. An aroused female cannot always bring a male to readiness for coitus, but an aroused male need not be concerned with the female's readiness for intercourse so long as she does not actively resist him. (It is true that a female may arrange the situation so that the male *wants* to take the initiative, but ultimately the initiative is still his.)

Having this natural advantage over the female, it is not surprising, although it is not laudable either, that the male has had an interest in ensuring that sexual initiative can be exercised at *his* convenience. Both his usually superior strength and the sexual initiative that is unavoidably his have secured for him the upper hand in sexual relations. This has presumably led to males' acquiring more power and authority over females in general and thus to the common tendency to restrict females to distinctly subordinate roles in society.

Avoiding Sexual Distraction

A second aspect of the sexual relationship requires mention as well. This is the fact that humankind's continuing interest in sexual pleasure ordinarily requires frequent (although not unceasing) opportunity for contact between the sexes. This is, of course, one of the major foundations of the marriage relationship (see Chapter 13, on the family). The other side of the coin, however, is that people may be distracted from an immediate task by the presence of members of the other sex. The result is that when tightly disciplined commitment to a complex task is required, there is a tendency to organize people into single-sex enterprises.

Whether the task is the building of a pyramid, the enactment of lengthy religious rituals, the waging of war, or the maintenance and exercise of political power, societies ordinarily seek to minimize the chance that sexual interests will distract those involved. This concern seems to lie at the root of the armed services' resistance to homosexuality; when a soldier is likely to be sexually distracted from his duties by another soldier, discipline is presumably weakened and the army's effectiveness lessened.

Only in rare cases (e.g., various religious orders) is sexual activity completely prohibited. More often, distractions due to sex are minimized by emphasizing a sharp division of labor between the sexes so that they have either relatively little contact with each other during engagement in goal-oriented activities or contact in relatively impersonal ways—usually achieved through clear-cut differences in authority. During nonworking hours, of course, the need for such barriers does not exist, and the sexes are free to mingle on a more personal basis.

This is certainly not to say that sexual interests do not exist within task-oriented social structures. The exploitation of females by males "on the job," facilitated by the males' typically greater authority, is probably as old as organized work itself. But it is also recognized as a danger to organizational efficiency in terms of both the direction of energies and the maintenance of formal authority. "No hanky-panky in the office" is one of the rules that (male) managers learn early, and even if the rule is systematically violated, its continued expression is evidence that people are aware of the dangers of sexual distraction.

The Outcome

Both the female's smaller average size and her capacity for bearing and nursing children have made it almost inevitable that males' and females' roles have been differentiated in certain specific ways in nearly all human societies. The physiology of sexual union and the potentially distracting force of sexual attraction have further reinforced the distinctions between the sexes' roles. The oucome has been, in most societies, the development of normatively enforced relations between the sexes in which the female's roles are characterized by fewer rights and more obligations than the male's.

With relatively few exceptions, women in nearly all societies have traditionally been expected to defer to male interest and initiatives; to leave major economic, political, religious, and even recreational activities in the control of males; and in general to adopt the attitudes and self-images appropriate to a condition of relative powerlessness. Almost everywhere in the world, restrictions on women's civil rights, their legal standing in regard to property and to political activity, and their opportunities for education and creative activities have been, until well into the twentieth century, clear evidence of their second-class citizenship or subjugation as a minority group.

The shaping of female sex roles has obviously not been based on sensible, conscious reasoning. Conscious reasoning entails the appreciation of individual differences, but the long historical development of sexual stereotypes has not been conspicuous by its acknowledgment of individual differences, talents, and desires. Instead, statistical tendencies have been translated into role definitions; what could reasonably be expected of *many* women (e.g., that women cannot be counted on to engage effectively in warfare) has been transformed into normative expectations of *all* women. The forces that have led to the development of distinctive sex roles have been nearly irresistible, however, because of the human need for roles keyed to status rather than to individuals, because there has been no third party to mediate the relations between the sexes, and because until very recently even the idea of defining sex roles differently was inconceivable to most people.

THE MAINTENANCE OF SEX ROLES

No discussion of role change is complete without a consideration of those factors that *resist* it. To the extent that role definitions are social rather than simply a recognition of individual differences, we must accept the fact that roles can change. The speed with which they change, however, and the particular ways in which they change apparently depend very much on the nature of the roles involved and how they fit into the larger society. Some of the factors that work to maintain the social definitions of roles, and thus to resist change in them, are particularly visible in the case of sex roles.

Socialization

Because virtually everyone is assigned a sexual status at birth and is thereafter treated as either a male or a female by everyone else, one's sex is extremely important in the formation of one's *self* (as discussed earlier). Socialization, in fact, is keyed more to sex than to either ethnicity or social class because one's sexual identity determines the nature of the earliest social relationships in which one is involved. The individual's self-definition, central to his or her sense of meaningful existence in relation to others, thus becomes habitual and extremely resistant to change.

Most of us are so accustomed to our sexual identities that we find it quite threatening to contemplate serious change in our sex-related roles. These roles form a large part of the ways that we confirm our identities, and the prospect of losing one's identity can be deeply frightening. One's sense of self, in fact, is so important that it may be irrational in certain situations, leading one to resist role change even at the cost of continuing to accept unwanted rights and onerous obligations or to reject new rights and relief from unpleasant responsibilities. A woman who is successful in business, for example, may feel that her femininity is threatened as she plays new roles (giving orders, engaging in hard-nosed bargaining), and she may even consider withdrawing from her position because of this.

Vested Interests

Although it may be said that the maintenance of self-identity is a vested interest itself, there are other, more obvious advantages that established sex roles carry with them. As described above, the status of "male" has almost universally given its occupants political and economic rights that have been denied to those occupying the status of "female." But the very absence of certain rights can be interpreted as an advantage. For instance, opponents of the Equal Rights Amendment (which would eliminate all legal differences between the statuses of female and male) have stressed that its passage would eliminate certain special rights that women now enjoy by virtue of their subordinate social position (rights to alimony, to avoid serving in the armed forces, etc.) and would subject them to obligations that they would not enjoy. Advocates of the "total woman" concept encourage women to take pride in their subordination and to find satisfaction in fulfilling expertly the traditional roles of woman as helper, admirer, mistress, and (unequal) partner of "her man."

Similarly, although a substantial number of men do not fully enjoy the obligations attached to the male status—responsibilities for leadership and initiative, restrictions on admitting emotionality and dependence—they still seem to find enough satisfaction in "the way things are" to resist, covertly if not overtly, attempts to change their traditional role relationships with females.

Vested interests, then, in the form of wishing to protect one's already established self, of preferring the habitual to the new, and of clinging to the tangible advantages conferred by current role definitions, can be seen as the main obstacles to the reformulation of sex roles.

THE REDEFINITION OF SEX ROLES

Despite apparently widespread satisfaction with sex roles as they have been traditionally defined, the past twenty years have seen growing public debate concerning the problem of whether—and, if so, how—sex roles should be changed. Because women's roles have been more onerous and restrictive, it is not strange that most attention has been focused on them rather than on male roles and that women have almost entirely taken the lead in raising the issue. Over the past century, several changes in American society and in Western societies more generally have clearly been responsible for this movement.

We can assume that traditionally defined sex roles have fitted the larger society's needs over much of history. Indeed, the sources of their stability, as discussed above, suggest that people will resist change even when new social conditions seem to require change. Yet people do come to sense, slowly and uncertainly, when their roles are out of joint with current circumstances and then to conceptualize their discomfort in terms that call for change. Our attention, then, should be directed first to those changes in American society which have produced in women an increased dissatisfaction with their roles.

Changing Social Conditions

Changes in the structure of economic activities in this country since the mid-nineteenth century have certainly had a major impact on the evaluation of sex roles. When the nation's population was primarily rural and engaged in agriculture, the division of labor between men and women was based on the assumption that each played a vital part in the family's survival. Close cooperation between them was necessary in most areas of everyday life, and the products of this cooperation—food, clothing, the education of children, social mobility—could be seen and appreciated. But with the advent of industrialization and the increasing separation of men's and women's daily activities, women had to assume more responsibilities in the household. These added role obligations, however, were not compensated by additional rights.

As universal public schooling was instituted during the latter part of the nineteenth century, the obvious similarities between the roles of "mother" and of "teacher" provided new opportunities for women to find employment outside the home. Nearly half of the public school teachers in 1880 were males, but by 1920, in a much-expanded educational system, women occupied nearly five-sixths of all teaching positions. The demand for better-prepared teachers required that the door to higher education be opened to women, and this slowly came to mean more than just teacher education. But although women more and more frequently attained the same educational achievements that men did, they were still usually denied the chance to make full use of what they had learned.

More and more women entered the wage-earning industrial labor force, too, but received lower pay. Women paid taxes, but were denied the right to participate in decisions that allocated tax funds. Their rights to buy and sell and borrow, to enter certain occupations, and to equal protection under the law in such matters as divorce and public welfare were also restricted.

At the same time, the population was growing and becoming more concentrated in the cities. Greater population densities meant more frequent contact with strangers (see Chapter 8, on communities), and in turn there was greater dependence on the law in settling disputes. The law's specific wording took on greater importance. As this occurred, it became increasingly reasonable to question whether the specific wording of a law actually embodied its manifest intent. So long as laws that used the words "man" and "he" were narrowly interpreted, they could readily be used to restrict women's rights; the law thus became a particular focus of interest for those seeking to redefine sex roles. If the Declaration of Independence, for example, proclaimed that "All *men* are created equal," it was fair to ask whether this didn't actually mean to refer to all *women* as well—and whether, then, women should not enjoy the same rights specifically granted to men.

These and other changes in American society sharpened the discrepancy between what women were in fact *doing* and the ways their roles were defined by norms that had developed in an earlier era. And there were additional factors contributing to the situation. The lengthening life span meant that women lived well beyond the years of intensive responsibilities for their children. The increasing availability of manufactured household necessities—clothing, prepared food, etc.—meant that the husband's money could be increasingly substituted for the wife's concrete contributions to the household. A vast number of changes in social conditions thus made the traditional female roles less and less appropriate to their new circumstances and activities. As both necessity and opportunity for new activities developed, women's sense of discontent with "woman's place" became more acute.

The Movement to Redefine Sex Roles

What we think of today as the "women's liberation movement" (or whatever other name is currently popular) can be traced in some senses to the late eighteenth century. But at different times and places, the "movement" has stressed very different aspects of sex-role change, and it is difficult to find substantive continuity in it beyond a continuing concern for *some* form of role change. We can, however, identify three reasonably distinct aspects of women's roles that have been the focus of attention at different times: political rights, sexual rights, and occupational rights.

The particular aspect of women's roles emphasized by "the movement" at a given time had important consequences for the tactics that were employed and also determined how much contemporary social conditions would affect the possibilities of success. Concentration on women's occupational rights, for example, was influenced very much by current economic conditions, whereas such conditions were of less consequence in the struggle to achieve political rights.

The movement is continuing, of course, so that no final judgments regarding success or failure are possible, but its story until now is a good illustration of how difficult and complex the process of role change can be.

Suffrage It is perhaps significant that the first aspect of sex-role change to receive concentrated, organized attention had very little to do with sexuality per se. The first demand that women be given the right to vote came in Mary Wollstonecraft's 1792 book, *A Vindication of the Rights of Women*. It is clear that a woman's participation in the electoral process would have very little effect on her other daily activities or on her relationships with men. The right to vote might eventually affect the distribution of power in society and perhaps the determination of certain social policies, but the emphasis was on woman as citizen rather than as a participant in the male/female relationship. A suffrage committee was formed in England in 1865, and its claims were strengthened by the publication in 1869 of John Stuart Mill's *On the Subjugation of Women*.

The Quakers in America had always accorded women equal rights in their activities. "Friends Academies" were coeducational from the beginning, and Quaker women were fully involved in the antislavery movement that began in the late 1830s. It was no coincidence that the first convention on women's rights in America, attended by some 250 women in Seneca Falls, New York, in 1848, was led by Lucretia Mott, a Quaker and veteran of the abolition movement.

American women, however, were excluded from the Fifteenth Amendment to the Constitution, which enfranchised black American males in 1870. Their first success came in the state of Wyoming, where they were granted suffrage in 1890. Other states followed the trend slowly, and by 1918 women had gained the vote in fifteen states. With the passage of the Nineteenth Amendment in 1920, American women were finally allowed to vote in all elections: "The right of citizens of the United States to vote shall not be denied or abridged by the United States or by any State on account of sex." In England women achieved full political equality with men in 1928, after having gained some rights as early as 1918.

Historians have noted that the "feminists" who were engaged in the campaign for women's suffrage were in other respects generally conservative in their views of female roles. Theirs was an attempt to add a particular right, but not otherwise to alter the place of women in the marriage relationship or in society at large. They were understandably unsettled, then, when after 1920 the movement took a direction that sought changes more directly related to sexuality.

Sexual expression   Although not the avowed goal of an organized movement, it was the question of women's sexual rights that came to the fore during the 1920s. The entire Victorian era, roughly from 1840 to 1900, had been characterized by what seemed to be an overwhelming fear of female sexuality. In extreme cases this had resulted in subjecting young girls to clitoridectomies; more generally it resulted in society's drawing a sharp distinction between the "ideal woman," who apparently tolerated sex only because of her husband's base and uncontrolled passions, and the "woman of loose morals," who because she was assumed to enjoy sex, was simultaneously ostracized and the object of intense masculine interest. But now that political equality had been achieved—in terms of voting, if not of election to political office—other aspects of "woman's place" came in for attention.

Sigmund Freud's new theory regarding the importance of the libido in human development (see Chapter 4, on socialization) was receiving increased attention in America, and the idea that women could have as much fun as men in anything they chose to do was slowly gaining acceptance. The thought of sexual pleasure was still too disturbing to be made the explicit subject of an organized movement. But the mass media, even if mentioning it only in terms of strict disapproval, gave the topic sufficient publicity so that it could become a focus of public attention (see the discussion in Chapter 17 of public opinion). Premarital intercourse increased in frequency during the 1920s, and the climate of opinion had changed sufficiently to make it possible for at least some women to discuss their own sexual needs openly with at least some men.

Interestingly, Freud's concept of female sexuality has come in for intense criticism by those women seeking "liberation" in the 1970s, even though we must give him much credit for introducing the topic for public consideration some fifty years ago. The current public interest in the details of both men's and women's sexual needs, expressed in the popularity of the many "how-to" books published since the 1960s, is evidence that questions in this area of sexual relationships have not yet been resolved.

Occupational interests   At the same time that the unorganized movement to redefine the sexual rights of males and females was going on, women were also moving hesitantly—and in the face of considerable male opposition—into new occupational spheres. The idea that a career could be as personally rewarding to a woman as to a man was barely recognized before the 1920s, and it is clear that it was still rejected by the vast majority of women during that decade. If a woman worked, it was because of simple economic necessity rather than for any kind of self-fulfillment; the ideal of "woman in the home, man at work" was not seriously challenged. Yet woman's right to take employment outside the home could not logically be denied if she were to enjoy other rights as a human being. It was simply that relatively few women wished to concentrate on this issue then.

The Depression of the 1930s slowed and even reversed initiative in this area as traditional sex roles were reemphasized under the lash of economic necessity. Many people believed that if men were out of work while women held jobs, the women should give up their positions so that men could continue to fill the role of family breadwinner. If the husband had to be supported by his wife's work, it was a sign of his personal failure to "be a man," as well as of her taking something (the job) that was rightfully his. The economic crisis undermined virtually all efforts to achieve sex-role change in the occupational sphere, and only the advent of World War II revived it.

With more than sixteen million males eventually serving in the armed forces between 1941 and 1945, the need for women to move into almost every type of occupation could not be avoided. The number of women in the labor force nearly doubled, reaching almost twenty million by 1945. Despite continuing problems both in the home and in the workplace, centered on how to conceptualize and legitimate the new role relationships that had emerged, the number of women in the work force did not drop after the end of the war.

Occupations still tended to be sex typed, however. *Doctor* Jones would be expected by nearly everyone to be male; *Nurse* Jones could only be female. There were post*men* and repair*men*, sales*girls* and *girls* Friday. Clearly, the tendency to restrict women to occupations that seemed particularly compatible with traditional female roles, and usually distinctly subordinate in terms of wages and authority, was still strong. Even in occupations to which both sexes were admitted without discrimination, job titles frequently indicated the individual's gender: actor and actress, waiter and waitress, author and authoress.

In general, the 1950s was a decade of confusion as far as sex roles were concerned. If more women were working, more were also glorifying the traditional household roles of mother and housekeeper; the "baby boom" of the 'fifties is ample evidence of how important such roles were to many women and to their husbands. It would be another ten years before Simone de Beauvoir's book *The Second Sex* (1953) would be joined by others, such as Betty Friedan's *The Feminine Mystique* (1963), and lead to renewed organizational efforts to deal with the confusion and injustice of the current state of sex roles.

The movement today   The idea of organizing to seek changes in sex roles was given tremendous impetus by the civil rights movement that took shape in the early 1960s (see Chapter 7, on intergroup relations) and by the growing protest against the Vietnamese War a few years later. Women had been deeply involved in both, but increasing disillusion with the roles that males expected them to play in these activities, especially in the civil rights movement, led them finally to recognize that a separate movement for women was necessary. Betty Friedan's National Organization for Women was founded in 1966, and by 1970 there were dozens of separate groups whose goals were one form or another of sex-role change. The complexity of the movement and its subsequent division in terms of political beliefs and specific objectives make it impossible to analyze here in detail. Yet the overall intent of the movement as a whole has been to achieve greater freedom—equality with males in all areas of life—through whatever tactics promise to be most effective.

Several specific issues were confronted successfully by the mid-1970s. Women's right to control their own bodies was the basic issue to be settled by the legalization of abortion. The broader problem of the right to different forms of sexual pleasure underlay the increasing activism of both male and female homosexuals. The rising divorce rate, currently at nearly one divorce for every two marriages each year, signaled the continued existence of problems in working out satisfactory male/female relationships. It testified also, however, to women's increasing ability and willingness to be independent of men and to put added pressure on state legislatures to make divorces easier to obtain.

But males' and females' interest in each other's company did not diminish at all. The development of more convenient and reliable contraceptives since the 1950s has made it possible for women to be much more certain that a sexual relationship would not result in an unwanted pregnancy. With conception now a matter of choice rather than chance, men and women were free to enjoy relationships without the risk of incurring long-term responsibilities. Accordingly, the number of unmarried men and women living together grew rapidly, with the result that such an arrangement has been less and less a cause for moral indignation. Newspaper etiquette columns, in fact, now give sober advice on the proper forms of address for one's "partner," "roommate," "friend," etc. Avoiding the legalism of marriage has apparently been in some cases an attempt to avoid old sex-role prescriptions so that new ones may be explored more freely, even though many such couples continue to play the traditional sex roles.

Two trends are particularly apparent now. First, the search for legal equality has resulted in systematic concentration on changing or reinterpreting many laws, culminating in the attempt to pass the Equal Rights Amendment (its passage is still in doubt at this writing). Second, in the realm of norms and values, the attempt continues, through experiment and persuasion as well as laws, to redefine a new complementarity of sex roles that will not be disadvantageous to either sex. Consciousness raising for both men and women is slowly being transformed from something faddish and unusual to a new, taken-for-granted perspective that is finding wider and wider acceptance.

The concrete details of new sex-related norms are by no means clear yet. But simply the awareness that others are seeking them has brought the topic to the point where exploring new relationships is not only tolerated but often applauded as well.

THE FUTURE OF SEX ROLES

We are obviously in the midst of change. Several factors, however, will slow the emergence of consensus on new role-relationships between the sexes. Sexual identity, first of all, is central to social structure. Therefore, changes in sex roles will have implications for all other sectors of society; working these out will take a long time. The courts are only slowly coming to play the part of a neutral third party in mediating changes in relations between the sexes. And there will be profound difficulties in finding a new fit between complete equality, on the one hand, and the instrinsic differences between the sexes, on the other.

It is apparent, though, that obstacles to change have weakened considerably in recent years. Legal support for distinctions between the rights of males and females has been falling steadily, and public opinion seems to have swung around to the point where the need for change is generally accepted.

There remain problems in both arriving at widespread agreement on the content of new sex roles and coordinating people's acceptance of them. Changes in norms are inevitably accompanied by uncertainty about not only what is "really right," but what others believe as well. John and Mary may agree that he should cook dinner and wash the dishes afterwards, but neither is certain of how the neighbors will react to this. Carmen and Julio may find it entirely satisfying that she hold a job while he looks after the children and the apartment, but their friends' response to this arrangement may be one of disapproval. Aaron may be happy to have a female boss at work, but is concerned that this may make him seem less "manly" to his friends in other companies.

We continue to attempt a redefinition of sex roles that will both take into consideration the intrinsic differences between men and women and encourage them to work together as complementary equals. (*Boston Globe* photo)

Developing new complementary sex roles, then, is not simply something that can be done privately by individual couples. New roles have implications for people's relations with others outside the dyad, and new norms are themselves subject to evaluation by others. John, for instance, may be late to the bowling league because of his new household responsibilities, so that his new relationship with Mary has real consequences for his other social relationships. Carmen may not have time to join the P.T.A., and yet the other mothers in the group may find it difficult to accept Julio as "one of the girls." And although whether Aaron's boss is male or female should make no difference in his participation in other social relationships, the very fact that he is subordinate to a woman at work will probably be evaluated negatively by some of his friends.

The Quest for New Norms

The thorough, unquestioned assumption that each member of a dyad knows fully what the other member should and actually does expect in the relationship is thrown into question when social support for this assumption is withdrawn. As it becomes obvious that others are questioning the assumptions that one has thought to be unquestionable, a sense of **anomie** (*normlessness*) develops. Each member's trust that he or she knows what the other wants—and that the other knows that this is known—is replaced by uncertainty and a sudden self-consciousness that undermines the spontaneity necessary for easy, satisfying interaction. Such difficulties, especially in the absence of a genuinely neutral third party to serve as referee, seem only to be heightened by attempts to solve them directly. Confronting uncertainty can only intensify it; being conscious that one is self-conscious simply adds to one's self-consciousness. The vicious cycle is intensified when two people are trying to attack the problem of their own relationship.

Writing individualized "marriage contracts" that specify each partner's rights and obligations is one way that people can try to resolve their mutual uncertainties. The contract becomes a kind of referee, to be called in when there are disagreements about the relationship. But even if the contract is obeyed by both parties, its existence unavoidably suggests that they do not fully trust each other. In the end, it confirms rather than eliminates the presence of uncertainty.

Yet conditions of uncertainty and potential conflict within dyads are intolerable for long periods. Simmel (1950) points out that to save such groups, the two members tend to concentrate on aspects of their relationship that are mutually accepted and to ignore or evade potentially disruptive issues. We may suppose that only when this practice becomes common will there be a chance for new norms to develop "naturally." To think objectively about norms, after all, is implicitly to question their legitimacy; it is those practices and mutual expectations that are taken for granted because they have *not* been examined objectively which, in the long run, provide guidance for effective, gratifying interaction.

Periods of self-questioning and explicit consideration of the need for new norms may well be inevitable during periods when the inappropriateness of traditional norms can no longer be ignored. It may be suggested, however, that this stage in the process must be followed by an implicit agreement to drop the subject so that new norms can develop by themselves without conscious planning and interference. We cannot see, for example, all of the subtle nuances and interrelations among the norms that guide our daily behavior, and attempts to plan them consciously are quite likely to fail as well as to hinder the development of more appropriate and workable norms.

In the present case, this second stage may be a long time in coming, for there is still much profit to be made in keeping the problem of sex roles in the public eye through the mass media and through organizational activities. Eventually, though, we may anticipate increasing boredom on the part of the public and increasing but unspoken agreement that the whole question of sex roles has been exhausted. Thereafter, new norms will slowly emerge, and it will be mainly the sociologists who keep track of them—until the new norms, too, become inappropriate and the cycle, in quite different terms, begins all over again.

The Content of Future Sex Roles

A large, complex society like our own has experienced steady differentiation in lifestyles, values, and roles. Because sex roles are so basic to social structure in general, however, they may be among the last to undergo this process. Yet we seem on the verge of considerably greater pluralism in this area of social life, and some vague predictions may be in order here at the end of this chapter.

In the legal sphere, it seems certain that individual rights will be steadily divorced from sexual identity. Males and females will become entirely equal before the law, particularly in their economic and occupational rights, so that the status of "human being" (or at least of "citizen") will be more important than that of "male" or "female" as far as the law is concerned. The rights to borrow, to enter into contracts, to be evaluated on the basis of merit alone, and many other rights will become completely sexless. In many areas this will mean simply the elimination of barriers that have hitherto denied certain rights to individuals on the basis of their sex alone. In other areas it will mean policies designed to restore equal footing to individuals who have previously been disadvantaged by the legal system. Current concerns with affirmative action and the conflict between using ability alone as the basis for admitting people to schools and occupations or else establishing quotas in order to redress past injustices are evidence that our legal system is going beyond the simple elimination of barriers in an attempt to ensure substantive as well as theoretical justice.

In personal lives it seems likely that different models of male/female relationships will develop among different social classes and ethnic groups and even in different parts of the nation. These models will afford both security for those who remain in these basic groups and an opportunity for change as others achieve vertical or horizontal social mobility. There will certainly be pockets of traditionalism to be found, and pockets of radical "unisexism" as well, but we may expect that the majority of the population will move slowly toward a more fundamental equalitarianism and at the same time greater tolerance of differences in individual relationships.

These changes will mean eventually that the importance of sexual identity and the place of sexual relationships in society will be significantly altered. In particular, greater emphasis on individual freedom will result in a greater variety of ways in which the sexes interact with each other, and we may expect a sharper distinction to be drawn between the area of private life (including sexual relationships) and the area of one's involvement in larger social structures.

What central characteristics may we expect to find in the new sex roles? For one, there will be acceptance of the right of both males and females to negotiate with each other in regard to sexual satisfactions. For a second, we can expect equal freedom for both sexes to enter into, and to break off, commitments to each other. And for a third, there will be increased mutual respect in the areas of political and religious debate, occupational achievement, and the right to homosexual preferences—the right, in other words, to deny that the male/female relationship is central to an individual's life.

Although it is unclear as to when these new "basics" will be established, both the changing nature of our society and the continuing emphasis on universalistic human rights (rather than "male" and "female" rights) suggest that they are inevitable in the long run. The paths to be followed in achieving them may be tortuous; abrupt changes in other parts of society may hamper or speed their achievement; and it may be many decades before clear evidence is available that a new consensus has emerged. But the process of role change is ongoing, and changes in sex roles, once begun, cannot be halted. All of us are "going along for the ride" whether we like it or not, and the sociological interest—even amazement—to be found in watching its course may be at least some compensation for the personal anxieties and societal disruptions that are likely to accompany it.

SUMMARY

Role change means changes in the norms that guide interaction between people occupying related statuses. Understanding role change thus requires that we know how people come to occupy statuses, how the roles "assigned" to these statuses develop, the conditions under which change occurs or is sought, and the mechanisms through which it is accomplished.

Change is more often sought in the case of ascribed statuses, for their occupants have little or no choice in the roles they are expected to play. This chapter has examined sex roles as a particularly revealing illustration of the process.

Both anatomical differences and the nature of sexual initiative and attraction have been of central importance in shaping traditional sex roles, with the more advantageous roles usually monopolized by males. Yet there has been considerable resistance to sex-role change on the part of both sexes because people have been so thoroughly socialized to them and because each sex can find important "vested interests" in its current roles.

As social conditions change, however, traditional roles become increasingly inappropriate. As values change, roles that were formerly satisfying may be reevaluated as undesirable. These things have occurred over the past century in this and other complex societies, and a many-faceted movement to achieve role change, led almost exclusively by women, has come into being.

The movement has concentrated on the achievement of equal political, sexual, and occupational rights for women: suffrage, the right of women to sexual pleasure, and increasing occupational freedom. Much has been accomplished, but it is suggested that after a period of intensive, explicit concentration on the need for sex-role change, a new consensus in this area will develop only after people turn their attention elsewhere and allow new norms to emerge "naturally."

As women come to be defined primarily as "citizens" rather than as "females," we may expect the achievement of full equality before the law for both sexes. There will be increasing tolerance of individuals' participating in different forms of sexual relationships, and the place of both sex and sexuality in the social structure of society will be significantly altered.

SUGGESTED READINGS

David, Deborah S., and Robert Brannon, eds., *The Forty-Nine Percent Majority: The Male Sex Role* (Reading, Mass.: Addison-Wesley, 1976). An excellent collection of articles and excerpts that examines the various meanings of "masculinity" and also the social and psychological costs that traditional male roles impose on men.

de Beauvoir, Simone, *The Second Sex* (New York: Knopf, 1953). An essentially materialistic interpretation of the reason for differences in sex roles, de Beauvoir's book was perhaps the first widely read attempt to conceptualize these roles and to point out their negative consequences for women.

Friedan, Betty, *The Feminine Mystique* (New York: Dell, 1963). In this book Friedan exposes the techniques that she claims have been used to keep women in "their place" by intentionally glorifying the traditional roles of mother, homemaker, etc. Whether it was because the times were different or because the protest was more vivid, through this book Friedan helped to inspire the current women's movement, whereas de Beauvoir's earlier work did not.

Filene, Peter Gabriel, *Him/Her/Self* (New York: Harcourt Brace Jovanovitch, 1975). This is a readable, wide-ranging review by a social historian of the reasons for, evidence of, and efforts to bring about change in sex roles in this country over the past eighty years. This chapter is particularly indebted to Filene's coverage of the "movement" in recent years.

Gornick, Vivian, and Barbara K. Moran, eds., *Woman in Sexist Society: Studies in Power and Powerlessness* (New York: Basic Books, 1971). With an emphasis on protest and the call to action, this book contains nearly thirty lengthy, well-researched articles on as many different aspects of women's "political repression."

Safilios-Rothschild, Constantina, ed., *Toward a Sociology of Women* (Lexington, Mass.: Xerox, 1972). This book makes a useful companion to *The Forty-Nine Percent Majority,* mentioned above, for it covers the making of women's roles and their consequences in much the same way. It is, though, perhaps more sociological than the former in that a number of well-known social scientists are included.

West, Uta, ed., *Women in a Changing World* (New York: McGraw-Hill, 1975). This book offers a sober assessment of the present state of women's roles through the writings of the editor and ten other authors, showing as much of the misery involved in changing sex roles as the triumph.

Glossary

Note: because this chapter serves as a kind of practical review of the concepts developed in the preceding three chapters, few new terms have been introduced here. For definitions of the major concepts, consult the glossaries of the preceding chapters.

Anomie A condition of "normlessness," or of people's shared awareness that there is little, if any, consensus among them on the details and strength of basic norms. The concept was first introduced by Durkheim in 1897 in his book *Suicide* (see Appendix 2, on sociological theory, for an extended discussion of this work). In the pure sense, *anomie* refers to a condition of the group itself and is thus a social fact; when the individual's sense of this condition is discussed, the term *anomia* is used.

Role change The process through which the norms governing the relations between two statuses are changed. Because role relationships are reciprocal (that is, one status's right is the other's obligation, and vice-versa), role change necessarily involves at least two roles. Role change may be initiated by the occupants of a more powerful status in order to enhance their advantages in interacting with those occupying a weaker status, it may be proposed because it will be of mutual benefit to the occupants of both statuses, or it may be sought by the occupants of the weaker status in reaction to the disadvantages they are presently experiencing.

II
SOCIAL CATEGORIES AND GROUPS

In this section of the book we take up the most tangible units of society—the various types of concrete groupings of human beings. Rather than emphasizing only the relations among social statuses, our interest here will be in the reasons that people come to occupy statuses in different types of groups and in the ways that such groups are influenced by their social and material environments.

Three major forms of human groups are identified on the basis of the principal reasons for their existence: *social categories, territorial groups,* and *purposeful groups.* A social category is a collection of people who have something in common that is recognized by others as important, whether or not those who are assigned to this category wish to be identified in this way. Skin color and other physical characteristics, religious customs, and language or accent are the major criteria by which social categories are identified, although their members need not have distinctive relationships with one another.

For certain purposes (the manufacture of clothing, for instance), it is important to treat fat people as one category and thin people as another. For other purposes, it may be important to treat all left-handed people or all those over the age of seventy as members of particular categories. For the most part, however, social categories play a significant part in social life only when they are based on the immediately recognizable characteristics of people that lead others to hold certain expectations about their social behavior.

In addition to the anatomical differences on which gender categories are based (discussed in Chapter 5), two other types of categories are particularly important in society. First, there are *social classes,* whose members share distinctive lifestyles because their members possess roughly equivalent amounts of "the good things of life"—wealth, power, and prestige. These are treated in Chapter 6, on social stratification. Second, there are *racial and ethnic groups,* whose members have in common distinctive physical characteristics and/or distinctive subcultures.

The relations among such categories, especially visible and having crucial conse-quences for their members, are treated in Chapter 7.

Territorial groups, the second major type, form because their members share the same living space and must necessarily develop patterned social relationships if they are to use this space with minimal conflict. They range from small rural hamlets to urban metropolises, but regardless of size they differ from social cate-gories and from purposeful groups in that they are the sites of people's physical existence. Such groups are discussed in Chapter 8.

The third major type is the purposeful group. Usually called formal orga-nizations, as in Chapter 9, such groups are ordinarily formed voluntarily by their members in order to achieve specific goals. Banks, hospitals, colleges, and armies are all formal organizations. Because their component statuses have been con-sciously designed to enable their occupants to work together in achieving organi-zational goals, these groups are quite different in character from either of the two preceding types. They tend to be the principal form of concrete human associa-tion through which economic, political, religious, and recreational goals are sought. (A different perspective on how people's individual and collective needs are served is developed in Section III, on social institutions.)

These different types, it should be stressed, are distinguished from one another on the basis of the initial reasons for their formation and in terms of the most important reasons for their continued existence. Each, however, may take on some of the characteristics of the others. A categorical group, for instance, can acquire a territorial identity (Little Italy, Harlem, a wealthy suburb), and it can organize itself to achieve particular goals (the N.A.A.C.P., the Polish-American Culture Society, perhaps a group intent on promoting class warfare). A territorial group, similarly, may be treated as a categorical group ("All New Yorkers are pushy") and may act as a purposeful group ("Let's all support the Podunk Boosters Association"). And most purposeful groups, of course, have specific geo-graphical locations, and their members may be explicitly categorized ("He's one of those Washington bureaucrats").

The family, as a concrete group, is categorical, territorial, and purposeful: "The Smiths, of 238 Appleton Way, are trying to earn a living and raise their chil-dren." The family, therefore, is the prototypical human group, as well as because it originally incorporated all of society's institutional functions.

Finally, membership in one type of group does not preclude membership in the others, and in fact nearly everyone includes memberships in all three types as parts of his or her status set. *Within* any given type, however, specific groups are often mutually exclusive. It is virtually impossible to belong to two racial groups at the same time, or to two social classes, or to live in two separate communities, or even to work full time for two separate organizations. Although such groups are all composed of concrete people occupying statuses, then, each type exists in time and space as a collection of specific individuals and can be treated as a dis-tinctive part of society.

Categories and groups are identified primarily by their existence as collec-tions of concrete individuals. They are thus most easily studied by means of the major sociological research methods (see Appendix 1). Most of the research liter-ature in sociology focuses for this reason on social categories and groups, and their investigation is ordinarily considered the "heart" of sociology.

6
Social Stratification

LIFESTYLE

The term **lifestyle** *refers partly to the tangible aspects of people's lives,* such as clothing, housing, and other possessions, *and partly to their behavior:* daily activity patterns, relationships with others, and preferences in recreation, entertainment, and even such things as food and sex. Because it covers so many different things, the term is difficult to define with precision.

Yet we recognize differences in lifestyles, and we often categorize people on this basis. We do this because the extent to which someone's lifestyle is similar to our own is a useful predictor of how much we have "in common" and thus of how easy and satisfying it will be for us to interact regularly with him or her.

Activities and preferences often reflect norms and values, so we can say that lifestyles are influenced by cultural (or subcultural) factors. But lifestyles are also influenced by material factors, since wealth and power determine the range of opportunities and relationships available to people. The two factors, of course, are interrelated. People not only "inherit" norms and values through socialization, but also modify them to suit the material conditions of their lives. And because people interact most intimately with others who share their backgrounds and material circumstances, they tend to develop common lifestyles which may set them apart from others.

To think of lifestyles as cultural is to think of ethnic groups and subcultures; to think of them in terms of their material aspects is to think of social classes. We usually evaluate subcultures in terms of how different they are from our own, but in the case of social classes we tend to look at them in terms of how much more desirable or undesirable their members' lifestyles are in comparison to our own. If society is divided horizontally by subcultures, then, it is divided vertically by social classes.

In either case, lifestyle is an important key to the division of society into various categories of people. The study of social stratification is essentially the study of both the causes and consequences of vertically ranked differences in lifestyles.

THE IMPORTANCE OF SOCIAL CLASSES

The study of social classes, or of social **stratification** (*meaning "arranged in layers"*) has long been a major focus of sociological investigation. Of central importance to people's relationships with others, stratification plays a major role in shaping social structures, and because it concerns the relationships among people and among groups, it is a uniquely social rather than psychological phenomenon.

In one sense, **social class** *is simply the outcome of the various factors that contribute to the development of a particular lifestyle.* One can imagine, for instance, that two families moving to two different agricultural communities in eastern Colorado during the early 1900s would have developed quite similar lifestyles simply because the conditions of their lives were so similar. But to the extent that social-class membership takes on a reality of its own—that is, that people become conscious of it and allow its existence to influence their behavior—it is more than simply a consequence; it becomes a cause as well.

Even without the additional complication of "class consciousness" (awareness of one's membership in a particular social class), we know that the various social classes are characterized by differences in not only immediately visible attributes such as clothing, but also their members' participation in social institutions and organizations, in where they live, in their values and self-images, in their physical and mental health, and even in their average life spans.

Because social stratification affects each of us personally—each of us is a member of one social class (and would probably prefer to be in a higher one)—and because it is so prominent an aspect of society, it was of interest to people long before the development of sociology as a discipline. The sociologists certainly did not *discover* stratification, then, but their systematic, societywide analyses of its causes and consequences have done much to put it in perspective for everyone.

The Individual's Perspective

As private citizens, we tend to deal with individuals rather than directly with the social categories that we call social classes. We come into contact with individuals whose lifestyles characterize them as members of different classes, but it is the ways in which their lifestyles influence our personal relationships with them that are of immediate importance to us.

We usually measure the relative desirability of different lifestyles on a vertical scale, meaning "better" when we say "higher" and "worse" when we say "lower." (Why we should do this is not altogether clear, but perhaps the natural advantages of height—being able to see farther, to avoid floods, and being less vulnerable to attack—were originally responsible for our favorable evaluation of height.) It is thus natural for us to talk of the "upper" and the "lower" classes and of others being "higher" or "lower" in class than ourselves. We look "up to" people we admire and "down on" those we do not.

Those who are at "the same level" with us are those with whom we can interact comfortably and with a sense of equality. There are others whom we suspect of thinking themselves "too good" to want to develop lasting, easy-going relationships with us, and still others we would rather avoid except in brief, impersonal encounters. A crude measure of who is higher or lower than we are in terms of social class can be found in how we answer the questions "Who is likely to reject *my* friendly advances?" and "Whose friendly advances am *I* likely to reject?"

We thus recognize social-class membership and will talk of "the social classes," but it is ordinarily the indicators of personal lifestyle that determine the ways we interact with others. People's dress, mannerisms, visible possessions, the situations in which we meet them, and such ascriptive attributes as sex, age, and color are usually more important than we realize in determining how we characterize others—and thus in our assumptions of how they will react to us.

In comparing these photographs of a street musician in Cambridge, Massachusetts, and the Prince and Princess of Monaco with Caroline and her husband, Philippe Junot, and his parents, one can conclude that social classes are characterized by basic differences in values, lifestyles, and self-images, identified by visible attributes such as clothing and possessions. (p. 132: Jack Prelutsky/Stock, Boston; p. 133: Rene Maestri/Sygma)

Because indicators of social class influence our perceptions of how enjoyable or profitable it will be to develop a personal relationship with someone else, it is clear that social-class membership provides broadly visible "behavioral boundaries" that subdivide our society into significantly different groups.

The Sociologist's Perspective

Because sociology focuses on society as a whole, the sociologist recognizes the centrality of social stratification in the organization of society as well as in the lives of its individual members. The sociological study of stratification thus has a number of different aspects. It is concerned with the determinants of social-class membership and with how these influence the lifestyles that are associated with different classes. It asks about the extent to which, and the reasons why, individuals remain in a single class throughout their lives or else move from one class to another. And it is interested in the different social standards by which people are ranked and in the consequences of those standards for the societies in which they are found.

It was noted in Chapter 2 that the term *status* is sometimes taken to mean "relative social-class standing" and that this is in some ways inconsistent with the way we use the term to refer to a social position. Yet the confusion does exist, and we may as well get used to it. The sociologist frequently substitutes "status" for the more meaningful term **socioeconomic status (SES)**, *which is the equivalent of "social class."* Thus "status" means both "social position" (e.g., wife, salesperson, student, grandmother, etc.) and "social class" (e.g., higher SES, middle SES, lower SES). Which specific usage is meant can usually be determined by the context in which the word is used.

Although sociologists are interested in individuals, their studies of stratification tend to be statistical or at least quantitative in nature. Social classes are large groupings of people, and their investigation thus focuses on the proportions of society's membership that fall into different classes, that share certain lifestyles, that remain in one class or move to others, and that are affected by the presence of other classes. Most often, then, the study of stratification is the study of *rates, characteristics,* and *distributions* rather than of individual life histories.

THE DETERMINANTS OF SOCIAL-CLASS MEMBERSHIP

We recognize social classes as categories of people that are distinguished in terms of the relative desirability of their members' lifestyles. The determinants of social class thus lie in the nature of whatever it is that enables people to live what we believe to be happy, satisfying lives.

Although nontransferrable characteristics, such as good health, good looks, and special talents, can certainly contribute to one's satisfaction with life, we find that the visible, generally accepted foundations of "the good life" tend to be those things that concretely influence our relationships with others. In particular, these are our abilities to obtain material goods and services from others, to influence or direct their activities, and to command their voluntary respect. Max Weber (1947) identified the three basic determinants of social stratification as "class, party, and status," and we refer to them today as *wealth, power,* and *prestige.*

Each of these things is "scarce." That is, each is something that can be gained or lost and is in relatively short supply. A dollar bill in *my* pocket cannot be in *yours* at the same time; if *my* preference for a particular political policy wins, *your* preference for a different policy loses; and if *I* respect you for having more of something or having done more of something than I have, *you* cannot return an equal amount of that respect. (If everyone were due the same amount of prestige, it would become meaningless; by definition, prestige is a measure of *un*equal respectability.)

People may thus be ranked in terms of how much of each of these things they have, even though it may be difficult to measure quantities of power and prestige in the same way that we can assess a person's monetary wealth. As noted above, people generally find it easier and more satisfying to establish long-lasting relationships—to form groups—with others who share the same lifestyle, and lifestyles are very much determined by how much of these three "good things of life" people possess. Let us look more closely at how wealth, power, and prestige influence one's lifestyle, and thus one's relations with others.

Wealth

Wealth is a bit more difficult to measure than one might think. It may mean the monetary value of the material goods one owns at a particular time, it may mean this plus the amount of money one has in cash and in bank deposits, etc., or it may mean how much money (and when) one expects to acquire in the future. Property and money, however, are of little value if others do not respect one's rights of ownership. (The concepts of property rights and of money as symbolizing abstract economic value are covered in more detail in Chapter 11, on the economic institution.) It is enough here to note that ownership, and thus wealth, is actually social in nature because it is based on others' acceptance of one's property rights.

Because human beings are physical organisms, material goods and services are necessary for physical survival. How much of them one is able to own or hire—one's wealth—can be of tremendous importance in determining how satisfying one's lifestyle is. In general, **wealth** *determines how much one may take for granted, in terms of not only possessions available for use now or easily obtained when wanted, but also the services one may obtain from others:* health care, entertainment, the performance of unpleasant jobs, transportation, and so on.

Power

More directly a kind of social relationship, **power** *refers to one's ability to determine others' actions.* In the simplest case, this may depend only on which individual is bigger, stronger, or tougher. But within the web of ongoing social relationships, the use of physical force is generally ruled out except in certain circumstances. Instead, power may be based on expertise, on holding obligations from others, on the ability to influence the actions of others besides those to whom one is giving direct orders, or on one's occupancy of an organizational or political office. The concepts of power and authority are covered in more detail in Chapter 12.

Power in the broad sense is usually based on a number of things, few of which can be measured precisely. It is a major component of the good life, however, for it determines the extent to which one can influence the actions of others so that they either benefit one directly or at least do not injure one's interests. If wealth is important first of all in determining how much of one's physical environment one can control, power is important because it determines how much one can control of one's social environment.

Prestige

The third factor that contributes to one's social-class standing is **prestige**—*the amount of respect, admiration, and deference one receives from others spontaneously or on a voluntary basis.* Expressions of respect gained through fear or calculation (an employee's "Sir" to the boss may come from fear of being fired or as an attempt to gain favor) certainly can be meaningful as they reaffirm one's power, but spontaneous respect has other benefits. It is intrinsically rewarding because it enhances one's sense of personal worth, and it can also be important in gaining access to those who rank high in terms of wealth and power.

The reasons that a person may be granted prestige are many and varied. It may come as added recognition that one *is* wealthy and/or powerful, since holding substantial amounts of these things is viewed in itself as being worthy of admiration. It may come as the result of a specific achievement, such as becoming a popular entertainer, winning a prize or setting a record, or being the first person to do this or that. It may reflect the extent to which one's occupation is viewed by others as being concerned with the good of society; doctors, judges, religious leaders, and teachers are usually accorded substantial amounts of prestige because they are supposed to be devoted to the welfare of others. And the amount of prestige one receives from others may be based on ascriptive factors such as age, sex, and ethnicity. An adult white male in American society is ordinarily given more respect than is a male of another racial or ethnic group, more than a female of any group, and more than either a child or an elderly person. By contrast, membership in any of these other minority groups may carry with it a certain amount of "negative" prestige or *dis*-honor, so that limits are set on the amount of prestige one may earn on the basis of any of the other criteria mentioned above.

It may be useful to clarify the distinction between prestige and a related word, **esteem,** which is usually used to indicate *the appreciation one receives for outstanding role performance, regardless of one's social position.* A short-order cook who produces particularly good hamburgers earns esteem, just as does a particularly effective governor, but these two individuals hold vastly different amounts of prestige. Prestige is geared to absolute social standards, then, whereas esteem is relative and has only an indirect bearing on one's social-class standing.

Because prestige may be based on so many different things, it may blend on the one hand into *esteem* and on the other into what is known as *notoriety* **Notoriety** is simply *the condition of being known to be the object of many people's attention, usually in a negative connotation* ("the notorious outlaw," "notorious for his extravagance"). Therefore, the term cannot be substituted for "prestige." If respect based on role performance becomes known outside the group qualified to judge this, it may contribute to one's prestige. A Nobel Prize winner in physics, for instance, may find that the esteem of his or her fellow physicists is transformed into prestige that is more widely acknowledged throughout society.

Prestige is often reflected in the use of honorific titles, such as Reverend, Colonel, Doctor, Judge—even Professor. Differences in wealth and power are often indicated by the ways people address one another, too. The higher someone is by any of these three measures, the more he or she tends to be addressed by a title as well as a name. Even "Mister," "Missus," and "Ms." connote respect as well as a degree of social distance. The mutual use of first names or last names alone usually indicates equality, but when such usages are one-sided, we can assume that meaningful differences in wealth, power, and/or prestige are present and are acknowledged by both people.

In the relations between children and adults, for example, adults address children by their first names, but the reverse is not generally true. In a factory the boss is "Mr. Jones"; the forklift operator, "Charlie." In these and other situations the apparent friendliness and informality suggested by the boss's use of Charlie's first name turn out to be actually a clear indication of his higher social position. The implications are even clearer when the son of an upper-class family calls the butler "Jeeves" and in return is adddressed as "Master Timothy."

Relations Among Wealth, Power, and Prestige

It should be obvious that the amounts of wealth, power, and prestige one holds are not unrelated. Wealth can buy power, power may be used to acquire wealth, and although both of these can influence the amount of prestige one has, prestige acquired independently can also enable one to gain additional wealth and power.

This means that for the most part, people generally hold roughly equivalent amounts of these three determinants of social class. If at some point in life a person has a significantly greater amount of wealth than of power or prestige, he or she is likely to try to use the leverage afforded by wealth to bring his or her power and prestige up to an equivalent level. One may use wealth to gain access to others who already have power—perhaps simply through joining an exclusive country club or perhaps through political contributions—and one may purchase the possessions that help their owner to "deserve" prestige. Similarly, wealthy and powerful people are often pleased to be associated with people who are prestigious, and those who have power will often be sought out by the wealthy and prestigious.

But being balanced in this sense is not a universal condition. There are those in society whose holdings of these three things are distinctly *un*equal, and their problems are worthy of attention.

Status consistency and inconsistency   The term **status consistency** refers to *a situation in which one holds equivalent amounts of wealth, power, and prestige.* Someone who has markedly different amounts of one or two of these things is said to be *status-inconsistent,* and this person tends to be uncomfortable about it. This discomfort stems from two sources: that one has been unable to use one's strong card in order to maximize one's holdings of the one

Fall from power brought status-inconsistency and exile to the Shah of Iran, shown here with the Empress in Egypt in January 1979. (P. Ledru/Sygma)

or two things that were low and that one's personal relationships with others are likely to be a bit difficult.

If we accept the idea that people interact most easily with others who have equivalent amounts of the same things they have—corporation presidents in terms of wealth, governors in terms of power, famous athletes in terms of prestige—it can be seen that they will experience some pressures to have equivalent amounts of the other things as well. During interaction, various topics may come into the conversation without being planned, and some strain will be experienced by both people if one of them is distinctly less wealthy or powerful or prestigious than the other, even though they are equals in other ways.

The governors of two states, for example, may have a great deal in common when they discuss their problems and responsibilities, but if one is independently wealthy and the other has nothing but his or her salary to live on, they may find it difficult to converse easily about their homes, hobbies, and plans for the future. Both are implicitly aware that their relationship would go more smoothly if they had roughly equal amounts of wealth as well as of power and prestige.

It is not difficult to find examples of people trying to achieve status consistency in their own lives. A successful racketeer may try to raise his power and prestige to a level equivalent to his wealth by buying a home in the right suburb, supporting and hobnobbing with important political figures, and sending his children to private schools. Teachers' unions in recent years have succeeded to some extent in raising educators' salaries to the point where they are roughly equivalent to the prestige traditionally associated with their profession. The elected office holder who is entirely dependent on a modest salary may be tempted to add to his or her income by selling political favors or perhaps only by employing political connections to get in on lucrative investments. There is more than greed involved in seeking status consistency; it is also a matter of ensuring comfortable social relationships with others.

It was noted above that prestige, more than wealth or power, may be greatly influenced by ascriptive factors. It is thus probably responsible for the majority of cases of status inconsistency. A wealthy black American or a politically powerful Hispanic will be especially aware that his or her ethnic identity seems to set a limit on the amount of prestige that can be acquired. A sense of frustration develops, then, not only because one feels personal insult in having negative prestige or dishonor ascribed to one, but also because one's ability to achieve status consistency is blocked by things beyond one's control.

Both adolescence and old age carry a certain amount of negative prestige in American society today. Despite the American idealization of youth, young people do not receive the respect that goes with adult responsibilities, and senior citizens lose prestige because they are no longer fully involved in productive occupations. With adolescents, of course, the higher prestige of adulthood lies in the near future, so they realize that their condition is only temporary. With those past their sixties, however, the prospect of increasing dishonor as they grow older can hardly be a cause for cheer.

To be "whole" in terms of one's relationships with others is to be status consistent, and ascriptive barriers to status consistency have increasingly become the targets of resentment and organized efforts to minimize their importance. Status consistency itself, of course, is of little satisfaction if one is low on all three measures of social class, but we may suppose that the movements to discredit racism, sexism, and ageism derive some of their energies from their participants' resentment of their status inconsistency.

EXPLANATIONS OF SOCIAL STRATIFICATION

As long as some people have what others want but do not have, there will be questions about how this situation arose. If everyone has been created equal, why is it that some are wealthy and others poor, some powerful and others powerless? What, in other words, accounts for the persistent, unequal distribution of the good things of life among the members of society—and is this fair?

Two principal explanations (or "theories"—see Appendix 2, on sociological theory) have been advanced to explain why all but the most primitive societies are stratified. Implicitly, these explanations seem to either justify stratification or else make it an object of deep indignation and perhaps justify active attempts to change or eliminate it.

The Functional Explanation

The functional theory of stratification holds essentially that it is not only inevitable, but also necessary for the survival of society. Differences in the amounts of wealth, power, and prestige that people hold are said to be related to differences in the value of their contributions to society. Accordingly, the person who invests many years of his or her life in training for a highly skilled occupation such as medicine or law should receive more social rewards than the person who has gone into a relatively unskilled occupation that requires little preparation. Without the prospect of a higher payoff later on, the former person would probably not have worked so hard to acquire a skill that others need, and society would be the poorer for lack of this skill (Davis and Moore, 1945).

The functional explanation thus sees social class itself as a reward. The prospect of attaining a higher social class motivates people to do more for society, so if a system of differential rewards did not exist, society would suffer from a lack of needed services. Despite much evidence that the stratification system is inefficient and that it is frequently subverted, this view holds that it is fundamentally necessary. Eliminating social classes, then, is not only un-achievable, but would actually be harmful to society if it could be done.

There is, of course, much to criticize about this explanation of stratification (Tumin, 1953). Members of the lower classes or of minority groups (see Chapter 7) who have special talents are often unable to develop them because they lack the resources for proper education and may even be barred from such opportunities simply because of their background. The stratification system is thus wasteful of talent. Higher-class people "take care of their own," too, which may mean that less talented people are put into responsible positions on the basis of personal connections rather than ability, which introduces a further degree of inefficiency. And there are certainly cases in which inherited wealth makes it possible for some people to do nothing at all for society. When faced with so many examples of how stratification *fails* to serve society's needs, it is quite possible to doubt the validity of the functional explanation.

The Conflict Explanation

If the possession of large amounts of wealth, power, and prestige is *not* due to the value of one's services to society, there can be only one other explanation: Some people have more because they have taken it away from others and then have used it to maintain their special privileges. Stratification is thus seen as the outcome of conflict. It serves no useful purpose for society, it perpetuates unfair inequalities, and the only obstacle to its elimination is the power that the upper classes have to defend their advantaged position (Dahrendorf, 1959).

Karl Marx's theory of history (discussed further in Appendix 2) provides much of the basis for the conflict view (see Bottomore and Rubel, 1956). Marx had been obsessed by the gross inequalities that were so visible among people during the midnineteenth century, when the Industrial Revolution was in full swing, and sought to explain them in terms of the repression of the working class by those who owned the "means of production." At the foundation of the distinction between the workers and the capitalists (or the *proletariat* and the *bourgeoise*) was the principle of property—the right of people to own things and to use this ownership (through investment) to acquire still more wealth. As the rich are able to get richer, so the poor must necessarily become poorer, and the stratification system is essentially unjust.

If the system is so obviously unfair, though, there must be some reason that the lower classes have not recognized this and revolted against it. Marx, of course, predicted that they would, and this belief is a fundamental tenet of the Communist ideology. But throughout most of history the working classes have *not* revolted, so this must be explained. Much of the conflict explanation of stratification, then, focuses on the ways in which the upper classes have been able either to "fool" or to coerce the lower classes into accepting their disadvantaged position in society.

Such explanations have included demonstrations that the upper classes do indeed control the mass media, that our schools and even our religions persuade us all that the status quo is just and reasonable, and have asserted that racism, sexism, and even "IQ-ism" are basically techniques through which the "haves" prevent the "have-nots" from challenging their privileges. And it is clear that the use of naked force, as in the industrial conflicts that erupted when unions sought to gain improved wages and working conditions, can be seen as a last resort when all attempts to hide the realities of class exploitation have failed.

But an all-out "conspiracy" theory of stratification is as difficult to accept as is a complacent "sweetness-and-light" theory. It is difficult to doubt that the prospect of greater rewards *does* motivate people to do more useful things for society; it is also difficult to doubt that advantages and disadvantages are both perpetuated in ways that have nothing to do with fairness or social value. How, then, are we to reconcile the two explanations?

Combining the Explanations

If the members of a society were suddenly and miraculously brought to perfect equality in terms of wealth, power, and prestige, it is not likely that this condition would exist for long. Some people would soon acquire greater amounts of these things, and others would have less. We can reason that the "winners" would have tried every technique in the book to do this. Some would have cheated or robbed or frightened others into giving up some of their possessions. Others would have sold their services at whatever prices they could get, and those whose services were both needed and in scarce supply would have been able to charge higher prices. The question, then, is which of these two methods of getting ahead would have been more prominent.

Since criminals are almost always in the minority and can usually be controlled by the majority, it seems unlikely that the illegitimate pathway to success would have been the more successful. Since the idea of a "war of all against all" is intolerable to most people, we might reason instead that initially at least, the principles embodied in the functional explanation of stratification would have accounted for the placement of most people in different social classes. Later on, however, as accumulated advantages enabled people to devote more of their energies to preserving their privileges at the expense of others, an accurate explanation of class differences would have to draw more and more on the conflict theory.

Indeed, there are indications that immediately after periods of great social change—revolutions, wars, depressions, etc.—merit and ability rather than inherited advantages are especially important in reconstituting the class system. After long periods of social stability, on the other hand, during which advantages are accumulated, lifestyles developed, and "class interests" more clearly recognized, it is clear that class membership becomes increasingly inaccurate as an indicator of the relative value to society of people's abilities and activities.

The validity of each explanation of social stratification, then, seems to depend very much on the historical period under examination, as well as on the values that are central to a society's culture. Because American culture emphasizes achievement over ascription, it is clear that despite much evidence to the contrary, Americans prefer a functional explanation of their own stratification system. It is to the nature of this system that we turn next.

THE AMERICAN SOCIAL-CLASS STRUCTURE

Given the American emphasis on equality, it is not surprising that we do not make social-class differences a major part of our outlook on life. Although obvious differences exist among people in terms of wealth, power, and prestige and in the lifestyles associated with these differences, Americans are probably less class conscious than are the members of most other societies in the world. This means that Americans are less certain about the characteristics of different classes, about where the boundaries between them lie, and even about the number of classes that exist in this society.

Sociologists have found that Americans usually have a vaguely defined idea that they are divided among three or perhaps four social classes: upper, middle, and lower, with "working" often inserted somewhere between the middle and lower classes. As many as six or seven distinct classes may be recognized in certain communities where the population is stable and people are pretty well aware of everyone else, but in metropolitan areas and areas of rapid social change, awareness of class lines tends to be less precise.

Despite our relative lack of class consciousness, it is possible to describe at least the major outlines of the American class structure. There are, however, enough complexities in the process of measuring social stratification to make it necessary to discuss some of them first.

Determining Social-Class Membership

It is easy to talk abstractly of how wealth, power, and prestige are related to the lifestyles that identify different social classes, but the task of measuring these characteristics empirically entails a number of problems. First, families rather than individuals are the real "units" of the stratification system. Not only would it be extremely difficult for members of the same household to have markedly different lifestyles, but it is natural that they should share a common lifestyle because they share in whatever amounts of wealth, power, and prestige are held by the head of the household. Occupation is probably the best single indicator of a person's social class, and it tends to be the adult male in the family who is most fully engaged in the occupational structure. The husband/father, then, largely determines the family's ranking because of the income, influence, and prestige that are associated with his occupation. (With the increasing number of women pursuing careers today, however, we may find that the family's total income is beginning to outdistance its rank in terms of power or prestige. The possible impact of this and other changes in American society on the American stratification system is discussed at the end of this chapter.)

Occupation is related not only to money, but directly to prestige as well. Two aspects in particular should be noted. First, since "being educated" is itself prestigious, an occupation that requires extended education commands a substantial amount of prestige regardless of the income it produces. The fact that such occupations typically command high incomes is due primarily to the relative scarcity of people who are able and/or willing to undertake the long education necessary to enter such occupations. And although it sometimes happens that certain occupations are monopolized by their practitioners through restricting entrance to medical schools, unions, etc., there remains the fact that out of 100 people who can dig ditches, only a handful of them might also be capable of becoming neurosurgeons or certified public accountants.

A second factor is that the *kind* of work one does helps to determine one's prestige. Manual, or "blue-collar," occupations, based on the use of one's muscles, are less prestigious than are nonmanual, or "white-collar" occupations, in which brains are more important than muscles. This fact seems to account for the occasionally glaring discrepancies we find between prestige and wealth, for a manual worker may earn considerably more than a white-collar worker and still be accorded less prestige. White-collar occupations probably command more prestige for two reasons. First, muscle power is probably distributed more evenly throughout the population than is brain power, so it is not so scarce. Second, physical labor is usually repetitive and physically tiring and tends to be avoided by those who have nonmanual talents that others need. Those who hold white-collar occupations thus demonstrate something enviable about themselves and are accorded more prestige.

The relative prestige of a person's occupation is ordinarily the only means we have to place him or her on the prestige scale. Power is even more difficult to measure. It is, in fact, frequently entirely *un*measured, or else researchers turn to indications of the person's participation and/or office holding in government and voluntary associations for an estimate of his or her rank on the power scale.

Wealth, too, is difficult to measure. A family's annual income may constitute all the wealth that it has, or it may be only a small part of its net worth. Money in checking and savings accounts, in stocks and bonds, and in real estate are the other major forms of wealth, but their actual cash value might vary a good deal over time. The distinction, further, between total net worth and disposable income adds still more complexity to the picture; some assets are easier to convert into cash than others are, and the tax laws affect different forms of wealth in different ways. Estimating a family's net worth, then, is neither as easy nor as precise as one might at first imagine.

Finally, there can be differences between subjective and objective measures of social class. Someone's own sense of his or her social-class membership may be at odds with the objective character of his or her lifestyle, particularly in a society whose ideology denies the importance of social class. Recent national studies, in fact, have shown that about three-quarters of the American population will identify themselves as "middle class" if offered a choice among only "upper," "middle," and "lower class" (Rossides, 1976, p. 250). By objective measures, of course, no matter how crude they are, Americans are ranged along the social class continuum in far different proportions.

The Size of Different Classes

Class lines are not sharply drawn in this country, and the correlations among various indicators of social class are sometimes weak. Nevertheless, it may be of some value to get a general idea of the proportions of the American population who belong to different classes.

For our purposes, it will be useful to think of five relatively distinct social classes: upper, upper-middle, middle, working, and lower. Table 6.1 suggests that although there may be only a moderately firm relationship between either

TABLE 6.1 DISTRIBUTION OF THE ADULT AMERICAN POPULATION ACCORDING TO THREE SEPARATE INDICATORS OF SOCIAL CLASS

Self-description[1] (percentage)		Years of education completed (1974)[2] (percentage)		Annual family income (1974)[2] (percentage)	
"Upper class"	3	More than 4 years of college	4	More than $40,000	3
"Upper middle"	17	College graduate	9	$25,000 to $40,000	9
"Middle class"	44	12 to 15 years	48	$10,000 to $25,000	53
"Working class"	34	5 to 11 years	34	$3,000 to $10,000	30
"Lower class"	2	4 years or less	4	Less than $3,000	5

[1]*Source:* Robert Hodge and D. Treiman, "Class Identification in the United States," *American Journal of Sociology* 73 (March 1968): 535–547. Data reprinted by permission of the University of Chicago Press.
[2]*Source: 1976 U.S. Fact Book* (New York: Grosset & Dunlap, 1976).

self-description and annual income or between self-description and educational attainment, the population can be divided into roughly equal segments along each of these scales. Of course, in the absense of very much explicit class consciousness among Americans, the best test of how meaningful these distinctions are must be your own sense of how realistic they are.

We may conclude from these figures, without fear of being seriously wrong, that less than one in twenty-five American families occupies the highest social class, perhaps one in ten can be classified as "upper middle class," nearly half of them probably deserve the term "middle class," one in three can be identified as "working class," and one of every twenty as "lower class." Raising the dividing line between the working and lower classes, of course, will increase the percentage of the population classified as lower class; indeed, many sociologists define as much as twenty-five percent of the population as members of the lower class (Rossides, 1976, p. 454). In 1975 the Census Bureau reported that twelve percent of the population fell below the "poverty level" (an annual family income of $5500 or less), but recent research at the University of Michigan has discovered that less than three percent of the population was consistently below this level between 1967 and 1975 (*New York Times*, July 17, 1977). The facts, however, that we have a reasonably high rate of **social mobility** (that is, *movement from one class to another over the course of a generation*—a topic covered in a subsequent section of this chapter) and that class lines are frequently blurred mean that this distribution of people probably has fewer consequences for Americans' perception of their society than would a similar distribution in a society characterized by greater class consciousness.

It should be remembered that these are *gross* figures. They do not take into account the consequences of minority-group membership for a given family's income or educational opportunities. They do not take into account regional differences in wage levels or in the relative importance of ascriptive factors in determining one's prestige ranking. They do not show how frequently a plumber with a fourth-grade education can earn $25,000 a year, whereas someone with a Ph.D. in English literature may be working in a department store at $6000 per year because of the recent decline in the demand for college professors. The table, then, gives only the crudest outline of the American social-class structure; it is something like one's first view of a mountain range thirty miles distant—it is far too simple to be a useful predictor of what will be found when one reaches an individual mountain.

Differences in Lifestyles

If social classes are distinguished basically by the differing amounts of control that their members have over their social and material environments, these should be accompanied by differences in values and in the perceptions of the world held by their members. At the upper end of the stratification ladder, for instance, people can take for granted most of the things that are increasingly problematic or unattainable for people at lower levels. A member of the upper class ordinarily takes it for granted that high-quality clothing and luxurious housing are always available, that adequate and even sumptuous food will never be lacking, and that travel, health care, and influence on public policies can be had whenever needed.

For the very poor person, none of these things can be taken for granted. He or she may worry about having enough to eat tomorrow, whether an old pair of shoes will hold out for another month, whether there is enough money to pay for a bus trip to visit a sick relative in a nearby city, and how to get the attention of a public health nurse at the clinic. There may be problems in getting the police to respond to an emergency call or in dealing with a child's schoolteacher. Such concerns are never far from the minds of those toward the bottom of the ladder, and they produce a perspective on life that is sharply different from that of those in higher classes. Although generalizations about social-class differences are just that—generalizations to which exceptions can always be found—enough research has been done in this area to enable us to draw up at least a rough picture of the major differences among social classes.

Having a good deal of control over one's "life space" is, of course, based on having substantial amounts of wealth, power, and prestige. More control means more ability to keep unwanted events out of one's life, as well as the ability to achieve more of one's goals. With more control, then, it is possible to take a more long-range perspective on the future. A person who can be confident that a particular dream can be realized in ten years can afford to ignore those immediate distractions which, if indulged in now, would undermine the achievement of that dream. But if one's confidence in the future is weaker because one has less control over the actions of others, there is less and less reason to give up immediate pleasures. The ability (if not always the tendency) to delay gratification thus usually increases with higher social class.

It is not clear whether one's readiness to delay gratification is the result of being socialized into a particular social class or is simply due to a realistic assessment of one's situation. Attempts to demonstrate the existence of a "culture of poverty" have not been entirely successful (Eames and Goode, 1973). For instance, even very poor people often give lip service to middle-class norms and values, which suggests that they would begin to exhibit behavior appropriate to higher social classes if their circumstances permitted it. Realistic responses to a condition of poverty and powerlessness may eventually become habits, but they apparently do not develop into a subculture that produces individuals who are entirely incapable of adopting different lifestyles.

Another aspect of delaying gratification is the tendency to keep one's emotions in check. Giving in to immediate passions, whether of anger or delight, is an immediate self-indulgence and is indeed more common at lower levels of stratification. This tendency, in turn, is apparently related to child-rearing patterns. Prompt physical punishment, a direct expression of rage or anger, is much more characteristic of the treatment of children in working and lower-class families. On the other hand, the "stiff upper lip" of the middle and upper classes is probably reflected in their tendency to rely more on the use of symbolic rewards and punishments such as giving or withholding love and approval.

One may assume also that having more control leads to greater self-assurance and is probably responsible for the finding that the amount of tolerance a person has for others' differing values and opinions increases with higher social class (Stouffer, 1955). Conversely, the lower one goes on the stratification ladder, the more dogmatic and authoritarian people tend to be. This may be partly a result of the strong relationship between social class and education, but it may also be a symptom of the higher level of distrust and suspicion of the larger society that is engendered by poverty and powerlessness.

Even though the higher classes are typically more tolerant of others' opinions, the fact that they have little more to gain (because they are already close to the top of the ladder) and a great deal to lose means that they tend to be more conservative in their political attitudes. Concern with maintaining or improving one's class position thus has a different set of consequences than does the relative amount of control one has over one's life.

At the very bottom of the ladder, people tend to be fatalistic about their situation, seeing little realistic hope of rising and believing that luck plays a large role in their lives. Working-class people, often barely above the lowest group, may be characterized as generally anxious about whether they can maintain their precariously held respectability. They show great concern for the things that distinguish them from the lower class: traditional sex roles, well-behaved children, a proper and "good" neighborhood, steady employment, etc. A college education for the children may be prized, but it is viewed very much as a ticket to a better job so that the next generation can reach middle-class status.

Those in the middle and upper middle classes, being farther from such problems, tend to emphasize achievement and the things that will enhance their ability to move upward. The values of competition and success become more important than those of respectability and propriety. A college education becomes training for a "better" lifestyle. At the upper end of the scale, finally, interest tends to be focused on preserving what has already been gained. Since there is little competition in terms of further achievement, the details of one's lifestyle, particularly in finding activities and possessions that will reinforce a high level of prestige, become increasingly important.

Finally, although an individual's sense of satisfaction with life can be considerably influenced by things that have nothing to do with social class, it is clear that one's overall sense of well-being is very much related to social class. With exceptions, of course, it can be said that the higher one's class, the greater one's happiness (Campbell, Converse, and Rodgers, 1976). With this as a basic human goal, it should not be surprising that Americans have a keen interest in how people move from one class to another.

SOCIAL MOBILITY

Social mobility, the movement from one social class to another, is usually measured in terms of an adult's family's position in relation to the position his or her parents' family occupied a generation ago. Mobility fascinates Americans, for nearly everything in our lives encourages us to get ahead, to improve our position in life. Getting ahead means moving *up* the stratification ladder, but the general concept of social mobility includes downward movement as well. Knowledge of the "rules of the game" is directly pertinent to our own aspirations, and the overall rates of upward and downward mobility are thought to be a useful measure of the extent to which the realities of American society reflect its ideals. It is understandable, then, that sociologists have paid a good deal of attention to this aspect of social stratification.

Systems of Stratification

The overall amount of mobility in a given society, and thus of one's opportunities to move upward or downward in social class, depends first of all on the relative weight the society places on ascription as opposed to achievement. In general terms, there are three major types of stratification systems, distinguished by the emphasis they place on ascriptive factors in determining one's social class.

A **caste (closed-class) system** *is one in which ascription is all-important. The individual's social ranking is determined almost entirely by his or her parents' rank*, so that social class is ascribed at birth. In traditional India, from which we get the word *caste*, there was no way for a person to move to either a higher or a lower caste, for individual character or achievement obviously could have no effect on who one's parents were. The system was essentially religious in its foundations, and the degree of "ritual purity" ascribed to each caste determined its relative prestige. Ranging from the Brahmans at the top of the hierarchy to the "untouchables" at the bottom, each caste dictated its members' occupations, religious practices, and lifestyle in general.

Until recently, the term "caste system" could be applied to many parts of the United States, where membership in a minority group was often the main factor in determining a person's opportunities for education, employment, political participation, etc. (Dollard, 1937). With the movement to extend civil rights, however, the term has become less and less applicable.

The idea of an **estate system,** not used so frequently in sociology today, is a useful way to describe *a society in which ascription is of substantial importance even though it is not directly supported by the religious or political system.* The term comes from medieval Europe, where the three principal "estates" were the clergy, the nobility, and the common people. People ordinarily remained in their estate for life, but some mobility was possible because even though the clergy made up a relatively small part of the populace, their celibacy meant that their ranks had to be replenished from the other estates. (The idea that journalists stand apart from the ranks of society, scrutinizing all with equal objectivity, accounts for their sometimes being called "the fourth estate.")

A good example of an estate system was to be found in nineteenth-century England, where until after the middle of the century the social classes were quite distinct, and their members generally accepted these differences as natural and proper. Family lineage was initially much more important than individual achievement, but as the Industrial Revolution progressed, wealth slowly came to supersede the prestige associated with one's family, so that opportunities for mobility increased.

The third type of stratification system is supposed to describe contemporary American society—in ideology if not always in actual practice. The American value system proclaims the **open-class system**—*the individual's mer-*

its and accomplishments should be the sole determinants of his or her class ranking—despite the obstacles posed by continuing racism, sexism, and the handicaps one inherits by virtue of being born into a lower class. Given this ideal, it becomes particularly important for us to understand the channels through which upward mobility takes place, the nature and importance of various obstacles to upward mobility, and the actual rates of upward and downward mobility today. The proportions of the population who have actually been upwardly and downwardly mobile in comparison to the previous generation should give us a good sense of how great the gap is between our professed ideals and our actual behavior.

Measuring Social Mobility

We have noted that families, rather than isolated individuals, are the units of social classes and that measuring a family's social class may be difficult. The same difficulties are encountered in trying to measure social mobility. An individual, of course, may be wealthy one day and bankrupt the next, but because lifestyle—which we have taken as the key to social class—does not change so rapidly, such short-term changes are not ordinarily thought of as social mobility. Instead, it is usually thought of in terms of twenty-five- to thirty-year spans, and thus it takes place against a background of broader social change.

One important difficulty, then, lies in trying to take into account society-wide changes in the objective conditions of life. Should we say, for example, that a person who earned $5000 per year in 1940 but had no antibiotics, television, or charter flights to Europe was equal in social class to someone today who earns $25,000 per year—or to someone who earns only $3000?

There is the additional complication that social mobility as well as social-class membership may be either subjective or objective. Subjective mobility occurs whenever a person *feels* that his or her social class has changed, regardless of whether there has been an objective change in his or her circumstances. A family whose income remains the same while those of the neighbors have all gone up substantially will probably feel a sense of downward mobility. On the other hand, if a person continues to earn the same salary while others have taken cuts in pay, he or she may well feel upwardly mobile. In this sense, mobility is certainly relative.

◄ Flamboyant costumes and outrageous behavior provided the vehicle of social mobility from obscurity to wealth and fame for Kiss, whose members gathered with their parents for a family portrait. (Ken Regan/Camera 5)

Whenever possible, however, sociologists use objective measurements of mobility because they are independent of private moods and can be verified by others. Measures of family income may be used after allowances are made for changes in the value of money from one generation to the next, and years of formal education provide another measure of mobility. But the most meaningful measure is probably occupation. The occupation of the head of a household gives a fairly good indication of his or her wealth, power, and prestige and is relatively easy to determine. Most studies of social mobility, then, compare the individual's occupation with that of the chief breadwinner in his or her parents' family, determine the relative prestige of each, and then identify the amount of mobility that has occurred.

Pathways to Upward Mobility

Behind most people's plans for the future is the question "How can I get ahead—how can I become richer, more powerful, more prestigious?" Although there are always some who reject society's standard definition of success, most of us have internalized our society's values to such an extent that we actually define success and happiness in terms of upward mobility. A discussion of those things that may either help or hinder someone in the pursuit of this goal is thus of intrinsic interest to most people as well as an important focus of sociological attention.

We can identify four distinct paths to success in terms of social class, although they are certainly not mutually exclusive. Table 6.2 classifies each of these paths according to whether or not it is available to all or to only a few and whether or not it requires the conscious effort of the person using it.

The pathway that most clearly embodies American values is based on education, work, and saving. Ideally, anyway, these things are open to all, and they clearly require sustained effort. With the American emphasis on

TABLE 6.2   THE MAJOR PATHWAYS TO UPWARD MOBILITY

	The pathway is open to:	
Utilizing the pathway requires:	All	Only some
Steady, conscious effort	Education Work Saving	Skill Talent Ability
Little or no effort	"Luck"	Inheritance and social connections

equality and activism, the "self-made" person who has taken this route to success is most honored, because he or she has apparently shown admirable amounts of motivation and self-discipline.

But not all people are born with equal amounts of talent, so the competition for success is not entirely democratic. As noted in Chapter 4, nurture is probably much more important than nature in determining the kinds of abilities (and the motivation to use them) that an individual will exhibit. Even if talent based on genetic inheritance were distributed randomly among the members of all classes, then, systematic differences in nurture according to social class would give the advantage to those in the higher classes. The fact that so many different types of talent are needed by society makes the competition *more* democratic, of course, but it does not guarantee that everyone begins with equal abilities or equal opportunity to capitalize on them.

Because it requires effort to perfect one's abilities, however, success based on talent is still an honorable path to upward mobility. This is true because an egalitarian, activist society admires talent regardless of its origin.

Perhaps because of the American emphasis on equality, the distinction between these two pathways is blurred. It was noted earlier that the amount of education a person has helps to determine his or her prestige. But Americans seem uncertain as to whether education (supposedly open to all) can actually instill talent or whether it only certifies the amount of talent that someone had to begin with. We are not sure of how separate these two routes to success really are.

Either way, education brings prestige. Because prestige is relative, however, and because the amount of formal education acquired by most people has been rising steadily, the amount of education needed to gain substantial prestige has also increased. In 1940, for instance, only about one-third of the nation's adult population had graduated from high school, and a high school diploma was considered an important prerequisite for upward mobility. By 1974, however, that figure had risen to sixty percent; thus that diploma necessarily commanded less prestige. More and more, a college degree is assuming the same importance for mobility that the high school diploma used to have.

The third pathway, "luck," is presumably random and thus equally available to all. Winning a lottery, accidentally finding a valuable old painting, etc., is presumed to be chance. More often, however, luck is something one must take advantage of if it is to lead to upward mobility. Being in the right place when a better job opens up, meeting someone by chance who will invest in your new money-making idea, or getting an opportunity to show your skills because someone else fell ill—these can be called "luck" in one sense, but are actually occasions to make use of the first or second pathways. Pure luck, then, is rarely a major means of upward mobility. Most often, it must be combined with one or both of the first two pathways, and then its importance in the process is difficult to measure. We can say, though, that the more that luck seems to have been responsible for someone's success, the less honored that person will be, for success has come without conscious effort.

Finally, although being born wealthy may be "luck" in the broadest sense, it is clearly not available to all once they have been born, nor has it required any effort. Achieving a high social class through birth, then, is perhaps the least honored route to success. The advantages acquired in this way—money, success-oriented childrearing, educational opportunities, and social connections—mean that inheritance is a particularly powerful pathway, regardless of how little it embodies basic American values. The pressure, then, is on such individuals to justify their good fortune through developing whatever talents they may have and through finding other socially acceptable ways to use their advantages.

Illicit upward mobility (wealth acquired through crime, power based on coercion, and prestige gained through lying about one's past and achievements) is probably equivalent to the first pathway discussed in this section, since it is presumably open to all and requires conscious effort. As soon as the foundations of this sort of mobility are discovered, however, all prestige is either lost or transformed into notoriety, and both wealth and power may be lost if the criminal-justice system becomes involved.

Obstacles to Upward Mobility

Although the lack of talent, motivation, or luck may account for failures to be upwardly mobile, several things may actively oppose someone's mobility as well. Ascriptive constraints on movement up the stratification ladder are considered in detail in Chapters 5 and 7 and need only be noted here. Two others require more discussion.

One of these is the active opposition of those in higher classes to people who seek to move up from lower levels. Sometimes this is conscious and organized, but a relatively high degree of class consciousness as well as clear-cut definitions of class membership are necessary before this can happen. Such has not ordinarily been the case in recent American history, even though it occurs here and there in particular communities and suburbs. More often, such opposition is simply the result of people's disinclination to associate with others whose lifestyles are different and characteristic of the classes below them. Dislike for the way "they" live is the reason given, rather than disdain for "their" lower social status. In addition to ascriptive characteristics, then, lifestyle may be a strong factor in determining who is accepted into which educational programs, who is hired for which sorts of occupational positions, who is admitted to which informal social circles, and who are deemed acceptable as marriage partners for one's children. Whether it is lifestyle or social class that is taken as the basis for discriminating among others, the effect is the same: a certain amount of active opposition to upward mobility by those higher on the ladder.

A second obstacle, completely impersonal, may be called *structural constraints.* These constraints are based on the relative size of the different social classes as they exist today, which is determined by the kinds of occupations a society needs, the amount of wealth available collectively for distribution and possession, and the degree to which power and prestige are concentrated in the hands of a few. The size of each class thus determines how many positions at that level there are to be filled by members of the next generation. Because changes in class size occur relatively slowly, structural constraints serve as the ultimate limit on the possibilities for upward mobility, regardless of the presence or absence of other constraints.

To take an extreme example, a society in which one percent of the people are in the upper class, ten percent are in the middle class, and the remaining eighty-nine percent are in the lower class could not possibly have a high mobility rate. Even if all the offspring of the upper and middle classes were to be downwardly mobile, only a bit more than twelve percent of the lower class could anticipate upward mobility—that is, only eleven out of every eighty-nine lower-class children could possibly find higher positions.

Such a society would look like a very flat pyramid, with the widest part (and the most people) at the bottom and very little of the pyramid's volume at the top. This approximates the distribution of social-class positions in most of the underdeveloped societies today and was probably an accurate picture of all societies in the past. Today, however, advanced industrialized societies tend to have a "stratification pyramid" that actually looks more like a diamond; the bulk of their populations is located at the middle levels, and only the very top and bottom of the diamond are tiny in proportion to the widest part. The possibilities for mobility are thus much greater.

This raises the question of how much mobility, both upward and downward, would be indicative of a completely open society in which one's class position as an adult depended entirely on his or her achievements and not at all on the social class of his or her parents. Knowing roughly how large each class is and assuming relatively little change over several decades, it is not difficult to determine what the mobility rates would be if the next generation's social class were determined by chance alone (or by assuming that all were born with equal amounts of luck, motivation, and talent and that there were no other constraints on mobility).

The amount of "pure-chance" mobility is, of course, determined by both the number of classes being considered and their relative sizes. In a three-class system with an equal number of positions in each, only one-third of the people could be expected to remain in the same class as their parents. With five classes of equal size, eighty percent would experience some mobility. Even if the relative sizes of five classes were 5-20-50-20-5, the random-chance rate of mobility would still be about sixty-six percent.

Obviously, no society in history has ever approached such high intergenerational mobility rates. The advantages passed on to their children by parents of higher-class families and the disadvantages similarly inherited by lower-class children put much more severe limits on the total amount of mobility that actually occurs. Nevertheless, it is of some interest to see how real American mobility rates compare with a model based on complete equality of both talent and opportunity.

Mobility in America

If we assume that the information contained in Table 6.1 gives us a rough approximation of the relative size of the five major social classes in America, we can develop an estimate of what the "pure-chance" or "pure-achievement" mobility rates would be. These figures are presented in Table 6.3.

The estimates of relative class size are, of course, open to dispute, but they are probably not off by more than five or ten percent at the most and thus will serve our purposes. By this model, almost two-thirds of the next generation should be either upwardly or downwardly mobile, with about one-third moving in each direction. The remaining thirty-six percent should remain stable.

The best estimates of actual American mobility today, on the other hand, tell us that close to fifty percent of the population have remained generally in the same class from one generation to the next. Further, approximately thirty percent have been upwardly mobile, and about twenty percent have been downwardly mobile (Lipset and Bendix, 1964). The differences between the two sets of facts are clear, but their meaning requires interpretation.

Although the amount of upward mobility seems close to what we would expect if there were nothing but structural constraints to limit it, the substantially smaller amount of downward mobility and the high level of nonmobility suggest that something else has been at work to influence the actual figures.

Since upward and downward mobility rates would be equal if the sizes of the various classes had not changed, we must conclude that the number of

TABLE 6.3   MOBILITY RATES BASED ON PURE CHANCE (OR IF TALENT WERE RANDOMLY DISTRIBUTED AND MOBILITY LIMITED ONLY BY STRUCTURAL CONSTRAINTS)

Original social class	Approximate percentage of population	Percentage from each class in this class after thirty years:				
		Upper	Upper Middle	Middle	Working	Lower
Upper	3	.09*	.36	1.44	.99	.12
Upper middle	12	.36	1.44*	5.76	3.96	.48
Middle	48	1.44	5.76	23.04*	15.84	1.92
Working	33	.99	3.96	15.84	10.89*	1.32
Lower	4	.12	.48	1.92	1.32	.16*

*Percentage of entire population who remain in same class as their parents (Total=35.62%).

positions above the bottom levels has increased, whereas those in the working and lower classes have decreased. This is in fact what has happened in the United States over the past fifty years and more. There has been a steady substitution of machines for human muscle, a decline in the agricultural population, and greater need for people to handle the "coordination" (that is, white-collar managerial and clerical jobs) required by an increasingly complex society. This means that the "pure-chance" upward mobility rate should be higher than the prediction in Table 6.3, that the downward mobility rate should be lower, and also that the "stability" rate should be lower as well, since a decrease in the number of positions to be filled at lower levels automatically produces a certain amount of upward mobility.

What are we to conclude from this? Faulty and suspect though our estimates may be for both the relative size of social classes and actual mobility rates, it looks as though there is a substantial—although not shocking—gap between the completely open-class society of our ideals and the facts about American society today. If the "pure-chance" or "pure-achievement" upward-mobility rate should be ten percent higher and the downward mobility rate five percent higher, it can be assumed that a minimum of ten percent of the population has encountered serious social rather than structural obstacles to upward mobility. Another five percent, further, has undoubtedly been "protected" against downward mobility by virtue of having been born into an advantaged situation, which would mean that another five percent has been prevented from moving upward to take their places.

Fifteen percent of the American population represents more than thirty million people. We cannot be sure, of course, that talent and motivation are indeed distributed randomly throughout our population. To the extent that they appear more often among the higher classes, our estimate that thirty million people have been unfairly denied the opportunity to move up may be too high. Yet if even half of this number have good reason to believe that "the system" is unfair, they present a powerful challenge to American ideals. What the future may hold for the American class structure is discussed briefly in the following section.

THE FUTURE OF SOCIAL STRATIFICATION

Probably the most important thing that will occur in the American stratification system over the next twenty or thirty years is a gradual reduction in the differences among the lifestyles of different social classes. A number of trends are in motion that make this likely.

First, although the poorest fifth of our population has earned no more than one-sixth of what the top fifth has earned—this ratio has remained constant since the 1940s (*U.S. Fact Book*, 1976, p. 392)—the wealth of those toward the bottom of the ladder has increased on an absolute scale. Despite inflation, the median income of the lowest fifth has more than doubled over the last thirty years. As the number of working wives increases, we may expect further advances in family incomes at all levels. And because wealth is certainly more important than power or prestige in determining a family's lifestyle, it is reasonably certain that the material aspects of lifestyles will be somewhat less differentiated in the future than they are now.

Second, power is probably becoming more widely dispersed as well. As interest groups multiply and as coalitions are increasingly necessary to bring policies through to implementation, it is apparent that more and more people will become at least indirectly involved in the exercise of power. As power contributes to lifestyle, then, another reason for sharp differences among them will diminish in importance.

The steady but slow-moving elimination of ascriptive barriers to the full use of talent in all areas means additional opportunities for upward mobility. As court decisions and governmental policies not only remove obstacles but also award compensation for past injustices, we may expect that individual achievement will become increasingly important in determining social class.

Because the tangible differences among lifestyles will decrease and because individual talents will be given wider scope, we can probably look forward to increasing emphasis on prestige as the basis for distinguishing among social classes. The nature of one's occupation will assume greater importance, but its capacity for generating income will become less important. There will probably be "fashions" in lifestyles; thus the types (rather than the value) of material possessions will receive more attention. And there will be more interest in how people spend their leisure time.

If these vague predictions are accurate, we can anticipate that social class will refer more and more to life*style* rather than to life *chances* and that style will slowly become more the expression of individual values than of how one must cope with harsh social realities. Extremes of poverty and of wealth will undoubtedly still exist, but a greater proportion of the population will be concentrated at the middle of the stratification ladder, and preferences rather than necessities will determine how people live their lives.

SUMMARY

The division of society into vertically ranked groups called social classes is made visible by the fact that different classes are characterized by different lifestyles. While also influenced by the norms and values of different subcultures, lifestyles are determined primarily by the relative amounts of wealth, power, and prestige that people have. Although analytically distinct, any one of these can be used to obtain more of the others. Most people, then, tend to be status-consistent, or to hold roughly equivalent amounts of each. A condition of status-inconsistency can be quite uncomfortable, so people have an understandable interest in achieving consistency. Enduring situations of status inconsistency are caused primarily by ascriptive limitations on prestige.

The existence of social classes has been explained in two different ways. The functional explanation views social class essentially as indicating the value of one's contributions to society and believes that the "reward" of higher social class is necessary to motivate people to do more for society. The conflict explanation, on the contrary, sees stratification as the outcome of continuing competition for wealth and power, with the "haves" continuing to exploit the "have-nots." The functional theory seems a more accurate explanation after periods of great social change, whereas the conflict theory seems to become more valid over long periods of social stability.

Although the American emphasis on individual equality and achievement denies the importance of social classes, it is possible to identify five classes in this country that have appreciably different lifestyles. By rough estimate, about three percent of the people are in the upper class, twelve percent in the upper middle class, forty-eight percent in the middle class, thirty-three percent in the working class, and the remaining four percent in the lower class. In particular, the extent to which their members have differing amounts of control over their material and social environments seems to determine their relative abilities to delay gratification and also their dominant hopes and concerns.

Social mobility—movement from one social class to another over the span of a generation—is determined primarily by the basis of a society's stratification system. In a closed-class, or caste, system, class is ascribed at birth, and there is virtually no opportunity for mobility. In an estate system, class membership is not prescribed by law or religion, but family background is so important that mobility is severely limited. In an open-class system like this country's, mobility is supposed to be based entirely on individual achievement. In America, of course, certain ascriptive barriers (race, ethnicity, and sex) continue to limit many individuals' opportunities to move upward.

Of the four major paths to upward mobility, work and saving are the most honored in an open-class system, whereas inheritance (almost the equivalent of ascriptive social ranking) is the least honorable. The uneven distribution of talent among the members of society means that mobility through ability is not equally open to all, but the confusion over whether talent leads to educational opportunities or education produces talent means that Americans do not clearly recognize the distinction between these two pathways. Luck, a fourth possible way to attain higher social class, plays a minor role in mobility, but is likely to be stressed by those to whom the other paths seem to be closed.

Serious obstacles to upward mobility include not only ascriptive barriers, but also the resistance of the higher classes to newcomers from below. Whether this is organized and explicitly class-oriented, or simply the working out of people's preference for others who share their own lifestyles, it can substantially reduce the amount of upward mobility in a society. Even more important is the absolute number of positions in each class that must be filled by members of the next generation. Both the number and relative sizes of a society's social classes must set final limits on how much social mobility its members can anticipate.

About fifty percent of the American population moved significantly up or down in social class from their parents during the last generation, but we can estimate that if this were a completely open society, the figure would be closer to sixty-five percent. So it may be argued that perhaps fifteen percent of Americans have been denied the chance to be mobile for reasons having nothing to do with their talents or motivations. This represents at least thirty million people and thus presents a serious challenge to American ideals.

Over the next quarter-century, this country may expect some decrease in the tangible differences among different classes' lifestyles and probably greater emphasis on those aspects of lifestyle which are related to prestige. Barring economic or other catastrophes, then, social class in America will slowly come to be more a matter of life*style* and less a necessary outcome of the relative ease or difficulty that different groups have in dealing with the harsh realities of life.

SUGGESTED READINGS

Bendix, Reinhard, and Seymour M. Lipset, eds., *Class, Status and Power,* 2d ed. (New York: Free Press, 1966). Although perhaps a bit outdated by now, the articles presented here by two leading students of stratification give an excellent idea of the various ways in which the topic has been studied and of the questions that remain to be answered.

Blau, Peter M., and Otis Dudley Duncan, *The American Occupational Structure* (New York: Wiley, 1967). This is probably as thorough a study of the importance of occupation in the American social class system as has ever been done. It is particularly rich in information on how education influences occupation and income.

Eames, Edwin, and Judith G. Goode, *Urban Poverty in a Cross-Cultural Context* (New York: Free Press, 1973). Using historical materials as well as data from around the world, the authors question the idea that there is a "culture of poverty" and explore the adaptive techniques developed by poor people in different societies to cope with the condition of having extremely limited resources.

Hollingshead, August B., and Frederick C. Redlich, *Social Class and Mental Illness* (New York: Wiley, 1958). An important study of the relationship between people's social class and the kinds of mental illnesses they suffer from. The authors find that different classes are characterized by different types of mental illness and that the treatment they receive varies as well.

Kohn, Melvin L., *Class and Conformity: A Study in Values* (Homewood, Ill.: Dorsey, 1969). Kohn's work focuses on the influence of social class, particularly the kinds of occupations associated with different classes, on family values and child-rearing practices.

Lenski, Gerhard E., *Power and Privilege: A Theory of Social Stratification* (New York: McGraw-Hill, 1966). This important analysis of the bases of social stratification includes much information on the relations among wealth, power, and prestige as they operate in different countries to determine both the nature of social classes and rates of mobility among them.

Lipset, Seymour M., and Reinhard Bendix, *Social Mobility in Industrial Society* (Berkeley: University of California Press, 1964). A broad overview of the topic, this volume offers a wealth of statistical information on the rates of mobility in many Western societies and explores their relationship to the ideology of equalitarianism.

Lynd, Robert S., and Helen M. Lynd, *Middletown* (New York: Harcourt, Brace, 1929) and *Middletown in Transition* (New York: Harcourt, Brace, 1937). Two pioneering studies of a small Midwestern city (Muncie, Indiana), one made during the "normalcy" of the 1920s and the other during the Depression of the 1930s, that show the pervasive influence of social class on all aspects of life in an American community.

Mills, C. Wright, *White Collar: The American Middle Classes* (New York: Oxford University Press, 1951) and *The Power Elite* (New York: Oxford University Press, 1956). Mills, certainly a representative of the conflict explanation of stratification, takes an activist position regarding the dysfunctions of stratification, showing both the unpleasant aspects of middle-class life and the way that he believes the various social elites cooperate to maintain their privileged positions in America.

Rossides, Daniel W., *The American Class System: An Introduction to Social Stratification* (Boston: Houghton Mifflin, 1976). An excellent text, well worth investigation for the reader who is interested in delving deeper into this topic.

Rothman, Robert A., *Inequality and Stratification in the United States* (Englewood Cliffs, N.J.: Prentice-Hall, 1978). This is a thorough, balanced examination of not only the current American situation, but also various perspectives on the topic—a very useful volume for those who want to know more about social classes in this country.

Warner, W. Lloyd, and Paul S. Lunt, *The Social Life of a Modern Community* (New Haven, Conn.: Yale University Press, 1941). Probably the most famous of the many investigations of stratification in America, this volume from the "Yankee City" series (actually, Newburyport, Mass.) reveals the six-class system of a conservative New England community.

Warner, W. Lloyd, et al., *Democracy in Jonesville* (New York: Harper & Row, 1949). Warner, an anthropologist who had previously studied Australian aborigines, here applies the "reputational" approach to identifying social classes in a small town in the Midwest.

Glossary

Caste (closed-class) system A system of stratification in which one's rank or social class is ascribed on the basis of birth, and mobility is virtually impossible. The word "caste" comes from ancient India. A caste is thus a hereditary class, and its members' lives are governed by the rights and obligations prescribed for them by the society's religious or political institution. A caste system is to be contrasted with an estate system and an open-class system (see below).

Estate system A system of stratification in which birth is more important than other factors in determining one's social class, but class boundaries are not directly maintained by religious or political prescriptions. In such a system a limited amount of mobility is possible. The term comes from medieval Europe.

Esteem The appreciation one receives for outstanding role performance. Esteem is thus relative to a specific status and is to be distinguished from *prestige* (see below), which is based on the amount of honor or respect given someone in comparison to other members of society, regardless of their particular statuses.

Lifestyle A term that encompasses such varied aspects of one's life as occupation, residence, daily activities, relations with others, and preferences in food, dress, recreation, etc. It is used to identify in a general way those themes and clusters of habits, common to certain people, that distinguish them from others. Differences in lifestyles due to different cultural backgrounds are associated with different racial and ethnic groups; those due to differences in wealth, power, and prestige are associated with different social classes.

Notoriety The condition of being known to be the object of many people's attention, ordinarily for reasons that are not respectable. For someone who craves public attention, notoriety may serve as a kind of substitute for prestige.

Open-class system A system of stratification in which ascriptive factors are of minimal importance in determining one's social class. Ideally, in other words, the individual's movement from one class to another is based entirely on his or her achievements (or lack thereof).

Power Strictly speaking, power is the ability to secure others' compliance with one's wishes or commands regardless of their initial willingness to do so (see Chapter 12, on the political institution, for a discussion of the bases of power). In relation to stratification, power (together with prestige and wealth, defined below) is one of the three analytically distinct scales on which individuals are ranked in relation to one another. It may be referred to more generally as "influence," or even as "clout."

Prestige The overall amount of respect or social honor one receives from others. It may be acquired on the basis of achievement (for example, occupational and educational attainments) and of ascriptive qualities (for example, membership in sex, age, and racial or ethnic categories). Prestige is measured against absolute standards, whereas *esteem* (see above) is relative to a particular status and is honorable, and *notoriety* (see above) is essentially dishonorable.

Social class A category of people who share roughly similar lifestyles, based on their command of similar amounts of wealth, power, and prestige, and whose lives are commonly thought for this reason to be either more or less enviable than the lives of people in different categories.

Social mobility Movement from one social class to another, either upward or downward, generally measured by contrasting the individual's social class as an adult with his or her parents' social class. (The term *lateral,* or *horizontal, mobility* refers mainly to movement from one occupation to another within the same class.) *Subjective* mobility is one's sense of mobility as it is influenced by the mobility of others (if they seem to move up while one does not, one *senses* downward mobility, and vice-versa). *Objective* mobility is based on changes in one's observable lifestyle or in the factors that contribute to this such as wealth, education, occupational prestige, etc.

Socioeconomic status (SES) One's status, or social position, as a member of a particular social class—upper class, working class, etc. It is with this usage that the word "status" as it refers to social position may be confused with "status" as indicating rank or relative prestige. See the discussions of this problem in Chapter 2 and in this chapter.

Status consistency A condition in which one holds roughly equivalent amounts of wealth, power, and prestige. Since holding a given amount of any of these things often helps one to acquire equivalent amounts of the others, status consistency (or balance) is a more common situation than its opposite, status *in*consistency (or *im*balance).

Stratification The organization of a society's population in "layers," or social classes, which are distinguished from one another by the relative advantages enjoyed by the members of each one. All but the simplest and most primitive human societies are characterized by the presence of two or more distinct classes, so that stratification is a feature of nearly every society on earth.

Wealth The determinant of one's lifestyle, and thus of one's social class, that is measured by one's relative control of material goods and services (see Chapter 11, on the economic institution, for a more general discussion of property and of money). Although one's wealth is visible in one's material possessions, it is also a function of one's present and anticipated income, one's savings and credit rating, and the current salability of what one owns. Even though it seems more readily quantifiable than either power or prestige, wealth is by no means either an easy or fully reliable indicator of one's social class.

7
Intergroup Relations

SOCIAL CATEGORIES

Because interaction with a stranger is never *certain* to be satisfying, people have a continuing interest in being able to minimize the chances of misunderstanding, frustration, and unintended conflict in their relationships with others. People want to know ahead of time, in other words, which others they can interact with easily and those with whom interaction is likely to be more difficult.

Two people are sure to have difficulty interacting if they do not share the same norms, and so indicators of foreignness (differences in physical appearance, language or speech habits, lifestyle, etc.) were probably among the earliest used by human beings as the basis for such predictions. Along with age and sex categories, the category of "stranger" was certainly among the earliest ascribed statuses used in human groups.

But someone who is a stranger to one group is almost always a member of another group. Such membership implies a degree of trust and preferential treatment within that group that is not extended to the members of other groups. To be categorized as a stranger, then, suggests not only that one may be more difficult to interact with easily, but also that this interaction may contain elements of competition or even hostility. This sort of suspicion is an almost inevitable consequence of the awareness of group differences.

It is also likely that once an ascribed status ("This person is a member of group X") has been identified and the characteristics of its occupants have been defined, people have a tendency to try to impose those characteristics on everyone who occupies it. We saw in Chapter 5 how this occurs in the case of the sexes. The relationship between an indicator of category membership (e.g., skin color) and the characteristics ascribed to that category may thus be reversed. Now skin color is used as the reason for forcing a person to fit the preconceived image others have of his or her ascribed status, rather than simply as a clue to what he or she is likely to be like.

As the differences among **social categories** *(people who share one or more visible or behavioral characteristics)* are accentuated in this way, the boundaries among different groups within society are drawn more sharply. The relationships among members of these different groups, further, are almost always characterized by an awareness of relative power and of how each group evaluates the others. As different racial, ethnic, and religious groups are identified within a particular society, then, there is likely to be some tension among them. Their differences produce distinctive patterns of interaction both within categories and among them, so that the existence of social categories has important consequences for not only their members' lives, but the structure of society as well.

SOCIAL CATEGORIES AND SOCIAL LIFE

Whenever we identify someone as a member of a racial or ethnic group—a black minister, a Jewish mother, a WASP businessman—we are assigning him or her to a categorical group. Thereafter, that person's racial or ethnic identity takes precedence over his or her characteristics as an individual because we have developed a set of expectations about all members of this category. Blacks have *these* characteristics, Jews have *those* characteristics, and WASPs are like *that*. Very simple. Now we think we know how to interact with this person, although we are really reacting to a category of people rather than to an individual. Why we should do this, and what its consequences are, is an important focus of sociological interest.

The topic of this chapter, intergroup relations, used to be called "race relations" by sociologists until perhaps twenty-five years ago, and the term is still in use today. "Intergroup," however, covers a broader range of social phenomena and seems more accurate because the same dynamics that underlie the relations among racial groups are also those that come into play when different ethnic groups (for instance, Jews and Christians, or Mexican-Americans and Italian-Americans) deal with each other. The basic dynamics of anti-Semitism are similar to those involved in white racism, and it is useful to have one term that will cover all of these things. (The "group" part of *intergroup*, it should be noted, clearly refers here to a social category rather than to a territorial or purposeful group, even though the category may often have a territorial or purposeful identity as well.)

Race versus Ethnicity

The relations between **races** (or between *groups whose members have readily visible physical similarities*) are still a predominant focus of sociological attention, primarily because this relationship seems most fraught with emotion and potential conflict in America today. But "race" is actually much more a social than a biological reality.

The broad human groupings that we ordinarily think of as separate races are large categories whose members share clusters of inherited, distinctive physical characteristics. But the different elements that make up these clusters—for instance, skin color, facial structure, type of hair, etc.—are not necessarily related to one another. There are many people in the world who have dark skins, thin noses, and straight hair—the inhabitants of India. There are those who have reddish skins, flat noses, and straight hair—the American Indians. The concept of race, as most people use it, has no biological reality as a sharp, permanent means by which humans can be divided into distinctive categories. It is particularly inaccurate, further, to believe that certain combinations of physical characteristics are innately related to particular psychological or behavioral characteristics.

Still, so long as "race" has some social reality—so long as physical characteristics enable people to categorize one another—it plays an important role in society. What is important, of course, is not "race" itself, but rather the tendency for distinctive clusters of physical characteristics to be associated with distinctive subcultures. Just as distinctive physical characteristics are passed down genetically through family lines, so *subcultures are passed down through the same lines by socialization* (**ethnicity**). If the former remain constant over several generations, it is not illogical to assume that there has been a comparable maintenance of the group's subculture, simply because the members of that category have not mingled intimately enough with the members of other categories to meld either their genetic or their subcultural heritages.

The important thing about "race" is that it is actually used as an indicator of distinctive subcultures; for practical purposes, then, different racial groups should really be defined as different ethnic groups, for it is each one's *ethos* (see Chapter 3) that is involved.

The problem of why and how categorical groups come to develop and maintain their differences and how these differences so often produce intergroup hostilities is a major focus of the study of intergroup relations. The other side of this coin, that is, how to prevent the buildup of intergroup tensions or to cool them down, is the "applied" aspect of this study.

Relations Among Social Categories

When we speak of intergroup relations, we usually think of tension, hostility, and conflict. This is not strange. For one thing, a situation of harmonious cooperation between the members of two categorical groups is not very dramatic, whereas conflict is more exciting and more likely to command our attention. For another, a group's boundaries are most clearly defined when it is in conflict with another group; two groups that do *not* make their differences important in their relationships may well come to look like one large group. (We *can* categorize blondes and brunettes, after all, but since the members of each category do not treat each other as being significantly different—haircolor advertisements notwithstanding—there is little to be gained in treating them as separate groups.)

The naturalness of intergroup hostility   The development of intergroup hostility can be traced to the operation of normal social forces. We need not look for purposeful evil on the part of one group or another or to "racial instinct" to explain the origin of such hostility. ("Evil," or at least selfishness, may play an important part in perpetuating hostility after it has developed, but evil is not the cause of its initial development.) Both the haters and the hated are the products—the victims, if you like—of perfectly natural social forces and processes. Although we may believe that people *should* be able to rise above these forces, it is probably more realistic to regard existing intergroup hostilities as the result of natural social processes rather than as the product of voluntary, conscious human decisions.

Ironically, the forces that produce intergroup hostility are the same ones that create and maintain groups. A group, after all, is identified not only because its members share a subculture and interact with one another in particular ways, but because it can be distinguished from its social surroundings. Membership ordinarily entitles one to a degree of intimacy in interacting with other members that one does not expect to enjoy with nonmembers. Further, since a fair amount of within-group interaction occurs for its own sake rather than as a means to some further end, it is important that members feel comfortable with one another. Our innocent phrase "to feel at home with someone" suggests the degree of mutual trust and intimacy found in the family; it is certainly expected more within one's socially defined groups than outside of them.

We already know that groups are of the utmost importance to us. They give us our social identities, they establish our norms and values, and they offer situations in which we can derive maximum satisfaction from our interaction with others. It is therefore important that we maintain and protect our groups. One of the chief ways we do this is by seeing that our groups' boundaries are clearly established, so that we know with some certainty who is and who is not a member.

Being aware that you may not know what a nonmember (someone from a different categorical group) expects of you, or how she or he will interpret your words and actions, is enough to make interaction with him or her potentially less rewarding—outside of impersonal, standardized situations such as buying groceries or attending a ballgame. There is thus a lower rate of interaction across group boundaries as compared to within-group rates. The lower rate of interaction tends, in turn, to lower the amount of mutual trust and understanding between the members of different groups.

The door is thus open to the development of false beliefs about other groups. The less a particular aspect of one group's behavior is known to another, the more likely it is that it will become the focus of unfavorable myths and fantasies. It is not unusual that religious and sexual practices are so often the subject of intergroup "tales," for they are the areas of group life that are least visible to outsiders.

Such beliefs, built up in the absence of genuine knowledge, are easily shaped in ways to belittle the other group. To maintain the attractiveness of one's own group, it is useful to make other groups seem less attractive, and so a potentially vicious cycle is begun. Members of the other group are said to be weak in terms of the abilities honored by this group, and at the same time they are believed to indulge freely in those fascinating pleasures which this group tries to deny its own members. As a result, interaction between members of the two groups decreases further, and each group has additional opportunities to elaborate its derogatory images of the other.

Stereotypes At this point, you will see that the term *stereotype* can be substituted for what was just mentioned as "derogatory image." A **stereotype,** in short, is *an image, or picture, that is assumed to fit every member of a social category* (Allport, 1954). It is a specific example of the broader concept of *prejudice,* which is discussed below.

Although a stereotype need not be negative—it is possible to have a *positive* stereotype of a category such as "teacher" or "minister"—the fact that it is applied indiscriminately to all members of a category, regardless of accuracy, is enough in itself to give the term a negative connotation. After all, American values encourage us to recognize differences among people by viewing them as unique individuals. Reliance on stereotypes also leads to inaccurate assumptions about people. This, in turn, can make our relations with them unsatisfying and even full of unnecessary conflict. Thus dependence on stereotypes both contradicts the value of individualism and is basically irrational.

Yet people continue to rely on stereotypes to guide their relations with others. A stronger group's stereotyping of a weaker group's members provides a cheap-and-easy, oversimplified guide to interaction in which errors are of little consequence for the former. A weaker group's stereotyping of a stronger group probably serves a defensive purpose—partly as a covert expression of hostility and partly as a warning that "they" can indeed be punitive if offended. Because stereotypes serve an immediately useful purpose, even though they distort social relationships, they are extremely difficult to get rid of.

The snowballing of intergroup differences As soon as "we" are clearly distinguished from "them," another obstacle to interaction across group boundaries appears. This is our fear that interaction with "them" will be defined as a sign of our lowered commitment to our own group or even as a willingness to bring outsiders into our group. Since neither of these prospects is likely to strengthen our relations with other members of our own group, we may be subjected to strong social pressures to avoid members of the other group. The old challenge "Would you want your daughter to marry one of *them*?" is an expression of the fear of bringing outsiders into the group, and it is found particularly in groups in which the family is an especially important part of the social structure—working-class neighborhoods, backward economic areas, and the like.

Intergroup competition for the scarce commodities of life, especially economic advantage and political control, may come either before or after the development of hostilities. Either way, it is clear that the development of a sense of "If my group doesn't get it, your group will" is guaranteed to heighten the tension. And if the competition is unequal, as it usually is because one group is superior in numbers or has some other advantage, the weaker ("minority") group usually loses. Thereafter, economic and political interests make it of practical importance for the winning group to ensure that it retains its dominant position.

The establishment of inequality   Once the boundaries between two cate-gorical groups have been drawn and derogatory images have been established, people come to view acceptance of them as a necessary part of membership in their own groups. Included in the definition of someone as a member of group P is that "he or she should believe X, Y, and Z about the members of group Q." Here we have **prejudice**, *the tendency to "prejudge," or to accept a generalized characterization (usually negative) of a group of people, and then to apply it indiscriminately to all members of that group.*

This sort of thinking is hardly realistic, of course; it reflects either the unthinking acceptance of a group-determined pattern of attitudes (which one may believe to be the only attitudes possible) or, in rare cases, a strong psy-chological need to hate. Either way, the group seems to tell its members, "It is good to dislike that group, for this clarifies and enhances our group's iden-tity—and if you need to hate someone, hate *them* so that your problems won't disrupt our group."

Prejudice represents a set of attitudes rather than a pattern of behavior. The behavioral parallel to prejudice is **discrimination**—*the systematic pref-erential treatment of the members of one's own group at the expense of the members of another group.* This distinction between attitude and behavior, or between motivation and action, is useful because it is obvious that they need not always go together. One may engage in discrimination without really believing that it is right and necessary, or one may be intensely prejudiced but afraid to express it in action. If the subculture of the group requires or legiti-mates discriminatory behavior, a member will probably engage in it whether or not there is a personal "need" for it; but if such behavior is defined as wrong, he or she can only express beliefs verbally or, at best, engage in covert discrimination (Merton, 1949).

Social distance   Prejudice lays out the attitudinal boundaries between groups, and discrimination makes them "real" by establishing behavioral boundaries. Together, they produce what sociologists call **social distance**—*the distance people would prefer to be from other groups in "social space"* (Bogardus, 1959). This may range from no social space at all (a willingness to marry a member of the other group), through willingness to eat with them, to work beside them, to have them in the same neighborhood, and so on, down to a

Prejudicial attitudes are made overt through discrimination, which establishes social distance. The result is segregation. These people are protesting the enforcement of social distance in restaurants. (Bruce Davidson/ Magnum Photos)

desire for such vast social distance that one is unwilling even to admit them to one's own country.

Social distance is usually implemented by spatial distance (when those desiring it have the power) through such devices as residential segregation, the segregation of public facilities such as schools, hotels, and restaurants, and discrimination in admission to religious, political, and occupational groups. Thus **segregation** *is the enforcement of spatial distance.* In some cases segregation may be voluntary and desired by both groups involved, but as soon as its imposition is unilateral and systematically denies meaningful opportunities to members of the other group against their wishes, it is being used as an instrument of oppression.

The group that is the more powerful—because of sheer numbers, prior establishment in a given locality, greater wealth, or even because its members actually owned the members of the other group at an earlier time—will usually seek to perpetuate its dominant position through the various methods of enforcing social distance.

Consequences of subordination If the dominant/subordinate (or majority/minority) relationship between two categorical groups lasts over several generations, the situation acquires a kind of "traditionalistic legitimacy" (see

Chapter 12). "This the way things have always been," the dominant group says, "and so it is morally right." And since the dominant group tends to control both the educational system and the mass media, its definition of the situation becomes part of the common culture that both groups share. (See Chapter 17, on public opinion and collective behavior, for a more detailed discussion of this process.)

The members of the subordinate group may thus come to share the dominant group's view of themselves and to discover that their feelings of deprivation have no public legitimacy. In such circumstances it is not unusual for them to be quite ambivalent about their own worth: If the "tools for thinking"—the symbols provided by the common culture—that refer to them all have negative connotations, it is extremely difficult for them even to think about themselves without "admitting" their own inferiority. Nothing could be more damaging to a person's self-confidence, ambition, and general sense of worth.

THE CIVIL RIGHTS MOVEMENT

Blacks versus Whites

For the past hundred years in this country, we have seen how hostilities between black Americans and white Americans, and the discriminatory practices that grew out of them, have fed into a vicious, self-perpetuating cycle. This cycle is based on the dominant group's using its position to acquire the largest share of the scarce commodities: wealth, power, and prestige. This ensuing poverty and powerlessness gave black Americans significantly less control of their environment. The result, as discussed in Chapter 6, is that they developed a set of values and patterns of behavior—a subculture—that differed markedly from those of white Americans, who have had much more control over their life situations.

The style of life associated with an extreme lack of control over the environment was characteristic of black Americans at the time of the Emancipation in 1863, for slaves had even less control over their lives than the most poverty-stricken free persons. Freedom itself, however, was not enough to do away with the subculture that had developed during slavery. Before the first free generation could begin to break out of the poverty culture, both legal and extralegal forms of segregation were imposed that condemned most black Americans to continuing poverty and deprivation.

Once segregation had been established, discriminatory behavior on the part of white Americans acquired a tinge of legitimacy. The distinction between lower-class and middle-class styles of life is, after all, one of differences in behavior, and in this country it has always been a person's right to say, "I don't want to associate with that person, because I don't like his or her behavior." For apparently self-serving reasons, the whites failed to see the illogic in reasoning from specific individuals to categories of individuals, and from there it was only a short step to the belief that it was a person's skin color rather than poverty that accounted for his or her lifestyle.

Once this belief was accepted—and it was, because it helped to justify the dominant group's position—discrimination in all forms could be justified on the basis that "these people are naturally inferior to us—they are ignorant, lazy, and immoral, and it is right that we should keep them apart from us." The blacks were powerless to prevent such attitudes from being written into law; now the norms of the white community could be enforced by the power of the state.

In fact, any group whose members have had little, if any, education, who live in a marginal economic situation, and whose family structure has been seriously weakened by these circumstances can probably be described as "ignorant, lazy, and immoral." Skin color and other physical characteristics have nothing to do with their behavior. The conditions under which most black Americans were forced to live during the century following Emancipation molded many of them to a lower-class style of life, and a self-fulfilling prophecy (see Chapter 17) was set in motion. "If these people are lazy and ignorant, there is no point in giving them a decent education or decent jobs"—and, lo and behold, the next generation of black Americans found themselves trapped in the same situation.

Only within the last thirty years or so has white America begun to listen to black Americans concerning the latter group's disadvantaged position in this society. Constituting only about twelve percent of the population as a whole, blacks could hardly hope to better their situation by the use of force alone, so (as discussed in Chapter 5) their main remedy was arguments based on American values and then the use of law.

The logical inconsistency between the words of the American Constitution and the discriminatory behavior of white Americans toward black Americans was emphasized by Swedish sociologist Gunnar Myrdal in *An American Dilemma* (1944), an important study of race relations in this country. Myrdal pointed to the serious gap between what white Americans *said* about human equality and what they actually *did*, even though most of them had managed to ignore their inconsistency or to explain it away by claiming that the Constitution had not meant to define Negroes as "men" in the same sense that Caucasians were so defined. Supposed biological differences were cited as well by whites to justify discriminatory practices.

Perhaps it was the renewed attention to basic values engendered by World War II; perhaps it was postwar affluence that made it easier for people to "afford" to worry about such things. For whatever reason, a slowly increasing number of whites came to agree with blacks that the present state of their relationship was intolerable. The dilemma would have to be resolved, and this would require changes in both attitudes and behavior, based eventually on changes in American laws.

In response to the newly perceived need to do away with this hypocrisy, President Truman took the first step toward desegregating the armed forces shortly after the end of the war, and in 1954 the Supreme Court ruled that it was no longer legal to provide "separate but equal" school facilities for children of different races, because such arrangements are inherently *un*equal. Thus began the national move toward **integration,** whereby two *social categories would attempt to interact without regard for their differences.*

Organization for protest   Black Americans' efforts to overcome the disadvantages imposed on them by virtue of their ascribed status go back to the earliest days of slavery. But only after the turn of this century did these efforts become effectively organized. An organization called the Niagara Movement was formed in 1905 to seek equal rights for blacks, and the National Association for the Advancement of Colored People was founded in 1909. During the early 1920s, Marcus Garvey's Universal Negro Improvement Association attracted perhaps as many as six million members, although it failed after he was deported to the West Indies after conviction of mail fraud.

During the first half of this century, despite all the barriers that had been erected against them, black Americans were gaining more education, more organizational skills, and more strength to protest the injustices that they were experiencing every day. With the moral support of some whites, even if not often with much practical support, the movement to secure full civil rights for blacks moved more swiftly after World War II. Following the 1954 desegregation decision, there was the bus boycott in Montgomery, Alabama, in 1955; the pressing of legal actions throughout the South to force local officials to implement the desegregation decision; increasing efforts to register black voters; and the beginning of nonviolent confrontations in the original sit-in at a variety store in Greensboro, North Carolina, by four black college freshmen in 1960.

The strategy of protest   Conceived originally by Mahatma Gandhi in India and symbolized in this country by Reverend Martin Luther King, Jr., **nonviolent protest** *is essentially the demonstration of one's willingness to endure physical suffering and deprivation for two purposes: to call public attention to the injustices one is protesting and to force the public to recognize its own inconsistency when it punishes the protester while at the same time giving lip service to the justice that he or she is seeking.* (Protest as a reason for deviant behavior is discussed further in Chapter 15.)

In one sense, since protest often involves violating the law (trespassing, unlawful assembly, etc.), it can be treated as criminal behavior, and appropriate legal sanctions can be applied. But when the protester is obviously making no personal "profit" from his or her actions and makes no attempt to evade these sanctions, those who apply them can hardly avoid wondering why he or she has broken the law. Indeed, the protester hopes that eventually they will come to wonder whether it is fair to impose punishment at all and whether the conditions that brought about the protest should not be changed instead. When nonviolent protest succeeds, it is because it has been able to make others face these questions and try to resolve them.

The civil rights movement today   With the achievement of a certain degree of progress toward full civil rights for black Americans and other minority groups and with a broadening of the movement, a different set of social forces has come into the picture in the last ten years. As some gains have been made, hopes for additional progress have been generated. This is sometimes called "the revolution of rising expectations," and it has heightened both the demand for speedier gains and the sense of frustration when they are not forthcoming. Out of this frustration in the late 1960s and early 1970s came new and some-times more violent efforts to change American society. At the same time, the officers of the more successful organizations began to substitute quiet, steady negotiation for uncompromising public rhetoric and thus appeared to become more conservative.

A variety of goals and tactics has developed, and there have been power struggles within different organizations. The question of who will lead whom, and where, no longer has a single answer for any minority group. Some leaders seek full equality and assimilation into the mainstream of American life through educational and economic achievements. Others have concluded that this goal is impossible and propose instead greater separation of the races—the creation of all-black communities or even states where the need to interact with whites will be minimized. And there remain others, typically younger and more impatient, who interpret the civil rights movement as a raw struggle for power and who anticipate eventually an all-out war with the larger white community.

Despite the lack of agreement on goals within the black community today, it appears that more and more reliance is being placed on "working within the system" to achieve equal rights and equal opportunities. Political organization and lobbying, together with economic organization and pressure, seem to be the most effective weapons today, and they are being employed in different ways in different places to overcome both current discrimination and the consequences of earlier discrimination.

The Other Minority Groups

Although only American Indians (or Native Americans) can claim to be the original inhabitants of this country, it was the earliest immigrants—primarily from northern Europe—who seized economic and political power in the new land and have largely maintained their position as the categorical groups against which other groups' differences must be measured. As people from other parts of the world emigrated to America, the extent to which they differed physically and culturally from the white Protestant "natives" determined the strength of the categorical boundaries that divided them from this "majority" group. This in turn determined the amount of time that would have to pass before the members of different groups could break away from the stereotypes originally assigned to them and achieve either **assimilation** *(taking on the characteristics of the majority group)* or at least full equality with the majority group.

Since physical differences are more immediately obvious than cultural differences and are more difficult to change, it should not be surprising that the categories identified by "racial" criteria have been more difficult to ignore than others. By the same token, the longer those groups most similar in appearance to the dominant white majority have been in this country, the less important it has been for others to categorize them separately. Today, Americans whose backgrounds are Scandinavian and German/Austrian (being both white and largely Protestant) are scarcely distinguished from those whose ancestors came from the British Isles. As shown in Table 7.1, these groups—known vaguely as White Anglo-Saxon Protestants—make up about thirty-five percent of the American population, or about seventy-eight million people (*Public Opinion,* Nov./Dec. 1978, pp. 32–34).

Being white but culturally different, usually in terms of religion, Americans from Irish, Italian, Eastern European, Greek, and other backgrounds—often called "white ethnics"—make up nearly thirty percent of the population. They still tend to be distinguished from the white Protestant group, although they are rarely the objects of systematic, overt discrimination that they once were. It is of interest to note that although such groups may still be the targets of "ethnic" jokes, the organizations that were originally intended to protect their members from discrimination are turning more and more to maintaining and celebrating their distinctive cultural heritages. A certain amount of categorization does heighten one's sense of personal identity and community, and so long as it does not entail systematic disadvantages, the members of these groups thus find it rewarding to emphasize their special cultural distinctions.

Recent surveys have found about one-fifth of the white population unwilling to claim a specific ethnic heritage, usually because their ancestors belonged to two or more separate categories (*Public Opinion,* Nov./Dec. 1978, p. 33). More than forty million Americans, then, must remain unclassified in terms of ethnicity, no matter how much this may frustrate our desire to find a neat pigeonhole for everyone.

Even more clearly different from the white majority are those groups whose members differ from it physically as well as culturally. The roughly twelve million Americans who come from Spanish-speaking cultures (the

TABLE 7.1 MAJOR RACIAL AND ETHNIC GROUPS
IN THE UNITED STATES TODAY

Origins	Millions	Percentage
	(approximate figures)	
Austria, England, Germany, Scandinavia, Scotland, Wales ("WASPs")	78	35
Eastern Europe, Greece, France, Ireland, Italy, Poland, etc. ("White ethnics")	63	28
Combined ancestries ("Unclassifieds")	42	19
Africa ("Blacks")	27	12
Caribbean (including Cuba and Puerto Rico), Central and South America, Mexico, Spain ("Hispanics")	12	5
China, Japan, Korea, India, Phillipines, etc. ("Asians")	2	< 1
North America ("American Indians")	< 1	< 1
	225	100.0%

Source: Public Opinion 1, 5 (Nov./Dec. 1978): 32–34. Figures used by permission.

Note: Because of the difficulties in categorizing people, these figures may be off by as much as five or ten percent. However, they provide a rough idea of the relative size of these different categories and should be viewed only with this in mind.

Caribbean area, Central and South America, and Mexico—known collectively as Hispanics, despite real differences among them)—tend also to have been more recent arrivals, and so stereotypes based on their initial characteristics often still include an assumption of linguistic as well as physical and cultural differences. (If the anticipation of language difficulties tends to sharpen categorical boundaries, it is unfortunate that the words "Spanish-*speaking*" should be used as the label for this group, for it may well perpetuate the stereotype.)

The ancestors of many Americans of Asian origin actually came to this country before 1900. Even after the disappearance of most linguistic differences, however, the physical characteristics and cultural heritages of more than two million Americans with Chinese, Japanese, Indian, Indonesian, Philippine, and Korean backgrounds have persisted and served to keep them

These Native Americans gathered before Mt. Rushmore near Wounded Knee, South Dakota, to protest discrimination and infringement of their rights. (Rick Smolan)

categorized as distinctly different from other Americans. But with their own values stressing education and work, they have been more than modestly successful by American standards.

Finally, there are today about 800,000 Native Americans in this country—perhaps less than a third of the number who were here before the first Europeans arrived. Their plight is still the most desperate of any minority group, but now they are beginning to organize themselves to seek an escape from poverty, discrimination, and the particularly onerous position of being the only group to be partially governed by a special branch of the federal government—the United States Bureau of Indian Affairs.

Fitting into American society Except for black Americans, whose cultural heritages were shattered and largely lost during the long period of slavery, each of these groups tends to be ambivalent about the extent to which it wishes to retain its separate cultural identity. For many of them, full retention of the parent culture tends to make them unfit for completely satisfactory participation in mainstream American society. In various ways their values, family structures, and economic practices work against the acceptance of those patterns of behavior which make up the lifestyle most valued by the dominant American culture. No easy answer has been found to the problem of how to retain one's full ethnic identity and still be happy as an American, but we may suppose that as tolerance of different lifestyles increases, this problem will diminish in importance.

For the sake of building such a distinctive ethnic identity, many black students today are seriously engaged in the re-creation of their own African heritage through various black studies programs. This and similar enterprises are foundation-building efforts, since establishing the details of a group's history leads to a sense of pride that can facilitate more effective organization and a more positive self-image. As black people begin to rescue themselves from the cultural oblivion to which they have been consigned for so long, their existence as three-dimensional human beings will become more clearly a part of all Americans' cultural map of the world. It will become more difficult for whites to indulge in blind prejudice, and it will be easier for blacks to seek and enjoy their rights without feeling that they are fighting the whole system by themselves.

Even with the positive sense of community that one's ethnic heritage provides, though, there remains the possibility that loyalty to a categorical group will supersede loyalty to the larger society. This could mean, in turn, a readiness to promote this group's interest at the expense of other groups, the intensification of intergroup hostilities, and a fragmenting of the larger social structure. If the preservation of each group's special identity is dependent in the long run on the preservation of society itself, it should eventually become clear that this identity can best be maintained if the members of other groups enjoy equal rights and opportunities.

THE FUTURE OF SOCIAL CATEGORIES

It is clear that American society is not the complete "melting pot" envisioned by earlier social commentators. The different racial, ethnic, and religious groups that make it up will not lose their separate identities through total assimilation. Nor, on the other hand, will they become completely separated. What, then, will be the state of intergroup relations in the future?

With neither full assimilation nor full segregation a realistic likelihood, we must expect that a situation of somewhat confused **pluralism** will characterize American society for the foreseeable future. This is *an arrangement in which categorical differences continue to be important in people's relationships, but do not carry with them systematic advantages or disadvantages like those we find in the relations between majority and minority groups.*

As noted in Chapter 5, there is a long-range tendency in this country for people to deemphasize the importance of one another's ascribed statuses (outside of situations where those statuses are directly relevant to their interaction). The makeup of an individual's status set, in other words, will be less limited in the future by the nature of his or her ascribed statuses than it has been in the past. Being female, for instance, will have less influence on whether or not one can also occupy the status of senator; being black will not rule out the possibility that one can also occupy the status of corporation president.

Barring war, economic upheaval, or other catastrophes, this trend will continue and will mean eventually that the disadvantages associated with membership in a minority group will largely disappear. This is not to say, however, that there will be complete tolerance or complete approval of intergroup differences, for one can hardly think one's own group the best without also thinking that other groups are less desirable. But we can predict that such sentiments will be more and more restricted to the private areas of life—marriage and family, choice of residence, and the choice of friends. For example, when where one chooses to live comes to be a matter of choice rather than of forced exclusion from other areas, we will find it easier to tolerate a certain amount of neighborhood segregation because it will be voluntary. A pattern of "daytime integration, nighttime separation" will certainly become more common, even though there will be many who choose residential integration as well.

It is possible, of course, that this prediction is overly optimistic. Some sociologists believe that discrimination against minority groups will continue in new and more subtle forms and that pluralism will become a slogan to mask the continued exploitation of some social categories by others. As a group, sociologists do not have a spectacular record of accurate social prediction. They do not yet understand, for example, the nature of the social forces that will tip the balance in favor of increasing or decreasing equality among different social categories.

But it is certainly clear that the social categories to which human beings assign one another have been of the most fundamental importance in shaping the structure of society and so in influencing the lives of their members. The practical question that sociologists must ask now is whether they will *continue* to be so important. Beyond this, the investigation of intergroup relations will be useful in helping us all to learn how the valuable aspects of social categories can be preserved at the same time that we are slowly eliminating their negative consequences.

SUMMARY

Readily identifiable differences between two people are often taken by each as indicators of their cultural or subcultural differences and thus of how easy or difficult it will be for them to interact. The assignment of people to racial and ethnic categories (that is, to ascribed statuses) is thus of some immediate practical value. It should be noted, of course, that the physical differences we define as "racial" are not intrinsically related to differences in character or ability, even though they may be associated with subcultural differences.

People tend to interact more with members of their own category than with those outside it and to develop a commitment to them. This leads them to disvalue the members of other categories, so some degree of intergroup hostility is difficult to avoid. Stereotypes are developed, and people react negatively to those who try to act "outside" the roles assigned to their ascribed statuses. The boundaries between categorical groups thus come to be important in determining a society's social structure.

Competition for wealth, power, and prestige comes to be viewed as intergroup competition, and the usual result is that a "majority" group wins out and then uses its advantages to prevent the members of "minority" groups from gaining an equal share of these scarce resources. Once established, such inequalities may come to be enforced by law as well as by terrorism; they come to be built into society's culture, and the members of the subordinate groups learn to view themselves as inferior.

Such a situation developed in American society, beginning with the importation of black slaves, but then defining other immigrants also as inferior social categories. The increasingly obvious discrepancy between professed American values and the actual nature of the American social structure, however, eventually led to the civil rights movement. Although this focused at first on the relations between black and white Americans, other disadvantaged groups (the "white ethnics," Asian-Americans, Hispanic-Americans, and Native Americans) have now joined the struggle for equality.

The task now is to eliminate systematic discrimination based on ascribed statuses while at the same time retaining the advantages that people find in their social categories—the sense of community and of special identity within the larger society. Although sociologists hold differing opinions of the future of intergroup relations in this country, perhaps as ascribed statuses become less important in the public areas of life (participation in the economic and political institutions), American society will be increasingly characterized by a kind of pluralism in which social categories are valued for their unique heritages, but do not entail either systematic disadvantages or advantages in relation to other groups.

SUGGESTED READINGS

Allport, Gordon W., *The Nature of Prejudice* (Reading, Mass.: Addison-Wesley, 1954). A thorough analysis of the sources and mechanisms of prejudice by one of America's outstanding social psychologists.

Berry, Brewton, and Henry L. Tischler, *Race and Ethnic Relations*, 4th ed. (Boston: Houghton Mifflin, 1978). This text is valuable especially for its analysis of the history of intergroup relations and for its coverage of the topic on a worldwide basis.

Feagin, Joe R., *Racial and Ethnic Relations* (Englewood Cliffs, N.J.: Prentice-Hall, 1978). This text is particularly valuable for its detailed coverage of the lifestyles as well as the present positions in American society of a number of different racial and ethnic categories.

Pettigrew, Thomas F., *A Profile of the American Negro* (Princeton, N.J.: Van Nostrand, 1964). A student of Allport's, Pettigrew provides here a detailed description of the black American community as it had been shaped through the 1950s by slavery, prejudice, and discrimination.

Pinkney, Alphonso, *Black Americans*, 2nd ed. (Englewood Cliffs, N.J.: Prentice-Hall, 1975). This is an excellent introduction to the facts of life as black Americans have experienced them, together with a sober evaluation of the chances for success of the civil rights movement. The book also contains extensive bibliographies.

Rose, Peter I., *They and We: Racial and Ethnic Minorities in the United States*, 2nd ed. (New York: Random House, 1974). Rose provides a brief but very useful review of the dynamics and effects of intergroup relations as they have affected the numerous minorities that make up American society.

Simpson, George E., and J. Milton Yinger, *Racial and Cultural Minorities*, 4th ed. (New York: Harper & Row, 1972). One of the best texts in the field, covering in extensive detail both fact and theory in the sociology of intergroup relations.

Williams, Robin M., Jr., *Strangers Next Door* (Englewood Cliffs, N.J.: Prentice-Hall, 1964). The final report on eight years of research on intergroup relationships in America, carried out by the Cornell Study of Intergroup Relations. Both Pinkney and Rose, cited above, participated in these studies.

Glossary

Assimilation The process through which the members of one social category (usually the weaker one) take on the characteristics of another category, to the point where there is no useful reason to distinguish between the two categories anymore. Because this means giving up those characteristics that have given members of the weaker category a distinctive identity, there may be considerable resistance to it, even though there are advantages to be gained through merging with the stronger category.

Discrimination The practice of systematically denying certain rights and privileges to the members of a minority group (a weaker social category), so that the members of the majority group (the stronger social category) enjoy specific advantages at the expense of those who are discriminated against. Discrimination may or may not be based on *prejudice* (see below).

Ethnicity The social identity of an individual or group as it is shaped by a particular subculture. The term is ordinarily used only in reference to minority groups, even though the majority group can be said also to have its own subculture (which has been made the standard against which other subcultures are identified) and thus its own distinctive ethnicity.

Integration A situation in which the members of two or more separate social categories interact without regard for their racial or ethnic differences. The term is relative to the situation, however, so that although it is possible to have integration in a school, there may still be discrimination in terms of housing or employment.

Nonviolent protest Norm-violating actions which, without injuring people or destroying property, are intended to call public attention to certain conditions which the protesters believe are unjust. Such actions are often against the law (loitering, trespassing, etc.), and the protesters show the sincerity of their cause by submitting to arrest without resistance. But since active cooperation with agents of the law may weaken the impact of their protest, they frequently go limp and force the police to carry or drag them away. This is also known as passive resistance. (See Chapter 15, on deviance, for additional discussion of protest.)

Pluralism A condition midway between *assimilation* (see above) and *discrimination* (see above). In other words, pluralism is a situation in which the differences among social categories continue to be recognized, but are not accompanied by systematic, enforced differences in the rights and opportunities of members of the different categories.

Prejudice The tendency to prejudge a person on the basis of his or her membership in a particular social category. Strictly speaking, prejudice may be positive as well as negative, but ordinarily it refers to a negative attitude toward a particular category (ranging from distaste to hatred). The "acting out" of prejudice can range from discrimination to genocide (the policy or practice of killing all the members of a specific group, usually a racial or ethnic category).

Race A category of human beings identified as being alike on the basis of one or more visible characteristics: skin color, facial structure, hair texture, etc. Although human beings can be broadly grouped in terms of such characteristics, there is no accepted evidence that these are related to psychological or behavioral characteristics. But as physical similarities persist from one generation to the next, it can be assumed that the group's subculture has also been maintained, and it is actually this that accounts for the social differences between one racial group and another.

Segregation The enforcement of physical separation in some or many circumstances between the members of two social categories, to the disadvantage of members of the weaker category. It may be an activity or a location from which they are excluded (an occupation, for instance, or a restroom). Total segregation would mean total separation of the two groups and thus the opposite of *assimilation* (see above).

Social category A collection of people who have been given a specific social identity by others (or who have claimed it for themselves) on the basis of one or more visible or behavioral characteristics they share. To belong to a social category is thus to occupy an ascriptive status, whether the ascription is based on physical appearance, language, religious practices, or something else. Membership in such a category is frequently an important part of one's sense of identity and is valued for this reason, but to the extent that it entails systematic denial by others of rights, or exclusion from opportunities, its value is weakened.

Social distance The relative amount of intimacy a person wishes or will accept in relation to a member of a different social category. It may range from willingness to marry such a person to a desire that the members of that category be completely excluded from one's own nation or society. Because such attitudes can be measured through interviews and questionnaires, it is possible to determine the social distance between any two social categories and to measure changes in such attitudes over time.

Stereotype An image, positive or negative, held by one individual or group and applied indiscriminately to the members of a particular social category. To the extent that it is used as the basis for one's attitudes toward every member of that category and for one's behavior in relation to each of them, it is the foundation of *prejudice* (see above) and perhaps also of *discrimination* (see above).

8
Communities

FOCUS:

POPULATION DENSITY

A human **community** *is a group that has formed because its members live (that is, regularly spend most of their time) in relative proximity to one another.* It is thus essentially a *territorial* group. On this basis, a single family in an isolated farmhouse is a community, just as is the population of a giant metropolitan area.

When large numbers of people live close together, however, the groups that they form will have many characteristics—some different, some entirely new—that distinguish them from smaller groups. In comparing communities of different sizes, then, the sociologist has an opportunity to see in sharp relief the ways in which social relationships are shaped by their specific settings: the number of people present in a given space and the physical characteristics of that space. **Population density,** *the number of people living in a given space,* is ordinarily expressed in the form of "X number of people per square mile," although "per acre" or "per block" can be used just as well.

As population density increases, two aspects of the community come to have an increasing influence on its members' social relationships. First, the question of how different parts of the community's land area are to be used—for business, industry, homes, recreation, etc.—becomes increasingly important. It is probably the need to work out solutions to this sort of problem that initially forces an aggregate of people in a given area to develop the relationships that make them a group—in the properly sociological sense. And once particular uses have been instituted (building a factory

185

here, a highway *there*), their presence may stimulate the development of new social relationships or the modification of old ones.

Second, as population density increases, there is a decline in the proportion of the group's members with whom any given member can interact directly; each member's personal acquaintance with others is limited to a smaller and smaller fraction of the group's total membership, and so the group is increasingly composed of strangers. There is greater need, then, to develop new types of social relationships through which the members' activities can be coordinated and controlled and also for clearer criteria by which membership itself is defined.

In the background, of course, is the fact that the population density of a territorial group is generally determined by the physical characteristics of both the area it occupies and the surrounding area and by its distance from other communities. Some of these characteristics, in turn, are determined in a practical way by the technology available to the group—the ways and extent to which the land's resources can be exploited, the modes of travel available, and the ways in which people are able to communicate with one another.

But these factors can be ignored for the present because our interest is primarily in understanding the ways in which social relationships change under conditions of varying population density. The sociologist's first job, in other words, is to describe the basic structure and dynamics of communities today rather than to discover their origins. Population density seems to be the concept most relevant to this task.

THE IMPORTANCE OF COMMUNITIES

The people who live in specific places—whether rural areas, towns, cities, states, even regions—have a special feeling for one another and the place where they live that is not found in connection with any other type of human

Where people live—"their" city, state, or even region—gives rise to special feelings the inhabitants have for one another and their community. (Leonard Freed/Magnum Photos)

group. Although people's homes have always held a special spot in their minds and hearts, in this urban age it is mainly the city that tends to be the object of these particular emotions. The affectionate nicknames we give our cities is one illustration of this: Windy City, The Big Apple, Golden Gate, Big D, City of Brotherly Love, Mile-High City, Steeltown, Beantown. We have civic pride in our towns and cities; we root for the home team; our city is the "home" of this or that; perhaps it is "first" in something or other; we have monuments parades, holidays, and slogans that celebrate our affection for these places; and we are proud or ashamed of our local economic and labor statistics, our crime and accident rates, and our collective educational accomplishments.

Whether we love or hate our communities, we treat them as something more than the sum of their present inhabitants. We think of them as entities, as beings with personalities of their own. Some bring a laugh when we think of them: Hoboken, Pismo Beach, Weehawken, Ho-Ho-Kus. Some are muscular, like Pittsburgh or Gary, Indiana. Others have a "high-class" character, like Scarsdale or Shaker Heights. New York and Chicago are "fast," whereas St. Louis and Milwaukee are sober and industrious. The name of a community, then, is more than just the name of a physical location; it is the name of a human group that has its own special characteristics.

Proximity

If anything will turn a number of individuals into a group, it is living close together over an extended period of time. They must learn to cooperate in the use of space; in doing so, they develop a division of labor that increases their interdependence, and they begin to assume a common identity. Because each one is affected to some extent by the actions of others, such as waste disposal, economic activity, and even traffic, there is considerable potential for conflict. To avoid this, the inhabitants of a place must work out among themselves a large number of stable patterns of interaction. This happens in nearly all territorial groups, and on a smaller scale the same thing can be seen among those assigned to the same barracks or ship in the armed forces and among students who live in the same college dormitory.

Continued physical proximity, whether by choice or assignment, almost always leads to the formation of a human group. One perspective on communities, in fact, terms this interdependence "human ecology"; it will be discussed in more detail below.

To be sure, neighbors in a large city apartment building may never get to know one another, but this is because there is little, if any, necessary genuine interdependence among them. The people with whom they need to interact—employers, merchants, relatives, etc.—tend to be located elsewhere. Although extreme crowding and a highly specialized division of labor thus seem to lead to exceptions to what has been said here about the relation between proximity and the formation of groups, this is a special case that does not contradict the general rule.

Vulnerability

There is a certain poignancy in the emotions that people invest in their communities. Formed primarily on the basis of physical closeness and dependent on the continued suitability of the area for habitation, territorial groups can be quite fragile. Their members are free to move from one neighborhood or city to another, and the frequency with which they do this in American society is quite high. It has been estimated that about one family out of five changes its residence each year (Lee and Bouvier, 1977). Territorial groups are thus losing members and replacing them with strangers more rapidly than their birthrates and deathrates might indicate. (For years, a resident of Washington, D.C., has been considered a social oddity if he or she admitted to having been born there, and this is becoming true of more and more cities.) The community retains its identity, then, even though its membership is continually changing, and with a decrease in the percentage of long-term residents, the amount of personal commitment to it as a meaningful group probably decreases as well.

A community can "die," too, even though its members do not. Rome "fell," and the event has been considered a tragedy for more than 1500 years. A mining town can be entirely deserted in a short time after the veins of coal, gold, or silver have been exhausted. Sometimes a small town must be inundated by a new artificial lake, so that its inhabitants are scattered and left with only a memory of the place and people they once knew as home. The extinction of a community by natural calamity—flood, fire, earthquake, or volcano—is an even more tragic event.

Although groups based on physical proximity may mean a great deal to their members, they are probably also the most easily disrupted. Categorical groups may never feel a sense of social identity, for they are identified more by others than by their own members, and purposeful groups such as business firms and voluntary associations are better organized and so usually able to deal with threats to their physical location; their identities are not necessarily tied to a single place.

Territorial groups are both aware of themselves and vulnerable to all sorts of disruptions, both natural and social. A new highway may be built through the center of a town, sharply altering the patterns of interaction that had been established. Economic conditions can drive a community's young people to make their homes elsewhere, so that it fails to replenish its population.

Despite these weaknesses, human communities—groups composed of individuals who live close together in space and who by necessity form social relationships and collective identities—do exist through time. Much of their continued existence is due to the virtual impossibility of eradicating their physical locations or eliminating all of the physical characteristics of a place that have made it a desirable place to settle. Even if a place is successively occupied by different groups, it retains its basic geographical identity, and the replacement of inhabitants is usually so steady that most human communities outlast their original inhabitants. At least eleven generations have been born and died in Boston, for instance, and yet it continues to be a single, identifiable human group. Communities are basic to human society (we all have to live *somewhere*), and they have been of considerable interest to sociologists since at least the early 1920s.

BASIC CHARACTERISTICS OF THE COMMUNITY

In order to study the sort of human group that develops on the basis of territorial proximity, the sociologist must have something more than vague emotional attitudes to legitimate this work. If a topic is to be studied as a "thing in itself" or as something about which reliable generalizations can be made, there must be reason to think that it is sufficiently distinct from other topics to make the study worthwhile.

Thus one of the earliest concerns of the sociologist was to determine the conditions under which the city or any other territorial group can be treated as a distinct social phenomenon. This was a central problem for the German sociologist Max Weber, who studied communities as well as politics, religion, social stratification, and bureaucracy. In the preface to an edition of Weber's classic little book *The City*, Don Martindale writes (1968, p. 59):

> Weber's general procedure was to review the concept of the city in terms of the evidence from world history. On this basis he established the concept of the urban community. Any community, including an urban community, is not an unstructured congeries of activities, but a distinct and limited pattern of human life. It represents a total system of life forces brought into some kind of equilibrium. It is self-maintaining, restoring its order in the face of disturbances. . . . The city, as a limited pattern, obeys its own laws.

For Weber, the problem was to specify what is necessary if this type of group is to contain within itself a substantial amount of the "causes" of its own future activities. There is not much point, in other words, in studying anything if it does not make up a reasonably "closed system" of interrelated elements.

Simplifying greatly from Weber's monumental scholarship, we can identify three basic characteristics that a territorial group needs if it is to be viewed as a social phenomenon worthy of investigation in its own right.

Membership

If a group is to exist, its members must be able to distinguish themselves from nonmembers. Membership in a group gives a person certain rights and obligations in relation to other members, so it is important that there be a way to identify the members of a community as well as of any other type of group. Since the community is first of all a territorial group, the basic criterion of membership must concern one's physical location or where one lives (that is, the location in which one spends most of one's time and keeps most of one's personal possessions).

When one cluster of homes is separated from others by stretches of sparsely inhabited countryside, the question of membership is hardly ever raised: Whoever lives *here* is a member of *this* group, and all others are *not.* But when communities increase in size, thereby filling the empty space between them, the matter of boundaries becomes more important. And when a community's members must be taxed and governed by its particular laws, there is further need to be able to determine just who is subject to these taxes and laws. The drawing of *political boundaries* is the solution, even though this is not always a good indication of the boundaries between other types of groups. In the end "legal residence" becomes the basic criterion of **citizenship**, which signifies *the individual's membership in a particular territorial group.*

Autonomy

Weber pointed out that when the inhabitants of a particular place owe greater allegiance to other groups (caste, kinship, religious, etc.) than to the territorial group, they do not form a genuine community. If the inhabitants' obligations to these other groups come before their obligations to the community, they resemble the passengers on a bus rather than the members of a human group: Although they are physically close, their interests and activities are determined largely by others who are outside the bus rather than by one another.

If the territorial group does not have a substantial measure of autonomy or a meaningful amount of control over its members' actions, it cannot be treated as "a distinct and limited pattern of human life," even though autonomy does not mean complete independence from all other groups. The modern **nation-state** is *the most completely autonomous territorial group there is,* but even nations find it advantageous to give up some of their autonomy in return for the benefits derived from military alliances, membership in the United Nations, and participation in international economic agreements.

Although the inhabitants of smaller territorial groups within the nation-state must be governed by the laws of that nation, they also have freedom to determine certain things for themselves. All American citizens must file a federal income tax return, for example, but individual states can determine whether or not they also wish to tax their residents' incomes. Individual states can establish the minimum age at which their residents can drive a car, drink beer, and get married. And smaller localities are free to establish their own traffic laws, so long as they are not in conflict with state and national laws.

The point is that even the lowliest community must have some independent control of its members. Otherwise, it begins to lose its identity to whatever larger group does have this control.

Self-Sufficiency

Autonomy, of course, is meaningless unless people have continuing reason to remain members of a specific territorial group. Collectively, its members must be able to obtain the basic necessities of life and to maintain the group's population through reproduction and attracting new residents. As in terms of autonomy, nation-states tend to rank highest of all territorial groups in self-sufficiency, even though few of them have such a complete range of natural resources that they can get along without developing regular economic relationships with other nations.

Within nations, separate territorial subdivisions may be much more interdependent (as an industrial city and an agricultural area are dependent on each other's products). But as long as the members of a particular community can support themselves by producing something that can be exchanged for what they need from other communities, that group can be considered self-sufficient.

The Trend Toward Urbanization

In addition to growing at an increasing rate, particularly since the eighteenth century, the world's population has been increasingly concentrated in cities. It has been estimated that whereas only seven percent of the world's people lived in communities of 5000 or more inhabitants in 1800, more than thirty percent of its vastly larger population did so in 1950; moreover, although less than ten percent of the United States population lived in communities of more than 2500 in 1800, more than seventy percent of them lived in "urban places" by 1960 (Hauser and Schnore, 1965). "Urbanism," or the character of life in cities, is therefore clearly of fundamental importance in modern societies. It forms the background for the large majority of social relationships that we observe today, and thus sociologists have devoted more and more attention to the social phenomena associated with *urban* groups.

Summing Up

Nations are the territorial groups that most fully meet the criteria of distinctive citizenship, autonomy, and self-sufficiency. To a lesser extent, communities within nations also have standards of membership, some control over their members, and the means to sustain their populations. Villages, towns, cities, counties, states, provinces, departments, and so on, have varying amounts of autonomy and self-sufficiency, but they invite sociological investigation simply because they continue to exist as separate human groups. As the world's population has become increasingly concentrated in areas of relatively high population density, attention has turned largely to studies of urban phenomena.

APPROACHES TO THE STUDY OF COMMUNITIES

Background

The communities sociologists have studied range in size from the countryside and its small rural villages to gigantic urban metropolises. Sociologists have used several different perspectives to examine these communities—as areas of the earth's surface that have been subdivided for various uses, as networks of social communication and interaction, and as combinations of various natural and social conditions that greatly affect the psychology of their inhabitants.

Perhaps the earliest focus of attention was the **rural-urban continuum,** *or the differences between rural and urban life.* The rural community is characterized by social relationships that resemble those existing in small, face-to-face groups, with the same individuals interacting in many different contexts and personalities often being more important than formal or "legal" relationships. The rural community also has a relatively high level of informal social control that ensures a high degree of conformity to group norms. The urban community, on the other hand, embodies the opposite characteristics: impersonal, formal, segmented relationships; little collective scrutiny of the individual's behavior; and a high degree of heterogeneity.

These differences have been summed up by various scholars in several different pairs of key words: sacred/secular, status/contract, folk/urban, *gemeinschaft/gesellschaft,* and even primitive/modern. More recently these

Paul Sample's painting *Janitor's Holiday* (1936) presents the small groups and informal, slow-paced atmosphere associated with the rural community. (The Metropolitan Museum of Art, Arthur H. Hearn Fund, 1937)

pairs of opposites, each covering roughly the same range of differences, have been used primarily in comparing whole societies rather than smaller social units and have also provided a framework within which the processes of societal evolution can be analyzed. This latter topic is taken up in more detail in Chapter 18.

The formal distinction between "rural sociology" and all other branches of the discipline, seen most clearly in some state universities where there are separate departments of rural sociology and of sociology, is apparently more an accident of history than a calculated division of labor. The former got its start in the land-grant colleges during the early years of this century, and the study of social life in rural areas provided a convenient justification for establishing sociology in agricultural schools. Naturally, they were called departments of *rural* sociology, and today there is a Rural Sociology Society that meets jointly with the American Sociological Association each year. Beyond these organizational differences, however, and the rural sociologists' central interest in rural social phenomena, there is no reason to distinguish between the two types of sociologist.

Human Ecology

Urban sociology, the logical counterpart of rural sociology, came into being as a major speciality at the University of Chicago in the early 1920s (Faris, 1967; Short, 1971). The city was there for the sociologists to study, and they took full advantage of their opportunities. The "Chicago School" was closely associated with the first systematic approach to the study of the city (which came to be called **human ecology**—*the study of the various ways in which human groups influence and are influenced by the physical settings in which they reside*) and paid major attention to the various uses of land within the city and their interrelationships. The ecology of larger areas—of regions and of nations and even of the planet as a whole—has come to be the province of the geographers rather than of the sociologists, but for the latter the term "ecology" still refers primarily to the study of land use within the city and how this is related to the city's inhabitants.

The central assumption underlying this perspective on the urban community is that the relatively high population density leads to competition for land. The more people who want to use a particular parcel of land for their own purposes, the higher its price or rent will be. In some cases an area is a highly prestigious one in which to live, so people will pay more for it as a residential location. In other cases the activities located in a particular area (especially businesses like a department store or theater) will be especially profitable because they are convenient to a large number of potential customers. The more a specific location promises prestige or profit to its owner or renter, the more it will cost. And as there is less competition for land in other parts of the community, those parcels of land will be used for less prestigious or profitable activities.

Most ecological theories identify three major types of urban land use: business areas, manufacturing areas, and residential areas; other uses such as education, religion, and recreation make up a miscellaneous category that is less important. Each of the major types is further subdivided into categories such as central and outlying business areas, light and heavy manufacturing areas, and residential areas identified in terms of social class—slum, working class, middle class, upper class, suburban, and commuter residential areas.

Working with these concepts, ecologically oriented urban sociologists have suggested several models to try to account for the patterns of land use that are found in cities (Harris and Ullman, 1945). The earliest of these was the **concentric-zone theory,** which assumed that *the single most important determinant of land use is its distance from the center of the city.* The center, after all, is devoted primarily to business activity because it is the most accessible from all other parts of the city, and business is the most profitable form of land use.

In the absence of distorting factors such as hills and rivers, there should thus be a pattern in the way land is used at greater distances from the center. For instance, since manufacturing activities are often associated with businesses and were often a basic reason for the city's original founding, areas of light and heavy industry should be located fairly close to the central business district. Outside of this, successive zones should logically be devoted principally to residential areas, with higher social classes typically located farther from the center. Since religious, educational, and recreational activities do not require enough space to form entire zones, they tend to be scattered, and their locations are less influenced by their distance from the center.

The basic principle determining changes in land use was initially assumed to be the city's growth and the ways that land owners acted in anticipation of this growth. Since a larger city requires a larger business area, the owners of residential structures just outside the center tended, for economic reasons, to allow their property to fall into disrepair because they expected to sell the land for new business use in the near future. This zone, then, should be a ring of slums—decaying residences with low rents that are inhabited largely by the poorest members of the community. As growth does occur, such blight can be expected to spread outward.

For some cities, e.g., Chicago, this model seemed not only logical but also fairly useful in describing the actual patterns of land use that were found. But when the model failed to describe other cities accurately, a different model was advanced. This was called **sector theory,** and its central assumption was that *a given type of land use will be repeated farther out in the same direction from the center of the city as the city grows.* Thus, for example, if the area to the southwest of the central business district consisted mostly of middle-class homes, the middle-class residential area would expand toward the southwest as the city's population increased.

Such a pattern could be accounted for partly by tradition, but probably more important would be the layout of major transportation routes, which tend to radiate out from the center of the city. The location of highways, commuter and freight railroads, and rivers should thus be at least as important as sheer distance from the center in determining land-use patterns within the city. Certainly the ways in which industries develop along railroad lines, certain types of businesses spread along major streets, and new residential developments appear beside superhighways at greater and greater distances from the central business district give some support to the sector model.

Today, however, a number of cities are the result of a growing together of several smaller communities that began with several centers rather than with only one. The **multiple-nuclei theory,** developed as an attempt to understand the consequences of this form of growth, stresses the fact that *once a*

*given parcel of land has been devoted to a particular type of use, this use—
and thus the associated uses of adjacent land—tends to continue over time.* If a
present-day metropolitan area (whether or not it is a single political unit) incorporates what were originally three smaller communities, it is more likely
that there will be three separate business centers than one central district. Patterns of residential differentiation by social class will not be those predicted by
either concentric-zone or sector theory, and reasons for the location of manufacturing areas and of transportation routes will appear quite mysterious unless the area's history is taken into account.

Land use, however, is less and less determined by the play of free economic and social-class interests. Zoning laws, the tax structure, and laws prohibiting residential segregation mean more and more that the growth and land-
use patterns of cities are being planned. As increasing attempts were made to
bring patterns of land use under conscious control, the ecological perspective
became more an applied aspect of sociology, and it has been relatively neglected by academic sociologists for the past thirty years or so. Today, however, as the fields of sociology and city planning find that they have more to
contribute to each other, it is likely that more sociological research in human
ecology will be carried out in the future.

Finally, at the "microsocial" level, there has been increasing interest recently in how *constructed* physical space influences social relationships. Such
things as the placement of walls, the width of sidewalks, the arrangement of
park benches, and the interior layout of business and apartment buildings
obviously have some impact on the development of small social structures because they influence the ease and frequency with which people can interact.
Such problems have been investigated by environmental psychologists as well
as a few sociologists (Michelson, 1970). Although no generalized theory of the
relationships between the small-scale physical environment and patterns of
social interaction has yet come to the fore, the topic merits our attention.

To begin with, people certainly cannot interact if they cannot see and
communicate with one another, and they will probably not develop patterns
of interaction if they are in one another's company only briefly. The usual
location of an individual—in a neighborhood, within an office building, or
even in a single room—may have a good deal of influence on the extent and
nature of his or her contacts with others. For example, people who live at the
intersection of two residential streets will see and perhaps get to know more of
their neighbors than will those located at the end of a dead-end street. People
working in an office that is next to the coffee dispenser will probably get to
know more of their co-workers than will people in other offices. And if someone's seat or desk in a room is out of eyesight of several others, she or he will
probably be less "in" the group than most other members.

To the extent that architects and other designers have social purposes as
well as economic and/or aesthetic criteria in mind when planning construction, they should have an interest in how specific features of constructed space

work with other variables (the number and variety of people who will use the space, the amount of time they will spend there, their purposes in being there, etc.) to influence the social patterns that will develop within that space. Additional factors, such as color, lighting, and the availability of nooks that are out of the mainstream of traffic and yet are not hidden, will also influence the kinds of relationships that develop. The general topic is only now coming in for systematic investigation, but findings in this area promise to be of considerable interest to citizens as well as to social scientists.

Social Organization

A rather different approach to the study of territorial groups, not so clearly focused as the ecological approach, has been to view the community as an arena in which many forms of social organization help to structure the activities of its inhabitants as they seek to satisfy many different needs. This approach focuses primarily on the many types of **voluntary associations**—*formal organizations* (see Chapter 9) *whose members join them out of personal interest rather than because the state requires it or because they provide the members' chief source of income.* These organizations range from neighborhood bridge clubs and gardening societies, through service and fraternal groups, to unions, large charitable organizations like the United Fund, and local political parties. This approach also pays attention to city governments and political processes, even though these are studied more often by political scientists.

These groups provide much of the "social cement" that makes a territorial collection of individuals into a genuine community. They have been described as standing midway between the individual and the power of the state, giving people a sense of participation in and a means of influencing the life of their community. They also make the individual's life more meaningful; membership in a bowling league, a business club, the PTA, or a church congregation gives the individual ties to other people that do not depend strictly on kinship, cash, or closeness (such as living next door or taking the same bus to work every morning). These organizations fill out the bare bones of the community—employment, residence, family, and necessary activities such as purchasing food and paying taxes—with relationships which, lacking any elements of coercion, are based on mutual interests.

A voluntary association can, of course, become as impersonal and bureaucratized as a corporation or a state agency. But if it does, it runs the risk of losing members because it no longer provides them with the personal ties that people need and enjoy. A person's commitment to the goals of a voluntary association must be very strong indeed if he or she is to continue as an active member after the amount of satisfaction from the social relationships found through participation in it begins to decline.

Research has shown that the higher one's social class, the more likely one is to be involved in voluntary associations and the more interested one tends to be in the affairs of the larger community (Hausknecht, 1962). Sociologists have found, too, that a much larger proportion of the social activities of working-class people involves family relationships (Berger, 1960). This should come as no surprise, for we know also that the children of middle- and upper-class families are more likely to move away from the communities in which they grew up. They move to the places where their better education and their specialized occupational interests can be best utilized, whereas those with less education have fewer reasons to move away from the community where their parents and relatives live.

We might even suppose that this is a kind of self-sustaining cycle. Being on the average farther away from other relatives, yet also wanting to be involved in a broad range of social relationships, middle- and upper-class individuals tend to seek voluntary associations in order to satisfy these needs, whereas the lower classes can more easily satisfy such needs through extended family relationships. Involvement in voluntary, nonfamily relationships would give the participants a greater concern for the community as a whole rather than simply for their kin, and so we would expect them to be more involved in community affairs—thus reinforcing their characteristics as members of higher social classes.

The formal structures of community governments have been largely an interest of political scientists, whereas sociologists have paid more attention to the characteristics and activities of the people within the community who seem to have the most influence on community affairs, regardless of whether they hold formal office. The findings of these studies are not always in agreement, but in general they suggest that few, if any, American communities are governed by monolithic, upper-class groups that seek principally to preserve the status quo for their own benefit. Rather, different issues attract different leaders (or "influentials") who are often middle class in origin and who often represent quite different interests. The evidence is unclear as to the relative roles played by talent, wealth, occupation, and family background in helping an individual gain access to the informal circles where so much real power and influence lie. And, no doubt, the picture is becoming even more confused as it becomes obvious that highly effective leaders can emerge from the ghettos of our larger cities. (See Chapter 12, on the political institution, for more on municipal power structures.)

The Social Psychology of the City

A third way of analyzing communities has been to look at the social-psychological consequences, for individuals and their relationships, of living in areas of varying population density. This approach attempts to investigate the effects on norms, values, and attitudes of living under different degrees of crowding. Here again, the city and the countryside serve as opposites.

Density itself can be important in several ways, affecting as it does the amount of waste on the ground and in the air, the contagion of diseases, and the economics of land use, but it is important sociologically as it influences the norms and organization of the group. At the psychological level it can be seen that our outlook on the world is strongly influenced simply by the number of strangers with whom we come into contact every day. The most important consequence of high population density for groups, however, is that it increases the pressures to specialize—economically, in the first instance, but also in terms of voluntary associations.

Just as competition for land within the city encourages the specialized use of land, so competition among people for living space and for success encourages specialization in their occupations. The best way to avoid ruinous competition with others, after all, is to find something that others need—a service or a product—and to provide it better or more cheaply than others can. As long as there are enough people in the vicinity to make up a reasonable market for this product or service, one has found a satisfactory niche in the community's economic structure.

Someone once suggested that a community is not really a *city* unless one can buy a good Chinese dinner there at three o'clock on a Tuesday morning.

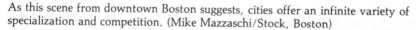

As this scene from downtown Boston suggests, cities offer an infinite variety of specialization and competition. (Mike Mazzaschi/Stock, Boston)

This is an exaggeration, to be sure, but it makes the point: A city is a place that has so many people within a limited area that some of them are bound to want Chinese food at every hour of the day, thus making it worthwhile for someone to provide it. The more people there are close at hand, the more it is necessary to specialize—and the easier it is to do this.

By its very nature, then, the city is a scene of great variety, whereas rural areas tend to be much less differentiated. By the same token, it is easier to be different in the city because most people will ignore you; in areas of lower population density, by contrast, each individual tends to be more tightly bound into a web of personal relationships and must pay more attention to others' opinions. (This statement, however, cannot be a hard-and-fast generalization. Within one's own neighborhood or profession in the city, the pressures for conformity can be quite strong, and in a rural area, once someone's differences are known and accepted—within limits—he or she is free to act as the village idiot or village intellectual without further difficulty.)

At the root of the difference between urban and rural areas seems to be the frequency with which one sees—and ignores—strangers every day. In the city a stranger may be a threat or merely a moving object that one must avoid bumping into on the sidewalk, but no one thinks it unnatural to see so many strangers during the course of a day. In a rural area a stranger tends to attract attention, and whether this is in the form of open hostility, cordial hospitality, or studied ignorance, he or she cannot expect the social invisibility that strangers have in the city.

These differences give greatly different qualities to rural and to urban life. In a small town or a farming area, one may feel terribly tied down by being continually the object of the neighbors' attention, whereas in a large city people's casual indifference to strangers means that one can feel terribly lonely. The city gives a person the chance to lead life as he or she chooses, and although this may be exhilarating for some, it can be painful or even frightening to others.

THE FUTURE OF COMMUNITIES

The future of communities is essentially the future of cities, for the concentration of people in areas of relatively high population density is increasing. In part, this urban concentration is due to the greater efficiency of modern agriculture, which now makes it possible for less than five percent of America's working population to provide food for the entire society (*U.S. Fact Handbook*, 1976, Table 589). At the same time, as noted above, higher population densities encourage (and also require) increased occupational specialization, thus providing increased opportunities for participation in the economic institution. Not only are rural areas less attractive in terms of employment, then, but cities become more attractive.

In addition to the economic factors which foster urbanization, there are also the noneconomic attractions of city life: more specialized services, more forms of entertainment, more personal freedom, and more variety and excitement. Despite the admitted (although sometimes exaggerated) drawbacks of urban life—higher crime rates, crowding, pollution, and impersonality—on balance it seems that cities will continue to be the home of an increasing percentage of the American population.

But with modern methods of transportation and communication, it is no longer necessary to live in the immediate vicinity of the city's opportunities in order to take advantage of them. A major trend in this country since the 1950s, in fact, has been a slow movement of the population from central cities to the suburbs, or smaller communities adjacent to major cities. The suburbs offer, at least to many, an attractive compromise between the isolation of rural life and the very high population density of the central city. Today, more than one-third of the American population can be defined as "suburbanites."

Not all of them commute to work in the city, by any means. As more people move into a suburb, more opportunities for employment open up there, and a higher proportion of the residents are employed locally. The central city continues to be attractive as a center of specialized services and entertainment, but its very high population becomes more and more a weekday characteristic rather than an unchanging condition.

Thus we may reason that there will develop a more even distribution of people throughout metropolitan regions (that is, areas that include both one or more central cities and their adjacent suburbs). One factor opposing this trend, however, may be more serious crises in the supply of energy. Basically, geographical mobility within metropolitan areas depends on energy, whether it is in the form of gasoline or electricity. As such forms become scarcer, their cost will rise, and people will try to economize on travel. The result, at least in the immediate future, may be a need to live closer to the opportunities that an area of high population density offers and so an increase in the population density of certain areas. This possibility can be offset, of course, if mass-transit systems improve and people are willing to rely on them rather than on individual transportation by private automobile.

Beyond the tendency for people to cluster together in areas of relatively high population density, we can predict also that the differences between the lifestyles of rural and urban populations will diminish. This will be due mainly to the influence of the mass media—particularly television—as they promote a greater degree of cultural homogeneity throughout American society. Originating primarily in urban areas, the contents of network television programs and of newspapers will supply our entire population with a common perspective on the world and an increasingly common set of values. Even though many American values originated during the eighteenth and nineteenth centuries, when our society was largely rural in character, the mass media are increasingly reflecting issues and concerns that are very much the products of urban life. (The role of the mass media in the development of public opinion is discussed in Chapter 17.)

Eventually, we may suppose that one's place of residence by itself will have less and less influence on one's values and lifestyle. The high rate of geographical mobility among communities we already have, together with the pervasive influence of the national mass media, will minimize the differences among people that would otherwise develop naturally from their experiences in living in areas of differing population density.

SUMMARY

Living in continuous proximity to others forces people to form groups, simply because they must avoid conflict in using the land that they occupy together. Although territorial groups, or communities, are important to their members as "home," they are particularly vulnerable to disruption. Members move, local resources are exhausted, natural disasters occur, and purposeful change in "the landscape" (damming rivers, building new highways, tearing down slum areas)—all can change or even eliminate social relationships in a given location.

To qualify as properly sociological groups, communities must have ways to identify their members, a substantial degree of autonomy (control over their own members), and must be self-sufficient. Without boundaries, members who are influenced primarily by the behavior of other members, and the prospect of continued existence, a territorial aggregate is not a group and is thus not worthy of investigation as a community.

Because the world's population is becoming increasingly urbanized and because this trend is much more pronounced in the United States, the study of communities is largely the study of cities. And since the conditions of urban life form the backdrop for most of our other social relationships, a number of approaches to this topic have been developed.

The human-ecology approach focuses on patterns of land use within the city, seeking the basic principles that seem to determine how different parts of the city's area will be used. The *concentric-zone theory* assumes that distance from the center of the city is the major determinant; the *sector theory* assumes that use is determined partly by tradition, but more by the layout of transportation routes and other physical features; and the *multiple-nuclei theory* seeks to explain urban land use on the basis of the prior existence of several smaller communities which have grown together. At the "micro" level, research is developing now on the relationships between the organization of "constructed" space and the patterns of interaction that develop within that space.

The high proportion of strangers in the city leads to the development of new forms of relationships—primarily voluntary associations—through which people can interact for reasons other than cash, kinship, or closeness. These groups bring people together to achieve common purposes outside the political structure and thus give structure to the "social space" that lies between the individual and the total group as a political entity. The city's political organization is important also to sociologists, even though it is more central to the interests of political scientists; studies of city leadership suggest that monolithic power structures are less common in American cities than is a pattern of varying alliances and contests among different interest groups.

Finally, the city's relatively high population density means that most of its inhabitants are strangers to one another. This leads to a tendency to ignore and to be ignored or else to limit relationships to formal, impersonal forms of interaction. This allows both greater heterogeneity in the community's members and a greater sense of personal freedom—although at the potential cost of considerable loneliness.

While the trend toward the concentration of population in urban areas continues, it is difficult to predict with certainty whether population densities will increase in central cities or will become more even throughout metropolitan areas that include both cities and their suburbs. The amount of energy available for transportation and the ways people use it seem now to be the prime influence on the degree of population density in our cities.

But differences in the values and lifestyles of rural and urban areas will continue to diminish as high rates of geographical mobility and the increasing influence of the mass media promote a more homogeneous culture. *Where* one lives, then, will be of less importance in the future in determining one's values and lifestyle.

SUGGESTED READINGS

Dahl, Robert A., *Who Governs? Democracy and Power in an American City* (New Haven, Conn.: Yale University Press, 1961). A political scientist's intensive study of the dynamics of municipal politics in New Haven in the late 1950s.

Hauser, Philip M., and Leo F. Schnore, eds., *The Study of Urbanization* (New York: Wiley, 1965). This volume contains a number of articles about urbanization as it has been viewed by the various social sciences. Although written at the professional level, it provides a good overview of both historical and present-day processes of urbanization, summarizing what is known of them.

Hunter, Floyd, *Community Power Structure* [1953] (New York: Doubleday/Anchor, 1963). In this investigation of the relations among forty top leaders in "Regional City" (Atlanta) in 1950–1951, Hunter demonstrates the complexity of urban political processes and the importance of interest groups.

Michelson, William, *Man and His Urban Environment* (Reading, Mass.: Addison-Wesley, 1970). One of the first books in sociology to concentrate on the relations between physical space and social organization, this one is a carefully written, stimulating guide to problems that have not yet been answered in this area.

Redfield, Robert, *The Primitive World and Its Transformations* (Ithaca, N.Y.: Cornell University Press, 1953). Almost a classic by now, this is an anthropologist's discussion of the nature of "folk society," which in many ways is the precise opposite of the urban society with which most of us are familiar.

Short, James F., ed., *The Social Fabric of the Metropolis: Contributions of the "Chicago School of Urban Sociology"* (Chicago: University of Chicago Press, 1971). This provides a comprehensive, valuable overview of the development of urban sociology and its leaders since the 1920s at the most important center of urban sociology in America.

Vidich, Arthur J., and Joseph Bensman, *Small Town in Mass Society* (New York: Doubleday/Anchor, 1960). A fascinating account of the ways, both effective and ineffective, in which the residents of a small, upstate New York community organize their lives and their perceptions of the "outside world" which increasingly controls them.

Warren, Roland L., ed., *Perspectives on the American Community* (Chicago: Rand-McNally, 1966). An eminent urban sociologist presents a collection of historical and current articles on the study of small and large territorial groups that give a well-rounded picture of the current state of urban studies.

Weber, Max, *The City* [1921], trans. and ed. by Don Martindale and Gertrud Neuwirth (New York: Free Press, 1968). Martindale's lengthy foreword helps to show the importance of Weber's work and provides a useful context for his historical analysis of the city as a human group in terms of both its central characteristics and the major types of cities to be found throughout history.

Glossary

Citizenship The social status that signifies membership in a territorial group, usually based on the fact that one's residence is located within the geographical boundaries of that group. Citizenship entails specific political rights and obligations in relation to that group and is thus a basic status in the political institution (see Chapter 12).

Community The term is used here to refer to any territorial group, regardless of size. Its most important feature is its members' common occupancy of a specific location in space, and it acquires the characteristics of a group because those who live in this space must work out patterns of interaction and agreements about allocating the use of this space. Communities may range in *population density* (see below) from very low (a rural hamlet) to very high (the center of a large city), and this fact has fundamental importance for the kinds of social relationships that develop within different communities.

Concentric-zone theory An explanation of land-use patterns in the city that assumes that the most important determinant of land use is its distance from the center of the city.

Human ecology The study of the relationships among human groups and the physical space they occupy. In addition to patterns of land use, human ecologists are also interested in the movements of populations within the community and in the broader reciprocal influences between human beings and the land they occupy.

Multiple-nuclei theory An explanation of land-use patterns that looks to the history of an area and views the initial uses of land (for example, the establishment of separate business districts in small towns that later grow together) as having a major influence on how patterns of land use develop later on.

Nation-state The political equivalent of a society. It is frequently almost identical with a society (for example, Mexican society and the sovereign state of Mexico), but is identified especially by its freedom from legal control by other groups and thus its equality with other nations in terms of autonomy. A nation-state is the most completely autonomous and self-sufficient of human groups, even though it must usually trade with other such groups in order to satisfy all of its members' needs.

Population density The number of people who occupy a given amount of space for at least a meaningful amount of time. It is usually expressed in terms of the number of people per square mile. The number of people who reside in a given area is the most common basis of this measurement, but it is also possible to compare a city's population density during working hours with its density during evenings or weekends. The concept is taken here as a fundamental determinant of the social relationships characteristic of communities.

Rural-urban continuum The dimension along which communities vary in their central social characteristics. The rural (low population density) end of the continuum is marked by the kinds of relationships one finds in groups whose members have known one another personally over an extended period of time, whereas the urban end (high population density) is characterized by impersonal, segmental social relationships among people who for the most part know relatively little about one another. Several pairs of contrasting terms have been devised to sum up these differences; they are noted briefly on p. 193.

Sector theory An explanation of land-use patterns based on the assumption that as a city grows, a given type of land will be extended outward from its center in the same direction. This theory also emphasizes the roles of both natural and constructed aspects of the landscape (rivers, valleys and hills, highways and railroads, etc.) in determining land use.

Voluntary association A type of formal organization (see Chapter 9) whose members join it for reasons of personal interest rather than because the state requires it or because it provides their chief source of livelihood. Within the community, it provides the individual with personal ties that extend beyond family, employment, and neighborhood. Although larger voluntary associations have salaried officers and staff, most members spend relatively little time occupying organizational statuses and often pay for the privilege of being members. (In some cases it may be difficult to avoid joining such an organization, as in the case of a closed-shop union, but the principle remains that no one is forced to join it.)

9
Formal Organizations

PLANNED SOCIAL RELATIONSHIPS

Whenever a job requires the cooperation of two or more people, they are likely to work out some division of labor. For something like moving a sofa, this may be no more than "You pick up that end and I'll take this one," and the coordination of responsibilities ends as soon as the sofa has been moved.

But if the job requires the continued coordination of effort, as when carpenters are building a house or an insurance company is handling a steady flow of paperwork, spontaneous verbal agreements about the division of labor will not do. The more complicated the job and the more people involved in it, the more it is necessary that someone *plan* the coordination of different activities, and the more important it is that these people follow the plans.

The outcome of this planning is the creation of consciously designed social statuses and consciously designed norms to guide their occupants' activities. To be effective, the descriptions of these statuses and the rules governing their occupants must be recorded and available to those involved, so that misunderstandings about responsibilities and relationships can be kept to a minimum. Further, there must be some means of ensuring that people will comply with these plans, which will be useless if they are not followed.

Collectively, the plans (or rules, since they are supposed to be followed) are known as constitutions, articles of incorporation, bylaws, company rules and regulations, manuals of procedures, and so on. They are the blueprints for human groups that are known as *formal organizations.* The rules may contain gaps and inconsistencies, they may be vague and in constant need of interpretation, and they may unintentionally create conflicts among the organization's members. They have, after all, been drawn up by human beings with imperfect knowledge of their consequences. Yet they are necessary, and the practical, or applied, aspect of studying organizations concentrates on how to improve them. This is the field of management science.

In the more purely sociological view, formal organizations are particularly interesting because they serve as natural "social experiments," in which certain hypotheses—the planned structure of the organization—are tested against the realities of social relationships. To the extent that an organization's planned structure is in error about these realities, the organization will be relatively unsuccessful in achieving its goals. Its members may quit, they may oppose one another in competing for certain objectives, or their actions may simply be uncoordinated. In any case, the organization will be less successful than it might have been, even though determining what complete success might be is the most difficult task of all.

More generally, sociologists have the task of describing different organizational structures, finding those characteristics of each that seem to occur together, and explaining why this happens. To the sociologist, then, a formal organization is not simply something to be improved; it is another type of human group to be studied for what it can tell us about social relationships in general.

THE NATURE OF FORMAL ORGANIZATIONS

There is a simple fact one should keep in mind in trying to do a job that requires the cooperation of others. One can organize many people for a few days or a few people for many days *without* having to rely on a set of written rules. But if one's purpose is to organize a large number of people for a long time in order to achieve a complex goal—to build automobiles, care for sick people, provide a college education, govern a city, or fight a war—it is absolutely vital that there be a set of rules to help them coordinate their various activities.

This unavoidable fact of social life accounts for the existence of **formal organizations,** *or groups that are formed in order to accomplish specific purposes.* Formal organizations are thus *purposeful groups* and are to be distinguished from *social categories* (to which people belong because they have been assigned to them by others) and from *territorial groups* (to which people belong simply by virtue of where they live). These latter types may have purposes, of course, but they have not come into being because of those purposes.

The word *organization* here refers to a set of consciously designed, interrelated statuses. The word *formal* means that this set of statuses has a definite form and thus does not change randomly or unpredictably. Its form is maintained by the existence of a set of consciously designed, explicit rules that guide the relationships among these statuses so that their occupants can work collectively toward the achievement of one or more goals.

A formal organization, in other words, is something like an incomplete, artificial society within the larger society. It has its own culture (the rules) and

its own social structure (the interrelated statuses described by the rules), but because it has only a limited range of goals, it is incomplete (that is, it does not serve all of its members' needs), and because it has been consciously created, we can say that it is "artificial."

The word *bureaucracy* is often used interchangeably with *formal organization*. Strictly speaking, however, a **bureaucracy** is only *the administrative part of a formal organization* rather than the entire group *and consists of the organizational positions responsible for policy making and for the administration and coordination of the activities of the other members.* (Max Weber pioneered in the study of bureaucracies as well as in the areas of political sociology, religion, and the city; his analysis of bureaucracies as symptomatic of the "rationalization" of modern society is treated in the following section.)

As a category, formal organizations include a vast number of different types of groups. Probably the type that comes to mind most readily is the business corporation, characterized by large office buildings, factories, and retail outlets. But a prison is also a formal organization, as are churches, universities, armies, and charitable groups. A government is a formal organization, as is a professional football league, a scientific society, and a Girl Scout troop.

Whenever the social statuses that make up a group have been planned and are described in writing, that group is a formal organization. This is true regardless of how many hours per week these statuses are actually occupied. Toward the "infrequent occupancy" end of this scale are voluntary associations, such as the Red Cross and a hobby group that meets only once a month; at the other end of the scale are groups that have been called "total institutions" because at least some of their members occupy organizational statuses twenty-four hours a day: a ship at sea, an army camp, a mental hospital, and a prison. The central characteristic of a formal organization, though, is that its statuses have been consciously planned.

ORGANIZATIONAL GOALS AND INDIVIDUAL GOALS

Making bobby pins, canning spinach, caring for delinquent children, and keeping records of a hospital's patients are not activities in which many people would voluntarily engage on a full-time basis. The performance of such tasks,

◄ The Radcliffe College lightweight crew, shown working out on the Charles River, constitutes a formal organization—a group that exists in order to accomplish a specific purpose. (*Boston Globe* Photo)

which are necessary if an organization is to achieve its goals, is rarely a central personal interest. Yet some occupational statuses require their occupants to spend seven or eight hours a day performing these tasks, and there are obviously people who occupy these statuses. The question of *why* people will do these things is taken up later in this chapter; for now, the point to be made is simply that organizational goals and individual goals are usually separate.

This fact raises serious problems for those who want an organization to succeed in achieving its goals. The nature of an organization's goals largely determines the statuses that must be included in the organization and the ways in which they should be related to one another. A coal-mining company, for instance, must have workers (that is, members) who can dig coal, and a department store must have salesclerks, merchandise buyers, people to keep the shelves stocked, etc.

Although this is obvious, it is by no means certain that the planned structure of an organization will automatically enable its members to be efficient and effective in helping the organization to achieve its goals. Those who draw up organization charts, decide how many coal miners or salesclerks will be needed, and write out job specifications do not necessarily have all of the information, experience, or wisdom that will guarantee their designing a successful organization. An overall perspective on organizations is needed to highlight the most important problems to be solved and to provide a general philosophy of management. A number of organizational theories have been advanced since the turn of the century to meet this need, and even though none has turned out to be the perfect guide to planning successful organizations, it is important here to review the basic assumptions of three of them.

Scientific Management

Toward the end of the nineteenth century, an American engineer named Frederick W. Taylor became concerned that the workers in certain industries were not using their newly designed tools as effectively as they should. His solution was to watch how these people did their jobs and then to devise new sequences of movements that would be less tiring and at the same time avoid all wasted motions. An emphasis on "time-and-motion" studies was the result, and this led to a larger philosophy of organizational management.

To justify asking workers to adopt new patterns of activity at the workbench, Taylor had to assume that they would want to do this if they saw that it was in their interest to do so. Out of this came the necessary belief that workers are motivated solely by the desire to earn money. If they could be made to see that doing their jobs "scientifically" would lead to higher wages, this should result in perfect harmony throughout the organization, because greater efficiency would lead to higher profits and thus to higher wages.

"Scientific Management" (also the title of a book published by Taylor in 1911) thus *concentrated on making workers into more efficient robots by planning precisely every bit of their organizational activities.* No allowance was made for the fact that workers, even on the job, have personal needs that they seek to fulfill. Instead, workers were viewed as machines whose operations could be made more efficient through scientific principles.

The Human Relations School

Beginning with some of Taylor's ideas in the mid-1920s, a group of researchers that included Elton Mayo, Fritz J. Roethlisberger, and William J. Dickson, undertook to study Western Electric's Hawthorne Works employees. The researchers' initial interest was in the effects of varied lighting and rest breaks on the workers' productivity. Their surprise at finding results contrary to their expectations (productivity went *up* as the light became dimmer, and it went *up* when fewer rest breaks were allowed) led eventually to their recognition of the importance of social factors in influencing workers' performance. The workers enjoyed being the object of the researchers' attention, and it was apparently this increased sense of their own importance to the company that led to higher productivity.

The Hawthorne studies also contributed the idea that workers' productivity is limited more by informal standards set by the work group than by the limits of their physical stamina. The concept of **informal organization**—*patterns of relationships that develop among the members of an organization without being described by the formal rules*—grew from this idea; the topic is covered in more detail later in this chapter.

From all of these observations came what has been called the **Human Relations theory** of management, which *stresses the importance of fulfilling workers' social and psychological needs, counting on the fact that a happy worker is a productive worker.* The best organization was thus one that its members viewed as a family, and this could be accomplished through sympathetic counseling, developing a friendly atmosphere, and letting the members know that their work was important and appreciated. Once this was achieved, the workers should be fully satisfied and productivity should be high, for there would then be no conflict between the organization's goals and those of its members.

(Recent *reanalysis* of the data from the Hawthorne studies suggests that Mayo and his colleagues were incorrect in their interpretation of their findings. Franke and Kaul [1978, p. 636], have found that closer supervision of the workers, the amount of rest they were allowed, and their increased worry about keeping their jobs during economic hard times were the factors that actually accounted for most of the variations in productivity. Correct or not, though, the original conclusions did serve as the foundation of the Human Relations school, and its importance as a theory of organization cannot be denied.)

The Weberian Model

Although Weber's analysis of bureaucracies was first published in Germany in 1922, little of his work was available in English until the late 1940s, and so both the Scientific Management and the Human Relations schools developed almost entirely without reference to his writings. In taking a broader view of formal organizations, however, drawing on both historical and cross-cultural materials, Weber came much closer to building a genuinely sociological picture of their central characteristics (Weber, 1947).

One of the basic trends he saw in modern society was what he called **rationalization,** or *the increasingly objective consideration of the relationships between means and ends and an increasing willingness to adopt those practices that promised the most efficient achievement of the ends being sought.* If *that* is the goal and if *this* is the most effective way to achieve it, there can be no question that we should adopt *this* means to *that* end. This single-minded concern with "technical rationality" can be seen in not only science and technology, but also the design of social organizations, and Weber foresaw that it would increase in importance.

Rationalization meant the subordination of personal to organizational interests. Even though he saw the dangers in this, Weber was interested in identifying the characteristics of the "ideal" bureaucracy—those which most clearly enhanced its rationality. Out of his lengthy discussion of the essential nature of such a bureaucracy, we can draw seven principles, each of which aims in one way or another at ensuring maximum effectiveness of the organization's members and minimum distraction by personal interests:

1. All organizational activities must be governed by *explicit, technical, abstract rules.* These rules, in other words, must be available for reference, they must cover activities rather than attitudes, and they must apply to the occupants of statuses rather than to specific individuals.

2. Each organizational position must have a particular, *limited sphere of responsibility,* marked out by the rules, so that there can be no question about accountability or about the members' rights and obligations in relation to one another.

3. Occupancy of an organizational position must be by *appointment on the basis of competence* to undertake that position's responsibilities, rather than through election or personal connections (such as nepotism) that are unrelated to technical competence. Likewise, promotion and removal should

be based entirely on competence. If this is the only rational standard, then, no irrelevant aspects of the individual should be taken into account in determining his or her fitness for office, so that an organization is being irrational when it evaluates prospective members on the basis of such things as race or sex.

4. Organizational positions must be organized in a clear-cut *hierarchy of authority* so that no member is left uncontrolled. In other words, the organization must be able to coordinate the activities of all of its members, and this can be accomplished only through having every position (except the top one) clearly subordinate to another. And since the exercise of some authority is both the right and the responsibility of all but the very lowest organizational positions, its use must be governed (and thus limited) by the rules that pertain to each position.

5. Not only the organization's rules, but also *the actions of its members must be recorded,* filed, and kept accessible for review. This facilitates the determination of accountability, provides a basis for rational planning, and ensures that each act can be judged in terms of whether it was in accord with the rules governing the member who did it.

6. As a further means of separating organizational and personal interests, the bureaucrat should be paid a *regular salary*—a certain amount of money per month or year—so that his or her actions are less likely to be influenced by the possibility of extra personal gain, as would be the case if the member were paid by the number of decisions made or the content of those decisions. (This principle clearly separates the "bureaucrat" from the "worker," who is almost always paid on the basis of the number of hours worked or the amount of work produced.) Additionally, the bureaucrat should not personally own the materials he or she uses in the course of carrying out organizational duties, for this would not only blur the distinction between the member's private and organizational life, but also complicate the process of moving people into and out of organizational positions.

7. Finally, the relationships among members of the bureaucracy should be *impersonal,* thus emphasizing their organizational statuses and in effect denying their identities as specific individuals. Again, the purpose is to minimize the intrusion of personal interests into organizational affairs.

In addition to these central characteristics of the fully rational bureaucracy, Weber spoke also of the desirability that membership in it should be regarded as a career that should confer tenure (the guarantee of lifetime employment after one's competence has been demonstrated). Tenure, however, seems less necessary to the efficient conduct of an organization than the seven characteristics listed above; only in the areas of public employment (Civil Service, etc.) and higher education is the granting of tenure a standard practice, even though today some unions are seeking its equivalent for their members.

As a final ideal, Weber pointed to the idea of a bureaucratic career as a "calling," or a vocation in which the individual finds personal fulfillment. This, of course, would mean a complete fusion of individual and organizational goals and cannot be treated as a realistic possibility in most cases.

Weber's understanding of the distinction (and potential conflict) between organizational and individual goals remains central to the modern sociological study of organizations. In particular, it has emphasized the basic importance of the various relationships that can exist between organizations and their members. In turn, this emphasis focuses attention on the question of *how* personal needs and organizations' goals are coordinated. How is it, in other words, that people somehow come to devote substantial amounts of time to activities that are quite unrelated to (or even in conflict with) their own interests? This problem is taken up in more detail after our discussion of the open-system model.

The Open-System Model

A more recent development in the study of organizations has been the adoption of the **open-system model,** which *views each organization as a system of interdependent parts that interacts with its environment.* Thus an organization is a system that must be open to exchange with its surroundings, just as an animal must eat, breathe, excrete, etc. This is a considerably more complex model than the others, if only because it requires the analyst to pay attention to many more aspects of the organization (Katz and Kahn, 1978).

The open-system model looks, for instance, at not only how members are related to one another, but also such things as cycles of communication and response within the organization and how the organization's output (products, services, etc.) affects its environment and then changes its relations with the environment. The model has been criticized as too unwieldy for effective use and as assuming more rationality within the organization than actually exists, but it gives promise of more comprehensive understanding of organizations in the future.

TYPES OF ORGANIZATIONAL CONTROL

Since individual and organizational goals need not be the same, they can be related in any of three ways: similar, merely unrelated, or in opposition. A research scientist, for instance, usually enjoys doing research and is thus likely to be very much in favor of the goals of the research group by which she or he is employed. It would be unusual, however, for an employee of a vacuum cleaner factory to be either very positive or very negative about the production of such machines, so his or her attitude toward the organization's goal is likely to be quite neutral. Finally, a person serving time in a prison is ordinarily definitely opposed to this organization's goal, which is to keep him or her locked up away from society.

The problem of securing members' compliance with organizational rules is thus even more important than the problem of designing an organizational structure so that its members can cooperate effectively in helping to achieve the organization's goals. Its members must be willing, for some reason or other, to accept the rules governing their organizational statuses, and how this willingness can be secured depends first of all on their attitude toward the organization and its goals.

In his *Modern Organizations* (1964), Amitai Etzioni distinguishes three basic methods of securing compliance by an organization's members, each one appropriate to a particular attitude toward its goals. These methods are based, respectively, on *coercive, utilitarian,* and *normative* types of power.

Coercive Power

Let us look first of all at those organizations whose members *disagree* with their goals. We would not ordinarily expect people to participate in such organizations at all, for they are definitely opposed to the achievement of those goals. But such organizations exist, and it is clear that their members are there only because they have been forced to be—they are in prisons, mental hospitals, concentration camps, and sometimes in the armed forces. And since they are there unwillingly in the first place, only the threat of physical punishment or deprivation can be effective in securing their compliance with the organization's rules. Their dislike of the organization precludes their being sensitive to the use of symbolic or material rewards, or even to symbolic punishments. **Coercive power**—*the concept of "Obey the rules or suffer physical punishment"*—is the foundation of control in such organizations. The offer of privileges such as extra food or access to recreational facilities in return for compliance, although it may appear to be the use of "rewards," is actually the offer of *less deprivation* and is thus still legitimately viewed as coercive.

One may ask, of course, whether a prisoner is actually a *member* of the organization, for he or she is treated more like a piece of raw material that is to be stored or processed by the organization. In this sense, the prisoner *is* the purpose of the organization's existence rather than a member working to help achieve this purpose. But because the prisoner is a human being and can be told the rules that must be obeyed, it is difficult to think of him or her as equivalent to a steer on a cattle ranch or a piece of lumber in a furniture factory.

Students in schools and patients in hospitals present a similar problem of definition. They differ from prisoners, since they *want* to avail themselves of the organization's services, but as the objects of these organizations' activities, they differ from the other members (teachers, counselors, doctors, and

Members of organizations that rely on coercive power usually belong because they have no choice. (Steve Hansen/Stock, Boston)

nurses). Although they are clients rather than full-fledged members, they do occupy organizational positions and are governed by organizational rules, so it is difficult to say that they do not belong to the organizations at all. Instead, they are best defined as partial, or transitory, members, and their lesser interest in the organization's future explains their limited authority to influence organizational activities.

Utilitarian Power

In an organization whose members are neutral in their attitudes toward its goals, people will give it their time and compliance only if they receive something valuable in return. The member here has an essentially calculating attitude toward participation—"What's in it for me?"—and so material rewards are necessary.

Utilitarian power, or *securing compliance in return for a reward*—usually in the form of wages—is so common that we rarely think of it in this light. The essential "bargain" is that the individual agrees to occupy an organizational position for so many hours a day and to comply with the rules governing it in return for a specified amount of money each hour, week, month, or year. The member is neither opposed nor committed to this organizational activity, but is willing to do it because the organization makes it worthwhile to do so. In a complex economic system (see Chapter 11), it is certainly easier for someone to give eight hours a day to an organization in return for the money with which to satisfy his or her private needs than it would be to try personally to grow, weave, and manufacture all the things needed to satisfy those needs.

Interestingly, the more direct the connection between work and wages, the lower in the organization a person tends to be. To receive a salary, as noted in the discussion of Weber's model of bureaucracy, is to be more trusted by the organization, and it is logical that those higher up in an organization are more committed to its goals—or at least to doing a professional job for whatever organization is employing them. The most purely calculative relationship between individual and organization, then, exists at the bottom of the hierarchy, where the work is typically least pleasant and control depends almost entirely on the "wages-for-work" bargain.

Normative Power

Last, there are organizations whose members belong to them because they are personally interested in helping to achieve the organization's goals. They *want* to do what the organization *needs* them to do. A church, a charity, a college, and a political party are examples of this type.

To be sure, such organizations' full-time members are paid: The minister of a church, the director of a charitable foundation, campaign managers for political candidates, and college professors must be paid so that they can continue to do their work without having to earn money elsewhere. But it is here, more often than in any other type of organization, that one can hear someone remark, "Isn't it nice that I'm getting *paid* to do what I *like* to do!" Wages here, in other words, are viewed as making it possible for people to work rather than as the major reason for their being members in the first place.

Since money is not the major motivator and coercion is not possible, the organization must often rely on **normative power**—*the use of symbolic rewards and punishments, principally in the form of indications that the member's work is helping or hindering the organization in achieving its goals*—to secure compliance with its rules. Because the member is personally committed to these goals, the idea is that his or her activities can be controlled simply by citing the relevant norms: "If you want to help this charity, you've got to be here at nine o'clock, do *these* things, and report to *this* person; otherwise, we can't collect the money we need." People who are not responsive to such controls, of course, must eventually be removed from membership, and it is assumed that such a threat—to sever them from a group that is trying to achieve their personal goals—should usually be sufficient to ensure compliance.

Mixed Controls

It should be stressed that each of these is an "ideal type," or a simplified mental model, for in real life no organization depends entirely on just one type of control. Prison guards are controlled by utilitarian power, a business firm will use pep talks to inspire its sales staff to greater compliance with its rules, and lectures on patriotism during basic training in the armed forces try to build the trainees' commitment to the goals of these organizations. In blue-collar industries, a foreman may occasionally find it necessary to back his organizational authority with his fists in order to keep workers "in line."

The distinction among coercive, utilitarian, and normative bases of control cannot give us a fully accurate description of actual organizations. It does, however, sensitize us to central trends and helps to make sense of some of the major differences we find among organizations.

LEADERSHIP AND AUTHORITY IN ORGANIZATIONS

Although an organization's rules guide its members' expectations of one another, rules themselves do not *do* anything. A "No Smoking" sign has never swooped down from a wall to put out someone's cigarette. Without someone present to *expect* others to behave in accordance with the rules—and to react appropriately when they do not—an organization could not function. Further, compliance with many rules is not "scheduled" in terms of the clock or the day of the week, but is called for whenever certain situations occur, especially when the situation involves an order from an organizational superior. And since meaningful response to one's behavior in an organization, in the form of significant positive and negative reactions, must come from someone higher in authority, it is clear that leadership is vital to the organization's continued successful operation.

Weber's idea of a hierarchy of authority is one of the more obvious requirements that an organization must meet, for no organization can survive long without one. Yet the components that make up effective organizational leadership are not fully understood. Why does one person inspire extra dedication and effort in his or her subordinates and another produce only grudging compliance and minimal effort?

Behind the organization's rules and the chart describing its hierarchy of authority are human beings. They have egos and reputations to protect and enhance just as much as they have economic needs, and they cannot be counted on to behave as though they are robots simply because they are occupying organizational positions. Organizational leadership, then, must consist of more than just "pressing buttons" or issuing orders in accordance with the rules. **Organizational authority,** of course, *is vested in the position, not the individual,* but *how* the occupant of a position plays his or her role can make a good deal of difference in how successful he or she is in securing compliance from subordinates.

The following list presents the kinds of ways in which organizational authority is used at different levels of the hierarchy. From the routine scheduling of subordinates' activities (toward the bottom of the hierarchy) to making changes in organizational goals (at the top), these responsibilities require the person to not only *tell* others what to do, but also *persuade* them. If a subordinate does not want in some degree to obey orders, the leader can elicit only the minimally necessary degree of compliance and may generate a certain amount of resistance to boot.

The Uses of Organizational Authority

1. Scheduling subordinates' activities

2. Ensuring subordinates' compliance with rules through:
   a) Training
   b) Applying sanctions (positive/negative, formal/informal)

3. Choosing among alternative courses of action for subordinates:
   a) Deciding which rules apply in a given situation
   b) Interpreting the rules in terms of specific implementation
   c) Resolving problems or conflicts not covered by the rules

4. Personnel decisions:
   a) Appointing new members to organizational positions
   b) Promotions, demotions, and horizontal transfers
   c) Removing (firing)

5. Changing the rules that govern subordinates:
   a) Changing individuals' responsibilities
   b) Changing the relations among subordinates

6. Changing or modifying organizational goals (policy decisions):
   a) Responding to crises
   b) Reorganization (initiating organizational change)
   c) Changing organizational goals

It should be noted that these actions concern only the official's relations with his or her subordinates; they do not cover coordinative relations with others at the same level of authority. To the extent that the official is also someone else's subordinate, his or her supervisor has the same set of responsibilities in relation to him or her. Also, the higher the official is in the organizational hierarchy, the more likely he or she is to be responsible for all of these uses of authority; the lower the official is, the more he or she tends to be limited to relatively routine uses of authority.

Gaining Subordinates' Compliance

We may define **leadership** as *the personal skills involved in eliciting compliance; authority,* by contrast, *is the right to give orders and to ask for compliance* that goes with an organizational office. Etzioni identifies three foundations of the ability to secure subordinates' compliance in an organization: leadership ability alone, authority alone, and leadership ability combined with authority.

A person with only leadership ability must be classified as an *informal* leader, since he or she does not occupy an office that confers the organizational right to give orders. An informal leader somehow motivates others to do as requested through the use of symbolic rewards and punishments—praise and criticism, to be specific—since she or he does not control the material rewards and punishments that someone with authority can use. (The informal leader of a group of junior accountants, for example, may be able to get fellow workers to follow suggestions, but he or she cannot change the size of their paychecks and does not have the power to hire, promote, or fire them.)

There is, on the other hand, the person who has *only* organizational authority—that is, who occupies an office that gives him or her the right to give orders but lacks leadership ability. Etzioni calls this person an *official.* Without the authority embodied in the rules governing this position, he or she would be unable to secure any compliance from others.

Finally, there is the individual who has *both* personal-leadership ability and organizational authority: a *formal leader,* in Etzioni's terms. He or she combines the two essential methods of securing the compliance of subordinates and thus can be expected to be particularly effective. Only the "content" of his or her orders—their being "right" or "wrong" in terms of helping the organization achieve its goals—is important now, since getting others to follow them is ensured.

Leadership in Different Types of Organizations

Although it would appear that a formal leader is needed by every type of organization, such a person would be wasted in a coercive organization, but is absolutely essential in a normative organization. The demonstration of why this is so shows further the value of Etzioni's classification of organizations.

Since the members (inmates) of a coercive organization are there against their will anyway, the ability to use symbolic rewards and punishments is quite irrelevant to one's success in getting them to comply with organizational rules. They must be motivated mainly by fear of possible material punishments. Therefore, such organizations tend to be led by officials rather than by formal leaders. There are informal leaders, too, but they show up among the inmates, who need a source of guidance to structure their relationships beyond those laid out by organizational rules.

In a normative organization, on the other hand, symbolic rewards and punishments are the chief means of securing the members' compliance. A person in authority who lacks leadership ability will be unable to make such symbols meaningful and thus will be ineffective. Someone who *can* use them but is *not* a part of the formal structure of authority, by the same token, must inevitably be viewed as a threat to the organization, for he or she may compete with those in positions of authority for the members' allegiance. The result is that the person with leadership ability will be either drawn into the organizational hierarchy or else eventually ejected from membership altogether. The case of a "popular" member of a local charity being asked to serve as chairperson for its annual drive illustrates the former tendency; the excommunication of Martin Luther by the Catholic Church in 1521 represents the latter.

The importance of formal leadership and the frequency with which informal leaders appear in utilitarian organizations seems to vary with the type of activity in which they are engaged. An essentially "blue-collar" organization, e.g., a steel company, probably has less need of formal leaders (because most of its members take a very calculating attitude toward it and are interested primarily in wages and other benefits). Here, too, informal leaders are likely to become involved in union activities, or else their influence on other workers is irrelevant to the matter of compliance with rules.

In a high-technology organization, where professional researchers and skilled technicians play important roles, there is a tendency to rely on normative controls even when by other standards it is a utilitarian organization. Here, for this reason, formal leaders are particularly needed and informal leaders are discouraged.

The concept of an informal leader, further, alerts us to the fact that not everything that goes on in a formal organization is described and governed by its rules. The "discovery" of informal organization, perhaps a major contribution of the Human Relations school of management, has led to greatly increased understanding of the nature of formal organizations.

INFORMAL ORGANIZATION

Not all of the patterned relationships found within formal organizations are described by the rulebook. When we think of our own experiences in organizations, whether in high school, a business office, or the army, we know what these are. They are the personal relationships that develop among an organization's members, unguided by specific rules because they are too subtle to be covered by explicit regulations or else are apparently irrelevant to the organization's purposes. Together, these patterns make up the *informal organization* that exists side by side with the formal organization.

These relationships develop for two reasons. First, although an organization's formal rules give its members general guidelines concerning what they are to do, the rules cannot prescribe *all* of the details of each person's job. People must develop informal rules to govern those aspects of their activities that are not covered in the rulebook. There is always room for some individual variation in how different people go about performing the same organizational tasks, and since these variations are likely to have consequences for the way that others must carry out their tasks, there are pressures to stabilize these variations so that everyone can do his or her job as easily as possible.

The second reason is that the members of an organization have individual needs that are not provided for by the formal rules. In the process of getting to know one another as individuals rather than as job specifications, they forge informal arrangements to take care of these "private" needs. Even when people are "at work" and are being paid to help the organization achieve its goals rather than their own private goals, they still need friendship, recognition from their friends, a sense of security, and the feeling that they are contributing something to their immediate group within the organization.

If they have any interest in making their work easier for themselves, they will begin to develop shortcuts in their work. They will telephone someone to order supplies or to convey information because this is quicker than sending the prescribed form "through channels." They will send the form along later, of course, so that their actions are properly recorded, but this sort of informal cooperation by telephone helps to make their work both easier and more efficient. Someone will check informally with a superior about a proposal to establish a new subdivision in his or her department, in order to make sure that it is worthwhile to go through the necessary paperwork that a formal proposal will require.

When done with the proper regard for formal rules, such behavior can be genuinely helpful to the organization. It can save time and money, while at the same time helping to reinforce the personal ties among employees through which they find the friendship and sense of belonging that the formal rules cannot provide. But because these networks of relationships are not covered by the organization's rules, they can also be a source of difficulty. Such informal groups begin to have needs of their own. Who will be the informal leader among the employees in the secretarial pool? What happens to the morale of the new employee in the stockroom if no one invites him or her to eat lunch with the others?

Occasionally two informal groups come into conflict with each other, as in a bitter rivalry between two departments. Their battle, carried out with organizational weapons, can interfere seriously with the overall efficiency of the organization. One department can be fussy in demanding that the other turn in nothing but perfectly filled-out forms, and the other in turn can be slow in delivering the materials that the former needs for its work. Such incidents show how important informal organization can be and also the futility of depending entirely on the formal rules to keep things running smoothly.

Further, an informal group may become a center of resistance to organizational change. Feeling that they have the support of their co-workers, people who feel threatened by change can resist it by slowing down their productivity or by making it difficult for their bosses to institute new ways of doing things. They can "lose" important papers, make purposeful mistakes to show that the old way of doing things was better, or sometimes simply ignore the new directives.

Furthermore, because the old way of doing things was important in helping the informal organization develop in the way that it did, change may threaten the foundations of the informal group. If one department is no longer supposed to report to another one, their members have lost their reason to interact regularly, and the informal organization that has grown up around their interactions is undermined. To the extent that the organization's members find their major satisfactions in informal groups, they will be more interested in protecting these groups than in putting their energies into helping the formal organization operate more efficiently.

Thus the people who manage formal organizations have a continuing dilemma in deciding how to deal with the informal organizations. To undermine all informal organization would be harmful to the organization's effectiveness, but to encourage or tolerate too much informal organization would be equally harmful. Most managers try, of course, to find the happy medium between too little and too much, but this is usually done on an *ad hoc* basis and without much sensitivity to the principle involved. In areas like this, management is definitely an art rather than a science, and neither management specialists nor sociologists have yet learned enough to offer detailed, foolproof guidance on managing the informal side of the formal organization.

SUMMARY

The need to coordinate people's activities for the achievement of a complex goal or for the performance of a continuing, complicated job requires the creation of "artificial" statuses and "artificial" norms to guide their relationships. These plans must be recorded and enforced if they are to serve their purpose. Any human group that exists to achieve a goal and is composed of such "created" positions, ranging from a neighborhood bowling team to the United Nations, is a formal organization.

Since such groups are designed and managed by people who have only imperfect knowledge of how to make them successful, there is a continuing need for an overall perspective to guide their activities; several theories of organization have been developed in response to this need. The earliest, Scientific Management, assumed that workers are motivated entirely by wages and concentrated on discovering the most effective ways in which they should do their work so that higher profits could produce higher wages. The Human Relations school, on the other hand, stressed the importance of social rewards in workers' satisfactions, assuming that if the organization takes care of their social and psychological needs, they will automatically be productive and happy to do what the organization needs them to do.

The sociological perspective on organizations, developed initially by Max Weber, takes it for granted that there can never be perfect harmony between an organization's goals and those of its members. Instead, it focuses on the ways in which organizations are structured to minimize such conflict. Weber's description of the ideal-type bureaucracy includes seven central principles of organizational design that serve this purpose.

The three major attitudes that members can have toward an organization's goals (negative, neutral, and positive) provide the basis for Etzioni's typology of coercive, utilitarian, and normative forms of power, through which organizations are able to secure their members' compliance with their rules. His review of the foundations of the ability to lead others—through personal leadership skills, occupancy of an office that confers authority, or both—yields three types: the informal leader, the official, and the formal leader. The fact that these seem to be systematically related to different forms of organizational power suggests that this is a useful approach to understanding organizations.

Finally, a consideration of the reasons for the existence of informal organization—patterned relationships among members that are not described by the formal rules—and of its potential for both helping and hindering the organization in the achievement of its goals, rounds out the chapter.

SUGGESTED READINGS

Blau, Peter M., and W. Richard Scott, *Formal Organizations* (San Francisco: Chandler, 1962). Two important students of formal organizations provide an extensive discussion of the types and dynamics of this form of human group. An extensive bibliography increases the value of the book.

Etzioni, Amitai, *Modern Organizations* (Englewood Cliffs, N.J.: Prentice-Hall, 1964). This brief volume, on which a good deal of this chapter is based, provides an excellent overview of the topic and introduces Etzioni's approach to organizational authority, control, and theories of management. His work has been expanded and illustrated with much empirical data in his *A Comparative Analysis of Complex Organizations,* revised and enlarged edition (New York: Free Press, 1975).

Goffman, Erving, *Asylums* (New York: Doubleday/Anchor, 1961). The world of "total institutions" (prisons, mental hospitals, etc.) is explored here in fascinating detail and with sympathetic insight by one of the most perceptive of contemporary sociologists. This one is a classic by now.

Moore, Wilbert E., *The Conduct of the Corporation* (New York: Random House, 1962). Moore writes with dry humor about the structure and problems of large-scale business organizations, providing an excellent, humanistic appreciation of their operations and foibles.

Selznick, Philip, *TVA and the Grass Roots* (Berkeley: University of California Press, 1949). This is Selznick's ground-breaking study of a government bureaucracy's attempt to establish a working partnership with its clients and of the problems that emerged in the process.

Sofer, Cyril, *Organizations in Theory and Practice* (New York: Basic Books, 1972). Oriented as much toward practice as theory, this is a British social scientist's discussion of the way large organizations "really" work. It is particularly valuable for its thorough coverage of various organizational theories and for its use of concrete illustrations.

Weber, Max, *From Max Weber: Essays in Sociology,* trans. and ed. by Hans H. Gerth and C. Wright Mills (New York: Oxford University Press, 1946). Pages 196–240 contain Weber's analysis of the essential characteristics of a fully rational bureaucracy as well as an overview of bureaucracies in different countries and at different times.

Glossary

Bureaucracy Strictly speaking, the administrative or managerial part of a formal organization. More loosely, the term is sometimes used to refer to an organization as a whole. The word comes from the Old French word for the coarse woven material used to cover writing desks and thus calls to mind the members of an organization who are principally concerned with paperwork. Bureaucracy, then, is "rule by bureaus, or desks," or by a system of managerial offices.

Coercive power Organizational control based primarily on the threat or actual use of physical force to secure compliance with organizational rules. It can be used only when the organization's members cannot avoid it and is thus appropriate only in organizations whose members are there against their will, as is the case in a prison.

Formal organization A group whose members occupy consciously designed positions and are governed by consciously designed rules so that, collectively, they can work to achieve one or more specific goals. The term *formal* is used to emphasize that the organization has an explicit structure (that is, its positions and rules are written out in detail). It is sometimes called a complex organization or, inaccurately, a bureaucracy.

Human relations theory The school of managerial thought that emphasizes the importance of satisfying workers' social needs. It thus focuses attention on styles of leadership, communication between workers and management, and the workers' social relationships on the job.

Informal organization The patterned social relationships that develop among the members of an organization outside those called for by the organization's rules. It develops primarily to satisfy needs that are not met by the formal organization and may be either helpful or harmful to the organization's ability to achieve its goals.

Leadership As used here, this term refers to the personal qualities that enable one individual to persuade others to do as he or she suggests. It is thus related to the concept of *charisma* (see Chapter 12). When a person with these abilities has organizational authority (see below), he or she can be said to be a *formal leader;* without such authority, the person is an *informal leader.*

Normative power Organizational control based primarily on the use of symbolic rewards and punishments (praise and criticism) to secure compliance with organizational rules. It is most effective when the members are personally committed to the organization's goals and have joined it for this reason.

Organizational authority The powers an organization's member has by virtue of the position he or she holds within the organization. Such powers are located in the office rather than the individual and so are to be distinguished from those on which *leadership* (see above) is based. Chapter 12, on the political institution, provides a discussion of rational-legal authority, which is the more general form of organizational authority.

Open-system model A relatively recent approach to the study of organizations that stresses the organization's relations with its environment (its clients, other organizations, the government, etc.).

Rationalization The quality of objectively determining the most efficient way to reach a goal and then following that path without regard to irrelevant concerns. Weber saw the increasing rationalization of Western society as a major reason for the growing importance of formal organizations.

Scientific management The theory, or school of organizational management, that stresses the rationally efficient design of both organizational structures and individual jobs so that the waste of energy is minimized. In viewing the organization's members primarily as parts of a machine, this perspective tends to assume that they are motivated only by money and to ignore informal organization (see above) and the members' social needs.

Utilitarian power Organizational control based primarily on the use of material rewards (ordinarily money) to secure compliance with organizational rules. It is most important when the organization's members are basically neutral toward its goals, for they will obey the rules only in return for something that is of concrete value to them.

III
SOCIAL
INSTITUTIONS

If society is to continue in existence, certain continuing needs of its members, both individual and collective, must be met. Its members must develop regular social relationships through which they can satisfy these needs, which are sometimes called *functional imperatives*. The arrangements people work out to satisfy those needs can be viewed as structures of interrelated statuses, and we find a separate structure concerned with each major need. These structures are called social institutions. In this section we shall examine in some detail the institutions through which four major social needs are met.

Those statuses through whose interactions the need for material goods and services is satisfied make up the *economic institution*. Those involved in meeting the need to organize collective action to achieve group purposes make up the *political institution*. The human need for intimacy, both psychological and sexual, and for care and support is met through the *family institution*. And the statuses people occupy while expressing their commitment to beliefs about the fundamental meaning of human existence make up the *religious institution*.

We should note here that sociologists do not completely agree about the essential nature or even the number of social institutions. Some sociologists use the term to refer to any established social practice, such as celebrating holidays, sending gifts to people on their birthdays, or holding wakes for the dead. Others use the term to mean any organized activity that involves large numbers of people. By the latter definition, a society's armed forces and its educational system are social institutions, for each has its own complex of interrelated statuses, millions of people participate in each, and each is recognized as a major part of society's overall structure.

But if we want to classify institutions in terms of the central societal needs that they serve, the military and educational systems do not qualify as separate social institutions. Instead, the military should be viewed as a specialized part of the political institution because its purpose is the legitimate use of force to protect society. By the same reasoning, the educational system should be viewed as a specialized extension of the family institution because of its concentration on two basic family functions—advanced socialization and the subsequent placement of young people in the social structure.

It comes down to a question of how one wishes to distinguish social institutions from other forms of social structure. The approach used here, that of identifying social institutions as structures through which distinctive major individual and collective needs are met, has been adopted because it is particularly useful in helping us to compare institutions and to grasp their common characteristics. Since the institutions discussed in this section are recognized by virtually all sociologists, regardless of the criteria by which they are defined, their analysis can be considered an important part of the standard sociological curriculum.

This section begins with a chapter on *social exchange*. Through an examination of *why* people want to interact and of the conditions under which *patterns* of interaction emerge, a model of social institutions as "exchange systems" is developed. The remaining chapters use this model in the analysis of each social institution in turn, suggesting that the central structure of all institutions is similar and that differences among them can be understood in terms of the distinctive characteristics of the needs they seek to satisfy.

10

Social Exchange and Social Institutions

FOCUS: *EXCHANGE*

No living thing can exist in isolation from its environment, for it must obtain from outside itself whatever is needed to sustain life. In the broadest sense every living thing thus engages in *exchange* with its environment, taking in some things and putting out others. The growing science of ecology concentrates on the complex systems of exchange through which different forms of life support each other's existence in a common habitat, as when earthworms aid the growth of plants by loosening the subsoil and in return are nourished by the remains of the plants' previous roots.

This sort of exchange need not be consciously planned by its participants, of course, for the actual existence of an exchange relationship does not depend on the participants' awareness of it. Human beings, however, are very much aware of their dependence on one another in many ways, and we can assume that they will do what they can to make sure that their exchange relationships are maintained.

This chapter examines the foundations of social interaction from an exchange perspective, assuming that people's awareness of their interdependence provides the motivation for them to work out stable patterns of interaction through which mutually satisfying exchange can take place on a regular basis. Further, the fact that people need a number of qualitatively different things from one another means that different patterns of interaction must be worked out to facilitate the exchange of each type. These different patterns form the basis of separate social institutions.

THE NATURE OF SOCIAL INSTITUTIONS

When using the term *institution,* a sociologist is not referring to a particular organization such as a bank, a school, or a prison, but to one of the major social structures that exists within society. In Section II of this book we covered three basic reasons for the development of patterned social relationships—occupancy of ascribed statuses, physical proximity, and common purposes. The first basis entails relationships with other ascribed statuses (male/female, upper class/lower class, black/white, Jew/Christian, etc.); the second leads to the formation of communities; and the third accounts for the existence of formal organizations. Social institutions develop for a fourth reason: people's continuing need to satisfy their individual and collective needs.

A social institution is thus a *functional* subdivision of society, which means that it is identified in terms of its contributions to the continued existence of society and its individual members. A review of the idea of *function* (noted in Chapter 1 and discussed at greater length in Appendix 2) will be useful at this point.

Functional Analysis

Functional analysis *is the process of looking at any pattern of interaction in terms of its functions,* that is, examining it with respect to *its consequences for the group or society in which it occurs.* If these consequences are largely beneficial, helping to maintain the group, they are called its *functions.* If they are largely harmful, tending to lead to the disorganization or breakdown of the group, they are called *dysfunctions.* The patterns of interaction that we call marriage, for example, are primarily functional; they minimize the potential for conflict over sex partners by limiting the rights of sexual access, and they also assign responsibility for care of the children who are born from this relationship. The patterns of interaction that make up terrorism, on the other hand, are dysfunctional, for obvious reasons.

Further refining the concept, sociologists also speak of *manifest* and *latent* functions, referring to whether or not the participants in a pattern of interaction are aware of its consequences. A social welfare program, for instance, has the *manifest function* of helping some of society's members to survive in at least minimum comfort, but it also has the *latent dysfunction* of identifying these people as poor, dependent, and powerless, thereby labeling them "inferior" and thus reinforcing their disadvantaged position. Organized crime, on the other hand, is *manifestly dysfunctional* because it violates the law, but it can have the *latent function* of providing a ladder of upward social mobility for certain groups who, for ascriptive reasons, are barred from most of the legitimate channels of upward mobility (Merton, 1957).

The identification of functions and dysfunctions is a complex task, for most patterns of interaction have many consequences for many other patterns, and it is by no means easy to determine which ones are the most important for the group as a whole. Yet functional analysis does provide a useful perspective on society, and it is particularly effective in helping us to understand social institutions.

Defining Social Institutions

The background of the word *institution* does not really suggest the use that the sociologist makes of it. To *institute* something means simply to establish it or to make it widely known and accepted. According to the dictionary, then, it would be reasonable to say that the practice of sending flowers to a sick person is "institutionalized" and that the patterns of behavior and meaning involved in this practice thus make up an institution. Indeed, some sociologists use the term in just this way. But to adopt this definition would have us applying it to so many different patterns of behavior, large and small, that its usefulness would be greatly diminished.

For our purposes, we shall define a **social institution** as *a complex of interrelated statuses whose occupants interact for the purpose of satisfying a basic personal or collective need.* In this chapter we shall be concerned with the foundations of all social institutions, concentrating on their general characteristics, the particular needs they seek to satisfy, and the general norms or principles that seem to govern their participants.

THE MOTIVATIONAL BASES OF INSTITUTIONS

To begin to understand the basic structure of institutions, we must go back to our definition of interaction as "the purposeful, reciprocal influencing of two or more people by each other." Here we must delve a bit deeper: We must ask where the purposefulness comes from, or why it is that people interact at all.

Admittedly, this is not a purely sociological question, for it concerns the motivations of individuals and thus belongs more properly to the psychologist. But to build a meaningful picture of society, we must take account of motivation.

Let us say, to begin with, that people engage in interaction because they want to—because, for some reason or other, it is worthwhile for them to influence and be influenced by another person. But instead of probing for unconscious needs and neurotic compulsions, let us assume simply that interaction is worthwhile to them *because they get something out of it.* Two people choose to interact with each other, in other words, because for each of them this is more pleasurable (or less painful) than doing something else at the moment.

To be sure, this is a pretty simple view. It ignores all of the cases in which people are in error about what they want to do—as when someone opens the door to interact with a friend, only to be confronted by a thug. It ignores the case of the person who doesn't really want to interact with the dentist, but decides that a little pain now is better than a big toothache later on. And yet, as will become apparent, this simple assumption is quite adequate for our purposes here.

To expand our answer to why people want to interact with one another, we must ask what it is that people obtain through interaction that *makes* it worth their while. To be adequate, our answer must take account of the fact that both parties to a pattern of interaction must "get something out of it" if it is to become a standard pattern of social interaction. If one of the parties did not get something satisfying from it, he or she would not be likely to engage in it the next time someone proposed it, and we would not observe it as a regular feature of social life.

Ordinarily, of course, we assume almost automatically that if someone initiates interaction with us, he or she not only wants something out of it, but also has something to give us in return. This may be no more than a thank-you in return for the time of day, or it may be as important as a promotion on the job in return for responsible performance.

Most of the time, the situational clues must be quite clear and unmistakable before a person will refuse absolutely to interact with someone else. Perhaps the most common example of such a situation occurs when a bum approaches a well-dressed person on the street and is totally ignored. Here the well-dressed person can see that there is nothing in the proposed interaction for him or her and so ignores the usual standards of courtesy and refuses even to acknowledge the existence of the other. (It is for this reason that the "con artist" must dress well if he or she is to persuade an intended victim that something valuable may be gained through participation in the proposed interaction.)

SOCIAL EXCHANGE

In considering why people want to interact, we have hit on the principle of *social exchange*, an aspect of interaction so fundamental that we rarely think about it. We may see the particular trees but fail to see the forest as a whole, even though our awareness of the importance of social exchange shows up in such common expressions as, "She is a very rewarding person to know," "He doesn't give very much of himself," and "You always get an even break with Lee." This way of looking at social relationships goes back at least to Plato, and the idea has been cast in a more modern form by sociologists such as George C. Homans, Alvin W. Gouldner, and Peter M. Blau (see Suggested Readings).

Social exchange—*interaction through which each participant obtains something of value from the other*—can be looked at in two ways: quantitatively and qualitatively. In examining the *quantitative* aspects of exchange, we are concerned with the "fairness" of the transaction, or with whether both parties to the exchange come away from it with the feeling that they have received equal value for what they put into it. To the extent that this does not happen, a situation of "structured inequality" exists. And we can also ask whether the exchange is "equal" by objective standards, regardless of whether both participants *think* that it is fair. A young stagehand, for instance, may spend half an hour finding a cup of coffee for a beautiful leading lady and be perfectly content to receive only a smiling thank-you in exchange. Or a share-cropper may toil in hot cottonfields for twelve hours in return for $5.00 or less, knowing that the exchange is distinctly unfair, but being unable to do anything about it.

Underlying this aspect of social relationships is what Gouldner (1959) has called "the norm of reciprocity," or the shared sense that social exchange *should* be equal. The areas of social life in which the quantitative analysis of exchange is most fruitful are those of social stratification and of power relationships in society.

But it is the *qualitative* aspects of social exchange that are more directly relevant to understanding the distinctions among social institutions. Here we use the term "qualitative" to refer not to value (as in "These shoes are of better quality than those"), but to distinct *differences in kind* among the various sorts of things that may be involved in social exchange. In other words, if there are marked qualitative differences among these things, there should also be different patterns of interaction that facilitate their exchange. To jump ahead of ourselves for a moment, consider the different norms that apply to getting a kiss and to buying a pair of socks. The conditions under which the first exchange takes place, and the understandings that must exist between the parties involved, differ considerably from those that characterize the second.

One more thing remains to be made explicit: the fact that patterns of exchange come to involve social statuses rather than concrete individuals. If the conditions under which the exchange of a particular sort of thing is carried out are determined partly by the intrinsic character of that thing, and if it is quite often the focus of interaction, then rules (norms) governing the relationship between the parties engaged in this exchange will develop—and, simplifying the procedure, the rules will be related to statuses rather than to specific persons. A young man may buy a pair of socks from a salesgirl in the afternoon and then kiss her in the evening, but it is the statuses they occupy at these different times that determine the sort of exchange they will engage in. A customer does not ordinarily kiss a salesgirl, nor does a girlfriend sell socks to her boyfriend when they are out together.

It is important, therefore, to look at the different kinds of things that people can obtain through interaction and that make their continued participation in different patterns of interaction worthwhile.

"COMMODITIES"

There is no end to the list of the specific things that people might want from one another. You and your friend may both be hungry, but you want to buy a hamburger and she wants to buy imported caviar. Or, you may both be dissatisfied with the government, but you want a socialist government and she would prefer a monarchy. Clearly, our analysis of exchange will get nowhere if we stay at this level of specificity.

We can, however, move to a more abstract level and talk about the different *categories* of things that people generally want. In the former example, we can include both hamburgers and caviar under the heading of "material goods" and include also such things as clothes, shelter, cars and roads, golf clubs and golf courses, and so on. Similarly, the desire for a monarchy or for a socialistic government can be seen as aspects of a more general need for effective social organization. Under this heading would come also such interests as protection from violence, responsible leadership, and a fair system of laws and courts.

There are two other general categories of human wants that we must take account of as well. One of these is the need for sex and affection—for intimate relationships, both physical and emotional. The other is a less clearly defined need, but perhaps it can best be described as a need for social support for the answers we have found to important but nonempirical questions. Such questions can range from "Why did I have to bet on *that* horse?" all the way to "What will happen to me after I die?" In the former case it will not be difficult to find people who agree with our sad conclusion that Lady Luck is indeed fickle. In the latter case we may develop, together with other people, an elaborate theology, complete with gods, demons, rituals, and sacrifices, to support our common belief that we will go to a happy hunting ground after we die—or to a blazing hell if we have been especially sinful during our lifetimes.

It is these general categories of things, which we shall call **commodities**, that are involved in most forms of human interaction. These are *the major types of things that are exchanged in the process of interaction,* and it seems reasonable to assume that the widespread and continuing interest on the part of most people in obtaining them throughout most of their lives can be viewed as the motivational foundation of the different social institutions. In other words, it is the exchange of material goods and services through interaction that forms the focus of the economic institution. It is people's mutual interest in maintaining order in their relationships and in being able to organize themselves to achieve collective goals that establishes the patterns of interaction that make up the political institution. The social arrangements through which most people's need for intimate sexual and social relationships is met form the institution of the family. And it is the ways in which people interact to sustain consensual support for their necessary but not empirically testable beliefs that make up the religious institution of society.

Here we have four commodities in which the members of society have a continuing interest. The need for these basic commodities, or **functional imperatives,** *must be satisfied if a society is to continue in existence.* Because they are all qualitatively different from one another, different patterns of behavior are required to facilitate their regular exchange. We turn our attention now to some of these differences.

Scarce and Joint Commodities

One particularly interesting aspect of the qualitative differences among these commodities lies in whether they are the *objects* of interaction or are themselves *produced through* interaction. Those which are the objects of interaction and are wanted for their usefulness later on can be said to be *scarce,* meaning that if they are possessed by one person or group, another person or group *cannot* possess them. This is clearest in the case of material goods: Two people cannot eat the same sandwich. But it is true also in the case of the need for collective action to achieve group goals. If one goal is decided on, its opposite obviously cannot be sought at the same time. If the policy is to wage war, those who would prefer peace are out of luck. If the decision for the group is to outlaw the sale of alcoholic beverages, those who wish to continue drinking have lost the battle. And because the winner of an important political office has more influence on which decisions are made than the loser, the office is also a scarce commodity. Thus material goods and services, and also the ability to determine political decisions, are scarce commodities, and this quality has important consequences for the norms that develop to govern their exchange.

The remaining commodities, on the other hand, which can be called *joint,* are essentially products of people's action. *Unless both parties obtain them, neither can.* The simplest example of this is a kiss. More generally, love and affection are genuinely satisfying only when both parties enjoy the interaction (exceptions to this rule are discussed in a subsequent section of this chapter).

In the area of basic beliefs, people give and receive mutual support for the importance and validity of their beliefs through engaging in activities that demonstrate their acceptance of those beliefs. Needing meaningful answers to

Material goods, which can be possessed by only one person at a time, are called scarce commodities; a joint commodity, such as a kiss, is the product of interaction and must be obtained by both parties simultaneously. (*Left:* Eric Kroll/ Taurus Photos; *right:* Jeff Albertson/Stock, Boston)

questions about the essential nature of human life ("Why did my friend die?" "Why must I suffer like this?"), we seek support for our answers to these questions in signs that others accept the same answers. It is for this reason that religion is essentially a social activity: We worship in groups periodically in order to reaffirm our faith, even though we also engage in private religious practices.

Thus the family and religion are organized around the exchange—in fact, the creation and sharing—of joint commodities. When we look at human groups as people drawn together through the need for social exchange, it seems no accident that primitive societies tend to have very highly developed family and religious institutions, whereas their economic and political activities are likely to be handled through the family and religious institutions rather than to be recognizably distinct patterns of interaction in themselves. After all, the first thing that is likely to draw people together and to provide the basis for regular patterns of interaction is their mutual interest in joint commodities. It takes two to tango, two to make love, and at least two to support each other's beliefs about things that are beyond their ability to test, and so we can understand why the family and religious institutions were the first to develop in early societies. It was only with increasing societal complexity that institutions based on the exchange of scarce commodities began to develop a high degree of autonomy; this topic is discussed further in Chapter 18, on social change.

MAINTAINING PATTERNS OF SOCIAL EXCHANGE

If regular patterns of social interaction are to develop, people must have some faith that others will be ready and willing to interact with them. If they view interaction as social exchange, they must be able to assume that others will be interested in obtaining what they *have* in return for something that they *want*. Without this assumption, few people would think it worthwhile to initiate interaction with others, for the frequency of frustration would be too high.

It is obvious that people do hold this assumption. One of the best ways to see it in action is to observe how people react when it is not born out. We can imagine someone's frustration and outrage if a storekeeper refuses to sell him or her a loaf of bread because "I don't like the way you comb your hair." In effect, this is denying that the storekeeper wants the customer's money, and the customer is left not only without the loaf of bread, but also with the frustration that comes when a basic normative expectation has been violated. One of the unpleasant aspects of being unemployed, aside from having no money, is the fundamental sense of being "unwanted"—or of wanting to exchange one's labor in return for wages, but finding that no one wants to engage in this exchange.

However, the acceptance of this norm is not sufficient to help people establish patterns of exchange. Because people have a number of different needs, they must develop more specific ways of determining *who* is interested in *what sort* of exchange. The solution to this problem, discussed at some length in Chapter 2, is the development of specific social statuses that "tell" others the types of social exchange in which their occupants are willing to engage. The statuses of buyer and seller, candidate and voter, priest and worshipper, and husband and wife would not have developed if there were not widespread and continuing interest in the commodities that are exchanged in the interaction between each of these pairs of statuses.

But people must also be *willing* to occupy these statuses, and so certain pressures develop to encourage people to do this. Behind these pressures lies the vague concern that the patterns of interaction making up society would be weakened if people were not ordinarily willing to participate in the kinds of exchange on which they are based. Despite our awareness that most people, most of the time, do want to engage in social exchange, we are reluctant to see anyone "drop out of the game" except under special circumstances, for in principle this seems to threaten the continued existence of these relationships. These pressures are expressed in three relatively vague but very general norms that can be called "the principles of social exchange."

THE PRINCIPLES OF SOCIAL EXCHANGE

There are three basic **principles of social exchange** that seem to *govern all social institutions or systems of social exchange,* no matter which commodity is involved.

The first principle is that people *should want* the commodity in question; they should want material goods, love and affection, and support for their beliefs. The second is that people should satisfy these wants *through exchange* with others rather than entirely by themselves or without giving equal value in return. Third, they should not try to obtain one commodity through behavior that is normatively appropriate to obtaining a different commodity. In other words, they *should not compromise* different systems of exchange.

Identifying these principles, of course, is not the same as asserting that the members of society hold them as conscious values or attitudes, any more than describing a planet's orbit around the sun implies that the planet "wants" to travel in that path. The first two principles simply describe what people must do, most of the time, if society is to survive, and the third is a recognition of the fact that different patterns of interaction are best suited to the exchange of different types of commodities. Yet these principles do show up here and there in people's attitudes, and it would be difficult to claim that they are completely unaware of them.

Wanting Commodities

The first principle, for instance, shows up in the economic institution in the vague suspicion many of us have of both the bum and playboy. The bum has obviously given up all interest in obtaining material goods and services beyond those minimally necessary to stay alive, and the playboy is not concerned with these things, because he already has so much money that he is not likely to be interested in acquiring more (through taking a job or selling his property). We cannot count on either one's wanting to interact with us on a regular basis as participants in the economic institution.

Clearly it is the principle that is at stake here rather than the immediate situation, but the feeling is based on the fact that someone who is not likely to be interested in interacting with us because of what we have to offer is somehow a threat to our expectation that "people will want what we have and will give us what we want in return."

Just as people are expected to want material goods—food, shelter, and so on—it is also felt that they should want money because it symbolizes material value. Likewise, people are seldom shocked to find that "every person has a price," and most people tend to agree with laws that require restaurants and other businesses to concentrate on making money by serving all customers, regardless of race or creed.

The same principle can be found in the political institution. It is felt that everyone should be interested in helping to determine who will lead the group: Everyone should get out and vote, everyone should make his or her opinions known, and anyone should run for public office if he or she seems to be able to do better than the incumbent.

In the family institution, bachelors, spinsters, and even young widows and widowers are often looked on with suspicion because by being presently unmarried, they seem to indicate that they are not interested in obtaining love and affection in the preferred way.

Finally, in the area of religion, we have all seen the posters that urge us to "attend the church or synagogue of your choice." People can urge us to do this only in a society that has religious freedom, but where there is an established national church, more concrete pressures may be used to get the people to attend services. Implicitly recognizing the importance of sharing religious beliefs, people do what they can to get others to join with them in supporting these beliefs through their actions.

Obtaining Commodities Through Exchange

The second principle, that one should satisfy one's needs for the basic commodities *through exchange with others,* can be similarly illustrated. Certainly, one should not obtain material goods, a satisfying form of social organization, or love, *without* exchange: Robbery, political rebellion, and rape are considered crimes in nearly every society. It is more difficult to find a parallel in the religious institution, except in those instances in which someone is forced to give lip service to a particular creed. Here the person is being forced to give support to others' beliefs without at the same time receiving support for his or her own, and in those societies in which the religious institution has been clearly separated from other institutions, such practices are felt to be wrong.

This same principle applies also to what we might call self-generated commodities. The do-it-yourself approach is all right up to a point, in the general view, but the hermit who lives alone and takes care of all his or her own needs is an object of suspicion because such a person obviously has no need to interact with others. One should not gain power over others by pointing a gun at them, either, for he or she has in effect seized control of the situation without the consent of the ruled rather than through an exchange that is mutually rewarding. The solitary satisfaction of one's sexual needs is felt to be wrong, too, and we do not really approve of the person who is a narcissist—who undertakes to provide privately all the affection and approval that he or she wants.

Finally, the person who develops a private religion is subject to some disapproval, both because this involves withdrawing from an interest in interacting with others to build support for mutual beliefs and because this obvious disagreement with others' beliefs may weaken their own faith in them.

Maintaining Separate Institutions

The third principle, that it is wrong to compromise different institutions by offering to exchange one commodity for a distinctly different one, is perhaps less often heeded in everyday life than are the first two. It still exists as a principle, however, and we can see its operation in a number of common situations.

Perhaps the most obvious illustration of the anticompromise principle is our feeling that political and economic institutions should not be merged into each other. We believe that it is wrong to exchange votes or political decisions for money and that the person who bribes a public official and the candidate who buys the votes necessary to be elected are committing moral as well as legal crimes. Political power and money, in other words, are distinctly different commodities; when they are exchanged for each other, the boundaries between these two institutions are weakened. More specifically, such compromises threaten people's faith that they can continue to obtain what they want, in terms of each commodity, in exchange for the things they have been accustomed to exchanging for them.

The same principle can be seen in the biblical injunction: "It is easier for a camel to go through the eye of a needle, than for a rich man to enter into the kingdom of God." Support for the basic beliefs, in other words, including "salvation," cannot be purchased with money; among other things, it was Luther's anger at the sale of indulgences that led him to begin the Reformation in the sixteenth century.

We find also that compromises between the family institution and the economic institution are generally felt to be wrong. Buying friends is not a good thing to do, and perhaps the opposition to prostitution that we find in all advanced societies is another reflection of this principle: One should not exchange love for money.

It is true that this third principle does not seem to operate so vigorously in less complex societies. This is because in more primitive societies, the major institutions are not so clearly differentiated from one another. The family in a primitive society is usually also the basic economic and political unit, and family relationships are indistinguishable from economic and political relationships. But as a society grows larger and as such undifferentiated relationships become less efficient in keeping things going, there is a tendency for each institution to become more clearly separated from the others and to emphasize its own "native" patterns of interaction and exchange. Only as this differentiation develops do we observe the third principle coming into play.

SUMMARY

Exchange is necessary for the survival of any form of life, and it is the need to engage in regular exchanges with others that motivates human beings to develop and maintain patterns of interaction. The different categories of things (or commodities) needed for the survival of its members and of society itself are the focus of different social institutions. A social institution is thus the set of interrelated statuses whose occupants' interactions are concerned with the exchange of a particular commodity.

Social exchange may be viewed either quantitatively or qualitatively. The former perspective emphasizes the conditions under which "fair" exchange is possible and also the processes through which "structured inequality" or stable patterns of *un*fair exchange develop. The latter, the qualitative perspective, takes account of the fact that the characteristics of the different types of commodities people obtain through social exchange require different patterns of interaction.

The commodities that are essential to society's survival can be thought of as social needs, or functional imperatives, and a different institution develops to serve each one. The economic institution is concerned with the production and allocation of material goods and services. The political institution is organized around the problems of mobilizing society's members for collective action, determining the nature of that action, and maintaining order in their relationships. Through the family institution, the need for physical and emotional intimacy is satisfied, and responsibility for the care of children is determined. The religious institution provides a structure through which people may develop consensual support for important beliefs whose validity cannot otherwise be demonstrated.

People need to be able to count on the fact that others will be interested in occupying the social statuses that are concerned with the exchange of each of these commodities. Three basic rules, or principles of social exchange, can be identified that encourage people to do this and that help to maintain the separate identity of each social institution. These principles can be expressed in the following "commandments": First, you should *want* the commodity; second, you should *obtain it through exchange* with others; and third, you should *not exchange one commodity for a qualitatively different one*.

These principles are not obeyed at all times, by any means. Yet in their absence, the patterns of interaction through which commodities are exchanged would become unpredictable and unreliable. Thus the vague (although occasionally quite specific) pressures that these principles embody continue to be needed.

Having established at least the bare bones of a model of social institutions, it remains for us to see how the particular characteristics of different commodities shape the institutions through which they are obtained.

SUGGESTED READINGS

Blau, Peter M., *Exchange and Power in Social Life* (New York: Wiley, 1964). This is an important effort to explain much of society in terms of exchange, reciprocity, and the power that grows out of imbalances in reciprocal obligations. Blau's work is thus very much devoted to a quantitative analysis of social exchange.

Gouldner, Alvin W., "Reciprocity and Autonomy in Functional Theory," in Llewellyn Gross, ed., *Symposium in Sociological Theory* (Evanston, Ill.: Row, Peterson, 1959), pp. 241–270. This article also concentrates on the quantitative aspects of exchange; Gouldner's concern is to show the compatibility of exchange theory with the tenets of functional analysis.

Homans, George C., *Social Behavior: Its Elementary Forms* (New York: Harcourt, Brace, 1961). Although some have accused Homans of attempting to reduce social behavior to the level of operant psychology, in this collection of essays he shows how a set of interdependent propositions about the quantitative aspects of social exchange can be put together with style and provocative challenge to other perspectives.

Merton, Robert K., "Manifest and Latent Functions," in his *Social Theory and Social Structure*, rev. ed. (New York: Free Press, 1957), pp. 19–84. This is probably the clearest and most comprehensive discussion of the bases and nature of functional analysis one can find. Merton is also frank in admitting the weaknesses of this approach.

Parsons, Talcott, *The Social System* (New York: Free Press, 1951). A landmark in the sociological literature, this was Parsons' first complete statement of his developing theory of society. Although avowedly functionalist, Parsons's analyses of social interaction and social institutions have implicit in them a strong hint of exchange theory.

Glossary

Commodity The term used here to denote a major type or category of things in which most members of society have a continuing interest. The commodities central to the economic and political institutions are *scarce,* in the sense that they cannot be completely shared, whereas those central to the family and religious institutions are *joint* because they come into existence through interaction.

Functional analysis The analysis of social phenomena in terms of their consequences for the continued existence of society. A particular pattern of interaction, for example, is *functional* if its consequences are generally beneficial to society; it is *dysfunctional* if its consequences are generally harmful. Those consequences that people recognize are *manifest;* those they are not aware of are *latent.*

Functional imperative A basic need of society, referred to here as a *commodity* (see above), which must be satisfied if society is to continue in existence.

Principles of social exchange The three vague but functionally necessary rules that apply to the participants in all social institutions. First, people should *want* the commodity (so that they will participate); second, people should obtain it *through exchange* (so participation will continue to be worthwhile for everyone); and third, people should *not compromise* different exchange systems (so the patterns of exchange in each institution will not be distorted by irrelevant considerations). These principles are not always obeyed by any means, but if no one obeyed them, society could not continue to exist.

Social exchange Interaction through which each participant obtains something that he or she defines as valuable, which means that each participant must also give something in return. It is presumably the prospect of a satisfying exchange that motivates people to engage in interaction, and it is their interest in maintaining stable, reliable patterns of exchange that underlies the development of social institutions.

Social institution A complex, or structure, of interrelated social statuses whose occupants' interactions are based on exchange that involves some aspect of a particular commodity.

11

The Economic Institution

FOCUS:

PROPERTY RIGHTS AND ECONOMIC VALUE

Human beings' need for material goods is continuous because food, clothing, and shelter are daily necessities; other goods and services may be needed almost as often. It would be almost a contradiction in terms, then, to conceive of a society whose members did not satisfy these needs through exchange with others. A society made up of economically independent hermits would hardly be a society at all, and its members would be poor as well, for they would lack the advantages gained through the **division of labor** *(dividing complex tasks into simpler parts and assigning them to different people for the sake of greater efficiency).*

Society's survival thus depends on economic exchange, and its members must work out patterns through which this can be accomplished with a minimum of conflict and a maximum of predictability. The nature of these patterns, though, must be determined to a considerable extent by the essential characteristics of the commodity being exchanged. Two such characteristics are particularly important.

First, there is the fact that material goods and services are scarce commodities. Two people cannot wear the same wristwatch at the same time, they cannot hire the same person to dig ditches in their separate backyards at the same time, nor can they drink the same bottle of beer. If one has it, the other cannot. Before patterns of exchange can develop, then, the idea of "ownership," or *property rights,* must be defined, and the methods by which it can be transferred must be worked out and accepted by the members of society. In other words, without assurance that economic exchange is reliable—that one can *continue* to own what has been obtained through exchange—there would be little motivation to engage in such interaction.

A second basic characteristic of material goods and services is that they are of differing amounts of importance, or value, to people at different times. The person who owns a good shovel does not need another one and thus will not be interested in offering another person very much for a second shovel; the person who has just eaten a full meal will not place very much importance on obtaining another meal right away. If people are to work out stable patterns of economic exchange, however, which requires the ability to anticipate others' interests, they must be able to distinguish between the immediate "value in use" of an item or service to specific individuals at specific times and its more general **economic value**—*its average value over time to a number of different people.*

As soon as this distinction is recognized and techniques are developed through which the two kinds of value can be systematically related, the system of economic exchange becomes much more predictable and dependable. To the sociologist, it is the ways in which human groups have developed different forms of economic exchange and the consequences of these forms for other parts of society that are of central importance in understanding the economic institution.

INTRODUCTION

The economic sector of society provides a good introduction to the study of social institutions, for it is probably the most familiar to us as a particular complex of social statuses. It has been the dominant institution in this country for many years—"The business of America is business," said Calvin Coolidge—and we are all familiar with the nature and uses of money and with the various statuses whose relationships center on the production and exchange of material goods and services or their monetary equivalents.

Industrial workers, farmers, salespeople, and merchants are those usually thought of first when we think of the economic institution. But since money represents the market value of goods and services, it is clear that the economic institution involves also such statuses as bankers, accountants, tax lawyers, and stockbrokers. Those who are concerned with the relations among different parts of the economy, even though they are sometimes located in the political institution, may be seen also as directly involved: labor leaders, economic analysts, and the statisticians who work for the Bureau of the Budget in Washington.

It is statuses like these that make up the economic institution. To understand its dynamics, though, we must look first at the foundations of this institution—at the nature of material goods and the basic idea of *property*.

PROPERTY

If there is to be an exchange of material goods and/or services, the participants must have a pretty good idea of *who* has *what* to exchange. It is clear, for instance, that John would not want to pay Bob $300 for a television set if Sam could seize the set later on the grounds that it had really belonged to him rather than to Bob. There must be some commonly accepted standards by which ownership is determined before trustworthy patterns of exchange can develop. So we must begin by looking at the various relationships that can exist between an individual and an object of economic value—the various forms of *ownership*.

The idea of ownership, of saying "This is my property," usually suggests physical possession at first. A good example is your wristwatch, a small article that you carry with you and over which you have exclusive physical control. Your ownership extends even to the right to smash the watch if you wish to. But if a bigger person could come along and take it away from you at any time without fear of punishment, your sense of ownership would be somewhat shaky. This possibility calls our attention to the fact that ownership does not consist simply in the physical possession of an item, but in the agreement of others that you have certain rights in relation to it.

Ownership does not consist in physical possession, but in others' recognition of an individual's rights in relation to an object of economic interest. (Robert V. Eckert, Jr./EKM-Nepenthe)

Ownership of a house consists of not simply living in it, but also having a deed to it—a piece of paper stating that you have gone through certain procedures to obtain the rights of ownership. The deed, in other words, should persuade others to agree that this is your house. Likewise, the sales slip you were given when you bought a box of pencils certifies that the store has given up its ownership of those pencils in return for a stated amount of money. In most cases, of course, physical possession itself is enough to convince others that something is indeed yours: No one challenges your ownership of the wristwatch that you wear. (But if you have twenty-five watches on your arms and in your pockets, someone might well ask for proof that they are your property. After all, only one watch is needed to tell what time it is.)

Types of Property Rights

If **property, or ownership,** *consists of rights rather than possession—of what others agree is yours rather than what you claim to own—*we can see that there are many different kinds of rights that may be owned. There can be many different aspects of things that others may agree that we own. For instance, we may become the owner of a section of lakefront property and wish to keep others off it, but we cannot carry this property around with us or destroy it at will. We may obtain the right to take oil out of the ground or to receive the profits from a song we have written; none of these are things that we can possess physically, and yet they are rights with respect to certain things, and they are rights that we feel it valuable to own.

So we can separate the different rights to something that can be possessed, and we can want to own some of them but not necessarily all. We cannot physically possess an idea, or an area of beach, or an oil pool lying miles below the earth's surface. We cannot physically possess the right to receive rental from a house or to use a private road. Yet these are rights that people may want to own, and the economic system has developed so that they can be acquired by people (that is, assigned to them by others) and later be transferred to others.

To own all of the possible rights to something, including the right of abuse or of using it up, would constitute "total ownership." But this kind of possession exists only in the case of small things such as watches, clothing, cigarette lighters, and so on. And even here, our rights of use are often limited in some fashion. You may own a gun, but you are not allowed to fire it inside the city limits; or, you may own land along a lake and even part of the lake itself, but this may not allow you to throw trash into the lake.

Different sorts of things have different potential rights inherent in them, and they may lack certain other rights. No one can own the right to use up an area of land, for no matter how much of it you cart away, the physical boundaries will remain. No one can own the right to the fruits or products of, for instance, a razorblade: It does not produce anything of value by itself in the way that an acre of farmland or a prize bull can.

We can also obtain a more restricted form of ownership, on a temporary basis, by borrowing or renting certain property rights. We can rent the right to occupy an apartment, but probably not the right to redecorate it as we see fit. We can rent a seat on a bus, but not the right to carve our initials in it.

In general, the more sophisticated a society is, the more likely it is that people's interests are specialized and that different property rights are distinguished from one another and treated as separate things to be owned or rented. Certainly the members of an aboriginal tribe in Australia would not think of owning just the mineral rights to an area of land, nor would they think it worthwhile to own the right to only a fraction of a business enterprise's profits—as we do when we buy stock in a corporation.

So we may conclude that property consists basically in *property rights* rather than in physical possession and that the exchange of these rights is the focus of the economic institution. The statuses that participate in this institution are defined by the roles they play in economic exchange.

Forms of Economic Exchange

Even after the problem of establishing property rights has been solved, there remains for every society the need to work out specific patterns of interaction through which these rights can be exchanged. As we shall see, the various forms of exchange that can be developed will determine the scope and effectiveness of a society's economic system.

Primitive societies did not solve two problems central to the development of more effective forms of economic exchange: coordinating different people's economic needs and enabling people to accumulate wealth so that investment is possible. Until the first problem has been solved, it is impossible for large numbers of people to participate in a single economic system. The second problem must be solved before the economic system can become sufficiently productive to support a very complex society. We can trace the development of successive forms of economic exchange, in fact, in terms of the progressive efficiency with which these problems have been solved. At the same time, we must also pay attention to the new problems which accompany each new solution.

We can conceptualize five relatively distinct forms of economic exchange, even though they are not actually so clear-cut and separate from one another as their analysis here might imply. The following sections thus concentrate on dominant trends rather than on forms of economic exchange that are mutually exclusive.

Gift exchange The most primitive form of economic exchange is **gift exchange,** or *the exchange between the individual and the group as a whole.* Gifts, by definition, are not given with the explicit understanding that something of equal value will be received in return immediately or at some specified time or even from the same person to whom the gift was given. Nevertheless, there is an *implicit* understanding that sooner or later the giver will receive other gifts in return, whether they are tangible or intangible, of approximately equal value (to the giver). Without this understanding, people would cease to give gifts, because they would not feel that it was worth it to them over the long run.

Take, for example, a group of girls who graduate from high school together and then get married, one after the other. Each receives gifts from the others before her wedding, without there being any formal agreement that she will give gifts of approximately equal value to the others. In the long run, though, each girl will have received roughly the same value of gifts from her friends. This is a simple example of gift exchange in modern society. The Social Security system in this country is a more complicated form. The original model of gift exchange comes from a sort of primitive communism in aboriginal tribes; each member contributes freshly killed game to the group and depends on others to do likewise when they can.

Such unspoken agreements can exist only when each member of the group has a high degree of faith in the others, and so they can operate effectively only in relatively small groups. As a group becomes too large for all of its members to know one another personally and to trust one another to play fair, other forms of exchange must become more important if the group is to stick together. It is perhaps for this reason that the idealistic principle "From each according to abilities, to each according to needs" has never formed a practical basis for organizing any sort of large group.

Barter   Just as gift exchange is the simplest exchange between individual and group, so **barter** *is the simplest form of individual-to-individual exchange.* Here, one specific item of material goods is exchanged directly for another, as when one person trades a bushel of apples to another in return for a bushel of corn. Services, too, may be exchanged in this way: You will help others put a roof on their new barn if they will help you dig some ditches on your land.

But this sort of exchange has serious drawbacks. First, it requires that you find someone who both *has* what you *want* and *wants* what you *have.* Since human needs and immediate possessions are so variable, it may be difficult for you to find such a person. Second, since many material goods are perishable, the question is not simply *whether* you can find this sort of person, but *how soon* you can find him or her. There may indeed be someone who wants the eggs that your hens laid this morning and who has the kind of knife that you want, but if you can't find that person until next month, you may as well eat the eggs today and forget about trading them for the knife.

Finally, barter usually requires some haggling before both parties are reasonably satisfied with the exchange. This can be quite time-consuming, and it slows down the pace of life altogether. Haggling may be fun, to be sure, but the thirty minutes you spend in agreeing how many eggs should be exchanged for a knife are thirty minutes that you cannot use in plowing your fields or working in your blacksmith shop. It is unlikely that any group ever got along for very long using a pure barter system. It is more likely that its members depended on gift exchange as well or else developed a more advanced type of barter.

Money barter   As soon as people came to agree that certain items—stone knives, clay pots, baskets of nuts, etc.—could always be used in exchange, they had begun to distinguish between the *generalized economic value* of an item and its immediate *utility.* Someone, for instance, might have been unable to find another person who was willing to trade a knife for a dozen eggs, but could find someone who was willing to accept the eggs in return for a clay pot. Even if the owner of the eggs did not need a pot at the moment, he or she knew that it would not spoil and that sooner or later someone with the right kind of knife would be willing to exchange it for the pot—not necessarily because the pot was needed, but because it could then be exchanged for something that the knife owner did need. The pot, in other words, came to be viewed not as something immediately useful, but as representing a certain amount of economic value that would always be of interest to others.

In this way, **money barter**—*the use of certain things as symbols of economic value rather than as items directly relevant to satisfying human needs* (in vaguely the same way we use money)—came into being. It is understandable that such items tended to be small and not likely to turn rotten or to break, so they could be carried about easily and depended on to retain their value. Ornaments in particular—bracelets, rings, jewelry—probably were used often in money barter because they possessed these special characteristics. Perhaps, too, their intrinsic aesthetic appeal made them appropriate for such use because it was so clearly divorced from utilitarian value. Among certain American Indian tribes, wampum (beads carved from shells and strung together in belts) was used quite explicitly as a kind of money. For many centuries, too, a king's wealth was measured in the sorts of things that a pirate's chest is supposed to hold: precious stones, silver dishes, golden necklaces, fine fabrics, and so on.

The advantages of treating some objects as embodying generalized economic value are clear. First, they allowed people to "store" economic value so that the problem of coordinating people's different economic needs was solved. One could turn eggs into their equivalent value and save it until needed without worrying that it would turn bad. This ability, in turn, greatly expanded the range of people with whom one could engage in economic exchange. And because value itself could now be stored, it became possible to accumulate wealth and to protect it; instead of owning twenty horses that might die or be stolen, one could own twenty gold necklaces and keep them hidden, knowing that they could be used in exchange whenever they were needed.

Having reached this stage, the next step needed was that of reducing these symbols of economic value to standardized units and then controlling their production.

Money economy The development of a **money-economy**—*the use of standardized symbols of generalized economic value (money) produced expressly for use in exchange*—must rank as one of the most important human inventions. At first, such units were simply small pieces of gold, silver, or other metals, and they were still assumed to be intrinsically valuable because of their durable beauty. But as the usefulness of *any* symbol of value became more apparent and as people found that they could depend on others to accept it in economic exchange without its having even aesthetic value, it became possible to substitute paper for metal. At first, of course, these were symbolic of gold or silver; they were "promises," in effect, that the holder could exchange them for the equivalent value in gold or other precious metal. However, as people developed increasing faith in one another's willingness to treat paper money as symbolizing economic value, even this connection was no longer needed. With the substitution in this country of Federal Reserve notes for silver certificates, paper money came to stand completely on its own as a medium of exchange that no longer required the backing of specific amounts of precious metal.

This is not the place to go extensively into economic theories, but a few aspects of money should be noted. First of all, as the use of money in economic exchange becomes habitual, it has an important effect on people's view of the world. As they come more and more to evaluate goods and services in terms of units of money, it becomes easier to compare anything with anything else. Now an individual can compare the cost of a month's vacation with the cost of an automobile and can thus plan his or her behavior more "rationally" in the sense of maximizing long-run material satisfactions (Weber, 1947).

The ability to store wealth in the form of money facilitates planning, too. It is possible, in fact, to see an important connection between the increasing use of money in economic exchange, which really began with the flow of gold from the New World into Europe in the sixteenth century, and the beginnings of "modern society" as it is characterized by increasing rationalization (in Weber's sense of the term; see Chapter 9) and economic growth. Certainly in this sense, the invention of money—and it was indeed *invented* by human beings—has had the most profound consequences for society.

It must be remembered, however, that the value of money—or what a unit of money is worth in terms of specific goods or services—depends on people's *agreeing* that it symbolizes a certain amount of "real value." This agreement, in turn, is determined largely by how much money there is in circulation compared to the amount of material goods and services available for exchange. If the amount of money rises, the prices of these goods and services (that is, their value expressed in terms of the amount of money people will exchange for them) will rise also. This is called *inflation,* meaning a lowering of the "real value" or "value in exchange" of each unit of money, and it is particularly harmful to people living on savings or fixed incomes, because they are depending on symbols which now have less buying power than formerly.

Conversely, a decrease in the amount of money relative to available goods and services is called *deflation,* and both prices and wages fall. Whereas those living on their savings or on fixed incomes are better off under these conditions, those depending on current incomes suffer, at least relatively if not more seriously because of increasing unemployment. When either inflation or deflation becomes serious, then, some part of the population will be hurt because of their society's dependence on a money economy. Although this fact is abundantly clear, no society yet has fully solved the problems of managing the production of money and regulating its flow so that its value remains stable. But the advantages gained through depending primarily on money as a medium of economic exchange obviously outweigh these dangers, and their solution lies in further economic innovation rather than in a return to barter or gift exchange.

Finance economy Growing along with the form of economic exchange we have called a money economy has been a fifth one, a **finance economy,** which is *characterized by the increasing importance of money itself as an object of* *interest because of its ability to generate more money.* A bank, for instance, makes its money produce more money whenever it loans (or, actually, "rents") the use of that money to a borrower for a certain period of time.

The relatively unchanging value of money (except in cases of runaway inflation or deflation), in contrast to the changing immediacy of human needs, makes it possible for someone to rent his or her extra money to someone else who needs it now—and who will presumably return the principal as well as the "rent" at a specific date in the future. The old idea that collecting interest (or *usury*) is immoral because money itself is "sterile" and cannot reproduce itself was gradually abandoned as it became clear that this could indeed happen.

This occurs through the process of *investment*, whereby accumulated wealth is used to buy and combine labor and raw materials to produce more goods at lower cost, thus increasing the amount of material goods available for exchange. These goods represent "real value," and so society's relative affluence is increased. (It is important, though, that the supply of money also increase so that prices do not decline to the point where further investment and production are discouraged. Whether this happens because more gold and silver come into circulation, as in previous centuries, or because the government prints more paper money, the value of money thus remains reasonably constant, and economic growth can continue.)

The invention of the *corporation*, a legal device that allows a group of people to act economically as a "legal person" to borrow, lend, enter into contracts, etc., was necessary as larger and larger amounts of capital were required for effective investment. The increasing importance of corporations in the economic system is due primarily to their control of larger and larger amounts of wealth relative to the wealth controlled by private individuals.

As larger and larger amounts of money are needed by organizations such as corporations and governments to cover short-term discrepancies between the dates of expected income and of necessary expenditures, these organizations must borrow from one another. And when millions of dollars are involved, the interest that their "owner" can receive for even a few hours' use of that money can be substantial. Thus banks and other lenders are quite ready to compete with one another for such business, and the management of interest rates becomes more important (Mayer, 1976).

An increasing amount of economic exchange, then, takes place between organizations rather than individuals. Although corporations and governments may act legally as individuals, it seems fair to characterize a finance economy as involving exchange between groups, with their individual members working *for* these groups. Over and above the production of material goods, then, a finance economy is increasingly one predominated by occupations that deal entirely with the ownership and management of money itself.

A second aspect of the economic system also becomes more prominent in a finance economy. This is the increasing importance of "credit," or one's ability to repay a loan later on. The tremendous amount of installment buying in the United States is based on the faith that many people *will* be able to repay loans in the future, and so goods and services are produced *now* in return for promises rather than for "hard cash." The amount of economic exchange thus increases just as though larger amounts of money were actually in circulation now. And although this can intensify economic growth through making possible larger accumulations of wealth, it also places more and more burden on the mutual faith that must underlie all economic exchange. When this faith fails, as it did in the Crash of 1929, the consequences can be disastrous.

Summing up   To conclude this discussion of the different forms of economic exchange, it should be emphasized that they are not so distinct in real life that they do not exist side by side in a particular society. As was evident in the example of the girls exchanging wedding gifts, we still find gift exchange going on in even the most advanced societies, and barter can be important on certain occasions as well, even though such exchanges make up only the tiniest part of the whole economic system. Different societies and different eras, then, can be characterized by the form of exchange that is dominant in each one, but we must not forget that even the most complex society employs primitive forms of exchange under special circumstances.

THE ECONOMY AND OTHER SOCIAL INSTITUTIONS

Thus far we have looked only at the central social structure of the economic institution. Since it is an abstraction from society, however, consisting of statuses and their interrelated roles rather than of concrete individuals, its nature and operations cannot be divorced from other institutions. The individuals who occupy statuses in the economic institution also occupy statuses in the family, political, and religious institutions as well, so it would be impossible to believe that what goes on in any one of these will not have consequences for what goes on in the others.

Mechanisms of Coordination

Perhaps the basic mechanism through which different institutions are coordinated is people's ability to *plan*—to look ahead and make sure that what they do in one situation (or while occupying one status) will not interfere with what they want to do in another situation. For example, a person is not likely to accept a job (a position in the economic institution) if it will require spending too much time away from his or her spouse and children, even if the job would be very desirable in terms of pay alone. The decision to take the job or not thus contributes to one institution's influencing the other. Similarly, a dedicated pacifist is not likely to take a job in a munitions plant, for there would be a conflict between his or her values (whether religious or political) and his or her economic activity.

Here we have two types of institutional coordination: the *physical* coordination of different activities and the *logical* coordination of the meanings of these activities. It is through these mechanisms at the individual level, together with such organized mechanisms as labor negotiations between cities and municipal unions, the impact of religious values on votes in Congress, and welfare programs that aid dependent children, that the institutions of society influence one another and are coordinated with at least modest effectiveness.

It is clear, though, that at different points in history, different institutions have been dominant; that is, they have influenced other institutions more than they have been influenced by them. In the most primitive human societies the family provided the basis for all social organization; economic, political, and religious activities were carried out largely as extensions of the family. As societies increased in complexity, it was often the religious institution—particularly as it included political functions as well—that dominated the other institutions. The conflict between church and state in medieval Europe can be viewed in this perspective as the slow, bitter separation of the political institution from the religious, resulting in the dominance of the political institution until well into the nineteenth century. Since then, it has probably been the economic institution that has called the tune for the other social institutions, even though with the growth of socialism, we are seeing a resurgence of the political institution.

But this topic falls more directly under the heading of social change, which is discussed more thoroughly in Chapter 18. Of more immediate interest here is a specific case of institutional relationships, one which has been of deep interest to sociologists and historians for three-quarters of a century.

Economy and Religion

The relationship between the economic and religious institutions, especially in the sixteenth and seventeenth centuries, has been the focus of a number of brilliant—and controversial—analyses. Perhaps the most famous of these is Max Weber's book *The Protestant Ethic and the Spirit of Capitalism*, first published in 1904. In it, Weber suggested that it was the **Protestant ethic**—*the particular combination of values and attitudes embodied in Protestantism*—that created the conditions necessary for the rise of modern capitalism during the sixteenth century.

The Protestant ethic, as Weber analyzed it, included a religiously inspired emphasis on hard work, saving, and self-denial as necessary (but not sufficient) conditions for religious salvation. Worldly activity was not carried out for the sake of profit or the luxuries that money would buy, but as a religious duty—as a "calling." And although worldly success might be a sign that one was "saved," it was not meant to be enjoyed. Translated into everyday activities, these beliefs led people to save and to reinvest the profits from their labors, since this was actually the only thing they *could* do with their money if luxuries were defined as sinful. Obviously, economic activity guided by these principles would become more and more profitable through the benign cycle of produce-save-invest-produce *more*, and so on. All of the economically rational means through which one could become more successful (even if not enjoying it personally) came to be defined as legitimate and worthy of full religious approval. Capitalism, then, was a specific economic consequence of innovations in the religious institution.

Weber's thesis, in other words, was that a change in the religious institution led to a change in the economic institution. However, there have been several countertheses. R. H. Tawney (1926) of England has argued the reverse of the Weberian thesis. As he analyzes the situation, it was the needs of a growing economic institution that required religious legitimation, and thus it was change in the *economic* institution that led to change in the *religious* institution. In his book *Religion and the Rise of Capitalism*, Tawney says essentially that changes in the social structure (the economic relationships) in this instance came *before* changes in the cultural structure (the way people interpret the world and guide their actions in it), even though there was continuing interplay between the two institutions which influenced the further development of each one. More recently, Amintore Fanfani (1955) has argued that Protestantism simply severed the ties between religious precepts and economic endeavor, so that capitalism was free to develop without interference from religious principles.

The entire argument, of course, is not one that can be settled once and for all, and we are not really in a position to decide which interpretation of the historical record is more acceptable today. We can, however, point to changes in these social institutions that led to changes in the family and in the political institution, just to demonstrate that no part of society is completely isolated from other parts.

Economy and Family

As capitalism developed, particularly after the Industrial Revolution got under way, the family was forced to become a smaller unit (not through producing fewer children, but through "discarding" grandparents, maiden aunts, cousins, and the like) for the sake of increased physical mobility. The breadwinner of the family had to be able to go where employment was to be had, and it is easier to move a nuclear family than one that includes others besides parents and children. The move from the land (farming) to industry also took the father out of the home for ten or twelve hours a day, too, so that the wife gradually had to take on more responsibility for the house and the children (Parsons and Smelser, 1956).

As the Industrial Revolution progressed, the economic institution also began to need more and more skilled workers. Both this demand and the Protestants' belief that individuals should be able to read the Bible for themselves led to the spread of public education during the nineteenth century, a movement which took some of the family's advanced-socialization responsibilities away from it and gave them to the schools. The family's functions were thus further reduced in scope by the needs of other institutions.

Economy and Polity

With the decline in supremacy of the religious institution in the more complex societies of the world, the two remaining major social institutions have been the economic and the political. They stand in a curious relationship. The political institution controls the right to use force (see Chapter 16, on social control, and Chapter 12, on the political institution) and thus has the power to establish and enforce the rules under which economic activities are carried on. At the same time, however, it must rely on the economic institution to provide the wherewithal to carry out its activities: tax monies to purchase arms, build highways, pay civil servants, institute welfare programs, etc. Neither could operate effectively without the other, and yet there are those who would relegate one or the other to a virtually powerless role in their relationship.

Some, for instance, would restrain the political institution—the government, in particular—to doing nothing more than preventing the use of force and fraud in the marketplace. This position, sometimes known as a *laissez faire* economic philosophy, would allow economic processes to develop without any hindrance at all. On the other hand, some would prefer to have all economic activities controlled entirely by the government, so that the self-interest which supposedly drives the economic system would be totally subordinated to the collective good. In extreme form, this is communism; somewhere between it and private enterprise, or capitalism, stands socialism.

At the root of the controversy lie differing conceptions of the relationship between private and public interests. Adam Smith's "invisible hand," described in his famous defense of the *laissez faire* idea, *The Wealth of Nations* (1776), was an argument that the private greed of individuals who are competing with one another in an open market would in the long run be good for society because it would "automatically" (as if guided by an invisible hand) lead to the best possible balance among price, quality, and quantity. The economic system would thus be maximally productive and maximally effective in satisfying people's needs. In isolation, greed is not an admirable virtue, but when greed is pitted against greed, Smith argued, the result is beneficial to all.

Smith, however, failed to see that the operations of an open market would lead to the accumulation of unfair economic advantage, to monopolies, and thus to a severe distortion of the "open market" conditions that he took for granted. At the other extreme, Karl Marx, a century later (see Appendix 2, on sociological theory), saw quite clearly the tendency for the wealthy to use their advantages to obtain control of the market for both goods and services so that they could further increase their wealth. He saw also that the economic and political institutions cannot remain separate so long as politicians want wealth and the wealthy want governmental policies that are to their advantage. Assuming an inevitable tendency for the rich and powerful to grow richer and more powerful at the expense of others, Marx argued that the very existence of "private property" was responsible for this and that the only humane solution would be to substitute collective ownership for private ownership. What Marx failed to foresee, however, was that the struggle for political power (especially as it would then entail economic power as well) could be just as inhumane and exploitive as the struggle for profit and property.

As long as the political institution is charged with maintaining the general welfare of society, it cannot escape at least minimal responsibility for trying to manage the economic system. And as long as the most dependable motivation for economic activity is private gain, the concept of private property and the

right to increase one's private wealth cannot be entirely undermined by political intervention in the economic process. Finding a suitable balance, however, between private acquisitiveness and its consequences on the one hand, and politically imposed constraints that seek to control those consequences on the other, has not been easy.

The solution that most nontotalitarian countries have worked out seems to be essentially one of giving private economic interests considerable leeway and then stepping in to redress the resulting imbalances through various forms of taxation, restrictions on economic competition, and programs that compensate some of those who have failed to succeed in the economic institution. The system is a patchwork quilt without a coherent philosophy; it is full of discrepancies that bestow favors and impose penalties seemingly at random on different parts of the population; and it is continually changing as new laws and new types of economic regulation are devised under pressure from different interest groups. Yet unsystematic as they are, such efforts are necessary to check the processes that would otherwise lead to an increasing maldistribution of wealth and thus to increasing dissatisfaction with "the system" by larger and larger proportions of society's membership.

To the sociologist, the relations between the economic and political institutions are of particular interest because they not only have such crucial practical consequences for society, but also illustrate the dilemmas that arise when tendencies toward institutional autonomy (embodied particularly in the third "principle of social exchange") run into the concrete realities of institutional interdependence.

SUMMARY

This has been very much a sociological examination of the economic institution, for it has ignored such things as the different forms of economic organization, the relative size of different parts of the economic system, and the consequences for individuals of involvement in different sectors of the system. Our concern has been with the basic structure of the economic institution, particularly as it is a necessary consequence of the essential nature of economic commodities.

◄ Government and the nuclear power industry are closely intertwined, with the industry being heavily dependent on government support and regulation, and the government seeking new sources of supplies of energy. But many politicians and citizens, such as these antinuclear demonstrators at Seabrook, N.H., oppose the use of nuclear power, arguing that its hazards outweigh its economic benefits. (© Eric A. Roth, The Picture Cube)

Property rights, rather than concrete goods and services, are the socially important focus of economic exchange, and these can be subdivided in many ways. Their differentiation has been an important aspect of the growing complexity of the economic institution. As this occurs, we can identify five major forms of economic exchange, even though they are by no means mutually exclusive.

Gift exchange, the most primitive form, involves exchange between the group and its individual members, but becomes undependable after the group increases beyond a relatively small size. *Barter,* the simplest form of exchange between individuals, involves the exchange of one concrete item or service directly for another, although the problem of answering the question "Who *has* what I need, and *needs* what I have?" places severe limits on the range of people with whom one can interact in this manner.

Money barter, in which certain objects serve as representations of economic value in its pure form rather than as the focus of utilitarian interest, is the first step toward a more efficient separation between "average value" and immediate personal need. The invention of money, the basis of a *money economy,* completes this separation. As there develops increasing acceptance of the trustworthiness of *symbols* of value, a higher and higher proportion of economic exchanges is carried out using money. This serves to cancel out discrepancies in the timing of individual needs, allows the number of people involved in a single economic system to expand enormously, facilitates rational planning and the accumulation of wealth, and thus makes possible more and more investment in increased economic efficiency.

Finally, with increasing amounts of wealth available, usually held by groups rather than individuals, a *finance economy* comes into being. This is characterized by a special interest in money as itself an income-producing commodity, the growing centrality of economic organizations in the structure and functioning of the economic system, and greater importance of loans and credit as a means of increasing the effective amount of money currently in circulation.

As structures of interrelated social statuses, institutions exist side by side in society and are coordinated chiefly by the fact that society's members usually occupy statuses in all of them. They must thus plan their activities in terms of both physical and logical integration, and this serves to coordinate different institutions; additional coordination is provided through organized negotiations between groups representing different institutions.

In examining interinstitutional relationships, the simultaneous rise of Protestantism and of capitalism in Europe provides an occasion to look at the analyses of Max Weber and others of relationships between the economic and religious institutions of society. The increasing subordination of the family to the economic institution is a clear case of one institution's dominating another.

Finally, the problems that have arisen in working out the relationship between the economic and political institutions show clearly the conflict between tendencies toward institutional autonomy and the realities of their actually intricate interdependence.

SUGGESTED READINGS

Fanfani, Amintore, *Catholicism, Protestantism, and Capitalism* (New York: Sheed and Ward, 1955). This book by a former Italian premier argues that the development of capitalism was at least partly due to the way in which Protestantism drew a sharp line between this world and the next—and then ignored this one.

Heilbroner, Robert L., *The Making of Economic Society* (Englewood Cliffs, N.J.: Prentice-Hall, 1962). An exceptionally readable account of the historical growth of the economic institution and its basic characteristics in modern society.

Maus, Marcel, *The Gift* [1925] (New York: Norton, 1967). One of the most distinguished pupils of his uncle, Emile Durkheim, Maus carried on the Durkheimian tradition in French sociology. In this book he analyzes the social conditions necessary for gift exchange and its continuing significance today.

Mayer, Martin, *The Bankers* (New York: Ballantine, 1976). This is an excellent introduction to the part of the present-day American economic system that deals directly with money as a commodity, ranging from checking accounts to the Federal Reserve system.

Parsons, Talcott, and Neil J. Smelser, *Economy and Society* (New York: Free Press, 1956). Analyzing the Industrial Revolution in England, Parsons and Smelser develop a sophisticated theory of the place of the economic institution in society.

Smelser, Neil J., *The Sociology of Economic Life* (Englewood Cliffs, N.J.: Prentice-Hall, 1963). For some reason, "economic sociology" has never become as important as "political sociology," although here Smelser shows what this special interest within sociology will probably cover when it has developed.

Tawney, R. H., *Religion and the Rise of Capitalism* (New York: Harcourt, Brace and World, 1926). Here, the British economic historian differs with Weber, arguing that economic developments in the sixteenth century had at least as much influence on Protestantism as the reverse, and perhaps a good deal more.

Weber, Max, *The Protestant Ethic and the Spirit of Capitalism* [1904–1905], trans. by Talcott Parsons (New York: Scribner, 1930). Weber's classic interpretation of the relationship between the Protestant Reformation and the rise of capitalism in sixteenth- and seventeenth-century Europe. Interestingly, the foreword is by R. H. Tawney.

_____, *The Theory of Social and Economic Organization* [1922], trans. by A. M. Henderson and Talcott Parsons (New York: Oxford University Press, 1947). Part II of this book, pp. 158–323, is particularly valuable as a detailed consideration of the forms of economic exchange and the importance of a money economy.

Glossary

Barter Economic interaction that involves the direct exchange of two items (goods or services) that have direct value in use to the participants.

Division of labor The separation of a complex job into its component parts, assigning each to a particular individual or group, and organizing their cooperation so that productivity per unit of human energy is increased because of the increased efficiency that comes with specialization. In the broader sense the term also refers to the development of occupational specialization throughout a society. (See Chapter 9, on formal organizations, and Chapter 18, on social change, for other aspects of this topic.)

Economic value The relative importance of a material good or service in comparison to the importance of other goods or services. When this importance is measured by someone's immediate need for it, it can be called *value in use*. When this measure is averaged over time and in terms of many people's relative need for the thing, it comes closer to the idea of *pure economic value*. The use of money as a reliable symbol of pure economic value makes it possible to assign a meaningful price to any object of economic interest, which facilitates economic planning and exchange.

Finance economy The most advanced system of economic exchange. In it, huge sums of money are controlled by groups, money itself becomes an object of economic interest because of the profit that can be made through loaning it, and credit becomes as important as the individual's or group's current wealth.

Gift exchange The simplest system of economic exchange, in which each member of the group contributes whatever he or she can to the group as a whole and in turn receives the necessities of life from the group. It approaches Marx's ideal of the abolition of private property, but probably depends too much on mutual trust and surveillance to work effectively in large groups.

Money barter The system of economic exchange in which durable objects that have intrinsic value in use (such as stone knives or gold ornaments) come to be treated also as symbols of pure economic value and are often accepted in economic exchange for this reason rather than for their ability to satisfy immediate needs.

Money economy The system of economic exchange in which there is a clear separation between the pure economic value represented by units of money and the value in use of specific goods and services. The increasing use of money (standardized units of economic value) can greatly enlarge the number of people who participate in a single economic system, encourage rationality in economic decisions, and facilitate the growth of wealth which can be used for investment.

Property The relationship of *ownership* between an individual or group and an object of economic interest. Although the physical possession of something seems the clearest form of ownership, it is a dependable relationship only to the extent that others agree that this relationship exists. The essence of property is thus *property rights.* Since rights can be subdivided, different aspects of a thing can be owned by different people. Economic exchange thus becomes really the exchange of these rights rather than simply of goods and services for each other or for money.

Protestant ethic The name Weber gave to the combination of attitudes and beliefs that characterized most Protestant sects, especially the Calvinists, in sixteenth- and seventeenth-century Europe. It included an emphasis on hard work, saving, and self-denial—all outgrowths of Protestant beliefs—and Weber argued that these attitudes were particularly conducive to the growth of capitalism.

12

The Political Institution

AUTHORITY

In order to survive, any group or society must be able to mobilize and coordinate its members' activities for defense and for the achievement of collective purposes. Survival requires that an assault by another group, and also deviant behavior by any of its own members, be countered by the group's collective response. Beyond this, promoting the general welfare often requires that the group's members obey certain rules. They must do certain things (for example, pay taxes, serve in the armed forces if drafted) and refrain from certain other things (for example, assaulting one another, poisoning the water supply) if the group is to remain in existence.

Since planning these rules and securing compliance with them is often a complex task that involves many specialized roles, it is clear that they must be directed by a particular individual or group. Human beings are not naturally programed for such activities the way that bees or ants are. And it cannot be assumed that all of the members of a group will *want* to take part in such activities or even agree that a specific collective goal *should* be sought. If collective action is to be effective, however, those people who disagree cannot be relieved of their responsibilities as members of the group. So leadership, or direction for group activities, is not enough; it must be direction that can be *enforced* if necessary.

To enforce an order is to compel someone to obey it by threatening to impose some sort of negative sanction (an unpleasant experience) on that person if it is not obeyed. In the most general sense **power** is based on *the ability to impose negative sanctions, without fear of retaliation, on one* *who disobeys.* But power is unreliable if its use is not supported by others. Leadership would be reduced to mere physical superiority in hand-to-hand combat if a leader could not call on others to assist in enforcing an order. And the others must give this assistance without having to be coerced; otherwise, the leaders would have more disobedience to deal with, and his or her power would be weakened further.

To ensure dependable leadership, and thus effective collective action, it is necessary that most of society's members agree voluntarily that a particular individual or group of individuals has the *right* to make decisions for the group as a whole—to provide directions for collective action—and also the right to enforce these decisions when necessary.

The right to use power is called **authority.** Its foundations, the ways in which it is allocated and limited, and the ways in which it is used and misused make up the central sociological characteristics of the political institution.

THE CONCEPT OF POLITICAL EXCHANGE

The political institution is that structure of interrelated statuses within society, and the norms governing the rights and obligations of their occupants, which together seek to meet two continuing social needs: the need for order in social relationships and the need for organized action to meet problems that face the group as a whole. If most of the members of a group or society were not willing on occasion to devote their energies to the achievement of collective goals rather than to their private interests, there would be no political institution—and no society, for that matter. But it is obvious that they do. They fight their country's wars, pay taxes for the support of its government's activities, and obey its laws even when it is inconvenient to do so. Why should they do this?

We can think of at least two answers to this question. First, they may serve their country out of sincere conviction that this is what they *want* to do, either out of long-range self-interest or a sense that their goals and society's goals are complementary or identical. On the other hand, as is perhaps more frequently mentioned, they may do it out of *fear* of the consequences of disobedience. From the individual's point of view, the second explanation may be more compelling: "They'll send me to jail if I don't pay my taxes!" But why the prospect of punishment for disobedience should be taken so seriously is something that requires further examination.

Punishment is reasonably certain only if its target cannot escape those who would impose it. If most third parties did *not* approve of its imposition, then, the "victim" might expect a reasonably good chance of escaping it. The "fear" argument thus seems valid only if most *other* people believe that the call to an action that will benefit the group (e.g., being drafted, having to file a tax return or serve on a jury, etc.) *should* be heeded. So we are still left with the question of why most people want to do what their groups need them to do—or at least want most *other* people to do these things—and this leads us back to the first answer to our original question: People do what their groups need them to do because in some way or other they *agree* that they should.

Commodities in Political Exchange

If people are to grant someone the right to make decisions for the group as a whole and to enforce those decisions, we assume that they must get something in return. What they get is directions for actions that will presumably benefit the group as a whole and thus each of its individual members. If, however, someone is granted authority only to make and implement *specific* decisions, his or her leadership of the group will be ineffective because it will be impossible to make long-run plans for the group, and the possibility that this authority may be withdrawn tomorrow can undermine his or her ability to enforce today's decision. (A good example of this sort of exchange is a pirate crew, whose members agree to obey their captain only so long as his leadership brings continued success in raiding other ships and ports.)

It is clear, then, that a leader must be able to count on continued authority if he or she is to be effective. Rather than agreeing to obey a leader only in return for guidance in particular activities, political exchange becomes more effective when this agreement becomes more generalized. When this happens we call it **loyalty,** and it constitutes *a readiness to accept the leader's directions (within limits, of course) regardless of the specific nature of those directions.* At the heart of political exchange is thus the exchange of the right to make decisions for the group (the allocation of authority to one or a few individuals that is supported by generalized loyalty) in return for decisions and guidance that will benefit the group.

At this point we come to a problem central to all political systems: *Who* shall determine the specific actions that will be required of society's members, and who, therefore, shall be given the right to enforce those decisions? Because the leader's decisions can be enforced, they will have important consequences for many people, and so the right to make them—or at least to participate in determining their content—is of continuing interest to the members of society.

The purest form of the "political commodity" would be the right to make and enforce decisions for the group without any regard for its members'

President Jimmy Carter looks on as President Anwar Sadat and Prime Minister Menachem Begin, representing the people of Egypt and Israel, sign the Egyptian-Israeli peace treaty on the lawn of the White House, March 26, 1979. (U.P.I.)

wishes, in the way that an absolute monarch or a totalitarian dictator is supposed to be able to decide what others must do. However, this right is almost impossible to exercise in practice, for even a dictator must consider the limits to which the people can be pushed. Therefore, the opportunity to *participate* in determining the content of decisions for the group must substitute for it.

In a democratic society the right to vote is the basic embodiment of this opportunity. It may not seem to us to be a scarce commodity, since over the past sixty years the franchise has been extended to nearly all adults. In the past, however, the opportunity to vote was much more restricted, and even today it is considered a form of punishment to deprive an individual of the right to vote. Beyond voting, the individual may seek a greater degree of influence on political decisions in a number of ways: trying to enlist others' sympathy for his or her cause, communicating directly with those currently responsible for decisions, and even seeking to occupy a decision-making status (that is, a political office). The position of "citizen" is the basic status involved in the political institution, together with all of the offices that make up the formal political structure. There are also informal statuses involved: member of an advisory group, influential political columnist, leader of an interest group, and so on.

Actually making decisions for the group may be entirely the prerogative of a dictator who is guided solely by a sense of what should be done and of what the people can realistically be persuaded or forced to do. It may be much more the act of someone who is representing the will of the people and who, as an elected leader, has little or no opportunity to act arbitrarily without regard for the wishes of his or her supporters. In each society, though, there is one individual or a small group of individuals who must finally make decisions for the group *official*—that is, to enact decisions so that at a certain time they become binding on the members of that society. *Der Führer* issues a decree, the *junta* makes a proclamation, the President signs a bill into law: These are the signals for others to begin doing something that they were not doing before (or sometimes to stop doing something that was previously allowed).

The chief obligation of this individual is to make decisions and to put them into effect. The chief right that the occupant of this status has is to expect others to accept and obey these decisions. Occupancy of the top political position gives an individual the greatest possible influence on the content of these decisions or of the commodity which forms the focus of the political institution. But since only one person at a time may occupy this position, the hope of gaining it is obviously not enough to keep the entire institution going. Rather, since even its occupant is not entirely free to choose courses of action for the society, it is, as we noted above, *the opportunity to influence* political decisions that serves as the basic commodity around whose exchange the political institution is organized.

All of the statuses that make up this institution, both formal and informal, are linked together through a common concern for the acquisition of this commodity, which is one form of *power.*

THREE BASES OF POWER

We may define *power* as the ability to get others to do what we tell them to do, even when they would rather not. There are several ways in which this can be accomplished (they are discussed briefly in Chapter 16, on social control), and it is important at this point to examine them systematically.

There are three basic ways we can change the "direction" of others' activities. First, we can offer a reward (either material or symbolic) in return for compliance with our wishes, or we can threaten to withhold something that they want if they do not comply. Second, we can persuade them that they can reach their own goals more effectively by doing as we suggest than by continuing in their present behavior. And third, we can use physical force to make them halt their current activity and can threaten to use more if they do not comply with our directions.

Contingent Rewards and Deprivations

The first type of power, the use of **contingent rewards and deprivations**, is, clearly, based on *the manipulation of the various sorts of "rewards"* that we control. We can offer money in return for service, offer to help a friend with homework in return for the use of a motorbike, or hold out the prospect of praise for a job well done. By the same token, we can threaten to withhold certain otherwise expected rewards: friendship and cooperation, respect, continued employment, etc. Because this form of power involves only the use of things that *we* control, it is available to everyone and is probably the chief form of power used in any group.

Its effectiveness, however, depends on others' wanting the rewards we can control, so it is not entirely reliable. The person who does not want our money or our friendship cannot be influenced by our wishes, and so we are powerless to influence his or her behavior.

Information and Inspiration

This second form of power depends on neither the manipulation of rewards nor the use of force. Instead, the use of **information and inspiration** as a basis of power *gets others to do as we wish by pointing out that they will profit by following our suggestion.* For instance, if I want someone to patronize my brother's shoestore, I can mention that he is having a special sale this week; if I want someone to stop parking in front of my driveway, I can point out a better parking place nearby. This technique, it should be noted, differs from the manipulation of rewards because it does not involve information about what *I* am going to do in the future. It is based simply on information about the situation in which others are acting.

It is also possible to get others to comply with our wishes by strengthening their commitment to a particular goal, as we do when we "inspire" someone to work harder, or by actually getting them to accept new goals. Those who seek to persuade others to share their religious beliefs are employing the latter technique, and when they succeed they have changed others' behavior by changing their personal goals.

Like the use of contingent rewards, power based on information and inspiration is available to anyone, but it too is unreliable. We may not have any information that is relevant to another's behavior, and we may be unable to influence his or her goals. Thus we cannot depend on this form of power in all cases to help us get others to comply with our wishes.

Physical Force

The use of **physical force** in dealing with others refers basically to *the restraint of physical movement and the infliction of pain.* Since the latter often depends on the former (one cannot spank a naughty child if the child cannot be caught), the former is the more important. The infliction of pain is effective primarily as a contingency ("*If* you do that again, I'll have to spank you;" "Mutiny at sea *will* be punished by flogging"), but it is not the most important thing about force as a basis of power.

Even the threat to inflict pain in response to disobedience is not entirely reliable. Some individuals refuse to reveal military secrets under torture, just as some children persist in misbehaving even though they know it will lead to a spanking. Not even the threat of death is always effective: Religious martyrs have preferred execution to giving up their beliefs, and homicide rates are not significantly influenced by the restoration of capital punishment (Bedau, 1964).

The only completely reliable use of physical force, then, assuming that it can be applied, is in restraining a person's physical movements. It is thus the most reliable form of power for making others *stop* doing certain things, even though it is less effective in making them *do* certain things. Being held in a prison cell can certainly prevent someone from robbing banks, but it cannot make that person paint a picture or even speak politely to the guards. To be sure, once someone cannot escape from a place or defend his or her person, other things can be done: Pain can be inflicted, property can be taken away, and things like reading materials, companionship, warmth, and even food and water can be withheld. The physical restraint of movement, then, is the basis on which all other forms of physical pain and deprivation depend, and it can be resisted only by the use of superior physical force.

All of us *could* use physical force in our dealings with others, of course, but then everyone else would be forced to use it too, and we would quickly find ourselves in a Hobbesian world where life is "solitary, poor, nasty, brutish, and short." Instead, we all have a vested interest in being assured that others will *not* use physical force whenever they feel like it. And although we cannot eliminate the possibility that they *might* use it, we can and have gone a long way in keeping the probability of its use down to a minimum.

What we have done, not so much through a formal and explicit social contract of the sort Locke (see Appendix 2) spoke of, but through a long cut-and-try process from which emerged those forms of social organization that are generally successful, is to see to it that the right to employ physical force against others within a group is clearly assigned to some people and withheld from all others. Further, we have defined the circumstances under which this right may be exercised: Except when force is needed for self-defense, we have agreed that it should be exercised only in the service of the group as a whole. The use of force in the service of private interests is thus vigorously discouraged (even if it cannot be entirely eliminated), because to do anything else would be to invite virtual chaos.

In discussing the use of physical force, then, we are led finally to the question of who is given the *right* to use it, rather than of who *can* use it. The distinction is similar to that pointed out in Chapter 11 between property and property rights. Our concern is with the social structures and processes through which this right is assigned to certain individuals and with the ways in which restrictions are placed on its use.

This third type of power entails the right to make people suffer through being deprived of property, health, freedom, or even life itself. Clearly, if someone does not want what you have, you cannot use rewards to influence his or her behavior. If you have no information relevant to the situation or cannot be "inspirational," you cannot influence his or her behavior. But if the group has given you the right to employ physical force whenever someone will not obey your orders (orders that presumably represent the group's wishes rather than simply your own), that person will find it impossible to ignore you. If your orders are not obeyed, you can impose some form of suffering whether that person likes it or not.

Authority

The right to give orders and the right to use force in seeing that they are carried out together constitute *authority*. This is essentially the right to make or to administer decisions for the group that are binding on all its members, backed up by the right to use force under specified circumstances in seeing that they are obeyed.

Only this type of power can form the foundation of political leadership and guarantee that at least a minimally acceptable level of order and of collective effort in the service of the group can be maintained. It is the only form of power that can make people do something they don't want to do, and the right to exercise it must underlie all formal political structures. It is the *right* of the police officer to use force if necessary (under conditions specified by law) to arrest someone who has broken the law; it is the *authority* of the government that gives the officer this right and that enables him or her to call on others for assistance if he or she cannot personally muster the amount of physical force necessary to do the job.

Most of the time, simply the fact that this right has been *assigned* to certain persons enables the government to maintain order; the right to *use* force does not need to be continually exercised. Knowing that all of the government's potential instruments of physical force lie behind the police officer's whistle and the order to "Pull over," we are usually willing to obey.

THE FOUNDATIONS OF AUTHORITY

In discussing the political institution, we are concerned with not only the nature of authority, but also the means by which people acquire this form of power. We are interested both in how someone comes to occupy a status that carries with it the right to use or direct the use of force and in how he or she acquires the right to participate in making decisions for the group that can be enforced this way. How do people get to be presidents or queens or chieftains? How do they persuade others that it is right for them and their associates to direct the use of physical force within their groups when necessary, while denying its use to others?

It is clear that there is considerable psychological gratification in being an acknowledged leader, even when this entails no special material gain. There is real satisfaction in being looked up to, even if one is unable to put into effect all the policies one believes would be best for the group. Thus many people would like to hold authority, or at least to participate closely in the exercise of authority, and we can say that authority is a scarce commodity for which there will always be competition. This means, in turn, that the group must develop some method through which authority is assigned to certain people—procedures that will produce a minimum amount of disagreement within the group about the fairness of the process.

Physical prowess alone might be sufficient to determine who will lead a band of apes or a gang of children, but since two small people can usually defeat a bigger person in physical combat, individual superiority in brute strength cannot by itself guarantee that someone will retain a position of leadership. Leadership must be accepted on grounds other than fear. There must develop some form of reasoning by which the members of the group or society can agree willingly that it is right for one individual to give orders, backed by the use of force when necessary, and that it would be wrong for someone else to give such orders.

This problem brings us to the heart of the political institution—the matter of the assignment of authority in such a way that most members of the group accept it. More specifically, this is the question of the various ways in which the assignment and exercise of authority are made *legitimate* or normatively acceptable to most people.

Here we must turn again to the work of Max Weber, the German economic historian and sociologist whose work *The Protestant Ethic and the Spirit of Capitalism* was discussed in Chapter 11. Weber also pioneered in the analysis of political systems, proposing three "ideal types" of authority, or three different types of reasoning that serve to legitimate the assignment of authority (Weber, 1947).

Traditionalistic Authority

Weber's first type of authority is called **traditionalistic**, meaning that someone is given *the right to rule mainly on the basis of tradition:* "This is the way things have always been." It is the most primitive type of authority and is probably rooted in early family relationships where the father was the authority simply because he was the oldest and probably the strongest member of that group. A child's unquestioning acceptance of the parents' right to give orders is a good illustration of what is involved in traditionalistic authority.

As far as society goes, such authority is presumably legitimated by the fact that once people know where it is located, or who has it, it is easier to keep things this way than to go through the turmoil of trying to reassign it to some-one else. Almost by definition, if the ruler's authority is based on tradition, there will be few if any clear-cut rules describing how it can be vested in any-one else while he or she is alive, so that the only way this can be done is through revolution.

A king is the king because his father was the king, even though it is rare that a traditionalistic ruler will base all claims to authority on this biological fact. Rather, divine justification will be invoked as well: "By the grace of God, King (or Queen) of England and Scotland, Lord Protector of Ireland . . ." etc.

There is no explicit bargain or terms of political exchange between ruler and ruled under traditionalistic authority, and in principle the ruler may act as arbitrarily and capriciously as he or she pleases. The ruler's subjects cannot point to any formal, explicit rights that they have to resist obeying his or her commands unless they actually create such rights—as was done by the English knights who forced King John to sign the Magna Carta in 1215 and later by the signers of the American Declaration of Independence. Even without developing such formal statements of rights, however, people can always try to resist a ruler's orders, using methods that range from being slow to obey, all the way to outright rebellion.

Thus, although there is no explicit statement of the rights of subjects under traditionalistic authority, there are nevertheless many unwritten restrictions on its use, and the ruler violates them only at some risk. Since it is extremely difficult to rule a large group on the basis of fear alone, there must be a substantial amount of agreement by the citizens that they should obey the ruler's commands, and this can be sustained only if those commands are within reason.

Charismatic Authority

The second of Weber's types, *charismatic authority*, is essentially what was discussed above as power based on "inspiration"; the word *charisma* means "gift of grace." A leader possessing **charisma** seems to *rule by virtue of personal qualities alone.* In Weber's initial formulation, charismatic leadership must initially be revolutionary in character, for it can appear only in opposition to an already established authority. The charismatic leader says, in effect, "It is written, but *I* say unto you . . . ," and certainly Jesus Christ is an excellent example of the charismatic leader. His authority was legitimated by the personal characteristics that he alone brought to the situation.

Like Christ in this respect, Adolf Hitler was a charismatic leader. Joseph Smith, founder of the Mormon church, was charismatic; Joan of Arc had charisma, and so did Mahatma Gandhi and Martin Luther King, Jr. We have all known people who have "magnetic personalities"—they have a bit of charisma in them. The quality of charisma thus lies in the individual or in the combination of individual and situation rather than in the type of actions that he or she persuades others to engage in.

We do not know specifically what goes into these personal qualities or how much their recognition depends on the situation rather than the individual alone, but we can talk about the operation of charisma. The charismatic leader is able somehow to persuade others of the "rightness" of the goals he or she is seeking, either by virtue of having received them from some supernatural source or because they are so undeniably "right" that they have only to be clarified in order to be accepted. In any case, there is something about this person that enables him or her to give others new goals—to inspire them—so that they "naturally" want to do what he or she wants them to do. It is as though such a leader has been able to figure out what they really wanted to do all along and is only reminding them of this now.

Charismatic leadership is not the sort of authority on which a stable political system can be established. It is unstable for two reasons. First, the charisma is an attribute of an individual rather than of an office, and so it can-

His charismatic qualities and leadership ability have enabled Caesar Chavez (center),
President of the United Farm Workers, to organize his people into a powerful union.
(Curt Gunther/Camera 5)

not ordinarily be passed along to someone else. Second, once the revolution
led by the charismatic leader has been won, the tasks he or she faces are quite
different. He or she must be concerned now with the day-to-day operation of
the government rather than with seizing control of it. Responsibility must be
delegated to others, who probably do not have charisma themselves, and the
leader may find also that people's enthusiasm for the goals will diminish as
they turn back to their own separate everyday problems and interests.

It is the process of trying to build a stable government on a charismatic
foundation that Weber called "the routinization of charisma," and he found
that this has usually been unsuccessful. The legitimation of authority is likely
to come to rest again on traditionalistic grounds (which may indeed come to
cite the original leader as a divine justification for established authority), or in
a few cases on the third type of legitimacy, which will be discussed below.

Today, of course, a certain amount of charisma can be created by the
mass media. Stalin was apparently quite successful in making himself charismatic in this way after he succeeded Lenin, and Khrushchev finally had to turn
to this technique in order to maintain his authority in the Soviet Union. We
have found the same thing with Castro and with Mao, not to speak of a num-

ber of other rulers of small countries who are trying to maintain themselves as dictators. The basic techniques through which some charisma can be created and maintained by use of the mass media are discussed in Chapter 17, on public opinion and collective behavior.

In connection with charisma, finally, it is worth noting that the kind of power based on the use of information can be viewed as a kind of "technical charisma." The expert is someone who has superior knowledge and experience in a particular area; when this expertise is recognized, people are usually willing to follow his or her advice because it is assumed that this will be the best way to achieve their own goals. The more general one's expertise becomes, and the more it expands to include the definition of goals as well as how to achieve them, the more it approaches Weber's concept of charisma.

Rational-Legal Authority

The third type of authority, most characteristic of large, modern societies, is **rational-legal authority.** It is distinguished from the other two types mainly by its *emphasis on the office of leadership, or the position in the social structure that carries with it the rights of leadership, rather than on the characteristic of the person occupying this status.* This person derives his or her authority from the position rather than from inheritance or personal qualities. This is indicated very clearly in our saying that we have "a government of laws." The leader's powers are defined by the office, rather than the office being defined by the powers of its occupant.

Weber calls this a rational-legal authority because the right to exercise authority is based in the legal system. Ultimately, this may be traced back in turn to a consideration of the relation between means and ends, whereby the legal system is itself legitimated by the fact that it is reasonably efficient in helping the members of society to achieve their own goals without undue frustration or disappointment. This is the rationality of the system, and it implies that a "rational stranger" could be persuaded of its legitimacy or its fairness on these grounds.

Another important aspect of this type of authority is that its rules are written down and made public. The terms of the bargain between ruler and ruled are made explicit. A traditionalistic monarch is not guided by a constitution, and a charismatic leader does not begin with a public set of rules that will limit his or her actions, but explicit rules are the defining characteristic of a rational-legal system. The rules exist before the leader does, and they lay out the rights and obligations of both ruler and ruled.

In such a system the ruler (or the government) can fairly expect the citizens to know what they *must* do, what they *may* do, and what they must *not* do, just as they know what the government may and may not do. When someone breaks the law, it can be logically assumed that this was done on purpose, because he or she must have known ahead of time what the law is. This legal expectation makes it fair for the government to impose penalties on the law breaker and, at least in principle, makes it impossible for him or her to claim that the punishment is unfair. We support this principle whenever we say that "ignorance of the law is no excuse." In this connection, you should recall from Chapter 3 the idea that membership in a group carries with it a responsibility to know and to accept the group's culture—and law is clearly an important part of its culture.

Basing a government's legitimacy on rational-legal grounds has a number of consequences. First, it means that a great deal of attention must be paid to developing a legal system and all of the social structures needed to implement it: courts, law schools, police departments, regulatory agencies, government bureaucracies, and so on. It requires also that the body of law be logically and systematically organized, since inconsistencies in it would undermine its rationality and thus its legitimacy. (It is the function of the Supreme Court, as discussed in Chapter 16, to decide whether such inconsistencies exist and, if they do, how they should be resolved.) The legal system must be able, in itself, to convince the citizen of its rationality and its fairness, and this requires both logical organization and impartial application to everyone.

Second, emphasis comes to be placed on "rational-legal" justice rather than on "substantive" justice. That is, justice comes to be seen as the technically defensible application of the law and its directives to a particular case, rather than as an emotionally satisfying assignment of punishment to fit the crime. The government must be able to prove conclusively the appropriateness of employing whatever physical force is needed to put someone in jail for two years for having stolen an automobile. Whether or not the person *actually* stole the car, the government cannot use its powers to punish him or her unless it can prove to a jury that the person did it—and that the government has been fair all along the line in conducting the prosecution.

The jury here, incidentally, represents the "rational stranger" mentioned above. Only when such a rational stranger can be convinced that what the government wants to do is indeed consistent with the overall goals of society and with the rules governing the government's actions is it allowed to employ the force it commands. When the murderer, cornered in an alley, snarls at the detective, "Sure I did it, but you can't *prove* it!" he or she is trusting that rational-legal justice will prevail over substantive justice.

Finally, given this emphasis on explicit, rational law, the citizen is encouraged to find loopholes that allow him or her to avoid taxes, escape punishment for crimes, and generally to emphasize his or her "legal" relationships with others. The frequency of lawsuits in this country provides some support for this latter contention. One price that we must pay for having a rational-legal form of government in our own society is the occasional outrage we feel when the law allows someone to escape what we think is well-deserved punishment for a crime that we are sure he or she has committed.

THE PROCESS OF POLITICAL EXCHANGE

Forms of Political Exchange

It was noted earlier that exchange in the political institution involves the right to influence decisions made for the group, on the one hand, and the benefits people obtain through collective action, on the other. As we saw in the case of economic exchange, however, there are several ways in which exchange can be carried out. Here, we will look briefly at several types of political authority and suggest that in important ways they parallel the forms of economic exchange discussed in Chapter 11.

The simplest type of political authority is one in which leader and followers are not aware that they are engaged in exchange at all. Gift exchange, the simplest economic system, does not involve specific consideration of who gets and who gives how much, and under charismatic authority there is no sense of an explicit bargain between leader and follower. Obedience is simply to the charismatic leader and is not contingent on the specific details of the leader's decisions or how the leader came to acquire his or her authority.

Barter in the economic institution is paralleled by what might be called **patronage politics** in the political institution, whereby *things of immediate value to each participant are exchanged directly:* a calf for a pig, or obedience only in return for specific decisions. When the Praetorian Guard literally sold the Roman emperorship to the highest bidder in the third century A.D., a barterlike exchange was clearly involved.

But neither barter nor patronage is well suited to a large, complex system of exchange. In barter there is no separation between the generalized economic value of an item and its immediate value in use to the person who acquires it. Similarly, in patronage politics no distinction is made between the generalized right to rule and the specific decisions that a ruler makes. Both forms of exchange are thus quite limited, for neither can coordinate the activities of large numbers of participants, and in neither is there the opportunity to build up large amounts of wealth or to establish a reliable center of political authority.

We can see also that traditionalistic authority is comparable to money barter, in that both forms of exchange make a *partial* distinction between the specific and the generalized forms of the commodity in question. When political authority is vested in the position of king or queen, there is recognition that the right to rule is associated with a particular social status. But since the citizens have no opportunity to determine who shall occupy this status, and thus no explicit power to influence the decisions made by its occupant, there can be no complete separation between the individual ruler (and his or her specific decisions) and the more generalized right to rule. In money barter, similarly, items that *can* have immediate utility are used to represent generalized economic value, but the fact that they can also be wanted for their value in use means that the two types of value have not been clearly separated.

Thus political exchange is not clearly recognized under traditionalistic authority, even though the citizen ordinarily receives a reasonable measure of social order and coordination of group activities in return for obedience to the ruler. Some citizens, of course, may suffer from the arbitrary exercise of such authority, but for most of them acceptance of the ruler's right to make decisions for the group is preferable to the unrest and probable bloodshed that would develop if there were no political authority or during a revolution attempting to overthrow the ruler.

Following this logic, we can suggest that the rational-legal authority is most comparable to a money economy. In each the distinction between the specific and generalized forms of the commodity is quite clear. Money represents generalized economic value, and a political office embodies the right to rule; in neither case is it specified what goods or services must be bought with the money or what specific decisions must be made by the office holder. Just as money can be acquired and then used as it is needed, so the right to make decisions for the group (based on holding political office) can be used in guiding the group as need arises.

There are several advantages to drawing a clear distinction between political authority and its particular uses. One is that investing authority in an office rather than an individual means that explicit procedures can be worked out to decide who shall occupy that office; it also means that the powers of the office will remain the same when one occupant replaces another. A further advantage lies in the way rational-legal authority ensures continuity of authority, thereby minimizing uncertainties about who is actually leading the group. The chances that power will be misused are not eliminated, certainly, but they are much smaller than under any other form of authority. (The major types of distortions of rational-legal authority are discussed later in this chapter.)

To complete this review of the parallels between different forms of economic and political exchange (see Table 12.1), we must ask whether the political institution has developed anything comparable to what was defined in Chapter 11 as a finance economy. In a finance economy the importance of money as it can produce *more* money (through being invested or loaned) becomes central. In the end, of course, money is important only as it can be exchanged for specific goods and services, and in the same way authority is important only as it can be turned into specific decisions for the group. Do we find that authority can be "invested" so that more authority (and thus more effective decisions) is created?

TABLE 12.1 INSTITUTIONAL EXCHANGE SYSTEMS: THE PARALLELS BETWEEN FORMS OF ECONOMIC AND POLITICAL EXCHANGE

Form of economic exchange	Central parallelism	Basis of political authority
Gift exchange	No explicit sense of exchange	Charismatic authority
Barter	Simple exchange of concrete forms of the commodity (goods and services, obedience to specific decisions in return for immediate benefit)	"Patronage politics"
Money barter	Partial distinction made between specific and generalized forms of the commodity	Traditionalistic authority
Money economy	Full distinction drawn between specific and generalized forms of the commodity	Rational-legal authority
Finance economy	The generalized form of the commodity becomes itself a central focus of interest, in that it can be "invested" to produce more of itself	"Power politics"
Specific form of the commodity: concrete material goods and services		Specific form of the commodity: obedience to specific decisions made by a particular individual
Generalized form of the commodity: money (embodying "generalized economic value")		Generalized form of the commodity: loyalty (embodying "generalized readiness to support decisions made for the group by anyone in authority")

The answer is yes. There are two ways in which this can be accomplished. First, a person can use his or her authority to support certain decisions; if others approve of them, that person may then be given greater authority (a monarch's powers may be expanded, a politician may be elected to higher office). Second, when authority is divided among several people, they can pool their powers to achieve a majority so that a proposal can be translated into action. When the engineering of such coalitions becomes important in itself as a kind of *power to create power,* or **power politics**, the parallel with exchange in a finance economy becomes obvious.

Although the foregoing analysis suggests that in an important sense, different social institutions exhibit comparable processes, it has not explained why the more advanced forms of political exchange have greater appeal for the members of complex societies. This is the topic of the next section.

The Importance of Political Exchange

The citizens' loyalty to a system of rational-legal authority rests mainly on their faith that it will afford them more opportunity than any other system to influence the decisions that are made for them. This opportunity lies in their ability to determine who will occupy the offices of government and exercise the powers of those offices. Candidates are ordinarily associated with general political principles (that is, the political philosophies or distinctive criteria they will employ in deciding among different courses of action), because no candidate or voter can foresee all of the situations in which decisions for the group will be needed. It is for this reason that a candidate's basic philosophy (liberal, moderate, conservative, etc.) is usually more important to the voters than any specific campaign promises.

In an election the voters are giving someone the right to exercise the powers vested in an office, and in return they expect to receive decisions that will satisfy them. If the occupant of an office fails to uphold his or her end of this bargain, however, there must be opportunity for the voters to make a new and, it is hoped, more satisfactory bargain with someone else. The working out of this exchange relationship gives us the major characteristics of the democratic political system: the secret ballot, specific terms of office and periodic elections, and the idea of majority rule.

All of these things are necessary if a political structure is to continue to command the loyalty of the citizenry. Without the secret ballot, the voter's exchange relationship with a candidate might be subverted by other considerations. Without periodic elections, the voter would lack the opportunity to withdraw support from an office holder who is not carrying out his or her part of the exchange. And without the principle of majority rule, there would be no way to decide which candidate has been elected to office or when a decision binding on society's members has been made by them or their representatives.

Margaret Thatcher, who became Prime Minister of England in May 1979, appealed to British voters because she represented the conventional, *laissez-faire* approach to government of the Conservative Party. (U.P.I.)

It is virtually impossible to establish a stable government, and to elicit more than grudging support for its decisions, on the basis of coercion alone. Instead, the members of a society must have some sense that it is to their advantage to support the political system voluntarily, regardless of whether they approve of a particular office holder.

The more complex a society becomes, or the greater the number of specialized statuses its members may occupy, the more freedom each one has because there are more different activities in which to engage. But more freedom also means more opportunities to misbehave, or to violate some of the laws and norms that govern society. It is important, therefore, that the smallest possible number of these citizens have reason to want to violate them. Instead, as many people as possible should feel that it is to their advantage to obey the laws. In the political sector this means that all citizens should be able to engage in some sort of exchange with their leaders and to feel that they have some voice in the decisions that are made for them. Periodic elections under a rational-legal system of authority make this possible.

In this respect the principle of majority rule is of particular interest. If a society is not split sharply into two or more groups but is instead characterized by **pluralism**—that is, *made up of a large number of partly overlapping groups*—and if two people vote together on one issue and oppose each other on another issue, then in the long run each of them should manage to be on the winning side more often than on the losing side. Even if each wins in a mere fifty-one percent of the total number of cases, the probability of his or her continuing to do so is statistically valid: If 100 marbles are sorted randomly, again and again, between one set of 49 slots and another of 51 slots, each marble eventually will have been in the 51-slot section more often than it was in the 49-slot section.

This conclusion is a matter of statistics rather than sociology, but it does ensure that within a pluralistic society each citizen will win often enough, or that his or her wishes will be respected often enough, to make it worthwhile to support this type of political system.

Only when a society is deeply divided, so that a minority of its citizens begin to lose on almost every issue, does support for a rational-legal, majority-rule type of political system begin to weaken. At any time, of course, there will be a few people whose deep commitment to a particular ideology convinces them that they must win on *every* occasion if society is to continue to deserve their allegiance, but most people are practical enough to be content with winning only some of the time. It is when a relatively large minority within society sees its needs continually ignored and its wishes continually frustrated that more serious problems arise. For the past thirty years, we have been witnessing the responses of one particular group—black Americans—to this sort of situation (see Chapter 7).

The typical outcome of such frustration is either attempted revolution or increasing dissatisfaction with the political system, which weakens its ability to govern effectively. Undesirable as either alternative is, they occur fairly frequently. The stability of any form of rational-legal political system is thus by no means assured. We now turn to an examination of some of the things that can go wrong.

DISTORTIONS OF THE POLITICAL-EXCHANGE SYSTEM

The power of a political office lies in the fact that the state, through its agents, will enforce compliance with decisions that have been legally made by the occupant of that office. Such decisions can have extremely important consequences for others. A change in the tax structure or the minimum-wage law will put more money into some people's pockets and less into others'. A decision to spend more money for defense may mean less spent on welfare programs. Even a municipal government's decision to purchase toilet paper from

Company A rather than from Company B is of serious concern to those involved. No wonder, then, that the specific content of political decisions is of continuing interest to the members of society.

Ideally, all such decisions should be made in the interest of society as a whole (with the principle of majority rule serving as a substitute standard whenever there is disagreement over what *is* best for the group). But because all political decisions benefit some people at the expense of others, there is always some concern that these benefits have been achieved unfairly or illegally. When office holders themselves benefit, we speak of corruption; when a particular segment of society seems to benefit regularly from governmental decisions, we suspect the existence of a power elite.

Corruption   Whenever *the powers of organizational office are used to enhance the occupant's private wealth,* **corruption** results. Corruption (from the Latin *com* and *rumpere,* "to break completely") may occur in private corporations as well as in political structures, but ordinarily the term is reserved for abuses of political office.

Beyond simple thievery (pocketing public funds or stealing public property), corruption most commonly involves "selling" political decisions in return for money or other considerations. Governments purchase supplies, contract for services, grant monopolies to utility companies, assess real estate values, set tax rates, and do a host of other things that have consequences for private citizens' economic interests. Decisions in these matters are made by individual office holders, whether elected or appointed, and relatively few are completely immune to temptation. If one can get away with it, why not give a big paving contract to the Jones Construction Company in return for a percentage of the profits (or a big campaign contribution, a job for one's uncle, or something else), even though the Smith Construction Company has put in a slightly lower bid?

Isolated cases like this, however, are not the same as organized corruption, which involves the acceptance of bribery and graft by many people—both office holders and their "clients"—on a regular basis. This is what is meant when we refer to a corrupt city or a corrupt state (O'Connor, 1975). To the beneficiaries of political favors, the extra costs may be accepted as simply another tax on doing business, even though this "tax" never gets to the public treasury. Although much of it increases the private wealth of those who receive it, a substantial part is used to ensure that the office holders will remain in office. Political campaigns, party organizations, and local party units all need funds, and corrupt office holders view money spent in this way as a "tax" on doing their business.

There is nothing to prevent the misuse of public money and property except the laws designed to prevent it. But someone must take the initiative in enforcing these laws. Certainly this will not happen if the corruption is not visible. Even if it is visible but those who should enforce the law find it more profitable to turn their backs (and do not believe that they will suffer because of this), nothing will be done.

It was noted in Chapter 9, on formal organizations, that the designers of organizations do not always foresee the problems that can arise from faulty design. This is true of governments as well, for they are also formal organizations. Some governmental structures, then, are more corruption-prone than others because they contain built-in opportunities to keep it hidden. If, for instance, the chain of authority between the purchasing and accounting departments of a city government is confused or consists of only one person, the chance to keep corruption hidden is increased. In fact, Steffens (1904) reports that around the turn of the century, some cities' governments were deliberately designed to facilitate corruption.

The system of checks and balances, which gives different parts of the government partial authority to veto the acts of the others, is the only organizational solution possible, but it is by no means foolproof. Citizen apathy—reluctance either to "throw the rascals out" or to reward those who would expose and prosecute corruption—can undermine this system as effectively as can poor design.

Perhaps it is no accident that both Adam Smith's concept of "the invisible hand" (see Chapter 11, on the economic institution) and the American system of checks and balances appeared toward the end of the eighteenth century. Both assume that the competition of selfish interests (for money in the economic system, for power in the political system), when properly organized, will produce the most efficient and effective institutions. But when selfish interests combine (in monopolistic economic practices or corrupt political practices), it may rest with other parts of society to limit the unequal distribution of either wealth or political advantage.

Power elites In Chapter 6, on social stratification, we saw that there is a tendency for people to hold roughly equivalent amounts of wealth and power and that one can be used to acquire the other. Toward the upper end of the scale, then, we are not surprised to find that political decisions often benefit the very wealthy. Rarely, however, is this the result of gross corruption in which members of the upper class literally "buy" these decisions on an *ad hoc* basis. Something else seems to be at work.

It has long been recognized that power is distributed unequally in all societies. The rulers are inevitably smaller in number than the ruled, the middle and upper classes are more active politically than the working and lower classes, and office holders are almost always more sympathetic to some groups than to others. The important question, then, is the amount of inequality that exists and the extent to which those who are more powerful cooperate systematically to maintain their advantages. Those who believe that there is a good deal of conscious cooperation among those who benefit from what the government does call these people the *power elite.*

An elite is a small group whose members are in some way superior to others. They have more of something or are better at something than most people. Scientists who have won the Nobel Prize constitute an elite, as do the professional tennis players who are ranked among the top twenty on a world-wide basis. A political elite is composed of those who occupy high political offices, and a **power elite** is thus *those who have the greatest amount of influence over governmental decisions (whether or not they occupy high office themselves).*

Prominent among sociologists who have argued that there is an organized power elite in this country are C. Wright Mills (1956) and G. William Domhoff (1967, 1971), who point out that there are strong personal connections among people placed highest in American economic, military, and political circles. These people share a common background (white, Protestant, Ivy League education, upper-class lifestyles, etc.) and have a common interest in perpetuating not only their personal advantages, but also those of others like them. The circulation of individuals among high offices in large corporations, the Pentagon, and the federal government suggests that the existence of an organized power elite is inevitable.

Behind this analysis is a good deal of indignation, for if ascriptive factors (birth into a particular ethnic group and social class) are so important in determining who actually has power in this society, the ideals embodied in a rational-legal political system have been seriously subverted. If money and social connections combine to give some people more influence than their single votes should allow them, the importance of others' votes is diminished. And if an organized, self-perpetuating power elite exists, it is clear that its members are systematically depriving others not only of meaningful participation in the political exchange system, but money and government services as well.

But not all sociologists agree with this analysis. David Riesman (1950) and Seymour Martin Lipset (1960, 1968) have argued that there are several power elites, each representing a distinctive interest and often in conflict with one another. This has been termed the *pluralist* perspective (see Chapter 7). A governmental decision, for example, to deregulate the cost of natural gas will benefit the fuel industry, but raise costs for manufacturers. A Pentagon decision to build more atomic submarines will mean less business for the aircraft industry. Conservative business policies may raise the level of unemployment and so weaken the incumbent party's chances for reelection.

It can thus be argued that rather than making up a homogeneous group, the power elite is composed of a number of different interests, with cooperation among its members being coincidental rather than a regular practice. Studies of different American cities have revealed different patterns. In Atlanta, Hunter (1953) found a partly organized power elite; in New Haven,

Dahl (1961) found a much more pluralistic structure; and in Chicago, Banfield (1961) found that the political machine of Mayor Daley was so tightly organized that there was little opportunity for any power elites to be influential.

At the national level, however, it is more difficult to determine precisely just how organized the "ruling class" is or what the balance between conflict and cooperation among its members actually is. In the absence of solid evidence, it is likely that arguments about whether or not America is ruled by a single power elite will reflect differences in theoretical perspectives and political ideologies more than they will describe the political structure itself.

SUMMARY

All groups need leadership—directions for collective action—if they are to survive. But leadership is ineffective if its decisions cannot be enforced. Enforcement is based on the use of *power*, and when the group assigns the right to make enforceable decisions for its members to one or more individuals, they are said to have *authority*. The exchange of authority in return for collective guidance is the social relationship at the foundation of the political institution.

There are three principal bases of power, or of the ability to get others to do what they are told despite initial resistance. The first involves the manipulation of rewards and deprivations, the second depends on the use of information or inspiration, and the third is based on physical force. The first two types of power can be used by anyone, but neither is entirely dependable. In the end, only the use of physical force (primarily to restrict a person's physical movements and only secondarily to inflict pain) can be counted on to enforce decisions. Political authority must thus be based on the right to employ physical force when necessary to see that decisions for the group are obeyed.

Max Weber identifies three distinct reasons that people are willing to grant authority to others. *Traditionalistic* authority is based on tradition ("This is the way things have always been"); a monarch illustrates this type. *Charismatic* authority is based on the leader's personal qualities and is most clearly evident when it arises in opposition to an established authority; Jesus Christ, Joan of Arc, and Adolph Hitler were charismatic leaders. *Rational-legal* authority, finally, invests authority in the office rather than the individual, with the rights and obligations of the office holder set forth in explicit form. Authority is thus granted to someone only as he or she is elected or appointed to office. This in turn implies the central characteristics of a rational-legal political system: periodic elections, the secret ballot, majority rule, and an emphasis on the legal relationships among people.

In a general way, the parallels between the various forms of economic and political exchange demonstrate the utility of an exchange perspective. These parallels are drawn in terms of whether the exchange relationship is explicit or not and, if it is, how clearly the distinction is made between the specific and generalized forms of the commodity.

Rational-legal authority is most appropriate for complex societies because it makes political exchange explicit and thus sustains its participants' commitment to the system. This commitment, however, will be weakened whenever one group consistently sees its needs and aspirations rejected by the majority or when it becomes clear that some people are regularly profiting from governmental decisions at the expense of others.

When office holders use their powers for private gain on a regular basis, a condition of corruption exists. Since all those involved profit from corrupt relationships, only a system of checks and balances can curb these practices—and this will be ineffective when citizens are apathetic about it.

Although sociologists agree that power and influence are distributed unequally in society, they do not agree that there is a unified, self-perpetuating power elite in America. Some point to similarities in background among those who hold the top positions in the economic and political structures as evidence that they do act as an organized group; others note that these people often have competing interests and so should be viewed as a plurality of elites.

SUGGESTED READINGS

Campbell, Angus, Philip E. Converse, Warren E. Miller, and Donald E. Stokes, *The American Voter*, abridged (New York: Wiley, 1964). This is a detailed report of research into the factors influencing American voting patterns from 1948 through 1956; the research was conducted by the Survey Research Center at the University of Michigan.

Gamson, William A., *Power and Discontent* (Homewood, Ill.: Dorsey, 1968). Winner of the McIver Award, this is a penetrating analysis of two theories of political power that shows how their synthesis provides a clearer understanding of political activity and conflict.

Janis, Irving L., *Victims of Groupthink* (Boston: Houghton Mifflin, 1972). This is an important study of the ways political leaders can both reinforce one another's beliefs and isolate themselves from counterarguments, leading to seriously unrealistic political decisions. The case studies are fascinating.

Mitchell, William C., *Sociological Analysis and Politics: The Theories of Talcott Parsons* (Englewood Cliffs, N.J.: Prentice-Hall, 1967). This book, by a political scientist, demonstrates the relevance of Parsons's work to the understanding of political systems and processes. It also provides an extensive bibliography.

O'Connor, Lee, *Clout: Mayor Daley and His City* (Chicago: Henry Regnery, 1975). This book provides a close look at the nuts and bolts of a municipal political machine and at the tenacity of governmental corruption.

Orum, Anthony M., *Introduction to Political Sociology* (Englewood Cliffs, N.J.: Prentice-Hall, 1978). This is an excellent textbook that covers the field thoroughly and clearly.

Weber, Max, *The Theory of Social and Economic Organization* [1922], trans. by A. M. Henderson and Talcott Parsons (New York: Oxford University Press, 1947). Section III of this book, pp. 324–423, gives Weber's analysis of the three ideal types of authority and of forms of government and political parties.

Glossary

Authority The right to make decisions that are binding on the members of a group and to impose negative sanctions on those who do not comply. In the political institution, these negative sanctions are backed by the right to use physical force if necessary in imposing them; in private organizations, they are generally limited to the right to withhold rewards that the organization can bestow (wages, promotions, entry to certain areas, etc.).

Charisma This term (meaning "gift of grace") refers to the personal qualities or characteristics of an individual that make others seem to want to follow his or her leadership without question. The *content* of the charismatic person's directives is unrelated to his or her *possession* of charisma (both Jesus Christ and Adolph Hitler had it). It is one of the three major foundations of authority (see above) identified by Weber.

Contingent rewards and deprivations One foundation of *power* (see below), based on offering a reward for compliance with one's wishes or threatening to withhold something another person wants if she or he does not comply. The reward or deprivation is contingent because its being given or withheld depends on whether or not the other person complies.

Corruption The systematic use of the powers of an organizational office for the office holder's private advantage. The term is usually applied to the abuse of political office, but can refer also to abuse in private organizations. Corruption involves the cooperation of one or more office holders and outsiders so that it is a matter of social relationships rather than simply individual greed.

Information and inspiration The foundations of power that rely on changing others' behavior by changing either their assessment of a situation through giving them new information about it (so that a different course of action becomes more attractive) or their goals so that they want to act in a different way. The former is the basis of power based on expertise, and the latter depends on something like *charisma* (see above).

Loyalty A generalized commitment to following the orders or suggestions of some person or group because of either their personal qualities or the office that they occupy. Loyalty is thus different from the *ad hoc* compliance with orders that is based on the prospect of a specific reward or punishment and is central to *patronage politics* (see below).

Patronage politics As used here, the type of political exchange that involves complying with a leader's directions only so long as each act of compliance is rewarded. At best, it is based on temporary loyalty to a leader because of that person's control of rewards rather than because of his or her personal qualities or the office he or she occupies.

Physical force The foundation of power that relies on the ability to use force in halting another's actions and to inflict physical pain (up to and including death). It is the most reliable foundation of power so long as sufficient force can be mustered to overcome opposition and is therefore the necessary basis of political power. When the right to use force in specific circumstances is granted someone, it becomes *authority* (see above).

Pluralism A situation in which power is divided among several different interest groups so that no one of them is continually able to determine the details of decisions made for the group. Shifting alliances among these groups, then, depending on the issues in question, assemble the power necessary to make binding decisions. A pluralistic power structure is ordinarily contrasted with a *power elite* (see below).

Power The ability, regardless of its foundation, to direct the actions of others even when they do not initially wish to comply. When others agree that someone has the right to direct their actions, he or she has *authority* (see above). When compliance is based solely on fear of deprivation or punishment, power tends to be illegitimate.

Power elite A small group of people within society who dominate the decision-making process in the political and economic systems, whether or not they occupy formal offices in these structures. As characterized by C. Wright Mills, the American power elite tends to be made up of those members of the upper class who share a common ethnic and educational heritage and who help one another move easily among the top positions in the political, economic, educational, military, and even religious structures of society.

Power politics The system of political exchange in which power becomes prized because it can be "invested" in return for additional power. Assembling alliances, influencing the behavior of important interest groups, and a readiness to manipulate the system itself (as in the sophisticated design of a candidate's television campaign) become of central importance in the political institution.

Rational-legal authority Authority based on people's allegiance to the political structure itself rather than to specific individuals. Loyalty is to the office, as its powers and limitations are defined by the legal system, rather than to the occupant who exercises these powers. Such a system is "rational," Weber proposed, because it is explicitly designed for efficiency and effectiveness and "legal" because it is rooted in the society's laws. Because it is not dependent on the parenthood or personal qualities of the individual leader, Weber said that rational-legal authority is ordinarily the most stable and thus best suited to complex, modern societies.

Traditionalistic authority Authority based on people's allegiance to a specific individual who has come to occupy the office of leadership (queen, czar, etc.) through birth rather than through election or because of personal qualities. Loyalty to this individual is thus based on tradition (which often gives the office certain charismatic qualities), together with a sense that it is better to accept this method of identifying society's leader than to let its acquisition be determined through unregulated intrigue and conflict. Traditionalistic authority is one of Weber's three major types of authority.

13

The Family Institution

FOCUS:

INTIMACY

The word *intimate* comes from the Latin *intimus* ("innermost" or "deepest"), and we use it to indicate a particularly close, long-lasting social relationship. The human need for intimate relationships is strong and enduring, for its roots are many: the need for material and emotional support, for sexual gratification, for self-affirmation, and for group membership.

One's first intimate relationship is with one's mother and then with other members of the immediate family. The term "family relationship," in fact, is almost synonymous with "intimate relationship." The importance of these relationships for the individual's emotional and intellectual growth were discussed in Chapter 4; with rare exceptions, the need for intimacy continues throughout life. Because closeness implies extensive trust, though, to be close to another person is to increase one's vulnerability to hurt and disappointment. It is probably the experience of this sort of "psychological injury" early in life that leads some people later on to deny their need for intimacy. A misanthrope is someone who is no longer willing to run the risks of intimacy, even though he or she may be deeply resentful of its loss.

If the need for intimacy is strong but at the same time entails serious risk, the only solution to the dilemma seems to lie in strengthening the mutual obligations of those involved through developing norms that reinforce them. This makes the maintenance of intimate relationships a matter of group concern and means that "outside" pressures will be brought to bear on those who violate their obligations. But since norms apply to statuses rather than to individuals, society must also be able to identify intimate relationships in terms of statuses and to determine how people come to occupy these statuses.

The prototypical intimate human group is, of course, the family, and we shall view it here as the set of interrelated statuses—the social institution—that has developed in response to people's continuing need for dependable intimate relationships.

THE FAMILY AS AN INSTITUTION

It may be difficult at first to consider the family a social institution, for we usually think of it as a small group. But the term *institution* becomes more appropriate when we recall that the family is distinguished from other forms of human association and that within any given society, most of these small groups exhibit the same general structure because their members are subject to the same general norms. And there is also the fact that individual family groups are linked to others through both biological and marriage relationships, so that very few such groups exist in complete isolation from other families.

The family may appear to be a relatively simple institution if we are thinking only of the typical American family—one that includes only the parents and their children in one household unit. But in broader perspective the family turns out to be much more complex. We shall examine the range of these complexities below, but at the outset we must ask how the family fits into our basic definition of *institution,* or how it can be viewed as a distinct exchange system within society.

Biological Bases of the Family

Although the need for intimacy includes more than just physical closeness, it is clear that most people need physical intimacy as much as they need emotional intimacy. Two fundamental biological facts, then, are of central importance in shaping the family institution: the sex drive and children.

The sex drive   First, there is the universality of the sex drive—"universal" in the sense that it is a continuing physiological need of both sexes rather than a periodic need governed by the calendar, as it is in nearly all other animal species. The widespread and continuing interest in sexual gratification provides one of the most compelling reasons for human beings to seek intimate relationships with one another. We can say, too, that the immediate purpose of nearly all sexual union is physical pleasure rather than a conscious, unemotional desire to propagate the species. Sex is viewed as an end in itself rather than as a means to something else; this assertion is even supported by the physiology of the situation, for the male must be physically aroused before sexual union can take place.

We can thus view sexual gratification as a "commodity" and see also that it is usually a *joint* commodity—something that (in the absence of force) neither party can obtain unless the other does too. This is not to say, of course, that both parties always find equal amounts of pleasure in sexual relations or that sexual gratification cannot also be found through masturbation or in homosexual relationships, but simply that for the vast majority of humankind a union between male and female is the most natural and gratifying form of sexual behavior. Given this fact, we can begin to understand some of the basic forces leading to the development of regular exchange relationships in this area of social life.

There is, first of all, an interest in securing a reliable source of this commodity through establishing a continuing relationship with a particular member of the opposite sex. In addition to this eminently practical motivation, there is also the fact that sexual union tends to bring out in each party what we shall call "particularistic" feelings—an interest in *this* man or *this* woman, rather than in men or women in general. Here, then, we have two sources of the motivation to enter into a continuing relationship (that is, of substantial duration, although not necessarily for life) with someone of the opposite sex.

Complementing this is the fact that the sex drive is an extremely powerful human need. Its expression, if uncontrolled, would be highly disruptive to many human relationships. So there is a collective interest in controlling its expression. Only the most powerful or attractive members of any group could ever be reasonably sure of continued success in finding a succession of sexual partners. Very few of us are Don Juans or Cleopatras. The majority of us are more likely to want to protect the relationships we have already established than to seek the freedom to compete continually with all others of our sex for the most attractive of the opposite sex. Such competition is ordinarily accepted only by the relatively young before marriage, when they have the energy and the ambition to enjoy this kind of excitement for a few years. Thereafter, most people tend to put pressure on their more physically or socially advantaged fellows to play by the same rules they do.

This does not mean, of course, that sexual relationships outside those sanctified by law and custom never take place. No societal rule has ever been strong enough to ensure absolute compliance. But such behavior is ordinarily defined as a violation of normative standards. Adultery is, almost by definition, a threat to established social relationships, and until recently premarital sex was "against the rules" for two reasons: It might result in pregnancy, and it was thought to lessen a girl's attractiveness as a spouse. These topics will be treated in more detail below.

The existence of the need for sex, then, also brings about a need to control its expression. Otherwise, the special commitment between marriage partners, symbolized by their exclusive sexual relationship, would be jeopardized, and others could no longer count on their staying together as a basic unit of society. Together, these needs are taken care of through the development of two particular social statuses and of norms governing their relationship. These are the statuses of *husband* and *wife*, and the reciprocal rights and obligations that make up their roles tend to satisfy the needs just mentioned. The marriage relationship, which establishes people in these interrelated statuses, makes it legitimate for a man and a woman to enjoy sexual union, and at the same time it is supposed to prevent them from finding sexual gratification elsewhere.

Ideally, if not always in fact, the wife is committed to an exclusive relationship with her husband, and he in turn is supposed to restrict his search for sexual gratification to his wife—or wives. Only in societies in which women occupy a position sharply inferior to that of men is it sometimes acceptable for a man to engage in sex with a woman not his wife. The marriage relationship, it should be noted here, may involve one or more men and one or more women; the numbers are not important, but the exclusiveness of the relationship between or among them is. As the marriage relationship is defined in every society, it provides for each member an acceptable sexual outlet and usually restricts each member to this outlet.

Children   We can turn now to the second basic biological fact that is important in shaping the family institution. This is simply that some sexual unions result in pregnancy and the birth of a child. At this point a new set of social forces is brought into play, forces that focus on the child.

A child obviously cannot be born into a social vacuum. Somehow it must be fitted into the ongoing social structure, and this is most easily accomplished by defining the child as the responsibility—and the heir—of the parents. A position derived from the parents is thus automatically conferred on the child so that everyone can be aware of their rights and obligations with respect to this new member of society. With a specific parent-child relationship established, it is clear who is responsible for the child's care, whom the child may (and may not) marry later on, and from whom he or she will inherit such things as wealth, power, and prestige.

It is ordinarily quite clear who the child's mother is, for pregnancy is almost impossible to conceal, and in many societies this fact alone is sufficient to place the child in society. Especially when the family is an **extended family** *(one that includes grandparents, uncles and aunts, cousins, etc., all living more or less in the same household)*, it is often enough for people to know who the mother is. The child can then be identified as a member of her extended family, and there are certainly enough adults present to ensure the child's well-being.

But in societies in which the male's position determines that of the other members of his family, it is usually more important that the child's father be identified. Whether the society is characterized by a **nuclear family** structure *(mother, father, and their children making up the household)* or a strong **patriarchy** *(a structure in which the eldest male has most of the power and responsibility in a more extended family)*, it becomes essential to the child's social identity that he or she have a recognized father.

The traditionally disadvantaged position of the orphan and the illegitimate child in our society demonstrates the importance of the child's having identifiable parents. Whereas the orphan is pitied for having no parents, the illegitimate child used to be the object of as much scorn as the mother. She had clearly violated the rules against sex outside the marriage relationship, and so the child was not only difficult to place in our social structure, but somehow also a living symbol of his or her mother's deviance. This is increasingly less true today, but the continued use of the word "bastard" as an insult today reminds us of how we used to respond to illegitimate children.

Actually, society does not so much need to know the *biological* father, as it needs to have *someone* occuying the *status* of father in relation to each particular child. In other words, the social and the biological aspects of fatherhood can be separated—and they are in many societies. In some societies it is the mother's brother who assumes the social role of father in relation to her child, even though the biological father is formally married to the mother. Socially, the father of an adopted child might operate as well as, or better than, the biological father for all intents and purposes, and the same holds true for a man whose wife has borne a child by artificial insemination.

So long as society needs to set limits on the expression of the sex drive and needs to fit the newborn child into the social structure, there will be a strong interest in the establishment of regular, lasting relationships between men and women—the institutionalized relationships that form the basis of the family.

Psychological Bases of the Family

A human being is not exclusively a biological creature by any means. In addition to physical needs, he or she has mental or psychological needs that are more than simple extensions of physiological characteristics. Some of these needs are particularly well satisfied in the marriage relationship.

One of them is the need for continuing affirmation of one's social existence and meaning in the world. This need is best satisfied through intensive, enduring patterns of interaction with one or a few others that cover nearly all aspects of life. One's sense of personal worth, or of the fundamental importance of one's existence, is supported as others depend on one. What one says and does can be seen to make a real difference to these others; one's health, happiness, and achievements are of evident concern to them; and seeing oneself reflected in others this way seems to be of considerable importance to one's overall well-being. Here we have a kind of joint commodity that parallels sex as something that each marriage partner expects to receive through the relationship, even though it is too intangible to be measured.

The opposite side of this coin is the need to be committed to something outside oneself. An exclusive concern with one's own private pleasures tends to produce a sense of disorientation or unreality, and even the pain of seeing a favorite political cause defeated or of seeing a loved one die seems preferable to the separation from reality that full-blown narcissism eventually produces.

Such commitment may be to political or religious ideas, but more frequently commitment to another person or to a few persons is more satisfying.

The family, like this one in Hong Kong, can provide the individual with feelings of commitment, intimacy, and a sense of personal worth. (Ken Heyman)

Individuals are concrete, whereas ideas are more difficult to hold onto; individuals provide concrete responses as one implements one's commitments to them, whereas ideas do not. In an era of individualism, commitment is usually to one other person (the Western ideal of romantic love expresses this in extreme form) or to this person plus the children that come from the union. In other societies commitment may be given more directly to the family as a group (rather than as a collection of specific individuals).

In addition, the marriage relationship provides mutual emotional support. Concern for each other's well-being is expressed through sympathetic interest in plans and ideas and through affirmations of the importance of each other's goals and achievements. As a private relationship, it also makes the home a place of refuge from external pressures and a shelter where the sting of frustration or defeat in the outside world can be eased. These emotional benefits are taken for granted in the parent-child relationship, but adults have the same needs and must depend on intimate relationships with each other to supply them.

We might guess that the psychological security and well-being which grow out of commitment to and continuing, intensive interaction with one or a few other people is what really cements the marriage relationship into a potentially more permanent arrangement than either the sex drive or social pressures can account for. These factors, sex and social pressures, typically come into operation before most individuals have attained the maturity—the patience and the insight—to recognize the psychological advantages that marriage provides. It must be recognized, though, that the psychological foundations of the family tend to sustain it after the biological factors have become less important.

Marriage Patterns

A marriage is always of some importance to others in addition to the husband and wife. The more important the family is as a key element in a society's organization, the more important is the question of who marries whom, for marriage is very important as a means for establishing a special relationship between two family units. It may serve to consolidate the land owned by the two families, or it may help the merger of two political factions or two business firms—or simply to resolve a family feud (recall Romeo and Juliet, or how the Hatfields and the McCoys ended their Kentucky mountain feud).

As the family declines in structural significance, the less important marriage becomes to anyone beyond those directly involved—the prospective spouses and usually their parents. The fact that two specific people will enter the marriage relationship is probably less important in this country today than it has ever been, anywhere in the world, because the relationship is of less consequence to other groups and relationships than it has ever been.

History records many loveless royal marriages that were entered into because of a need to establish or reinforce friendly relationships between the ruling families of different nations, rather than because the bride and groom cared for each other personally. Among the higher classes in many countries, marriages have frequently been "arranged" in this way in order to consolidate wealth, to extend property holdings, or to resolve conflict. Throughout most of history, families as groups have gained or lost power, wealth, and prestige according to whom their offspring married. To have a child marry "beneath his or her station" was regrettable and sometimes a scandal, whereas "marrying up" was an occasion for celebration.

The more one's parents and other relatives are involved in the selection of one's spouse, the more the marriage is said to be "arranged." Beyond the question of the social class of each spouse, the principles by which such arrangements are made are usually referred to as *endogamy* and *exogamy*. **Endogamy** *is the practice of requiring one to marry someone from within the specific group or category to which one belongs,* such as one's own ethnic, religious, or social-class category. **Exogamy,** by contrast, *specifies the group or category from which one's spouse may* not *come.* For instance, someone in the United States is not allowed to marry a close relative, and frequently there is considerable sentiment against marrying a member of another ethnic or religious group.

Despite such rules and preferences, however, the desire to help one's children "marry up" persists, especially in open-class societies (see Chapter 6, on social stratification). One might assume that since in the past, and to a lesser extent today, it is the husband rather than the wife who determines the social class of the newly formed family, it would be easier for a woman to marry up than for a man. He would have less to lose by marrying someone from a lower class than she would.

But recent census data and other research reveal little to support this argument (Scanzoni and Scanzoni, 1976, p. 116). It has been suggested elsewhere, in fact, that similarity in educational achievement is more important than family class background in influencing people's readiness to marry each other (Blau and Duncan, 1967, p. 359). For both men and women, then, it is likely that there is equal opportunity to marry up rather than an extra opportunity for women.

In this regard, though, the belief still persists that a "nice girl" (i.e., a virgin) has a special advantage in finding a suitable husband—an argument often cited in support of premarital chastity. We may suppose that this belief developed during a period when men looked on women more as property than as equals, reasoning that they would be more valuable if their commitment to a husband were complete and not marred by previous experience. Now that sex roles are changing (see Chapter 5) and contraceptives are quite reliable, however, it will be of interest to see how attitudes toward virginity may change in the future.

MAJOR FAMILY FORMS

Monogamy/Polygamy

There are several major types of family structure found throughout the world. Seeing why it is possible to view marriage as an exchange relationship, after all, does not tell us anything about the ways in which this relationship may be worked out in detail or about other natural and social factors that influence these details.

The most important distinction is that between *monogamy* and *polygamy*. **Monogamy**, the arrangement with which we are most familiar, is *one man, one woman;* in **polygamy** the arrangement is that *one of the marriage partners has more than one spouse.* Thus polygamy does not refer only to one man with several wives; it can also mean one woman with several husbands. More strictly speaking the former sort of polygamy is called *polygyny*—many wives—and the latter is called *polyandry*—many husbands.

Most people in modern societies tend to look on anything besides monogamy as somehow wrong; it may be interesting, but it is not fully legitimate. This feeling simply shows how strongly bred into us our own society's rules of marriage can be, for so long as all of the parties to a marriage relationship agree that it is acceptable, it is not wrong to them. There are, however, factors beyond the agreement of those personally involved in the relationship that seem to determine whether a given type of marriage can actually be a stable, long-lasting pattern within a given society. Let us look briefly at some of these factors.

The least prevalent form of marriage is polyandry, in which one woman becomes the wife of several men. Given the usual dominance of men over women, polyandry is likely to occur only under unusual conditions—when there is a severe shortage of women in a society. If, for instance, a society has a strong tradition of female infanticide (the practice of putting female infants to death right after birth because the parents believe female children to be worthless), polyandry may be the only alternative to bachelorhood for many males.

This practice has been found in only a few societies, and they have been typically quite poor. Even here, though, the tendency is for the husbands to be brothers, so that the problems of sharing a wife are mitigated by the husbands' family obligations to one another.

For the sake of completeness, it is necessary to mention here a theoretically possible type of marriage—**group marriage,** or *marriage involving several men and several women simultaneously*—and to remark that evidence is very much in doubt as to whether this form of marriage has ever existed except as isolated experiments. We have some suggestive evidence from India that group marriage has existed, but this information is not sound enough to let us conclude that group marriage has ever been a stable part of human society.

The major remaining alternative to monogamy is *polygyny*, or what we usually refer to as polygamy. This is found, at least in principle, in many parts of the world, and it even existed in this country among the Mormons in Utah in the second half of the nineteenth century. In practice, however, the large majority of marriages throughout the world tend to be monogamous, even where polygyny is permitted.

The reason that relatively few men take advantage of the opportunity to marry several women is that it is quite expensive to support more than one wife. Statistically, too, the approximately equal number of men and women in all societies would make it impossible for even a majority of the men to have more than one wife unless a substantial number were barred from marriage altogether. In many polygynous societies, however, a wife will encourage her husband to take a second wife if possible, because this will lighten her own household responsibilities. But a poor camel driver or a humble rice farmer cannot afford to support more than one wife, no matter how much the society may permit and even encourage it.

Even when a man is wealthy enough to maintain two or more wives, it should not be supposed that he does this primarily for the sexual advantages it might provide. In many societies the first wife decides when he will sleep with whom, to ensure that none of the wives is ignored. Among the Mormons, sexual relationships were limited to those times when a wife wished to become

Top: The men and women of this California commune have chosen to share sexual privileges, living quarters, and collective responsibility for child rearing. (Bob Fitch/Black Star)

Bottom: The Mormons who settled in Utah during the late 1800s permitted men to take more than one wife. (Culver Pictures, Inc.)

pregnant. Maintaining order within such a family requires considerable constraint, and a polygynous marriage is never the riot of sexual indulgence that most Americans seem to imagine it to be (Leslie, 1976).

The legitimacy of polygyny, if not its actual prevalence, seems to be closely related to the position that women occupy in a society. Their position may be influenced by religious teachings, the economic structure, or many things at once, but it almost always involves women's being "second-class citizens" in several respects. Laws governing the inheritance of property, the custody of children, and the right to sue for divorce, among other things, are much less generous for women than they are for men in such societies. In many instances an adult woman has almost no civil rights at all.

Under such circumstances, and in the absence of a romantic-love ideal (the belief that a powerful emotional attraction between two individuals is the only basis for marriage), polygyny makes a good deal of sense as far as women are concerned. It is to their advantage to be able to divide up the household chores, to spread the responsibility for childcare, and to be protected by a wealthy husband. If the intimacy between husband and wife is less, it seems to be compensated for by membership in the larger group and by the greater security it affords each member.

Although polygyny may be compatible with certain types of societies, it is not appropriate to the more universalistic type of equality among individuals that characterizes the most complex societies of today. It might be speculated, although it is not an established sociological finding, that the emphasis on monogamy in Judaism and Christianity was one of the important factors in making it possible for the societies that adopted these religions to advance beyond others in terms of complexity. Certainly an important barrier to the idea of equality in exchange is absent when monogamy is preferred, so that fewer obstacles stand in the way of building a society on the basis of voluntary acceptance of norms and laws. And this, as was suggested in the previous chapter, seems necessary if a society is to develop beyond a certain level of specialization.

Rules of Residence and Family Organization

Two other types of variation in family structure should be mentioned, even though we cannot explore them fully here. One of these is the *rules of residence* that govern the families in a given society. These are the rules, or at least the ideals, that encourage a newly married couple to live with the husband's family, with the wife's family, or to live apart from both of them. These three forms are called, respectively, *patrilocal, matrilocal,* and *neolocal* types of residence.

It is actually the rules of residence in a society that seem to have the greatest influence on the other characteristics of the family, despite our own greater interest in variations along the monogamy/polygamy dimension. Rules of residence are closely related to the rules governing inheritance, for one thing, and to the monogamy/polygamy distinction also. Matrilocal residence, whereby the young couple takes up residence with the wife's parents, is most often found in settled agricultural societies in which the women are largely responsible for the production of food. Family lineage here is traced through the wife's descent, so it is obvious that polygyny would be impossible. (Which one of his wives' families would the husband go to live with, and how could he justify removing his other wives from their families?)

Where the basic economy is one of hunting and fishing or where there is a good deal of warfare among different social groups, we find patrilocal patterns of residence almost exclusively. If the man's greater physical strength is important to the group, men are likely to call the tune. Polygyny is compatible with patrilocal residence and is more closely associated with it than with neolocality.

The **neolocality** pattern seems to be found mainly in societies in which a small group—*father, mother, and children alone*—can be relatively self-sufficient. Such a society is typically one with a complex, advanced economic system, even though traces of matrilocality or patrilocality may continue to be found in rural areas.

There is a third dimension of variation in family organization that quickly becomes quite complicated and need not concern us a great deal here. This concerns the different ways in which the extended family may be organized—how the entire group, consisting of grandparents, uncles and aunts, parents, children, nephews and nieces, etc., is structured as a social group. Both the internal organization of such a family and its relations with other extended families living in the same vicinity have been found to exhibit a large but comprehendible number of forms of organization. In the detailed analysis of these forms we meet such terms as *clan, sib, stem family, joint family, moiety,* and *totem,* and each would easily be worth a chapter in itself. Any good text in introductory anthropology can provide an extended treatment of this aspect of family organization.

THE FAMILY IN SOCIETY

Up to this point, we have looked at the psychological and sociological foundations of the family as an institution and have tried to capture the flavor—if not all the details—of the various forms that families may take under different circumstances and in different societies. The family was certainly the basic unit of primitive society, and as such it had to take on responsibility for not only the control of sexual behavior and the care of children, but also the organization of economic, political, and religious activities. For the anthropologist studying primitive cultures, the term "social structure" is frequently equivalent to what we have been speaking of as family structure. In a very important sense, a primitive society tends to be primarily an elaboration of the extended family.

As a society increases in size, though, and as its members invent and occupy more and more specialized social statuses, the various social institutions tend to become separate from one another and to become the sort of semi-autonomous exchange systems that we find in our own society today. The study of this process of evolution, or of "structural differentiation," is discussed in more detail in Chapter 18, on social change; it is really just beginning in sociology now, and so our comments about the "evolution" of the family can be only tentative. But since the concept of structural differentiation seems to be the most useful framework for explaining some of the characteristics of the modern American family, we must do our best with it.

As various activities are removed from the family's responsibility, there is less need for it to be a complicated structure. As the economic system becomes more clearly a distinct complex of statuses and their interrelations, the family no longer needs to be entirely self-sufficient in producing its own food, clothing, and shelter. As society grows larger and its political problems become important to many families at the same time, the family patriarch can no longer make all the major political decisions for his descendants.

As soon as the main breadwinner can earn a living away from the family and when the changing character of the economic system requires him or her to be able to move to where the work is, the advantages to be gained in breaking away from the extended family become obvious: A nuclear family finds it easier to move, both geographically and in terms of social class. The shift from extended family to nuclear, neolocal family is under way as soon as the family seeks to adjust itself to these changes in its social—especially the economic —environment.

A progressive shedding of functions by the family seems to be a self-perpetuating process, at least up to a point. But at the same time that structural differentiation is occurring, a complementary trend toward increasing interdependence between the family and other parts of society is taking place. Today the nuclear, neolocal family depends on others to produce its food, educate its children, bury its dead, and defend it against thieves and invaders (Winch, 1971).

The gradual shedding of these responsibilities, which has characterized the typical American family over the last two centuries, has been the subject of a good deal of worry by social critics. They have suggested that this process has resulted in a serious weakening of the bonds that unite family members, with such unpleasant consequences as delinquency, divorce, and forms of psychological misery such as alienation and anomie. It can be argued, though, that these things are the price we pay for the advantages we gain: better food and material goods, better education for our children than we could provide for them by ourselves, and more public facilities that many families can take advantage of. Yet it cannot be denied that these slow and apparently inexorable changes have brought new problems to the American family. The sociological context of the family described in the preceding pages may be useful in an examination of these problems.

Problems of the American Family

For more than a century, the American family has been ceding a number of its traditional responsibilities to other institutions. In addition, changes in society have brought traditional family norms increasingly into question. In particular, we may cite increasing affluence (which makes it easier for individuals to be economically self-sufficient), the trend toward greater freedom and equality for women, and of course "the pill" and other trustworthy methods of contraception as well as the legalization of abortion. No longer must the woman depend on the man for economic security, as she did in the past; no longer is it "dishonorable" for an adult woman to live by herself, earning her own livelihood and leading her own social life; and no longer must the fear of pregnancy serve as a barrier to sexual relationships outside the marriage contract.

The legalities of marriage, then, are becoming less "sacred." Further, as discussed in Chapter 5, on changing sex roles, there is increasing confusion within the marriage relationship over the legitimacy of each partner's traditionally defined rights and obligations. Among these current difficulties, two problems stand out with particular clarity.

Divorce   The dissolution of the husband-wife relationship is essentially the breaking of a legal contract which has united two people. Having entered into this relationship, each partner is subject to a number of laws that enforce his or her obligations to the other, and it is to withdraw from the statuses subject to these laws that one or both parties seek a divorce. In this light, arrangements for alimony, child support, etc., can be seen as ensuring that neither party is "injured" by the dissolution of the contract—or at least that the "injury" is not unequal.

Today in the United States there are approximately twice as many marriages per year as there are divorces. This does not mean, though, that half of all marriages end in divorce, for the number of married couples at any given time (those who *might* divorce) is far greater than the number of single people who might marry. Instead, it has been estimated (*Newsweek*, May 15, 1978) that about sixty percent of the adult population will marry once and remain married; another sixteen percent will marry, divorce, and then remarry for good; and an additional twelve percent will go through divorce at least twice. Since four percent of the adult population never marry, another eight percent remain single after one divorce, and about eight percent are widowed, we can say that probably eighty percent of all American adults are married at any given time.

These are of course gross figures. Higher social class is clearly related to higher marital stability (Scanzoni and Scanzoni, 1976, p. 463), which means that the working and lower classes have slightly higher divorce rates. Part of this is due to economic problems and part to the fact that the divorce rate is higher among those who marry young, both of which are characteristic of the working and lower classes.

It is no secret that the divorce rate has been increasing steadily since the nineteenth century. Currently, about one-third of all marriages end in divorce; less than half that proportion did so in 1960. With the continuing high "currently married" rate, however, this simply means that married adults are more likely to change partners now than in the past.

This means, in turn, that at present about two of every five children under eighteen will live in a one-parent home during some part of their youth. Although two-thirds of all American children now live with both of their natural parents, another one-sixth live in one-parent homes, and almost that many more live in homes where a natural parent has been replaced by a stepparent. The remaining three percent of American children are living with relatives or in institutions (*New York Times*, Nov. 27, 1977).

Because close to half of all current American divorces involve children, it is legitimate to be concerned with their reaction to the separation of their parents. The breaking of intimate relationships, no matter what the reason, is always traumatic for spouses as well as for children, and it is usually more than a year before feelings of resentment, self-doubt, and anger begin to disappear (Trotter, 1976). There is good reason, then, to agree that divorce is undesirable. Children are better off when brought up by parents who care for each other as well as for their offspring, but it is not clear that children suffer more from divorce than from being reared in a home torn by dissension. In many cases divorce may be the lesser of two evils (Nye, 1957). The undeniable fact is that changes in American society have increased the family's vulnerability to disruption.

As it has given up its various responsibilities to other, more specialized groups and institutions (schools, hospitals, the entertainment industry, etc.), the American family has become more clearly a consumer rather than a producer. Its members need one another now more for emotional reasons than for economic reasons. Thus they have less reason to stick together when their emotional needs are not being satisfied. In former days sheer economic pressures (not to speak of social pressures and the difficulty of obtaining a divorce) kept couples together long after the relationship was emotionally dead.

The economic and religious forces binding families together today are weaker. It is easier for a woman to support herself now, it is easier for a man to run a household without a wife, and the stigma attached to divorce has diminished a great deal. So the decision to separate is more strongly influenced by emotional factors now. Are the partners' emotional needs being satisfied by the marriage? If not, divorce seems an increasingly reasonable alternative.

The marriage relationship, in other words, has become more clearly an exchange relationship. And, just as in other types of exchange, one participant may want to back out of it if he or she doesn't feel that it is a fair exchange. Thus when marriage is more frequently defined by both partners as an exchange relationship based on mutual emotional satisfaction, it is logical that those who enter into it should be allowed to break off the relationship if they are not getting a fair return on their investment.

To be sure, divorce does bring up a number of other problems—the adequate care of the children being the most important—but it can be argued that these problems, too, are a part of the price we pay for the other advantages we receive through a society that shapes the family in this way. And even if we feel that this is too high a price, the way back to an earlier or less divorce-prone type of family is by no means easy to find.

Adolescents and the elderly   Divorce is not the only major problem brought about by the predominance of the nuclear, neolocal family in American society. Two other problems are also becoming more evident, and they have to do with the relatively narrow "fit" of this type of family structure with certain periods in the lives of their members. Our present type of family is most appropriate to the period when the adults are, say, between twenty and fifty and when their children are still dependent on them and in the home. Two age groups, on the other hand, seem to be particularly unfitted for this type of family: the older adolescents and the elderly.

The young person between the ages of fifteen and twenty or so is torn between his or her own physical maturity and the pressures of society on him or her to remain socially dependent and relatively uninvolved in the mainstream of adult life. Those in this age group are supposed to postpone marriage and real independence for the sake of the advanced education that is thought to be necessary for later success as an adult. Encouraged, however, to train for adulthood, to learn independence at the same time that they are asked to remain dependent on their parents, these young people are likely to be quite dissatisfied. They may be confused, sense a lack of direction or of real participation in the world, and they are often ready to join in all sorts of fads or causes that offer temporary certainty and direction for their lives.

The elderly face a different problem. The neolocal, nuclear family is not prepared to contain grandparents on a comfortable basis, and yet as they retire from active participation in the economic system and become less self-sufficient, the elderly frequently need somewhere to go and someone to care for them. Rest homes, senior citizen communities, Medicare, and many other programs and facilities have been developed by public and private agencies in response to this problem. To judge by the continuing high level of concern for our older citizens, however, it is apparent that these remedies have not yet been completely successful by any means.

The future If these various problems can all be seen as byproducts of the changes in family structure brought on by the increasing complexity of society, can we look forward to a brighter future for the family? Perhaps the best guess is that we are presently at a stage of the differentiation process which places a particularly heavy strain on the family and that further changes in other parts of society will alleviate much of it.

For instance, there is slowly being developed a "service ethic" for adolescents, one which promises to give rise to new organizational structures that will give this period of life much more meaning and a real sense of participation in the world. The Peace Corps and Vista are two important examples. Within the next few decades, too, there seem likely to develop new values that will enable us to accept and enjoy more fully the increasing amounts of leisure time that our affluent society will afford us, so that retirement from active involvement in the economic system will be much less a sudden transition from purposeful activity to boredom and a sense of uselessness. And finally, the development and widespread use of genuinely effective contraceptives is leading gradual adoption of a new view of sexual activity.

Along with a clearer distinction between sexual union for immediate gratification and the long-term relationship that includes the conscious desire to have children, there will develop a redefinition of why people should get married. The steady increase in the proportion of our population that has experienced premarital sex and the increasing number of people who are "living together" without the formalities of marriage suggest that we are indeed coming to draw a clearer line between these two aspects of sex. As we begin to accept normatively the distinction between early sexual exploration and the acceptance of responsibility for children, we shall probably see a decline in the divorce rate.

Part of this will be due to the fact that fewer marriages will have been contracted so early or so casually. We are already seeing, in fact, a rise in the average age at which both men and women enter their first marriages, and there is also a current trend for married couples to delay having children.

Although today we are also seeing some experimentation in "communal marriages," in which several men and women share living quarters and sometimes sexual access as well, such arrangements generally end up as separate couples with their own children rather than as genuine group marriages. The fact that the anthropological literature is almost devoid of true cases of group marriage suggests that this is a highly unstable family form and is unlikely to exist for long under any circumstances. Over the long run, we may guess that knowledge of such "experiments" will serve to focus attention on what is really essential in the marriage relationship and will thereby free most people from some of the beliefs and practices surrounding it that are no longer relevant. It is almost certain, however, that our society will continue to be characterized by monogamous, nuclear families.

SUMMARY

People's continuing need for intimacy, both physical and social, is a need for a *joint* commodity because it is necessary that at least two people enjoy it if it is to be satisfied at all. And because intimacy is both needed and risky, it is important that norms governing such relationships be developed and that the statuses to which these norms apply be identified. We may thus view the family institution as the set of interrelated statuses through whose interaction the "commodity" of intimacy is acquired.

The human sex drive is an important foundation of this institution, for it requires a close, continuing relationship between at least two people, nearly always one male and one female. Rights of sexual access, too, must be limited if this basic human need is not to disrupt other social relationships. But people enter into intimate relationships for psychological reasons as well, and these turn out to be a more reliable foundation for the family than does the partners' interest in sexual gratification.

The more central the family is to a society's overall social structure, the more a particular marriage will have important consequences for others besides those who come to occupy the statuses of husband and wife. Other considerations—economic, political, social class—will thus play a larger role in determining who marries whom, even to the point of giving the marriage partners' private wishes no credence at all.

A marriage need not consist of only one male and one female *(monogamy)*. The family structure that includes one husband and two or more wives *(polygyny)* is actually approved by the majority of the world's societies, even though only a minority of their male members can afford to acquire more than one wife. A marriage involving one wife and several husbands *(polyandry)* is quite rare, and *group marriage* is so inherently unstable as to be more a theoretical possibility than a reality anywhere in the world.

These various family forms are closely related to other family practices: rules governing where a newly married couple should live, *family authority being invested in the female* (**matriarchy**) or the male (**patriarchy**), the way that property is inherited through the male line *(patrilineality)* or female line *(matrilineality)*, and the many forms of extended family and kinship organization. These practices, in turn, are influenced by economic and religious factors.

As an institution, the structure of family statuses is shaped by the functioning of other social institutions. Over the past 100 years and more, the family (particularly in America) has gradually given over a number of its traditional responsibilities to other institutions, so that by now it has been reduced primarily to a consummatory rather than a productive group. Today, people form families more for what they get *in* the family relationship than because they need it in order to survive. This situation, together with increasing equality for women and the availability of trustworthy contraceptive techniques, has meant the development of several serious problems for the modern American family.

The divorce rate is extremely high compared to that in past generations, even though more than four-fifths of the population eventually finds a satisfactory marriage. The fact that about one-third of all first marriages are likely to end in divorce is symptomatic of the fact that the exchange relationship on which the family is based is becoming clearer: With fewer "external" pressures to remain married, there is little reason why someone should not be able to break off a relationship after he or she finds the exchange no longer satisfying.

The fact, however, that the family is for this reason now adapted primarily to the needs of the two parents and their young children means that it is not well suited to the needs of either older adolescents or the elderly. But we may predict that the development of new norms and forms of organization (in particular, increased skills in and acceptance of leisure activities, benefiting the elderly, and an emerging "service ethic" for younger people) will slowly resolve some of these problems.

The changes that do come about in family structure will not occur without corresponding changes in other institutions, and the resistance of some of them to change (the economic institution, the educational system, bodies of religious beliefs, and so on) will doubtless slow the rate of change in the family. But so long as people continue to need intimate relationships, and try to guarantee their maintenance, the family as an institution will not disappear. The sociologically interesting aspect of this institution will continue to be the way it adjusts to both changes and rigidities in the other parts of society.

SUGGESTED READINGS

Christensen, Harold T., ed., *Handbook of Marriage and the Family* (Chicago: Rand McNally, 1964). Contributions from many specialists in the sociology of the family make this a comprehensive and authoritative review of the entire field.

Goode, William J., *World Revolution and Family Patterns* (New York: Free Press, 1963). This is Goode's prize-winning study of the effects of industrialization on family structure; he uses research materials from many different societies.

_____, *The Family* (Englewood Cliffs, N.J.: Prentice-Hall, 1964). This brief text provides an excellent worldwide perspective on the nature of the family and its problems.

Murdock, George Peter, *Social Structure* (New York: Macmillan, 1949). In his analysis of anthropological materials on some 250 societies, Murdock winnows out the central characteristics of all human family systems and identifies the factors which make for differences in family organization.

Reiss, Ira L., *The Family System in America* (Homewood, Ill.: Dorsey, 1971). This collection of articles provides a good survey of perspectives on the family, drawing particularly on historical and anthropological materials.

Scanzoni, Letha, and John Scanzoni, *Men, Women, and Change: A Sociology of Marriage and Family* (New York.: McGraw-Hill, 1976). One of the better textbooks in this field and one that makes a serious attempt to apply sociological theories to explaining both structure and change in the family.

Winch, Robert F., *The Modern Family*, rev. ed. (New York: Holt, Rinehart and Winston, 1971). This text is particularly insightful in its examination of the relationship between the family and other social institutions.

Glossary

Endogamy The practice of selecting a spouse from among the members of one's own social group. A marriage that must involve members of the same ethnic, religious, or tribal group is said to be *endogamous*.

Extended family A family, generally occupying the same household or adjacent households, that includes not only the spouses and their children, but also other relatives such as grandparents, uncles and aunts, brothers and sisters, cousins, nieces and nephews, and grandchildren.

Exogamy The practice of forbidding the selection of a spouse from among the members of one's own social group. When an individual is forbidden to take a spouse from among his or her own ethnic, religious, or tribal group, the marriage is said to be *exogamous*.

Group marriage A marriage relationship that involves two or more husbands and two or more wives. This form of marriage is so rare that its existence as a realistically possible one (that is, stable enough to last over several generations) may be seriously questioned.

Matriarchy Literally, "rule by the mother." The term generally refers to an extended family group in which the oldest female is acknowledged to be the head of the household.

Monogamy The marriage relationship that involves one member of each sex—one husband and one wife, rather than having two or more individuals occupying one of these statuses. In a society with a monogamous marriage pattern where divorce and remarriage is frequent, the relationship may be termed *serial monogamy*.

Neolocality The family residence pattern in which newly married spouses establish a household apart from that of either of their parents so that neither lineage is given preference. If the spouses customarily go to live with or near the wife's parents, the pattern is *matrilocal;* if they live with or near the husband's parents, the pattern is *patrilocal.*

Nuclear family A family in which the household is ordinarily inhabited only by the spouses and their children. This is in contrast to the *extended family* (see above), and societies can be classified in terms of which pattern is the more prevalent.

Patriarchy Literally, "rule by the father." The term generally refers to an extended family group in which the oldest male is acknowledged to be the head of the household.

Polygamy The marriage relationship in which there is one wife and two or more husbands, or vice-versa. When the husbands are plural, the marriage is *poly-androus,* and the pattern is called *polyandry;* when the marriage includes one husband and two or more wives, it is *polygynous,* and the pattern is called *polygyny.* Although a large majority of societies around the world *permit* polygyny (and a tiny minority permit polyandry), the most common marriage relationship is actually monogamous.

14

The Religious Institution

BELIEF

To believe something is to feel certain that a particular idea, or "mental construct" in one's head, is a valid representation of its referent—that it is an accurate picture of the thing it supposedly represents. But we ordinarily use the word *belief* to refer to values and their justifications, and here the sense of validity (their *truth*) is qualitatively different, for we cannot test empirically the truth or falsity of values.

It was pointed out in Chapter 3 that culture is the shared "blueprints" that the members of society use as a guide to interaction and that there is a continuing need for these blueprints to be accurate. The parts of culture that picture "what *is*" can be tested for accuracy through sensory experience just as though they were scientific hypotheses to be tested by experiment. Those that picture "what *should be*," however, have no external, empirical points of reference. Here, moral authority must substitute for empirical test.

Still, there are parallels. Just as sensory experience enables one to assess the accuracy of his or her knowledge of what *is*, so the personal experience that we call revelation or intuition can help one determine the validity of a belief about what *ought to be*. The accuracy of a roadmap can be determined by whether or not it helps one reach a particular destination, and the validity of a belief can be established by praying for guidance. Although they are quite different, in both cases the individual measures validity through immediate personal experience.

But in neither case is direct personal experience enough. We must depend a good deal on others for information about the empirical reality that lies beyond our own experience, for it would be impossible for us to test personally every item of information about the world that is relevant to our daily activities. As discussed in Chapter 17, on public opinion and collective behavior, one must often rely on a substitute for personal experience in establishing the validity of such information. The process of **consensual validation**—*when we see that others believe something, it is easier for us to believe it too*—makes this possible.

Similarly, the personal experience of revelation is too infrequent to provide full support for our acceptance of a belief. Here, too, we must depend on the testimony of others to reinforce our sense that our values and priorities are valid. But because values are not facts or specific events, they cannot be validated simply by others' reports of what they have observed. Instead, others' support of the validity of beliefs must be more frequently in the form of behavior that indicates, both directly and indirectly, their own acceptance of the truth of these beliefs. Collective affirmations of faith and participation in rituals that symbolize faith are thus needed to supply the same degree of consensual validation for beliefs that, for instance, the mass media provide in the case of empirical knowledge about current events.

Because a shared, organized set of values is just as necessary to the maintenance of stable patterns of interaction as is accurate knowledge of the empirical world, people have a continuing need to maintain the sense that their beliefs are both valid and shared. The social relationships through which this need is satisfied make up the religious institution.

THE SOCIOLOGICAL STUDY OF RELIGION

It should be made clear at the beginning of any sociological analysis of religion that the sociologist's purpose is not to answer religious questions or to determine the truth of particular religious beliefs. By their very nature, such beliefs are not subject to empirical test or demonstration. Sociologists study the ways in which people's behavior is influenced by their beliefs and also the ways in which their beliefs are influenced by other aspects of their lives, but the truth or falsity of these beliefs is never at stake.

Sociologists ask the same sorts of questions about religious behavior that they ask about political and economic behavior. The sociological study of religion, then, is the attempt to describe and understand the patterns of social relationships that are associated with religious beliefs; it is not at all interested in *evaluating* these beliefs.

The Religious Impulse

We begin with the assumption that people interact—and thus develop patterned social relationships—because they want to. With reference to religion, as with other types of relationships, we ask at first about the motivations that seem to underlie people's continuing interest in taking part in these relationships. Voltaire quipped, "If God did not exist, people would have to invent Him"; our question is, "If God did not exist, *why* would people invent Him?"

A number of answers to this question have been proposed. Some have suggested that religion is an outgrowth of magic, or of practices that were initially intended to influence natural phenomena for practical reasons: curing an illness, bringing rain, attracting fish to one's net, destroying an enemy, etc. (Malinowski, 1954). Others have supposed that the experience of dreaming, particularly dreams in which the dreamer talks with friends who have died or seems to be somewhere else, led people to distinguish between the physical body and the "soul" and thus to develop an idea of the supernatural. There have also been psychological explanations of religious beliefs and practices as attempts to resolve unconscious conflicts and to deal with the inevitability of death (Freud, 1957). Other attempts to identify the roots of the religious impulse have included Marx's assertion that religion was invented to keep the lower classes content with their lot and Durkheim's theory that the impulse is actually people's response to the mysterious moral power of society itself.

Regardless of its specific origins, we know that the outcome of this impulse is the development of sets of explicit, shared beliefs—and the patterns of interaction through which they are expressed—that define and explain the world and humankind's place in it. To the extent that such beliefs satisfy a need, we may look at them as answers to questions.

Human beings are able to *ask* questions even if they do not have the ability to *answer* them. A question comes to mind whenever we find a gap in our explanation of an event or in our mental picture of the world around us. The more clearly we can identify this gap and the more important to us it is, the more energetically we seek an answer to fill it. We may answer our question—fill the gap we have discovered—by personal investigation, by asking others for the answer, or by such less dependable means as intuition. If the question is important, we will find some way to answer it.

If, however, the question is not very important to us, or if we have some quick-and-easy way to answer it (as when we explain something odd by saying "It is only a coincidence"), or if we are afraid of the answer we might find, we will not search so hard for an answer. We do not have to answer a question just because we can ask it, and often it is easier to forget a question than to answer it.

But some questions cannot be forgotten. They follow us around, nagging and bothering us because they *are* important, regardless of whether they can be answered in ways that allow us to test empirically the validity of our answers. It is the most fundamental of these nonempirical questions that become the focus of people's religious activities. It took thousands of years for us to learn how to test an answer to the question of why fire burns, but eventually this became an empirical question. The question of what happens to us after we die, however, will probably never be a matter of empirical test, and so we must find a different way to validate our answers to this and similar questions.

The way people have been able to validate their answers to such questions has involved what may be called "consensual validation," and it is this that enables us to view the religious institution, like other institutions, as a social structure organized around the exchange of a unique commodity in which human beings have a continuing, widespread interest.

Beliefs and Social Exchange

Whether or not we think that the answers people have found over the centuries to their nonempirical questions are correct, we can agree that most people are "weak" and require the support of others to help them keep on believing in their answers. If one cannot find an empirical demonstration of the truth of one's belief in, say, the Virgin Birth or the Eight-Fold Way, the only alternatives are private intuition (which may be difficult to depend on over a long period) or the testimony of others that they also hold this belief. For better or worse, very few people have received direct revelation of the truth about such things as what happens to us after death; the great majority of us need instruction in a satisfactory response to such questions, and we need continued evidence that our fellows accept these answers along with us. Our faith, in other words, usually requires frequent social reinforcement.

This interdependence, our mutual need for support in our basic beliefs, provides the basis for a system of exchange. The process focuses on the joint commodity of mutual affirmation or support and involves an implicit agreement: "I will support your beliefs by saying and doing those things that indicate *my* acceptance of them, if *you* will do the same for me." The social positions and role relationships that make up the religious institution seem to be organized so that each of us can both give and receive this type of support for our religious beliefs. The clearest example of this is, of course, the weekly worship service, although beliefs can be demonstrated in other ways as well: through service as a medical missionary, contributions to charity, volunteer work for the "Y," and so on.

Further on, we will look at some of the different types of social organization through which such mutual reinforcement of beliefs is achieved. First, though, we will examine the basic questions that seem to underlie the religious impulse and thus motivate people to engage in these relationships. In general, these can be reduced to two distinct questions that are asked by nearly everyone. The first concerns the far reaches of time, both past and future, particu-

Organized worship services provide social reinforcement for most people's basic religious beliefs and faith. (Nicholas Sapieha/Stock, Boston)

larly in terms of the *origin* of the world and of humankind and of ultimate *ends*. The second is the problem of *evil*, a term used here to indicate the central "stuff" that characterizes all the threats, frustrations, and anxieties to which people are heir, including death. The two questions cannot be completely separated, since all instances of evil (and its opposite, good) are located in time, but for now it will be useful to look at them individually.

Origins and ends   It was noted in the previous chapter that kinship groups form the central social structure of most primitive societies. In such societies one's relationships to others are determined primarily by the ties defined by blood and marriage; knowing who one's ancestors were is thus of vital importance to everyone. No matter how far back one can trace his or her genealogy, however, there must come a point beyond which nothing is known for sure. But since it is logical that there must have been ancestors all the way back to the beginning of the species, myths and legends are created to fill this void. These ordinarily include a creation story.

Every society having any traditions at all has such a legend. It almost always involves beings with superhuman powers, since such powers must have been necessary to bring humankind and the world out of nothingness. Ordinary people cannot create something from nothing, and yet we must have come from *somewhere*. Thus in their search for ultimate ancestors, primitive people had reason to conceive of beings with powers far mightier than their own. Out of the logical implications of their need to know their remote history might well have developed people's first appreciation of the supernatural.

Such legends, being unprovable by any other means, required collective agreement to make them continually believable. In this light we can begin to understand the origins of tribal ceremonies that celebrate (and thus reaffirm the reality of) the imaginary forebears of the tribe, their powers, and their influences on the tribe today.

The power to create implies generalized power over natural events, and this is one point at which the concern for origins links up with the concern over evil, since a good deal of evil is caused by such events as forest fires, hurricanes, tidal waves, and landslides. This problem will be taken up in more detail in the next section.

Besides looking at the remote history of their race, people also look to the future. The future may be viewed as what lies ahead for either one person or the group. In the former perspective the question is usually couched in terms of what happens to the individual after death; in the latter it becomes the broader question of the group's future and may focus on a promised land, a future Armageddon, or a Second Coming. Because the future is different in quality from the past—the past has already happened in a certain way, whereas the future cannot be predicted with any real certainty—it is not surprising that most bodies of religious belief have less to say about the future of the tribe or society than about its past.

Only when the fate of the individual is involved is there any comparable elaboration of beliefs. The nature of the soul, the form in which the afterlife will be experienced, and even the location of the afterlife are questions of deep interest to most individuals. The extent of concern with these questions seems to depend very much on how people define evil, and so this is another point at which the two major origins of the religious impulse become intertwined.

Evil, and also good   Evil was defined above as that which is common to all instances of pain, frustration, loss, defeat, and failure, including death. People have been able to conceptualize it as a tangible "thing" and thus to ask where it comes from and why it is visited on them in such unwelcome quantities. And with the identification and reification of evil, people also come to conceive of its logical counterpart, good, as something equally real. They ask the same questions about it: Where does it come from? Why is there not more of it in my life?

In a very important sense the problem of understanding evil comes to be a question of explaining the relationships between it and good, particularly the question of why there seems over the long run to be a balance between good and evil in the world. Since both of these things come into our lives over and over again, it is logical that people should wonder why it is that neither of them every completely "wins out" over the other.

Historically, humankind has worked out three major explanations of this balancing process, with ideas about the origins of good and evil as a part of each.

The first and simplest is **dualism,** *the idea that there are two independent powers in the universe, one standing for good and the other for evil.* In Zoro-astrianism, the former was *Ahura Mazda,* which in more contemporary terms can be thought of as God, and the power working for evil was *Aingra Mainyu;* in the Judeo-Christian tradition this is represented by the Devil. The balance between good and evil is explained by the belief that these two powers are continually battling each other, intruding almost randomly into people's lives, but in roughly equal amounts. Even though we may believe that eventually good will win out over evil, our experience and many of our religious accounts portray them as being about evenly matched.

A second explanation of the balancing process is that of **Karma,** a Hindu term that describes *a more abstract relationship between good and evil, relating both more directly to the individual's behavior.* Here the experience of evil is viewed as punishment for prior misdeeds, whereas good fortune is defined as the reward for proper behavior. The balancing between good and evil takes place in terms of the individual's existence, sometimes over several lifetimes, and focuses on his or her long-run position in society rather on particular incidents. Although *Karma* emphasizes free will as far as future rewards and punishments are concerned, it involves a kind of fatalism about the immediate present.

This view of the relation between good and evil is, of course, central to the Judeo-Christian view, even though in some cases elements of a dualistic interpretation of the problem are involved. Ill fortune, for instance, may be defined by some as an obstacle designed to test us, in the way that Job's faith was tested. It may be defined as the result of "original sin," in which case the individual's past behavior can have been only partly responsible for his or her present troubles. Ill fortune may even be viewed as a particular example of the Devil's work. Present-day explanations of evil may involve more than one of these major approaches to the problem.

The third explanation of the origins of good and evil is actually *denial* that the problem is a realistic one. This takes at least two forms. The first is found in the Eastern teachings associated with the Buddha (Buddhism in its various forms, Confucianism, and Shintoism), which say essentially that evil is simply the misery one experiences because one has not apprehended the world correctly and that the solution lies in attaining a kind of passive wisdom that enables one to experience the world as it really is.

The other form of denying that good and evil are relevant probably reached its purest form in the Calvinistic branches of Protestantism in the sixteenth century. Here the doctrine of **predestination** was central; it proclaimed that *one's ultimate fate had been determined before one was born, and so there could be no meaningful relationship between one's behavior in this life and one's fate in the afterlife.* If there was no connection between this life and the next and if the afterlife was what one should really be concerned with, it was wrong even to wonder about the successes and failures that we experience here on earth. The good and evil that people met in this life were utterly unimportant; the question of where they came from and how they were balanced was dismissed simply by denying that anyone should have any reason to ask it in the first place.

It should be noted that this view of good and evil was difficult to maintain. Even the strictest theocracy could not quell people's curiosity about their fate by saying, "Don't worry, it's already been taken care of." But without knowing *how* things had been taken care of for the individual, he or she was continually searching for signs, for some hint or indication of whether he or she was destined for Heaven or for Hell. Eventually there developed the idea that success in this life might be such a hint, a sign of grace, even though success had to be a pretty dry thing, because it was immoral to pay too much attention to this life and its pleasures.

To enjoy one's success would indicate a lack of proper concern for the afterlife, so the wealth that someone acquired could only be plowed back into the business—which then usually worked to make him or her even more successful. This attitude of perseverence, frugality, and hard work was called the "Protestant ethic" by Max Weber, and its economic implications were explored in more detail in Chapter 11 as one influence on the economic institution.

MAJOR WORLD RELIGIONS AND THE BALANCING PROCESS

Different world religions have explained in various ways the problem of how good and evil are balanced. The two major details to be considered in distinguishing among explanations are, first, whether the balancing takes place for the individual or for the group as a whole; and second, how long a period of time is involved. The former question asks whether the individual or the group is more important, and the latter asks whether the balancing will take place before or after the lifetime of the present generation.

Charting these pairs of alternatives along two sides of a fourfold table, we can fill in the cells with different religions, as in Table 14.1. In the upper left-hand cell is the *civil state*, which is the only agency that can ensure that an individual receives his or her just deserts in this life. Unless the state vigorously enforces its laws, it is possible that some murderers will live long, happy lives and that some genuinely saintly people will have short, tragic lives. Supernatural justice sometimes takes too long, and the state must intervene to see that good is rewarded and evil punished.

Probably the major illustration of this form of religion was the Roman state, particularly when the emperor was worshipped as a god. Perhaps Fascist Italy and Nazi Germany were of the same type, as the state itself became an object of virtual worship. Societies organized under a Marxist system of thought—the Soviet Union and the People's Republic of China—might also fit in this cell, for communism has often been called a "secular religion."

In the lower left-hand cell, where the focus is on the individual and the balancing takes place after death, we find most of the major world religions. In

TABLE 14.1 HOW WORLD RELIGIONS HANDLE
THE BALANCING OF GOOD AND EVIL*

	The focus is on:	
The process takes place:	Individual	Group
Before death	Civil State	Judaism
After death	Christianity Hinduism Islam	(Zionism)

*Religions denying that the problem is realistic: Calvinistic Protestantism, Buddhism, Confucianism, Shintoism.

each of these, although particular details differ, it is the individual who will pay or be rewarded in the next life for his or her behavior during this one.

We find only one major religion in the upper right-hand cell, where the balancing process takes place for the group as a whole, and the process is generally viewed as occurring during this life. This, especially in its pure historical form, is Judaism, which began supposedly as a contract between a tribe and Yahweh, or God. Much Jewish ritual throughout history has been concerned with the group itself rather than with its individual members, and concepts of the individual's afterlife have been a relatively unimportant part of Judaic theology.

Because the Jews have been a persecuted minority for most of the last 2500 years, it is not difficult to see how this focus on the group itself survived among them. The particular crimes of an individual are more likely to result in the persecution of the entire group if he or she is a member of a minority, and so it has been quite reasonable for Jews to view good and evil as pertaining first of all to the group rather than to its individual members.

The only religion that seems appropriate to the lower right-hand cell is actually a particular aspect of the Jewish faith and of some Christian sects. Zionism, until the state of Israel was established under United Nations auspices in 1947, was little more than a faith that someday the Jewish people would again have their own promised land. This faith reached peaks of intensity during and immediately after periods of severe persecution of the Jews, such as the Eastern European pogroms of the nineteenth century and again during the Second World War. When the balance had obviously turned toward evil for the group as a whole, the only possible explanation (if balance were to be maintained over the long run) was that sometime in the future probably after most of the present generation had passed away, the group itself would experience as much collective good as it was experiencing evil at present.

Although the Judaic form of Zionism has today become largely a form of political support for Israel, there are a few other religious groups that may appropriately be assigned to this cell. The Church of Jesus Christ of Latter Day Saints (Mormons) believes in the literal restoration of Zion on the American continent, and both the Seventh Day Adventists and the Jehovah's Witnesses hold similar convictions that Christ will return to earth. Because these groups also pay attention to the individual's salvation, however, they are not such pure examples of this type.

THE SOCIAL STRUCTURE OF RELIGIOUS ACTIVITY

Having explored some of the motivational and cognitive forces involved in the development of religious activity, we turn now to its social structure. Recall that the mutual affirmation of beliefs, like the quest for intimacy, is a *joint* commodity—one that both parties must obtain through exchange if either one is to enjoy it—and that the special role relationships organized to facilitate this type of exchange probably developed earlier in human history than did those involving *scarce* commodities (material goods and services, the right to make or influence decisions for the group).

This means, among other things, that activities related to religious beliefs were probably better organized than those involving political matters by the time that a given society had grown large enough to need a special institutional structure to deal with the latter. It is perhaps for this reason that political authority and religious leadership tended to be fused in the early stages of societal development. This was certainly the case in ancient Egypt and India. Rome, as an empire built on many conquered societies, did not illustrate this principle quite so clearly, because it had to deal with a multitude of different religions. The most striking example of the fusion of religious and political power in modern times has been Japan, which until 1945 maintained at least the fiction that the emperor was the divine head of both the religious and political structures of that nation. The historical tendency has been for political interests to develop and work through existing religious structures until they were ready (after considerable struggle, usually) to assert their own autonomy within society.

Here, however, we are concerned with the organization and activities that make up the religious institution itself, and for the sake of clarity we will try to view it as though it exists in isolation from other social institutions.

Participation

In its simplest form **religion** *involves two or more people who are engaged in mutually acceptable demonstrations of their acceptance of and commitment to certain beliefs.* This definition does not cover individual activities such as private prayer, of course, but we may view such private acts as being carried out with reference to an unseen audience—either the individual's fellows or the deity—and we may assume that participation in organized religious activities always precedes the individual's desire for and knowledge of how to engage in private worship.

Organized activity of any sort requires a blueprint (e.g., the order of worship, the sequence of actions involved in a rain dance) and a schedule (e.g., Friday evening or Sunday morning, the vernal equinox) so that it can be carried out with some order and regularity. When large numbers of people are to be involved, further, leadership of these activities becomes necessary; out of this need has grown the status of "priest," "rabbi," and so on. As the members' activities become more specialized, the group must assume the characteristics of a formal organization (see Chapter 9). As long as organized patterns of interaction are needed to implement the religious impulse, the elaboration of social organization is inevitable.

Participation in such activities is not always motivated directly by religious interest, of course. People may participate in order to demonstrate their commitment to the group or in order to gain others' approval, even when the activities themselves mean little to them. Yet participation would not be meaningful even in these terms if there were not some general sense that people "should" participate—and so we must still conclude that the religious impulse is at least indirectly responsible for such participation.

In the mid-1970s about forty percent of America's adult population participated in organized religious activities each week, and perhaps half of them also engaged in additional activities such as prayer meetings, Bible study groups, and the like (*New York Times*, January 4, 1976). Further, more than one in every ten adult Americans was active in new forms of religious behavior: transcendental meditation, Yoga, the "charismatic" forms of worship usually called Pentecostalism, and the practice of various Eastern religions (*New York Times*, November 18, 1976). Of those belonging to a Christian faith, about one-third said that they had experienced a "born-again" episode in their lives, nearly forty percent said that they take the Bible literally, and almost half of them had, at one time or another, tried to persuade others to accept their beliefs (*New York Times*, September 26, 1976).

With the exception of the growth of various new forms of religion in the United States, the rate of participation does not seem to have changed significantly over the last twenty years, even though different segments of the population differ sharply in this respect. A bit more than half of the Roman Catholics report having attended a religious service within the last week, less than forty percent of the Protestants say this, and about one-fifth of the Jews report such participation (*New York Times*, January 4, 1976).

The extent to which people take part in organized religious activities is apparently determined by four distinct factors. The first of these is simply individual need—the personal importance an individual attaches to participation and the amount of satisfaction she or he gains from this. This in turn is influenced by both the individual's agreement with the beliefs held by his or her religious group and the experience of personal crises in which only religion can provide some solace. In this respect it is apparent that an increasing number of Catholics have ceased active participation in the Church, as its firm stand against contraception and abortion (reaffirmed in 1968) has come into direct conflict with their personal needs and beliefs (Greeley, 1976). It has also been suggested that the long-term decline in the *importance* of religion in America (if not in religious participation) has been due to the decreasing frequency with which Americans have had to deal with the early death of friends and loved ones (Berger, 1967).

A second influence on participation is social pressure, or the importance that one's family, friends, and neighbors place on regular participation. Although social class is definitely related to *which* religious group one belongs to (*Gallup Opinion Index*, 1971), it apparently does not influence one's rate of participation (*New York Times*, January 4, 1976).

The third factor is the extent to which other activities compete with religious services for people's participation. The enactment of "blue laws" in this country, prohibiting many economic and recreational activities on Sunday, was clearly an attempt to eliminate as many distractions as possible from church attendance.

Finally, we may suppose that if there are alternative ways in which basic beliefs may be reinforced, some of the need for specifically religious activity will be reduced. One such "functional alternative" (a different structure or process that performs the same function for society) seems to be the mass media, particularly television. In the media's selection of topics to be presented and in their handling of them, they provide much support for basic American values (see Chapter 17 for a discussion of how this works) and may thereby be weakening to some extent people's need for organized religion.

The question of who participates *with whom* is also of some interest. Because attending a local church or synagogue involves membership in a concrete group, it is usually the case that the members find it more satisfying to worship with others who are "like themselves." It should not be surprising, then, to find that membership in specific religious groups is correlated with social class, race, and ethnicity. Despite the dominant conviction that "all people are equal before God," the consensual validation of belief is more easily found in groups whose members are similar to one another in these respects, because some of the satisfaction found in organized religious activities is lost when the others involved are significantly dissimilar.

Forms of Religious Organization

The ways in which an organized religious group is related to the rest of society and its relationships with other religious groups provide another way to analyze the social structure of religion. Sociologists have identified four ideal types of religious organization; we can distinguish them in terms of whether they *accept* or *reject* secular concerns and whether they are *tolerant* or *intolerant* of other religious groups. A fourfold table embodying these distinctions is given in Table 14.2

The type of religious organization in the upper left-hand cell, called an **ecclesia,** is *generally accepting of secular affairs, but is intolerant of other religious groups.* This type is allied with the civil state, as was the Roman Catholic church in medieval times, and it typically includes nearly all citizens of the state in its membership. It is easy to see that such a group would have to be

TABLE 14.2   THE MAJOR FORMS OF RELIGIOUS ORGANIZATION

Attitude toward other religious groups:	Attitude toward this world:	
	Accepting	Rejecting or ignoring
Intolerant	Ecclesia	Sect
Tolerant	Denomination	Cult

sympathetic to secular concerns because of its close connections with political authority, and also that it would be intolerant of other religious groups, because the state has given it a monopoly on religious authority so that it does not need to tolerate rivals.

When a society is characterized by the separation of church and state, however, so that no single religious group has the formal support of the state, we are likely to find the **denomination**. This, like the ecclesia, may have quite a large membership, but *since it has no special political support in gaining members, it is not likely to be the only religious group in a society.* So whereas the ecclesia is accepting of secular concerns because of its necessary collaboration with civil authority, the denomination must be ready to compromise with secular interests if it hopes to attract a large number of members.

(The term *denomination* is one of the terms in sociology that is taken from everyday usage, and there is no need to go into detail in defining it. Baptists, Presbyterians, Unitarians, and Christian Scientists are all members of Protestant denominations in this country; none of them are given special favors by the government, and all seek new members in open competition with other denominations.)

The third cell in Table 14.2—the **sect**—*is characterized by both an intolerant attitude toward other religious groups and a tendency to reject the secular world.* This type of religious group tends to be much smaller than either the ecclesia or the denomination, and it ordinarily places so much emphasis on its own special teachings and practices that it must necessarily shun other religious groups. Frequently a sect is a group that has broken away from a denomination, as in the case of the Amish of Pennsylvania, who split off from the Mennonites, or the Molokan Brotherhood of California, which broke away from the Russian Orthodox Church. In other cases a sect may represent the continuance of a cult after its original founder has died or left it.

The sect's teachings are intended to encompass every aspect of its members' lives, and so it cannot allow them to be open to the temptations of secular society. Consequently, a sect's members often emphasize poverty and simplicity in their lives, and the group is usually ready to take care of their needs so

In November 1978 some 900 members of the Jonestown cult in Guyana committed mass suicide under the direction of their leader, Jim Jones. (Wide World Photos)

that they need not depend on assistance from the corrupt world that exists outside its own boundaries. Children raised within a sect, thoroughly indoctrinated with its teachings and isolated from people with different beliefs, grow up to carry on the sect's traditions. It is no wonder that sects are often stable, long-lasting groups.

Finally, and really a kind of catch-all, there is the **cult,** *whose members' loyalty to a charismatic leader provides them with immediate emotional satisfactions.* Since the incident in Jonestown, Guyana, when some 900 members of a cult committed mass suicide or else killed one another in November 1978 at the direction of their leader, cults have been the focus of a great deal of public attention and concern. One important difference between a sect and a cult is the presence in the latter of a charismatic leader who, for good or evil, persuades a number of people that his or her guidance promises them the only "salvation" they can find. In extreme cases this guidance may require the members to surrender their worldly goods to "the church," to abandon friends and relatives, and in rare cases even to die or kill others at the leader's command.

Such leaders' power over their followers is difficult to explain, for the essentially mysterious nature of charisma precludes any final answer to why it is that some people follow them so blindly. We may guess, however, that a combination of the members' alienation from society and the leader's hypnotic self-confidence, together with what has been called "groupthink" (the development of a set of beliefs which includes the central assumption that all who disagree are enemies—see Janis, 1972), can account for this. In extreme cases induction into the cult may also entail procedures so rigorous that they resemble brainwashing (see the section on adult socialization in Chapter 4).

In less extreme (and more common) cases the members' involvement is less extensive, often involving no more than participation in services once or several times a week. In this country the term "cult" can be applied to such groups as "The Great I am," "The Moorish Science Temple of America," Father Divine's following in the 1930s, many of the independent "holiness" churches, and most of the store-front-and-neon-sign churches that are found in the run-down areas of our larger cities.

These groups tend to ignore rather than to reject the secular world. And since it is the presence of a charismatic leader rather than of an extensive, organized set of beliefs that holds their members' loyalty, they tend to be relatively tolerant of other religious groups. This seems to be true also because cults concentrate on the immediate arousal of religious enthusiasm and thus emphasize emotional rather than intellectual satisfaction.

Table 14.2, we should remember, does not mean to suggest that a particular religious group cannot change from one form of organization to another. Christianity, for example, began as a cult during the first century of the Roman Empire and over the next three centuries became a sect. Under Constantine the First, it became the official state religion in 486 and thus an ecclesia. Finally, after the Reformation in the sixteenth century, which undermined the Church's position as an ecclesia in most European countries, it broke into a number of denominations. In this country the Roman Catholic Church resembles a denomination more than anything else, although in Spain it remains an ecclesia.

It is difficult at the present time to decide whether the Unification Church of the Reverend Sun Yung Moon is more like a sect or a cult, and this problem is a useful reminder that the four types of religious organization discussed here are "ideal types" rather than models to which real groups always correspond. They emphasize certain important ways in which religious groups differ from one another and are useful for this purpose rather than because they describe existing religious groups in complete detail.

RELIGION AND SOCIETY

To conclude this introductory discussion of the religious institution, it is important that we look at its relationship to the other institutions of society. The basic functions of religion *for society* lie in its legitimating the foundations of society's culture and its integration and transmission of the basic beliefs and values that give social life meaning and purpose. The ultimate justification of anything, whether it be political authority, standards of sexual conduct, or tragic misfortune, seems to most people to lie beyond the realm of empirical reason and sensory evidence. Only religion can provide meaningful interpretation of the world at this level.

It was noted in Chapter 12 that the religious institution has an extremely important relationship to the political institution, providing as it does the basis for political legitimacy under both traditionalistic and often charismatic forms of authority; even in a rational-legal system, as we have found in this country, it is virtually impossible to keep the two institutions entirely separate.

Under communism, to be sure, the basic justification of political authority is not found in a shared concept of the supernatural, but instead in an elaborate picture of the inevitable movement of history. It is not unreasonable, then, to think of communism as a "secular religion," since in many ways Marxism and its various modifications do perform many of the functions of religion. Its failure to replace religion completely, however, suggests that communism does not provide satisfactory answers to *all* of the questions that make religion so universally important to human beings.

Just as it is important to the political institution, religion performs legitimating functions for the economic system, as we saw in the relationship between the Protestant ethic and the rise of capitalism, and for the family in its sanctioning of the marriage relationship. Finally, almost by definition, it is the religious institution that has "custody" of the fundamental justifications for the patterns of behavior that make up society, and thus it stands behind the continued stability of the other institutions of society.

The Future of Religion

Is there a chance that religion as we know it today may die out altogether as a recognizable social institution? If, as has been proposed here, religion performs certain functions for people and their societies that no other institution does, and if these functions are really needed, the disappearance of all social structures that perform these functions is extremely unlikely. But the particular details of these structures are always subject to change, and it may happen that radical changes will occur.

Criticism versus collaboration   The autonomy of organized religion is weakened whenever it falls too much into line with other institutions. To the extent that it comes to be a "wholly owned subsidiary" of the political or the economic institution and serves merely to justify the status quo in those institutions, it begins to lose its claim to being an independent source of truth and of the values that should guide people's behavior. Perhaps some of the anguish we see today in the clergy of all faiths reflects their sense that the gap between the central teachings of religion and the nature of contemporary society is widening. They are torn between teaching the truth as they see it and losing members whose interests are vested in the status quo—and possibly even losing their own positions within their particular churches and synagogues.

Innovation versus tradition   The fact that more than sixteen million American adults now participate in one or more new forms of religious activity is evidence of both people's continuing need for this institution and the fact that the affirmation of faith can take many forms. Two things seem to characterize most of the new religious movements. One is an increase in the amount of active, often spontaneous participation by those involved, instead of the relatively passive, ritualized activities of those who take part in more traditional religious services. Although spontaneity has long been associated with many of the fundamentalist Christian groups, growing public interest in it over the last fifteen years has led many of the more "proper" denominations (including the Roman Catholic Church) to incorporate such practices into their own forms of worship. Glossolalia ("speaking in tongues"), faith healing, and "witnessing" are among these types of active participation.

Also evident is an increased concern for immediate, private religious sensation, in contrast to the emphasis in traditional worship services on **ritual**—*stylized activities whose purpose is essentially symbolic rather than practical.* The sensations sought range from the relief of specific emotional or physical difficulties (in which case the line between religion and magic becomes blurred), through the inner peace that is the goal of Eastern religions, to the ecstasy of the "born-again" experience.

These two characteristics do not always go hand in hand. The quest for inner peace is essentially passive and ritualized, and the pentecostal or fundamentalist forms of worship emphasize public professions of faith as much as they do the participants' inner feelings. Some of the new forms of religion, further, are clearly sectlike in organization: Members of the Unification Church and the Hare Krishna followers devote themselves full-time to their beliefs and have developed tightly knit organizational structures in association with their blends of Eastern and Western doctrines. The transcendental meditation movement, on the other hand, is almost entirely without a theology or structure; it can be argued, in fact, that this practice barely qualifies as a "religion" at all—except that the needs it satisfies seem to be more religious in character than anything else.

Emphasizing inner experience and active involvement in its creation, these new forms of religion seem to provide a new way through which the basic religious commodity—the mutual support of belief—can be obtained. Perhaps the increasing sense of disorientation that accompanies rapid social change (see Chapter 18) has increased people's need for more direct and meaningful participation in religion; perhaps it is simply that the more traditional religious practices have become so overintellectualized that they no longer satisfy the essentially emotional need for religion. But there is no reason to predict that traditional religious structures will wither away entirely. Instead, in order to survive as groups, they will slowly adopt some of the newer practices (slowly and uncertainly, to be sure, and often without explicitly recognizing it), and we will certainly continue to have organized religious groups in society.

We can predict, however, that for some time to come, religious groups will be less fully integrated into the rest of society than they have been. There will be some groups that seek more fervently to justify the status quo, others that serve as centers from which detailed criticisms of society will come, and still others that are concerned primarily with their members' immediate peace of mind and so ignore the rest of society. At a minimum, we shall see a broader spectrum of "teachings" and, perhaps to afford a common ground on which these more differentiated groups can agree, a greater emphasis on what has been called "civil religion"—a relatively undetailed acknowledgment of the existence of God and faith that American ideals are in keeping with the ideals of virtually all religions (Bellah, 1967).

SUMMARY

The religious institution has developed in response to people's need for consensual support of their *beliefs*, or the sense that their values and priorities are "true," for by definition beliefs are not subject to sensory or empirical validation. Although the sociologist has no interest in the truth of particular religious beliefs, he or she is very much interested in how beliefs both influence and are influenced by social relationships.

The individual's need for belief lies in the desire that his or her behavior have meaning and justification beyond mere personal whim, and it is necessary also that values be shared so that society's members can develop predictable, stable patterns of interaction. We may view beliefs about the ultimate nature of the human condition (out of which grow convictions about how people *should* behave) as a necessary consequence of people's ability to ask questions. They ask about the origins and ends of human existence and about the reasons for the presence of both good and evil in their lives. To answer these questions, all societies have developed "genesis" myths, explanations of what will happen in the future to both individuals and the group, and accounts of how good and evil seem to be almost evenly balanced. The idea of *dualism* posits separate forces of good and evil, *Karma* assumes that good and evil are the result of the individual's or group's previous actions, and some religions are characterized by a *denial* that the experience of good and evil is at all realistic. It is possible, in fact, to categorize the major world religions in terms of how they deal with the apparent balance between the amounts of good and evil that are experienced by individuals or by groups (Table 14.1).

Participation in religious activities or rituals—in symbolic affirmations of belief—requires scheduling and leadership, and religious organizations are the result. Participation in them varies according to a number of variables, although we can say generally that about forty percent of the American population takes part in religious services each week. It is possible to distinguish four major types of religious organization—the *ecclesia, denomination, sect,* and *cult*—depending on whether they are tolerant or intolerant of other religious groups and whether they accept or reject secular concerns (Table 14.2).

In answering the need to validate religious beliefs, the religious institution also serves to legitimate the values that underlie behavior in other social institutions. Religious values sanction political authority and economic activities, and they confirm the marriage relationship.

Yet religious organizations are probably more influenced *by* other social institutions than they influence them, so that the details of the future of the religious institution are quite unclear. It seems fair to say, though, that no other institution is fully capable of fulfilling the particular needs that it answers. Thus even though the contents of religious beliefs may change somewhat and the forms of religious organization may change still more, it is certain that the religious institution will continue to be a basic part of even the most modern and complex societies.

SUGGESTED READINGS

Bellah, Robert N., *Beyond Belief* (New York: Harper & Row, 1970). Bellah has been remarkably innovative and wide-ranging in his studies of religion, and this book provides an impressive look at his work.

Durkheim, Emile, *The Elementary Forms of the Religious Life* [1912] (New York: Free Press, 1947). Here Durkheim presents his influential argument that the source of organized religion is the awe that society itself inspires in people; although his basic data (on totemism among the Australian aborigines) are not always sound, the ideas he draws from them have played a major role in the sociology of religion.

Faulkner, Joseph E., ed., *Religion's Influence in Contemporary Society* (Columbus, Ohio: Merrill, 1972). This reader contains thirty-four articles on all aspects of religion, ranging from empirical studies of beliefs to theoretical analyses of the place of religion in modern societies.

Glock, Charles Y., and Robert N. Bellah, eds., *The New Religious Consciousness* (Berkeley: University of California Press, 1977). The editors conclude this collection of articles on the new religious movements with essays of their own that draw together the findings that have been presented and provide a rich sociological understanding of what is occurring in religion today.

O'Dea, Thomas F., *The Sociology of Religion* (Englewood Cliffs, N.J.: Prentice-Hall, 1966). A relatively brief but comprehensive introduction to the topic, this text is a good example of the functionalist approach to the analysis of religion.

Pope, Liston, *Preachers and Millhands* (New Haven, Conn.: Yale University Press, 1942). The classic study of religion in a Southern mill town. It is especially noted for its development of the distinction between the sect and the denomination and the processes by which the former becomes the latter.

Robertson, Roland, ed., *Sociology of Religion* (Baltimore: Penguin, 1969). An excellent collection of excerpts from major works in the field, together with research reports, that offers a comprehensive review of the sociological and anthropological study of religion.

Stark, Rodney, and Charles Y. Glock, *American Piety: The Nature of Religious Commitment; Volume I: Patterns of Religious Commitment* (Berkeley: University of California Press, 1968). The authors draw on extensive survey data to show the wide variations in belief that characterize different American Protestant groups—variations that often separate them more sharply from each other than they are typically separated from Catholics and Jews.

Swanson, Guy F., *The Birth of the Gods* (Ann Arbor: University of Michigan Press, 1960). This is an important comparative analysis of materials from a large number of primitive societies, showing some of the relationships between particular social variables and particular aspects of religious beliefs.

Weber, Max, *The Sociology of Religion* [1922], translated by Ephraim Fischoff (Boston: Beacon Press, 1963). Written after his intensive work on the religions of China, India, and ancient Judaism, this work sums up Weber's analysis of the nature of religious activity and its relations with other parts of society.

Glossary

Consensual validation The process through which two or more people confirm each other's faith in the validity of a belief by actions that demonstrate their own acceptance of its meaning. The process may involve matters of empirical fact as well, but is important primarily as it sustains people's faith in values and the untestable beliefs that are at the heart of religion.

Cult A type of religious group, usually organized around a charismatic leader, whose members' loyalty is based mainly on the immediate emotional satisfactions they find through participation rather than on commitment to a complex, systematically organized body of beliefs.

Denomination A type of religious organization that is ordinarily much larger than a cult, with its members belonging to many separate units of the organization such as local churches or temples. It tends to be based on an extensive body of beliefs and is unrelated to society's political institution. In a society that emphasizes the separation of church and state, there tend to be many denominations, each of which may compete with the others for members.

Dualism A belief in the existence of two separate supernatural powers, one embodying good and the other evil.

Ecclesia A type of religious organization that is allied with society's political institution as the official state religion. In extreme cases membership in it is a necessary aspect of citizenship, and those who do not belong to it may suffer serious disadvantages.

Karma The type of religious belief that views a person's present fortunes as divinely determined rewards or punishments for previous behavior. When a society's culture emphasizes the present rather than the future, the focus is on how one's current situation is a consequence of one's acts during a previous existence; when emphasis is on the future, the focus is on how one's behavior today will result in rewards or punishments in the next life.

Predestination The religious belief that the course of history, and thus of every individual's past and future, has already been determined by an omnipotent deity. Whether one will be among the elect (those going to heaven) or the damned (those going to hell) is thus predetermined, although no one can know his or her own fate. The anxieties caused by this belief, Weber suggested, led to a search for signs of one's fate in measures of worldly success and contributed eventually to the rise of capitalism.

Religion Organized social activities that have as their purpose the maintenance and reinforcement of beliefs that answer basic questions about human existence: origins and ends, good and evil, and the supernatural agencies related to them.

Ritual A pattern of behavior whose purpose is essentially symbolic rather than utilitarian, although it may aim quite "practically" to influence the specific actions of one or more supernatural beings.

Sect A type of religious group whose members are characterized by strong commitment to its beliefs, together with some suspicion and avoidance of the secular society around it and of other religious groups. The members of a sect typically form a very close-knit group and prefer to depend on one another rather than on assistance from outsiders. In some cases, sect members attempt to spread their beliefs to others through some form of missionary activity.

IV
MAJOR SOCIAL PROCESSES

Although people engaged in interaction can never predict one another's behavior with total accuracy, it is important to distinguish between routine, highly predictable types of interaction and types that are more unpredictable. The former can be called *patterns* of interaction; they occur again and again, their participants enter them voluntarily because they expect to gain something, and the presence of shared norms enables the participants to cooperate in achieving their goals. Buying something in a store, campaigning for political office, getting the kids off to school in the morning, and taking part in a worship service all involve patterned social relationships. Together, such patterns of interaction make up the institutional structures of society.

But there is much social interaction that lacks these characteristics. In these cases not all of the participants want to be involved, an outcome satisfactory to all participants is rare, and either there is disagreement on what norms should apply to the situation or else none seem relevant at all. A bank robbery, a police raid on a terrorist group, people fleeing a flash flood, and the current efforts to develop new sex roles are examples of relatively unpredictable types of interaction. They are marked by conflict, or at least confusion. For want of a better term, we shall call these types of social relationships *social processes*.

Although the participants in social processes have difficulty predicting one another's actions or the outcome of their interaction, the sociologist believes it possible to discover regularities in them. In this section we will see how the sociological perspective can be useful in finding the regularities that exist below the surface of the major social processes that occur in society.

Deviant behavior—acts that frustrate, upset, or injure others—is clearly unpredictable in any concrete sense. If people could predict when and where such acts would occur, they would be more successful in preventing them. The relationship between someone engaged in deviant behavior and the person who suffers because of that behavior is a conflictful relationship, with the latter usually believing that the former has violated one or several social norms. Chapter 15 covers the major types of deviance, the kinds of situations that generate deviant behavior, and some important theories of deviance.

If deviant behavior involves people who "get out of line" in society, the process of social control represents society's attempts to protect itself against the disruptions caused by deviance. Chapter 16 introduces the major forms of social control and the various methods (with varying degrees of success) by which they are implemented.

The various forms of behavior that occur when there are no norms relevant to the situation or when relevant norms are collectively ignored are considered in Chapter 17, on public opinion and collective behavior. The process through which public opinion is formed provides a model for understanding behavior in other unstructured situations: panics, riots, fads, social movements, and so on.

Chapter 18, finally, discusses the broader topic of social change. Defining the topic as change in the form or frequency of social relationships, the chapter surveys the various sources of change and the major attempts to delineate the central forces and directions of social change throughout history. The chapter concludes with a consideration of current attempts to control the process of change.

15
Deviant Behavior

THE VIOLATION OF EXPECTATIONS

If we toss a coin ten times and it comes up heads ten times, we may be surprised or amazed, but we will not be angry at the coin. Only our "statistical expectations" have been violated. But when another person does something unexpected and thereby upsets our plans, we may well become angry. We had been counting on him or her to do as we expected—to behave in accordance with the norms that we believe should govern people in this situation—and our anger is rooted in the feeling that this person chose to violate those norms. Our *normative* expectations have been violated.

Social relationships, whether they involve specific interaction (ordering a meal in a restaurant, for instance) or noninteraction (strangers in an elevator consciously avoiding one another's eyes), are based on shared norms. Each of us plans his or her behavior on the basis of these expectations. "If I ask the waiter to bring more water, he will." "I won't stare into that stranger's eyes because she will think I'm trying to establish a personal relationship." We assume, further, that others plan their behavior with the same normative expectations in mind, for they are presumably members of our society and share its culture. Thus the patterns of social relationships that make up society depend largely on our continuing to live up to one another's expectations.

Yet there are many occasions whey people fail to abide by norms and so fail to live up to others' expectations. In the concrete sense they have thereby injured others' interests, directly or indirectly. But in the broader sense they have undermined others' generalized faith that the members of their society can be counted on to behave in accordance with the normative standards contained in their culture.

The violation of expectations, then, is something that is important well beyond its immediate, concrete consequences. For the citizen, it is not only a matter of personal safety and security, but also a concern for the general reliability of social relationships. For the sociologist it is central to the basic question of how society can continue to exist.

Together, the ways in which normative expectations can be violated make up a topic that is of intense personal interest to everyone and of fundamental theoretical interest to the sociologist. The broadest term we have to encompass all the forms of behavior that violate expectations is *deviance,* or *deviant behavior.*

The study of **deviance**—*individual and collective failure to abide by accepted norms*—is a prominent part of sociology and represents a major heritage from the days when sociologists were concerned largely with social amelioration, or betterment. The study of deviant behavior has become more systematic and much less tinged with disapproval than it was fifty years ago, for deviance is simply another type of social behavior to be studied in its own right. A major advance in this area has come as sociologists have recognized that the standards by which deviance is defined are themselves social phenomena and that these standards deserve study, just as do those acts that society defines as illegal, immoral, or antisocial.

But it will be easier to begin with all those forms of behavior that we ordinarily define as deviant—delinquency, vice, blasphemy, embezzlement, assault, robbery, murder, treason, and so on. We need to look more closely at what is common to them and thus allows us to include all of them under a single heading.

THE CONCEPT OF DEVIANCE

Aspects of Deviance

All of the various acts or patterns of behavior we call deviance have three different aspects that seem to justify our putting them into the same conceptual category.

Statistical deviance   First, most "deviant" acts are *statistically abnormal*, at least in the sense that we believe they occur much less often than such nondeviant acts as going to work, kissing one's spouse, buying a pair of shoes, or attending a religious service. If we were to list all of the different relationships that could possibly exist among people in a given situation, those that tend to occur least often would by this criterion be defined as deviant. To define deviance simply as "statistically abnormal behavior," however, would require that we also include in this category exceptionally "good" (or outstanding or successful) behavior. The student who always gets straight A's, or the person who gives half of his or her income to the poor, or one who always loves one's enemies would be as deviant as the rapist or the burglar. A purely statistical definition thus seems to include more kinds of behavior than we really want to deal with, even though some sociologists have used it and have done some interesting work along this line. (For example, people who are especially saintly or successful may elicit negative responses from others, just as "real" deviants do, even though their only "crime" is to turn in a better role performance than most other people.)

Although most members of our society consider violent behavior deviant, violence may be an acceptable way for members of a juvenile gang to seek revenge or to achieve a "rep" with other members. (Michael Abramson/Camera 5)

Normative expectations   The definition of deviance as "statistically abnormal" turns on the matter of *empirical* expectations. A second characteristic of all forms of deviance is that they violate society's *normative expectations.* It is difficult to draw a hard and fast line between these two types of expectation because they shade into each other. What begins as a purely empirical or statistical expectation—"Betty always knows what tomorrow's algebra assignment is"—may turn into something like a normative expectation as soon as other people come to base their own behavior on this expectation: "I didn't write down the assignment because I expected Betty to get it—she *ought* to have gotten it."

Most normative expectations, of course, are based on cultural prescriptions and proscriptions rather than on privately observed statistical regularities, and it is their violation which elicits "moral outrage" in the observer. This criterion for identifying deviance is probably the one most frequently used by sociologists today, even though the question of why and how such expectations have developed has not yet received the scrutiny it deserves. But for many purposes it is sufficient to take these expectations as given, especially when they are embodied in law, and to concentrate on who violates them and why.

Harmful consequences, real or in principle   The third aspect common to all of the forms of behavior we think of as deviant is that their consequences are commonly thought to be undesirable. All of them, in principle if not actually in each specific instance, seem to threaten harm to society. No single act of deviance, of course, is going to harm all of society's members, but society tends to view each such act as a potential precedent for others' behavior: "If this went on unchecked or if everyone started doing it, what would be the consequences for us and for society in general?" It is on this basis, clearly, that the state justifies its concern with deviance and assumes responsibility for the control of many forms of deviant behavior.

It should be noted that this third method of defining deviance gives us more freedom than is generally available with definitions based on empirical or normative expectations. First of all, it is not concerned with motivation, so it can include acts which are not purposefully harmful or consciously in violation of norms. Second, it is not based directly on laws or moral standards, so it can include acts which are not proscribed by law—and can sometimes ignore those which are. Third, this approach is broad enough to include as deviance the kinds of behavior that seem to threaten society simply because they have been declared illegal, regardless of whether the behavior itself is actually harmful. Whenever a society puts itself "on record" as being opposed to a particular type of behavior by formally declaring it to be illegal, it forces those who engage in this behavior to demonstrate a positive lack of commitment to society and its culture and thus in principle to threaten the sense that this culture (of which law is an important part) is shared and accepted by everyone.

Defining Deviance

When we see that the foundation of definitions of deviance consists in the anticipation that deviant behavior will harm society, we are forced to admit that specific acts of deviance are "deviant" mainly in relation to particular societies. No group or society can tolerate random violence among its members, but beyond this minimal standard it becomes clear that deviance exists only in relation to the "normal" expectations contained in a particular culture. This fact may offend our feeling that deviance is, or ought to be, absolutely rather than relatively wrong, but it does give us a broader perspective. "Harm" in a given society often depends on how social relationships are defined by its culture, so that we cannot always say that a particular form of behavior is harmful. Copying the answers to a test, for instance, would not be a "bad thing" if it were not for the expectations present in the situation that determine the importance of tests and how they are to be taken.

It is true that some deviance becomes harmful only because the behavior involved has been *defined* by others as deviant, even though people are not always correct in determining which forms of behavior *would* actually harm society if they were to be adopted by more and more people. *Most* societies throughout history, however, have been reasonably successful in identifying *most* of the types of behavior that would actually harm them and in acting collectively to control them. It seems reasonable to assume that the collective anticipation of injury to society lies at the basis of all definitions of deviance. But this is certainly related to the other two definitions—statistical abnormality and violations of normative expectations. We can see the relations among these criteria in the following way. If behavior is defined as harmful to society, it will sooner or later be proscribed by norms; if behavior is thought to be normatively wrong, it will usually become relatively rare in fact, since it is violations of normative expectations that are most frequently identified and punished by society's members.

For our purposes, then, we can conclude that the essential characteristic of all forms of behavior that are defined as deviant is their potential for harming society, whether directly or indirectly. We can thus define as **deviance** *an act or series of acts which, if continued, would lead to the weakening or dissolution of society—in the opinion of most members of that society.* We can also make this definition applicable to smaller units of society by substituting "group" for "society," so that it can be used also in the analysis of deviance within families, voluntary associations, communities, and other types of groups.

Deviance, Social Problems, and the Sociologist

Because deviance is in one way or another considered a threat to society, it is important that we discuss its relationship to the closely related concept of "social problem." There is no complete agreeement among sociologists as to how these two terms should be distinguished, but for our purposes it will be useful to limit the definition of deviance to actions which in themselves are potentially harmful to society. Deviance, then, certainly *is* a social problem, but does not cover all situations that we may define as **social problems**—*those social conditions generally considered undesirable and perhaps correctable.*

It is not deviant to drive into the city, to have children, or to be out of a job, but when too many people do these things or share certain undesirable characteristics, we have traffic jams, the population explosion, and unemployment. Homicide is a form of deviance *and* a social problem, whereas poverty and unemployment are scarcely intentional conditions that can be forbidden by norms. As certain problems, such as air pollution and overcrowding in slum areas, come to be defined as threats caused by specific acts (factories failing to install pollution controls, landlords who subdivide tenements into too many apartments), those acts can be declared illegal and thus forms of deviance. But when the problem is essentially one of "behavioral congestion," as is a traffic jam or an overcrowded camping area, society must choose whether it is more important to abridge certain individual rights or to tolerate such problems.

This distinction between deviance and social problems at least locates the former as one category of the latter and should make it possible for us to approach deviance with a clearer and perhaps more useful perspective. *How* the sociologist approaches deviance is worthy of comment at this point.

As a citizen, the sociologist is, of course, concerned about the problems that beset society. But there is debate within the profession today over the extent to which sociologists *as sociologists* should take public positions on current issues. The more traditional belief has been that moral neutrality rather than partisan advocacy of or opposition to, say, the decriminalization of marijuana, is more appropriate for one who professes to study society dispassionately. This position assumes that active involvement in trying to resolve a problem might interfere with the sociologist's ability to study it without bias. And because not all sociologists hold the same views on particular social problems and how they should be solved, it is wiser not to risk the discipline's reputation through public debate over which solution should carry its official blessing.

But many sociologists today say that it is impossible to avoid all bias and that it is more honest to make known one's political and social preferences than to pretend absolute objectivity. It is only a short step from this belief to saying publicly, "As a sociologist, I think we should [support X, oppose Y, work for Z, etc.]." In more extreme form, some sociologists say that *not* taking an active part in the resolution of social problems is itself unethical: "If you're not part of the solution, you're part of the problem."

I disagree. Whether or not an individual sociologist can be free of all bias, a basic article of faith in any science is that the critical professional give and take among scientists will keep bias to a minimum. Further, to divide all of society into "good guys" (those active in trying to solve a social problem such as poverty) and "bad guys" (those whose inaction seems to represent approval of poverty) is a vast and unscientific oversimplification.

There is no intent here to criticize the desire to help resolve society's problems, but experience suggests that a dispassionate analysis of what is wrong with society—and why—will probably produce more effective action than will an emotional commitment to "do something about it right now."

In addition, not all sociologists study deviance or other social problems because they want to help solve them. As a citizen, a sociologist may be appalled at the spread of heroin addiction in society; as an applied sociologist, he or she may want to propose effective countermeasures; but a "basic" sociologist may be interested in addiction simply as a distinctive type of social behavior whose study may lead to a more detailed understanding of society as a whole.

So the sociologist does not usually sound in writing as though she or he is very worried or upset by a particular type of deviance or social problem. A sociologist's analysis of bank robbers, prostitutes, or poor people may even sound cynical—or at least show less moral indignation than many people think should be shown. Yet he or she ordinarily believes that effective analysis requires emotional detachment and so places professional obligations ahead of his or her attitudes as a citizen. The goal is the understanding of a type of social behavior, whether this is for practical reasons or for the sake of extending theoretical knowledge, and it should not be surprising that the sociologist does not take an evaluative position with respect to every example of this behavior that is under investigation.

THE MAJOR TYPES OF DEVIANCE

Before looking into the various origins of deviant behavior (motivations, situations, and so on), we ought to know more clearly just what we are dealing with in this chapter. With deviance defined as behavior which would threaten society if it were to continue unchecked, it will be useful now to identify the different types of deviance according to *how* they seem to be potential threats.

There are two distinct aspects of society that deviance may threaten: the "real world" of concrete patterns of interaction and the "symbolic world" of interrelated values and symbols—its culture. The two are closely linked, of course, but some types of deviance tend to threaten *first* people's ability to engage in their regular social activities (as an assault might put someone in the hospital or the theft of your car would make it harder for you to visit a relative), whereas other types pose their initial threat to the culture that these people share (a politician's saying one thing and doing another, for instance, can create a "credibility gap" that is actually a threat to the validity of culture, and someone's shouting obscenities during a religious service can be defined as threatening the integrity of the worshippers' shared "definition of the situation"). No form of deviance is a threat to only *one* of these aspects of society, but for the sake of conceptual clarity it is important to distinguish between them and to recognize as well a kind of middle ground in which are found the kinds of deviance that pose an equal threat to both social structure and culture.

Threats to Culture

As any act of deviance violates expectations, it threatens culture in the sense that it raises the question of how widely shared and thoroughly accepted these expectations are. To the extent that people's faith in the sharedness of their culture is shaken, their own commitment to it will be weakened (because it will seem a less reliable guide to effective interaction), and so they will be more hesitant about interacting with others; consequently the pace of life in society will be a bit slower, and there will be less integration and interdependence among its parts. Thus a form of deviance which is first of all a threat to culture will, by causing some harm to the foundation on which interaction is based, also have harmful consequences for other aspects of society.

What sorts of deviance can be identified as posing an initial threat to culture? What sorts of acts seem to threaten the sharedness, or the organization, or the accuracy of a group's culture?

Lying poses a clear threat to the validity of culture because it inserts false ideas into our picture of the world. An individual who lies to escape punishment for something, to misdirect someone else, or for the sake of improving his or her own reputation is disturbing the "culture" of only a small number of individuals. But when outright lies or half-truths are disseminated through the mass media by politicians or advertisers, the potential harm is more substantial. In either case these false ideas sooner or later come into logical conflict with other elements of culture, so that lying tends also to weaken the organization of culture.

A more direct threat to its organization is found in blasphemy, obscenity, and other forms of "verbal naughtiness." Part of the strength of any culture's organization depends on keeping aesthetically or emotionally dissonant elements apart from each other in conceptual space. When the sacred and the profane, the pure and the dirty, or the refined and the vulgar are juxtaposed in the same thought or are presented to us simultaneously in the same situation, we sense that our culture's structure of meaning has been distorted. Some of the relief from pain or anger that we find in cursing, in fact, may come from our sense that we have indeed been aggressive, even though we have not seen that our culture is the object of this assault.

Finally, there is censorship—the purposeful withholding of information or symbolic experiences from part or all of the members of society. This obvious threat to the sharedness of culture is usually carried out by the government or other organized groups to "protect" society, either by withholding information (e.g., military secrets) that others might use against society or by trying to prevent the disorganization of meaning that public display of sacrilegious or openly sexual materials would presumably cause. The "protection" provided by censorship, however, must be balanced against both the harm introduced by lowering the level of a culture's sharedness and the possibility that censorship may be employed for the benefit of the censors rather than of the public. Although it is not ordinarily considered a form of deviance—probably because it is usually done "officially" and supposedly for the good of the public—censorship does represent a potential threat to the sharedness and accuracy of culture.

Threats to the Social Structure

All forms of deviance that have individual victims—people who are injured in some way by the actions of others—can be said to threaten social structure immediately and culture only secondarily. This is because, so far as society is concerned, the victim's ability to continue participating in normal social relationships has been impaired. The victim's own feelings about the matter, of course, concentrate on his or her private sense of injury. The pain of any injury to the victim, however, cannot be measured objectively, so that the social rather than the personal consequences of such deviance become important in demonstrating the existence of a deviant act and its seriousness.

We may assume that every member of society has a basic need to feel in control of his or her body and that this need extends to nearby "personal space" and to personal property. Any purposeful action that violates this need thus violates a basic social norm and, except under special circumstances, is defined as deviant. The police may have a right to use force in controlling a suspected criminal, for instance, and a parent may have the right to spank a naughty child, but ordinarily we treat such "invasions of the person" as acts of deviance.

The loss of money or property through theft or damage is certainly the easiest injury to assess, because these things can be measured in terms of economic value. The value of a stolen car, a broken window, or the amount of money lost in a holdup can usually be established to everyone's satisfaction. The psychic injury to the victim, or the sense of dismay and loss, is ordinarily ignored in identifying the nature and seriousness of the deviance that caused it. Norms concerning property rights rather than injury to the ego are those said to have been violated.

Although physical injury involves pain, only its social consequences can be measured: To what extent has the victim's ability to continue participating in normal social relationships been impaired? Murder is the extreme here, for it prevents its victim from further participation in *any* form of behavior and thus has the most serious consequences for all those who had expected to interact with and to depend on him or her in the future. Otherwise, the seriousness of deviance resulting in physical injury tends to be measured in terms of how long the victim is kept "out of circulation" and the kinds of activities in which future participation will no longer be possible.

Psychic pain, or injury to the ego, is the most difficult to measure. This may come through physical pain (especially when it is purposefully inflicted) or through embarrassment, humiliation, or fright. But because it is impossible to demonstrate its existence directly, difficulties arise sometimes even in establishing the occurrence of a deviant act, not to mention its relative severity. There are, unfortunately, ways to inflict physical pain that leave no marks and so cannot be shown to have happened at all, and the other forms of psychic injury leave no visible traces at all. Further, because there may always be suspicion that the victim has a vested interest in claiming to have experienced *more* psychic pain than actually was felt, charges of deviant behavior that resulted only in injury to the ego have always been difficult to deal with.

Regardless of how difficult it may be to prove "victimization," though, the forms of deviance that produce injury to others are direct threats to the ongoing social relationships that make up society and are ordinarily viewed as more serious than those which threaten primarily the organization or accuracy of culture.

Threats to the Organization of Values

It was pointed out in Chapter 3 that a high level of agreement on the relative importance of different values is necessary if culture is to provide guidance in social relationships. *Behavior,* then, *which reverses generally held value priorities* constitutes a third form of deviance called **vice,** even though it does not threaten the accuracy or logical organization of culture and does not have victims.

Among the forms of deviance labeled as vice are gambling, prostitution, drug addiction, and various sexual "perversions" such as pornography, homosexuality, transvestism, and sadomasochism. Each generally requires the willing cooperation of two or more people. No one is forced to join a floating crap game, to visit a prostitute, to take heroin, or to engage in a homosexual relationship, so it is rare that either party will complain. (To be sure, it is possible that involvement in such activities can make one vulnerable to certain forms of injury-producing deviance—robbery, assault, blackmail, etc.—but these are not intrinsic to the vice itself.)

Each of these types of deviance seems to demonstrate that its participants are reversing or "perverting" the relative importance of two cultural values. In gambling, for instance, the function of money as a medium of economic exchange is made less important than its use as an object of recreational interest. The turn of the cards or fall of the dice determines the transfer of money without its ever generating any contributions (goods and services) to society. The allocation of goods and services is thus distorted by severing the relationship between money and economic activity, and so in principle, gambling is a threat to the higher priority ordinarily given to work than to play.

A chief objection to prostitution has always been that it threatens the foundations of the family, even though there is no evidence whatsoever to support this charge. The impersonal sale of sexual services, however, does involve a definition of the sex relationship that is in sharp contrast to the "preferred" view that it is an expression of love between two people. By making sex an essentially economic rather than personal interaction, prostitution distorts the value that "places" sex in the family as a privileged relationship based on enduring mutual concern and support. The topic is discussed at greater length in Chapter 13, on the family, and also in Chapter 10, on social exchange.

Serious addiction to any substance that changes one's behavior tends to alter one's value priorities. While "under the influence," whether of alcohol, heroin, or a hallucinogen, the person is ordinarily not interested in engaging in normal patterns of interaction and so becomes "untrustworthy" in the eyes of others. If, further, need for the substance increasingly dictates one's behavior,

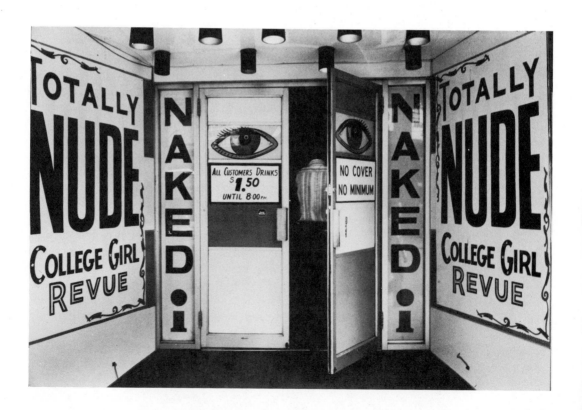

his or her values become more distorted. Honesty with others, respect for others' property rights, and even self-respect become less important than doing whatever is necessary to get the next "fix," and the addict thus becomes a threat to others. Even if all drugs could be obtained free and on demand, the addict's withdrawal from participation in many of the normal activities that make up society would still demonstrate his or her "perverted" scale of values.

Finally, although it is increasingly accepted that sexual alternatives of all kinds do not threaten society so long as they are private and involve consenting adults, there will probably continue to be a tendency to define them as deviant on the grounds that they conflict with our culture's definition of "normal" sex. Homosexuals and transvestites clearly violate the norms associated with ascribed sex roles, pornography completely depersonalizes the sexual relationship by substituting a film or a book for a real individual, and other "perversions" are usually viewed as incomprehensible ways to achieve sexual gratification: "People who get their kicks *that* way are *weird*—and who knows what other crazy things they might do!"

The vices, then, are defined as deviant because their participants seem to be guided by value priorities that conflict with those contained in our culture. This means that vice is very much determined by the way a society's culture is organized, and we know that each one of the forms discussed here has been tolerated and even approved in other societies at other times. To remove the stigma from vice would thus require changes in the culture or else greater toleration of discrepancies between our values and our behavior. The latter seems a likely trend at the moment, but perhaps at the cost of decreasing agreement on values and thus decreasing societal integration.

DEVIANCE-GENERATING SITUATIONS

Many factors go into producing deviant behavior. Biological, psychological, social, and cultural factors may all be involved in producing a particular instance of deviance, and each one has been tested in one theory or another as the dominant cause of deviance. Although one may be more important than the others in producing a given case or even a certain type of deviance, it is clear now that there is no simple, monocausal explanation of why people engage in deviant behavior.

◄ Vices, such as pornography, are difficult to define, for what is illegal in one society may be tolerated or even approved in others. (Stephen J. Sherman)

Because each deviant act is *chosen* by an individual, if only out of ignorance, misperception of the situation, or desperation, its immediate source is always within the individual. But no choice is ever made in a vacuum. It is always influenced by culture (as the individual has internalized it) and by the immediate circumstances, as well as by the individual's personal needs and goals. Thus the immediate source of deviance is psychological, but the tendency today is to look at the broader situation. The sociologist is more interested in predicting rates of deviance than in explaining specific cases; the best approach for us, then, is to identify the different types of deviance-generating situations and then to examine the processes that produce those situations.

We can identify six reasonably distinct deviance-generating situations, plus a seventh that will be treated later. Since not all of these involve conscious motives, it seems better to think of them as "sources" of deviant behavior and to avoid the implication that all deviance is chosen purposefully or rationally.

These situations can be ranged along a continuum. At one end is the set of circumstances that makes us believe that the person did not wish to engage in deviance and is highly unlikely to repeat that behavior. At the other end are the circumstances that suggest that the person both wished to violate a norm and will do so again whenever possible. The question of intent, then, plays a large role in our reaction to an act of deviance, along with its specific consequences (Marshall, 1968).

Desperation

The first point on our continuum can be called *desperation.* It covers those acts of deviance which an individual cannot reasonably avoid committing. The man who runs naked into the street because his house caught fire while he was in the shower, the person who shoots someone in self-defense, the unemployed woman who steals from a grocery store to feed her children, and the soldier who commits suicide to avoid torture at the hands of the enemy—all have committed acts which under other circumstances would be considered deviant. But because all were committed in the service of a "higher value" (stay alive, protect yourself, take care of your family, defend your country), we assume that each act is completely forgivable. To accuse these individuals of willfully threatening society (even if only through setting undesirable precedents) would imply that the "higher" values are not so important after all.

It is for this reason that many people, when accused of deviant behavior, will try to justify their actions by reference to some sort of desperation. The boy who steals a car may say, "But I had to have it so I could take my girl out." The prostitute will explain: "There was no other way to earn enough money to pay my mother's medical bills." The man who embezzles money from his employer will claim: "He really owed it to me—I work a lot harder for him than he pays me for." Needless to say, such private value hierarchies rarely help these individuals escape the legal penalties called for by their acts; if such defenses were ordinarily accepted, no one would ever be penalized for any act of deviance.

Ignorance

The second point on the scale is best termed *ignorance.* It is the kind of situation in which deviance is committed simply because someone did not know that it was illegal or did not foresee its consequences. This is the explanation we usually assign to the retarded fellow who didn't fully understand that it was wrong to break into an unoccupied house and to the person who didn't see the "no trespassing" sign. It presumably also covers cases of inadvertent injury to others, as might occur when a child is hit after darting suddenly in front of a car, even though the "ignorance" here is simply failure to predict the child's action.

Because "ignorance of the law is no excuse," this is not offered as a defense when someone is accused of deviant behavior. A person may not be severely punished if ignorance was obvious, but we ordinarily believe that at least a mild slap on the wrist is called for, to warn the person again against further ignorance or carelessness.

Impulsiveness

Impulsiveness is the third point on our continuum, and here it becomes worthwhile to look for the motivations that produce the deviance as well as the situation. Neither desperation nor ignorance accounts for very much of the deviance that occurs in society, and beyond educational measures there seems little that can be done about deviance originating in these sources. Impulsiveness, however, is a more serious problem.

Deviance due to impulsiveness seems to be committed by people who place a higher value on the gratification of momentary emotional needs than on the achievement of more distant goals. A "crime of passion," such as a man's killing his wife during an argument, is best viewed as the result of impulsiveness, as is the deviance committed by the man who gets into a tavern brawl because someone insulted him, the teenage girl who "can't resist" swiping a piece of costume jewelry from a department store, and the man who finally rapes his playfully teasing girlfriend. These people know what is considered deviance and what is not, but they give in to their own immediate desires in certain situations.

Impulsiveness can be traced to an individual's upbringing, to a culture or subculture that condones impulsive acts, or to the absence of clear-cut rules.

governing the situation. The psychological explanation of impulsiveness is that the person has somehow failed to develop an adequate set of inner constraints; he or she is said to have a weak superego. Some cultures or subcultures tend to value the immediate satisfaction of emotional needs, so that people are not trained or encouraged to develop inner controls. Finally, regardless of psychological development or culture, a person may act impulsively if he or she enters a new and relatively unstructured situation such as a war, a civil disorder, or a natural disaster (see Chapter 17).

Risk Taking

Fourth on the continuum is a category that we can call *risk taking.* It involves simply a willingness on the part of a person to become involved in a situation whereby he or she might possibly become involved in deviance, depending on chance and events over which he or she has no control. Such an action may involve no more than a person's writing a check against insufficient funds, hoping to deposit more money in the account before the check is cashed, or it may be a youngster's decision simply to "go out with the gang" and let things develop spontaneously—perhaps just going to a movie, perhaps breaking into a candy store.

Because deviance originating in risk taking implies more rational motives than impulsiveness, it is presumably more likely to be repeated. Thus it must be countered with more severe sanctions. But because it is not entirely rational, in the sense of being planned as a regular activity, we feel that it is somewhat less reprehensible than is the kind of deviance that stems from calculated selfishness, the next category on the scale.

Selfishness

This fifth category implies that the individual is consciously aware of the decision to violate a normative standard, whether it is a law or not, and that he or she does so for personal gain. This type of deviance requires planning, both to be successful and to avoid punishment, and the existence of planning is itself the principal evidence that the individual knew that the behavior was "wrong." The deviant has clearly placed his or her own interests above the good of the larger group and has thus signaled the intention to engage in deviant behavior as often as it seems possible to get away with it.

Professional criminals, whether small-time pickpockets or millionaire vice lords, are thought to have selfish reasons for their deviance. They make their living from their deviant activities and offer a direct threat to the welfare of others and to the general faith that society's norms and values are accepted by everyone. Premeditated murder, too, is by definition the result of selfishness, even though the "gain" is not always monetary.

For these reasons, deviance originating in *selfishness* is a clearly unforgivable form of activity; ordinarily it is thought to deserve the most severe sanctions. This severity seems reasonable, our thinking goes, since it is the individual who has in effect set the terms of his or her relationship with society, having calculated the cost of possible penalties against the benefits of continued deviance and decided that the balance is in his or her favor. One obvious thing for society to do, then, is to increase the penalty until the risk is no longer reasonable. But most cases of selfish deviance involve money and property rather than human life or health, and thus they are not so serious as to deserve such extreme sanctions as execution, life imprisonment, or astronomical fines. Collectively, then, society must find the degree of severity that will discourage most cases of calculated deviance without at the same time being so severe that there is nothing more severe to use in more serious cases. This subject is treated more fully in the next chapter.

"Pure Evil"

The extreme end of our continuum is rather difficult to accept at face value. This is the category of *pure evil,* and it serves primarily as a kind of residual category into which we can put anything not covered by the other five. It is useful to describe any kind of deviance which is not rationally understandable to others. During periods of history when people accepted the idea of unadulterated evil as a real presence in the world, in the form of men being possessed by devils or women being genuine witches, this category was actively employed as an explanation of deviance. Those whose deviance was assumed to be the expression of pure evil were defined as the absolute enemies of humankind and were ordinarily executed as promptly as possible. Today, however, we no longer accept "evil" as a rational motive and so place the apparently motiveless deviant in a mental hospital, deciding that his or her action came really from a special kind of desperation or impulsiveness that we term mental illness.

Unless we assume that it is rational for some people to enjoy being destructive and bringing misery to others, we have no alternative but to relate such apparently purposeless deviance to insanity. About the only kind of deviance today that is sometimes explained as the result of pure evil is vandalism—destruction apparently for the sake of destruction itself. But even this, particularly in the case of juveniles, tends now to be viewed as the outcome of impulsiveness or risk taking, even though it is possible also to see it as a kind of symbolic protest against the frustrations that always beset adolescents.

This sixth category on our continuum, then, stands today more as a historical monument than as a useful explanation of deviance, even though it seems conceptually necessary to round out the set of categories.

Protest

There is, finally, a seventh identifiable "reason" for deviance, even if it cannot be readily placed on the continuum that contains the first six. This is *protest*—deliberately engaging in deviant behavior for the sake of achieving some particular change in society. The purpose of deviance that originates from this motive is not, as protesters make very clear, private gain of any sort. Instead, the object is the improvement of society along lines identified by the protesters' values, a topic discussed in Chapter 7 in connection with the civil rights movement. Because their deviance is symbolic rather than immediately gratifying (in anything other than a moral sense), society finds it difficult to decide just how to respond to protesters.

The protesters hope that in forcing society to punish them, they will expose the wrongness of the norms they have violated or else dramatize the issue for which they are making this sacrifice. Although nonviolent protests (sit-ins, marches, boycotts, and so on) are essentially attempts to persuade society to change through clarifying and dramatizing certain problems, violent protest seems to escalate this to a form of blackmail. Assaults on property and even persons call for more severe responses from society. Only after such protests continue for some time is it likely that society will find it necessary to do something about the basic conditions that sparked the violent acts.

Protest is thus the attempt to turn society's mechanisms of social control against itself in order to achieve change. The phenomenon is really too new (or until recently it has been too rare) for sociologists to have achieved any systematic understanding of the circumstances under which protests succeed or fail, but it is clear that its prevalance today is calling into question the traditional assumption that a democratic society has enough built-in mechanisms of self-correction to make massive, continued protests unnecessary.

THEORIES OF DEVIANCE

Although the preceding discussion of deviance-generating situations gives us an idea of the immediate origins of specific acts of deviance, it does little to explain deviance in broader terms. In this final section of the chapter we turn our attention to the major attempts that have been made to account for the existence of deviant behavior.

All such attempts have their practical aspects. An effective theory of the origin of deviant behavior may help us prevent it, but even if this cannot be done, it is important that we be able to explain it so that its existence does not pose a direct threat to the legitimacy of society's norms. The discrepancy, after all, between what the norms call for and concrete violations of those norms may as easily throw the norms into question as it can lead us to condemn their violators. To sustain the moral authority of society's normative structure, we thus prefer specific explanations of why certain people in certain circumstances do not obey the norms.

Beyond these practical purposes, theories of deviance can offer additional insight into the nature of society itself. In different attempts to explain deviance, four distinctive aspects of society have been taken as the principal source of the motivation to violate norms: the biological, psychological, cultural, and social-structural components of society.

Biological and Psychological Explanations

Probably the earliest attempts to explain deviance were based on biological factors. We can understand the course of such reasoning. If the violation of norms is "bad" and yet the members of society are assumed to accept its norms, perhaps deviant individuals are actually physically or mentally different from those who do not engage in deviance. The deviants must either have a built-in tendency toward deviance or else be somehow unable to understand and accept social norms.

The first "scientific" effort to develop and support a biological theory of deviance was made by Cesare Lombroso (1835–1909), an Italian physician. He believed that criminals tend to be "throwbacks" or *atavists*—people genetically like primitive human beings who exhibit their supposedly greater tendencies toward selfishness and aggression. Other attempts to explain certain forms of deviance as the result of biological factors have emphasized hereditary feeblemindedness, epilepsy, somatotypes (particular body structures—thin, muscular, and obese—based on the relative proportions of muscle and fat), and, more recently, the XYY chromosome (an accident of inheritance in which the individual has received two male, or "Y," chromosomes instead of one).

Although the concept of deviance covers such a wide range of behaviors that no biological factor can account for all of them, there do seem to be demonstrable correlations between specific physical characteristics and, for example, certan types of juvenile delinquency (Cortes and Gatti, 1972). But the linkage is still complex and indirect, and the idea that genetic factors directly determine one's readiness to violate norms cannot be accepted.

Attempts to locate the causes of deviance in people's psychological characteristics have ranged from the idea of "moral insanity" through a vaguely defined concept of "psychopathy" to the assumption that most antisocial behavior is actually an expression of unconscious needs and conflicts. Although it is clear that individual motives are often influenced by the unconscious, so that to some burglars theft may be actually a symbolic attempt to get something they were denied in childhood, psychological explanations of deviance are difficult to link to the structure of society. Attempts to locate the causes of deviance entirely within the individual, as both biological and psychological theories do, produce only incomplete explanations at best, since deviance does not occur in a social vacuum. (For an excellent review of such theories, *see* McCaghy, 1976.)

Cultural Explanations

Many forms of deviance must be learned: They involve interaction with others, specific goals being sought, and definitions of when they can be engaged in. Since much of what people learn comes from culture, perhaps an important cause of deviance can be found here. As with psychological theories, cultural theories take individual motivation to be the immediate cause of deviance, but view it as influenced more by one's culture than by one's individual experiences.

Cultural theories have generally taken two forms. The first assumes that a substantial number of people who live together in similar circumstances may develop a subculture that includes norms and values which predispose these people to certain acts that are considered deviant by other members of society. The concepts of a "culture of poverty" (Lewis, 1966) and of "lower-class subculture" (Miller, 1958) develop this idea as they identify particular values and attitudes that characterize such groups. These include an emphasis on personal honor and the importance of defending it, negative attitudes toward the police and higher social classes that may encourage law breaking, and a tendency to honor those who are skillful in "beating the system." But it is unclear whether these should be viewed as elements of a genuine subculture that totally determine people's outlooks or whether they are adopted more consciously as rational responses to particular life circumstances (Eames and Goode, 1973).

A second explanation in this vein does not assume the existence of distinctive subcultures; rather, **differential association** *looks to the people with whom an individual associates as they influence the individual's definitions of appropriate and inappropriate behavior.* This theory was developed by Edwin H. Sutherland (1883–1950), who argues that a person engages in deviant behavior because he or she has been exposed to an excess of opinions or definitions that favor the violation of laws. The nondeviant, then, has presumably experienced a surplus of opinions or definitions that favor law-abiding behavior. Rather than viewing culture itself as the source of an individual's tendency to violate norms, Sutherland thus concentrates on the concrete social relationships through which one develops a set of norms and values (Sutherland and Cressey, 1974).

Logically, this explanation makes a good deal of sense. But as soon as we remember that not everyone's opinions carry equal weight with us, we discover that predicting the tendency to violate norms on the basis of whom one associates with becomes almost impossible. How, for instance, are we to measure an "excess of definitions" of one sort or another when usually one particular individual's opinion may be more than enough to offset the opinions of ten other people in the same situation? Differential-association theory, then, ends up as a kind of *post hoc* explanation of deviance that has serious weaknesses as a predictive instrument. A more serious flaw in the theory is that it does not offer a systematic understanding of how some groups come to provide their members with attitudes encouraging deviant behavior, whereas others do not.

Social-Structural Explanations

Cultural theories of deviance rest essentially on an awareness of subcultural differences within society, whether these are related to social classes, ethnic groups, or simply to the individual's circle of associates. Social-structural theories, on the other hand, tend to assume that cultural norms are widely shared and look instead to the person's location within the social structure (that is, social class, occupation, rural or urban residence, etc.) for an understanding of his or her tendency to violate norms. Here we shall examine two prominent theoretical perspectives that attempt to explain deviance as caused by social-structural factors.

The first was proposed by Robert K. Merton in 1938 in a now-famous article titled "Social Structure and Anomie" (Merton, 1957). It distinguishes between the goals that a society endorses and the socially approved means by which its members may achieve them. The individual, reasoned Merton, may accept or reject either one as a guide to conduct. The vast majority, of course, accept both: The **conformist** *both adopts the goals valued by society and seeks those goals through activities approved by society's norms.* In this society, for instance, wealth is a legitimate goal, and earning it through participation in the economic system is the approved way to achieve it.

But there are many people who, although they accept the goals approved by society, find themselves unable to achieve them in the approved ways. They lack the necessary education, encounter discrimination, become unemployed during an economic slump, or for other reasons cannot reach the goals they seek through normatively appropriate means. Out of this frustration comes the search for alternative—illegitimate or deviant—pathways to success. If one cannot earn wealth, one can steal it; if one cannot win an election honestly, one can bribe voters or spread false accusations about one's opponent. Merton calls these people *innovators,* and they make up the bulk of what we usually think of as deviants. Committed to society's goals but not to its norms, they seek shortcuts through a social structure that would otherwise prevent them from gaining what society tells them they should want. In this perspective the prostitute, the racketeer, the embezzler, and the rapist are all innovators.

In addition to these categories, Merton also identifies three others. People who accept society's means but reject its goals, "going through the motions" without a sense of their purpose, are called *ritualists*. The teacher who lectures but is not interested in whether the students learn anything represents this type, as does the fussy bureaucrat to whom properly filled-out forms are more important than the reasons for which they are filled out. Such people are not deviant in the sense that their behavior actually violates norms, but in the broad sense their defection from society's values distinguishes them from conformists.

A smaller proportion of society's members reject both its goals and its norms—the *retreatists*. The hobo, the alcoholic, the drug addict, and the drifter manage to stay alive through whatever means they can find, legal or not, but they do not seem to have much more than this in mind to give direction to their lives.

Finally, Merton characterizes the *rebel* as an individual who, although uncommitted to either the norms or the values of society, has devised *new* goals and *new* means through which to attain them. Individuals who devise new religious beliefs and new political ideologies, trying to persuade others of their validity and either ignoring or attacking the established social structure, are members of this category.

In this theory, deviance is explained largely as a natural response to a gap between culturally approved goals and the social structure through which they are supposed to be achieved. To the extent, however, that these goals are not uniformly shared by all members of society, the theory fails to explain all instances of deviance, and of course it fails to explain those forms of deviance which are essentially irrational or neurotic in character. Nevertheless, the theory has played an important role in the sociological analysis of deviance and continues to stimulate both research and more theory.

The second social-structural explanation of deviance, called **labeling theory,** *begins with the assumption that no behavior is deviant until it is labeled* as such. In this perspective, deviant behavior is thus *created* by society; instead of asking why someone has committed a deviant act, we should ask who decided to define this act as "deviant" and why.

There is merit in this approach. For one thing, the unequal application of justice in society means that an act may or may not be defined as deviant, depending on who committed it. For instance, the children of wealthy parents may well get off with just a warning if caught vandalizing a school, whereas children from a ghetto area are much more likely to be convicted of delinquency for precisely the same behavior. If "delinquency is in the eye of the beholder," its explanation must lie at least partly within the beholder (Erikson, 1964). In particular, this insight cautions us that official crime statistics may be quite misleading because they consider only those people who have successfully been labeled as deviant—members of the lower classes and of minority groups, who lack the power to resist being labeled (Cicourel and Kitsuse, 1963).

In their efforts to achieve equal voting rights for women and to convince others of the validity of their cause, the suffragettes defied the established social structure in order to achieve their goal. This woman, being arrested by two London bobbies in 1905 for her suffragist activities, might have been classified as a rebel. (The Bettmann Archive)

Going beyond this point, labeling theory also argues that being labeled increases the likelihood that an individual (now labeled "thief," "prostitute," "homosexual," etc.) will repeat his or her behavior. After someone has been publicly labeled, others are likely to react to him or her on the basis of this label, which comes to serve as an undesirable ascribed status. To avoid the disadvantages this carries with it, the individual tends to limit his or her social relationships as much as possible to others who have been similarly labeled. Subsequent deviance, either as a direct reaction to being labeled or as the result of increased association with other "deviants," is called *secondary deviance* (Lemert, 1972). The labeling process may thus create additional deviance by making it more difficult for the person to find a nondeviant career.

The need to rationalize their disadvantaged situation (that is, to protect their self-images) and to develop effective ways to deal with "straight" society may result in these people's developing a counterculture (see Chapter 3). Here, certainly, the theory of differential association is directly relevant to understanding the sources of secondary deviance.

Labeling theory, however, tends to be weak in explaining the *initial* reasons for someone's deviant behavior and in helping us understand why certain forms of behavior *can* be labeled deviant (even if labels are not uniformly applied). But in drawing our attention to the fact that deviance as a phenomenon is a product of social definition and to the snowballing process initiated by the labeling process, this theory adds much to the sociological understanding of deviance.

SUMMARY

The importance of shared normative expectations in the continuity of social relationships means that their violation can have critical consequences for society. The study of deviance is thus of personal interest to everyone and of central theoretical importance to the sociologist. Although deviant behavior is defined primarily as the violation of norms, this is due ultimately to the fact that norms develop to prohibit those forms of behavior that people believe will have harmful consequences for society.

There are three major ways in which deviance may harm society. The first is through weakening the accuracy and/or logical organization of culture; the second is by impairing people's ability to participate in ongoing social relationships; and the third is by demonstrating through one's actions a serious disagreement with (or perversion of) society's values. In the last case the activities that we call *vice* embody this sort of threat.

The identification of seven relatively distinct "deviance-generating situations" offers another perspective on the topic. Six of them, ranging from *desperation* through *pure evil*, seem to determine how likely it is that the deviant act will be repeated and thus influence the severity of society's response to it. The seventh, *protest*, poses difficult questions for society because it cannot easily be placed on this continuum.

Finally, there have been numerous attempts to identify the causes of deviant behavior and to see its relations to other aspects of society. Those that assume the causes to be located entirely within the deviant individual, whether concentrating on biological or psychological causes, are unsatisfactory because they ignore the social context of deviance. Theories that emphasize cultural factors (the existence of subcultures within society, the tendency to learn attitudes and values through differential association with others) come closer to being helpful. Social-structuralist theories seem even more promising.

Merton's "means/ends model," although paying little attention to subcultural differences, draws our attention to the fact that not everyone who accepts culturally approved goals, or ends, has equal opportunity to achieve them through socially approved means. A more recent perspective, labeling theory, recognizes that deviance is a matter of social definition and emphasizes the fact that its understanding must include an awareness of who does the labeling and what purposes this serves. It also makes clear that the labeling process frequently stimulates those who are labeled to engage in further deviance.

Our consideration of deviant behavior is rounded out in the next chapter, with a consideration of the various ways in which the members of society respond to deviance with social control.

SUGGESTED READINGS

Bell, Robert R., *Social Deviance*, rev. ed. (Homewood, Ill.: Dorsey, 1976). This is a solid text, complete with much reference to empirical research findings, that covers just about all of the major forms of deviance.

Goffman, Erving, *Stigma* (Englewood Cliffs, N.J.: Prentice-Hall, 1963). In one of the first works to explore the process of secondary deviance, Goffman here analyzes the effects on individuals of physical stigmas (ugliness, being crippled, etc.) as well as the stigma of being labeled "deviant" by society.

Lemert, Edwin M., *Human Deviance, Social Problems, and Social Control* 2d ed. (Englewood Cliffs, N.J.: Prentice-Hall, 1972). A stimulating collection of Lemert's articles in which he examines the problems raised by "labeling theory," the effects of deviance on those who engage in its various forms, and the basic problems involved in defining and identifying deviance in the first place.

McCaghy, Charles H., *Deviant Behavior: Crime, Conflict, and Interest Groups* (New York: Macmillan, 1976). Effectively organized and more readable than most texts in this area, this book serves as an excellent introduction to many of the topics that could be covered only briefly in this chapter. Highly recommended.

Merton, Robert K., "Social Structure and Anomie," pp. 131–160 in his *Social Theory and Social Structure*, rev. ed. (New York: Free Press, 1957). Since its original publication in 1938 and throughout subsequent revisions, this article has undoubtedly been the most important single contribution to the sociological analysis of deviance.

Merton, Robert K., and Robert Nisbet, eds., *Contemporary Social Problems*, 3rd ed. (New York: Harcourt Brace Jovanovich, 1971). This collection of lengthy, authoritative articles on the major forms of deviance and other social problems is one of the most popular texts in the field today.

Nettler, Gwynn, *Social Concerns* (New York: McGraw-Hill, 1976). Rather than simply reviewing what has been said about various social problems, Nettler speaks directly to the reader about the nature of "social concerns" ranging from happiness to war, marshalling both empirical findings and sympathetic wisdom in providing a meaningful perspective. This one is difficult to put down.

Sutherland, Edwin H., and Donald R. Cressey, *Principles of Criminology*, 10th edition (Chicago: Lippincott, 1978). This important text is built around Sutherland's major contribution to the understanding of deviance—the concept of differential association.

Glossary

Conformist   In Merton's terminology the *conformist* is the person who accepts both the goals defined by the values of his or her society and also the legitimate pathways it makes available to achieve these goals. The *innovator* is the person who accepts cultural goals, but employs illegitimate means to achieve them. The *ritualist* behaves in accepted ways, but rejects or ignores the goals toward which they lead. The *retreatist* is uncommitted to both culturally approved ends and means. The *rebel,* finally, is the person who actively seeks new goals, often through new means which others find unacceptable.

Deviance (or Deviant behavior)   An act or series of acts which, if continued or emulated by others, would lead to the weakening or dissolution of society—in the opinion of most members of that society. For some sociologists, behavior is deviant only when it violates an established norm; here, it is assumed that, more importantly, behavior is defined as normatively wrong because it somehow threatens or actually disrupts either patterned social relationships or the organization of cultural symbols and values.

Differential association   A term used by Edwin H. Sutherland to refer to the process through which a person's definitions of right and wrong are shaped by his or her intimate association with others. The "differential" refers to the relative proportion of others who encourage respect for the law, in relation to those who teach one both disrespect for it and the techniques for violating it.

Labeling theory   The perspective that views the term "deviant" as a label that is applied to some people by others and that thereafter influences their behavior. To the extent that a propensity toward further deviant acts is strengthened as a result of being so labeled, resulting in *secondary deviance,* the perspective sensitizes us to the interplay between deviance and social control. Taken to extremes, some sociologists argue that deviance does not exist until it is labeled by the members of society, so that deviance is actually *created* by society.

Social problem   A condition of some part or aspect of society that is generally considered undesirable and perhaps correctable. The term is thus broad enough to include more than deviant behavior, for there are many undesirable conditions— unemployment, poverty, the energy shortage, etc.—which are not due to the violation of specific norms.

Vice   An activity that seems, directly or indirectly, to reverse or "pervert" the relative importance of cultural values. More commonly, the word refers to an immoral habit, often so powerful that a person cannot stop indulging in it. But the immorality seems to lie in either the excessive importance that such habits assume in people's lives or, more clearly, in the ways that they are practiced in contexts that distort the meanings normatively attached to them. Whenever a specifically pleasurable activity comes to dominate someone's life or is obtained through normatively inappropriate means, it can be considered a vice.

16
Social Control

SOCIAL ORDER

Today the idea of order in society tends to carry political connotations. "Order" hints of a conservative, authoritarian, "law and order" mentality. Yet the concept of order need not be tinged with ideology. If society itself consists in the existence of patterned (orderly) social relationships, the important issue is not whether order itself is good or bad, but the *kind* of order someone has in mind and in *how* it is maintained. Order enforced against people's wishes is undesirable—except when their wishes would disrupt the kind of order that *I* prefer. The democratic ideal is voluntary order based on the fact that most people, most of the time, find enough satisfaction in their social relationships to want to maintain them.

Two separate questions must be asked about this ideal. One concerns the standards by which people decide that their social relationships are worth maintaining. These standards can vary, of course, and it is always possible to charge that people have been misled into accepting a lower level of satisfaction than is necessary. But the question of "social justice" is a matter of evaluation rather than of description, and the sociologist is more interested in a second question: What is social order, and how is it maintained?

A simple description would identify social order as "the maintenance of stable social relationships." Looking at *how* people are able to engage in such relationships, however, we can see that *predictability* is often more important than the specific details of their relationships. Shared, reciprocal expectations enable people to engage in particular social relationships again and again, and if change in expectations can be predicted, people can continue to interact smoothly even though their concrete behavior changes. *The essence of* **social order,** *then, is located in the continued, effective "meshing" of people's actions* rather than in the lockstep repetition of the same actions time after time.

As noted in the previous chapter, however, deviance occurs in all societies, even though rarely to the extent that they are actually destroyed. Thus the maintenance of order, or of people's continuing to share norms so that they can anticipate one another's actions, cannot be taken for granted. Conflicting expectations develop; mistakes are made; people violate norms on purpose. There is always some degree of unpredictability in society and therefore a threat to the maintenance of social order.

It is clear that if order cannot be taken for granted, yet is maintained for the most part, there must be something at work to prevent the spread of deviance and the disruption of society. Accompanying the sociologist's interest in the forms, extent, and causes of deviance, then, is a companion interest—the nature of the social activities and structures that counteract the disruptive consequences of deviance. This is the topic of *social control.*

THE NATURE OF SOCIAL CONTROL

Defining Social Control

It is convenient to identify the area of social behavior covered by the term "social control" as the mirror image of what we have discussed under the heading of deviance. That is, we shall define social control here as society's reponses to internal threats to its continued smooth functioning. These responses may be formal or informal. They may or may not be successful. But for the sake of efficiency, we shall limit our attention to *responses* rather than let the topic expand to include everything that might *possibly* be thought of as social control.

For instance, it would seem to make sense to define as social control all of the rewards that society normally offers in return for conformance to its rules. The idea of social control can also be expanded to include consideration of "internalized controls," or the prohibitions against deviance that people learn through the process of socialization. To extend the definition so widely, though, would have us examining not only socialization, but also education, the economic institution, and the religious institution, among other things, for surely these provide, in different ways, support and inducement for "proper," or normative, behavior. To look at everything the concept of social control *might* cover, then, would require the study of virtually every aspect of society, and we would lose the advantages that are gained through subdividing sociology into smaller, more manageable areas of interest.

There are, further, considerable differences between the activities that serve to maintain conformance and those that seek to correct nonconformance. To put them all into the same category and to treat them all as aspects of the same social phenomenon would pose formidable problems of analysis and generalization for us. If, for instance, we were interested in what keeps automobiles from running off the highway, we would not want to spend time studying how gasoline motors are made or what makes people want to go from one city to another. We are interested only in what happens when someone drives off the road—what is done about that person, the automobile, the road surface, and so on, so that a repetition of the event is less likely.

Motivational Foundations of Social Control

If no one ever patched up a house and if no one ever tried somehow to discourage "wrong" behavior by another member of a group, both the house and the group would sooner or later disintegrate. Each would become harder and harder to distinguish from its surroundings, and eventually both would lose their identities as particular organizations of parts (roof, walls, and doors—or statuses having special relations to one another). Given people's tendency to be lazy and often to prefer to "let things slide," it may seem remarkable that society is generally kept in a reasonable state of repair. But people do spend a good deal of time and energy in catching criminals, applying therapies, and otherwise correcting those whose behavior they interpret as threatening to their groups.

The various institutions in which human beings participate and the groups to which they belong—the entire fabric of social relationships that makes life meaningful—are of such importance that we are frequently willing to forego our own immediate interests for the sake of the group's apparent needs. To be sure, people's private needs sometimes lead them to do things that disrupt relationships with others. But at any given moment, there seem to be more people who are concerned with keeping their normal relationships intact than there are people who are ready to disrupt them. We might reason, then, that the amount of social energy available for social control is almost always greater than that which goes into deviant behavior.

In a reasonably stable society, people's reasons for wanting to protect their normal patterns of behavior lie primarily at the level of unreflective habit. Having internalized the rules of their culture—having made these rules part of their own personalities—most of us simply define the violation of these rules as "wrong" and therefore as something to be eliminated. But when we think consciously of why we want to oppose such threats, our thoughts are probably something like the following: "In general, I like things the way they are. But if others begin to do X too often [e.g., assault people, rob bank vaults], I can predict that eventually my chances to participate in my usual relationships with others will be reduced. I will not like this. Therefore, I will try to repair whatever damage has been done to these relationships and to ensure that such threats will occur less often in the future."

As soon as an injury to society has occurred—whether it be a fire in an apartment building, a rock tossed through a window, obscenity uttered in church, or a murder—nothing can be done to prevent it. It has already happened. Two necessary courses of action remain. First, we must pick up the pieces as best we can and restore the status quo. Second, if sufficient energy remains, we must try to prevent the recurrence of the injury.

The sociologist is interested in the organized patterns of behavior that people have developed to implement these tasks. The rest of this chapter is devoted to a survey of the main types of social controls we find in society and the principal social structures through which they are implemented.

FORMS OF SOCIAL CONTROL

We must distinguish, first of all, between those forms of social control that are backed by legitimate force and those that are not. Legitimate force implies the power of the state and thus the existence of rules to govern its use. (This topic is discussed at greater length in Chapter 12, on the political institution.) **For-**

mal social **controls** are *the organized techniques used by society to protect itself; they include all of the controls that are mandated by law and exercised "in the name of the state"* by the police, court system, prisons, federal regulatory agencies, and so forth. Society maintains these specialized parts of its political institution on a continuing basis so that they are ready to cope with threats to society as they occur.

Informal social **controls,** on the other hand, are *those exercised spontaneously, or on an ad hoc basis, by private citizens who do not have the legal right to use force.* When a man uses force—say, a baseball bat—in trying to control his neighbor during an argument, he has himself become deviant in the eyes of the law. Informal controls, then, differ in character from formal controls and are used under different circumstances.

How are we to know when informal social control is aimed at making someone stop violating normative expectations rather than at forcing someone to do as the "controller" wishes without regard to norms? There is no objective way to make this distinction, unfortunately, partly because even the most self-seeking scoundrel will try to justify attempts to control another by casting his or her purposes in terms of norms. Once we rule out the use of force, however (unrealistic as this may be sometimes), we find that the techniques are the same whether the goal is the enforcement of norms or private gain at the expense of another.

Techniques of Informal Control

A private citizen's attempt to halt another's deviance is a more complicated process than one might imagine. An instance of informal social control, for one thing, does not begin with the act of deviance itself—say, someone's crowding into line ahead of another, or trespassing in another's yard, or playing the stereo too loudly nextdoor—but with the "injured" person's *announcement* that the other's behavior is offensive. There is an important but unrecognized etiquette involved here (Goffman, 1967).

Whether or not the offender seems aware that his or her action is "wrong," the victim of this behavior must act as though the offender is *not* aware of this. It is important for the future course of the relationship that the victim first call attention to the offense in a cool, neutral voice: "I beg your pardon, I believe I was in line ahead of you." This gives the offender a good opportunity to back out of the situation without either admitting guilt or risking a more unpleasant confrontation: "I'm so sorry—I didn't see that there is a line here." On the other hand, if the victim skips this step and immediately employs an aggressive response—"Hey, stupid, can't you see the end of the line is back there?"—the offender can claim offense also: "What right have you to yell at me? I didn't see there was a line here!" The victim's "innocence" in the situation is thus compromised and neither party has the clear-cut "moral superiority" that might otherwise allow a quick solution to the problem.

If, however, the victim's complaint is rejected ("What's it to ya?" or "So make me!" for example), several techniques are available for use in trying to bring a halt to the offender's deviance. The lack of much "folk wisdom" concerning techniques of informal control probably testifies to the ineffectiveness of most of them, especially when one is dealing with a stranger, but a general review of the possible "tactics" of informal control will shed some light on this type of social relationship. There are seven major techniques of informal control available to almost anyone, even though few of us are aware of all of them or can decide on which may be the most effective when we are faced with the immediate necessity to act.

To ignore another's offense, or to grit one's teeth and accept the defeat entailed in letting someone "get away with it," is probably the most common reaction to deviance, even though it cannot properly be classified as an effort at control. Nor can we define as control an act which, although it may serve as "revenge" (say, "innocently" jabbing someone with an elbow after having been elbowed oneself a moment earlier), is not clearly an attempt to halt someone else's offensive behavior. (This reminds us, incidentally, that *completed* acts of deviance are more difficult to deal with than ongoing ones; an apology may be easy to obtain after someone has spilled coffee in your lap, but obtaining compensation for the subsequent cleaning bill can be extremely difficult.)

The least aggressive technique of informal control is to supply the deviant with *additional information* about the situation—information which one hopes will persuade him or her to stop. A young lady being annoyed by a stranger at a bus stop, for instance, might tell him: "A cop comes by here about this time every day, Mister, and if you don't stop bothering me, he'll arrest you!" The difficulty with this technique, of course, is that one may not *have* any additional information that is relevant to the offender's interest in continuing the offense or that it may not be believed.

The victim can also think of offering a *reward* for compliance with his or her request that the offense be stopped. We may think it foolish to offer a material reward in return for a halt to the bothersome behavior, because this is the same as paying blackmail, but it is a possibility. The offer of a symbolic reward, though, may be more effective: "I really admire a person who plays fair in a situation like this."

The opposite of a reward is the victim's threat to *withhold* something of value that the offender would otherwise anticipate receiving as a matter of course. Again, this can be symbolic or material. The victim might say, for instance, "I think that anybody who keeps on doing this is despicable!"—implying that all respect will be withheld if the offense is not stopped. Or, if the two parties know each other and expect to interact again in the future, the victim can threaten to withhold friendship, cooperation, or anything else that the offender might otherwise be counting on. The statement "If

In this famous scene in *Public Enemy*, James Cagney exerts informal social control by introducing a small amount of force into the situation—shoving a grapefruit into Mae Clarke's face. (Culver Pictures, Inc.)

you don't stop that, I'll never speak to you again!" is a common example of this tactic.

Distraction is a technique often used with children, but rarely by adults in relation to other adults. It is common to break up an argument among kindergartners by distracting them ("Oh, see what Sandra is doing over there!"), but because we fail to think of it or else do not believe that it will work, we make little use of it in trying to halt an adult's offense. One might, of course, feign a heart attack in order to foil a holdup or bring up something quite irrelevant to the deviant's behavior in trying to develop a new "definition of the situation" so that his or her behavior is no longer appropriate. But because this is a fairly creative tactic, it is apparently more difficult to employ on the spur of the moment.

A more aggressive tactic is the introduction of additional *unpleasantness* into the situation, with the implicit understanding that it will be halted as soon as the deviance stops. Cursing, yelling, and crying are common examples, and such things as teasing, sarcasm, and personal criticism fall into this category as well. The driver who leans long and angrily on the horn is also depending on unpleasantness to make someone stop blocking the street.

Even though the most risky, the victim may resort to *force* or the threat of force in attempting to halt another's deviance. The use of force by private citizens violates the general principle that the right to use force (except in self-defense) should be a monopoly of the state, but despite its illegality, it remains a technique available at least to some people. Its most prominent use, of course, is in physical discipline as it is applied to children, but it is also common among younger males and, with increasing frequency, among females as well.

Finally, the victim may *appeal to a third party* for assistance, and in certain situations this is probably the most popular technique. One can call an usher, the manager, or a police officer if one is nearby, or one may try to involve friends and neighbors in the confrontation. The goal is to enlist the aid of an agent of formal social control, to muster a greater show of strength if there is a question of the informal use of force, or else to threaten the imposition of additional withholding on the offender by altering his or her relationship with others in the future. When fully successful, this technique can result in the offender's being ostracized or rejected by others; to the extent that the deviant believes that this might occur, it can be a highly potent technique of informal control.

It should be noted that all of these techniques of informal control, with the exception of force, are based not on doing something directly "to" the deviant, but on changing his or her social circumstances in some way. Adding information, making rewards available or withholding them, introducing something unpleasant (but not physical force), and changing the ways in which others will interact with the deviant in the future are all methods that depend on making it more sensible for him or her to stop than to continue being offensive.

In each case, of course, the would-be controller's success depends entirely on how sensitive the deviant is to the rewards, information, or punishments that are offered. The more self-sufficient the target of the controls is, the less likely he or she is to be influenced by informal social controls when they are exercised by a single person. The occasional arrogance of the upper class, for example, may be due largely to its members' greater degree of self-sufficiency (see the discussion in Chapter 6 on social class and its relation to one's control over the environment). Self-sufficiency leads to some insensitivity to informal social controls.

When these various strategies are combined and elaborated, however, and particularly when other people are brought into the situation, informal controls can be much more effective. The discussion of the social psychology of the city in Chapter 8 alludes to this fact indirectly. If a person expects to continue in personal contact with most of the people who make up his or her social environment, as in a small town, it is clear that these people can cooperate in making life more or less comfortable in the future, depending on how one behaves now. In the city, where relatively few people in any public situation expect ever to see one another again, informal controls based on planned future actions will be almost entirely ineffective. Under these circumstances, people tend to rely much more on *formal* social controls.

Strategies of Formal Social Control

Unlike informal controls, formal control represents society's *collective* efforts to protect itself, using duly appointed agents who have the right to use force in carrying out their responsibilities. Even if only a single individual has been injured by an act of deviance (a robbery, for instance), the act is defined as a threat to society itself so that the collective strength of society can be used to halt the deviance. Even if there is no victim to complain, as in the case of vice, society may decide, through its legislators, that such behavior still constitutes *in principle* a threat to society. The deviant, in other words, represents a source of real or potential disruption of the system, and the system must act to repair whatever damage has been inflicted and to lessen the chances of similar damage in the future.

Our problem at this point is to see what strategies the system may employ in protecting itself. A simple illustration will help us get at the central ideas involved. Let us imagine a platoon of soldiers getting ready to march in a parade before a visiting general. Their sergeant, anxious that the soldiers look as sharp and professional as possible, has one problem. Private Jones, who has never really gotten the hang of marching, is out of step now.

The first thing that comes to the sergeant's mind is to have Jones fall out and return to the barracks. The would leave the platoon one person short, but at least everyone would be in step.

Instead, however, the sergeant sings out the command, "Private Jones, *skip-step!*" A skip-step is a little maneuver, only slightly complicated, in which the soldier takes three quick steps instead of two, thus changing from a right-left, right-left pattern to a left-right, left-right pattern. Unfortunately, this is another aspect of marching that Jones has been unable to master. The plan fails. The platoon, with Jones still out of step, is rapidly approaching the parade ground.

Finally, in a burst of inspiration, the sergeant gives the command, "Everyone *except* Private Jones, skip-step!" There is a concerted skipity-skip by all of Jones's buddies, and by the time the platoon marches past the reviewing stand, everyone is neatly in step. The sergeant gives a silent sigh of relief. This effort at "social control" has been successful.

Now, letting the platoon represent any group, or society itself, and letting Private Jones represent a threat to the orderliness of the group, what social-control strategies can we see in the sergeant's three attempts to make the platoon look good? The essence of the sergeant's first idea—sending Jones back to the barracks—was that of removing the disruptive element from the system. In the most general sense we can think of this strategy as **insulation**—*the type of control society employs whenever it executes, exiles, or imprisons a person.* The second strategy—getting Jones back into step with the other soldiers—can be called **reintegration,** which includes *all attempts to get the deviant to start behaving properly again:* techniques that range from torture to psychotherapy. Finally, there is **adaptation,** *which occurs when society discovers that the only way to avoid disruption by a particular form of deviance that cannot be halted is to change itself so that the deviant behavior will no longer be threatening.*

These three strategies are highly abstracted, of course, and it is difficult to say that any concrete method of social control used by society represents a pure case of any one of them. Imprisonment, for instance, is usually viewed as punishment (supposedly a method of reintegration) as well as a way to "protect society" (insulation); the strategy of adaptation is rarely so complete that all change is made by society and none by the deviant. The more typical pattern, if adaptation is involved at all, is for society to make some changes and the deviant to make changes in his or her behavior as well. Between reintegration and adaptation, then, lies a broad area that may best be called *compromise.* Even though these three ideal-type strategies of social control are analytic rather than descriptive, it will be useful to keep them in mind as we examine the organization and history of formal social control.

THE STRUCTURE OF FORMAL SOCIAL CONTROL

Formal social control can be distinguished in two ways from informal controls. First, it is based on the *right to use force;* second, it is *organized.* The role of force in society is considered in detail in Chapter 12, on the political institution; here, we shall be content to recognize that force is the most reliable technique for controlling people and is at the same time something whose misuse can have the most serious consequences for the maintenance of social order. The members of society thus regard the control of force as of the utmost importance. In the end, it is difficult to avoid the conclusion that the right to use force must be restricted to the state for use by its agents, the police (except under temporary circumstances when self-defense cannot wait for the arrival of the police). At the same time, there is much concern that this right be strictly controlled.

There are only two ways to control the use of force: the use of superior force or self-control by those who have to means to use it. Self-control, in turn, is possible only through commitment to a set of principles that determine the circumstances under which the use of force is proper. The former method promises ultimate civil war if not unending guerrilla warfare throughout society, and no society has ever achieved social order on this basis alone. Chapter 12 covers the ways through which reliance on the second method is achieved; here, our attention is on the nature of the principles or rules to which commitment has been achieved.

If the defense of society against disruption is of concern to its members, they must somehow reach agreement on the circumstances under which force may be used in their collective defense and on who may use it. The statements that describe these circumstances and determine who has the right to use force in them are called *laws*.

The Nature of Law

When a **law** is passed—that is, agreed to by those who have the right to make laws—it becomes *a formal public promise of what the state will do (through its agents), using whatever of its resources are necessary, under a particular set of circumstances*. The phrase "using whatever of its resources are necessary" clearly covers the use of physical force. Certain laws, in fact, are explicit descriptions of when force may and may not be used as one of the state's "resources."

In *The Lawyers* Martin Mayer (1967, pp. 121–122) provides a particularly insightful perspective on the nature of law:

> [L]aw clearly does not "prohibit" anything—words can no more prevent a possible human action than King Canute could stop the tides. Nor does law in fact seek to prevent actions in themselves—there is nothing you may not safely do, without risk of interference from law, if you are alone in the middle of the desert. What law says is that if you act in specified ways, in a range of circumstances, you may be liable, upon completion of specified legal procedures, to suffer specified unpleasant consequences.

In order to fulfill its promises, of course, the state must be able to use force, its only means for ultimately ensuring that someone will indeed "suffer specified unpleasant consequences." The important thing, of course, is not that the state always succeeds in carrying out its promises, but that it *tries*. And in order to do this, social structures must be established whose members are devoted to carrying out these promises on a full-time basis.

Laws, then, guide and legitimate actions, are backed by the right to use force, and seek to implement society's desire to maintain order among its members and to promote their common welfare. Although there are several varieties of law—laws that cover different areas of behavior and human concern—we need identify only three major types.

The kinds of behavior that are defined *a priori* (ahead of time) as direct threats to society are covered by *criminal law*. These laws require the police or other agents of the state to take the initiative in seeking to apprehend those who have engaged in certain forms of behavior. As soon as a burglary or a murder has been discovered, for instance, the police undertake an active search for the perpetrator; it is not necessary that a citizen bring suit before they become involved.

A second type of law, *civil law*, covers those relations among the members of society which, although involving personal conflict, are not defined as intrinsically threatening to society. Here, for instance, is the area of *torts*, or "civil injuries," as when a customer claims to have been cheated by a merchant. Without the customer's going through specified procedures, the police will not intervene spontaneously.

A third, more diffuse type of law can be referred to as *administrative law*. Laws of this type concern the government's own organization and actions, such as establishing or reorganizing certain agencies and undertaking or modifying programs such as the war on poverty, agricultural research programs, and the development of new weapons systems. These laws are least relevant to an understanding of formal social control, but since they are backed by the state's right to use force, they must be recognized as one aspect of the overall structure through which social order is maintained.

The Courts

"The prophecies of what the courts will do in fact, and nothing more pretentious, is what I mean by the law," said Justice Holmes. What the trial or lower courts do, essentially, is *apply the law*—that is, determine whether a specific concrete act or series of acts was indeed the action referred to in a law as an occasion for the state to act and whether responsibility for that act can be assigned to a particular individual. Evidence is taken, witnesses are heard, and finally a determination is made whether there actually *was* an act that is covered by law and, if so, whether a specific person can be demonstrated to have committed that act. These are the "specified legal procedures" referred to in the quotation from Mayer above.

But because the state's ability to impose "specified unpleasant consequences" on individuals is so awesome, backed as it is by the state's right to use whatever force may be necessary to do this, meticulous care must be taken to see that this power is not abused or applied arbitrarily. Many laws, therefore, are procedural in nature, in that they specify the rights of the accused as clearly as they do the rights of the state. The Bill of Rights is, of course, the chief example of this, and laws governing the admissibility of evidence, the ways in which prisoners must be informed of their rights, etc., are also intended to guarantee that the state will not abuse its powers.

Laws are only "written promises," of course, so in themselves they cannot prevent the police from using unnecessary force or judges from handing down capricious sentences. The old question "Who will guard the guardians?" has no ultimate answer. But by giving some courts the responsibility for seeing that due process has been carried out in other courts—and the right to declare a lower court's conclusion invalid—we have generally been able to hold such abuses of the law to a tolerable level.

There are thus two major types of courts, arranged in something of a "check-and-balance" system. Those in which cases are initially heard—*municipal, trial, or lower courts*—*have primary responsibility for applying the law in specific cases. Higher (or appellate or supreme) courts, on the other hand, deal with questions of whether the proceedings in the lower courts were themselves within the law and with the resolution of inconsistencies between different laws.*

Like culture, the body of laws that govern a society (they are actually a part of society's culture) cannot be inconsistent. It would be intolerable for the state to "promise" that a specific act is perfectly legal and at the same time to state that its commission will result in punishment. And because laws have logical implications that go beyond their specific wordings, it is not infrequent that laws do come into conflict with each other. If law A, for instance, logically implies Q, while law B logically implies *not-Q,* an inconsistency has been located which must be resolved. It is ordinarily the task of a state's or the nation's appellate courts to arrive at such a resolution, and because final answers to these problems are absolutely vital, their decisions cannot ordinarily be questioned in yet another court. The buck must stop *somewhere.*

The Police

Viewed in this perspective, the police are very much "the servants of the court." Although in practice they handle a good many problems that never reach the courts—controlling traffic, settling family disputes, carrying out inspections, etc.—in theory their responsibility is to apprehend those who are suspected of engaging in acts to which the law applies and to "bring them to justice"—that is, to ensure their appearance in court so that specified legal proceedings can take place.

Because there are so many *more* police than there are judges and other courtroom personnel and because the police are the people who are actually equipped with nightsticks and guns, they often appear to be an autonomous part of the formal social-control system. Indeed, the study of police forces—of the organization of police departments, of police procedures, of the problems of inefficiency and corruption that beset such organizations as they do all other human organizations, and of their specific role in the community—is the subject of a complete college education in police science and is too complex to

be dealt with here in detail. Yet the police would be without legitimacy and without function if the courts did not exist. They are, then, a specialized part of the social structure through which formal controls are implemented.

The Penal System

The last component of society's formal social-control system administers the "specified unpleasant consequences" imposed on those who have been convicted of violating the law. The penal system includes municipal, state, and federal jails and prisons; special arrangements for particular groups such as juvenile delinquents, drug addicts, and the criminally insane; and the entire apparatus that administers probation and parole. Like the police, it is a complex system, complicated by overlapping political and functional jurisdictions, and a detailed analysis of its organization and operations is beyond the scope of this book. Something of its development, however, is covered in the following section.

THE DEVELOPMENT OF FORMAL SOCIAL CONTROLS

A relatively primitive group or society tends to use an either/or strategy of social control: The deviant is either expelled from the group or hardly punished at all. The group simply lacks the level of political organization needed to employ a wider range of controls. But as a society becomes larger and more complex, there is need for controls that are more flexible because a

◄ As specialized agents of the courts, the police have the right to use force in enforcing the law and apprehending lawbreakers. Here police officers are subduing some of the thousands who protested in New York City in December 1977 against American investment in South Africa. (Keler/Sygma)

larger number of deviant behaviors is possible. This need seems to have been met first by the development of a series of methods of inflicting physical pain on the deviant, in amounts corresponding roughly to the seriousness of his or her deviance.

The ancient *lex talionis* (law of retribution) embodied a kind of "barter system" in determining what physical punishment was the appropriate response to a particular kind of deviance. This kind of law involved primarily personal injuries; for example, a man would be allowed to break the leg of the person who had broken his leg. However, the principle was used by the state as well. A pickpocket's hand might be amputated, or a cheating merchant might be given a public whipping.

There were difficulties with this system. Although pain is impossible to measure (see Chapter 12), different people can tolerate different amounts of pain, and it was almost impossible to work out a dependable "pain scale" that could be tied neatly to a scale measuring the seriousness of different types of deviance. Still, punishment was apparently needed, even though its efficacy as a deterrent was never as great as might have been hoped. It will be useful at this point to examine some of the "theories of punishment."

Theories of Punishment

All societies impose **punishment**—*negative sanctions applied to those convicted of deviant behavior*—and several explanations have been offered of *why* they do so. The simplest of these sees in even the most elaborate punishment the spirit of revenge or retaliation. If the frustration one experiences after being the victim of deviance leads to aggression, as psychologists since Freud have suggested in several theories (Berkowitz, 1968), punishment may be viewed as the collective acting out of this aggression—the infliction of some sort of pain on the cause of the frustration. In this view, the purpose of punishment is the relief of the victim's and others' discomfort that accompanies the sense of frustration. The *revenge* theory of punishment, then, emphasizes humankind's primitive emotional processes.

But because emotional relief is an end in itself, without any reference to the prevention of future deviance, the expression of anger seems merely a "selfish passion" (Berns, 1979) and too illogical to justify punishment. A more acceptable explanation is that the purpose of punishment is to deter future deviance, both in the person being punished and in others. The *deterrence* theory, however, must assume that the potential deviant is rational, aware of the punishment that may be incurred by deviance, and can calculate his or her chances of being caught. If these conditions are present, it makes sense for us to ensure that apprehension will be so certain and punishment so unpleasant that the potential deviant will give up his or her plans on the grounds that "crime does not pay."

Unfortunately, much deviance is *not* planned (particularly murder), and the faith that one can "get away with it" often borders on the irrational. There is little assurance, then, that the effectiveness of punishment as a deterrent is as impressive as this theory assumes. It is clear that the "success" of punishment in lowering the frequency of deviant acts cannot account for its continued use around the world.

Another explanation of why society punishes wrongdoers was suggested by the French sociologist Emile Durkheim in 1893 (Durkheim, 1964). He pointed out that through the punishment of someone who has violated society's norms and values, its members collectively reinforce their commitment to those standards of behavior by giving concrete expression to their abhorrence of the deviant's act. Without occasional actions to implement values, Durkheim argues, the values begin to lose their meaning, and the validity of culture begins to suffer.

In agreeing to the punishment of a criminal, the members of society assure one another that they *are* angered by what he or she has done. In this sense, the imposition of punishment has the same intent as does the enactment of a religious ritual (see Chapter 14), for it aids in the consensual validation of cultural values. For this reason, we may call this theory the *value-reinforcement* theory of punishment.

Finally, parallelling on the cognitive level the emotional balancing that is highlighted in revenge theory, it may be suggested that the infliction of punishment also serves to keep the cultural record properly balanced. For instance, an act of deviance is "recorded" in our culture: "On March 18, Harry robbed John." This brings a certain amount of inconsistency into our collective picture of the world, for our culture also contains the fundamental assertion that robbery is wrong. Since the act cannot be undone, the only way to restore consistency to our culture is to *add* to the record the fact that *Harry was punished for his act.*

Because Harry has been forced to experience something unpleasant to a degree roughly equivalent to the "profit" he expected to gain through his deviance, society has balanced the books symbolically. Here the urge to punish is seen as being rooted in our collective need to rid our culture of inconsistencies, and we may call this the *symbolic-balance* theory of punishment.

To some degree, each of these four theories must be a valid explanation of why human groups everywhere punish their deviant members, even though none can account for it alone. The predominant methods of punishment, however, vary considerably around the world. Over the last century or so, the amount of simple physical pain administered by the state as formal punishment has decreased almost to the vanishing point (except in totalitarian societies and in less complex societies). Instead, the state has come to rely almost entirely on two forms of "indirect pain"—imprisonment and monetary fines. How this came about is important to our understanding of the nature of formal social control.

First of all, as noted above, the subjective experience of pain is impossible to measure; therefore, it does not fit easily into a rational, systematic program of social control. Second, it may lead to the unintended death of the victim, after which it is impossible to make amends for any injustices that may have been involved in the original sentence. And third, there has been increasing public distaste for the savagery that the infliction of pain implies. Indeed, the propriety of society's inflicting the "ultimate" pain, death, is being questioned more and more seriously.

Imprisonment

The use of imprisonment as punishment has been common in Western civilization only since about the seventeenth century. It was used in ancient times, of course, but only as a way to make sure that the person who was to be executed, exiled, or physically punished would be available when the time came to carry out the sentence. Throughout most of history, societies have simply not been able to afford the luxury of maintaining people in prison for long periods of time (Tappan, 1960, Chapter 20).

Further, it has always been difficult to justify imprisonment in terms of insulation alone. If the person to be imprisoned is really a threat to society, why not just execute or at least exile that person permanently? Either way is cheaper than supporting someone in prison for life, and it would be foolish to imprison someone for less than life if he or she is likely to threaten society again as soon as the term is ended.

Imprisonment for a specific period of time makes sense only if it is defined as having some reintegrative value—if the loss of liberty is itself painful enough to persuade the individual that continued deviance "isn't worth it." As well as combining temporary insulation with a method of reintegration, imprisonment has the further advantage of being measured in terms of time, a continuous variable that applies equally to everyone, so that ten years in prison can be said to be twice as "painful" as five years in prison. It is thus a more rational form of punishment and at the same time apparently more humane than physical pain.

Monetary Penalties

Just as imprisonment deprives the individual of physical freedom, the imposition of a monetary fine deprives him or her of some freedom to participate in society; without money, one cannot purchase some of the things or services one might have otherwise. Because the two forms of indirect punishment can be compared in this way, we often find that one is substituted for the other. The traditional sentence imposed by the judge, "Thirty dollars or thirty days," shows this clearly: The state believes that the punishments are equivalent and that it is irrelevant which one is chosen.

Reintegrative Controls

Beyond these modern forms of punishment, there are nonpunitive methods of reintegration that can be used to direct the deviant back into normal patterns of behavior. There are many kinds of half-way houses that try to help ex-convicts and ex-addicts. Vocational training is intended to remove a person's need to engage in deviant behavior because he or she lacks the skills needed to earn an honest living. Plastic surgery sometimes helps a person to participate more easily in normal social relationships by changing an excessively ugly or bizarre appearance.

On the whole, reintegrative controls are much more costly to society than any technique of pure insulation. They require a greater investment of money and time to achieve their goals and also a greater willingness by society to suffer whatever injuries may be inflicted on it later by those whose reintegration has not been successful. But the psychic or cultural cost to a society of insulation, particularly execution, is extremely high when that society stresses the absolute value of all human life, and a relatively affluent society seems willing to spend more material resources on social controls when this promises to spare it the cost of a serious gap between its values and its behavior. (The fact that our prisons fail almost completely as an effective means of reintegrating deviants does not contradict this statement: it only shows that we do not yet understand how to spend our resources effectively on reintegrative controls.)

Adaptation as Control

Adaptation is even more costly to society than reintegration because it involves changing society itself. Whenever a particular threat to society cannot be controlled, or when its source cannot be identified so that controls can be applied, society must adapt to its presence. The patterns of behavior and interaction that make up society must be rearranged so that they are no longer vulnerable to this particular threat.

During Prohibition, for instance, the number of people who systematically violated the law was so great that eventually it became "cheaper" to change society (that is, to repeal Prohibition) than to keep on trying to control a type of behavior that apparently could not be eliminated. In fact, the very existence of Prohibition created opportunities for other forms of deviance as well.

When the specific identity of a threat cannot be determined, as was the case with the "Boston Strangler" and the "Son of Sam" in New York City, people must adapt privately to ward off the threat. They buy burglar alarms, stronger locks for their doors, and police dogs; they restrict their movements and become more suspicious of strangers.

In terms of both psychic and monetary costs—the prices people pay in anxiety, uncertainty, and stress when they must develop new patterns of behavior, as well as the money they must pay—adaptation is clearly more expensive to society than either insulation or reintegration. Although it is frequently used, it is certainly the least systematized. It is, further, distasteful to many people because it seems to represent a surrender to deviance—almost a form of paying blackmail. Because adaptation requires us to accept deviance by changing ourselves to accommodate it, we use this strategy of control only in desperation and with the greatest reluctance. For this reason it is rarely a popular strategy for protecting society from disruption, and it is not usually regarded as a distinct type of social control.

Adaptation does not fit easily into the definition of formal control because it does not necessarily depend on the potential use of legitimate force. Occasionally it involves explicit social policy, but more frequently it consists of unorganized individual responses to vaguely defined threats, and only later does it become clear that adaptation has taken place.

By now, it may have become apparent that the strategies of formal control are applicable also in the analysis of society's responses to external threats: floods, fires, earthquakes, droughts, the exhaustion of natural resources, and aggressive acts by other societies. The same strategies are, in fact, used for defense by any living system whether it be plant, animal, group, or culture. Finally, you may have recognized that since adaptation involves changes in society itself, it might better have been treated under the heading of social change.

There is merit in this idea, and after the next chapter, on public opinion and collective behavior, we will explore the relevance of adaptation to social change.

SUMMARY

The maintenance of social order is just as interesting to the sociologist as are the various forms of deviant behavior. But rather than seek to cover everything that might be defined as promoting order, our attention here has been limited to the ways in which people respond, individually and collectively, to actions that threaten social order. It is assumed that individuals engage in social control out of a desire to protect the patterns of interaction that they find satisfying.

When social control is attempted on an *ad hoc* basis by private citizens who do not have the right to use force in their dealings with one another (except in self-defense), it is *informal* social control. Several different techniques of informal control are available, ranging from the offer of new information about the situation (which might alter the offender's motives) to the illegal use of physical force and the enlistment of others' assistance. With the exception of force, however, the success of informal control depends largely on how sensitive the offender is to its use rather than on the nature of the control itself.

Society's *formal* social-control system is organized and based on the right to use force under certain circumstances in defense of the group as a whole. There are three major strategies society can use to protect itself against disruption by its own members: *insulation* (preventing further disruption by imprisoning, exiling, or executing the deviant), *reintegration* (getting the deviant to stop behaving disruptively), and *adaptation* (adjusting the rest of society so the deviant's behavior can no longer disrupt it).

Since the use of force in social relationships can be a threat to order, but is necessary at times, the question of who can use it and when is of considerable importance. Limitations on its use are embodied in law, which may be viewed as public promises of what the state will do (through its agents) in specific circumstances, no matter how much opposition it encounters. *Criminal law* specifies the circumstances under which its agents will take the initiative in apprehending persons suspected of engaging in certain activities and in holding them for trial. *Civil law* specifies procedures in resolving conflicts between private citizens that do not fall under the criminal law; the state's agents (the police) do not intervene unless requested to do so by one of those involved. *Administrative law*, finally, concerns the operations of the government itself, as in establishing new departments, regulations for the letting of contracts, etc.

Trial, municipal, or *lower courts* determine whether a law has been violated and whether a specific individual committed the violation. Appellate, supreme, or *higher courts* are concerned with the legality of the state's own acts, particularly in whether or not due process has been followed in the lower courts, and with the internal consistency of the legal system.

As agents of the court, the *police* are responsible for bringing people accused of crimes into court so that it may be determined whether they are indeed the individuals on whom specified punishments should be inflicted. All of the other activities of the police—directing traffic, guarding parades, counseling citizens about crime prevention, etc.—should be seen as logically necessary extensions of this central responsibility.

The *penal system*, through which state-imposed punishments are carried out, is composed of the local, state, and federal prisons, the administration of parole and probation, and special facilities for delinquents, addicts, the criminally insane, etc. Although its organization and operation are too complex to be covered here, the reasoning that accounts for its existence is of interest.

Several theories have been advanced to explain why all human groups *punish* (whether through inflicting pain, imprisonment, or the confiscation of property) those who violate their standards of behavior. Although it is difficult to believe that the idea of *revenge* alone is sufficient to account for the elaborate system of formal controls we have today, a frequent explanation is that the prospect of punishment serves to deter people from future deviance. But since much deviance is impulsive (and thus not influenced by the rational assessment of its potential cost) and many deviants repeat their acts even after being fined or imprisoned, the *deterrence* theory does not seem to account fully for the continued practice of punishing deviants.

Durkheim proposed instead that the infliction of punishment reaffirms others' commitment to the norms that the deviant has violated, so that its chief function is that of *value-reinforcement*. And there is also the idea that punishment helps to *balance* the symbolic record by cancelling out the logical inconsistency that would otherwise exist between the statements "We do not want anyone to do X" and "Harry did X and got away with it."

Because pain is difficult to measure and thus to standardize, modern societies have moved increasingly to employ either imprisonment or monetary fines as their major methods of punishment, with longer prison terms or higher fines imposed for more serious crimes. Imprisonment is primarily a form of insulation, even though the faith that it can deter future deviance leads us to think of it also as having reintegrative aspects. Other forms of reintegration—therapy, vocational rehabilitation, etc.—are more costly than imprisonment, and when society must use adaptation (because a source of disruption cannot be identified or halted), the total cost is even higher.

SUGGESTED READINGS

Bedau, Hugo A., ed., *The Death Penalty in America* (Garden City, N.Y.: Doubleday/Anchor, 1964). An extremely useful collection of writings concerning the rationale behind capital punishment and research findings on its lack of effectiveness as a deterrent.

Black, Donald, *The Behavior of Law* (New York: Academic Press, 1976). This brief book presents a challenging series of propositions concerning the relationships between the extent to which formal social controls are used and a number of other aspects of society. Original and highly stimulating.

Bordua, David J., ed., *The Police: Six Sociological Essays* (New York: Wiley, 1967). These essays, especially written for this book, probe the nature of police responsibilities, operations, and control by the community.

Bowers, John W., and Donovan J. Ochs, *The Rhetoric of Agitation and Control* (Reading, Mass.: Addison-Wesley, 1971). A frank exploration of the uses of language in both rebellion and its suppression.

Chambliss, William J., and Robert B. Seidman, *Law, Order, and Power* (Reading, Mass.: Addison-Wesley, 1971). A full-scale text providing thorough coverage of the place of law in society.

Durkheim, Emile, *The Division of Labor* [1893] (New York: Free Press, 1947). Durkheim's first book, this contains his theory of the functions of punishment and explanation of the ways in which law becomes more restitutive and less punitive as society becomes more complex.

Goffman, Erving, *The Presentation of Self in Everyday Life* (Garden City, N.Y.: Doubleday/Anchor, 1959). This appealing study of the dramaturgy of daily life is particularly valuable in its analysis of the subtle, informal controls we all use in ordinary social interaction.

Mayer, Martin, *The Lawyers* (New York: Harper & Row, 1967). This is an excellent popular survey of both the legal profession and the nature of law itself, providing a useful background for anyone interested in law as a principal foundation of social control.

Niederhoffer, Arthur, and Abraham S. Blumberg, *The Ambivalent Force: Perspectives on the Police.* 2d ed. (New York: Holt, Rinehart and Winston, 1973). A collection of relatively brief articles on many different aspects of the police force and its role in society.

Glossary

Adaptation The strategy of social control (in the broadest sense of protecting society against disruption) that involves alterations in society so that behavior which was formerly disruptive can no longer harm it.

Courts The specialized part of the political system whose function is to determine the applicability of law in particular cases, to ensure that this process has itself been carried out within the law, and to resolve inconsistencies between laws. The first of these tasks is the responsibility of trial (or lower) courts; the latter two are undertaken by appellate (or supreme, or higher) courts.

Formal control The organized actions by agents of the state, backed up by the right to use force under specified circumstances, that seek to protect society against disruption by the actions of its own members. The rights and responsibilities of these agents (judges, police, federal agents, etc.) are set forth in society's body of criminal and civil law.

Informal control The *ad hoc* actions of private citizens in seeking to halt deviant behavior by others. The use of information, rewards and the withholding of rewards, unpleasantness, and the assistance of others who have some formal authority in the immediate situation are all legitimate techniques of informal control. The private use of force is not legitimate, but in fact is often used in attempts at informal control.

Insulation The strategy of social control that involves removing the deviant from the system through exile, imprisonment, or execution so that his or her actions can no longer disrupt the activities of others.

Law The body of formal public promises by the state of what its agents will do in specific situations, regardless of others' resistance. Because there may indeed be resistance, the right to use force if necessary is required if these promises are to be implemented.

Punishment The imposition of an unpleasant experience, ranging from verbal criticism to death, on someone as a consequence of his or her previous behavior. The chief reason for punishment has been variously thought to be simple revenge, deterrence against future deviance, value reinforcement, and a symbolic balancing of the record of human activities.

Reintegration The strategy of social control that concentrates on changing a person in some way so that she or he will no longer want or need to engage in deviant behavior. The deterrent theory of punishment assumes that punishment is reintegrative, because it persuades the deviant that further deviance will result in too much unpleasantness to be worthwhile. Other methods of reintegration include rehabilitation, therapy, and perhaps ways to change people's motives like religious conversion.

Social order The existence of stable social relationships, based more on people's being able to predict one another's actions than on endless repetitions of the same forms of interaction. Change in social relationships thus does not mean disorder unless it is unpredicted.

17

Public Opinion and Collective Behavior

FOCUS: *BEHAVIOR IN UNSTRUCTURED SITUATIONS*

It has been stressed that a clear distinction should be made between concrete human beings and the social statuses they occupy. But social statuses, together with the norms that guide their occupants' relationships, exist only as people are aware of them and agree that they should guide behavior in specific situations. The range of human needs, however, goes beyond those that are conveniently provided for by established structures of interrelated statuses. An **unstructured situation** *exists when people find themselves wanting or needing to behave in ways that are "outside" the established structures, or that cannot be effectively guided by established norms.*

People's behavior in such unstructured situations may seem essentially random with respect to normative (predictable) patterns of interaction. Yet we find regularities even here. The process of developing new expectations in such situations, so that the participants can avoid working at cross-purposes with one another, is central to their relationships and provides a way to discover these regularities.

In the broad sense, sociologists call these emergent relationships *collective behavior.* At their foundation, though, are the processes through which people learn what to expect of one another when established norms cannot provide guidance. This can be seen most clearly in the formation of *public opinion,* and its understanding is necessary for a systematic analysis of the various forms of collective behavior.

When behavior common to a number of people cannot be accounted for by their obeying established norms, we must ask why and how this has occurred. This question in turn raises several others. Under what circumstances do people jointly conclude that established norms are no longer relevant in a particular situation? How do they come to develop new expectations of one another? How can we explain why one type of collective behavior occurs rather than another?

The degree to which a situation is unstructured may, of course, vary from nearly zero to one hundred percent; no pattern of social interaction is *entirely* predictable, but in everyday life the degree of unpredictability tends to be quite low. And we have many ways of reestablishing structure after it has been threatened momentarily: We ignore a disruption, apologize for nonnormative behavior, or work out compromises to settle differences of opinion. In one sense, then, collective behavior is only the tip of the iceberg, distinguished from more ordinary behavior simply because it is a response to an extreme amount of social unpredictability or unstructuredness.

But the major forms of collective behavior, ranging from riots to social movements, are recurring social phenomena, and their investigation can do much to help us understand more fully the relationships between human beings and social structures.

THE NATURE OF COLLECTIVE BEHAVIOR

In contrast to the complex, differentiated patterns of interaction that make up the enduring structures of society, **collective behavior** *refers to people's participation in forms of behavior that are not guided by established norms and that are primarily the same rather than different and interdependent.* A number of people running from a threatened explosion, for example, are doing the same thing; a number of people buying the latest fashion in footwear, similarly, are doing the same thing. There is very little "division of labor" here, or complementarity of roles, even though large numbers of people may be involved. If established social statuses and their interrelationships make up the more routine and predictable structure of society, then, the various forms of collective behavior—fads, mobs, panics, social movements, etc.—become highly visible against this stable background.

The study of collective behavior is thus the study of temporary, relatively undifferentiated patterns of behavior that are not (at least in the beginning) guided by shared norms. In this sense participation in collective behavior takes people out of their everyday statuses and involves them in actions which, for one reason or another, cannot be predicted by referring to established norms. This behavior may violate norms that "should" be relevant, or it may occur under circumstances to which no established norms are relevant in the first place. An instance of collective behavior can be quite dramatic, as is a riot or a wave of mass hysteria, or it may be quiet and relatively unremarkable, as is a change in fashion. But because all of these forms of behavior occur "outside" the established structure of interrelated social statuses, they are all classified as collective behavior.

Whenever people are responding to a common stimulus (a threat, a shared sense of injustice, a chance to be "in," or even a change in one another's behavior), they have something in common—their response. It is this that makes their behavior *collective* and allows us to treat it as a distinctive social phenomenon. More important, virtually all collective behavior is greatly influenced by people's awareness (or at least assumption) that others are *also* responding to the same stimulus. A fashion, after all, would hardly be worthwhile if people did not assume that others would approve of their taking it up; panic would not occur in a smoky theater if only one person decided to leave. As we shall see, it is the ways through which people develop expectations about one another's actions—current and anticipated—in unstructured situations that are crucial to understanding collective behavior.

First, under the heading of *public opinion,* we will discuss the development of mutual expectations among people concerning aspects of their current situation. Then we will go on to consider more systematically the various characteristics of unstructured situations and how they are related to the major forms of *collective behavior.*

PUBLIC OPINION

Public opinion *refers to the attitudes of the members of a public toward an event or issue to which their attention has been drawn.* A public is thus a category of people who have in common the fact that they are all aware of a particular event, person, issue, condition, etc., and view it as relevant to their interests. There is a public for sports news, a public for fashions, and another for information about the stock market. There is a public for news of an impending flood or hurricane (composed of just about everyone in a given area); in November 1963 the entire American population became a single public in the aftermath of President Kennedy's assassination.

The idea of a public helps us to recognize that different people may become involved in different instances of public opinion. Because it is focused on current events, which are always new and thus require the formation of new attitudes, public opinion constitutes one type of collective behavior.

Initially, we usually think of public opinion in terms of the proportions of people who hold different opinions on a particular issue. For instance, we might read: "Fifty-nine percent of the voters favor Candidate Smith, thirty-five percent favor Candidate Jones, and six percent are undecided." The opinions of people, however, are important only as they help others to predict how they are likely to act in the future. In this case we would predict that a majority of the voters will vote for Smith and can guide our own behavior accordingly. Similarly, believing that others will approve of a particular type of clothing, we may buy it rather than a different type. Being aware that most of our neighbors are in favor of capital punishment, we may be hesitant to voice an opinion against it.

The importance of public opinion thus lies in people's awareness of one another's attitudes (Davison, 1962). It involves a number of people—a public—whose attention is focused on a particular issue or event, who have formed an opinion of it, and who believe that they know what others' opinions of it are. Knowledge of others' opinions is important because it gives us an idea of how they will behave in relation to that issue or event.

Readiness to respond in one way implies disapproval of alternative responses. The voter who favors Candidate Jones may show some disapproval of those who say that they intend to vote for Candidate Smith, for their behavior might prevent Jones's election. In the same way, someone who has just bought a new eight-cylinder automobile will be less than pleased with people who say that such a vehicle is a symbol of selfishness or foolishness rather than something to be admired. We are thus interested in others' opinions because they give us an idea of how others will react to our own behavior.

In an important way, then, public opinion operates like social norms, for it involves preferences and judgments. Just as the violation of a norm can draw disapproval from others, so the expression of one opinion can annoy those who hold a differing opinion of the same issue. And just as the acceptance of certain norms is a condition of membership in a particular group, so the holding of certain opinions may also be viewed as incumbent on a group's members. Both for practical purposes (our need to be able to predict others' behavior) and for symbolic purposes (indications of group membership), we have a continuing interest in others' opinions. How we come to learn of their opinions is thus of some importance.

The Origins of Public Opinion

Our sense of what most people are thinking—or, more precisely, what those people with whom we interact are thinking—tends to be a generalization rather than a precise headcount. It is based on hints and clues of various types, and on this basis we develop an idea of what most of our acquaintances are thinking about particular issues. We take pains to learn the opinions of our spouses, roommates, and close friends in some detail, but beyond them we are usually content with a more general idea. There are four main ways in which we develop an awareness of public opinion, and they can be ranged roughly in order of their importance in influencing our everyday relations with others.

Direct experience   First, of course, is our hearing others' opinions and seeing their actions. These are likely to be the people with whom we interact frequently, and we are ordinarily interested in their opinions because we want to maintain amicable relationships with them. After all, it is usually more important for us to get along with our relatives and our friends in the office and neighborhood than for us to offend them unnecessarily over something that has no direct bearing on our day-to-day relationships. If someone knows, for instance, that a friend is deeply committed to the "right to life" movement, he or she will usually refrain from expressing approval of abortion unless the topic cannot be avoided. Why stir up unnecessary controversy?

One significant consequence of the natural human tendency to avoid disagreement over "irrelevant" issues occurs when people have the impression that most of their acquaintances hold a particular opinion. Through reluctance to take an apparently unpopular stand when it is not immediately necessary to do so, they tend to remain quiet about their own opinion—and thus strengthen everyone else's impression that the popular opinion is even more widely shared. Through this process, public opinion can build to the point where it becomes an important criterion of group membership, thereby making it even more difficult to resist. The "bandwagon" effect can thus be based on group pressures as well as a desire for personal advantage (that is, a desire to be with the majority). It is for this reason that politicians seek endorsements, advertisers seek to persuade people that a new fashion will be admired by everyone, and a rumor can sometimes produce mass hysteria.

To be sure, individuals are not always reluctant to disagree with what they perceive as "majority opinion." In addition to those who are simply honest and forthright in expressing themselves, there are some who enjoy arguments, others who wish to draw attention to themselves, and a few who delight in upsetting people. And whenever an issue directly affects someone's personal interests, we can expect him or her to speak up about it regardless of others' opinion. There may be widespread agreement, for instance, that improvements in the state highway system are needed, but if it is proposed that a new superhighway be built through *your* backyard, your opposition is likely to be quite vocal, despite what you think your friends' opinions are.

The general rule here is that the closer an issue is to someone's own life, the less he or she will take others' attitudes into account when forming a personal opinion of it. Conversely, the more distant from one's personal interests an issue is (for example, controversy over a political scandal in another state), the more likely one's opinion of it is to be influenced by what one believes others' opinions are. It can also be said, however, that the more a topic is relevant to someone's personal interests, the less likely it is to be of *general* interest—and so the less likely it is to be an object of *public* opinion. So if public opinion ordinarily concerns topics that are of direct, immediate concern to only a small proportion of the people who are aware of them, we can see why it has the "snowballing" tendency noted above.

Indirect evidence A second source of our awareness of others' opinions is our acquaintances' reports of what *their* acquaintances are thinking about current issues. We know, of course, that people sometimes exaggerate things ("Nobody in my dorm likes the new counselor!") and that they are more likely to report others' opinions that agree with their own than those which do not. We may well be wary of such second-hand indicators of public opinion, then, but in the absence of any information to the contrary, we tend to assume that they are essentially correct. They are at least better than no information at all.

The mass media Television, radio, movies, newspapers, and magazines make up the **mass media**, *the major forms of mass communication through which information is carried to large numbers of people at about the same time.* The media constitute a third and particularly important way through which people become aware of one another's opinions. In general they do not tell us specifically *what* others are thinking, but through reporting current events (regardless of accuracy or completeness), they provide the basis for at least guessing what others' opinions will be. The process works as follows.

First, we assume that most people are exposed to the mass media. Other people read newspapers, watch television, etc., and so are likely to be aware of current events at the same time we learn of them. Second, we assume that we share with these people most of our culture's central values. It is the application of these values to current events that produces opinions, and in this sense they serve as the major premises in a series of syllogisms.

A *syllogism* is a pattern of reasoning that goes, in the classic example: "All men are mortal; Aristotle is a man; therefore, Aristotle is mortal." This is sheer logic: All of the members of category A have characteristic X; Q is a member of category A; therefore Q must have characteristic X. The first statement is the *major premise,* the second is the *minor premise,* and the third is the *conclusion.*

Our culture provides us with a vast number of major premises, such as "Murder is bad," "People should try to get ahead," and "Cannibalism is revolting." We all share these major premises because they are part of our common culture. The mass media then give us a number of *minor* premises every day: "Prominent attorney murdered," "Jane Smith elected to Congress," "Survivors lived on human flesh."

Knowing the major premise relevant to each event and being given the minor premise in a headline, we come almost automatically to conclusions (in the form of opinions). The murderer should be caught and punished; Ms. Smith deserves congratulations; and the people who survived the plane crash were in desperate circumstances. Further, *we assume that everyone else who has seen these headlines will have come to the same conclusions.*

A **cultural syllogism** can be thought of as *the process whereby the mass media shape public opinion by disseminating information to which people apply cultural values and assume that others have done likewise.* Thus the mass media create "instant public opinion" by making it possible for each of us at the same time to develop expectations about others' opinions of current issues and events. If we meet an acquaintance later in the day, then, we are likely to behave in accordance with these expectations. Even in the absence of any direct evidence of his or her opinion of a particular topic, we have already *assumed* that he or she holds a certain opinion of it, and we will act on this basis. Although we may have personal reasons for adopting a different opinion, we may be reluctant to express it if we believe it likely to generate an "unnecessary" argument; therefore, as noted earlier, our silence may actually contribute to others' impression that everyone in fact holds what is assumed to be the majority opinion.

It is because of this unique power of the mass media to *create* (rather than simply to reflect) public opinion that totalitarian governments insist on close control of all mass media. By the same token, it is the reason that a free press is so important to the maintenance of a democracy.

Public opinion polls   The last source of our information about others' opinions is the public opinion poll or survey (see Appendix 1 for more information on survey research). As such reports usually appear in the mass media, we learn that "forty-two percent of the state's citizens are in favor of more funds for the state university, thirty-eight percent want to cut its budget, and the remaining twenty percent have no opinion." We usually have no reason to question the accuracy of these figures as they sum up the opinions of a very large number of people, but we are not at all sure that they are accurate in describing the opinions of our immediate acquaintances. We are unlikely, then, to use such information as a guide to interaction with the people we see every day.

It tends to be those who are concerned with the attitudes of thousands or even millions of people—primarily advertisers and politicians—who have a practical interest in public opinion polls. For the rest of us, such reports may be interesting and may give us a pretty good idea of, for instance, who will win an upcoming election, but we rarely depend on them for information about our own circle of acquaintances.

It must be admitted, however, that the information provided by polls can in some situations influence our opinions and thus our behavior. A poll can help a candidate shape his or her campaign so as to appeal to a larger number of voters. A survey of consumer preferences can lead to the development of a new product—or of a new package for an old product—that will attract more customers. And to the extent that knowledge of a candidate's relative strength early in a campaign can encourage or discourage supporters, a self-fulfilling prophecy (see below) can be set in motion.

But it can be argued that these are special and relatively rare cases. For the most part, our expectations about the opinions of those with whom we interact regularly are influenced by our own direct experience, by their reports of others' opinions, and by our assumption that they will respond in predictable ways to the contents of the mass media.

The end result is always a general impression of what other people are thinking about some current issue or event and thus a generalized expectation of how they are likely to behave in relation to it. No matter how we acquire this information, we need it in order to guide our own behavior effectively. Public opinion is continually developing in response to current events, and it is thus of continuing interest to all of us.

Prophecies: self-fulfilling and self-destroying If someone's current opinion indicates what she or he is likely to *do* in the future with regard to a particular issue (contribute to a particular candidate's campaign, argue with those who favor other candidates, vote for that candidate, etc.), others will use it to predict his or her future behavior. Yet we are not always correct in our assessment of others' opinions, even though we are influenced by what we *think* their opinions are. When people are collectively wrong in thinking they know others' opinions, some interesting things can occur.

If we think of expectations as prophecies—as predictions of what others will do under certain circumstances—we can see that in some cases *people's expectations, even though inaccurate at first, can literally make themselves come true* (**self-fulfilling prophecies**) and that in other cases *expectations can actually prevent themselves from coming true* (**self-destroying prophecies**) (Merton, 1957). It is only necessary that a number of people believe that others hold a certain opinion.

A self-fulfilling prophecy operates in the following way. Suppose that someone invites a number of people to a party, but for some reason each of them believes that the party will be a flop because none of the others intends to go. Perhaps a story has circulated that the host is likely to become drunk and abusive, and each of these people assumes that the others believe it. At any rate, even if privately each guest would *like* to go, he or she predicts that no one else will be there and so decides not to go after all. As a result, the party is indeed a flop, even though public opinion was incorrect in its portrayal of the guests' personal attitudes. The prophecy, or the shared expectation that no one will attend the party, has fulfilled itself.

The same process can operate on a much larger scale. Merton points out (1957, Chapter 11) that white Americans' shared belief that black Americans were intellectually inferior led them in the past to deny many educational and occupational opportunities to blacks, thus producing a situation in which this "prophecy" seemed to come true (see Chapter 7, on intergroup relations). Similarly, if the members of one group come to believe that they are about to be attacked by another group, their preparations for defense may appear so warlike to the other group that its members decide that they must attack first in self-defense. The expectation of an attack has made the expectation come true.

The key to the self-fulfilling prophecy is each person's belief that he or she will be disadvantaged if he or she does not do what others are expected to do. If, for example, a rumor spreads through a small town that there is going to be a shortage of sugar in the local grocery stores, many people will try to get an extra supply before their neighbors buy it all. The result, of course, *is* a temporary shortage of sugar. The collective expectation of a shortage has made everyone predict that everyone *else* will be buying up sugar, and so it becomes important that they do this too.

The *self-destroying prophecy* has the same dynamics, except that in this case people believe that it will be to their disadvantage if they *do* engage in the behavior they expect of others. An example is found in the following incident. Prior to the opening of the New York World's Fair in 1964, a group of civil rights activists announced their plan to hold a "stall-in" on opening day. The mass media carried the story that they were going to have a number of old cars run out of gas on the roads leading to the Fair, causing a monster traffic jam and calling attention to their demands. The public's response to the prediction of a traffic jam was a collective decision to stay away from the Fair. The highways were almost empty on opening day. As a result, opening-day receipts were considerably lower than had been expected, and no traffic jams developed. Publicizing the prophecy led to behavior which prevented it from coming true.

Public opinion can thus be viewed as an independent force in social relationships, generated by people's need to know one another's opinions. What people believe about others' opinions of current issues and events and how they arrive at these beliefs, regardless of their accuracy, provides the foundation for understanding all forms of collective behavior.

The Public Opinion Process and Collective Behavior

Although public opinion ordinarily refers to the opinions of large numbers of people on issues that are widely known, the processes through which it develops lie at the foundation of all forms of collective behavior. We can say this for the following reasons.

First, collective behavior is by definition behavior that occurs in *unstructured situations*—that is, when people's behavior is *not* guided by established norms that define interrelated roles. Second, also by definition, collective behavior involves a number of people. (Only in fancy can we conceive of a one-person riot, a one-person fad, or a one-person social movement.) If, then, a number of people are behaving in similar ways but without normative guidance, they must obviously be responding to something in the present—to some sort of stimulus other than ordinary normative expectations. The stimulus can be something "outside" the group (a fire, word of an impending flood, etc.), or it can be the actions of other people (seeing some people begin to act hysterically, hearing others boo an umpire, etc.). The important thing is that a number of people have become aware of the stimulus at roughly the same time, each one knows that others have also become aware of it and are likely to respond to it, and each one recognizes that previously established norms are either irrelevant or else are for some reason inoperative in the present situation.

Our first question, then, if we are to develop a systematic understanding of collective behavior, must concern the ways in which situations may become unstructured.

UNSTRUCTURED SITUATIONS

Since social life is for the most part fairly orderly and predictable, it is clear that something must happen before there is shared recognition that a situation—that is, a context within which people are interacting—has become unstructured. There are essentially two ways in which this can happen.

One is when a new stimulus appears that makes established norms and patterns of behavior irrelevant. The appearance of smoke and flame in a theater makes it obvious to everyone that the previously applicable norms concerning audience behavior are now inappropriate. The survivors of a tornado, as they emerge from the wreckage, recognize that the norms governing everyday community life are now quite irrelevant to their immediate needs. But the situation becomes unstructured only if people do not share an alternative set of norms appropriate to the new situation.

If people have been trained through participation in fire drills or civil defense emergency exercises to be familiar with an alternative set of norms relevant to the new situation, the situation will remain structured, and no collective behavior will ensue. An important aspect of such drills, in fact, in addition to people's becoming acquainted with the procedures to be followed "in event of emergency," is that they become aware that *others* are *also* acquainted with these procedures. It is this awareness that enables people to switch to the new norms and thus to keep the situation structured.

The other way in which a situation can become unstructured occurs when there are increasing indications that people are ignoring the norms that

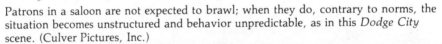

Patrons in a saloon are not expected to brawl; when they do, contrary to norms, the situation becomes unstructured and behavior unpredictable, as in this *Dodge City* scene. (Culver Pictures, Inc.)

"should" govern their behavior. For example, take a crowd that has gathered outside a jail, curious about a murderer who has just been captured and is being held there. If a few stones are hurled at the jail's windows, everyone sees that at least some members of the crowd are prepared to ignore the usual prohibitions against damaging public property. As more stones are tossed, the impression quickly spreads that *no one* is going to heed these prohibitions. And as it becomes obvious that some norms are being disregarded, people become less certain that other norms will continue to be obeyed. Through the observation of others' behavior, and in the absence of indications that their "deviance" is going to be countered by any form of social control, the members of the crowd may well come to the common conclusion that the situation has become unstructured.

Yet, as has been pointed out, people continue to need to be able to predict others' behavior. When it becomes clear that previously established normative expectations are no longer useful for this purpose, because either there are none that pertain to the new situation or everyone else seems to be disregarding the norms that should be relevant, people must turn to the immediate situation for information about what to expect. This is the only remaining way the individual has to develop expectations about what others are going to do—and thus to decide how he or she can behave more effectively.

We have all been in a situation in which someone suddenly asks, "Hey, do you guys smell smoke?" Alerted to possible danger, others begin to sniff and to explore and then try to reach agreement on whether something is indeed burning and, if so, whether it poses an immediate threat. Rarely does someone simply announce, "I smell smoke—I'm getting out of here!" Such behavior would not only imply a lack of concern for others, but might also draw their disapproval or ridicule—"You're crazy, there's no fire!" People ordinarily seek group support in the identification of something that seems to require redefinition of the situation, partly to confirm their own perceptions and partly to legitimate their own responses to it (which might otherwise appear irrational or deviant).

This sort of incident illustrates people's need to achieve some sort of mutual agreement that the situation *does* justify unusual behavior. The more quickly such agreement is reached (or, in the participants' minds, *seems* to be reached), the more dramatic is the ensuing collective behavior.

Different individuals, of course, may require different amounts of evidence before they decide that the situation *has* become unstructured, and those who reach this conclusion first may later be defined as leaders of the collective behavior that develops in the absence of established norms. (And indeed they have led it, at least in the sense that their concrete actions provided the evidence needed to persuade others that the situation had become unstructured. Those who actively encouraged others to join in the new behavior are, of course, more deserving of being called leaders.)

If a new, shared definition of the situation does not emerge, however, nothing in the way of *collective* behavior will occur. At best there will be random actions by different people, an unresolved sense of confusion, and probably a return to the acceptance of whatever norms seem most relevant to the situation. When the sheriff in a typical Western movie stands before a potential lynch mob and persuades its members to return peacefully to their homes, he has succeeded because he has not simply reminded them of their duties as citizens, but also undermined each member's sense that the others will approve of violent, lawbreaking behavior. And it has been his authority, perhaps demonstrated by knocking down the mob's ringleader, that has suggested to each member that all of the others will take him seriously.

The Time Factor

All forms of collective behavior occur in unstructured situations and are guided in the absence of established norms by their participants' newly developed expectations about one another's attitudes and probable behavior. We have already discussed the two major reasons that situations become unstructured; here we shall look at the importance of *how quickly* people become mutually aware that this has happened.

The speed with which a number of people become aware of one another's sense that established norms are either irrelevant or inoperative in their current situation is determined largely by how easily they can communicate with one another and by the apparent urgency of the need for new forms of behavior. Further, these two factors interact with each other. If, for instance, several people become aware separately of a possible threat (say, a forest fire a mile away), they will quickly seek contact with one another because the need is urgent. If, on the other hand, they are already together in a crowd, they can see almost immediately how others are responding to a threat, and this makes it more urgent that they redefine the situation. In either case the shared sense of unstructuredness develops fairly rapidly.

When people are not together, and when evidence of unstructuredness does not suggest an urgent need for action, the forms of collective behavior that develop are far less dramatic. They develop more slowly and usually involve much more limited aspects of their participants' lives. Fads, fashions, and social movements are the principal forms of collective behavior that emerge under these circumstances.

We can identify three categories of the relative rapidity with which situations become unstructured: those in which this happens almost immediately, those that require between a few hours and a few months for this to happen, and those that become unstructured only over periods extending beyond several months. Since rapid unstructuring can occur only when people are together, we shall turn our attention first to the nature of *crowds*.

Crowds and Collective Behavior

In sociological terms, a **crowd** *is a temporary gathering of otherwise unrelated people in a particular area for some purpose.* A crowd may be made up of the curious onlookers who gather at the scene of an automobile accident. It may be people in a city street who are taking advantage of a sale, celebrating a holiday, or merely seeking cooler air on a hot summer evening. It may be an audience at a movie or concert. The members of a crowd, in other words, have gathered for some reason other than simply to create a crowd, even though other people may be attracted to a crowd in order to find out why it has formed.

Sociologists talk about four major types of crowds (Blumer, 1951), although not all are necessarily examples of collective behavior. *Casual* crowds are made up of members who gather only accidentally—to watch something unexpected such as a collision, a fight in a schoolyard, or even a cat stuck in a tree. The act of gathering is itself a type of collective behavior in this case—individuals responding in the same way to a particular stimulus in the immediate situation—but the crowd itself is not.

The members of a *conventional* crowd have planned ahead of time to be in a particular place in order to see a play, hear a concert, watch a baseball game, or attend a wedding. Such crowds tend to be passive, and their members ordinarily assume that the situation will be structured by established norms.

An *expressive* crowd is a gathering for the purpose of enabling its members to express their feelings about something together. It may be a rally preceding a college football game, a demonstration in front of City Hall, or a religious revival meeting. If a conventional crowd becomes particularly vocal in reacting to, say, a great opera performance or a referee's decision, it may be briefly transformed into an expressive crowd. And if its members begin to do more than express their feelings—to throw things, destroy property, or assault one another—it becomes an acting crowd.

An *acting* crowd's members are *doing* something, whether it is cleaning up a park, lynching a horsethief, or looting a burned-out warehouse. Their actions may have developed "on the spur of the moment," as a sports audience may begin to riot, or they may have been planned ahead of time. To the extent that planning is involved and the participants' actions are organized, the crowd does exhibit structure, but whether it qualifies as a case of collective behavior depends on whether the participants' actions are in violation of established norms. A lynch mob, for instance, may have planned for some time, with specific roles assigned to particular individuals, but it is a type of collective behavior because its members are collectively violating certain norms—something they would not do as separate individuals.

Behavioral contagion   Being a member of a crowd increases one's sensitivity to others' behavior for several reasons. First, the fact that one is physically in the midst of a large number of people means that their actions may have direct consequences for one's own well-being. Second, because most of them are strangers, one is less confident that established norms can be relied on to predict their behavior. And third, there is ordinarily a mutual awareness that social controls are less effective in crowds, both because of the anonymity that people feel when they are among strangers and because even formal controls are difficult to apply to large numbers of people (Schultz, 1964).

Behavioral contagion *occurs when, rather than relying fully on established norms for guidance in what to expect of the other members of a crowd, one is at least prepared to depend more on immediate evidence of what others are actually doing, regardless of norms,* if this seems necessary. There is thus a tendency to concentrate on the immediate situation rather than on the long-term consequences of behavior and, if the situation becomes unstructured, to act in ways that are similar rather than complementary to the actions of others. Without normative guidance for more complicated patterns of interaction, the tendency is to respond in the same way to a particular stimulus or to the behavior of others. Because under such circumstances people begin to imitate one another's actions, collective behavior by crowds is often described as the result of behavioral contagion.

But different crowds vary in terms of their members' susceptibility to behavioral contagion. Two factors seem particularly important in determining people's readiness to "expect the unexpected." One is the apparent size and expected duration of the crowd. The larger it is, the more people feel hemmed in by one another; they sense that it will be more difficult to get away from the crowd presence, and so it becomes more important that they pay attention to one another's behavior. Similarly, a larger crowd is likely to last longer, and there is thus more opportunity for its members to develop a shared sense of unstructuredness.

The second factor is the extent to which a crowd's members define the situation as normal and thus governed by established norms. When there is a clear understanding of why they have gathered and of what will go on during the time they are together (a play, an athletic contest, a series of speeches), a crowd's members are unlikely to anticipate the situation's becoming unstructured. The stronger the reasons to believe that the situation is structured, then, the lower the chances that behavioral contagion will occur.

Although collective behavior by crowds can be classified in terms of apparent purpose, this approach does not get at the central sociological characteristics of different forms of collective behavior. Rather than develop an elaborate list of purposes, then, we shall restrict ourselves here to a discussion of the basically different forms of collective crowd behavior in terms of the relationships among their participants.

Combining the "time" categories with the two basic reasons for unstructuring, we can devise a table that seems useful in arranging the various forms of collective behavior so that the reasons for their differences become clear. They are arranged in Table 17.1.

TABLE 17.1   THE MAJOR FORMS OF COLLECTIVE BEHAVIOR

Why the situation has become unstructured:	How rapidly people recognize that the situation has become structured:		
	Few hours or less	Few hours to few months	Few months or longer
Appearance of a new, "outside" stimulus (established norms no longer relevant)	Public opinion* Panic Response to disaster	Hysteria	Social movements of all types (initial causes difficult to classify)
Failure of established norms (increasing signs that others are ignoring them)	Mob Riot	Fad Fashion Craze	
Typical duration before behavior ceases altogether or new norms are established:	Less than a week; often less than a few hours	From a week to a year or two	From a year to a decade or more

*By definition, current events are new stimuli, and responses to them develop rapidly through the use of cultural syllogisms.

THE MAJOR FORMS OF COLLECTIVE BEHAVIOR

Our next task is to examine the characteristics of different situations in which collective behavior occurs—the ways in which they have become unstructured and the ways in which new mutual expectations have developed to replace established norms. Through this we can get some idea of how the major forms of collective behavior are related to one another, despite wide differences between them in terms of the specific kinds of behavior that are involved.

Panics, Riots, and Mobs

A **panic,** as the word implies, *is a sudden collective response to an immediate threat.* Whether it is a fire in a theater, a sniper shooting into a parade, or a rabid dog loose in a crowded park, people respond simply by trying to get

away from the threat. The situation becomes unstructured almost immediately. Fear of the threat is heightened if people see that others' efforts to escape are likely to impede their own, and a vicious cycle of desperation inciting
greater desperation is set in motion. The results can be catastrophic. More
than 500 people died in the Iroquois Theater fire in Chicago in 1903; nearly 500
died in the Coconut Grove nightclub fire in Boston in 1942; 164 people were
killed in a supper club fire in Southgate, Kentucky, in 1976. It is impossible, of
course, to determine how many people would still have died in those fires if
the crowds had been orderly and not blocked the exits, but it is certain that the
number of deaths would have been greatly reduced.

A rare exception to the rule that rapid unstructuring can take place only
when people are together is the case in which many people learn separately *but
at the same time* of an immediate threat. This happened during the famous
"invasion from Mars" broadcast by Orson Welles in 1938. This radio drama
was produced in such a way that many listeners believed that the country was
actually being invaded by monsters from Mars. In their panic, the listeners
tried to drive into remote areas, to warn their neighbors, or to barricade themselves in their homes. But because not many others were similarly agitated
(many people had not heard the broadcast, and many others knew that it was
fiction), genuinely *collective* behavior did not last long. By the next morning
the scare was over (Cantril, 1940).

Because only an outside stimulus is likely to undermine a strongly shared
sense of structure, the panic is almost the only form of collective behavior that
is associated with conventional crowds. (Casual crowds, being more transitory in membership and ordinarily of briefer duration, are probably the least
likely to develop any form of collective behavior.)

Whereas panic is always a response to a threat (even though it may exist
only in people's imaginations), *riots* and *mobs* seem to result from people's
awareness that others are disregarding established norms. Although there is
not complete agreement among sociologists on the differences between a riot
and a mob, it is generally accepted that a mob is more organized than a riot. A
mob *is a group that has a common purpose to act*—to inflict violence on a particular victim or group of victims, to destroy a particular object, to loot an un-
protected business area—and its members act in ways that seem cooperative
rather than at cross-purposes. Leaders are more frequently associated with
mobs than with riots, then, because concerted action often requires some sort
of guidance.

A **riot,** on the other hand, *is made up of people whose actions are directed
against one another or at random targets.* In this respect what appears to be a
riot (a so-called race riot, for instance) might better be viewed as two mobs
attacking each other, or a mob might simply be a number of rioters who have
agreed temporarily on a common target for their actions. Whether a case of
collective behavior should be classified as a riot or a mob is thus not always

easy to determine, for the extent to which those involved are organized may change from one moment to the next.

Necessary preconditions   Whereas a panic is a "natural" response to a sudden threat, neither riots nor mobs can develop in the absence of certain necessary preconditions. In his *Theory of Collective Behavior* (1962), Neil Smelser has presented a systematic analysis of these conditions. He lists six characteristics that must be present before norm-violating collective behavior can occur:

1. *Structural conduciveness,* or the presence of the components necessary for collective behavior: the existence of a crowd, the readiness of one group to resist the actions of another, means of communication, etc. Other necessary components could be the factors that facilitate the gathering of a crowd, such as reasonably good weather and open space.

2. *Structural strain,* or a shared sense by those involved that the existing situation is in some way unsatisfactory. This has usually taken some time to develop—a sense of frustration or deprivation related to living conditions or a fear that something important may be lost—and people are ready to expect expressions of this dissatisfaction.

3. *A generalized belief about the source of this strain.* This is necessary if people are to be able to define and to recognize certain acts as responses to the strain, for otherwise there would be no agreed-on forms of behavior through which to express dissatisfaction and no opportunity for them to become contagious. Such a belief need be nothing more complicated than, say, a minority group's agreement that its members are exploited by the local police or a belief by students at one high school that those attending another school are "out to get them."

4. *A precipitating factor*—either an outside stimulus that is related to the general belief (for example, an incident in which a student from one high school is beaten up by a group from the other school) or the sight of several people apparently acting to express their shared sense of strain. The *rumor* of a specific incident, whether it is true or false, can serve as a precipitating factor if enough people are aware of it and know that others are also aware of it.

5. *Mobilization for action.* This refers to either the actions of a leader who initiates and directs the behavior of others or simply the behavioral contagion discussed earlier. In the latter case it is the specific action by one or a few members of the crowd that is progressively emulated by others.

6. *Perceived weakening or absence of formal social controls.* This can develop in several ways, particularly when circumstances seem to make the application of social controls less likely. During a blackout, for instance, the police will obviously have a much harder time spotting and apprehending looters and vandals; a similar effect is achieved if there is evidence that the police do not intend to enforce the law. At times, too, the very existence of a large crowd can give its members the feeling that they can overwhelm any opposition to their actions, whether it is organized or not.

With all of these factors in place, collective behavior has come into existence. Smelser's formulation of the necessary preconditions and current circumstances is applicable primarily to various types of mobs and riots, but a panic differs only in that steps 2 through 5 in his analysis are telescoped into a very brief time. The appearance of flame in a nightclub, for example, initiates a sudden sense of strain, is at the same time clearly the source of the strain, and is also the precipitating factor; individual responses to it then serve to mobilize others' actions.

Hysteria

A hysteria can be thought of as a panic in slow motion; indeed, such slower-developing phenomena as the collapse of a stock market and the spread of anxiety about the presence of a supposed "mad rapist" in a community are often called panics. But since neither of these types of collective behavior develops in crowds (although both may lead to the gathering of crowds), it will be easier to refer to them as hysterias.

A **hysteria** *comes into being as people begin to share the belief that they are faced with a severe but unidentifiable or unstoppable threat.* If *everyone* had heard and believed the "invasion from Mars" broadcast, for instance, a brief but genuine hysteria would have resulted. The threat to which hysteria is a response tends to be relatively distant, in that its impact does not seem immediate and its precise form is unspecified; the fear of Communist subversion, of economic disaster, or of an enemy invasion is the sort that may produce hysteria. As people become aware that others are taking it seriously and are prepared to react to it, they develop a sense of the forms of behavior that will be appropriate and accepted by others.

The less a specific threat can be identified, the more people search for something that can "represent" it and can serve as a focus of their response. "Scapegoats" are usually found—old women who can be identified as witches, people who can be identified as secret agents, or the members of a minority group. As people see one another treating these scapegoats as the source of the threat, collective violence toward them is often the result.

If, on the other hand, the threat is a slow-motion parallel to a theater fire, leading people to believe that others' responses to it will make their own responses less effective, the sense that urgent action is needed will increase. (See the discussion of the self-fulfilling prophecy earlier in this chapter.)The "bank runs" of the early 1930s, in which people hurried to withdraw their money from banks before others could do so, fearing that otherwise the bank would run out of cash, seem to stand midway between a genuine panic and a hysteria. They did not originate in crowds, but developed more quickly than many forms of hysteria and turned into self-fulfilling prophecies.

Crazes, Fads, and Fashions

These forms of collective behavior develop more slowly than do those which occur in crowds and ordinarily last much longer. Further, they do not involve direct violations of established norms, but instead are forms of behavior that develop in areas of social life that are by nature relatively unstructured. Finally, they tend to be responses to opportunities rather than to threats.

A **craze,** for example, *develops when people begin to believe that others have come to place an unusually high value on a particular object of economic interest.* In the attempt to make money by getting in on the anticipated "boom" early, they begin to pay higher prices for whatever it is—tulip bulbs in midseventeenth century Holland, parcels of land in Florida during the 1920s, etc.—and thus confirm one another's expectations. For a time, these mutual expectations become a self-fulfilling prophecy, for others *are* willing to pay higher and higher prices for the commodity. Eventually, however, people begin to recognize that the boom exists *only* because they expect others to be willing to pay still higher prices for the commodity rather than because it is intrinsically valuable. As they conclude that they must sell *now* in order not to lose the money they have invested, a crash results, prices drop swiftly to normal levels, and many people are left with worthless investments. A craze may last for a few months or for several years, but the cycle is inevitable.

A **fad** *represents the appearance of a new activity or object of interest* (a game, a hobby, a form of entertainment, a type of food, etc.) *in which large numbers of people become quickly interested.* It may involve owning something new—a hula hoop, a skateboard, a "pet rock," a record by a new rock group, a portable tapedeck—or it may be participation in a particular activity—sitting atop flagpoles, swallowing goldfish, playing a new game, or dancing a new step.

The motivation to participate in a fad seems to be the desire to be "first" by local standards or else to share a new interest or experience with others so as not to be left behind. Whereas a craze is based on the assumption that others will pay more for a particular commodity, a fad is based on the assumption that others will "pay" in the form of admiration or envy in response to one's

The movie *Animal House* precipitated the national fad for toga parties. In this example of collective behavior, people responded to a common stimulus (the movie) and the desire to be "in." (Ira Wyman/Sygma)

having or doing the new thing. Knowing about the fad and perhaps becoming an expert in it becomes a temporary requirement for group approval, and this can develop only as people become aware that others are prepared to honor this. And, as with a craze, people eventually recognize that others are becoming tired of the fad; little is to be gained from continued participation, and the fad dies away.

Fashions *involve styles or changes in form that are not central to the thing in question.* We usually think of "fashion" as referring mainly to clothing, but there are also fashions in music, in cooking, and in automobile design, etc. (Klapp, 1972, Chapter 10). Fashions are like fads, then, except that they involve changes in style rather than new interests in unrelated objects or activities. For this reason, they develop more slowly: Adopting a new fashion requires giving up the old one, and there will be many reasons to resist this. Some people may simply have an economic investment in the previous fashion—a closet full of wide-lapel jackets, for instance, or of square-toed shoes—and others may prefer not to be identified with those who are taking up the new fashion ("Only hippies wear their hair long").

Yet change does occur, and when there are intrinsic limits to the ways in which styles may vary, fashions tend to go in cycles. Women's skirts, for instance, tend to go from short to long and back again; hair may be worn short, then long, and then short again. Only rarely, however, is a new fashion adopted rapidly and by everyone, for even though consensus may slowly develop about the desirability of a new fashion, not everyone can afford to "keep up," and not everyone approves personally of what he or she believes "most people" have come to admire. As a form of collective behavior, then, fashion is probably the slowest and most incomplete and thus the least dramatic.

Social Movements

If a hysteria is a panic in slow motion, a social movement can be viewed as a mob in very, *very* slow motion. *Having a common purpose and in the beginning behaving "outside" the everyday structure of social relationships, a* **social movement** *ordinarily develops over months and even years* rather than in the space of a few hours or less.

We can speak of *general social movements,* such as the slowly mounting dissatisfaction with traditional sex roles (discussed in Chapter 5) and of *specific social movements,* which are organized attempts to bring about or to prevent a particular sort of change in society. The former may take a century or more before large numbers of participants are involved. It will follow Smelser's model, moving slowly from "structural strain" to "generalized belief," and the next stage—mobilization for action—is where specific social movements take form. A specific social movement, whether it is the Women's Christian Temperance Movement or the Socialist Labor Party, is an organized effort to deal with the source of strain.

Within its own organizational structure, then, a specific social movement can hardly be said to be unstructured. As with the case of mobs, however, the unstructuredness lies in the broader situation within which this form of collective behavior emerges. To the extent that this behavior is not normatively predictable on the basis of current expectations, it is "outside" of present social structures and thus deserves classification as collective behavior.

Specific social movements tend to be classified in terms of their purposes, or relationship to the existing social structure. Some are *reactionary,* attempting to get society to return to an earlier set of values or social relationships. An organization seeking to restore traditional women's roles or to delegalize labor unions is an example of this type. Some movements are *conservative,* in that they are trying only to maintain the status quo by resisting further change. Organized attempts to prevent the legalization of abortion or the decriminalization of marijuana are examples of conservative social movements.

Reform movements advocate specific types of social change, as do groups concerned with civil rights and with women's liberation; these may be further subdivided in terms of how extensive their goals are and the tactics they use. Some have relatively narrow purposes (say, the passage of laws concerning welfare benefits) and employ respectable tactics such as advertising and lobbying. As goals become more sweeping and tactics more violent, social movements become *revolutionary* in nature (the American and French revolutions

The Imperial Wizard, head of the Invisible Empire, directs Ku Klux Klansmen as they gather for a rally in Decatur, Alabama, in June 1979. A reactionary group, the KKK has recently begun to revive its activities in the South and elsewhere. (U.P.I.)

of the late eighteenth century, and the Russian revolution in 1917, are good examples). Finally, *utopian* movements seek essentially to escape from society and to restructure only the lives of their own members.

Because social movements take a relatively long time to develop, they are obviously not responses to *suddenly* unstructured situations. Rather than concentrating on the causes of social movements, then, studies of this form of collective behavior tend to concentrate on two other aspects of their development: the types of people who participate in them and the stages through which they evolve.

Participation in social movements There have been several theories of the particular psychological characteristics that seem to make an individual especially likely to join social movements. Personality syndromes, such as the "authoritarian personality" of Adorno and his associates (1950) and the "true believer" of Hoffer (1951), have been proposed to explain the readiness of certain people to accept unquestioningly others' leadership, particularly when it justifies aggressive attitudes and acts against other racial, religious, or political groups. Individuals like these tend to be especially prone to anti-Semitism and other prejudices and thus to make willing recruits for right-wing movements such as the Nazi party and the Ku Klux Klan.

Although some people are more willing than others to follow certain types of leadership, however, social movements vary so much in terms of their goals and structures that it is difficult to think of a single type of person who is *generally* prone to join social movements. Because "joining" is not something that takes place in a vacuum, other factors must also be considered. The individual's social circumstances—being a member of a disadvantaged minority, being status inconsistent (see Chapter 6), having a particular amount of education, one's community and family relationships, etc.—probably carry more weight than do specific personality characteristics in determining the individual's readiness to participate in social movements.

Stages in social movements   In terms of development over time, most social movements exhibit a similar pattern, although not all of them manage to evolve through the entire cycle. In the beginning, or what students of social movements often call the *incipient* stage, there must be some type of structural strain—an unsatisfactory social condition experienced privately by a number of people. As these people begin to recognize that their feelings are shared by others, they become more prepared to think about acting to correct the situation and more ready to approve of such actions by others. This is termed the *popular* stage.

During the popular stage, and often after some experience with unorganized attempts to achieve change, people learn that correcting the problem will take a long time and will require the coordination of many people's efforts. Now the movement has reached the *formal* stage; leadership becomes important, different jobs are assigned, efforts are made to recruit new members and to influence public opinion, and actions are more carefully planned. Since people have joined the movement because of their commitment to its goal, the type of leadership that usually emerges is charismatic in nature—the leader must embody personally the goals and values of his or her followers, depending on example and inspiration for the right to lead rather than simply on the occupancy of an organizational office. (See Chapter 12 for a discussion of charismatic leadership and Chapter 9 for the relationship between leadership and organizational goals.)

Depending on a number of factors—sustaining its membership's enthusiasm, gaining new members, achieving some success, not arousing strong opposition, etc.—a social movement may remain in existence long enough to reach the final, or *institutional*, stage. At this point it has become reasonably well integrated into the broader social structure of society and has become so normatively structured that it ceases to be identifiable as collective behavior. Labor unions, evangelical religious groups, and socialist political parties (especially in Europe) are social movements that have reached this stage. It is possible, however, for a social movement to disappear before reaching this stage because it has been entirely successful in achieving its goal. The women's suffrage movement and the Vietnam peace movement, although well organized during the formal stage, had no reason to continue in existence after they had accomplished their aims, and so have gone out of existence instead of becoming institutionalized.

SUMMARY

The term *collective behavior* refers to all forms of social behavior that develop in unstructured situations—that is, when normative guidance is lacking or relevant norms are for some reason being ignored. The participants in collective behavior tend to behave in similar rather than complementary ways, and their involvement is ordinarily temporary rather than long-lasting.

The development of *public opinion*—the members of a public becoming aware of one another's attitudes toward a current issue or event—is a basic form of collective behavior. The more distant an issue is from our immediate personal concerns, the more our opinion of it will be influenced by how we think others are responding to it. There are four major ways through which we develop a sense of public opinion. In order of their influence on our own opinions, these are: direct observation of others' attitudes, people's reports of others' opinions, figuring out how others will respond to the contents of the mass media (through the application of "cultural syllogisms"), and public opinion polls.

Even when people's perceptions of others' attitudes are incorrect, public opinion can play an important role in influencing their behavior. When a number of people mistakenly believe that others hold a certain opinion and thus will behave in a certain way, *and* when it seems necessary to engage in the same behavior in order to avoid trouble or loss, a *self-fulfilling prophecy* occurs. If, on the other hand, people think that it will be *dis*advantageous to engage in the actions that each expects of everyone else, the prophecy (that is, the shared expectation of what other people will do) becomes *self-destroying*.

People become mutually aware that established norms or values are not an adequate basis for predicting others' behavior under two conditions: when something new appears in the situation that makes established norms irrelevant (smoke and flame in a theater, for example) or that calls for evaluation (an event reported in the mass media) and when it becomes obvious to people that others are ignoring the norms that should govern their behavior (as when fistfights begin to break out during a political rally). In either case those involved must develop new ideas about what to expect of one another. This must be done by paying attention to the new stimulus and determining how others are likely to react to it or by watching others' actions and deciding how to respond to them.

In addition to the *reasons* that situations become unstructured, the *speed* with which this occurs is a determinant of the forms of collective behavior that develop. If a number of people are to become mutually aware at the same time that the situation has become unstructured, they must be within sight and hearing of one another—gathered in a *crowd*. Sociologists identify four types of crowds. *Casual* crowds (people gathered temporarily, for instance, to watch a street musician) are least likely to develop collective behavior. *Conventional* crowds (such as theater audiences) are likely to respond with collective behavior only when an immediate threat is discovered. *Expressive* crowds (such as a political demonstration) are particularly open to behavioral contagion, and *acting* crowds are by definition examples of collective behavior. The types of collective behavior that develop most rapidly are thus associated with crowds and are usually the most dramatic.

Panics, riots, and mobs are the principal forms of collective crowd behavior. Whereas a panic is the crowd's reaction to an immediate threat and is precipitated by it alone, riots and mobs generally do not develop unless their participants share (in Smelser's analysis) a sense of structural strain and a common belief about its source. Then, when a precipitating factor appears and social controls seem ineffective, mobilization can occur: A riot can erupt or a mob can go into action.

When the people involved are not initially together in a crowd, shared awareness of unstructuredness develops more slowly, and responses to it are usually less urgent. The exception to this is the hysteria, in which people are responding to a threat which seems highly dangerous but is unspecified in terms of when or in what form it will appear. Crazes, fads, and fashions, on the other hand, develop more slowly and in response to perceived opportunities (for profit or social approval) rather than to threats.

Social movements, finally, are the slowest form of collective behavior to develop, although Smelser's model applies to them as well. A *general* social movement comes into being as more and more people sense some specific type of structural strain. This may take years or decades, developing into a *specific* (or consciously organized) movement only after the strain has become a focus of shared attention and people feel that collective efforts to do something about the source of the strain are needed. After these *incipient* and *popular* stages of development, the *formal* stage is reached; leadership appears and action is organized to prevent or achieve some sort of social change.

In terms of their goals, social movements are categorized as reactionary, conservative, reform, revolutionary, or utopian in purpose. If they succeed in their aims, they are likely to disappear. If, however, they continue to work toward their goals and become more broadly integrated into the ongoing social structure, they reach the *institutional* stage and can no longer be viewed as collective behavior.

SUGGESTED READINGS

Adorno, T. W., *et al.*, *The Authoritarian Personality* (New York: Harper & Row, 1950). Originally focused on characterizing the anti-Semitic personality, this important study has led to much additional work on the relations between personality and social structure. It is by no means accepted as the final word on the topic, but stands as an excellent example of research on a challenging problem.

Hoffer, Eric, *The True Believer: Thoughts on the Nature of Mass Movements* (New York: Harper & Bros., 1951). Hoffer, an iconoclastic California longshoreman, is no longer the focus of attention that he once was, but this book generated a good deal of controversy when it first appeared. His ideas are still worth considering.

Klapp, Orrin E., *Currents of Unrest: An Introduction to Collective Behavior* (New York: Holt, Rinehart and Winston, 1972). Although this text pays relatively little attention to collective crowd behavior, it offers a broad and thoughtful coverage of the other, longer-lasting forms. It also offers an exhaustive bibliography of books and articles on the topic.

Lang, Kurt, and Gladys Engel Lang, *Collective Dynamics* (New York: Crowell, 1961). The authors stress the conditions under which social situations become unstructured and the ways in which responses to this are systematically influenced by different types of "structural strain."

Smelser, Neil J., *Theory of Collective Behavior* (New York: Free Press, 1962). Smelser's theory, on which much of this chapter has drawn, stands as probably the most useful framework available for the analysis of the conditions under which collective behavior is likely to occur. It is much more extensive and tightly reasoned than the part of it used here, and the book deserves careful study.

Turner, Ralph H., and Lewis M. Killian, *Collective Behavior*, 2d ed. (Englewood Cliffs, N.J.: Prentice-Hall, 1972). Combining text and readings, this is an excellent introduction to recent thinking on the causes and forms of collective behavior. In emphasizing the immediate "rationality" of behavior that in long-range perspective seems quite "irrational," the authors make an important contribution to the sociological understanding of behavior in unstructured situations.

Glossary

Behavioral contagion The process through which the intensity with which people engage in a particular form of behavior is strengthened by their seeing that others are also engaging in it. The best example is a *panic* (see below), in which people's attempts to escape from an enclosed place spur others on to more and more frantic efforts to escape.

Collective behavior Participation in a form of behavior that is guided not by established norms, but instead by the current behavior of others. In such cases people tend initially to copy one another's behavior so that they are generally doing the same thing rather than complementary things. The term covers phenomena ranging from an instantaneous panic, through fads and fashions, to slowly developing social movements.

Craze A form of collective behavior in which the immediate incentive is profit, inspired by the assumption that a particular commodity will become increasingly valuable because others will want it more and more. A craze is a form of *self-fulfilling prophecy* (see below), except that it inevitably ends when people recognize that the commodity cannot continue to increase in value indefinitely.

Crowd A temporary gathering of people, generally unrelated to one another, in a particular area for some purpose. Sociologists identify four major types of crowds: *casual, conventional, expressive,* and *acting* and recognize that a particular crowd can change from one type to another.

"Cultural syllogism" The process through which people apply cultural values to information carried by the mass media, come to an opinion about it in this way, and then assume that others (also exposed to the mass media) have come to the same conclusions. Thus the mass media can create an atmosphere of mutual expectations concerning current events, which constitute the major focus of public opinion.

Fad A wave of interest in a novel object or activity, inspired by the assumption that others are also interested in it, so that possessing or participating in it will be approved and perhaps envied by others. Its dynamics are similar to those of a *craze* (see above), except that the "profit" here is social rather than economic.

Fashion Interest in a style or particular difference in form that is not central to the basic purpose of an object or activity. Because fashion can change without interfering with this purpose (as when the width of men's neckties changes), fashion can become something like a fad. The difference is that there are limits to the amount of variation possible, and fashion does not involve entirely new objects or activities.

Hysteria A shared sense of fear focused on a vaguely identified threat that is assumed to be serious and unavoidable. It spreads through *behavioral contagion* (see above) and can be compared to a panic in slow motion, in that it mounts as people see one another becoming more fearful.

Mass media Vehicles of communication that reach large numbers of people at about the same time. Newspapers, television, and radio are the major media, with magazines and films being perhaps less important in the creation of public opinion through the operation of *cultural syllogisms* (see above).

Mob An acting crowd whose members have a common purpose, generally something unacceptable by normative standards.

Panic A sudden, collective response to an immediate threat. It is dominated by fear and an attempt to escape the threat rather than to oppose it, and it escalates rapidly through the process of *behavioral contagion* (see above).

Public opinion The attitudes of the members of a public (those who have a common interest in a particular topic) toward a current issue or event that they define as relevant to their own interests. The important thing is that they are aware, rightly or wrongly, of one another's attitudes, so that these mutual expectations have an important influence on their behavior in relation to that issue or event (and thus in relation to one another).

Riot An acting crowd whose members' actions are directed destructively against one another or at random targets. When it involves two distinct groups fighting each other, it might better be viewed as two mobs in interaction. A pure form of riot would be people engaged in random violence against things or against one another.

Self-destroying prophecy An expectation shared by a number of people about what the others will do at some point in the future, which for this reason persuades each of them *not* to engage in it. Its very existence as a shared expectation destroys the chance that it will come true.

Self-fulfilling prophecy A shared expectation concerning people's future behavior which is itself responsible for their subsequent participation in it. An expectation that a town's grocery stores will run out of bread, for instance, can encourage everyone to stock up on bread as soon as possible so that the stores in fact *do* run out of it.

Social movement A form of collective behavior, relatively slow to develop, in which the participants first come to recognize a threat or problem, then become aware of others' concern about it, and finally organize to do something about it. There are four stages through which social movements pass—the *incipient, popular, formal,* and *institutional* stages—but not all go through the entire cycle. Depending on the nature of their goals, social movements can be classified as *reactionary, conservative, reform, revolutionary,* or *utopian* in purpose.

Unstructured situation A situation in which people come to recognize, rapidly or slowly, that established norms cannot be depended on for guidance in anticipating how others will behave. This may be due to the appearance of something new that changes the nature of the situation (e.g., a fire or a sniper) or simply to evidence that others are no longer obeying the norms that should govern their behavior (e.g., a sports audience that begins to riot after in unpopular decision by a referee). All collective behavior develops in unstructured situations.

18
Social Change

FOCUS: *PATTERNS IN HISTORY*

Because it is important to us that our mental pictures of the world be organized, we have to believe that the world itself is organized. We have faith that beneath the apparent confusion and randomness of current events, somehow there can be found order, structure, and regularities that make human existence understandable and thus meaningful. A faith in order underlies religion, and it is also at the foundation of all science, including sociology. It is the foundation of our search for the regularities that must lie beneath the confusing surface of everyday experience.

These regularities must be found in sequences of events, for without the passage of time they could be only spatial (as in a printed design or a sculpture). Regularities in everyday life are not difficult to find: Most students come to class regularly, most professors show up on time, holidays are celebrated annually, etc. But finding regularities that seem to hold true for large populations over long spans of time can be difficult. Yet it seems unlikely that short-term regularities could exist if, over longer periods of time, things occurred only at random. The logic of experience, then, tells us that there must be some sort of order to be found in even the longest stretches of human history.

The distinction between today's patterns of social relationships and yesterday's *different* patterns is obvious to all of us, even though in past centuries it may have been only historians who noted such differences. The ways in which we lead our lives seem to be changing more rapidly now, and it requires almost a conscious effort of will to avoid wondering how this has come about and where it will lead.

In its broadest form, the study of social change is the search for patterns in history—for the basic causes and principles of change that can transform the sense of fundamental uncertainty about the world into a confidence that there is order in human experience. The discovery of such patterns will serve to link our lives today in a meaningful way to both the past and the future. As the search progresses, it will also provide a firmer foundation for every aspect of sociology. The attempt to understand social change is thus the most challenging and the most important task the discipline can undertake.

THE IMPORTANCE OF STUDYING SOCIAL CHANGE

There is a feeling in many parts of the world today that the old order of things is changing so rapidly and so extensively that tomorrow will be radically different from today. As the population grows larger, as new forms of technology are introduced, and as norms and values change, there is increasing uncertainty about what life will be like even a few years from now. Whether it will offer greater freedom or more regimentation, increased equality or greater inequality, and whether it will be characterized by more violence or less are questions we cannot answer with certainty.

It may be, in fact, that *less* change is taking place than we think. Perhaps the sense that our lives are changing with such giddying speed is largely a product of the mass media, which often cater to the public's insatiable interest in novelty and signs of "progress." Part of the problem is that we are not certain of what is meant by "change." Everyone can predict that his or her life will be quite different in ten years from what it is today, but it is difficult to tell how much of this will be due simply to having grown older and acquired a different status set and how much will be due to changes in society itself.

It should be noted here that the sociological study of social change is more than simply the projection of trends. It is not necessary to be a sociologist in order to see that the percentage of this country's population who are over sixty-five will continue to increase. It does not require sophisticated sociological analysis to understand that our reserves of traditional sources of energy are dwindling. It is for the sociologist, rather, to try to determine how the social relationships that make up society will themselves be changed by these trends.

One would assume that an understanding of social change should have immense practical value, because it will help us to anticipate what the future will hold and thus to prepare for it. As we shall see, however, the more comprehensive the study of social change becomes, the more likely it is to deal with such broad generalizations and such lengthy time periods that it can offer little in the way of specific guidance for the immediate future.

But there are certain "impractical" advantages to be gained through the analysis of social change. Even the vague assurance that there is some sort of pattern to human history may strengthen the sense that there is meaning in life, despite the occasionally wrenching changes that we seem to encounter almost at random. And a general understanding of the nature and processes of social change can provide a broad, systematic framework within which sociological knowledge of the more immediate aspects of society can take on more certainty. In both ways the study of social change can be valuable even if it does not yield solid predictions on which to base social policies, economic investments, or successful career planning.

With the prospect of these impractical advantages in mind, we shall need more than a vague idea of what social change is if we are to study it effectively.

The term itself, for instance, does not indicate the *aspects of society* that are involved in change, the *magnitude* of this change, or the *period of time* that is involved. To get on with the job, we shall thus need to specify the definition of social change in terms of these questions before we can develop some understanding of the causes, processes, and consequences of social change.

DEFINING SOCIAL CHANGE

To the individual, social change means essentially a change in what he or she can expect of others and probably changes in his or her own behavior as well. Not all such change is based on changes in norms. A rise in a neighborhood's crime rate, for instance, will produce changes in what people expect of one another and thus in their patterns of interaction (less trust of strangers, more cooperation for self-protection), even though the norms against mugging and theft have not changed. On the other hand, the recent changes in the relationships between men and women represent the acceptance of new norms.

But a person experiences changing expectations whenever she or he begins to occupy a new status. One's first day in college is often tinged with anxiety because one is unsure of the new obligations that go with the new status. A change in the *individual's* social relationships, however, is not the same as

change in the relationship between *social statuses.* The status of college student is part of the established social structure, and its relationships with other statuses (professor, roommate, librarian, etc.) have remained fairly stable for a long time. Coming to occupy a new status, then, is not a form of social change.

People, of course, are continually changing, both physically and in terms of the statuses they occupy. As they move through the life cycle, life clearly changes for them, even though the social structure does not. In many peasant societies an individual is likely to live very much the same kind of life that his or her grandparents did, and movement through the same series of statuses is evidence that the cycle itself has not changed.

Social stability, the baseline against which we identify social change, therefore cannot be the concrete experiences that make up our day-to-day existence, for they change frequently. Instead, we must look to things that have relatively longer-lasting stability—the *patterns* of social relationships that link different statuses. As long as these remain roughly the same, even though different individuals move in and out of them, we can say that nothing has changed *socially.*

Identifying Social Change

A change in a social relationship means that there is a noticeable difference in its specific details from one point in time to another. It would certainly be easier to talk of social change if we could discover a period of time during which patterns of interaction had *not* changed and after which they *did,* but discovering a period of nonchange is virtually impossible. All the sociologist can do, then, is to establish a relatively artificial baseline (say, the divorce rate in 1960 or the percentage of the population engaged in agricultural work in 1930) and to measure change against that.

How noticeable change should be, however, and what period of time should be involved before we are sure we indeed have a case of social change are difficult questions to answer. The average American worker, for instance, spent almost fifty-five hours per week on the job in 1910, as compared to about thirty-nine hours per week in 1960 (de Grazia, 1964). This represents a decrease of sixteen hours in the average work week—certainly a noticeable change to anyone reviewing the figures—but this is an average decrease of less than twenty minutes per week each year and might not be especially visible to the workers themselves.

◄ Because of strict adherence to their religious beliefs, these Pennsylvania Mennonites have resisted the outside influences of modern society. Their values and lifestyle have changed very little from one generation to another. (Mark Chester/Stock, Boston)

If change occurs at a fairly slow, steady pace, relatively few people will view it as alarming or as worthy of concentrated attention. But when it happens so rapidly that most people can say, "Things have changed a lot over the past few years," this awareness itself can play a role in how people plan for the future and thus in their current behavior. Whether things are expected to change for the better or for the worse, people will behave differently than if they did not anticipate change.

But from the sociologist's point of view, the *rate* of change is simply one aspect of the phenomenon. Whether change is rapid and visible to many or slow and noticed only by specialists, the problem of analyzing its causes and charting its future remains the same.

What about social change that is visible but apparently only temporary? If, for example, the average age of college undergraduates increases substantially, as it did just after World War II, but we have reason to believe that it will drop back to its previous level in a few years, shall we define this as social change? For the sociologist the answer must be no, for to include temporary change within the definition of social change would require us to analyze such things as the alternation between summer and winter forms of recreation and every fluctuation in the unemployment rate. Simply for reasons of intellectual economy, we must restrict our definition of social change to changes which are apparently irreversible.

Quantitative and Qualitative Change

When looking at society as a whole, we can see two major types of social change. One is a change in the *frequency* with which certain social relationships occur. For instance, when an increasing proportion of society's members some to occupy certain statuses (say, white-collar occupations or the status of "senior citizen"), there will be a corresponding increase in the frequency with which the roles associated with these statuses are played. This is *quantitative* change in society, even if there has been no change in the norms governing these statuses.

The second major type is *qualitative* change, or the appearance of new forms of interaction governed by new norms. This may involve change in the norms describing the relationship between two existing statuses (see Chapter 5, on changing sex roles), or it may be the development of new statuses and forms of interaction as new needs or opportunities arise. As a larger proportion of the population lives past retirement, there will be an increased need for services tailored especially for those people. In recent years we have seen the rise of specialized "retirement communities," and we can imagine that new norms have developed to guide their residents' relationships. As more and more people live to see their grandchildren reach adulthood, we may see new family norms emerging to regulate these relationships. The social status of computer programmer had to be invented when the new opportunities made possible by large-scale computers were recognized, and we are still working out certain problems in connection with this status—whether "software" (sets of instructions for the computer) can be patented, how to guard against embezzlement by computer, etc.

We cannot really separate quantitative and qualitative forms of change, for one leads to the other. A shift in the frequencies of different forms of interaction may produce a need for new norms, as when increasing numbers of automobiles made it necessary to pass new traffic laws. When a new opportunity arises, such as when gold was discovered in California in 1849, there was an increase in the number of people occupying the status of prospector. But for analytical reasons it is useful to make the distinction, for it gives us a clearer idea of what we are trying to understand.

At this point we can boil these ideas down to a concise definition: **Social change** *is change in the form or frequency of specific social relationships, of sufficient magnitude to be clearly visible, and of such nature as to be apparently irreversible.*

Our next task is to develop a systematic understanding of *why* social change occurs.

SOURCES OF SOCIAL CHANGE

If a pattern of interaction is a series of concrete events that we can observe, we cannot look to the interaction itself for an explanation of change in that pattern. Instead, we must turn to those things that influence people's participation in patterns of interaction: the culture that they share and the material circumstances in which their interaction takes place. If there is a change in either or both of these, we can assume that a change in the pattern of interaction will follow.

Take, for example, a small agricultural community that has been relatively stable for a long time. After the introduction of network television, the community's younger residents may adopt certain new norms and values— say, about the relations between the sexes—and so their patterns of interaction will change. Or suppose that an improved variety of corn becomes available that requires a shorter growing season and adds to the farmers' profits. New patterns of interaction will develop among the farmers as they alter their work schedules and as the additional money enables them to buy better equipment and to take longer vacations. In the former case, changes in one aspect of the community's culture has led to changes in social relationships; in the latter, changes in the community's material circumstances (the production of more corn and then the other changes made possible by more money) have similarly led to changes in patterns of interaction.

TABLE 18.1   THE MAJOR REASONS FOR SOCIAL CHANGE

Its source is:	The immediate cause is in society's:	
	Culture	Material circumstances
Immanent	Working out the implications of values, norms, discoveries, etc.	Development of new technology Population growth Purposeful change in the environment Etc.
External	Diffusion (the adaptation of norms, values, knowledge, and artifacts from other societies):	Natural catastrophes War Disease Changes in climate Etc.

Another aspect of these sources of social change will add more detail to our picture of them. This is the distinction between changes in either culture or material circumstances that are the result of something that happened earlier within a given society, and changes that could not have been predicted on the basis of that society's history.

The former can be called an *immanent* source, for it is a consequence of previous developments within the same system and, in principle at least, could be predicted for this reason. The latter can be called an *external* cause—a change in the culture or material circumstances of a society that is due to something outside it. An example of the former would be the development of transistors and other microelectronic devices that has made possible the large-scale computers which have radically changed our methods of handling information. The sudden appearance of a plague, on the other hand, or an unexpected attack by a neighboring country could not have been anticipated on the basis of earlier events within society, and so these must be classified as external causes of social change.

These aspects of social change are summed up in Table 18.1, which gives us some idea of how specific sources of change are related to one another. In the following sections, each source will be covered in more detail.

Changes in Culture

Although culture (see Chapter 3) has certain dynamics of its own—principally, the continuing pressure for its contents to be accurate, organized, and shared—we know very little about the processes through which new values emerge and others change, how the relative priority of different values changes, or how "cultural perspectives" alter so that people perceive the world about them in a different way. There is some reason, in fact, to think that the symbols and values making up a culture would not change at all if it were not for changes in the material and social reality to which they refer. After all, symbols and values are not physical things; they are not subject to erosion or the wear and tear of use, and we find it difficult to think of "spontaneous" change in culture.

But to take this argument to its logical extreme, making the contents of culture entirely dependent on the physical aspects of society, would have us ignore that fact that the rules by which culture is organized (verbal logic and the means by which consistency among values is maintained) seem to be independent of material factors. We must remember, too, that it takes *time* for human beings to work out the implications of logical and evaluative relationships. We tend to assume, for example, that the logical relationship among certain symbols exists instantaneously, so that the equation $10,437 \times 2.94 = 30,684.78$ "happens" all at once and is unrelated to the passage of time. But it takes a certain amount of time for someone to work out the answer to this multiplication problem, even with the help of a pocket calculator. In more complicated cases it can take generations for people to work out all of the implications inherent in, say, a set of religious beliefs or a particular scientific theory.

The result is that culture can certainly seem to change "by itself" without there being any significant change in the material circumstances of society. And even if one could ultimately trace changes in culture back to changes in the physical setting of society, the chain of causes and effects would be so long and so tangled that there seems little practical use in insisting that culture cannot change independently. Instead, the process of human creativity, the ways in which public opinion develops (see Chapter 17), and even the ways in which errors in communication can have important consequences require consideration as more immediate causes of culture change.

Change due to immanent reasons is by no means the only way a culture may be altered. Knowledge, values, and practices developed elsewhere are frequently "imported" by a society as its members see that these will be useful or meaningful. This general process is called **diffusion,** and it covers *the adoption of artifacts* (things made by human effort) *as well as cultural materials from other societies.* By now there has been so much contact among the different societies of the world that it is estimated there are few, if any, societies today whose cultures contain less than ninety percent of materials originally developed in other societies (Linton, 1936).

Diffusion can occur under many circumstances. It may be the result of one society's conquering or being conquered by another; it may take place as explorers bring news of another society home with them; it may result from the emigration of people from one society to another; and it may accompany economic exchange between different societies. In recent centuries diffusion has often been forced on societies by their colonial rulers, particularly in the area of religious beliefs, but also in economic and educational practices and in the colonialized societies' legal systems.

Due to the need to keep their culture internally organized and consistent, however, the members of a society do not ordinarily adopt everything that they might from other societies. Unless coercion is involved, diffusion usually occurs only when the new item fits reasonably well into the established system of beliefs, values, and social relationships. Americans, for example, are not likely to adopt the practice of polygyny from another society, because it conflicts with our values; another society might not adopt some of our agricultural practices, because they would interfere with the social structure its members have built on the basis of their own practices.

Occasionally, of course, something may be picked up through diffusion without a full understanding of all its consequences, and by the time they

Social change may result from the diffusion of artifacts and technology, which in turn affect cultural values and practices. (Cary Wolinsky/Stock, Boston)

appear—perhaps seriously disturbing other parts of the society's culture or social structure—it may be too late to reject what has been adopted. White (1962), for example, suggests that the adoption of the iron stirrup by European societies early in the Middle Ages made the knight on horseback a much more effective warrior. This eventually laid the foundations for feudalism, which in many ways was a form of social organization especially suited to provide knights for the rulers' armies. (For some examples from the anthropological literature, see Linton, 1936, pp. 347–354, and Sharp, 1977.)

In this respect it should be noted that the diffusion of artifacts and of technology probably occurs more often than the diffusion of more specifically cultural items such as values and religious beliefs. This is because value systems tend to be complete in themselves and thus resist adding or substituting new values, whereas practical material items are easier to welcome whenever they seem to make it easier to realize those values. The subject of technology will be taken up in more detail in the following section.

At this point we must ask how important it is that we be able to describe in detail the ways in which *culture* changes. Our interest is in explaining *social* change—change in actual social relationships—and too much concern with the causes *of causes* will dilute our attention. In this sense the relationship between cultural change and social change is comparable to that between material change and social change, and an understanding of, say, how soil erosion occurs is not usually thought of as vital to an understanding of social change.

Suffice it to say, then, that *as* culture changes, patterns of interaction are likely to change also. It is true, too, that culture sometimes changes in order to justify new patterns of behavior, as Tawney suggested in his analysis of the relationship between Protestantism and capitalism (see Chapter 11). But this would be a consequence rather than a cause of social change and, again, is not immediately relevant to our interest at the moment.

Changes in Material Circumstances

By material circumstances we mean everything in the setting of social relationships that is not cultural. The term thus includes the physical features of the environment (both natural and constructed), the climate, the natural resources, the artifacts in use, and even the number of people who are involved. Change in any one of these things, either by making an established pattern of interaction less effective in satisfying its participants' needs or by making available new opportunities to achieve their goals, can bring about changes in social relationships.

Change in a society's material circumstances is immanent whenever it results from the activities of that society's members. Whether it is the depletion of a natural resource, the clearing of forestlands for crops, or pollution of the air by industries, it can clearly be traced back to the actions of those members. The construction of highways, dams, buildings, and harbor facilities is another type of immanent change, and population growth falls into this category as well.

A society's material circumstances may also change without human causation. A natural catastrophe such as an earthquake, volcano, plague, or a tidal wave can permanently change the material circumstances in a particular area. Slower forms of change—in the climate or the ecology of an area—can also occur without being due to the past or present activities of society's members. Although sudden natural change is usually countered by efforts to restore the previously existing situation, gradual change in material circumstances is sometimes difficult to perceive. People make individual adjustments to it without a clear awareness that their ways of life may be changing permanently. Explicit collective recognition that change has taken place usually comes only later, when it is too late to do much about it.

In the past, most material change was due to natural causes or was the unforeseen result of people's activities. For the last century and more, however, it seems safe to say that the greatest amount of material change has been due to **technology,** or to *humankind's ability to make systematic use of natural phenomena in order to achieve specific goals.*

The essence of technology is knowledge, even though the application of this knowledge is physical in form. The knowledge that exposing clay pots to heat would make them more durable and waterproof enabled people to produce artifacts that they could use to transport and store liquids and foodstuffs more easily. Today, the knowledge that silicon crystals with certain characteristics can be formed through a particular process enables us to produce the microtransistors used in computers. Technology thus represents a particularly close link between cultural and material factors as they cause social change.

Earlier in history, technological knowledge developed as people discovered things about nature by accident. The discovery that metals could be obtained from certain rocks by heating them must have been accidental. Because they have lower melting points, copper and tin were discovered before iron, and the fact that blending the two would produce a harder metal —bronze—must also have been an accident. But since the emergence of modern science in the seventeenth century, the relationship between knowledge and its application has been reversed.

Science—the systematic, cumulative search for knowledge about the way nature works—has made knowledge an end in itself, with concern for its practical application only a secondary consideration. Humanity's collective store of scientific knowledge has been growing at a fantastic rate; Price (1963) estimates that it has been doubling every fifteen years since 1660. This means that there has been a larger and larger number of specific facts available for use in developing new means of manipulating natural phenomena in the service of human needs and thus an increasing rate of technological progress. The overwhelming importance of technology in producing social change today has been made the basis of a particular theory of change—the theory of *cultural lag* (discussed in the next section of this chapter and in Chapter 3).

More than anything else, then, the social "invention" of science as a full-time career devoted to the search for knowledge of empirical phenomena has been responsible for most of the changes in the material circumstances of society over the last hundred years. New methods of communication, new sources of energy, new ways to help the injured and diseased, new materials for the construction of practically everything we use, and even new techniques for discovering still more about nature—all have led to vast changes in our relations with the physical environment and have accelerated the pace of social change.

As noted earlier, scientific and technical knowledge is more easily diffused than other elements of culture, for it concerns new ways to achieve goals rather than the nature of those goals. A Saudi Arabian can appreciate a technological advance in methods of desalting seawater as readily as can an Israeli; an Australian aborigine can see the advantages of steel knives over stone knives as easily as can an American. Whether it is the knowledge itself or an artifact produced by applying that knowledge, better ways to manipulate nature can be appreciated by everyone. They are thus more likely to be adopted from other societies than are norms and values.

The fact that scientific and technological research is now a planned human activity means that we are conscious that it can indeed lead to changes in our material circumstances. The control of technology, or attempts to ensure that it does not produce unwanted social change, is thus of growing concern to us. This aspect of it is taken up in more detail in a later section of this chapter.

To sum up: Change in patterns of social interaction results from changes in either the participants' purposes (which we think of as changes in culture) or the physical setting of those patterns. We can classify the sources of these changes on the basis of whether they result from the activities of society's members, have been adopted from other societies, or (in the case of material change) are due to natural events that have not been caused by human activity at all.

Analytically, this is all very neat. But since all of these types of cultural and material change are going on all the time, and since their combinations and interactions can be so complex, our analysis gives us little in the way of a foundation for concrete predictions about social change. We can project trends some distance into the future, we can make intelligent guesses about how they will influence one another, and we can apply established sociological knowledge in interpreting how people will respond to certain cultural and material changes, but we cannot be certain that our predictions will be correct. The development of *social indicators* (discussed later in this chapter) will certainly strengthen our ability to foresee social change more accurately, but "random" events (political scandals and assassinations, droughts, the actions of other nations, etc.) will still play such an important role in what actually happens that dependable, detailed predictions may never be possible.

Still, this prospect has never discouraged people from speculating about the topic. Perhaps more for sheer intellectual satisfaction than for practical reasons, a number of attempts have been made to discover the essential character and direction of social change. It is to these theories of social change that we now turn our attention.

THEORIES OF SOCIAL CHANGE

Despite the fact that detailed, accurate forecasts of social change are almost impossible to make, the desire to make sense of human history has inspired numerous attempts to discover the key principles that can explain why and how society changes. Probably the earliest theories were religious, viewing history as being determined chiefly by the actions of one or more supernatural beings or else as directed toward divinely appointed ends. But with the increasingly secular perspective that has developed in the West since the eighteenth century, religious explanations have been largely discarded in favor of those that concentrate on empirical factors. Although sociological theories are covered in greater detail in Appendix 2, it will be useful here to survey briefly the major theoretical analyses of social change.

These theories can be categorized most easily on the basis of the *direction* of change that they consider fundamental. Those which find social change moving in a single direction are called *evolutionary* theories; those which find history repeating itself are called *cyclical* theories. Within these categories, theories differ chiefly in terms of the central forces they take to be responsible for the movement of history.

Evolutionary Theories

The idea of **evolution** *implies systematic change over the course of many generations toward a condition that is in some way superior to one which existed at an earlier time.* It is ordinarily used in reference to biological populations (including humankind), but can be applied also to changes in art, music, mechanical devices, and even games. Early evolutionary theories of social change usually assumed that humankind is moving toward greater and greater perfection, and most of them believed that the present age or the very next stage of history would be the pinnacle of this process. Rousseau (1712–1788), Condorcet (1743–1794), and Comte (1798–1857) believed that the energy behind social change was the increasing power of human reason. During the eighteenth and nineteenth centuries, humankind's intellectual development seemed its most prominent characteristic, and it was difficult not to be optimistic about where it would lead. With this in mind, these early theories asserted also that all societies should pass through roughly the same stages of development, moving from "primitive" to "modern" conditions as successive generations accumulated more and more knowledge of the world and of themselves.

By the time Charles Darwin's *Origin of Species* was published in 1859, the Industrial Revolution was well under way and the British Empire was at the peak of its power. Rather than the simple power of reason, then, it was apparent that political and economic power were the mainsprings of social evolution. So the idea of *natural selection* ("survival of the fittest") replaced reason as the driving force behind social change. Herbert Spencer (1820–1903) argued that social change came about as new social practices enabled the groups that adopted them to win out in competition with other groups (Spencer, 1971), and his ideas were taken up in this country by William Graham Sumner (1840–1910) (Sumner, 1906). Both men believed that since social evolution is due to "natural" forces rather than to human reason, purposeful intervention in the process (for example, efforts to alleviate poverty) should be viewed as not only doomed to failure, but probably harmful as well.

Karl Marx (1818–1883) developed the idea of "dialectical materialism," a process through which the basic material circumstances of a society (in particular, the chief "means of production" in use at a given time and who owns it) tend to generate opposing forces. Out of the ensuing conflict between these forces (the "dialectic") develops a new set of material circumstances—which then produces *its* own opposition. Marx's theory of social change was evolutionary in that he foresaw an eventual end to this process in the final emergence of a Communist society in which private ownership would no longer exist, and thus material inequalities could no longer play a role in human history.

Cyclical Theories

The horrors of the First World War seemed to call an end to the development of optimistic theories of social change. Shock and despair at the failure of earlier dreams of peace and progress were apparently the emotions that underlay the main theories to emerge between 1920 and the 1940s. If not downright pessimistic, they were essentially resigned to the idea that history is a slowly revolving wheel rather than a ladder leading upward and onward.

In 1922 Oswald Spengler (1880–1936), a German philosopher and historian, published *Der Untergang des Abendländes* (*The Decline of the West*), in which he proposed that all civilizations undergo a natural life cycle that ends in death. He saw parallels between the histories of ancient and modern civilizations and, asserting that history is guided by "fate" rather than material or cultural factors, predicted that contemporary Western civilization would end in "death," just as previous civilizations had.

Pitirim Sorokin (1889–1968), a Russian emigré who taught at Minnesota and then Harvard until his retirement in 1955, was only slightly less pessimistic about today's world. In his four-volume *Social and Cultural Dynamics* (1937–1941), he identified a pattern of alternation in history between an "idealistic" and a "sensate" configuration of cultural values and social organization. The former is characterized by a stress on religious beliefs and absolute moral codes; the latter emphasizes material things and sensory pleasures. The transition from one to the other, Sorokin said, occurs as the system of symbols which expresses a civilization's values begins to lose meaning and an alternative set of symbols, embodying different values, arises to take its place. He identified the Roman Empire at the time of Christ as a fully sensate civilization and the Christian societies of medieval Europe as dominated by an idealistic civilization. Between the two extremes, he believed, lay an intermediate stage called the "ideational"—a desirable but unstable blend of the characteristics of the other two. He argued that Renaissance Europe was an ideational civilization and that the advanced societies of the twentieth century are again in the depths of an overly sensate condition.

William F. Ogburn's concept of *cultural lag,* although less than a complete theory of social change, is relevant at this point. As Ogburn (1886–1959) analyzed social change, it is increasingly due to advances in technology. A society's culture is reasonably well integrated over the long run, he reasoned, but in the short run parts of it are continually out of joint with one another because some parts are always changing more rapidly than others. He stressed *technology as particularly likely to change more rapidly than social norms, creating a* **cultural lag** *that can be quite disruptive until the norms "catch up" with the change in material circumstances.* For example, he pointed out that automobiles are manufactured to travel much more rapidly than the law allows or than most highways can handle. The construction of the interstate highway system was one response to this lag, although today the nationwide speed limit imposed because of the energy shortage again has produced a conflict between potential speed and allowable speed.

The advances in technology which have made contraceptives safe and reliable have made possible new relationships between the sexes (see Chapter 5), but the traditional norms and values governing these relationships developed during a time when birth control was much more difficult and when the family was a more important part of the social structure. The current confusion over how men and women should relate to each other may thus be viewed as another example of cultural lag.

Ogburn posited an increasing accumulation of knowledge and thus a greater tendency for technology to change more rapidly than other parts of culture, but he did not sketch an overall direction of social change. Rather, his analysis approaches a cyclical model, since it focuses mainly on how different parts of society are continually adjusting to changes in other parts.

Finally, the British historian Arnold J. Toynbee (1889–1975) analyzed twenty-one major civilizations in terms of how they responded to various "challenges." He believed that a civilization would not change unless it was challenged—by its environment, another civilization, an internal crisis, etc.— and then devised an adequate response to that challenge. An adequate response, usually originating in a creative individual or a creative minority, would somehow free additional energy which could be used for growth. A civilization that failed to encounter a challenge would remain stagnant, and one that met an overwhelming challenge would either be arrested in its development or begin to disintegrate as an integrated social system. Toynbee did not believe that history could be viewed in terms of predictable cycles, because challenges and creative responses to them cannot be predicted, but he believed that he had found the key process through which social change occurs.

Neoevolutionary Theory

A more recent theory of social change, associated particularly with Talcott Parsons (1902–1979) and the functionalists (see Appendix 2), focuses on *structural differentiation,* or the progressive specialization of social structures within society (Parsons, 1977). This approach assumes that societies will increase their control of the physical environment if they can, but does not say that this is inevitable. Those societies that can control greater amounts of physical energy will grow in size and complexity, becoming more differentiated; those that cannot will not change very much; and those whose supplies of energy decrease will become *dedifferentiated,* or simpler in terms of structure. With increasing differentiation comes the need for more effective ways to integrate society's parts or to coordinate their activities. (See Chapters 11 and 12 for discussions of how this has been done in the economic and political institutions.)

Structural differentiation   Because increasing size and complexity is a major aspect of social change in all of the theories discussed above, we will examine it in some detail at this point. Let us look, for example, at the process of structural differentiation in a small business firm. Suppose that in the beginning there is only one man who is making ceramic ashtrays; he not only makes them, but also sells them, orders the raw materials, cleans up around the shop, and handles the bookkeeping. This is a very simple social system, for all of these jobs—social statuses—are handled in sequence by the same person, and coordinating them is usually easy.

Suppose now that the man becomes very successful. Instead of selling twenty-five ashtrays a week, he can sell five hundred. To meet the customers' demand, he must expand: He must hire someone to do the selling and deliveries, someone else to do the office work, and a third person to handle supplies and cleaning up, for all of his time must now be devoted to manufacturing the ashtrays. To succeed at this higher level of complexity, he must have enough money coming in to pay his new employees, and he must make some effort to coordinate their activities so that the production and sales operations fit smoothly together. His business has experienced some structural differentiation.

Now let us suppose that orders come in so fast that our ceramicist has the opportunity to sell five *thousand* ashtrays per week. To meet this demand, he needs to hire some people to assist him in production, more salespeople, more office workers, perhaps a supervisor, and so on. And to coordinate their activities, he must switch from his accustomed informal, word-of-mouth technique to a set of rules, a system of interoffice memos, and a lot more paperwork. Here, he has not so much added new statuses to his group as he has had to switch to more efficient techniques for coordinating everyone's activities. (Recall here the discussion of formal organizations in Chapter 9.)

Whereas additional *energy* is needed if structural differentiation is to occur (in the form of more food, more money, or better sources of mechanical power), at the same time there is need for better means of *coordination,* or *integration.* Otherwise, it would become increasingly difficult to hold a more complex set of activities together within a single human group. In the example of the ashtray factory, more energy came in the form of more money from customers, and better coordination came in the switch to more formal, bureaucratic techniques of running the business.

This is not to say that structural differentiation will inevitably occur whenever additional energy becomes available to a society. To the extent, however, that increased energy produces population growth and at the same time frees a greater proportion of this population from direct dependence on the land (that is, from subsistence-level agriculture), we may expect the society to move along the path of greater differentiation. Without additional energy, we have a vast, sprawling peasant society like that of India, but with energy we can have a much smaller but more complex society like that of Denmark or Switzerland. And without increasingly effective techniques of coordination, we will see either the splitting of a group into smaller, semiautonomous groups or a great deal of inefficiency in the use of whatever energy is available to the group.

The problem of developing a pool of surplus energy is perhaps the most important problem faced today by the developing nations of Africa, South America, and the Far East. It accounts for the extreme emphasis in the Soviet Union and the People's Republic of China on depriving the civilian population of consumer goods in order to build up heavy industry and agriculture. If surplus energy is not "naturally" available, after all, a totalitarian government can create it by preventing the population from using as much energy as it might otherwise like to.

Just as a small farmer might scrimp and save for years, foregoing all purchases beyond those absolutely necessary for survival, and then invest the savings in more land and a tractor, so a society can do the same thing. And once "economies of scale" have been achieved—through the fact that a larger and better-organized farm or factory can produce more at a lower cost per unit—the farmer or the society can reap the benefits of the investment. The purpose of saving is to reach that ill-defined take-off point at which each unit of additional investment begins to pay off more and more.

For the developing countries, economic growth is the principal focus of planned social change, but for the industrialized and the postindustrial nations, attention begins to turn to the quality of life. Once a society's material needs are well in hand, there is time to worry about its members' psychological well-being: civil rights, the fair distribution of goods, services, and opportunities, a clean environment, and all of the other things that enable each individual to live a satisfying life. Policies aimed at either type of goal are, of course, instances of consciously initiated social change, which we shall discuss below.

TAKING CHARGE OF SOCIAL CHANGE

Almost anything about human societies that can be measured quantitatively and charted over time shows a sharply rising or a sharply falling path as we move through time to the present. Whether it is life expectancy or infant mortality, the average distance an individual travels during his or her life or the average time it takes one to travel a given distance, the amount of energy consumed per capita or the hours of labor needed to buy a pair of shoes, the lines on the chart assume an increasingly upward or downward slope as we get past the first quarter of the twentieth century. The amount of social change that has taken place during the life of today's college students (if it can be summed up at all) is probably more than twice the amount that occurred during their parents' first twenty years, and it is probably several times the amount that occurred while their grandparents were reaching maturity.

The rate of social change, in other words, is speeding up sharply. Having gotten past the take-off point for continued economic growth, the ensuing increases in population, the use of technology, and the proportion of people engaged directly in activities that produce further growth have meant that each succeeding year sees more social change than the previous one. A number of people, in fact, are saying today that change rather than stability will be the central fact of life from now on and that members of the most advanced societies will have to "shift gears" mentally if they are to cope with the rapid pace of change (Toffler, 1970).

As its pace quickens, social change becomes more visible and thus a topic of collective concern. And because social change now is apparently caused primarily by advances in technology, something which is under our conscious control, it has become increasingly evident that we should be able to control the rate and direction of social change.

But acting now to ensure that the future will be better (or at least no worse) than today requires accurate predictions of not only what the future will be like if we simply continue our present patterns of behavior, but also the impact our conscious attempts to alter the future will have. In neither case, however, have we been remarkably successful in making such predictions. Still, we continue to want to control the future, for without any expectations of what it will be like and of how our present actions will affect it, we would have no basis for rational behavior at all. Despite the difficulties involved, the growing practical concern for predicting and guiding social change has led to two major activities in this area.

Social Forecasting

As far as the collective good is concerned, the only reason to change our behavior in order to influence the future is the assumption that without a change of some sort, the future will be less desirable than it could be. The prediction, for example, that we will experience a severe shortage of petroleum in a few years if we continue to use it at our present rate may persuade us to try to reduce fuel consumption now. We may also have private reasons for wanting to know what the future will be like. If it is predicted that the average work week will be shorter in the future, manufacturers of products used in recreation may step up productivity in order to take advantage of anticipated increases in demand for their products. Either to forestall an undesirable situation, then, or to take advantage of coming changes, it is important that we get the best possible picture of what the future will be like.

The only way to do this is to collect information about the past and present and then to project these trends into the future, modifying them on the basis of additional knowledge whenever possible. But there are literally thousands of different aspects of society which might be measured for this purpose, and although many of them are routinely covered by the U.S. Census, the Departments of Labor and of Commerce, and other agencies, we are not yet clear about which ones carry the greatest weight in determining the direction of social change. Economic measures are quite important, of course, and the field of economic indicators is well advanced by now. The developing area of research called **social indicators,** which *measures noneconomic aspects of society,* has only recently come to be a focus of serious attention (Boruch and Riecken, 1975).

Regardless of how accurately we may be able to forecast social trends, there remain two problems which we may be incapable of solving. One is the fact that many individuals and groups issue predictions, but they are not always in agreement. Sometimes predictions seem to be self-serving, as when

Klaytu, an electronic robot, does the housework, walks the dog, welcomes guests, goes to the market, and speaks several languages. What projections might you make about the effect on our society of our increasing dependence on computer technology? (J. P. Laffont/Sygma)

the oil industry predicts an energy shortage unless additional tax incentives are granted to encourage more exploration for new oil fields. Whenever the maker of a prediction seems likely to profit by what others might do on the basis of that prediction (no matter how realistic the prediction is), others are likely to doubt its accuracy for this reason.

Even with the most honest of intentions, people can still differ in their predictions, and we have no sure way to decide which of them is more accurate. To be sure, a successful record of accurate predictions in the past may give us reason to believe one person or group more than others, but there are pitfalls even here. Those who have a vested interest in getting others to accept their predictions may try to discount their previous failures and to play up their successes in order to increase their credibility (as do astrologers and other professional "psychics"). The task of determining who has made dependable social forecasts in the past, then, may be more difficult than it seems.

In addition to both of these problems is the fact that some people stand to gain and others to lose, no matter which policies are devised to deal with anticipated future conditions. Thus there will always be some people who question the accuracy of *any* predictions that might lead to new policies. Although we might hope that only the most accurate predictions will emerge from public debate over them, it is more often the case that the public comes to doubt *all* predictions and is reluctant to support any but the most moderate actions based on them. Only the gradual development of a group of professional social forecasters—people whose vested interest in their predictions is limited to pride in their accuracy—seems likely to help us out of this dilemma.

Planned Social Change

Regardless of the problems that currently beset social forecasting, we cannot avoid having to act in ways which we *hope* will be most effective in protecting or enhancing our interests in the future. People have always done this on an individual level, of course, but it is evident that today we are undertaking planned social change on a much larger scale and with the collective welfare of society in mind.

The chief problem here lies in how well we can predict the consequences of new policies. In the recent past, programs to eliminate poverty, decrease drug abuse, and improve the quality of city life have often been unsuccessful. Programs to ensure equal opportunities for the members of minority groups have been only partly successful. It is clear that we do not yet know enough about how to introduce social change effectively and also that we have not been able to foresee accurately all of the indirect consequences of such programs. In many instances the side effects of planned change, such as the social disorganization which accompanies urban redevelopment (Gans, 1962), may create bigger problems than those it was intended to solve.

But there is growing awareness that planned change in one area of life will have consequences for many other areas and that these must be assessed before plans are put into action. For example, a plan to improve access to the center of a city by building new highways into it will have consequences for the social character of certain neighborhoods, for store owners in outlying business areas, for the quality of the city's air, and for the need for police services. Particularly when tax money is to be used for such programs, citizens are beginning to demand that more attention be paid to the indirect consequences of planned social change before it is implemented. The introduction of laws calling for the submission of environmental impact statements before new construction plans are put into effect is one example of this tendency.

When distinctly new programs are proposed, there is *a tendency now to try them out on a small scale first as* **social experiments.** The idea of a "negative income tax," whereby families below a certain income level are given money sufficient to bring them up to the lowest income thought adequate in their area, has been the subject of this sort of research recently (*New York Times,* Feb. 5, 1979). Careful studies of the direct and indirect effects of the plan have been carefully evaluated to determine whether it will in fact produce the desired results and avoid undesirable side effects.

It is clear that both *predicting* what will happen in the future and *making* it happen require accurate knowledge of the ways in which social change comes about. As social scientists come to understand more about the process, as we learn to project current trends more realistically, and as social experiments add to our knowledge, we should be able to look forward to more effective control of social change in the years to come. But specific policies are always hammered out in the political arena, not in the quiet halls of universities and research organizations, and the most detailed knowledge of social change will be ignored if it is not believed. Those who look to sociology and the other social sciences to help us make life more satisfying for everyone in the future must thus pay attention not only to the content of their findings, but also to how it is received by others.

Sociology and Social Change

Does the accelerating pace of social change mean that what sociologists have discovered up to now is wasted? One may legitimately wonder whether knowledge of society developed in the past is going to be relevant in the future when change, both planned and otherwise, is so much more the order of the day. Perhaps most of what is contained in the sociological literature will be only of historical interest by the year 2000.

But this need not be the case. The knowledge that physical scientists acquire under calm laboratory conditions helps them to understand the causes and effects of hurricanes; the facts gained from careful chemical experiments tell us what to expect from explosions and from corrosive acids. Why, then, should not the knowledge of society gained in less turbulent times be of value when social change is all around us?

The problem, of course, is to learn more about the relative significance of the different social variables involved and about their actual interactions. The sociologist will not become irrelevant to the problems of the future by any means, nor will the store of sociological knowledge built up in the past be useless. However, additional efforts by new recruits to the profession will be necessary if the discipline is to make the kinds of contributions we will need to help us to understand the new world that we are creating for ourselves.

SUMMARY

At present the study of social change is not advanced enough to enable us to predict the future with much accuracy. But we cannot avoid the belief that there must be regularities in human history which, when discovered, will help us to see what lies ahead. Finding patterns in history will be important as they both strengthen our sense that human existence is meaningful and provide a framework for other types of sociological knowledge.

Social change refers to either change in the frequency with which certain forms of interaction occur or the development of new forms of interaction; it can thus be either *quantitative* or *qualitative* in nature. But forms of interaction cannot explain changes in themselves, so for an understanding of why change happens we must look to the things that influence their participants. Social change, then, may be due to changes in *culture* (in norms, values, or knowledge) or to changes in the *material circumstances* in which interaction takes place. We may further distinguish among the sources of change by classifying them as *immanent* (growing out of the previous actions of the members of a society) or *external* (being due to something outside that society, either another society or a natural event such as an earthquake).

Although changes in culture may be ultimately due to changes in material circumstances, culture seems to contain sources of change in itself, especially the pressure toward organization or internal consistency. This means that people are continually working out the implications of what is already contained in their culture—religious beliefs, scientific knowledge, etc.—so that it is useful to think of culture change as a separate source of social change. The introduction of cultural components from other societies through *diffusion* is today another important reason for cultural change.

Changes in material circumstances may be purposeful, as in the application of technological knowledge; it may come about through the adoption of material artifacts through diffusion; or it may be due to natural changes in the environment. As humankind's store of scientific and technical knowledge accumulates, speeding up the rate of invention, changes in the material circumstances of society that result from new technology are the chief causes of social change today.

Despite the difficulty of producing accurate predictions of social change, people have speculated on the broad course of change in human history for centuries. In general, theories of social change can be classified as either *evolutionary*, in which change follows a single path, or *cyclical*, in which it repeats itself. The ideas of social change developed in the eighteenth and early nineteenth centuries were generally optimistic, viewing advances in human reason as the main cause of change and assuming that all societies pass through similar stages in the course of becoming more and more ideal. Later evolutionary theories substituted the Darwinian principle of the survival of the fittest for reason as the force behind social change. Cyclical theories, less optimistic than those which assumed that societies evolve toward some sort of perfection, have sought patterns of alternation between different states of civilization, positing either a kind of life cycle for every human society or else swings between extremes in the central focus of different societies' cultures.

More recently, *neoevolutionary* theory has stressed the process of *structural differentiation* as the key to understanding change. This concentrates on the ways in which societies become more complex as they achieve more control over their physical environments and find more effective ways to coordinate their more specialized parts.

The acceleration of social change, due mainly to technological innovations, has been accompanied by a decline in people's faith that their normative expectations are shared by others and by a sense that a more abstract set of "ground rules" will be needed if we are to avoid increasing social disorganization. The psychological parallel is the problem of sustaining confidence in the meaningfulness of the world. When change takes place too rapidly, people begin to lose faith in their ability to know what they can expect of others, and vice versa. And without this, their sense of priorities and of control over their own lives is seriously weakened.

Growing awareness of change has led also to more concern that we try to control it. There is increasing interest in social forecasting based on the collection of *social indicators*, even though predictions of the future face obstacles to their acceptance for several reasons. Efforts to implement planned social change have rarely been fully successful in the past, although small-scale trials of new programs in the form of *social experiments* may improve our ability to develop more effective methods of planned social change.

Perhaps the best immediate solution we can find to the problems posed by an increasing rate of social change will be the development of a more abstract set of rules governing human relationships, within which different generations and different groups within generations can "agree to disagree." Failing this, we may face an increasingly divided and disorganized society, one that has been undermined by its own successes and by its inability to understand what is happening to itself.

SUGGESTED READINGS

Applebaum, Richard P., *Theories of Social Change* (Chicago: Markham, 1970). This is a brief, useful survey of the basic assumptions of four types of theories of social change: evolutionary, equilibrium, conflict, and rise-and-fall.

Baldock, Cora V., *Australia and Social Change Theory* (Sydney, Australia: Ian Novak Publishing Co., 1978). In addition to a sophisticated and highly readable review of theories of social change, concluding that a neo-Marxist theory is superior to others, Baldock provides a stimulating application of these theories to the recent history of Australia.

Lenski, Gerhard, and Jean Lenski, *Human Societies: An Introduction to Macrosociology*, 3rd ed. (New York: McGraw-Hill, 1978). This text follows the development of human society from its earliest forms, providing a cogent picture of how societies grow and change, but avoiding excessive concentration on the search for simple explanations.

Lauer, Robert H., *Perspectives on Social Change*, 2d ed. (Boston: Allyn and Bacon, 1977). Lauer provides here an excellent, detailed survey of the major theories of social change, with extensive coverage of different mechanisms and patterns of change as well.

Parsons, Talcott, *The Evolution of Societies* (Englewood Cliffs, N.J.: Prentice-Hall, 1977). In this book, edited by Jackson Toby, Parsons explains his use of the principle of structural differentiation to help us understand both the history and the current state of societies around the world. It is a profoundly illuminating analysis for the serious student of long-range social change.

Toffler, Alvin, *Future Shock* (New York: Random House, 1970). Toffler marshals evidence that the pace of social change is increasing beyond our comprehension and offers some imaginative suggestions for coping with the disorganization and confusion that rapid social change produces.

White, Lynn, Jr., *Medieval Technology and Social Change* (Oxford, England: Oxford University Press, 1962). White, a historian, gives an account of the importance of such simple inventions as the iron stirrup, the horse collar, and horseshoes in the development of European society. It is an impressive illustration of the way in which technology can bring about massive social change.

Glossary

Cultural lag William Fielding Ogburn's term for a situation in which one part of culture has changed more rapidly than another, leading to confusion and frustration as both parts continue to influence people's behavior. Ogburn singled out as the chief cause of cultural lag today technological change because it is cumulative and thus moves faster and faster. He cited the automobile as an example, a product of technology which is made to go faster than our highways can safely handle and which has required the development of new norms to govern parking, licensing, and traffic control in order to diminish the lag that emerged as it came into widespread use.

Diffusion The process through which one society adopts something from another. Voluntarily or through coercion, a society may adopt such varied things from other societies as a tool, a type of clothing, a new food crop, scientific knowledge, a political ideology, or a religious belief.

Evolution Movement by something toward a condition that is somehow superior to its previous condition, usually by means of small changes from one generation to the next. The term is usually applied to biological species, but seems applicable also to human societies. For the most part, being superior means an increased ability to survive and grow, but when applied to art forms it may mean greater aesthetic excellence, and with machines it may mean increased efficiency. Movement in the opposite direction is sometimes called *devolution*.

Social change Change in the form (*qualitative*) or frequency (*quantitative*) of specific social relationships, of sufficient magnitude to be clearly visible, and of such nature as to be apparently irreversible. It may be due to change in society's culture or in the material circumstances of its members' lives and may be due to previous events within the same society (*immanent* causes) or to events occuring outside of it (*external* causes).

Social experiment A relatively small-scale, practical test of a new social policy, designed to provide information on how well the policy might succeed in achieving its goals and on what unexpected side effects its implementation might produce. As with any social research (see Appendix 1), close attention is paid to the design of the experiment and to the systematic collection of information about its consequences, but its aim is policy-relevant knowledge rather than answers to purely scientific questions.

Social indicators Measures of various trends over time in society that can be used to help predict specific aspects of society in the future. Just as trends in the gross national product can be used to help predict the future state of our economic system, so trends in such things as patterns of migration, suicide rates, and the uses of leisure time can help to indicate how various noneconomic aspects of social life may change in the future.

Technology Humankind's manipulation of natural phenomena (e.g., the fact that a magnet passing close to a wire will generate an electric current in it) in order to help it achieve its goals more effectively. Although the essence of technology is knowledge, its embodiment in physical form is the purpose of this knowledge. Today, advances in technology are probably the chief cause of social change.

APPENDIXES: RESEARCH AND THEORY— THE MEANS AND ENDS OF SOCIOLOGY

The two appendixes in this section focus on topics central to sociology as a professional discipline. Although they form the background of our understanding of the specific aspects of society covered in the preceding chapters, their treatment must necessarily be more abstract and less directly relevant to the student's interest in the nature of society itself.

As a social science, sociology depends on research-based information for its understanding of social relationships and of the structures and processes that make up society. The specific procedures that sociologists employ in developing valid statements about these things may thus be viewed as the *means* of sociology: the foundation of reasoning and practice that underlies the empirical content of the discipline.

Without a framework within which to organize research findings, however, so that they can be combined to support a more coherent and generalized understanding of society, research is without purpose. Sociological theory, then, constitutes the *end*, or ultimate purpose, of sociology, for it is the attempt to reduce our knowledge to a series of interrelated generalizations that can economically and systematically describe the essential nature of society.

Appendix 1 discusses the nature of science and its basic assumptions and then proceeds to explain the major methods of research sociologists use in carrying out their work. Appendix 2 covers the history and current state of sociologists' efforts to make sense of what they have found—the central concerns of sociological theory, its history, and the several theoretical perspectives that guide sociological thinking today.

Appendix 1
Sociological Research

FOCUS:

VALIDITY

The basic product of science is not gadgets, medicines, or weapons, but rather words and numbers. But they are important or worthwhile only to the extent that they are *valid* descriptions and measurements of physical, biological, and social reality. All sciences, in other words, can be defined as collective efforts to develop *accurate* "verbal pictures" of various aspects of reality. They are concerned with identifying the "units" of reality that are of lasting importance (e.g., the pi-meson, the gene, the process of photosynthesis, the group, the quasar) and with developing generalized statements about the composition and qualities of these units and the relationships among them.

However, because a statement about reality is not the reality itself, there is always a chance that a statement will be a *mis*leading picture of reality, so that it fails to help us to make accurate predictions or to enable us to understand why something has happened. The heart of scientific research, then, is the techniques all scientists use to ensure that their generalizations about reality are valid. This appendix deals with the various ways in which sociologists gather information that will enable them to make valid descriptions and generalizations about the social relationships that make up society.

THE NATURE OF SCIENCE

In all of its complexity, the universe (all of "empirical reality") simply *is*. It does not tell us how it is organized or what it is doing, and the painstaking labor (both mental and physical) of thousands of people has been required to produce our present understanding of "how things work." This labor is called research, and its product is accurate, generalized, *public* statements about reality. (By its very nature, science can be neither a collection of individual secrets nor a private, mystical understanding of the *is-ness* of reality. If it were either of these, we would not recognize it as a social activity, and it certainly could not make much progress in terms of adding new knowledge to what is already known.)

The word *science* comes from the Latin *scientia,* meaning "knowing." Since the 1840s, however, when the word *scientist* was coined, science has come to refer almost exclusively to humankind's collective attempts to produce valid statements about empirical reality.

Although science*like* activities have been carried out by human beings throughout history, social awareness and acceptance of scientific research as a specific pattern of interrelated activities have existed for barely 500 years. We generally think of "modern" science as beginning in 1543, when Copernicus published *De Revolutionibus Orbium Coelestrium* (*On the Revolution of the Heavenly Spheres*—the first reasoned proposal that the earth revolves about the sun, rather than vice-versa) and Vesalius published *De Humani Corporis Fabrica* (*On the Fabric of the Human Body*—the first accurate work on human anatomy). Since the middle of the nineteenth century, humankind has come under the same kind of objective scrutiny, and we now talk of the *social* sciences as well as the physical and biological sciences.

Although *public*—which actually means *published*—statements about reality are the goal of scientific research, we must be careful not to think of science as an activity that is basically different from other human activities. After all, a child's interest in a frog—in finding out how hard it must be poked with a stick before it will jump—is an attempt to acquire knowledge of one part of reality. The child will probably not record any observations and may not try to generalize from this frog to other frogs, but the fundamental purpose of the child's activity is the same as that of the scientist.

Scientific research is a special realm of human activity because it involves a systematically organized *series* of many ordinary activities: seeing, thinking, writing, and so on. What makes research different from other human behavior, and what has made it so successful in discerning how reality is organized, lies in the way that these different activities have been linked together and pursued steadily with an explicit goal in mind: the publication of generalized, logically interdependent, valid statements about the units, qualities, and relationships of which reality is composed.

Three distinct aspects of science may be singled out for special attention: (1) the men and women who carry out scientific research—the scientific community; (2) the products of their research—the bodies of knowledge, or statements about reality, that are found collectively in the books and journals that make up the literature of science; and (3) the various activities that make up the process of research. It is the third aspect of science, the process of research (and the thinking that lies behind it) that will be the focus of this appendix.

The Scientist's Approach to Reality

If scientists are to cooperate in their research—as they must, for no single individual has the time or energy to study *all* aspects of reality—they must agree at least on the ground rules of their common enterprise. Although there is no need here to undertake a thorough survey of the philosophy of science, certain basic assumptions about the nature of reality and the scientist's relationship to it should be explored. These assumptions provide the underlying rationale of science, and their logical consequences provide the basic guidelines for the research process.

Regularity At the heart of the scientist's perspective on the universe is the assumption that reality is neither capricious nor simply a figment of one's imagination. Reality is assumed to exist independently of human perception and to be *invariant* in its basic relationships. That is, scientists assume that a truly valid statement about reality (say, the statement that water [always] freezes at 32° Farenheit) will describe this aspect of reality without regard to *where* or *when* it is applied. If this were not so, there would be no point in trying to make *generalizations* (statements that are valid descriptions of two or more separate events) about water, for otherwise it might freeze at 50° in North Carolina and at 15° in South Carolina or at 40° on one day and 25° the next—without there being any way to predict these specific figures.

In actual practice, of course, we might find at first that the freezing point of water *does* vary somewhat. But because we assume that reality is, at base, invariant, this finding leads us to look for the causes of the variation; it does *not* lead us to conclude that the freezing point of water varies randomly. We will look, then, for such things as impurities in the water, changes in atmospheric pressure, or even difficulties with our thermometer, and as soon as we have identified them, we can modify our basic statement to read: "Pure H_2O, under a specific atmospheric pressure, freezes at 32° Farenheit, according to a standardized measuring instrument."

Units, Qualities, and Variables

The experience of being "at one" with the universe—transcending the division between "self" and "everything else" and perceiving reality as an unbroken wholeness—may be emotionally satisfying, but science cannot work this way.

Instead, the scientist assumes that reality can be divided into identifiably different "units" and that the purpose of science is to describe them and the relationships among them.

A unit, as the term is used here, is any *thing* or *event* that we can distinguish from other things or events and that we can identify over and over again. It may *exist itself* over a significant period of time, as does the moon or a particular human being; it may *occur again and again,* as thunderstorms and presidential elections do; or it may *occur in many "copies,"* as bacteria, pigs, diamonds, and human groups do. These are the "nouns" of science, the aspects of reality which have a continuing or repeated existence and are therefore worth studying.

Not all such units are immediately apparent to us (as atoms, statuses, and planetary orbits are not), and there is certainly no single best way to divide reality into separate units. What the sociologist treats as a unit, for instance, the psychologist will treat as a collection of different units—the group, as contrasted with its individual members. Yet if we are to make statements about reality that have lasting validity, we must assume that it can be broken down into different units.

A good deal of science is devoted simply to identifying the units of reality that participate in regular relationships with other units. Much of a student's introduction to any field of learning consists of learning the names and identifying characteristics (or qualities) of the units that are of particular interest to that discipline: Groups, roles, norms, and values are some of the basic units that sociologists have identified; novels, poems, styles, and moods are some of the units important in literature courses.

After several units have been identified with reasonable precision, the scientist is interested in making statements about their characteristics and relationships. This brings us to the concept of *variables.* We can think of a variable as either a *quality* of a unit that may vary while the unit still retains its identity (such as the weight of a watermelon, the loudness of a sound, the amount of violence that occurs during a riot, or a person's attitude toward abortion) or a *relationship* between two or more units that may vary (for example, the distance between two planets, the amount of trust between two people, or the balance of power among several nations).

The term *variable* is also used (somewhat more loosely) in scientific statements to mean *any* aspect of reality that is being referred to. In talking *about* the statement: "Education plus motivation, in the presence of opportunity, produce success," each of the four nouns mentioned may be referred to as a variable. In this case education and motivation are called *independent* variables, opportunity is called an *intervening* variable, and success is the *dependent* variable. Thus the independent variables are what you start with, the dependent variable is what you end up with, and the intervening variable is something that comes between the two and influences their relationship.

Taking a stricter definition of "variable," it should be pointed out that a unit for one scientist may be a variable for another, and vice-versa. A scientist who is interested in the effect of sunspots on climate may treat rainfall as a unit that can vary in quality between zero and 200 inches per year. In another case a scientist may treat rainfall as a variable quality of different units (perhaps as one characteristic of American cities, in terms of which they differ from each other). Similarly, whereas an individual male may be a unit of study for the psychologist, the percentage of males in a population may be viewed as a variable by the demographer.

In the end it boils down to what the scientist wants to treat as *un*varying and what he or she wants to view as possibly *varying* from one situation to another. A unit, by definition, does not vary over time, whereas qualities of units and the relationships among units may. So long as this is clear and the difference between the strict and the loose usages of the term *variable* is understood, there should be no difficulty in handling these concepts and using them correctly.

Relationships: Co-occurrence, Sequential Occurrence, and "Cause"

The statements that scientists make about the qualities of and the relationships among units are of two major types. First, there are statements that describe a situation as it existed at a single point in time or that exists through time without change. Such statements describe *co-occurrence:* Palm trees *grow* in tropical climates; large hotels and department stores *are* usually located close together in the center of a city; an exploding firecracker *emits* both light and sound. Such statements simply record the presence together *in time* of two or more units and/or qualities and carry no implication of what preceded them or of how they may otherwise be related.

Second, there are statements that describe the relationship between two or more things at different points in time, or *sequential occurrences.* Such statements take into account the passage of time and indicate a difference between what was observed at time 1 and at time 2:

A. At ten o'clock John got hungry, and *later* he ate lunch.

B. A moment *after* the hard puff of air was directed at the candle, the flame went out.

C. *Following* a rise in temperature, the snowbank melted.

It would be easy to rearrange these statements so that different sequential occurrences are described:

A. A ten o'clock John got hungry, and *later* the snowbank melted.

B. A moment *after* the hard puff of air was directed at the candle, John ate lunch.

C. *Following* a rise in temperature, the flame went out.

These statements might be just as valid (in terms of describing what did happen at time 1 and at time 2) as the first three, but we would reject them as meaningless. We can find no reason to connect these pairs of events by including them in single sentences. A statement that does no more than describe *something* at one point in time and something *else* at a later point in time, then, may be quite useless. There must be some connection between the two events, a sense that this particular sequence of events is not simply a coincidence but was to be expected, before we think it worthwhile to make a statement that links them in this way.

Statements of co-occurrence and of sequential occurrence are both forms of *correlation,* a term used more generally to refer to the existence of a regular relationship between two or more things. It is useful, however, to distinguish between co-occurrence and sequential occurrence, because the concept of *cause* is explicit only in the latter.

Whenever we link separate events at two points in time, we are implying that event X is usually followed by event Y (or that Y would not have happened if X had not occurred first); we are asserting that "X *caused* Y." Our belief in—and our experience of—regularity in the universe actually requires us to believe that causal relationships must exist. If they did not, everything would occur randomly, without any dependable (that is, repeated or predictable) relationship to anything else, and the universe would be in a state of utter chaos. To talk about the regularities that underlie our perceptions of reality, then, we must have a concept of causality: We must assume that events are both *caused by* prior events and that they in turn *cause* future events. We cannot, of course, assume that *everything* that occurred at time 1 has been equally responsible for the occurrence of a single event at time 2, and so we are left with the problem of tracing out the specific "chains of causes" that must exist among the units and qualities that make up reality.

It is probably a mistake to believe that causal connections can be treated as phenomena in themselves. The attempt to find a tangible linkage between, say, the appearance of a television commercial and your subsequent purchase of a certain toothpaste or even between the swing of a bat and the flight of a baseball through the air leads to philosophical quandaries that we need not wrestle with here. It will be easier to take the concept of cause to mean simply the existence, under specified conditions, of an *inevitable* sequence of events.

This definition of cause provides the criterion by which generalizations about relationships can be based on observations. To speak of an inevitable relationship between X and Y, or to say that X *causes* Y, one must have observed that whenever X occurs, Y always occurs later (within, of course, a particular area of space and span of time). If X is not always followed by Y, we must assume either that X is not "the" cause of Y (so that Y must be caused by either X in combination with something else or something else altogether) or that something else in the situation occasionally *blocks* the occurrence of Y. It is, ultimately, in the exploration of why Y does not *always* follow X, even when most of the time it does, that new relationships are discovered and that scientific knowledge advances.

The Importance of Quantification

In describing qualities and relationships, scientists cannot be content to talk simply in terms of "more" and "less." Such vagueness would make the comparison of units and the description of their relationships very crude indeed. Precise descriptions of reality require, sooner or later, that *standardized units of measurement* be used; the use of such measures is generally called *quantification* (from the Latin *quantus,* meaning "how great").

No unit of measurement exists *in* the phenomenon being measured, of course, but instead has been devised (or, as in the case of the year, recognized) by human beings. The important thing about any particular unit (whether it is a centimeter, a minute, a kilogram, or a volt) is that it be standardized, both so that many people may use it to achieve the same measurement and that mathematics may be used in making sense of the relations among measurements. In building a doghouse, for instance, it is important not only that you be able to order a four-foot board by telephone and be assured that it will fit precisely into the four-foot space you have measured, but also that you be able to reason that two *two*-foot boards will do the job just as well.

A great many different units of measurement are used in science, ranging from common measures of extension, duration, and weight to such esoteric units as the gauss (a measure of magnetic flux density) and points on the Richter scale (a measure of the intensity of earthquakes). Because quantification is crucial to precise descriptions of reality, scientists in all fields often seek new, better ways to measure the phenomena in which they are interested.

Sometimes, particularly in the social sciences, a unit of measurement may not seem at first to make much sense. A measure of "social distance," for instance, or one that ranks people in terms of how "alienated" they are, may seem quite artificial or even a travesty on "real" methods of measurement. But as such measures become standardized and offer meaningful comparisons of different individuals and groups, they serve the purposes of social scientists in the same way, and just as usefully, as measures of heat and density serve physical scientists.

Summing Up

In this section we have covered the basic rationale of science, or the reasoning about reality that underlies and justifies the scientific enterprise. If reality were not characterized by *regularity,* there would be no point in trying to develop generalized descriptions of it. If it could not be subdivided into *units* and *qualities,* there would be nothing to describe (other than everything at once). If we did not have a conception of *cause*—no matter how slippery it is—we could not generalize about changes in qualities of relationships, for we would have no assurance that our generalizations would have any lasting validity. And if we could not eventually *quantify* our descriptions, they would be too vague to enable us to make the fine distinctions on which valid generalizations about relationships must be based.

The scientist's assumptions about reality are thus the product of not only actual experience (that is, of repeated observations of regular relationships in "nature"), but also logical reflection on what must *necessarily* be the basic character of reality. With this as background, we can go on now to discuss more concretely the process of scientific research and then the particular methods of research used by sociologists.

THE RESEARCH PROCESS

Recording Observations

Science works only indirectly with reality itself. Instead, scientists work primarily with *recordings* of what has happened at specific times in various parts of reality. A recording may be what the scientist writes about what he or she has observed, it may be the squiggles on a kymograph drum, it may be a check mark on a questionnaire, or it may be a bubble-chamber photograph. Whatever form it takes, however, it is the basic material of research. Events themselves occur and then are gone; even though a scientist may have seen them happen, they are lost forever unless some record of those events has been made. (Remembering is a form of recording, certainly, but memory is much more subject to loss or at least to distortion than is a recording that exists apart from memory—on a piece of paper or a magnetic tape.)

A recording is necessarily an *abstraction* from the reality that existed when the record was made. It preserves only a small part of the original situation. But without some reliable way to preserve those aspects of the situation in which she or he is interested, the scientist's ability later on to analyze and to compare different events is seriously limited.

It is not overly simple to say that research is essentially the job of arranging efficiently for the recording of certain aspects of reality which the scientist has reason to believe are related to one another in some way. Research thus involves both thinking ("What events do I need a record of, and why?") and acting ("How can I find or create these events, and how can I record them?"). With these practical questions in mind, we can concentrate now on what scientists *do* in the concrete process of research.

What to Look for: Hypotheses

No matter how one originally came to be interested in a particular phenomenon, one must eventually pay *systematic* attention to it if one's goal is the production of valid generalizations about it. Specific, interrelated questions must be asked so that one can know what to look for.

Most often in science, such questions grow logically out of what is already known. If it is known, for instance, that A turns green when mixed with B and also that C turns green when mixed with D, it seems logical to wonder whether B and D have something in common. If so, A might turn green when mixed with D, and C might turn green when mixed with B. Stated in a way that will give specific guidance to our research activities, we can say, "I think that after I mix A with D, A will turn green."

Here we encounter the idea of *hypothesis*. A hypothesis is no more than an educated guess that has been stated in the form of a prediction: "A will turn green after it is mixed with D." A good hypothesis is a prediction that we believe *ought* to come true because it seems a logical extension or consequence of some other generalizations that we believe are valid. The better the hypothesis, in terms of the reasoning on which it is based, the more it is worthwhile for us to test it—to arrange or to find a situation in which A *is* mixed with D and to make a record of the outcome.

To test a hypothesis, then, is to find out whether it is an accurate prediction: *Does* A turn green after being mixed with D? The more complex the hypothesis, however, and the more difficult it is to determine what one has found after carrying out the research, the greater the chance of misinterpreting one's findings. Since most scientists like to be correct in their predictions—it is always disappointing to find that one's carefully constructed hypothesis is wrong—the more common error is to believe that one's findings support one's hypothesis, or turn out as predicted, when in fact they do not. This is called a Type I error. (As discussed in Chapter 7, the belief held by white Americans that black Americans were inherently "inferior" was a Type I error, for they mistakenly interpreted the consequences of their *own* actions as proving that their belief was correct.)

If a scientist concludes that his or her hypothesis is incorrect, when in fact it *is* correct, a Type II error has been made. Although less frequent, Type II errors usually are made when the scientist does not see that the connection between X and Y (stated by the hypothesis) is being blocked by the presence of an unrecognized third variable. For instance, one might hypothesize that adding a certain substance to the soil will make plants grow taller. But if some sort of poison is accidentally mixed with the substance without the scientist's knowledge, it will appear that the substance kills plants rather than aids their growth. He or she will then reject the hypothesis, even though the substance by itself would indeed have made the plants grow taller, thus acting as the hypothesis predicted.

Since the purpose of research is the production of valid knowledge, one way to look at research procedures is to view them as designed to eliminate both Type I and Type II errors. This will become apparent in subsequent sections.

Where to Find It: Observation and Recording

Once a scientist has decided on the kind of event that should be observed, the next question is that of arranging to be there when it occurs. Here, two possibilities exist. In many cases the scientist must simply wait for the event to occur "naturally." In others, he or she may be able to make the event occur whenever there is need to observe it. Whereas an astronomer must wait for an eclipse of the sun, a chemist can put two substances into a test tube whenever it seems important to observe their interaction. Whereas a sociologist must wait for an election before observing the relationship between campaign oratory and voters' choices, it is possible to ask someone's opinion about something whenever this kind of information is needed.

In some instances, then, the scientist must simply try to be on hand whenever and wherever the kind of event specified in a hypothesis seems likely to occur. In others, however, the scientist can *arrange* for the occurrence of an event by applying a stimulus to some part of reality. In the catalog of different methods of research, as we shall see, this distinction is of considerable importance.

"Controlling" the Situation

Since most hypotheses involve some variation on the basic idea that "X causes Y" (with "X" often meaning a combination of several specific things), the most direct way to test a hypothesis is first to find or create an instance of X and then to see whether Y follows it. For one reason or another, however, it is often impossible to follow this plan:

1. It may be impossible to find or create a situation in which *only* X is present (so that it will be difficult to be certain that the subsequent appearance of Y was caused by X rather than by something else);

2. X may happen "naturally" only rarely, or it may be very difficult to "produce";

3. The length of time between the appearance of X and the appearance of Y may be longer than the scientist wishes to wait.

Fortunately, scientists have developed ways around these problems. They fall under the general heading of "control."

To a scientist, *control* means determining whether or not certain variables (units, qualities, or both) exist or have played a part in producing the situation that is or will be observed. Control may involve ensuring that a hypothesized cause (X) or effect (Y) is present (but not both, for then there could be no *test* of the association between X and Y). It may involve techniques designed to ensure that "irrelevant" variables (all those *not* mentioned in the hypotheses) are at least partially excluded from or have played relatively little part in producing the observed event. It may involve both types of control.

The only way to be *sure* that Y has been caused by X is to make sure that nothing *but* X could have caused Y. To do this, the scientist must either physically exclude all other possible causes of Y from the situation or try to see to it that all potential causes but X are at least partially cancelled out so that, logically, X remains the *most likely* cause of Y.

An example of the first method, *physical control,* is the chemist's sterile test tube. He or she puts a mixture of compounds A and B into the test tube and assumes that the walls of the tube will keep out all other substances. If Y (say, a new compound) appears in the test tube later, the interaction of A and B is thus the only possible cause.

Arranging things so that all possible causes but X are at least partially excluded is a more complicated method, usually employed when physical control is not possible, as in the social sciences. Here, the scientist's basic assumption is that no other variable will be correlated as strongly with Y as is X, so that no matter whether other variables (which may be present) work to help or to hinder the appearance of Y, Y should appear more often (on the average) if X appeared earlier than if X did not. This method may therefore be called *statistical control.*

In employing statistical control the scientist must find or create a number of cases in which X is present and a comparable number which are similar in other respects, but in which X is absent. The two groups of cases are then compared at a subsequent time in terms of how often Y has appeared in each group. (Conversely, cases may be found in which Y is present or absent, and the scientist then looks for how often X appeared earlier in each group of cases.)

To the extent that Y appears more often in the X-present cases than in the X-absent cases (or that X appeared earlier more often in the Y-present cases than in the Y-absent cases), there is some reason to believe that there is a "real" (rather than coincidental) connection between X and Y. The "deviant" cases (that is, X present but Y absent, or X absent but Y present) have presumably been produced by the influence of other, unidentified variables. Since, however, none of these other variables is assumed to be more closely associated with Y than X, the connection between X and Y should still show through the tangle of other relationships. (If it does not, of course, the scientist may find it necessary to conclude that the initial hypothesis linking X and Y was incorrect.)

Statistical Significance

There is still, of course, the problem of determining how likely it is that the different frequency with which Y appeared in the X-present and X-absent groups was due simply to coincidence, or "chance." Depending on certain assumptions about the variables being studied and the way in which other variables are distributed, a particular statistical test is selected and performed on the findings. Interpreted properly, it should tell the scientist how likely it is that he or she would have found the same results even if there were no actual relationship at all between X and Y.

Ordinarily, a sociologist feels justified in saying that a "real" connection has been found between X and Y only when "statistics prove" that the same results could have been due to chance alone in only one out of twenty or more repetitions of the same research. (One chance in twenty is the standard usually chosen as the cut-off point for proof. This is referred to as the ".05 level of significance," meaning that only in five of one hundred repetitions of the same research would one expect the connection between X and Y to be this strong by chance alone.) If the test shows that the same difference would occur by chance alone *more* often than once in twenty repetitions, the sociologist usually assumes it to be too risky to assert that a real relationship has been found.

Statistical significance should not be confused with the more popular meaning of the word "significance." It may be found, for example, that X "really" accounts for only three percent of the variance of Y; this may be highly significant in statistical terms (that is, the relationship should be found only once in a thousand times by chance), but it is hardly amazing, portentous, or a major reason for either worry or joy. When someone says, "This finding is statistically significant," it means only "This finding is quite unlikely to have been merely a coincidence, or due to chance alone."

Summing Up

We have, then, two basic dimensions of the research process: (1) whether or not the researcher *arranges* for the occurrence of the phenomenon he or she wishes to observe; and (2) whether or not the researcher *controls* the situation (and, if the situation *is* controlled, whether this is by physical or statistical techniques). Putting these aspects of the process together, we can produce

TABLE 1   MAJOR METHODS OF SOCIOLOGICAL RESEARCH

			Does the sociologist *control* the situation being observed?	
		NO	YES Post-facto (statistical) control	Current (physical) control
Does the sociologist *arrange for* or produce the situation being observed?	NO	I Observation	II Content analysis, unobtrusive measures	Control group
	YES	III Interview	IV Survey analysis	Experimental group

(left vertical label: Participant Observation) (right bracket label: Experiment; V bridges the two "current control" cells)

Table 1. Not surprisingly, we find that each of the six cells can be filled with one or more of the standard methods of sociological research. In the next section, each of these methods is discussed in more detail.

THE MAJOR METHODS OF SOCIOLOGICAL RESEARCH

Observation (Cell I)

In its purest form, research based on observation calls for the sociologist to act simply as a talented "camera," recording the details of a particular scene, activity, or event and doing nothing to influence what is being observed. The aim is to make a record of something in its natural state, with no controls whatever being imposed on it. (In principle, of course, it may be impossible for an observer to have *no* influence on what occurs, but his or her influence can often be minimized to the point where it is likely that nothing different of any importance would have occurred if the observer had been absent.)

What the observer looks for and makes a record of may be determined by the particular hypothesis that she or he has in mind. Often, however, the observer's purpose is simply to describe a group, a setting, or an activity in as much detail as possible, not in order to test a hypothesized relationship, but to provide a full picture of the subject. The result may be an ethnography (such as an anthropologist's report of the life and social organization of a jungle tribe); it may be a description of the patterns of behavior in a blue-collar bar, a report of social change in a particular group or neighborhood, or an account of a particular individual's activities over a given period of time. The subject matter of observational research is limited only by what an observer can see and hear.

The report of an observational study can be rich in detail, but this very richness means that the researcher may have a difficult time developing generalizations that will be valid beyond the particular subject matter that was observed, if only because it is unlikely that this entire combination of variables will occur again in different times and places. The usual term for such a report is *case study*, and its value lies primarily in its potential for generating hypotheses and for use by other researchers.

Since it is the observer who does the actual recording, his or her "field notes" are of critical importance, particularly in terms of *what* is recorded, but also in terms of format and preservation. (Obviously, field notes that are disorganized or partly illegible are difficult to use later on, especially in retrieving specific facts; it is unfortunately true, also, that fledgling observers are often careless about *saving* all of their notes.) The question of what to make a record of must always be answered before observation begins, even if it is no more than a general decision to record "whatever looks interesting." Ordinarily, however, the observer will at least have an idea of the sorts of things that will be relevant to his or her interests: indications of dominance and subordination, the coordination of activities, the topics of casual conversations, etc.

This does not mean that the observer cannot develop new ideas during the course of the research about what is worth recording. Frequently, in fact, it is only after a good deal of observation that the researcher finds a particular aspect of the subject matter that stands out as especially worthy of attention. To the extent that this happens, some or most of the earlier records will likely turn out to be wasted because they do not cover the newly discovered focus of the research. But this is almost inevitable, and no one who has had experience with observational studies worries about it.

Related to pure observation is the method called *participant observation* (spanning cells I and III). Here, the researcher takes part in the activities that are being studied, giving up any pretense of having *no* influence on them, but trying instead to act as a normal member of the group. The participant observer refrains from attempts to lead the group or to introduce anything novel, for this could change the naturalness of the situation. As a normal member of the group, the researcher naturally can get closer to his or her subject matter and is free to ask others about what they are doing and why. To be sure, this involves arranging for certain events to occur (answers to the researcher's questions), but it is ordinarily assumed that such intervention in the situation will not materially alter its essential character. And if one loses something in terms of complete naturalness, this can be more than made up for in the greater amount of detail that can be gathered and perhaps also in the greater insights that can be gained.

After a series of observations, either "pure" or "participant," have been made of the same topic, it is possible to compare them. For example, if the interactions among the members of a particular group have been observed over a period of several days or weeks, it may be useful to compare the records made when a particular person was present with those made when he or she was absent. If any systematic differences show up, it may be supposed that the presence or absence of someone to play this person's role in the group was at least partially responsible for them. Once the researcher has moved to this stage of the research process, the methods of analysis become more and more like those employed in cells II and IV of Table 1.

Content Analysis and Unobtrusive Measures (Cell II)

Cell II includes those methods used in research on phenomena which have naturally left records of themselves. Printed matter, for example—books, magazines, newspapers, even personal letters that have been preserved—is not ordinarily produced for the purpose of being studied by sociologists, but because it remains in existence long after its initial appearance, a researcher may study its contents at a later date. The use of unobtrusive measures (information recorded for one purpose which the sociologist may use later as a measure of a particular variable in which he or she is interested) involves the same general strategy. Here, such things as stock market reports, records of business transactions, committee minutes, and even records of variations in the volume of water flowing through a municipal water system can be of use to the sociologist.

In neither case has the sociologist arranged for the occurrence of these phenomena, and in neither case does he or she record observations of them, for they already exist as records of something or other. To these recorded data, the sociologist brings primarily a hypothesis and a method of analysis that will produce findings relevant to that hypothesis.

Content analysis involves analyzing the meaning of written materials: short stories in magazines, advertising copy, novels, and so on. The contents of radio and television broadcasts may be studied also, but usually only after they have been described and/or transcribed on paper. A sociologist might, for instance, be interested in whether attitudes toward conservation are influenced more by political ideologies or by the state of the economy. Taking a sample of newspapers published every five years between 1950 and 1975 and published in different parts of the country (say, Denver, Chicago, Atlanta, and Boston), the researcher would look for indications of attitudes toward conservation—editorials, reports of campaign promises and of organized activities focused on conservation issues, etc. She or he would also look for references to more general political attitudes and for information on the local unemployment rate. Properly classified and arranged, the resulting associations among these three variables might show or at least give some support to the assertion that attitudes toward conservation are more closely related to economic conditions than to political ideologies. Further analysis of the materials might even enable the researcher to suggest that a concern for the environment *is* related to political attitudes, but only when the economy is functioning well.

In using unobtrusive measures for a study, the sociologist might be interested in the relationship between social class and personal vanity. To provide a crude indicator of relative social class, he or she might turn to local tax records (say, the average assessed valuation of owner-occupied homes in different parts of a city). A useful measure of personal vanity might be the dollar value of deodorants sold in the same areas during a given month. The unobtrusive measures used are thus tax records and sales figures.

Taking ten or twenty different areas of the city and ranking them in terms of the average value of the homes in each one, the researcher would then obtain figures on deodorant sales for each area as well. If the hypothesis states that the higher one's social class, the greater one's personal vanity, then the rank-ordering of areas in terms of deodorant sales should come close to matching the rank-ordering of average housing value. Using a test of statistical significance, the researcher should be able to state whether or not the hypothesis has been borne out by the findings. (If it is not, of course, one can conclude that either the hypothesis was incorrect or these particular measures do not "really" measure the variables under consideration. If there are compelling reasons to believe that the hypothesis *should* have been correct—on the basis of theory or of others' previous findings—the researcher may wish to devise a different test of the hypothesis before rejecting it as untrue.)

It should be noted that the controls used in both cases are imposed *post-facto* (after the fact) by the researcher. He or she did not arrange for the newspapers to be published or for the tax and sales records to be kept, but instead categorized news items or ranked different areas of the city afterwards. The logic of seeking and testing relationships thereafter was the same as that used in other forms of research, but because the basic "facts" were in existence before the research begins, we identify content analysis and the use unobtrusive measures as basically similar research methods.

Interviews and Questionnaires (Cell III)

A question, either asked directly by a researcher or printed on a questionnaire which the respondent fills out, can be thought of as a stimulus: It elicits a kind of behavior (an answer) that the individual probably would not otherwise engage in at this particular time and place. The researcher is thus arranging for the occurrence of the phenomenon that he or she wishes to observe and record. However, the researcher in this case has no control over the various other things, past and present, that may influence the respondent's answers (other than who the respondent is, how the questions are asked, and sometimes the setting in which they are asked). There is simply no way for the researcher to ensure that a respondent does not have a hangover, did not win a lottery yesterday, or is not anxious to make a good impression, yet each of these other variables may influence the answers that a respondent will give.

The questions addressed to a respondent can cover an extremely broad range of topics. In general, they may be divided into three major categories: *factual* (age, sex, occupation, education, and other facts that in principle could be independently verified); *plans* ("Do you plan to buy a new car within the next year?" "Would you go on strike if your union voted to do so?"); and *attitudes* ("Which is more important, money or happiness?" "About how satisfied are you with your present job?" "Would you rate this teacher as poor, average, or excellent?"). It is ordinarily assumed that *factual* questions yield the most reliable answers (that is, the same individual will answer them the same way next week), *plans* questions yield somewhat less reliable answers, and *attitudinal* questions elicit the least reliable answers.

If, however, we are interested in the "average" attitudes of several hundred respondents, we will find that this average is more reliable than are the answers provided by the individual respondents. That is, if twenty-five percent of the group is highly in favor of increased defense spending one week, this percentage should not change very much if the same question is asked again next week, despite the fact that a number of individual respondents may have changed their minds during the week. When dealing with large numbers of respondents and with their "average" responses, then, the researcher can usually assume a substantial amount of *reliability* in his or her data.

But reliability is not necessarily the same as *validity*, or how "true" the respondents' answers are. Here again, questions dealing with *facts, plans*, and *attitudes* probably yield decreasingly valid answers, even though the sociologist rarely assumes that even a modest minority of respondents purposely gives false answers. There is, of course, nothing the sociologist can do about people's honesty, but she or he can try to maximize the validity of their answers by making sure that questions are phrased as neutrally as possible and that the *same* questions are used with all respondents (to ensure that all have actually been exposed to the same stimulus).

Being aware that the *way* in which a question is asked can influence how a person answers it and also that the *order* in which a series of questions is asked may influence the answers to some of them, sociologists devote a good deal of time to designing their interview schedules (lists of questions to be asked) and questionnaires. One would not expect, for instance, that a valid indication of the respondent's opinion would be obtained after the question: "Do you prefer delicious Brand P or foul-tasting Brand Q?" And one might expect an older female to become annoyed with an interviewer who first asks, "How many children do you have?" and *then*, "Are you married?"

The point here is that an interview is basically a kind of social interaction, and the respondent reacts to the interviewer as well as to his or her questions. To a lesser extent, this is true also of self-administered questionnaires, even though in this case the problem is more that the respondent will not return the questionnaire at all than that invalid answers will be recorded. If a respondent becomes bored, impatient, or offended by either an interviewer or a questionnaire, his or her answers will be influenced by these emotions—and an undesirable new variable has entered the situation.

An interview may last only a minute, or it may last four hours or more. It may be "structured" (that is, it employs a specific set of questions that are to be read to all respondents in the same words) or "unstructured" (an unstructured interview is one in which the interviewer is free to phrase questions in the way that seems most effective with a particular respondent and to probe to find out why a respondent has given a particular answer).

Obviously, there is no such thing as an unstructured questionnaire, although some provide "precoded" answers to be checked or circled (for instance, "What is your marital status? ____single, ____engaged, ____living together, ____married, ____separated, ____divorced, ____widowed"), whereas others are "open-ended" (for example, "What is your opinion of the present Mayor? _____"). Any particular questionnaire, of course, can contain both kinds of questions.

The construction of interview schedules (questions to be asked by interviewers) and the design of questionnaires is an art rather than a science. There is, however, a good deal of accumulated experience in this area (recorded principally in textbooks, some of which are cited at the end of this appendix), and the person planning an interview or questionnaire for the first time will be wise to take advantage of this store of wisdom.

A single interview, particularly if it is at least partly unstructured and allows the interviewer to cover a topic in some depth, can be a productive source of hypotheses. But few, if any, reliable generalizations can be based on a single interview. The same is true of questionnaires. Thus the analysis of the information collected through these methods must wait until a substantial number of interviews have been made or questionnaires collected. Then cases may be grouped and compared in whatever ways the researcher wishes. This process is usually called survey analysis.

Survey Research and Analysis (Cell IV)

A survey is essentially a broad look at a situation: A farmer *surveys* a field, or a political candidate *surveys* his or her chances for election. In sociology the word refers to the collection of the same sorts of information from a number of people through interviews or questionnaires and also to the analysis of these data. Beyond what has been discussed in the preceding section, three aspects of survey research are of particular importance: (1) the purposes of survey research; (2) who is surveyed and how they are reached; and (3) the techniques used in analyzing large quantities of survey data.

We usually think that a survey's purpose is to describe some aspect of reality, such as the number of people in the total population who were victimized by crimes last year, the percentage of votes that each candidate can expect in a forthcoming election, or the proportion of children who prefer green-tinted over pink-tinted toothpaste. This is the sort of information that commercial polling organizations tend to gather, and they generally do a highly effective job of it.

But a survey can also aim at identifying the relationships among two or more variables without regard to the actual frequency of these relationships in a given population. It may be of sociological interest, for example, to know whether blue-collar workers' attitudes toward their jobs are influenced more by their wages or their supervisors' behavior; the *total number* of blue-collar workers who are particularly sensitive to each variable is irrelevant to the purpose of the research.

There is, then, a distinction between a "descriptive" survey and an "analytical" survey. Whereas the former hopes to provide an accurate picture of how certain variables are distributed within a particular population (or "universe"—for example, the universe of all cigarette smokers, or all married women, or all teenagers in the city of Sacramento), the latter is concerned more with the extent to which X is related to Y than with how often X appears in a particular population.

A successful (that is, accurate) descriptive survey depends very much on how the researcher selects the respondents who will be interviewed or questionnaired. The most foolproof way, of course, would be to obtain information from every member of the population in which one is interested. Almost always, however, considerations of time and money make this impossible. Fortunately, thanks to statisticians and to actual experience, we know that a completely random sample of about 1500 people will provide a miniature "picture" of an entire population, whether it includes 20,000 or 100,000,000 people altogether, that is accurate to within two or three percent.

Complete randomness—which means that every single member of the population has precisely the same likelihood of being included in the sample—is easier to describe theoretically than to achieve in practice. Although a detailed discussion of the different techniques of drawing samples (and of their various advantages and disadvantages) is beyond the scope of this appendix, suffice it to say that several sampling techniques are available that enable the researcher to *approximate* complete randomness. For our purposes, it is enough to note that the sampling process is of fundamental importance when the survey's purpose is descriptive and of somewhat less importance if its purpose is primarily analytical. In the end, of course, it is always desirable to be able to say not only that X *is associated* with Y, but also that X occurs *with a certain frequency* in a particular population.

After the sample has been drawn and the desired information collected by means of interviews or questionnaires, the researcher begins to analyze the data, or to find out which variables are associated with which other variables. For instance, if a high proportion of respondents who say that they have graduated from college *also* say that their incomes are above $16,000 a year, whereas very few of those who report only a grade school education say that they have incomes above this figure, the correlation between "high education" and "high income" is clear: X is almost always accompanied by Y, whereas non-X is hardly ever accompanied by Y.

Having found this relationship, the researcher may next wish to find out whether the respondents' membership in various ethnic groups affects it. This is done by separating both the "high-education" and "low-education" groups according to ethnicity and then comparing these groups. Here one may discover that the relationship between education and income is weakened among the members of certain ethnic groups and strengthened in others, and the analyst is now faced with the problem of explaining why this is so. In this case ethnicity has been viewed as an intervening variable, or something that affects the relationship between the independent and dependent variables. In another case ethnicity might be used as the independent variable and education as an intervening variable; *how* the relationships among variables are handled depends on the analyst's hypotheses and interests. (Never, of course, is a variable that is obviously located *earlier* in time than another, treated as though it were a possible *effect* of the other.)

Indexing concepts   Sociological concepts (e.g., alienation, social solidarity, structural differentiation) are themselves abstractions, and their referents do not exist in any single concrete form. The researcher's problem, then, involves relating *specific data* (for instance, people's reports of how often they visit relatives) to *general concepts* (in this case, perhaps "family solidarity"). The sociologist is thus interested in not only the validity of individual respondents' answers to questions, but also whether those answers can be meaningfully used to represent, or "index," the concepts that make up the hypothesis being tested. This is essentially the problem of interpreting survey findings.

The researcher's hypothesis might propose that family solidarity is higher in times of economic depression than in times of affluence. One important part of testing the hypothesis will depend on developing a measure of family solidarity. Using only people's reports of how often they visit relatives as an index of this concept is a possibility, but a more reliable index (that is, one which gets closer to the central meaning of the concept) should probably be based on answers to several questions: frequency of visiting relatives, frequency of writing or telephoning them, frequency of lending money to relatives, frequency of helping out in times of illness and childbirth, etc. Attitudinal questions about the respondents' feelings toward relatives might be used as well.

Since each of these behaviors or attitudes presumably reflects one aspect of family solidarity, it is reasonable to assume that a score or scale based on several of them will yield a more trustworthy measure of the amount of solidarity present in the various respondents' families. The development of such measures and of other techniques for turning "raw data" into indices of generalized concepts has been an important part of the history of sociological research. Over the past thirty years, the introduction of punch cards (on which data are recorded) and of large computers that can process masses of data rapidly and accurately has made surveys the major method of sociological research. Increasingly sophisticated techniques of indexing concepts and of analyzing relationships have been developed, too, so that today survey research and analysis is also the most "technical" method of research employed by sociologists. The complexity of this method, however, should not obscure our awareness that it, like all other methods, is basically a means of collecting information from people and of looking for and interpreting relationships among the answers they have given.

The Experiment (Cell V)

The classical experiment involves some form of physical control of the research subjects and the comparison of two supposedly identical subjects, only one of which has been exposed to the causal variable that is being tested. A researcher in nutrition, for instance, might take two rats from the same litter, put each into a sealed, sterilized cage, and give each of them identical amounts of the same food for a month. Then one of the rats would be given a particular vitamin in addition to its food. At the end of another month, the weights of the two rats would be compared.

If the rats were indeed identical at the beginning of the experiment, the researcher would be able to say with assurance that the difference in their weights at the end of the experiment was due entirely to the presence or absence of the vitamin in the rats' diet. The rat that received the vitamin served as the "experimental subject," and the rat that did not receive it was the "control subject." Because no two rats are *precisely* identical, however, the experimenter would probably have used a number of rats (say, twenty in the experimental group and another twenty in the control group) and would assume that the use of statistical as well as physical controls would improve the validity of the findings. The dependent variable, then, would be the *average* weight of the rats in the experimental group, as compared with the average weight of those in the control group.

In sociological research it is virtually impossible to find individuals or groups that are identical, and it is also extremely difficult to manipulate people in the way that one can manipulate rats. Instead, the sociologist who wants to carry out an experiment must seek subjects who are naturally matched and must also persuade them to cooperate in the experiment. For example, if he or she wanted to carry out an experiment on the influence of radio versus television in shaping people's attitudes, the formation of matched experimental and control groups would be the first order of business. Perhaps the students in a large lecture class would be asked to fill out a questionnaire that asks about personal background and political attitudes; on the basis of their answers, perhaps ten students could be found who have in common such things as sex, ethnicity, grade-point average, social class, political preference, and so on.

Five of these students would be selected at random to serve as the control group, and the other five as the experimental group. All would be tested initially to determine their attitudes toward a particular public issue. Then, while the control group is exposed to only the "audio" part of a debate by experts on the issue, the experimental group views the same debate on television. Afterwards, their attitudes are tested again, and the researcher can assume that any differences in attitude between the groups have been caused by the difference between the sources of the subjects' information about the issue.

The logic here, of course, is the same as that employed in research using post-facto controls: comparing individuals who have been exposed to certain variables with others who have not. In the experiment, however, the researcher applies the stimulus *now* and does as much as possible to maintain physical control over the presence or intrusion of "irrelevant" variables.

The "natural experiment"   Basically, a natural experiment is one in which the experimental and control groups occur naturally rather than having been formed by the researcher. A sociologist might, for instance, discover two small towns that are similar in terms of population, ethnic makeup, economic base, and distance from other towns, but that differ because one of them has recently suffered a severe flood. The sociologist thus has found a remarkable opportunity to study the consequences of the flood, perhaps in terms of how the disaster has influenced the social solidarity of the town's citizens.

It might be hypothesized that the citizens of the flooded town, having faced a common danger together, will rate higher on measures of social solidarity than the citizens of the "control" town. Employing the same questionnaire or observational methods in both towns, the sociologist can gather data relevant to the concept of solidarity and can then compare the results from each town. If the hypothesis is correct, a higher level of solidarity will be found in the "experimental" town—the one which suffered the flood.

It might turn out, of course, that hostilities stemming from people's failure to help one another during the flood, or from the belief that relief funds were distributed unfairly, have actually *lowered* the sense of solidarity in the flooded town. If this is found, the research will at least have discovered that increased solidarity comes not simply from exposure to common danger, but from how people have responded to it.

Natural experiments are comparatively rare, simply because the circumstances that make them possible are rare. Nevertheless, when one can be found, it can be immensely useful in the sociologist's attempts to learn more about the relationships that make up social reality.

The experiment, then, is by no means the principal method of research used by sociologists. The difficulties of controlling human beings and of applying stimuli to them make the experiment inappropriate or impossible in many cases, even though the basic logic of the experiment is duplicated as closely as possible in content analysis, the use of unobtrusive measures, and in survey analysis. Experiments are conducted much more often when the focus of attention is individuals or small groups, and in many cases it is the major method of research used by psychologists and social psychologists.

ETHICS IN SOCIOLOGICAL RESEARCH

No discussion of research on human beings can be complete without considering the ethical aspects of the process. Ethical behavior may, ideally, mean "acting in accordance with certain basic principles or standards of behavior, regardless of others' wishes," but in practical terms it boils down to behavior that does not violate others' *trust*. Because sociologists deal with human beings, and because the research subject's cooperation (answering an interviewer's questions, filling out a questionnaire, taking part in an experiment) is *voluntary*, the same assumption of mutual trust is present in the research relationship that underlies any other sort of voluntary social interaction.

This means that the social status of "sociological researcher" is subordinate to that of "adult human being," so that the sociologist's obligations as a human being are assumed to override any special rights that he or she may claim as a sociologist. In agreeing to cooperate with the sociologist, then, the research subject ordinarily views the relationship as one in which his or her normal rights as a human being will be respected.

Two particular expectations are involved, whether or not they are made explicit. First, the subject assumes that the researcher has been honest in explaining why the subject should be willing to participate in the research. Second, the subject assumes that he or she will not suffer any injury as a result of cooperating with the researcher. But the "research relationship" is unique in certain respects. The researcher ordinarily does not know the subject personally and may indeed view the subject simply as a "case" or a store of information. Further, the impersonality that the researcher assumes in trying to make sure that the subject's responses are not biased may increase his or her tendency to forget that this *is* a social relationship. Therefore, the researcher may sometimes fail to remember that expectations regarding "common decency" are still in force as far as the subject is concerned; sometimes, too, these expectations may be violated inadvertently.

The former obligation of the researcher, that of being honest in dealing with research subjects, is sometimes difficult to live up to. One would assume, of course, that the sociologist has a fairly clear idea of why he or she is doing the research and that this purpose can be clearly explained to the people whose cooperation is sought. But sometimes it is not fully clear to the researcher just *how* the data will finally be used; sometimes the subject cannot fully understand the researcher's purposes; and sometimes the validity of the subject's answers, or the naturalness of the subject's behavior, might be biased if the specific purpose of the research were known.

These ethical problems are generally grouped under the heading of "informed consent," and they are particularly important when the researcher is dealing with people who by definition are unlikely to be able to give free, informed consent to participation in research. Children, the mentally ill and retarded, and penitentiary inmates (who may be under some pressure to cooperate) pose serious problems here, especially when there may be some risk involved.

Research that requires some initial deception of research subjects in order to produce valid findings raises a different problem. A sociologist, for instance, may believe that people will not give honest answers about their attitudes toward different ethnic groups if they are asked directly, but will reveal their real attitudes if they are not aware that such information is being sought. Subjects might be recruited, then, with the explanation that they will be asked to evaluate the work of several artists, in a study of aesthetic judgment—even though the way their judgments are influenced by the artists' ethnicity is the actual information the researcher is looking for. In principle this is deliberate deception by the researcher, and even when there is no apparent risk to the subjects at all, it is unethical.

In practice, of course, vagueness can be substituted for misstatement, and when virtually no risk to the subjects is involved, many sociologists will justify deception on the grounds that the importance of the information to be obtained is sufficiently great to excuse this sort of violation of trust. When deception must be used, though, it is generally important to explain it later on to the subjects so that in the end, the researcher will have been completely honest with his or her subjects.

The researcher's latter obligation, to ensure that a subject will not be harmed through his or her cooperation, is even more important. Rarely in sociological research is there risk that the research process itself may be physically harmful, but there is always a chance that participation in a stressful experiment, or even being reminded of painful experiences by an interviewer's questions, can upset a subject, and this would constitute harm. Whenever research subjects are to be placed in new and perhaps disturbing situations as part of the research, even when they have volunteered to participate, the researcher cannot avoid responsibility for making every effort to see that all possible risks are minimized.

Another source of potential harm to the subject lies in the chance that information given to the researcher might be revealed in a way that could injure the subject's relations with others. An employee's opinion of the boss, for example, should obviously not be relayed to the boss in any way that might allow the employee to be identified. Further, to transmit information obtained from subject A to subject C, even anonymously, when it would ordinarily go from A to person B and *then* to C, might indirectly damage the normal relationships among these three individuals.

As a matter of professional principle, then, any information obtained from a research subject that is not already "in the public domain" must be treated by the researcher as private and confidential, just as one would treat a secret revealed by a friend. The information then can be made public only in aggregative form (that is, as percentages or numbers) or in quotations whose sources are securely disguised.

This is not simply a question of whether a subject whose trust has been violated can get back at the researcher; it is a matter of professional integrity and of the overall reputation of social researchers in general. To the extent that one sociologist violates his or her subjects' trust, the ability of other sociologists to gain people's cooperation in the future will be slightly diminished. One researcher's unethical behavior can injure not only the subjects of a particular research project, but also the discipline itself.

Summing Up

The obligations of all researchers who work with human subjects are clear: to be as honest as possible in securing their cooperation and to make sure that they will not be harmed by either the research process itself or subsequent misuse of the information they have provided. Careful attention to possible risks to subjects—whether these lie in the breach of faith caused by deception, in the questions asked or the actions called for by the research, or in the chance that the information obtained may later be used by someone to the subject's disadvantage—is thus the clear ethical obligation of everyone engaged in any form of social research.

It should be noted, finally, that some social scientists are now calling for behavior that is even more ethical than that described above. They propose that findings based on information provided by research subjects be actively shared with them, with a view toward helping them in whatever ways seem needed. This position recognizes that the researcher owes something positive to his or her subjects and goes well beyond the attitude of noninterference or "leave things just as they were," which has been the foundation of more traditional ethical standards. But the extent to which research subjects *want* such help, or indeed *can* be helped, varies so much from one situation to the next that it is unlikely that this will become a standard ethical obligation of all social researchers.

It is, however, worth bearing in mind. The social researcher is a human being, first of all, interacting with other human beings, and the basic principles of exchange that underlie all patterns of social interaction cannot be ignored simply because one is "doing research."

SUMMARY

The logic by which actual relationships among different qualities and units of reality are discovered underlies all methods of research. All methods focus ultimately on identifying associations between units and/or qualities that occur because of some causal relationship rather than by chance. These associations may be only those of co-occurrence, but ordinarily scientists seek to identify sequential associations in which, by knowing what occurred *first*, one can predict the occurrence of something else later on.

Because, however, different hypotheses raise different problems in terms of how the relevant variables are to be located, recorded, and controlled, a number of different research methods are required. Table 1 combines the distinction between whether or not the sociologist creates the event that he or she wishes to observe (and to make a record of it) and the distinction between whether or not the effects of other variables on the hypothesized relationship are controlled. The six cells of this table enable us to see the basic relationships and distinctions among the five major methods of research employed by sociologists: observation, interviews and questionnaires, content analysis and the use of unobtrusive measures, survey research and analysis, and the experiment.

Beyond implementing the logic of science through these various methods, the sociologist must also be aware that social research is a form of social interaction. Since research subjects in effect volunteer to help the researcher, their rights as human beings—that they will not be deceived or harmed through their cooperation—must be respected, and the social researcher must assume responsibility for seeing that ethical standards are observed before undertaking his or her research.

Nearly all departments of sociology offer a course in research methods and usually require students majoring in the subject to take at least one semester's intensive exposure to the theory and practice of sociological research. This appendix can do little more than introduce the reasoning that underlies research and to show how this reasoning, in combination with different topics and problems, has produced different methods of research.

Involvement in research can be arduous, sometimes boring, occasionally frustrating, and even, at times, dismaying or frightening. But the end result is usually a deeply satisfying sense that one has found something real in society and that one can make some statements about this "something" with firm confidence. Such statements are the fundamental goal of science, and to participate in adding to the store of sociological knowledge is not only an adventure, but can often be a source of solid intellectual pleasure as well.

SUGGESTED READINGS

Comprehensive Texts on Research Methods

Cole, Steven, *The Sociological Method* (Chicago: Markham, 1972).

Goode, Wiliam J., and Paul K. Hatt, *Methods of Social Research* (New York: McGraw-Hill, 1952).

Hammond, Philip E., ed., *Sociologists at Work* (New York: Basic Books, 1964).

Phillips, Bernard S., *Social Research: Strategy and Tactics* (New York: Macmillan, 1966).

Riley, Matilda White, *Sociological Research: A Case Approach* (New York: Harcourt Brace and World, 1963).

Sanders, William B., *The Sociologist as Detective*, 2d ed. (New York: Praeger, 1976).

Selltiz, Claire, Marie Jahoda, Morton Deutsch, and Stuart Cook, *Research Methods in Social Relations*, rev. ed. (New York: Holt, Rinehart and Winston, 1962).

Observational Studies

Humphries, Laud, *Tearoom Trade: Impersonal Sex in Public Places* (Chicago: Aldine, 1970).

Loffland, John, *Analyzing Social Settings* (Belmont, Calif.: Wadsworth, 1971).

Liebow, Elliott, *Tally's Corner: A Study of Negro Streetcorner Men* (Boston: Little, Brown, 1967).

Content Analysis

Berelson, Bernard, *Content Analysis* (New York: Free Press, 1952).

Thomas, Wiliam I., and Florien Znaniecki, *The Polish Peasant in Europe and America* [1919] (New York: Octagon Books, 1971).

Unobtrusive Measures

Webb, Eugene, Donald T. Campbell, Richard D. Schwartz, and Lee Sechrest, *Unobtrusive Measures: Nonreactive Research in the Social Sciences* (Chicago: Rand McNally, 1966).

The Interview

Hyman, Herbert, *et al.*, *Interviewing in Social Research* (Chicago: University of Chicago Press, 1954).

Merton, Robert K., M. Fiske, and Patricia L. Kendall, *The Focused Interview* (New York: Free Press, 1956).

Survey Analysis

Davis, James, *Elementary Survey Analysis* (Englewood Cliffs, N.J.: Prentice-Hall, 1971).

Rosenberg, Morris, *The Logic of Survey Analysis* (New York: Basic Books, 1968).

The Experiment

Mill, John Stuart, *A System of Logic* [1843] (London: Longmans, 1961).

Swingle, Paul G., ed., *Social Psychology in Natural Settings* (Chicago: Aldine, 1973).

Appendix 2
Sociological Theory

FOCUS:

SCIENTIFIC THEORY

The discovery of regularities—of "clusters" of events that repeatedly occur close to one another in time and space or that form predictable sequences over longer periods of time—is the first task of any science. As soon as one seeks to describe the relationships *among* such regularities, however, one has moved beyond the direct description of reality and into the realm of what may be called theory. This is as true for sociology as it is for physics.

The task of sociological theory is thus to lay out an ordered description of the *bases* of social regularities. It seeks to find and make clear the broader principles that are illustrated in the regularities found through research. In the physical sciences it is generally accepted that the laws of motion, of thermodynamics, and of gravity (many of which are subsumed under the even more basic theory of relativity) enable us to grasp the central principles that govern physical events. At present, sociology and the other social sciences are nowhere near such confident understanding of their own subject matter. But the urge to seek underlying principles persists, and an understanding of the current state of sociological theory is necessary if one is to appreciate the discipline itself.

Sociologists today are by no means in agreement on the assumption that society can be viewed as an integrated whole, much less on the basic "laws" that might underlie its central characteristics. But social regularities, ranging from the dynamics of small groups to the development of social institutions, are generally recognized. Given this reason at least to *think* that

477

there must be generalized principles underlying social regularities, a number of attempts have been made to identify them. This appendix provides an overview of the history and current state of sociological theory.

THE MEANING OF "THEORY"

In the usual scientific sense a theory is a body of interrelated generalizations, based on empirical evidence, that describes the central characteristics of a particular type of phenomenon. Theory is thus the goal of any science, for it is the organized summing up of that science's knowledge of its subject matter.

An ideal theory would be one that describes in a few statements the relationships among all the things, qualities, and processes that constitute the subject matter of a particular science. It would enable scientists in that field to identify a concrete example of their topic, to note its present characteristics, and then to predict its characteristics at some point in the future.

Such a theory, however, is unlikely ever to be achieved. Although the basic desire of scientists in any discipline is to acquire *more* knowledge of their subject matter, this does not necessarily mean that they will ever reach the goal of *complete* knowledge. Human interests change, new phenomena appear that require explanation, and new questions can be raised about existing knowledge. This means that theory is always *being built* and thus that there are various types or stages of theory now in existence.

In the beginning, theory is often little more than *ad hoc* speculation, as when someone says, "I have a theory that Bob hates dogs because he was frightened by one when he was small." This is really a hypothesis, or a statement of a relationship that one *thinks* exists, but in everyday speech we sometimes call it a theory.

A more organized type of theory comes into existence as scientists discover more and more empirical regularities and devise generalizations that describe systematic linkages among them. As statements of such general relationships are proved to be correct time after time, they may come to be called scientific laws. We may refer to theories developed in this way as "natural science" theories.

But the quest for generalizations need not wait for the discovery of unvarying empirical relationships. Instead, because theory is composed of symbols—formed into statements that are not themselves the parts of reality to which they refer—it is possible also to build theories that are essentially *conceptual schemes*. That is, one may begin with the symbols (or concepts) that represent all of the important aspects one can think of concerning the subject matter in which one is interested and then work out the various logical relationships that must exist among these symbols.

If, for instance, human interaction *must* involve shared expectations that focus on reciprocal rights and obligations, we can develop a set of concepts that refer to each of the important components of interaction (norms, values, roles, statuses, and so on) and try on the basis of logic to describe the relationships that should exist among them. Our sense of the correctness of this sort of theory depends more on the standards by which we judge the relationships among symbols to be logically complete than on the extent to which the relationships they describe are actually found in reality.

In the end, of course, a conceptual scheme must be tested against research-based evidence before it can be accepted as embodying genuine scientific knowledge. But such evidence is often difficult to obtain, either with sufficient precision or in sufficient amounts to facilitate a definitive test of the conceptualized relationships. As a result, there is a strong tendency to pay more attention to the logical coherence and *apparent* accuracy of the theory than to its demonstrated ability to produce valid empirical predictions.

A science whose subject matter is particularly difficult to study directly and fully, then, is perhaps more likely to develop conceptual schemes than is one in which empirical research is easier to conduct. As we shall see, this has clearly been the case with sociology. For the most part (although often facing sharp disagreement from those who prefer the "natural science" model of theory), sociological theories at present are conceptual schemes, based on partial or even anecdotal evidence, rather than bodies of generalizations founded on firm research findings.

THEORIES OF SOCIETY: AN OVERVIEW

Naming and defining something does not necessarily mean that we have identified something real (witches, sea monsters, and leprechauns have been named and described, but not found in reality) or something that can usefully be treated as a phenomenon worthy of study in its own right (the general concept of mental illness, for example, apparently covers a variety of quite unrelated mental states). Yet there is widespread consensus that something called "society" exists and is worthy of study. If it exists, there must be something central to its nature that enables us to identify it.

Almost by definition, this central nature is *social order,* for if regularities did not exist in social relationships, there would be nothing "out there" for us to identify except for randomly behaving individuals.

But accepting the existence of social regularities is one thing; accounting for them is quite another. All of us know that the behavior of others is reasonably predictable; our lives would be chaotic if we could not depend on others to behave largely as we expect them to. We also know, however, that people sometimes fail to behave as expected and that even when people do what they should do, they may not want to. The existence of social order is thus problematic in two senses: it is clearly not in evidence one hundred percent of the time, and it is not always the product of immediate human desires.

A theory of society, therefore, must try to account for the conditions under which social order develops, is maintained, changes, and disintegrates. Since any theory must first be *induced*—that is, generalizations derived somehow from a few concrete cases must at first be assumed to apply to other cases as well—its basic principles must at first be *assumptions*. (As these lead to accurate predictions, they come to be treated more and more as "truths" rather than as assumptions, but they are always assumptions in the beginning.)

The sociologist's knowledge of society is incomplete, both because the discipline is relatively young and because its subject matter is so broad. In building sociological theory, then, the tentative nature of our assumptions about the bases of social regularities is especially clear. This means that several *different* assumptions are possible and that there is no easy way to determine which one is more valid than the others.

Explaining Social Order

Although a number of basic assumptions may be used in explaining the persistence of social order, it is possible (at risk of considerable oversimplification) to identify two fundamental questions that every theory must answer either directly or by implication. The ways in which they are answered provide the foundations, or the central assumptions, on which different sociological theories have been constructed.

The first of these questions is whether it is the physical or the cultural aspects of society that are more important. Which of these two aspects, in other words, should be emphasized if we are to develop the most accurate description of society?

Theorists who emphasize the physical aspects of society tend to concentrate on the material interests of human beings, especially their economic concerns and the social structures through which their material needs are met. Those who emphasize the cultural dimension of society tend to take for granted that at least minimal material needs are satisfied and to pay greater attention to socialization, symbol systems, and to the meaning of interaction to people.

The second question is more abstract and perhaps more a matter of philosophy than of empirical truth: Is order in social relationships natural, or is it problematic? If one assumes it to be natural, there is no need to concentrate on how it comes into being; the important phenomena to be explored are the ways in which disorder is controlled and the various ways in which order is worked out in society. On the other hand, those theorists who do *not* take order for granted must of necessity emphasize the processes through which order is imposed on an otherwise *dis*orderly situation.

Combining these two questions and the alternative answers to each one, we can get a view of four reasonably distinct traditions in sociological theory. This is certainly not the only way in which different theories may be distinguished from one another, nor does it mean that there is only one theory associated with each combination of answers. It does, however, provide a

TABLE 1   CENTRAL SOCIAL RELATIONSHIPS
EMPHASIZED IN DIFFERENT SOCIOLOGICAL PERSPECTIVES

Society is essentially:	Order is: Natural	Problematic
Physical	Exchange (exchange theory)	Conflict (conflict theory)
Cultural	Coordination (structural-functionalism)	Communication (symbolic interactionism, ethnomethodology)

meaningful starting point from which to examine the central characteristics of several important sociological theories.

It should be noted, incidentally, that the names of different theories are not always indicative of their basic perspectives. Some are named after their principal developers, others on the basis of their central concerns, and still others by a key phrase taken from their founders' initial statements. Marxist and Parsonian theories were named after their major proponents (although they are viewed today as important representatives of conflict and structural-functional theories, respectively). Exchange theory and symbolic-interaction theory are named for the central phenomena in which they are interested, and perhaps "Social Darwinism" illustrates the third way in which theories may be named. This means that the names of theories are not always useful guides to how they should be categorized. Table 1 identifies the central social relationships that are taken as the focal points of different theories, depending on how the basic "assumptional" questions have been answered.

The Four Traditions

If human beings are thought of primarily as physical organisms, their physical needs stand out; if there is a natural tendency toward order in their relationships, these relationships must be based on *exchange*. A focus on exchange thus leads to an emphasis on people's "selfish" interests, their "rationality" in calculating costs and benefits in their relations with others, and the process of bargaining. As the focus moves from individuals to groups, the natural order that Darwin found in *The Origin of Species* (1859) is reflected in sociological theories that have come to be termed "Social Darwinism." Here, although conflict ("the survival of the fittest") is important, it is assumed that the outcome of conflict is natural order.

When it is assumed that order is natural and that human beings are essentially guided by norms and values rather than by biological needs, the social phenomena of interest tend to be the relationships among different social regularities. The development and maintenance of coherent sets of norms and values, the ways in which different social patterns fit together and support one another, and how the various needs of "society itself" (as an integrated system) are taken care of, call for particular attention to the *coordination* of social relationships.

When the physical aspects of society are stressed but there is no assumption that order can be taken for granted, one must accept as the central characteristic of society the inevitability of *conflict* over the necessities of life. This leads to an emphasis on the role of power in social relationships and on the inequalities that develop and are maintained through the use of power.

Finally, if human beings' minds are more important than their bodies as far as social relationships go—if they are more cultural than physical—but order in their relationships is problematic, the foundations of order must lie in the ways in which people work out agreements in the realm of meaning and of shared definitions of situations. *Communication* is thus the major problem to be emphasized by a theory that begins with this particular combination of answers to the basic questions, and we have yet another range of social phenomena to be explored as the central "stuff" of society.

As we shall see later on in this appendix, each of these four perspectives can be associated with one or more "named" sociological theories, even though this scheme for organizing them, like any other, must result in oversimplification and will hide many things that are common to two or more of them. Before coming to the present-day array of theories that embody these four perspectives, however, it will be useful to look briefly at the prehistory of sociological theory and then in more detail at the "founding fathers" of sociology.

SOCIOLOGICAL THEORISTS

The Prehistory of Sociological Theory

Although we think of the discipline of sociology as beginning with Auguste Comte (1798–1857), who coined the word about 1836, we may trace attempts to theorize about society back at least to the classical Greeks. Only gradually, however, did the emphasis shift from *pre*scription to *de*scription. And only gradually did such theories expand from the realm of political philosophy to broader and more objective considerations of the whole of society.

Plato (ca. 427–347 B.C.), for instance, gave us perhaps the first detailed utopia in *The Republic,* in which he described the ideal state as one in which only the wisest rule and all change is prevented as much as possible. But his conclusions were essentially pessimistic, for he anticipated continual movement away from this idea; still, his approach and the aspects of society he singled out for attention continue to influence Western thought.

Aristotle (ca. 384–322 B.C.) is known for his assertion that "man is a social animal." In his *Politics,* he describes the ideal state as a kind of small city (by our standards, not much more than a small town) in which happiness—the ultimate purpose of human life—is to be found in political compromise between the rich and the poor, with a kind of limited democracy (political influence being based on merit and ability) as the most satisfactory form of government.

More than a millenium later, the Arab historian and statesman Ibn Khaldun (A.D. 1332–1406) undertook a much more objective approach to the problem of interpreting history. In his monumental *Kitab al-'Ibar* he surveyed the history of the Arabic world and thought he saw a cyclic pattern alternating between primitive and civilized culture. In particular, he stressed the influence of physical environment on social organization, but also made room for the presence of occult or mystical abilities such as prophecy and magic. His methodology, almost "scientific" in the modern sense of the word, was probably his most important contribution; it is unfortunate that his work did not become available to Western scholars until the 1800s, or perhaps the social sciences would have developed somewhat more rapidly.

To the extent that politics was almost universally taken to be the cornerstone of social order, Niccolo Machiavelli (1469–1527) stands as one of the earliest social theorists in the West to take at least a reasonably objective (albeit cynical) view of the foundations of political order. In *The Prince,* a book of advice to the ruler of Florence, he suggested that humankind is essentially selfish and shortsighted and that these characteristics could be manipulated by the ruler in such a way as to ensure the safety and well-being of the state.

Thomas Hobbes (1588–1679), John Locke (1632–1704), and Jean-Jacques Rousseau (1712–1778) are usually thought of together as "social contract theorists," in that all of them posited an initial, unorganized "state of nature" and then saw human beings joining consciously into civil groups in order to preserve their lives and property by giving up some of their natural freedoms in return for the protection of the state. Charles Louis Montesquieu (1689–1755), in *The Spirit of the Laws,* took a more sophisticated view of the relationship between "natural law" (that is, those principles of behavior that should be obvious to all people through the proper use of reason) and the human laws on which the state is based. He argued that a society's "spirit" (we would say its culture) is critical in determining the kind of social and political organization it will have, and he believed that order is best guaranteed by the existence of a plurality of interest groups within society because their competition would serve to check the self-seeking tendencies of each one. Both Comte and Durk-heim looked to Montesquieu as the single most important forerunner of sociology.

Another influence on Comte was the Marquis de Condorcet (1743–1794), who is known today primarily for his "optimistic" theory of human progress. His *Essay on the Progress of the Human Spirit* described nine stages through which human civilization had passed and predicted that the next one would bring the perfect society. He believed, with most of his predecessors, that the human faculty of reason was responsible for human progress and that con-scious efforts to encourage the use of reason would speed the coming of a more satisfying social order. It is one of the ironies of history that he died in prison during the French Revolution.

To summarize this brief review of the forerunners of sociological theory, we may say that prior to the middle of the nineteenth century, social theory was primarily: (1) political in orientation, in that it focused on the knowledge needed by rulers in order to maintain a successful (that is, orderly) state; and (2) *pre*scriptive rather than *de*scriptive, in that the practical consequences of their analyses were more important to these authors than the ideal of knowl-edge for its own sake. Since the time of Comte, however, and particularly after Weber (see below) laid the philosophical foundations for a sharp distinction between descriptions of what *is* and what *ought to be,* sociological theory has become more objective and free of the personal preferences of its developers.

(Prescriptive theories continue to be produced, of course; we need only recall Marx's *Communist Manifesto* and B. F. Skinner's *Walden II* to see that such theories are very much alive today. It is true also that the objectivity of theorists is not beyond question. The supporters of different theories often ac-cuse one another of being subtly influenced by both personality and social-class interests, even though such charges cannot be taken as proof that the theories themselves are invalid.)

After an examination of the principal contributions of the "fathers" of sociology, we shall review the current state of sociological theory.

The Founding Fathers: Comte, Marx, Durkheim, Simmel, Weber

The history of sociology before 1900 is almost exclusively European. Indeed, it was not until the decade of the 1920s that Americans began to contribute to the discipline in any substantial measure, even though such pioneers as William Graham Sumner (1840–1910), Lester F. Ward (1841–1913), Albion W. Small (1854–1926) and Charles Horton Cooley (1864–1929) had made sociology vis-ible in American academic life well before then. After about 1930, with the decline of free scholarship in Europe because of the rising tide of fascism, soci-ology became largely an American specialty. Today, however, the field has re-gained its international quality, and contributions come as readily from Amsterdam and Adelaide as they do from Berkeley and Boston.

Nevertheless, sociologists worldwide look to nineteenth-century Europe for the foundations of the discipline. The following sketches of the most important "first-generation" sociologists cannot, of course, cover their theoretical contributions in detail, but are offered here as an introduction to the history of sociological theory.

The Bettmann Archive

Auguste Comte (1798–1857)   Comte is recognized as the "father of sociology" because he coined the word itself and, in spirit at least, laid the basis for the scientific study of society. In his six-volume work *Cours de philosophie positive,* published between 1830 and 1846, Comte developed the idea that humankind has developed both socially and intellectually through three distinct stages. In terms of thought, these stages are the theological (or "fictitious"), the metaphysical (or "abstract"), and the scientific (or "positive"). He did not name the corresponding stages of social organization, but identified them roughly with, first, all history prior to the Middle Ages (when warriors and priests held most of the power); second, the period between about A.D. 1000 and 1700 (when members of religious and political bureaucracies were the principal leaders); and third, the period beginning in the eighteenth century, when scientists would come increasingly to provide guidance in what is good and realistically possible for society.

Comte's "law of three stages" stands today only as an historical curiosity, but his conception of a hierarchy of the sciences (with sociology, naturally, at the top of the ladder) was of considerable importance in encouraging the systematic study of society. Comte mixed this vision of sociology with a good deal of utopian fervor, and toward the end of his life he believed that he had founded a new scientific religion that would pave the way to a more perfect society.

The distinction between *is* and *ought* is not always clear in Comte's work. As with earlier social theorists, he attempted to derive the latter from the former, and the faith that this is possible is a major component of his philosophy of "positivism." Positivism holds that scientists *can* be absolutely objective in their observations of reality and thus that empirically valid knowledge comes only from science ("positive" knowledge being possible only through observation, experiment, and comparison). The other major tenet of positivism is that it is only on the basis of scientific knowledge that an effective system of values can be constructed, so that scientists will be able to determine not only what *is* but what *should be* as well.

It remained for the generations after Comte to recognize that absolute objectivity is nearly impossible and that scientific findings cannot tell us what values we should hold. To characterize a sociologist today as a positivist is often viewed as an insult, implying a lack of sophistication in his or her appreciation of sociology. Today positivism is appreciated mainly for the impetus it provided in the beginning for the scientific study of society.

The Bettmann Archive

Karl Marx (1818–1883)   Only over the last twenty years or so has the name of Karl Marx been separated sufficiently from the doctrines of Soviet communism to allow us to study his works without being thought unpatriotic (or even traitorous). It is clear, though, that Marx's analysis of history has had a profound effect on sociological thought as well as on world politics during this century.

Briefly, Marx saw human history as a struggle, rooted specifically in the relationship of human beings to the ways in which they sustain their physical existence. If the main trend of sociological and philosophical analysis before him had concentrated on the mind—the stress on reason as the path to social order was one theme, and Comte's three stages of thought was another—Marx reversed this by arguing that material (or economic) considerations lie at the root of all social relations. Instead of finding the essence of human existence in thought (Descarte's *Cogito, ergo sum*—I think, therefore I am—expresses this neatly), Marx would say that it lies in the physical foundations of life (perhaps *Appetitio, ergo sum*—I hunger, therefore I am—might be an appropriate summary of his viewpoint).

Because of economic scarcity, life *is* a struggle, and the core of human history is the various arrangements that have been worked out to keep this struggle under control while at the same time ensuring that there would be sufficient economic productivity to keep most people alive. The struggle, however, Marx believed, is not between individuals but between *classes*, and a person's class membership is determined solely by his or her relationship to the "means of production" (that is, the arrangements through which the necessities of life are produced). In general, the chief dividing line between classes is that between those who own and profit from the means of production and those who work for and are exploited by the profiteers. As long as some people get *more* and others get *less*—and as long as these advantages and disadvantages are perpetuated by the way in which society is organized—the overriding characteristic of society is *class struggle*.

The struggle, however, is not always apparent. Marx believed that culture (belief systems such as religion, ideology, even aesthetics) is rooted in economic relationships and that its content is often shaped by the ruling class to make the lower class accept or even be unaware of its exploited condition. His concept of "false consciousness," or of the lower classes' distorted perception of their disadvantaged position, helped him to explain why revolt against the ruling class had occurred so rarely in history.

But there is more to Marx's thinking than a view of conflict and economic exploitation. He was genuinely concerned for how people's feelings were influenced by their place in the class structure. In particular, he made much of how human beings are increasingly *alienated* from the world around them—from their work and the products of that work, from the community, and even from themselves. A sense of belonging and of meaningful involvement in life—the opposite of alienation—seemed to him to grow weaker as society becomes more complex. Personal relationships become narrower and more impersonal as jobs are subdivided into smaller ones for the sake of efficiency and as economic relationships come to dominate other reasons for interaction. But Marx also saw alienation as a source of energy leading to social change, for he believed that when people come to understand why and how the economic system leads to this unpleasant condition, they will seek to change the system.

Marx viewed social change as essentially change in the makeup of social classes, which in turn depended on change in the most important means of production. In ancient times, when muscle was the major element in economic production, the most important class line was between free people and slaves. During the feudal period, when serfdom replaced slavery, the most important distinction was between the nobles and the serfs, or between who owned the land and who worked it. After the Industrial Revolution, machines became the major means of production, and the crucial class line was drawn between those who owned and those who worked the machines. It was now the capitalists, the owners of the factories, against the working class.

Although these changes could be viewed as the results of technological advances, Marx took a broader view and concerned himself with the social context that led people to make and adopt such advances. Within each major mode of production, the conflict between the exploited and the profiteers led to the development of new classes that could profit from a new mode of production. Thus the economic entrepreneurs, the budding capitalists, emerged during the feudal period and themselves became the dominant class as the Industrial Revolution came about, relegating the land-owning class to a lesser position.

Although Marx believed that the final test of social theory is its implementation in practice, a clear distinction should be drawn between his own analysis of the dynamics of history and its adoption as the theoretical foundation of communism. His contributions to the study of social classes, of the relations between knowledge and social structure, and of the effects of economic organization on the psychological characteristics of the members of society have become important foundations of modern sociology. The discussions, arguments, and countertheories that his ideas have generated mark him as one of the major figures in the development of modern sociology.

The Bettmann Archive

Emile Durkheim (1858–1917)   Throughout his academic career (he was the first person to hold a "chair" of sociology in France), Durkheim worked to demonstrate the uniqueness of the subject matter of sociology. If human groups and societies are to be the focus of a special field of scientific research and theory, he believed, there must be something about them that cannot be traced back to biology, psychology, economics, or the physical environment.

In works published between 1893 and 1912, he offered several versions of the nature of this unique character of society. In *The Division of Labor* (1893)

Durkheim conceptualized this in terms of two forms of societal integration: *mechanical solidarity* and *organic solidarity.* The former is found in relatively undifferentiated (that is, simple) societies in which all of the members and groups are related to one another in much the same way that the parts of a machine are related: All of the parts move at the same time. A more differentiated, or complex, society, on the other hand, is characterized by organic solidarity. Much like the different organs of an animal, the different parts of society are partly autonomous but functionally interdependent, and coordination among them is based on reciprocal needs and responsibilities. Instead of being oriented to a single goal or event, as the peasant farmers who make up a simple agricultural society are all oriented to the changing seasons, the members of an organically integrated society are coordinated through their interdependence. An example would be the way in which the economic and political institutions of a complex society influence each other, even though they remain organizationally separate.

Later, in 1895, Durkheim published his *Rules of the Sociological Method,* in which he emphasized the concept of *social facts.* Facts pertaining directly to society itself, he said—such as degrees of integration, the rates at which various phenomena occur, and forms of organization—must be explained by their relationship to other social facts rather than in terms of facts about individuals. In his famous study *Suicide* (1897) he demonstrated that variations in suicide *rates* cannot be explained by reference to mental illness, climate, or poverty, but are instead related to variations in the degree of societal integration.

In *Suicide* he conceptualizes three distinct relationships between the individual and society and identifies a particular type of suicide with each one. First, there is *altruistic* suicide; here the individual is so thoroughly integrated into society that she or he places the unquestioned dictates of society above individual survival. Ritual suicide, such as *hara-kiri,* and the heroic self-sacrifice of a soldier who dies to save others represent this type. Second, there is *egoistic* suicide, which occurs when the individual feels estranged from society. The sense of being cut off from society, as may come from having been exposed as a criminal or failing in one's career, explains this type of suicide.

Finally, there is *anomic* suicide, which is due to the absence of any integration into society because there is, in effect, no coherent society into which the individual *can* be integrated. This occurs during a state of *anomie,* or "normlessness." Suicides during times of social upheaval, when people feel that there are no guidelines for behavior or standards by which to choose among goals, tend to be anomic in nature. A comparable situation on the individual level might occur when someone suddenly achieves vast wealth; all of the former economic restraints on behavior are now meaningless, and anomic suicide would be one response to this massive disorientation.

Continuing his efforts to identify the foundation of social order and thus the unique subject matter of sociology, Durkheim eventually developed the concept of the *conscience collective* and explored it in his analysis of primitive religion (*The Elementary Forms of the Religious Life*, 1912). The central importance of the *conscience collective* is not its similarity to the more general idea of culture, but its "coercive" effects on the members of society. Briefly, Durkheim sees humankind being guided and constrained unknowingly by the "rules" that are generated through social interaction. In their attempts to recognize the source of these constraints, which people are aware of even though they cannot identify their origin, the members of society develop the idea of "the sacred" as embodying this supernatural power and impute sacredness to various symbols, objects, and places. The beliefs and rituals that are focused on "the scared" serve to unite the worshippers and to sustain the integration of their norms and values, but they are actually the worship of society itself.

Thus, Durkheim argues, the power of society, becoming real as it constrains people, is the basic origin of religion. He went on to suggest that as we come to recognize this, we can substitute a sociological appreciation of the relations between individuals and society for the myths and ceremonies that constitute religion today. (In this belief Durkheim represents a further working out of the faith in human reason underlying so many of the earlier social theories. He did not, however, go so far as to try to establish a new "religion" along these lines, as Comte did, but was apparently content to know that his ventures into understanding society could produce this as well as other insights into the question of social order.)

Because he not only labored so diligently and so effectively to establish the foundations of sociology as a distinct science, but also made an academic career of his work, it is fitting that we think of Durkheim as the first *professional* sociologist.

Georg Simmel (1858–1918)   A contemporary of Durkheim, Simmel's most important contribution to sociology was his detailed exploration of the "forms" of social relationships. He avoided thinking of society as a superorganic whole, but viewed it instead as a network of social relationships which could, when properly analyzed and understood, be reduced to a relatively small number of prototypical forms. For this reason, his work is often referred to as *formal* sociology.

He believed, for instance, that competitive relationships, whether between business rivals, suitors, or nations at war, should be essentially similar in terms of the assumptions, attitudes, and strategies that characterize them. Similarly, dominant/submissive relationships should exhibit the same underlying characteristics, whether they involve the relations between a sergeant and a private or those between a parent and a child. Working along these lines, he developed generalized descriptions of "the stranger" and of "the poor person" as distinctive "social types." In more modern terms we would say that he concentrated on the analysis of social statuses and on the norms, roles, and processes that apply to relations among different types of statuses.

In other works Simmel pioneered in the analysis of how the *size* of human groups influences the relations among their members. For instance, the essential difference between a *dyad* (two people) and a *triad* (three people) lies in two facts that are related entirely to the numbers involved rather than to individuals themselves. First, the withdrawal of one member from a dyad terminates that group's existence altogether; to the extent, then, that its continued existence is important to both members, they will develop ways to compromise their differences and to skirt or ignore issues that might generate conflict. In a triad this is not the case. When three people are involved, coalitions are possible, so that any two members may unite against the third and thus determine the course of group activity on the basis of power rather than of individual interest. As groups grow larger, of course, more combinations and permutations of such relationships become possible.

Simmel published relatively little in the way of books, but contributed several important articles to American sociological journals. Perhaps his most important book was *Soziologie* (1908); excerpts from it are to be found in several sources today.

Because he gave a prominent place in his analyses to the presence of struggle and conflict in social relationships, Simmel is ordinarily taken to be one of the forerunners of conflict theory, the current status of which will be treated in the next section of this appendix. In his emphasis on the importance of numbers in determining the character of social groups, he can also be seen as a pioneer in the growing interest in developing mathematical models to describe interaction patterns and organizational change. Although he did not contribute an all-encompassing "sociological synthesis" in the way that Marx or Durkheim did, Simmel's close attention to some of the finer details of social relationships marks him as lastingly important in the development of sociology.

Brown Brothers

Max Weber (1864–1920) Along with Durkheim, Weber is seen today as one of the true giants in the history of sociology. (Marx's place in this pantheon may be still open to debate, but more and more sociologists agree that he deserves equal billing as a "giant.")

Perhaps the central thrust of Weber's work, even though he did not achieve an overall synthesis of his ideas, is that sociology must be concerned with the *meaning* of social action. He believed, in other words, that society cannot be understood without reference to the motives of social "actors," so that the interplay between human purposes and social organization is the central phenomenon with which sociology must be concerned. It was from this conviction that Weber developed the concept of *Verstehen,* or "standing in the place of"—a kind of "sympathetic" research method which involves the attempt to understand the social situation as the actor in that situation sees it.

With this idea in the background, Weber's wide-ranging explorations of many different topics—largely through the use of historical materials—begins to make sense. Rejecting Marx's insistence on the primacy of material factors, he examined the role of religious ideas in several societies (China, India, ancient Palestine, and Reformation Europe). As an aspect of what he saw as the increasing "rationalization" of Western society (that is, the increasing awareness of and emphasis on effectiveness and efficiency in the relations between means and ends in human endeavors), Weber analyzed the foundations of political authority and the nature of bureaucracy. And in connection with the broader problem of power in society, he also investigated cities as unique human groupings and the various foundations of social stratification. (Because his ideas have been so seminal in so many areas of sociology, his contributions are taken up in greater detail in several other chapters of this book [6, 8, 9, 11, and 12]; there is thus no need to attempt an intensive examination of them here.)

Weber also made important contributions to the philosophy of the social sciences. His insistence that human values cannot be derived from the objective analysis of society (an antipositivist position) stands as a landmark in the development of sociology as a science. Another aspect of this position was his distinction between the motives of the researcher (which may well be influenced by personal interests and cultural values) and the potential validity of the researcher's findings; interests and values can certainly influence *what* someone chooses to study, but this fact should have no bearing on the procedures through which that person's findings are evaluated as true or false.

Finally, Weber's emphasis on the distinction between the social and the physical sciences—resting essentially on the fact that we can understand the perspectives and motives of other human beings in a way that we can never understand animals or chemical elements—gave further impetus to the claim that sociology and the other social sciences have a legitimate, distinctive place within the realm of academic scholarship.

SOCIOLOGICAL THEORIES TODAY

Americans have not been particularly noted for the development of "grand" theories of society. Instead, given what is often seen as the practical, fact-oriented nature of American character, it is understandable that their contributions have been much more often in the nature of sophisticated research techniques and empirical studies. It is perhaps for this reason that the period during which Americans dominated sociology (between approximately 1930 and 1955) was, with one major exception, largely devoid of fundamental theoretical contributions.

Still, theory is necessary if research findings are to be fitted together into a larger whole. Whether or not an individual sociologist chooses to engage in "theory" as a central endeavor, he or she senses the need for a conceptual background from which meaningful questions can be drawn and against which the meaning of research findings can be assessed. But because the works of the "fathers" filled this need for the most part, few American sociologists have apparently felt it necessary until recently to devote their major energies to the extension of existing theories or to the building of new ones.

The major exception to this tendency was Talcott Parsons (1902–1979). Born in Colorado, the son of a Congregational minister who later became a college president, Parsons took his undergraduate work at Amherst, his graduate studies at Heidelberg, and began teaching at Harvard in 1927. He retired from Harvard in 1973. Although his structural-functional theory of society was certainly *the* sociological theory of the 1950s and early '60s, it has come under increasing attack (or at least increasing distinterest) as other schools of theory have engaged the interest of more and more sociologists.

Harvard University

Drawing heavily on what he saw as convergences among the central insights of Weber and Durkheim (and of the Italian theorist Vilfredo Pareto [1848–1923] and the British economist Alfred Marshall [1842–1924]), Parsons's initial contribution, *The Structure of Social Action* (1937) sought to link the "meaning" of Weber with the organic model of Durkheim to provide a model of social interaction within a cultural context that could be analyzed as a system. With the publication in 1951 of *The Social System*, Parsons's structural-functional model became the only full-fledged American sociological theory on the scene. Because the alternative theoretical perspectives that have become prominent since the 1960s have generally been at pains to point out their differences from "Parsonian" theory, it will be useful to begin this final section with a consideration of what they differ from.

Structural-Functionalism

This approach to theory clearly assumes that order is natural and that humankind's "culture-carrying" capacity is more important in the analysis of social order than human beings' physical existence and material interests. Order implies the existence of a system—a set of interrelated, interdependent components that continues to be distinguishable from its surroundings—and calls attention to the problem of how these components are interdependent and how their activities are coordinated so that they can continue to exist as a system.

The origins of this perspective lie in analogies to living systems such as animals and plants, and for this reason it is sometimes called an "organic" theory. The analogy has an ancient history and was expressed in modern form first by the British social anthropologists A. R. Radliffe-Brown (1881–1955) and Bronislaw Malinowski (1884–1942). Just as an animal eats and excretes, reacts to danger, and seeks safety and comfort, so any other living system should have "needs" and "parts" that specialize in satisfying these needs. Society thus has its own functional needs—those that must be fulfilled if it is to continue in existence—and it should be possible to identify specific social structures that fulfill these needs. (The meaning of the hyphenated term "structural-functional" reflects this assumption: Social structures develop to satisfy functional needs, so that structure reflects function. Further, since structure can be seen but function must be deduced, the obvious strategy is to identify structures first and then to determine their contributions to the ongoing system.)

Parsons has written voluminously, and it would be impossible to do justice here to the range and sophistication of his work. It may be briefly remarked, however, that the emphasis in his theorizing changed over the years, moving from a consideration of the patterned variations in social actors' perceptions of one another as they are appropriate to different types of interaction, to classifying the four basic functional needs of the social system and relating them to different social structures, and then to exploring the "generalized media," such as money and influence, through which different functional sectors of society "communicate" with one another and are thus coordinated. More recently, Parsons focused his attention on the evolution of societies. This evolution is viewed as a process of structural differentiation in which structures (and thus responsibility for meeting functions) become increasingly specialized and require new means of coordination. (In the absence of sufficient energy, or course, or more effective techniques of coordination, a pattern of *de*differentiation may occur, so that Parsons's neoevolutionary theory is by no means unilateral. It does not, in other words, predict inevitable progress, as did Comte and Condorcet.)

The other American sociologist most prominently associated with functionalism is Robert K. Merton (b. 1910). Merton has not worked at such a high level of abstraction and generality as Parsons, but his discussions of the functionalist approach and his illustrations of its applicability to many aspects of society, beginning in the 1930s, probably did more to make functionalism the foundation of what has been called "standard American sociology" (Mullins, 1973) than any of Parsons's writings. Merton introduced and systematized the concepts of *manifest* and *latent functions*—respectively, the recognized and unrecognized consequences of social actions and structures as they contribute to the functioning of groups and of society—and of manifest and latent *dys*functions (consequences that are harmful to functional needs). Since the late 1950s, he has concentrated much of his attention on the study of science as a unique sector of society and is generally recognized as the father of the sociology of science.

The chief criticism of functionalist theory has been that it assumes more order than actually exists in society. It therefore is said to be unable to deal effectively with social conflict and social change and thus is inadequate to the task of analyzing society in all of its varied aspects. Ideologically, too, it has been the target of substantial criticism. By emphasizing order, it is claimed, functionalism promotes a kind of complacency about the status quo which may block efforts to bring about improvements in justice and equality and which must necessarily define protest and other attempts to change "the system" as dysfunctional and therefore as wrong.

Despite these charges, structural-functionalism remains the major theoretical perspective for a substantial number of sociologists (and indeed has provided whatever theoretical unity may be found in this book; the preceding chapters, then, provide a more extended review of the functionalist viewpoint).

It will be useful next to look at an "assumed-order" perspective that treats human beings essentially as physical beings rather than simply as the occupants of social statuses embedded in a cultural system.

Exchange Theory

Functionalism takes account of social exchange—that is, the exchange of money for goods, of votes for political decisions, etc.—but sees it in a context dominated by cultural values and the functional needs of society. When exchange is taken as central to social relationships, however, it leads the sociologist in rather different directions.

Exchange theory is by no means as fully developed or as ambitious (in the sense of seeking to explain all of society) as functionalism, and it has gained prominence only within the last fifteen years or so. The principal insight it has to offer is that people need things from one another and that humans' exchanges are not necessarily equal. Its focus is thus on the quantitative aspects of exchange (Who gets more out of the relationship and under what circumstances?). Being aware of the possibility of unequal exchange, and thus of exploitation, human beings in this perspective are expected to be selfishly rational in calculating how best to achieve a maximally favorable exchange relationship and to try to establish circumstances in which they will regularly win rather than lose in exchange.

Out of these considerations one may turn to a basically psychologistic model, as has George C. Homans (b. 1910) or to a concern with the social-structural consequences of "patterned bargaining," as has Peter M. Blau (b. 1918). Homans, in *Social Behavior: Its Elementary Forms* (1961), takes up the stimulus-response model of psychologist B. F. Skinner and applies it to the behavior of people in groups; he finds that exchange is "rewarding" and thus "reinforcing" in the development of social relationships. Blau, in *Exchange and Power in Social Life* (1964), invokes a "norm of reciprocity," or a basic human sense that both parties to exchange should get equal value from it, and then suggests that social power grows out of and maintains situations in which exchange is not equal.

Both treatments of social exchange, however, seem to assume that order is natural in social relationships. Its task, then, is to explain the ways in which exchange helps to account for this and the ways in which it is fundamental to larger social structures. Ideas of reciprocity, though, or of fair exchange, scarcely represent the full range of cultural norms and values that must eventually be treated in a full-scale sociological theory.

Complementing the *quantitative* analysis of social exchange, then, must be a concern with its *qualitative* aspects, or the question of what sorts of things are appropriately exchanged for what other sorts of things. Chapter 10 of this book suggests, for instance, that although people need various qualitatively different things from one another—not only goods and services, but also power, love, and support for beliefs, among others—these are not all appropriately exchangeable for one another. We tend to frown, for example, on the exchange of sex for money and on using political power to promote a particular religious belief. Out of such reasoning is developed an idea of the foundations of social institutions and some of the basic rules that govern them as exchange systems.

It is apparent that exchange theory is a promising approach to the analysis of society. With its emphasis on individual needs and the structures through which exchange takes place, it has certain important elements in common with conflict theory (to be discussed below); with its assumption of order and the integration of different human needs, it is not entirely unrelated to functionalism. It may, then, provide in the future a bridge between two major theoretical perspectives which seem at present to be sharply in conflict with each other.

Conflict Theory

Based very clearly on the insights of Karl Marx, conflict theory today shares with exchange theory an emphasis on struggle and competition among people for the scarce necessities (and luxuries) of life. It differs, however, in rejecting the assumption that order is natural; instead, it takes for granted that order comes about only when it is imposed by one group on others, whether this domination is economic or political or both, and that inequality is an inevitable consequence of this. Since society's class structure is the most visible evidence of continuing inequality, it tends to be the focal point of conflict theorists' investigations.

Underlying the systematically unequal distribution of the necessities and luxuries of life is *power*. Contemporary conflict theory defines power in the broadest sense, covering not only the potential exercise of physical force (whether legitimate or not), but also power based on the possession of wealth and prestige. It is only power that resolves conflict and imposes order, and it is most effective when it is invisible.

The widespread existence of order, then, is in the end due to the various ways—not all of them conscious or manipulative—through which the more powerful groups or classes in society secure power to themselves and persuade others of its legitimacy. Competition and conflict between different elements of the exploited classes may be encouraged to a limited extent as one way to distract attention from the upper classes' power and privileges.

Another way in which this is accomplished is through the dissemination of an ideology (a shared view of the way things ought to be) that justifies the present conditions of inequality so that the lower classes are content with their lot. (Although current views are more sophisticated, Marx's statement that "religion is the opium of the people" illustrates this idea.)

There is some contradiction between this view and the basic assumption that the objective material conditions of their lives determines people's norms, values, and definitions of the situation, an idea central to the field known as the sociology of knowledge. This assumption flows naturally from the idea that if culture is to be useful, and thus maintained, it must be an effective guide to behavior, and behavior always takes place in material circumstances. Therefore, culture must be rooted in these circumstances and subordinate to them, rather than an independent influence on social behavior.

The contradiction, however, is explained as a relatively temporary condition. Through their control of the mass media, the educational system, and even religious institutions, the more powerful groups in society can encourage "false consciousness" for a period of time. But as material conditions change, and as social theorists discover the reality of the situation, the false picture of the world becomes increasingly inadequate as a guide to behavior and cannot continue indefinitely to blind the masses to their objective disadvantages.

Although C. Wright Mills (1916–1962), in his analysis of the ruling class in America and his critique of functionalism (*The Power Elite*, 1956, and *The Sociological Imagination*, 1959), clearly paved the way for a revival of conflict theory, Ralf Dahrendorf's *Class and Class Conflict in Industrial Society* (1959) is usually taken to have signaled the revival of the Marxist perspective in contemporary sociology. Another leading conflict theorist has been Lewis A. Coser (b. 1913), although his work (*The Functions of Social Conflict*, 1956, and *Continuities in the Study of Social Conflict*, 1967) does not make conflict so central to social life as does that of others. In drawing on the work of Simmel, Coser also shows that the roots of conflict theory go back to more than just a single individual.

Because it concentrates on the reasons for structured inequality in society, conflict theory seems almost inevitably linked with active efforts to redress such injustices. If a social structure is demonstrably unfair to some groups in society, it is difficult to avoid becoming morally indignant and then seeking to correct the situation. The connection, in fact, between conflict theory and "radical sociology" (an activist sociology that stresses improving society through the immediate use of sociological knowledge) is thus quite natural, even though it is not usually the theorists themselves who are deeply involved in political action.

Although its link to political activity may make conflict theory especially attractive to some and especially threatening to others, this cannot be taken to demonstrate either the validity or the falsity of the theory itself. Without the political passions that now surround the theory, it is possible that sociologists would have an easier time keeping it in perspective *as a theory* and making greater progress in finding how it and other theories can contribute to a more comprehensive and empirically valid understanding of society.

Symbolic Interactionism and Ethnomethodology

Although representatives of these two perspectives would probably deny any close connection between them, it is useful to link them here because of their predominant concern with how human beings symbolize their experiences and cooperate in "constructing" social reality. Both theories emphasize the individual's assessment of the social situation and stress the importance of learning how shared definitions of the situation (including the participants' purposes and relationships) are developed and modified.

Symbolic interactionism has been called "the loyal opposition" in American sociological theory (Mullins, 1973) because, although it has provided a base for persistent criticisms of structural-functionalism, both perspectives share a number of central concepts. Its most notable representative today is Herbert Blumer (b. 1900), who has elaborated the ideas developed by William I. Thomas (1863–1947) and particularly those of George Herbert Mead (1863–1931; see Chapter 4, on socialization, for a discussion of Mead's contributions).

To the symbolic interactionist, the most important social phenomenon is the fact that individuals define (or conceptualize, or "symbolize") the situations in which they interact and then behave in response to the meanings that they have attributed to those situations. Perhaps this central focus is best summed up in Thomas's famous dictum: "If men define situations as real, they are real in their consequences" (that is, the situations *as defined* by humans become real *because* they have real consequences—people's responses to what they have "seen" in the situation). Thomas's original illustration of this idea was an anecdote about a paranoid man on a bus: *Believing* that the other passengers were his enemies, he pulled out a gun and shot one of them, thus demonstrating that it is the way we define a situation (rather than the situation itself) that influences our behavior (Thomas, 1928, p. 384).

From this point of view, society exists simply because people believe that it exists and then behave on the basis of this belief. Social structures, then, cannot be understood without an awareness that they are the creations of their participants, and this awareness shows us also that the same processes that produced these structures can also change them.

The importance of this insight cannot be denied; indeed, it is central to the discussion of public opinion in Chapter 17. At the same time, however, it has not yet been able to serve as the foundation of a more comprehensive theory of society in the way that the basic assumptions of the functionalists have. The symbolic-interactionist perspective is particularly adapted to the understanding of microsociological topics (behavior in small groups, deviance), but has had relatively little to say about such macrosociological topics as social institutions and social stratification.

Despite the fact that it has been paired here with symbolic interactionism because of its emphasis on communication, ethnomethodology (literally, "the study of the methods of the people") differs significantly from symbolic interactionism. For one thing, its roots are primarily in European philosophy rather than in American sociology, even though the perspective itself is almost entirely an American specialty. The word itself was coined by Harold Garfinkel (b. 1924) in the 1960s to identify a particular area of questions and research methods centering on the ways in which people in everyday life "negotiate" common understandings of their situations, actions, and purposes in order to sustain a shared sense of meaning and order in social life. The philosophical importance of such questions was developed by Edmund Husserl (1859–1938), Ludwig Wittgenstein (1889–1951), and Alfred Schutz (1899–1959) in their works in a branch of philosophy called phenomenology. All were concerned in one way or another with the ways in which human beings construct reality symbolically and thus impose order on the universe.

More specifically than the symbolic interactionists, ethnomethodologists seek to discover the hidden rules that govern communication among people and ways in which they account for their actions and for unexpected events. They are looking, in other words, for the "syntax" of verbal interaction and explanation in the same way that linguists look for the rules that structure language itself. The ways in which people signal their intentions to one another (often without being aware of it), the rules that seem to govern the order in which participants speak during informal interaction, and such processes as bidding at auctions are examples of the specific topics in which ethnomethodologists are interested. (As a simple illustration, we usually can sense without being explicitly aware of it that when someone begins a sentence with "*Well* . . . ," he or she is thinking of ending the conversation.)

Some other perspectives within sociology that have been strongly influenced by phenomenology include phenomenological sociology itself (illustrated in the work of Peter Berger, George Psathas, and Jack D. Douglas) and in what has been called "dramaturgical sociology" (in which social relationships are viewed as being "staged" for various audiences). The well-known books by Erving Goffman illustrate the latter.

It is clear that meaning and communication, rather than the physical aspects of society, are central to both symbolic interactionism and ethnomethodology. The assumption that social order is problematic rather than natural, however, is more closely associated with the latter. In concentrating on how shared definitions of the situation are *negotiated*—that is, developed anew in each instance of interaction—the ethnomethodologist must of necessity assume that order has to be created rather than simply discovered. The symbolic interactionists, on the other hand, more often seem to take order for granted and concern themselves with how people come to perceive it.

Yet both perspectives employ Weber's method of *Verstehen*, acknowledge the contributions of Marx to the sociology of knowledge, and have undeniably seized on certain phenomena that cannot be ignored by any sociological theory. Neither one pretends to explain society as a whole, however, and so more than the other theories discussed above, they must be viewed as incomplete. Precisely how either one might contribute to a future theoretical synthesis is not yet clear, but the student of sociological theory can certainly look forward to continued efforts by their proponents to extend their application to more aspects of society.

SUMMARY

Scientific theory is the summing up of a field's knowledge in the form of interrelated generalizations that describe relations among the regularities that are found in its subject matter. In sociology, with its particularly complex subject matter and imperfect information about society, theory tends to be in the form of conceptual schemes rather than rigorous deductions from research findings.

In the construction of conceptual schemes, assumptions must be made which are not themselves directly testable, even though they may reflect a good deal of the theorist's personal experience. The ways in which two fundamental questions about the foundations of social regularities are answered seem to provide four reasonably distinct theoretical perspectives within contemporary sociology. These questions ask whether the physical or cultural aspect of society is more important and whether social order is natural or problematic.

Although social thought prior to the middle of of the nineteenth century was concerned largely with the practical and the political, the "founding fathers" made giant steps between 1880 and 1920 in expanding the sociological perspective and turning its development away from the practical toward the more abstract character of science. Marx and Simmel stressed the physical aspects of society and took order to be problematic; Comte, Durkheim, and Weber, the forerunners of functionalism, placed more emphasis on the cultural nature of society and seemed to accept social order as natural.

Today, although functionalism (particularly in the form of Parsons's structural-functionalism) has lost the dominant position it held twenty years ago, it remains perhaps the most fully developed sociological theory we have. It is challenged now on both ideological and empirical grounds: that it tends to promote acceptance of the status quo and that it is unable to deal adequately with social change. Conflict theory, its chief challenger, is based principally on the work of Marx and is seeking to build a theory of society based on the assumption that order is problematic because of the continual struggle among human beings to satisfy their material needs.

Two promising but less well-developed theoretical perspectives that are attracting increasing attention from sociologists concentrate on social exchange and on the social construction of reality. The former emphasizes analyses of the social patterns through which various human needs are satisfied through exchange, whereas the latter concentrates on discovering the rules that underlie the communication practices through which people construct shared meanings and definitions of social reality.

There is clearly a lack of consensus within sociology today over which of these perspectives is the most promising foundation for genuinely adequate theory of society. Unfortunately, discussions of sociological theory tend to become intertwined with ideologies, so that moral and political concerns may impede the cautious, systematic extension and testing of different theories. Yet because theory is so important to science, and because valid empirical predictions are the ultimate test of the "goodness" of any theory, we may anticipate that at some point in the future a synthesis will be forged which incorporates the major insights of each perspective. In the meantime, conflict among theories can only be functional for sociology itself.

SUGGESTED READINGS

Comprehensive Texts on Sociological Theory

Coser, Lewis, *Masters of Sociological Thought*, 2d ed. (New York: Harcourt Brace Jovanovich, 1977).

Duke, James T., *Conflict and Power in Social Life* (Provo, Utah: Brigham Young University Press, 1976).

Mullins, Nicholas C., *Theory and Theory Groups in Contemporary American Sociology* (New York: Harper & Row, 1973).

Ritzer, George, *Sociology: A Multiple Paradigm Science* (Boston: Allyn and Bacon, 1975).

Rossides, Daniel W., *The History and Nature of Sociological Theory* (Boston: Houghton Mifflin, 1978).

Turner, Jonathan H., *The Structure of Sociological Theory*, rev. ed. (Homewood, Ill.: Dorsey, 1978).

Representatives of Classical Theoretical Positions

Durkheim, Emile, *The Rules of the Sociological Method* [1895], translated by Sarah A. Solovay and John H. Mueller, ed. by George E. G. Catlin (Chicago: University of Chicago Press, 1938; reprinted by Free Press in Glencoe, Ill., 1958).

Marx, Karl, *Selected Writings in Sociology and Social Philosophy*, edited by T. B. Bottomore and Maximilien Rubel (New York: McGraw-Hill, 1956).

Simmel, Georg, *On Individuality and Social Forms: Selected Writings*, ed. by Donald Levine (Chicago: University of Chicago Press, 1971).

Weber, Max, *The Theory of Social and Economic Organization* [1922], trans. by A. M. Henderson and Talcott Parsons (Glencoe, Ill.: Free Press, 1947).

Representatives of Contemporary Theoretical Positions

Berger, Peter L., and Thomas Luckmann, *The Social Construction of Reality* (Garden City, N.Y.: Doubleday, 1966).

Blau, Peter M., *Exchange and Power in Social Life* (New York: Wiley, 1964).

Blumer, Herbert, *Symbolic Interactionism: Perspective and Method* (Englewood Cliffs, N.J.: Prentice-Hall, 1969).

Coser, Lewis, *The Functions of Social Conflict* (Glencoe, Ill.: Free Press, 1956).

Dahrendorf, Ralf, *Essays in the Theory of Society* (Stanford, Calif.: Stanford University Press, 1968).

Garfinkel, Harold, *Studies in Ethnomethodology* (Englewood Cliffs, N.J.: Prentice-Hall, 1967).

Homans, George C., *Social Behavior: Its Elementary Forms* (New York: Harcourt, Brace, 1961).

Merton, Robert K., *Social Theory and Social Structure*, rev. ed. (Glenco, Ill.: Free Press, 1957).

Mills, C. Wright, *The Sociological Imagination* (New York: Oxford University Press, 1959).

Parsons, Talcott, *The Evolution of Societies* (Englewood Cliffs, N.J.: Prentice-Hall, 1977).

Psathas, George, ed., *Phenomenological Sociology: Issues and Applications* (New York: Wiley, 1973).

Bibliography

ADORNO, T. W., et al., *The Authoritarian Personality* (New York: Harper & Row, 1950).

ALLPORT, Gordon, *The Nature of Prejudice* (Reading, Mass.: Addison-Wesley, 1954).

ARIES, Phillipe, *Centuries of Childhood: A Social History of Family Life* (New York: Vintage, 1962).

BANFIELD, Edward C., *Political Influence* (New York: Free Press, 1961).

BECKER, Howard W., Blanche Geer, Everett C. Hughes, and Anselm L. Strauss, *Boys in White* (Chicago: University of Chicago Press, 1961).

BEDAU, Hugo Adam, *The Death Penalty in America* (New York: Doubleday/Anchor, 1964).

BELL, Robert R., *Social Deviance*, rev. ed. (Homewood, Ill.: Dorsey, 1976).

BELLAH, Robert N., "Civil Religion in America, " *Daedalus* (Winter 1967): 1–21.

_____, *Beyond Belief* (New York: Harper & Row, 1970).

BENDIX, Reinhard, and Seymour Martin Lipset, eds., *Class, Status and Power*, 2d ed. (New York: Free Press, 1966).

BERELSON, Bernard, *Content Analysis* (New York: Free Press, 1952).

BERGER, Bennett M., *Working Class Suburb* (Berkeley: University of California Press, 1960).

BERGER, Peter L., *Invitation to Sociology* (New York: Doubleday/Anchor, 1963).

_____, *The Sacred Canopy: Elements of a Sociological Theory of Religion* (New York: Doubleday, 1967).

BERGER, Peter L., and Thomas Luckmann, *The Social Construction of Reality* (Garden City, N.Y.: Doubleday, 1966).

BERKOWITZ, Leonard, "Aggression: Psychological Aspects," in David L. Sills, ed., *International Encyclopedia of the Social Sciences*, Vol. 1 (New York: Macmillan and Free Press, 1968), pp. 168–174.

BERNS, Walter, *For Capital Punishment: Crime and the Morality of the Death Penalty* (New York: Basic Books, 1979).

BERRY, Brewton, and Henry L. Tischler, *Race and Ethnic Relations*, 4th ed. (Boston: Houghton Mifflin, 1978).

BLAU, Peter M., *Exchange and Power in Social Life* (New York: Wiley, 1964).

BLAU, Peter M., and Otis Dudley Duncan, *The American Occupational Structure* (New York: Wiley, 1967).

BLAU, Peter M., and W. Richard Scott, *Formal Organizations* (San Francisco: Chandler, 1962).

BLUMER, Herbert, "Collective Behavior," in Alfred McClung Lee, ed., *New Outline of the Principles of Sociology* (New York: Barnes and Noble, 1951).

——, *Symbolic Interactionism: Perspective and Method* (Englewood Cliffs, N.J.: Prentice-Hall, 1969).

BOGARDUS, Emory S., *Social Distance* (Yellow Springs, Ohio: Antioch College Press, 1959).

BORUCH, Robert F., and Henry W. Riecken, eds., *Experimental Testing of Public Policy: The Proceedings of the 1974 Social Science Conference on Social Experiments* (Boulder, Colorado: Westview Press, 1975).

BOTTOMORE, T. B., and Maximilien Rubel, eds., *Karl Marx: Selected Writings in Sociology and Social Philosophy* (New York: McGraw-Hill, 1956).

BROWN, Dee, *Hear That Lonesome Whistle Blow* (New York: Holt, Rinehart and Winston, 1977).

CAMPBELL, Angus, Philip E. Converse, Warren E. Miller, and Donald E. Stokes, *The American Voter* abridged ed., (New York: Wiley, 1964).

CAMPBELL, Angus, Philip E. Converse, and Willard L. Rodgers, *The Quality of American Life* (New York: Russell Sage Foundation, 1976).

CANTRIL, Hadley, *The Invasion from Mars* (Princeton, N.J.: Princeton University Press, 1940).

CHOMSKY, Noam, *Language and Mind* (New York: Harcourt Brace Jovanovich, 1972).

CHRISTENSEN, Harold T., ed., *Handbook of Marriage and the Family* (Chicago: Rand McNally, 1964).

CICOUREL, Aaron, and John J. Kitsuse, "A Note on the Use of Official Statistics," *Social Problems* 11 (1963): 131–139.

COLE, Stephen, *The Sociological Method* (Chicago: Rand McNally, 1972).

COOLEY, Charles Horton, *Human Nature and the Social Order* [1902] (New York: Schocken, 1964).

CORTES, Juan B., and Florence M. Gatti, *Delinquency and Crime: A Biopsychosocial Approach* (New York: Seminar Press, 1972).

COSER, Lewis, *The Functions of Social Conflict* (New York: Free Press, 1956).

——, *Continuities in the Study of Social Conflict* (New York: Free Press, 1967).

_____, *Masters of Sociological Thought*, 2d ed. (New York: Harcourt Brace Jovanovich, 1977).

CRESSEY, Donald R., ed., *The Prison: Studies in Institutional Organization and Change* (New York: Holt, Rinehart and Winston, 1961).

DAHL, Robert A., *Who Governs?: Democracy and Power in an American City* (New Haven, Conn.: Yale University Press, 1961).

DAHRENDORF, Ralf, *Class and Class Conflict in Industrial Society* (Stanford, Calif.: Stanford University Press, 1959).

_____, *Essays in the Theory of Society* (Stanford, Calif.: Stanford University Press, 1968).

DAVID, Deborah S., and Robert Brannon, eds., *The Forty-Nine Percent Majority: The Male Sex Role* (Reading, Mass.: Addison-Wesley, 1976).

DAVIS, James, *Elementary Survey Analysis* (Englewood Cliffs, N.J.: Prentice-Hall, 1971).

DAVIS, Kingsley, *Human Society* (New York: Macmillan, 1948).

DAVIS, Kingsley, and Wilbert E. Moore, "Some Principles of Social Stratification," *American Sociological Review* 10 (April 1945): 242–249.

DAVISON, W. Phillips, "The Public Opinion Process," in Reo M. Christenson and Robert O. McWilliams, eds., *Voice of the People: Readings in Public Opinion and Propaganda* (New York: McGraw-Hill, 1962).

de BEAUVOIR, Simone, *The Second Sex* (New York: Knopf, 1953).

de GRAZIA, Sebastian, *Of Time, Work, and Leisure* (New York: Doubleday/Anchor, 1964).

DeVOS, George A., "Suicide in Cross-Cultural Perspective," in H. Resnick, ed., *Suicidal Behaviors* (Boston: Little, Brown, 1968).

DOLLARD, John, *Caste and Class in a Southern Town* (New Haven, Conn.: Yale University Press, 1937).

DOMHOFF, G. William, *Who Rules America?* (Englewood Cliffs, N.J.: Prentice-Hall, 1967).

_____, *The Higher Circles: The Governing Class in America* (New York: Random House, 1971).

DOUGLAS, Jack D., ed., *Introduction to Sociology: Situations and Structures* (New York: Free Press, 1973).

DUKE, James T., *Conflict and Power in Social Life* (Provo, Utah: Brigham Young University Press, 1976).

DURKHEIM, Emile, *The Division of Labor in Society* [1893], translated by George Simpson (Glencoe, Ill.: Free Press, 1964).

_____, *The Rules of Sociological Method* [1895], translated by Sarah A. Solovay, John U. Meuller, and edited by George E. G. Catlin (Glencoe, Ill.: Free Press, 1958).

_____, *Suicide* [1897], translated by J. A. Spaulding and George Simpson (Glencoe, Ill.: Free Press, 1951).

_____, *The Elementary Forms of the Religious Life* [1912], translated by Joseph Ward Swain (Glencoe, Ill.: Free Press, 1947).

EAMES, Edwin, and Judith G. Goode, *Urban Poverty in a Cross-Cultural Context* (New York: Free Press, 1973).

ELKIN, Frederick, and Gerald Handel, *The Child and Society: The Process of Socialization,* 2d ed. (New York: Random House, 1972).

ERIKSON, Erik H., *Childhood and Society* (New York: Norton, 1952).

ERIKSON, Kai T., "Notes on the Sociology of Deviance," in Howard S. Becker, ed., *The Other Side: Perspectives on Deviance* (New York: Free Press, 1964).

ETZIONI, Amitai, *Modern Organizations* (Englewood Cliffs, N.J.: Prentice-Hall, 1964).

_____, *A Comparative Analysis of Complex Organizations,* rev. ed. (New York: Free Press, 1975).

FANFANI, Amintore, *Catholicism, Protestantism, and Capitalism* (New York: Sheed and Ward, 1955).

FARIS, Robert E. L., *Chicago Sociology, 1920–1932* (San Francisco: Chandler, 1967).

FAULKNER, Joseph E., ed., *Religion's Influence in Contemporary Society* (Columbus, Ohio: Merrill, 1972).

FEAGIN, Joe R., *Race and Ethnic Relations* (Englewood Cliffs, N.J.: Prentice-Hall, 1978).

FEDERICO, Ronald C., *Sociology,* 2d ed. (Reading, Mass.: Addison-Wesley, 1979).

FILENE, Peter Gabriel, *Him/Her/Self* (New York: Harcourt Brace Jovanovich, 1975).

FRANKE, Richard H., and James D. Kaul, "The Hawthorne Experiments: First Statistical Interpretation," *American Sociological Review* 43 5 (Oct. 1978): 623–643.

FREUD, Sigmund, *The Future of an Illusion* [1927], translated by W. D. Robson-Scott (New York: Doubleday, 1957).

FRIEDAN, Betty, *The Feminine Mystique* (New York: Dell, 1963).

FRIEDL, Ernestine, "Society and Sex Roles," *Human Nature* 1, 4 (April 1978): 68–75.

GALLUP OPINION INDEX, "Religion in America" (Report Number 70, April 1971).

GAMSON, William A., *Power and Discontent* (Homewood, Ill.: Dorsey, 1968).

GAMST, Frederick C., and Edward Norbeck, eds., *Ideas of Culture: Sources and Uses* (New York: Holt, Rinehart and Winston, 1976).

GANS, Herbert J., *The Urban Villagers* (New York: Free Press, 1962).

GARFINKEL, Harold, *Studies in Ethnomethodology* (Englewood Cliffs, N.J.: Prentice-Hall, 1967).

GLOCK, Charles Y., and Robert N. Bellah, eds., *The New Religious Consciousness* (Berkeley: University of California Press, 1977).

GOFFMAN, Erving, *The Presentation of Self in Everyday Life* (New York: Doubleday, 1959).

_____, *Asylums* (New York: Doubleday/Anchor, 1961).

_____, *Stigma* (Englewood Cliffs, N.J.: Prentice-Hall, 1963).

_____, "On Face-Work," in his *Interaction Ritual: Essays on Face-to-Face Behavior* (New York: Doubleday/Anchor, 1967).

GOODE, William J., *World Revolution and Family Patterns* (New York: Free Press, 1963).

GOODE, William J., and Paul K. Hatt, *Methods of Social Research* (New York: McGraw-Hill, 1952).

GORNICK, Vivian, and Barbara K. Moran, eds., *Women in Sexist Society: Studies in Power and Powerlessness* (New York: Basic Books, 1971).

GOULDNER, Alvin W., *The Coming Crisis of Western Sociology* (New York: Basic Books, 1970).

_____, "Reciprocity and Autonomy in Functional Theory," in Llewellyn Gross, ed., *Symposium in Sociological Theory* (Evanston, Ill.: Row-Peterson, 1959), pp. 241–270.

GREELEY, Andrew, "Council or Encyclical?" in *Review of Religious Research* **18** (Fall 1976): 3–24.

HAMMOND, Philip E., ed., *Sociologists at Work* (New York: Basic Books, 1964).

HARE, A. Paul, Robert F. Bales, and Edgar F. Borgatta, eds., *Small Groups*, rev. ed. (New York: Knopf, 1965).

HARRIS, Chauncey D., and Edward L. Ullman, "The Nature of Cities," *Annals of the American Academy of Political and Social Science* **13** (November 1945): 7–17.

HAUSER, Philip M., and Leo F. Schnore, eds., *The Study of Urbanization* (New York: Wiley, 1965).

HAUSKNECHT, Murray, *The Joiners* (Towata, N.J.: Bedminster, 1962).

HOCKETT, Charles F., *The State of the Art* (The Hague, Netherlands: Mouton, 1968).

HOFFER, Eric, *The True Believer: Thoughts on the Nature of Mass Movements* (New York: Harper & Bros., 1951).

HOMANS, George C., *The Human Group* (New York: Harcourt, 1950).

_____, *Social Behavior: Its Elementary Forms* (New York: Harcourt Brace, 1961).

HUMPHRIES, Laud, *Tearoom Trade: Impersonal Sex in Public Places* (Chicago: Aldine, 1970).

HUNTER, Floyd, *Community Power Structure* (New York: Doubleday/Anchor, 1953).

HYMAN, Herbert, *et al.*, *Interviewing in Social Research* (Chicago: University of Chicago Press, 1954).

JANIS, Irving L., *Victims of Groupthink* (Boston: Houghton Mifflin, 1972).

JENCKS, Christopher, *et al.*, *Inequality: A Reassessment of the Effect of Schooling in America* (New York: Basic Books, 1972).

KATZ, Daniel, and Robert L. Kahn, *The Social Psychology of Organizations*, 2d ed. (New York: Wiley, 1978).

KLAPP, Orrin E., *Currents of Unrest: An Introduction to Collective Behavior* (New York: Holt, Rinehart and Winston, 1972).

KOHN, Melvin L., *Class and Conformity: A Study in Values* (Homewood, Ill.: Dorsey, 1969).

KROEBER, Alfred L., and Clyde Kluckhohn, *Culture: A Critical Review of Concepts and Definitions* (New York: Vintage Books, 1963).

LANG, Kurt, and Gladys Engel Lang, *Collective Behavior* (New York: Crowell, 1961).

LEE, Everett S., and Leon F. Bouvier, "Endless Movement: America as a Nation of Migrants," *Population Profile Series* (Washington, Conn.: Center for Information on America, 1977).

LeMASTERS, E. E., *Parents in Modern America* (Homewood, Ill.: Dorsey, 1970).

LEMERT, Edwin M., *Human Deviance, Social Problems, and Social Control*, 2d ed. (Englewood Cliffs, N.J.: Prentice-Hall, 1972).

LESLIE, Gerald, *The Family in Social Context* (New York: Oxford University Press, 1976).

LEWIS, Oscar, "The Culture of Poverty," *Scientific American*, 215 (1966): 19–25.

LIEBOW, Elliott, *Tally's Corner: A Study of Negro Streetcorner Men* (Boston: Little, Brown, 1967).

LINTON, Ralph, *The Study of Man* (New York: Appleton-Century-Crofts, 1936).

LIPSET, Seymour Martin, *Political Man* (New York: Doubleday, 1960).

———, *Revolution and Counterrevolution* (New York: Basic Books, 1968).

LIPSET, Seymour Martin, and Reinhard Bendix, *Social Mobility in Industrial Society* (Berkeley: University of California Press, 1964).

LOFFLAND, John, *Analyzing Social Settings* (Belmont, Calif.: Wadsworth, 1971).

LYND, Robert S., and Helen M. Lynd, *Middletown* (New York: Harcourt, Brace, 1929).

———, *Middletown in Transition* (New York: Harcourt, Brace, 1937).

McCAGHY, Charles M., *Deviant Behavior: Crime, Conflict, and Interest Groups* (New York: Macmillan, 1976).

MacLEAN, Charles, *The Wolf Children* (New York: Hill and Wang, 1978).

MALINOWSKI, Bronislaw, *Magic, Science and Religion* (New York: Doubleday/Anchor, 1954).

MARSHALL, James, *Intention in Law and Society* (New York: Funk and Wagnalls, 1968).

MAUS, Marcel, *The Gift* [1927] (New York: Norton, 1967).

MAYER, Martin, *The Lawyers* (New York: Harper & Row, 1976).

———, *The Bankers* (New York: Ballantine, 1976).

MEAD, George Herbert, *Mind, Self and Society* (Chicago: University of Chicago Press, 1934).

MERTON, Robert K., "Discrimination and the American Creed," in Robert M. McIver, ed., *Discrimination and National Welfare* (New York: Harper & Row, 1949), pp. 99–126.

———, "The Self-Fulfilling Prophecy," in his *Social Theory and Social Structure*, rev. ed. (New York: Free Press, 1957), pp. 421–436.

———, "Social Structure and Anomie," in his *Social Theory and Social Structure* (*Ibid.*), pp. 131–160.

MERTON, Robert K., M. Fiske, and Patricia L. Kendall, *The Focused Interview* (New York: Free Press, 1956).

MERTON, Robert K., and Robert Nisbet, eds., *Contemporary Social Problems*, 4th ed. (New York: Harcourt Brace Jovanovich, 1976).

MICHELSON, Williams, *Man and His Urban Environment* (Reading, Mass.: Addison-Wesley, 1970).

MILL, John Stuart, *A System of Logic* [1843] (London: Longmans, 1961).

MILLER, Walter B., "Lower Class Culture as a Generating Milieu of Gang Delinquency," *Journal of Social Issues* **14** (April 1958): 5–19.

MILLS, C. Wright, *White Collar: The American Middle Classes* (New York: Oxford University Press, 1951).

———, *The Power Elite* (New York: Oxford University Press, 1956).

———, *The Sociological Imagination* (New York: Oxford University Press, 1959).

MITCHELL, William C., *Sociological Analysis and Politics: The Theories of Talcott Parsons* (Englewood Cliffs, N.J.: Prentice-Hall, 1967).

MOORE, Wilbert E., *The Conduct of the Corporation* (New York: Random House, 1962).

MULLINS, Nicholas C., *Theory and Theory Groups in Contemporary American Sociology* (New York: Harper & Row, 1973).

MURDOCK, George Peter, *Social Structure* (New York: Macmillan, 1949).

MYRDAL, Gunnar, *An American Dilemma* (New York: Harper & Row, 1944).

NETTLER, Gwynn, *Social Concerns* (New York: McGraw-Hill, 1976).

NEWSWEEK MAGAZINE, "Special Report: Saving the Family" (May 15, 1978): 63–90.

NEW YORK TIMES, "Young Adult Church Attendance Found Stabilized in a Gallup Poll" (January 4, 1976).

———, "Poll Finds 34% Share 'Born Again' Feeling" (September 26, 1976).

———, "Meditation, Yoga, Mysticism Said to be Gaining Popularity in U.S." (November 18, 1976).

———, "Poverty is Found Less Persistent but Wider Spread than Thought" (July 17, 1977).

———, "The Family in Transition: A Challenge from Within" (November 27, 1977).

———, "Test in Seattle Challenges Minimum Income Plan" (February 5, 1979).

NYE, F. Ivan, "Child Adjustment in Broken and in Unhappy Unbroken Homes," *Marriage and Family Living* **19** (November 1957): 356–361.

O'CONNOR, Len, *Clout: Mayor Daley and His City* (Chicago: Henry Regnery, 1975).

O'DEA, Thomas F., *The Sociology of Religion* (Englewood Cliffs, N.J.: Prentice-Hall, 1966).

OGBURN, William F., *Social Change* [1922] (New York: Viking, 1950).

———, *On Culture and Social Change*, edited and with an introduction by Otis Dudley Duncan (Chicago: University of Chicago Press, 1964).

ORUM, Anthony M., *Introduction to Political Sociology* (Englewood Cliffs, N.J.: Prentice-Hall, 1978).

PARSONS, Talcott, *The Social System* (Glencoe, Ill.: Free Press, 1951).

———, *The Evolution of Societies* (Englewood Cliffs, N.J.: Prentice-Hall, 1977).

———, ed., *American Sociology: Problems, Perspectives, Methods* (New York: Basic Books, 1968).

PARSONS, Talcott, and Neil J. Smelser, *Economy and Society* (New York: Free Press, 1956).

PETTIGREW, Thomas F., *A Profile of the American Negro* (Princeton, N.J.: Van Nostrand, 1964).

PHILLIPS, Bernard S., *Social Research: Strategy and Tactics* (New York: Macmillan, 1966).

PIAGET, Jean, *The Construction of Reality in the Child* (New York: Basic Books, 1954).

PINKNEY, Alphonso, *Black Americans,* 2d ed. (Englewood Cliffs, N.J.: Prentice-Hall, 1975).

POPE, Liston, *Preachers and Millhands* (New Haven, Conn.: Yale University Press, 1942).

PRICE, Derek J. de Solla, *Little Science, Big Science* (New York: Columbia University Press, 1963).

PSATHAS, George, ed., *Phenomenological Sociology: Issues and Applications* (New York: Wiley, 1973).

Public Opinion 1, 5 (Nov./Dec. 1978): "American Ethnic and Religious Groups" pp. 32–34.

REDFIELD, Robert, *The Primitive World and Its Transformations* (Ithaca, N.Y.: Cornell University Press, 1953).

REISS, Ira L., *The Family System in America* (Homewood, Ill.: Dorsey, 1971).

REYNOLDS, Larry T., and Janice M. Reynolds, eds., *The Sociology of Sociology* (New York: McKay, 1970).

RIESMAN, David, *The Lonely Crowd* (New Haven, Conn.: Yale University Press, 1950).

RILEY, Matilda White, *Sociological Research: A Case Approach* (New York: Harcourt Brace and World, 1963).

RITZER, George, *Sociology: A Multiple Paradigm Science* (Boston: Allyn and Bacon, 1975).

ROBERTSON, Roland, ed., *Sociology of Religion: Selected Readings* (Baltimore: Penguin, 1969).

ROSE, Peter I., *They and We: Racial and Ethnic Minorities in the United States,* 2d ed. (New York: Random House, 1974).

ROSENBERG, Morris, *The Logic of Survey Analysis* (New York: Basic Books, 1968).

ROSSIDES, Daniel W., *The American Class System: An Introduction to Social Stratification* (Boston: Houghton Mifflin, 1976).

_____, *The History and Nature of Sociological Theory* (Boston: Houghton Mifflin, 1978).

ROTHMAN, Robert A., *Inequality and Stratification in the United States* (Englewood Cliffs, N.J.: Prentice-Hall, 1978).

SAFILIOS-ROTHSCHILD, Constantina, ed., *Toward a Sociology of Women* (Lexington, Mass.: Xerox Publishing Co., 1972).

SANDERS, William B., *The Sociologist as Detective,* 2d ed. (New York: Praeger, 1976).

SCANZONI, Letha, and John Scanzoni, *Men, Women, and Change* (New York: McGraw-Hill, 1976).

SCHEIN, Edgar H., *et al., Coercive Persuasion* (New York: Norton, 1971).

SELLTIZ, Claire, Marie Jahoda, Morton Deutsch, and Stuart Cook, *Research Methods in Social Relations,* rev. ed. (New York: Holt, Rinehart and Winston, 1962).

SHORT, James F., ed., *The Social Fabric of the Metropolis: Contributions of the "Chicago School of Urban Sociology"* (Chicago: University of Chicago Press, 1971).

SCHULTZ, Duane P., *Panic Behavior* (New York: Random House, 1964).

SCHUTZ, Alfred, *Collected Papers, I: The Problem of Social Reality* (The Hague, Netherlands: Martinus Nijhoff, 1962).

SELZNICK, Philip, *TVA and the Grass Roots* (Berkeley: University of California Press, 1949).

SHARP, Lauriston, "Steel Axes for Stone Age Australians," in James P. Spradley and David W. McCurdy, eds., *Conformity and Conflict,* 3rd ed. (Boston: Little, Brown, 1977).

SILLS, David L., ed., *International Encyclopedia of the Social Sciences* (New York: Macmillan and Free Press, 17 vols., 1968).

SIMMEL, Georg, *The Sociology of Georg Simmel,* edited and translated by Kurt H. Wolf (New York: Free Press, 1950.

_____, *On Individuality and Social Forms: Selected Writings,* edited by Donald Levine (Chicago: University of Chicago Press, 1971).

SIMPSON, George E., and J. Milton Yinger, *Racial and Cultural Minorities,* 4th ed. (New York: Harper and Row, 1972).

SKINNER, B. F., *Walden II* (New York: Macmillan, 1948).

SMELSER, Neil J., *Theory of Collective Behavior* (New York: Free Press, 1962).

_____, *The Sociology of Economic Life* (Englewood Cliffs, N.J.: Prentice-Hall, 1963).

SOFER, Cyril, *Organizations in Theory and Practice* (New York: Basic books, 1972).

SOROKIN, Pitirim, *Social and Cultural Dynamics* (New York: American Book Company, 4 volumes, 1937–1941).

SPENCER, Herbert, *The Evolution of Society: Selections from Herbert Spencer's Principles of Sociology,* edited and with an introduction by Robert L. Carneiro (Chicago: University of Chicago Press, 1967).

_____, *Structure, Function and Evolution,* edited and with an introductory essay by Stanislav Andreski (New York: Scribner's, 1971).

SPENGLER, Oswald, *The Decline of the West, Volume 1,* translated by Charles F. Atkinson (New York: Knopf, 1926).

STARK, Rodney, and Charles Y. Glock, *American Piety: The Nature of Religious Commitment: Volume I: Patterns of Religious Commitment* (Berkeley: University of California Press, 1968).

STEFFENS, Lincoln, *The Shame of the Cities* [1904] (New York: Hill and Wang, 1957).

STOUFFER, Samuel A., *Communism, Conformity, and Civil Liberties* (New York: Doubleday, 1955).

SUMNER, William Graham, *Folkways* [1906] (Boston: Ginn, 1960).

SUTHERLAND, Edwin H., and Donald R. Cressey, *Principles of Criminology*, 9th ed. (Chicago: Lippincott, 1974).

SWANSON, Guy F., *The Birth of the Gods* (Ann Arbor: University of Michigan Press, 1960).

SWINGLE, Paul G., ed., *Social Psychology in Natural Settings* (Chicago: Aldine, 1973).

TAPPAN, Paul W., *Crime, Justice, and Correction* (New York: McGraw-Hill, 1960).

TAWNEY, R. H., *Religion and the Rise of Capitalism* (New York: Harcourt, Brace and World, 1926).

THOMAS, William I., *The Child in America* (New York: Knopf, 1928).

THOMAS, William I., and Florien Znaniecki, *The Polish Peasant in Europe and America* [1919] (New York: Octagon Books, 1971).

TOFFLER, Alvin, *Future Shock* (New York: Random House, 1970).

TOYNBEE, Arnold J., *A Study of History*, abridged by D. C. Somervell (New York: Oxford University Press, 1947 [vols. 1–6], 1957 [vols. 7–10]).

TROTTER, Robert J., "Divorce: The First Two Years are the Worst," *Science News* (October 9, 1976): 237–238.

TUMIN, Melvin M., "Some Principles of Social Stratification: A Critical Analysis," *American Sociological Review* **18** (August 1953): 387–397.

TURNER, Jonathan H., *The Structure of Sociological Theory*, rev. ed. (Homewood, Ill.: Dorsey, 1978).

TURNER, Ralph H., and Lewis M. Killian, *Collective Behavior*, 2d ed. (Englewood Cliffs, N.J.: Prentice-Hall, 1972).

TYLOR, Edward B., *The Origins of Culture* [1871] (New York: Harper, 1958).

U.S. FACT BOOK: THE AMERICAN ALMANAC (New York: Grosset and Dunlap, 1976).

VIDICH, Arthur J., and Joseph Bensman, *Small Town in Mass Society* (New York: Doubleday/Anchor, 1960).

WARNER, W. Lloyd, *et al.*, *Democracy in Jonesville* (New York: Harper & Row, 1949).

WARNER, W. Lloyd, and Paul S. Lunt, *The Social Life of a Modern Community* (New Haven, Conn.: Yale University Press, 1941).

WARREN, Roland L., ed., *Perspectives on the American Community* (Chicago: Rand McNally, 1966).

WEBB, Eugene, Donald T. Campbell, Richard D. Schwartz, and Lee Sechrest, *Ubobtrusive Measures: Nonreactive Research in the Social Sciences* (Chicago: Rand McNally, 1966).

WEBER, Max, *From Max Weber: Essays in Sociology*, translated and edited by Hans H. Gerth and C. Wright Mills (New York: Oxford University Press, 1946).

_____, *The Protestant Ethic and the Spirit of Capitalism* [1904–1905], translated by Talcott Parsons (New York: Oxford University Press, 1947).

_____, *The Theory of Social and Economic Organization* [1922], translated by A. M. Henderson and Talcott Parsons (Glencoe, Ill.: Free Press, 1947).

_____, *The Sociology of Religion* [1922], translated by Ephraim Fischoff (Boston: Beacon, 1963).

WEST, Uta, ed., *Women in a Changing World* (New York: McGraw-Hill, 1975).

WHITE, Leslie A., *The Evolution of Culture* (New York: McGraw-Hill, 1959).

WHITE, Lynn, Jr., *Medieval Technology and Social Change* (Oxford, England: Oxford University Press, 1962).

WILLIAMS, Robin M., Jr., *Strangers Next Door* (Englewood Cliffs, N.J.: Prentice-Hall, 1964).

_____, *American Society*, 3rd ed. (New York: Knopf, 1970).

WINCH, Robert F., *The Modern Family*, rev. ed. (New York: Holt, Rinehart and Winston, 1971).

WOLLHEIM, Richard, *Sigmund Freud* (New York: Viking, 1971).

Index

Note: Terms in boldface type are defined on the page in boldface type.

Christianity, and good and evil,
324
origins of, 331
See also Religion
Church of Jesus Christ of Latter
Day Saints, 325
Cicourel, Aaron, 362
Cities, concentric-zone theory
of, 195–196, 203
feelings about, 188
future of, 201–203
and human ecology, 195
multiple-nuclei theory of,
196–197, 203
sector theory of, 196, 203
social psychology of,
199–201
urban redevelopment, 440
Citizenship, 205
criterion of, 191
City, The, 190
Civil law, 378, 386
Civil rights movement, 105,
118, 149, 181
and American society,
178–179
blacks vs. whites, 172–174
and minority groups,
175–178
organization for, 174
strategy of, 174–175
See also Social movements
Class. *See* Social class
*Class and Class Conflict in
Industrial Society,* 497
Clothing, and interaction,
33–34
Coconut Grove nightclub fire,
406
Coercive power, 217–218, **227.**
See also Power
Cognitive development, 77,
82–83, **97.** *See also*
Development
Collective behavior, 3, 31, **417**
brawl, 400–401
of crowds, 403–405

major forms of, 405–414
nature of, 392, 414
public opinion process and,
399
See also Social movements
Commodities, 236–239, 243,
244
intimacy as, 312
obtaining, 241–242, 243
political, 269–270
in political exchange,
268–271
scarce and joint, 237–239
sexual gratification as, 296
wanting, 240–241, 243
See also Economy
Commune, 304
Communication, 6, 483, 500
and social change, 431
and urbanization, 202
See also Mass media; Social
exchange
Communism, 332, 433
Communist Manifesto, 485
Community, 3, 185, **205–206**
autonomy of, 191–192
basic characteristics of,
190–193
future of, 201–203
importance of, 187–190
membership in, 191
religion as, 326
self-sufficiency of, 192
and social change, 425
study of, 193–201
vulnerability of, 189–190, 203
Competence, and management,
214
Competition, 497
Computers, increasing
dependence on, 439
and social change, 425, 430
Comte, Auguste, 14, 19, 490,
494, 501
on social change, 432
sociological theory of, 483,
485, 486

Concentric-zone theory,
195–196, 203, **206.** *See also*
Ecology
Conceptual schemes, 479
Concrete operations stage, of
development, 83. *See also*
Development
Condorcet, Marquis de, 485,
494, 432
Conflict, 483
family, 89
between informal groups,
224–225
role strain, 48
status, 45–47
value, 60
Conflict theory, 19–20, **28,**
496–498, 501
Simmel's, 491
of social stratification,
141–142
Conformity, 89. *See also*
Deviance
Conformist, 361, **366**
Confucianism, 323
Consensual validation, 317,
319, **336**
Conservative social
movements, 411. *See also*
Social movements
Construction, and social
change, 431
Consummatory orientation, 25,
26. *See also* Commodities;
Economic exchange
Content analysis, 463–464
*Continuities in the Study of
Social Conflict,* 497
Continuity, and socialization,
89–90. *See also*
Evolutionary theories
Contraceptives, 118, 313, 434
Contraculture, 64, 68, **69**
Conventional crowd, 404, 414.
See also Crowds
Converse, Philip E., 149
Co-occurrence, 453, 474